LANGUAGE

ITS STRUCTURE

AND USE

EDWARD FINEGAN
University of Southern California

NIKO BESNIER
Yale University

HARCOURT BRACE JOVANOVICH, PUBLISHERS

San Diego   New York   Chicago   Austin   Washington, D.C.
London   Sydney   Tokyo   Toronto

ISBN: 0-15-549175-X
Library of Congress Catalog Card Number: 87-82787
Printed in the United States of America

Cover: © 1979, Ted Spiegel/Black Star

PREFACE

For the past 2,500 years, philosophers, rhetoricians, and grammarians have described the structures of human language and the uses to which those structures are put in the high and low affairs of women and men. Building on these millennia of observation and reflection, linguists working in this century have further broadened our understanding of languages and of language use. As physicists have revised our understanding of atoms and space explorers our knowledge about the satellites of Uranus, so linguists have contributed to a burst of new insight into the nature of language. In *Language: Its Structure and Use* we present a glimpse of language as it is understood in the 1980s.

Despite the pace at which the twentieth century has added insight into the nature of language, many questions remain unanswered, and the realization that some of today's insights replace those of yesterday serves as a reminder that tomorrow's insights will replace today's. There is far more yet to be learned about language than we currently know, and exciting and important work remains for future generations. As our subtitle indicates, we have given substantial attention both to language *structure* and to language *use*. In both these arenas there is much yet to be learned, and we invite you, our readers, to participate in advancing our knowledge of language—the single most important and powerful tool of human endeavor and one, remarkably, that is available to all humans equally.

A WORD TO STUDENTS

Throughout this textbook you will find words in **boldface** type. When an important word is first discussed (though not necessarily when first mentioned), it is set in **boldface** to indicate its importance and to highlight the fact that it is defined in the Glossary (beginning on page 523) whenever you need a reminder of its meaning. For ease of reference as you read the chapters and do the exercises, there are tables of English vowel and consonant symbols on the inside front cover and a table of all consonant symbols used in this book on the inside back cover. When you want to learn more about a topic, the Suggestions for Further Reading and the References at the end of each chapter will steer you in the right direction.

A WORD TO INSTRUCTORS

This book includes more topics than can normally be covered in a one-semester course. We expect that most instructors will wish to cover the first six chapters and select from among the remaining chapters according to their own interests and the needs of their students.

We invite comments and suggestions about any aspect of this book that may benefit future readers on either side of the desk. We are eager to hear about materials that prove particularly useful or valuable to students, and about discussion or exercises that prove too perplexing.

ACKNOWLEDGMENTS

In writing this book, we have drawn on the work of countless scholars whose analysis and writing over the centuries have given us a footing from which to address the questions discussed here. The References at the end of each chapter give only a clue to the range of scholarship we have relied on. Our indebtedness is no less to those who are not cited than it is to those whose work we recommend to our readers. We are also indebted to many colleagues for helpful comments about various parts of the book as it was in preparation: at the University of Illinois at Urbana-Champaign to Larry Bouton, Yamuna Kachru, and Erica McClure; at the University of Southern California to Joseph Aoun, William Brown, Allan Casson, Bernard Comrie, José Hualde, Larry Hyman, Audrey Li, and Douglas Pulleyblank; to Dede Boden of Washington University and Robert R. van Oirsouw of the University of Utrecht. For helpful reviews of the initial proposal and for comments on draft chapters, our appreciation to: John Algeo, University of Georgia; Carlo Coppola, Oakland University; David Dinneen, University of Kansas; James Nattinger, Portland State University; John Oller, University of New Mexico; and Anthony Woodbury, University of Texas, Austin. We are grateful for data received from Zeina el-Imad Aoun, Du Tsai-Chwun, Liou Hsien-Chin, Yeon-Hee Choi, Jin Hong Gang, José Hualde, Yong-Jin Kim, Won-Pyo Lee, Mohammed Mohammed, Phil Morrow, Masagara Ndinzi, and Minako Seki. To our students at USC and the University of Illinois who used drafts of the book and offered comments we are also appreciative. To José Hualde we are grateful for his work on the index. To Bill McLane, Catherine Fauver, Merilyn Britt, Sarah Randall, and the other staff at Harcourt Brace Jovanovich we are appreciative for help at every stage, as well as to Dan Hammer for his incisive editing. Finally, a very special word of thanks goes to Doug Biber, our colleague and friend at USC; his comments have suggested improvements throughout the book, and we appreciate his sensitivity and generosity.

Edward Finegan
Niko Besnier

CONTENTS

Part II   *LANGUAGE USE*

LANGUAGE STRUCTURE AND LANGUAGE USE

1

LANGUAGE AND LINGUISTICS

What Is Human Language?

Language has been a focus of people's curiosity and intellectual probing for millennia. Like other inquiries that are central to human experience, questions about language and how it functions are not new to the twentieth century. As old as speculation on any subject, the nature of language occupied Plato, Aristotle, and other Greek philosophers. In some areas of grammatical analysis, they made contributions that have remained useful for two thousand years.

In the nineteenth and twentieth centuries the field of linguistics emerged to answer the question: What is language and how do languages develop? This book aims to provide a modern context for asking and answering this question. Ensuing chapters will provide views of language as it has come to be understood toward the end of the twentieth century; nevertheless it is useful here to make some general observations about the nature of language and to offer a framework for our journey through the various aspects of its structure and use.

Perhaps the most basic observation about language is that it faces in two directions. The fundamental task of every language is to link voice to meaning—to provide words for the expression of thought and feeling.

Language is therefore like a coin whose two sides are **expression** and **content**.

Traditionally, language has been viewed as a vehicle of thought, a system of expression that mediates the transfer of thought from one person to another. To view language solely this way, however, is to confine oneself to an exceedingly narrow perspective. In everyday life language serves a great many more social and affective functions than the cognitive ones commonly associated with it. The widespread and traditional view that language is principally a vehicle for expressing thought is thus unsatisfactory. For one thing, we know very little about thought—and most if not all of what is known has been learned through language. Hence, definitions of language that involve thought run the risk of being circular. Thought isn't easily objectified or easily characterized.

To be sure, the notion of thought is a very familiar one. "I was just thinking . . . ," we say to friends, or "I think I'll skip the game on Saturday." Such statements, frequent as they are in conversation, pass unnoticed with respect to the verb *think*. Language and thought are so intimately entwined that we tend to equate them. Still, as speakers and writers struggling to find words to match our thoughts, we tacitly acknowledge that thought and language are distinct. From time to time, each of us recognizes better and worse "fits" between our thoughts and the words we use to express them—better fits between content and expression.

Content encompasses *what* we are attempting to say; expression encompasses the way we articulate this content; and language is the mental code that links the two. To enhance students' ability to find an adequate and suitable fit between written expression and various kinds of content—narrative, description, argument, and especially exposition—colleges traditionally require writing courses, whose aims are essentially practical. Courses in linguistics are less traditional and less practically oriented. While these, too, focus on the expressive side of language, they do so not to provide a practical tool for discovering and conveying one's thoughts but as an inquiry into the organization of language and the uses to which its forms are put in speaking and writing.

Linguistics thus addresses itself to two fundamental arenas of human experience: the mental and the social. Linguists are interested in how language is organized in the human mind and in how the social structures of human communities shape language to their own purposes, reflecting those social structures in language use. To be sure, knowledge of the ways languages are organized and used can be helpful in our interactions with members of our own society and with members of other societies, but the main goal of this book is not a practical one. It aims to provide an understanding of how language is organized mentally and of how it is put to work in social interaction.

We will not attempt to define the content side of language, although we will discuss the semantics of words and sentences in Chapter 6. Instead, we will rely on common-sense notions of linguistic content and will use phrases such as "X means Y" to suggest in "Y" the content side of the coin. We will also discuss at some length what we can infer about the content side from an analysis of language structure and language use; but bear in mind that content is the far side of the coin for linguists, despite its being the reason for the very existence of the expression side.

Signs and Symbols

Signs   We often use the word *sign* in everyday conversation. We commonly talk about signs of trouble with the economy, no sign of a train coming into a railway station, someone's vital signs at the scene of an accident, and so forth. A *sign* is an indicator of something; in the cases we've specified, the indicator is inherently related to the thing that is indicated—it is a *nonarbitrary* indicator. That is to say, there is a direct, usually causal relationship between the indicator and the thing indicated. Smoke is a *sign* of fire, and clouds are a *sign* of impending rain. **Signs**, then, are nonarbitrary indicators of the things they signal, the things they are signs of.

Symbols   In thinking about language, it is crucial to distinguish nonarbitrary signs from indicators that are partly or wholly arbitrary. *Arbitrary* indicators of something else are called **symbols**. Common symbols in the workaday world include traffic lights, railroad crossing indicators, flashing red or blue lights on police vehicles, wedding rings, and national flags. With these, there is no inherent connection between the symbols and the things they symbolize. For example, no property of the color red is inherently associated with stopping; yet red lights and red signs are used conventionally in traffic codes to indicate that cars or pedestrians must stop. Being arbitrary, a strictly symbolic indicator can be present without the thing indicated (as with a wedding band on an unmarried person). There is nothing causal in the relationship between a symbol and what it symbolizes. Nor is there anything in the nature of an arbitrary symbol that makes it inherently better (or worse) than other potential representations for the same thing. Societies are free to select various symbols to represent particular notions or things. If, for example, a national transportation department decided to use the color blue as a signal for traffic to stop, nothing would prevent that department from doing so. Being only conventional representations, symbols can be changed. In contrast, it is impossible to change the relationship between smoke and fire or clouds and rain, because these are nonarbitrary relationships.

Some essentially arbitrary symbols are not entirely arbitrary, of course. Sometimes a symbol directly suggests its meaning to some degree. Such symbols as ☼ to represent the sun, or the Roman numeral III to represent the number three, or a skull and crossbones to indicate poison, are not entirely arbitrary. But there is no inherent connection between the symbol and the symbolized even in these cases; the symbol can be present without the symbolized, and vice versa. Such basically arbitrary but partly related symbols are called **representational** (or **iconic**) symbols. Linguistic examples of iconic symbols might include the words *meow* and *trickle*, for it is commonly supposed that these words have some nonarbitrary relation to the things they symbolize. (Iconicity, or representational symbolization, has played a role in the development of writing; see Chapter 11.)

Besides the kind of iconicity captured in words—as when the sound of the word *meow* seems to echo the vocal sounds of a kitten—iconic expression appears spontaneously in ordinary speech. For example, one of us once telephoned the home of friends and had a brief conversation with the four-year-old who answered. We were trying to reach the boy's mother, but he reported that she was showering at the time. As the matter was of some urgency, we told the child that we would call back in a few minutes. He indicated that calling back soon would do no good; his explanation was this:

My mother is taking a <u>long</u>, <u>long</u>, <u>long</u> shower.

The repetition of the word *long*—making the expression longer to reflect the content—illustrates the potential for iconicity in human language. Iconic language is expression that in any fashion mimics or directly suggests its content. The boy stretched out the expression itself in order to underscore the salient part of the semantic content of his message.

Similarly, certain aspects of grammar appear to be influenced by iconic principles. English, for example, has two ways of expressing conditional sentences:

If you behave, I'll bring you some candy.

I'll bring you some candy if you behave.

In other words, we have a choice between placing the conditioning part (*if you behave*) before or after the consequence of the condition (*I'll bring you some candy*). Though contextual factors sometimes influence the choice of alternatives, speakers and writers show a strong preference for the first pattern (condition followed by consequence) over the second pattern (consequence followed by condition). This preference, also found in many other languages, is most apparent in speech. Why might the first pattern be preferred to the second pattern? The answer has to do with the order of occurrence of the events described by conditional clauses. In this example, the hearer must *first* behave, and *then* the speaker will bring the candy. So the events described by the preceding sentences are ordered in time, and this order is reflected in the preferred linguistic order of condition first, consequence second. There is thus an iconic explanation for preferring the order condition–consequence to the order consequence–condition in conditional sentences: with the first order, the expression side reflects better the temporal sequencing of events in the content side. In some languages, only the first pattern (condition–consequence) is allowed; but there is no language, as far as we know, in which conditional sentences can be expressed only with the noniconic order consequence–condition.

Despite such occasional iconic characteristics, human language is not fundamentally representational. It is fundamentally and essentially arbitrary. The form of expression is generally independent of its content except for the meanings that have been established by social convention and by frequent association. The fundamental arbitrariness of human language is unaltered by the fact that certain symbols come to be so closely associated with what they represent that reaction to the symbol—to the expression—can be as strong as reaction to what lies behind it—to the content. Burning a flag, for example, can in some cases provoke reactions nearly as strong as would betraying one's country. Though the important difference between arbitrary and nonarbitrary representations is sometimes overlooked in common parlance, we will reserve the term *sign* for reference to nonarbitrary representations or icons and will use the word *symbol* to refer to representations whose meaning is assigned in a partly or wholly arbitrary manner.

We can illustrate the arbitrary nature of linguistic symbols with an example. Imagine a parent cooking dinner and trying to catch a few minutes of the televised evening news. Suddenly a strong aroma of burning rice wafts into the TV room. This aroma, an unmistakable *sign* that the rice is burning, will send the parent scurrying to salvage dinner. Compare this nonarbitrary sign with the words of a youngster in the kitchen who sees the smoke and shouts, *The rice is burning!* Like the aroma, this utterance is likely to send a parent scurrying, but there is a world of difference between the two modes of communication. The aroma—a direct result of the rice burning—will convey its message to anyone who has previously experienced it. There is nothing conventionalized about the aroma; it is thus a *sign*. The words of the child, on the other hand, are arbitrary. It is a fact about English—agreed to conventionally by generations of English speakers—and not a fact about burning rice that enables the utterance to do the work intended by the child: alerting the parent to the situation. The utterance is thus a *symbol*.

Other languages convey the same message differently: Korean by the utterance *pap t^{h}anda*, Swahili by *wali inaunguwu*, Arabic by *yahtariqu palruzzu*, and so on. The forms of these utterances have nothing to do with rice or its chemistry, or with the manner in which it is cooking, or with anything inherent in the situation; they are not iconic. Instead, they have to do solely with the nature of the systems of symbolic expression that we call English, Korean, Swahili, and Arabic.

Hence the utterances, unlike the aroma, can and do differ from culture to culture. Moreover, they can be uttered—and convey their message—whether or not rice is in fact burning. Young pranksters seeking an opportunity to change channels to their favorite TV show, or looking for attention from a busy parent, or being jocular or cantankerous, might use the same utterance regardless of the situation in the kitchen. Signs, on the other hand, are not arbitrary and do not exist independently of what causes them. Only by an elaborate ruse could a sign of burning rice be devised independently of an actual occurrence.

Because the relationship between symbols and what they symbolize is arbitrary, the meaning of a given symbol can differ from culture to culture, and different cultures usually evolve different symbols to represent the same thing. Even words that mimic natural noises are cross-linguistically distinct. Cats don't *meow* in all languages (compare Korean *yaong*, for instance).

To repeat, one central fact about language is that the connection between the things signified and the words used to signify them—between signified and signifier, or symbolized and symbol—is arbitrary. In English, we refer to the stuff that bakers make as *bread*. The French call it *pain*, the Russians *xleb*. In Chinese, the word is *miàn bāo*; in Fijian, it is *madrai*. Not only can one and the same thing be symbolized differently in different languages; even in a single language several symbols can represent the same entity or notion. We purchase *a dozen* or *twelve* bagels for the same price. We can write *12* or *XII* for the same concept, as well as *TWELVE*, *twelve*, or *Twelve*. Thus, to represent even a straightforward numerical concept, English permits several alternative symbols. For more complex content, the variety of possible expressions in phrases and sentences often seems limitless.

Languages as Rule-Governed Structures

Precisely because the relationship between linguistic symbols and the things they represent is arbitrary, languages must be highly organized systems if they are to function as reliable vehicles of expression and communication. If there were no pattern to the way we voiced our thoughts and feelings, listeners would face an insuperable task in determining what we meant. If language were not a highly organized and patterned system, listeners would find it impossible to unravel its arbitrary symbols for the messages they encode. It is not surprising, then, that languages have evolved over centuries into extraordinarily complex systems, so complex that we have yet to uncover many of their basic properties.

We have said that language is rule governed. It follows observable patterns that obey certain inherent "rules." Such rules are not imposed from the outside, and they do not specify how something should be done. Instead, they are merely the regularities that we can observe being followed when people talk and write. In other words, the linguistic rules described in this book are based on nothing more than the observed regularities of language behavior and—equally important—of the underlying systems that we can infer from such language behavior. Linguistic rules are thus more like the patterns describing how the digestive tract or the circulatory system works than like the kinds of rules that prescribe what clothes to wear to a formal dinner or how to behave when visiting a foreign dignitary.

A language is a set of elements and a system of rules for combining those elements to form patterned sentences that can be used to do specific jobs: Utterances report something, greet someone, invite a friend to lunch, request the time of day, make a wisecrack, poke fun at someone, argue for a particular course of action, make inquiries, express admiration, propose marriage, create fictional (and science-fictional) worlds, and so on in an endless list. And languages do this using a finite system of elements and rules that a child normally masters in a few short years. The mental capacity that enables speakers to form grammatical sentences is called **grammatical competence**.

Speech as Rule-Governed Language Use

There is more to the ability to speak and write than grammatical competence. Knowing the elements of a language and the patterns for putting them together into well-formed, or grammatical, sentences falls far short of knowing how to accomplish the work that speakers do with language; it falls short of native-speaker fluency. To be fluent in a language requires not only mastery of its grammatical rules but also competence in the appropriate use of the sentences that are structured by those rules. Fluency requires knowledge of how to put sentences together in conversations, for example, and of how to rely on nonlinguistic context and previous linguistic context in shaping appropriate utterances. The point is that fluency presumes two distinct kinds of competence: knowledge of how to form sentences and knowledge of what those sentences are capable of doing and of when and how to use them appropriately (as well as how to interpret them when uttered in particular contexts).

The mental capacity that enables us to use language appropriately is called **communicative competence**. It enables speakers to weave utterances together into conversations, apologies, requests, directions, descriptions, sermons, scoldings, or jokes and to do the myriad things we do with language when it is appropriate to do them. When asked by an inquiring visitor the whereabouts of the campus bookstore, a student who replied *There's a great show on television tonight about California condors* would certainly be greeted with raised eyebrows, though no one could point to ungrammatical English as the culprit. We would say that the student's grammatical competence was fine, but his or her communicative competence was sorely lacking. Knowing a language—being a fluent speaker—presumes both communicative competence and grammatical competence. Neither one is sufficient by itself to constitute fluency in the full sense of the word—in the sense that encompasses both structure and use. Grammatical competence and communicative competence are needed together.

We can summarize by saying that grammatical competence is the native speaker's implicit knowledge of vocabulary, pronunciation, sentence structure, and meaning, while communicative competence is the implicit knowledge that underlies the appropriate use of grammatical competence in various situations of language use. Different speech communities may have different grammatical competences or different communicative competences; most commonly, both differ. The rules that govern the appropriate use of language differ from one speech community to the next, so that even a shared grammatical competence may not be adequate to make one a fluent speaker in another community, at least in some situations. Joke telling is not the same cross-culturally: members of one culture may find jokes about other people's misadventures funny, whereas members of another culture may find such jokes offensive. In fact, the very concept of joking (as distinct from telling "funny stories") seems not to exist in certain societies. Likewise, even within the English-speaking world, what is considered impolite in one place might be routine interaction elsewhere. For example, a difference in rules for speaking to strangers explains why some visitors to the Big Apple think New Yorkers are brusque or impolite when giving directions, though the same utterance that provokes an unfavorable judgment in an outsider will be interpreted by a native New Yorker as routinely polite.

What Is Linguistics?

With this background, we take up the question: What is linguistics? We can define linguistics as the scientific inquiry into human language—into its structures and uses and into the relationship between them. The scope of linguistics as discussed in this book includes both language structure (and the grammatical competence underlying it) and language use (and its underlying communicative competence).

Linguists acknowledge that, despite significant strides in our understanding of human language in recent years, not enough is known to provide a complete understanding of language. In fact, language is so complex and multifaceted that any attempt to define it in a few words is doomed. Linguistics is best regarded as an enterprise whose principal objective is to provide an increasingly adequate understanding of particular facets of languages, thereby gradually building our understanding of the nature of language itself.

In many discussions of the subject, language is defined as an arbitrary vocal system used by human beings to communicate with one another. This very common definition of language is useful as far as it goes, but it downplays one important element that philosophers have brought to the forefront of current thinking. Speech is more than grammar; it is action. A language is a grammatical system that has work to perform, a system that speakers exploit purposefully. Language is used to do things, not merely to report them or talk about them.

As mentioned earlier, people have been interested in the nature of language structure and use for over two thousand years. Plato and Aristotle discussed language in the fourth and third centuries B.C., and from them we have inherited several of the categories generally recognized today in grammatical analysis. Nouns and verbs were identified by the Greek philosophers, whom we also credit with establishing the grammatical genders of masculine, feminine, and neuter (that is, 'neither') and with recognizing that verbs have tenses, such as present and past. More than a century before Plato and Aristotle, grammatical analysis was underway in India, where a sage named Pāṇini wrote a description of Sanskrit that some scholars regard as one of the finest grammars ever produced for any language. Both the Greeks and the Indians were concerned with the question of the relationship between symbols and the things signified by them—an issue that still warrants attention, as we have already seen.

Today, the empirical and scientific study of language has taken on additional importance in an age where communication is as important to social, intellectual, political, economic, and moral concerns as ever before. Linguistics—now augmented by insights from psychology, sociology, anthropology, philosophy, and rhetoric as well as from communications engineering and other sciences—has become a prominent academic discipline in universities throughout the world, alongside departments of language and literature.

There are many branches of the field of linguistics, and new ones continue to develop. Historically, the central branch is grammar, and probably most linguists today are engaged in the study of grammar—of the principles of sentence formation, of the systems of human vocal sounds, of word structure, and of meaning. Some are interested in the description of particular languages, some in uncovering the patterns across languages and explaining universal patterns in psychological or sociological terms.

Other linguists are interested in language variation: variation across different speech communities or within a single community, variation across time, variation at one time and in a single community across different situations of use—differences between conversational structure, for example, and sports announcer talk. Like grammarians, linguists interested in variation seek two kinds of explanation—those that are essentially psychological and have to do with the constraints on the human language-processing capacities and those that are essentially sociological and have to do with the structure of societies and the interaction of people. Ultimately, of course, much of what is found will best be explained by a combination of psychological and sociological approaches.

A third group applies the findings of the discipline to real-world problems, especially in the educational arena, to the acquisition of literate aspects of language (reading and writing), and to the acquisition of second languages and foreign languages. Other applied linguists address problems in language policy at national and local levels: what languages to allow for use in what situations—in the schools, the courts, the voting booth, and so on; what kind of writing system to aim for; what regulation of existing language is needed, as in the Plain English movement in the United States or in the development and production of the tools of standardization such as dictionaries and grammars.

ANIMAL COMMUNICATION

To what extent is the ability to communicate through a language restricted to the human species? When we observe animals in groups, it doesn't take long to realize that they too interact: dogs display their fangs to communicate displeasure or aggression; bees appear to "tell" each other where they have found flowers; male frogs croak in order to attract female frogs. It is only natural to ask: How do the forms of communication used by animals differ from human language?

Animal communication—or "animal language," as it is sometimes called —has fascinated human observers for centuries. People sometimes speak of porpoises, chimpanzees, gorillas, dolphins, whales, bees, and other animals as though they had language systems similar to those of humans. Almost any week, television programs show people trying to communicate through music with apes, alligators, or turkeys (turkeys gobble when a particular note is played on a wind instrument). There is no doubt that most, and presumably all, species of animals have developed systems of communication with which they can signal such things as danger and fear, hunger and the whereabouts of food, rutting instincts and sexual access. We now know a good deal about what, why, and how bees communicate. More recently, chimpanzees, with their extremely limited vocal apparatus, have been raised as human infants and taught sign language so as to skirt the difficulties or impossibility of their speaking.

Communication Among Animals in Their Natural Environment

People had wondered for a long time how bees were able to communicate to one another the exact location of a nectar source, and there was speculation about a "language" that bees must possess. After years of careful observation and hypothesizing, Karl von Frisch demonstrated that honeybees have an elaborate system of dancing by which they communicate the whereabouts of a honey supply. Various aspects of the dance of a bee returning to a hive indicate the distance and the direction of a nectar source. The quality of the source can be gauged by sniffing the discovering bee. Von Frisch's careful analysis demonstrated that the kind of creativity that is characteristic of a child's speech is lacking in the bee's dance. Bees do not use their communicative system to convey anything beyond a limited range of meanings (such as "There is a pretty good source of nectar in this direction"). Analogies between bee dancing and child language are therefore far-fetched and misleading.

The same lack of creativity characterizes the communication that takes place between other animals. Beyond a limited repertoire of meanings, even intelligent mammals like dogs do not have the mental capacity to be communicatively creative. They use a set communicative system, never venturing beyond the boundaries of this system.

Furthermore, much of the communication that occurs between animals relies on signs rather than symbols. When gazelles sense potential danger, for example, they flee and thereby signal to other gazelles in the vicinity that danger is lurking. The communicative function of the act is almost incidental compared to its more pressing survival function. Similarly, a dog signals its wish to be let inside the house by barking and signals the possibility that it might bite momentarily by displaying its fangs. These acts are not arbitrary symbols; rather, they are signs that accompany desires and possibilities.

Vocalizations that might be construed as symbols of various sorts in different animals are usually accompanied by gestures. One study found that only 3 percent of the signals among rhesus monkeys were not accompanied by gestures. Whatever animals express through sounds seems to reflect not a logical sequence of thoughts but a sequence accompanying a series of emotional states. Animals' communicative activities thus seem to differ from human language in that they consist essentially of signs, not arbitrary symbols.

Teaching Human Language to Chimpanzees

The situation with chimpanzees is more complicated and more interesting. In the wild, chimps use a limited nonlinguistic communicative system similar to that of other mammals, though more sophisticated. However, because the intelligence of chimps comes closest to that of humans, there have been several attempts to have chimps learn and use human language in laboratory settings. There is considerable disagreement among researchers as to whether and to what degree chimps can achieve humanlike linguistic competence.

The earliest chimp to get some notoriety for her communicative prowess in the laboratory was named Vicki. After being raised for about seven years by psychologists Keith and Catherine Hayes, Vicki could utter only four words—*mama, papa, up*, and *cup*—and only manage these with considerable physical strain. Chimps are simply not equipped with suitable mouth and throat organs to enable them to speak.

Though chimps do not have the *physiological* capacity to speak, the question remains: Do they have the *mental* capacity to learn language? After viewing a film of Vicki trying to vocalize human language with her limited vocal apparatus, Allan and Beatrice Gardner began to conduct their own research on chimp language. Sensitive to the fact that the normal disposition of chimpanzees is to be silent, the Gardners decided to teach a chimp human language by the use of gestures instead of vocalizations.

In 1966, they gave a home to a ten-month-old chimpanzee named Washoe, which they raised as a human child in as many ways as possible. Eventually, Washoe came to eat with a fork and spoon, to sit at a table and drink from a cup, and even to wash dishes after a fashion. She wore diapers and became toilet trained; she played with dolls and showed affection toward them. Like human children of her age, Washoe was fond of picture books and loved having her human friends tell her about the pictures in them.

Ingeniously, the Gardners decided to conduct all communication with Washoe in American Sign Language (also known as ASL or Ameslan), which they also used to communicate between themselves and with their research team whenever Washoe was present. ASL is a system of signing used by the hearing impaired in North America. It consists of both representational and arbitrary gestural symbols—called signs—that can be combined in accordance with rules that resemble the rules of grammar of ordinary spoken language.

The Gardners were keen observers of the kinds of simplified communication that human parents commonly provide for children. Like parents talking to human babies, they used repetition and simplified signing in talking with Washoe. The results? In the first seven months in her very human environment, Washoe learned four signs. In the next fourteen months, she mastered an additional thirty signs. After fifty-one months, Washoe had acquired 132 signs that describe objects and thoughts, and she understood about three times that many. Washoe used the signs not only for particular objects but also for classes of objects. She used the sign for *shoe* to mean shoes in general; she used the *flower* sign for flowers in general, and even for aromas like the smell of tobacco. Washoe signed to everyone, even to dogs and trees. She asked questions about the world around her, the world of objects and events. After mastering the use of only eight signs, Washoe started combining signs to make complex utterances: YOU ME HIDE; YOU ME GO OUT HURRY; LISTEN DOG (when a dog barked); BABY MINE (referring to her doll); and so on. After just ten months in her foster home, Washoe made scores of combinations of three or more signs, such as ROGER WASHOE TICKLE and YOU TICKLE ME WASHOE.

In subsequent work with four other chimps (Moja, Pili, Tatu, and Dar) who arrived at the Gardners' laboratory within days of birth, the Gardners demonstrated that chimps who are cross-fostered by human adults replicate many of the basic aspects of language acquisition characteristic of hearing and hearing-impaired human children, including the use of signs to refer to natural language categories such as DOG, FLOWER, and SHOE. Remarkably, when these chimps subsequently moved to another laboratory, an infant chimp named Loulis acquired at least forty-seven signs that had no other source than the signing of his fellow chimps.

In cross-fostering Washoe and her chimpanzee playmates, the Gardners had made the simple but crucial assumptions that human language is acquired by children in a rich social and intellectual environment and that such richness contributes to the cognitive and linguistic life of a child. The Gardners are convinced—and have convinced other observers by their research with their cross-fostered chimpanzees—that there is no absolute difference between human language and the communicative system that such animals as chimps can learn. They believe there is a continuum between human and nonhuman communication, a continuum about which there remains a great deal to be learned.

The language activities of other celebrity chimps were neither vocal nor gestural but visual. Sarah used plastic chips as symbols for words and showed considerable ability to put them in sequence. Lana used an appropriately marked computer terminal to create series of symbols similar to the plastic ones used by Sarah.

The Failure of Project Nim   Certain psychologists have voiced skepticism about the various projects to teach chimps human-style language. Some critics believe that the individual words that the chimps select in the various modes could have been triggered in some instances by inadvertent clues from the researchers. As a result, they claim, the sequences of strings produced by chimps are not productive sentences parallel to those that human children create. Other critics doubt that chimps have the ability to use language to make comments, ask questions, and express feelings as humans do.

In an effort to provide more control on the effort to teach language to a chimp, a very rigorous experiment was carried out at Columbia University. It sought to avoid many of the objections to previous research (though, inevitably, it introduced new problems of its own). The chimp on which this research was conducted was named Nim Chimpsky, after the distinguished linguist Noam Chomsky of the Massachusetts Institute of Technology, a proponent of the hypothesis that the nature of human language is very different from that of animal communication. In the course of his education Nim had several linguistic accomplishments, reflecting in part repetitions of the achievements of his predecessors. However, after five years of work with Nim, psychologist Herbert Terrace concluded that chimpanzees are not in fact capable of learning language as children do. Even with elaborate training, Nim produced very few longer utterances and displayed little creativity and spontaneity in his use of signs. Unlike Washoe, Nim would sign only when researchers prompted him and would never initiate interactions. These characteristics, Terrace contends, clearly distinguish what Nim was able to learn from what children do with language.

Some critics of Project Nim are convinced that the fact that Terrace employed some sixty-odd research assistants over the five years may have contributed importantly to the limitations in Nim's linguistic achievements. Moreover, the assistants were instructed to treat Nim not like a human baby but in a detached fashion. They were forbidden, for example, to comfort Nim even if he cried out during the night. The question arises as to how similar Nim's learning environment was to the environment in which a normal human child acquires language. Critics maintain that the research conditions of Project Nim had a fatal impact on Nim's emotional and linguistic education.

Conclusions and Implications   What sense can we make of the seemingly contradictory conclusions of these researchers? What is clear is that chimps can learn to symbolize and to use such symbolization as a tool for achieving other ends. It is also clear that chimpanzees are more intelligent than had previously been suspected and that their intelligence may be only quantitatively different from that of human children. With respect to chimps' acquisition of language, it would appear that the exceptional success of the Gardners' cross-fostering may be due in large part to their efforts to encourage the acquisition of signing in heavily contextualized circumstances approximating those normally provided for infant children. The Gardners have in fact been critical of those researchers who attempted to teach language to chimps in what were essentially laboratory training sessions. Similar exercises and drills have proved woefully inadequate in teaching foreign languages to human beings in schools and colleges and would presumably fail equally to foster first-language acquisition in children in the absence of a rich, natural, and socially and emotionally interactive home life.

We have described several attempts to teach language to chimps, whom most observers thought the most likely candidates to demonstrate that animals could acquire something akin to human language. Research with porpoises and monkeys has rather consistently failed to provide convincing evidence that animals could develop anything closely resembling human language, although some success with a gorilla named Koko has aroused renewed interest in this perennial question. The consensus of opinion at the present time seems to be that animal expression is usually tied directly to the animal's emotional state at the time of utterance, but that the evidence produced by the Gardners and other psychologists working with chimpanzees raises serious questions about the extent of this generalization. It is clear to many that Washoe and her chimpanzee friends learned to communicate in ASL about as well linguistically as human children two to three years old.

LANGUAGE ACQUISITION

The natural acquisition of language distinguishes humans from animals. In normal circumstances, human beings manifest an innate disposition to speak and to acquire language spontaneously, while animals do not. The language of children and its seemingly effortless acquisition have been a subject of increasing interest among linguists and psychologists during the past few decades. A good deal is now known about the patterns of acquisition within certain languages, and our understanding of how these patterns are similar and different across cultures is increasing. In this section we will introduce some of the basic findings on children's language acquisition.

Principles of Language Acquisition

First, it is important to recognize that any child who is capable of acquiring some particular human language is capable of acquiring *any* human language. Though there is a remarkably impressive predisposition in every child to acquire language, there is no biological basis—not in the lips or the brain—for preferring one particular language over any other. In light of the difficulties many of us have in trying to learn a foreign language, it may be perplexing to realize that children find all languages about equally simple to acquire as a native tongue. This is not to say that particular aspects of a particular language may not be more difficult to acquire than the equivalent parts of another language. The acquisition of definite articles in a language like German, with its many different forms corresponding to different "cases" (for subject, object, and so on), "numbers" (singular and plural), and "genders" (masculine, feminine, and neuter), is manifestly more complicated and more difficult than to acquire the English definite article, which completely lacks variation in number, gender, and case. (English speakers use the same form, *the*, in the phrases *the boy, for the daughter* and *to the lions*, which in German would have different forms.) But on balance it is accurate to say that all languages are about equally challenging to acquire as a mother tongue when considered in their entirety.

Some general observations about child language acquisition are useful here. First, we know that all children except those with mental or physical impairments acquire their native language in childhood, whatever their culture and whatever their level of intelligence. The ability to acquire a language is a fundamental human trait. Second, by about age six children the world over have acquired most of what they need to know about their language to speak it fluently. Because of the universality of these facts, linguists and psychologists are increasingly convinced that children come to the task of acquiring a language with a genetic predisposition to do so. There is little doubt that, at the very least, children are born with certain mechanisms or cognitive strategies that help in the task of language acquisition, though we do not yet know the precise nature of those mechanisms.

Third, linguists and psychologists are convinced that language is not acquired by imitation—certainly not solely and probably not principally by imitation—although exposure to a language is an essential ingredient in the process of acquiring it. We have all heard even very young children make up sentences that they are very unlikely to have heard before. Children have an undeniable capacity to be creative with language, and they certainly don't wait to hear a particular sentence before using it. They also go through periods when they make predictable mistakes. For example, many children use the form *goed* instead of *went*, rationalizing that the past tense of verbs is generally formed by adding an *ed* ending. Even children who have no contact with other children make the same mistake; and, since adults never use this form, children cannot be imitating it.

It is the task of children to construct a system of rules for expression and communication that will enable them to utter sentences and larger chunks of discourse appropriately and to make sense of utterances made by others. Children must do this with little, if any, explicit teaching by parents; they are constrained by exposure to limited and sometimes defective data, and they must acquire their mother tongue in a way that will enable them to produce and understand sentences they have never heard before. In other words, children acquire an entire grammatical system that enables them to produce and understand a potentially infinite number of utterances—and they achieve this in the first few years of life. It has been estimated that by the time a child arrives in school perhaps 80 percent of the structures of its language and more than 90 percent of its sound system have been mastered. Leonard Bloomfield, a distinguished linguist of the first half of the twentieth century, said that acquiring language is "doubtless the greatest intellectual feat any one of us is ever required to perform." Fortunately, language acquisition is an intellectual feat that all normal human beings are equally well adapted to and at which we are equally successful. Even intellectual geniuses have no advantage over others in acquiring a first language.

Two aspects of general maturation are crucial to a child's ability to acquire language: the ability to symbolize and the ability to use tools. We have stressed the symbolic nature of language—it is an arbitrary representation of something else, of other entities, experiences, feelings, and so on. In order to acquire language, a child must first be able to hold in mind a symbolic realization of something else. Even if it is no more than a mental picture of an absent object, such symbolization is a prerequisite to language acquisition.

The second ability—more wide-ranging than its application to language—is the ability to use tools to accomplish goals. Language is a tool made up entirely of symbols. It is an arbitrary vocal system that performs work—a symbolic tool that has evolved to accomplish such things as getting fed, being lifted up, being handed a toy, and getting cuddled. From quite an early age, children use language to accomplish such things. It is this purposeful activity that we are calling tool use; language is the most effective tool that people have for accomplishing work of almost any sort. Given the extremely limited ability of children to achieve their goals physically, the psychological motivation to develop a more powerful linguistic tool must be very strong indeed—probably in every child as well as in the evolution of the human species. The great effectiveness of language as a tool provides relatively helpless children with a strong motivation for language acquisition.

Adult Input in Language Acquisition

Stating that language acquisition is not a process of imitation does nothing to diminish the critical importance of exposure to some kind of linguistic input. As witness to the importance of adult input in language acquisition, there is the case of "Genie," a child who was not exposed to any language while she was growing up and who subsequently did not acquire her native language. Genie's parents locked her away in a dark attic for the first thirteen years of her life and never spoke to her. When she was discovered, in 1970, Genie was unable to speak. Linguist Susan Curtiss tried to teach her English, but the attempts were not very successful. When a child is deprived of linguistic input in the first few years of life, language acquisition is severely stunted.

On the other hand, it is important to realize that parents do not generally go about teaching language to young children. Instead, children spontaneously *acquire* language on the basis of the input they receive. In fact, some researchers have shown that conscious attempts to teach correct forms of language to children lead nowhere. Children simply ignore instructions and go on acquiring a native tongue at their own pace. In natural settings, parents rarely correct children's grammatical mistakes; they correct utterances that are false rather than those that violate rules of grammar. A child who says *Kitty's hands are pink* may be told *No, Kitty doesn't have hands; Kitty has paws.* But if a child asks *Where Kitty go?* (for 'Where did Kitty go?'), adults seldom correct the utterance. To a very great extent, then, children acquire the grammatical rules of their language without direct instruction from adults.

Of course, certain aspects of language use are taught to children in a conscious manner. When very young children go trick-or-treating on Halloween (to take the example of a context in which politeness becomes a salient aspect of linguistic interactions), they do not produce the appropriate utterances like *hi*, *thank you*, and *goodbye* unless prompted by their guardians (*Say thank you! What do you say?*). So they need to learn certain rules of language use consciously, and adults typically provide the necessary instruction to guide the learning of these politeness rules.

Even when adults are not explicitly teaching children the rules of language use, they frequently modify their speech, adapting it to what they think children will readily understand and acquire. We have all witnessed mothers using *baby talk*, or "motherese"—the language used in addressing babies.

> Ohhh, what a biiiig smiiile! Baby is smiling at Mummy? Baby is smiling at her Mummy? Yeah! Baby is happy to see Mummy! Now, open wiiide . . . Hmmmm! That's good! We like soup, don't we?

This example, uttered slowly and with exaggerated intonation, is typical of the kind of linguistic input that English-speaking American mothers give young children.

Baby talk differs from normal adult language in a number of characteristic ways. Adults' voices frequently take a higher pitch than usual when they address babies and young children. They also exaggerate their intonation and speak very clearly and slowly. Repetitions (*Baby is smiling at Mummy? Baby is smiling at her Mummy?*) are frequent in baby talk. Sentences are short and simple, and pronouns like *I* and *you* are replaced by personal names (*Baby, Mummy*). Utterances addressed to babies and young children frequently include special baby-talk vocabulary, including words like *doggy*, *kitty*, and *din-din* that are more easily perceived but do not normally occur in adult talk, and the choice of baby-talk words is more restricted than in normal speech. Finally, baby talk includes a high proportion of questions, particularly for small children (*Baby is smiling at Mummy?*). Adults, then, modify their utterances systematically when addressing small children; these modifications simplify the linguistic input that young children hear, making it easier to perceive.

It is interesting that the features of baby talk are found in many cultures. When Berbers of North Africa address their babies, they simplify their language in the same way that Americans do. Although not all cultures modify their speech to children, modification is widespread. Children themselves acquire baby talk very early in life, and it is not uncommon to hear four-year-olds using baby talk when addressing dolls or younger siblings.

The extent to which baby talk helps children in acquiring language is difficult to assess, but we know one thing for certain: children who grow up in cultures where baby talk is absent (as it is in Samoa, for example) do not acquire their native language more slowly than children who are exposed to baby talk. So we must conclude that baby talk is not essential to successful language acquisition.

Still, baby talk does seem to have other functions. First of all, it exposes small children to simple language, which may be helpful in the task of unraveling the rules of grammar. Since children have to figure out so many different features of the grammar of their mother tongue, selective input (fewer words, few complex sentences, many repetitions) may facilitate their task. Baby talk may even teach children certain rules of language use, the rules of conversation in particular (see Chapter 10). By asking many questions of small children, adults may communicate subtly that there is a question-answer sequence of utterances in conversation. Even before a child learns to speak, adults adapt their utterances to alternate with a child's babblings; the implicit message is to alternate your utterances with your interlocutor's.

While it is clear that children do not acquire language through imitation, they need a certain amount of input in order to acquire the rules of grammar and language use. There are few contexts in which adults consciously teach children these rules. But even when conscious instruction does not occur, adults in many cultures help foster acquisition by adapting their language in a way that seems easier for a child to understand.

Stages of Language Acquisition

Whatever the nature of the input they receive, children go through several stages in the process of acquiring their native language. Starting at about age one, children are heard uttering single words like *mama, papa,* and *up.* Many of the first words that children utter refer to familiar people (*Mama, Papa*), toys and pets (*teddy bear, kitty*), food and drink (*apple, milk, juice*). Typically, they use the same word for things that have a similar appearance. A child may begin using the word *kitty* for the family cat and then apply the same word to all cats. Children are thus able to generalize the meaning of words. Sometimes this process gives rise to overgeneralizations, as when the word *kitty* is applied to all animals.

Attentive observation of children's utterances at the one-word stage indicates that children are not rehearsing simple words; rather, they are using single words as complete utterances. A child uses the word *papa,* for example, to mean different things in different contexts: 'Here comes Papa' (upon hearing a key in the door at the end of the day); 'This is for Papa' (when handing Papa a toy); 'This is where Papa usually sits' (when looking at Papa's empty chair at the kitchen table); or 'That shoe is Papa's' (when touching a shoe belonging to Papa). In different contexts, a child may give the same word different intonations. Holding a shoe and uttering *Papa,* a child is not merely naming the object of its focus but is using a fairly simple expression for a relatively complex message.

From the one-word-utterance stage, children move on to utterances like *Papa come, Shoe mine,* and *Apple me.* The transition from the one-word stage to the two-word stage occurs at about two years of age (or a bit younger). At this stage, children show a preference for a nounlike element and a predicatelike element in each utterance. They tend to verbalize in propositions—to name something and then say something about it: *Papa,* [he] *come*[s]; *Shoe*, [it's] *mine; Apple*, [give it to] *me*. One striking fact about the two-word-utterance stage is that children from all cultures appear to express basically similar things in their propositions at this stage.

We don't know whether the disposition to verbalize in propositions is a tendency of the language process itself or is tied to aspects of perception. But children seem to be trying from the start to express propositions, not words, even with a single word. It is not that children at the two-word stage are attempting to *communicate* more by using two words instead of one; in fact, two-word utterances convey the same meaning as one-word utterances. Rather, two-word utterances *express* more of the information than one-word utterances.

By the time a child is about two and a half years old, utterances have become more complex, as in the following examples of a boy at age two years, five months:

[about a past action by his brother]
Mimo hurt me.

[to an adult whispering in his ear]
No do that again. (*'Don't do that again.'*)

[bumping his arm into a door]
Oh! hurt meself.

Yeah, money Neina. (*'Yeah, the money is Zeina's.'*)

[showing a toy to his uncle]
That's mine, Uncle Ed.

[refusing to accept a messy piece of candy]
No! Yucky.

Me put it back. (*'I'll put it back.'*)

It is interesting to consider some of the things that a child must know in order to utter these and similar sentences. In the first place, the child knows English words: *money, mine, yucky, that's*. Second, since they were used in appropriate contexts, it is clear that the child knows what the words can be applied to. Third, the child knows the part of speech (or word class) for at least some of these words. The phrase *this money* indicates knowledge that *money* belongs to the class of nouns—words that take modifiers like *this, that*, and *the*. Given the contexts in which the utterances occur, it is also apparent that the child is uttering propositions, however incompletely they may be encoded and however much they differ from adult formulations of the same propositions. More noteworthy than the fact that several of these sentences match what an adult grammar would produce is that the child appears to be using language in a systematic fashion. The structure of the utterances is governed by rules of grammar that stay constant from one utterance to the next.

By age five, children's utterances average about 4.6 words per sentence, and their vocabulary is increasing by about twenty words each day. Utterances like *But that isn't yours*, *But that doesn't belong to you*, *Guess who's visiting me*, and *Do you know what I did at school today?* are common. Estimates of the number of basic words known by schoolchildren of age six run about 7,800, counting as single words each of the following sets: *cat, cats, cat's, cats'* and *walk, walks, walked, walking*. If we count derived forms like *dollhouse* as a third word besides *doll* and *house*, then 13,000 words seems to be a reliable figure. Two years later, by age eight, a child's vocabulary has increased to 17,600 words (or 28,300 words including derived forms). This represents an average increase of more than thirteen basic words or twenty-one words and derived forms each day. Of course, a word isn't acquired in its semantic fullness on a single occasion; rather, its full range of meaning is generally acquired in stages over a period of time.

THE RELATIONSHIP BETWEEN LANGUAGE AND THOUGHT

From the moment that children begin to utter their first words, language and thought appear to go hand in hand. That this should be so is not surprising, given that one of the functions of language is to express thought. But the exact nature of the relationship between language and thought is far from straightforward. In this section, we will address the question: To what extent does the language that we speak shape the way we think?

When children are young, the boundary between language and thought is shadowy. When we observe children at play, we find that they often talk to themselves. A five-year-old working on a jigsaw puzzle might be heard saying the following:

> Okay, the blue one. Goes here. Now, this one. This one fits here. The rabbit is here. It goes here. Another blue one, here it goes. And where does this one go?

This sort of verbal activity of children is referred to as *egocentric speech* (or self-directed speech). Children produce it whether or not they have an audience, and they produce it more frequently when the tasks that they face increase in complexity. So, for example, when children are asked to work on difficult jigsaw puzzles, they produce more egocentric speech than when working on easier ones.

Egocentric speech thus resembles adults' thoughts in more than one way:

Egocentric speech and thought are self-directed.

Egocentric speech and thought become more intense during problem-solving tasks.

In fact, many adults revert to egocentric speech when they have to make difficult arithmetic calculations, for example. It is likely that egocentric speech in children and thought in adults are related, although the exact nature of the relationship is not clear. The great Russian psychologist Lev Vygotsky suggested that egocentric speech is a precursor of thought; as children grow older, egocentric speech gradually becomes internalized and turns into thought in the young adult. The process of internalization begins very early, according to Vygotsky, and this accounts for the fact that young children can think, albeit in more limited ways than adults. Whether or not egocentric speech and language are related so directly, there is nevertheless some connection between the development of thought and the development of language in children.

But how tight is the "fit" between language and thought? In particular, to what extent are our thoughts shaped by the way we express ourselves in our native language? Note that Vygotsky's proposal to treat thought as internalized egocentric speech does not necessarily mean that thinking is subservient to what can be expressed in the adult's native language. Once egocentric speech becomes internalized and turns into thought, speech and thought do not necessarily remain similar.

As everyone who has tried to learn a foreign language knows, certain things can be expressed more conveniently in some languages than in others. While one language may have a special word to refer exclusively to a particular object or notion, in another language this object can be described only by using a whole phrase or sentence. For example, in Tuvaluan, a language spoken by the Polynesian inhabitants of a group of islands in the Central Pacific, there are different words to refer to many different types of coconut, which need to be described at great length in English. Here are a few examples:

pii: drinking coconut, with little flesh and much water, at a stage when the water is maximally sweet

mukomuko: young coconut with some flesh in it, before it has become too solid

uto: coconut at the stage when its husk can be chewed on and its water is still sweet

motomoto: same as *mukomuko*, but with firmer flesh

niu: coconut ripe enough for its flesh to be grated

uttanu: mature coconut whose sprout has already pierced through the husk and whose water has turned into an edible spongious solid kernel

Similarly, French speakers often note that English has more words for sounds (*crash, splash, roar*) than French has. The question then arises: Do these differences between languages mean that people from different cultures think differently or perceive the world differently?

In the first part of the century, three great scholars—Franz Boas (known as the "father of American anthropology"), Edward Sapir, and Benjamin Whorf—advanced a theory that the way people think is determined by the structure of their native language. Their proposal is usually referred to as the *Sapir-Whorf hypothesis* (or the theory of linguistic determinism or linguistic relativity). Marveling at the intricacies of the structure of American Indian languages (which the average Euro-American had previously considered "primitive" and "inferior"), Boas, Sapir, and Whorf maintained that we are mental prisoners of the structure of the language that we speak natively.

For example, Whorf noticed that in the Hopi language tense (such as past and present) is not a grammatical category as it is in English. Instead, every Hopi statement has to be marked as to whether it is a statement of unchangeable truth (*Water is fluid*), the report of an event that the speaker has witnessed (*I arrived yesterday*), or a hypothesis (*I assume that he'll be here tomorrow*). These categories are marked in the same way that tense is marked in English verbs (*talk* versus *talked*). Whorf maintained that the difference between the structure of Hopi and the structure of English explains certain differences in the cultural character of Hopi society and of Euro-American society. The Hopi, according to Whorf, are typically suspicious of hypotheses and conjectures and are very sensitive to the source of information. Euro-Americans, in contrast, pay much more attention to the passing of time than the Hopi do. According to the Sapir-Whorf hypothesis, these differences in the thought patterns of members of the two cultures are a direct consequence of the grammatical structures of Hopi and English.

While the Sapir-Whorf hypothesis is an attractive one, there are some problems with it. First of all, if thought were determined by language, it would be difficult to imagine how people from different cultural backgrounds could communicate at all. Second, many people in the world are bilingual or multilingual from a very early age. Would we want to say that these people have different "thought compartments" in their brains, each one associated with a different language? Obviously not. Third, the fact that a particular category does not exist in a language does not mean that native speakers of that language cannot understand (and, hence, think about) the category: the grammatical system marking the source of information in Hopi can be explained in English (as demonstrated in the previous paragraph) even though it does not exist in English grammar. Finally, the lexicons and grammars of all languages share many universal patterns, even though at first glance the languages of the world differ so strikingly from one another. Sapir and Whorf overestimated the variability in the structure of languages.

Today, few scholars take the Sapir-Whorf hypothesis literally. Many linguists take the position that language may have some influence on thought but thought may also influence the structure of language. So the interaction between thought and language is a two-way street rather than an absolute cause-and-effect relationship. Language and thought do appear to be closely connected in various ways. Their interaction is a complex one about which we still have much to learn.

MODES OF LINGUISTIC COMMUNICATION

We have at our disposal several different ways of communicating. We can, for example, communicate our feelings and moods with gestures, as dancers do. We can also draw sequences of figures, as on a cryptic treasure map, or we can convey moods and emotions through painting or music. These types of artistic communication do not rely on language; they belong instead to the realm of nonlinguistic communication, and as such they lie outside the scope of this book.

In linguistic communication, in contrast, language is the primary vehicle through which meaning is conveyed. There are three basic **modes** of linguistic communication: oral communication, which relies on the use of speech and hearing organs; writing, a visual representation that was invented about five thousand years ago; and signing, another visual representation, which many hearing- and speech-impaired people (and their friends) rely on for communication. In this section we briefly review some of the characteristics of these three modes of linguistic communication.

Speaking

To observe a group of human beings engaged in a conversation is to witness several kinds of communication. There is first of all the voice, with all its complexity and richness of intonation and other modulation. There is also a tapestry of gestures, including hand waving of various sorts, body stance, and facial movements. These combine to communicate intentions—not only the seemingly obvious ones encoded in utterances themselves but also more subtle ones like the participants' wish to speak or to let someone else speak.

The primary vehicle of linguistic communication is the voice, and speech is the primary *mode* of human language. That this is so is hardly surprising, for speech has several advantages over other potential vehicles of human communication. It is extremely valuable to have a vehicle whose use interferes minimally with other life-sustaining activities. Because speech does not need to be seen, it can do its work as effectively in darkness as in light, around corners, and in other visually inaccessible spots. Although in nature it cannot span time, its physical reach is much greater than arm's length. Unlike signing, speech leaves the eyes and the hands free for other work. We can both talk and listen while looking at things besides our interlocutors. In the development of speech in the human species, when hands and eyes were occupied in hunting, fishing, and food gathering—the manual activities of work and play—speech was free to do other work: to report, point, ask for and give directions, explain, promise, bargain, warn, flirt, threaten, and deceive. Eating is one thing that people can't do well while talking, but even eating doesn't preclude speech—as the lunchtime din in any college cafeteria will demonstrate.

Speaking has still other advantages. For one thing, the human voice is a complex vehicle, with many channels. It has variable volume, pitch, stress, and speed: it is capable of wide-ranging modulation. Take a simple sentence like *Isn't that sad?* and consider the various utterances created by different voice modulations. With different modulations, we can express irony—suggesting that it isn't sad at all. Or sarcasm. Or humor. We can make an assertion, ask a question, poke fun, be teasing, or express sympathy in a relatively straightforward way. This variation in expressive power through modulations of the voice occurs at the level of language that is called *phonology*.

We also have other linguistic channels, including vocabulary and sentence structure, which subsequent chapters will cover in detail. Speech is not a single-band channel. It has intonation and stress, as well as the more familiar grammatical levels. Besides a set of sounds, speech takes advantage of the organization of those sounds—of their sequencing into words and sentences. Like writing, speech can take advantage of word choice and word order. In many ways, speech is even more versatile than writing. Intonation, stress, and volume are privileges of the spoken mode, but not of the written.

Writing

Long before the invention of writing, people had been painting stories on cave walls or exploiting other kinds of visual symbols to record events and other matters. Such *pictograms* were independent of language—a kind of cartoon world, in which anyone with knowledge of the lives of people but without specifically linguistic knowledge could come along and reconstruct the depicted story or event. Pictograms are language independent. When shown to adult speakers of different languages, the depicted stories can be told in Japanese, Arabic, English, Swahili, Indonesian, or any other language. Pictograms tell a story or provide information that can be understood in any language: they are a direct, nonlinguistic symbolization, like a silent film or the road signs used internationally to indicate a curved roadway ahead or the availability of food and lodging.

If we decide to associate such drawings not with the objects they represent but with the *words* that refer to the objects they represent, then we have a more sophisticated system. The system of representation becomes *linguistic* communication because it relies on language for communication. There is ample evidence that writing was invented about five thousand years ago by some ingenious souls who chanced upon an occasion or a need to use pictograms to represent spoken words instead of the objects that they customarily represented. For example, while it is very difficult to express with pictograms a message containing reference to abstract objects (hunger or danger, for instance), the task becomes possible if the graphic symbols represent words. Once someone recognized—at least implicitly—that a written symbol could serve to represent a linguistic symbol, the first step in the development of writing had been taken. People came to realize that the possibilities of the new system of linguistic communication were immense.

It should be clear that speech and writing are related in different ways to the world they symbolize. Speech, which preceded writing by a very long time in human history, is a symbolic system that represents entities in the real world—things like sun, moon, fish, grain, woman, and man. Writing, on the other hand, does not directly represent this same world. A written sentence like *John cooked dinner* is a secondary symbolization; the written symbols represent the spoken words, not the entities themselves. One way to picture the relationship between speech, writing, and the "real" world is shown in this diagram:

writing $\longrightarrow$ speech $\longrightarrow$ "real" world

Writing in its various types and the relationship of writing to speaking will be investigated in greater depth in Chapter 11.

Signing

The third mode of linguistic communication is *signing*, the exclusive use of gestures to communicate messages. Of course, when we speak, we use gestures and facial expressions to convey some of what we mean. But these gestures differ from signing because they serve merely to support oral communication. They could not be used by themselves for communication. Signing, in contrast, can be used as the sole means of conveying messages.

Two kinds of signing are possible. One consists of spelling out words by "drawing" with the hands the shape of written symbols (such as letters) that are used in writing to represent sounds. Like writing itself, this method depends on the prior existence of a spoken language; it also requires a form of written representation. Thus, any signing system that relies on the modeling of letters (such as the one used by the deaf and blind Helen Keller) is two steps removed from the linguistic system that hearing and seeing children acquire.

The other kind of signing is independent of the spoken word and could be used cross-linguistically provided users understood the code. In this type of signing, particular gestures stand for particular words. The fact that these words may be pronounced differently from one language to another is not important, because the gesture does not make any reference to the sound of the word in any language. Such a system was traditionally in use among certain American Indian nations in the western United States and among certain Australian Aborigine nations. It is also what underlies certain signing systems in use today for the hearing impaired.

Like writing, signing is a secondary symbolic system in which signed symbols represent words, which in turn are symbols for objects, concepts, and feelings. Signing differs from writing in that its users must be in full sight of one another for it to function successfully. In this sense, signing is more similar to speaking than to writing.

Speaking, Writing, Signing: Modes of Linguistic Communication

Speaking, writing, and signing are the three primary modes of linguistic communication, each with its own advantages and limitations. For example, speech is the only mode of linguistic communication that is possible when visibility is impaired. It is also the only mode in which the communicator's hands and eyes are left free to do other things. People signing to one another must be in view of one another and, in effect, facing one another. Speech has limitations, too, some of which are shared by signing. Both speech and signing have an evanescent character and vanish upon being uttered. Neither spoken nor signed utterances can be retrieved after they have been uttered, unless they were tape-recorded or filmed. Writing, on the other hand, has evolved to meet other needs. It can be preserved, sometimes for millennia, as with the words of Homer, Plato, Aristotle, and Jesus—all of whom were public speakers whose words were written down by others. Writing has another advantage over speech and signing: it can transcend space. One can send a written message anywhere on earth. With technology, of course, this advantage of writing over speaking and signing is decreasing.

In this book we will focus primarily on language as it is represented in spoken and written communication. It is important to remember that writing is a secondary mode of linguistic communication and that speaking is the primary mode.

SUMMARY

Language is, first of all, a system of grammatical rules that govern its structural organization in sentences. Equally important is the role of language as a tool that we use to communicate with each other. Structure and use—the two facets of language—go hand in hand and correspond to the dual function of language: as an integral component of our mental functions and as a tool in the regulation of social interaction.

Human language is primarily a system of arbitrary symbols, rather than a system of nonarbitrary signs of meaning. This fact distinguishes human language from the communicative systems that animals use in their natural environment, which are more akin to a system of signs. While humans are the only species that has evolved the innate ability to use language, it is unclear to what extent animals (chimpanzees in particular) are able to learn human language in experimental settings. Some experiments have demonstrated that chimps are capable of learning and using sophisticated systems of symbols, while other experiments have concluded that language is the exclusive property of humankind.

Children do not acquire their native language through conscious instruction by adults or through mere imitation of what they hear adults say. While a child must receive some linguistic input in order to acquire language, input is not the sole factor that accounts for the development of the ability to produce and understand language. Rather, children are born with the mental capacity to acquire language. The process of acquisition consists of assembling the rules of grammar into *grammatical competence* and of language use into *communicative competence*. Three stages of the process can be identified, distinguished by the amount of information the child is able to package into each utterance.

Language as a mental process is closely linked to thought, as witnessed by the fact that children's egocentric speech resembles the thought processes of adults. The exact nature of the relationship between language and thought is still largely unclear. In adults, the structure of language and the structure of thought appear to influence each other, but the particular language we speak does not determine our thought processes.

Communication that involves language can take place in any of three modes: speaking, writing, or signing. Of these modes of linguistic communication, speaking is auditory and primary; writing and signing are visual and secondary.

EXERCISES

1. Most linguists would claim that animal languages are fundamentally different from human languages. In what ways are animal communication and human language different? In what ways can they be said to be similar or the same?

2. In what sense are computer "languages" like natural languages? Is there any similarity in the way that computer languages are learned and natural human languages are acquired? What about computer languages and foreign languages? Are there similarities in the ways that computer languages and human languages evolve?

3. Below is a list of characteristics that describe linguistic communication through speaking, writing, and signing. Discuss which of these characteristics apply to the three modes of linguistic communication, and provide examples to illustrate your claim. Pay particular attention to the different types of spoken, written, and signed communication; some of these characteristics might apply to some but not others. Also pay attention to the impact that modern communication technology has had on these characteristics.

   (a) A linguistic message is ephemeral—that is, it cannot be made to endure.
   (b) A linguistic message can be revised once it has been produced.
   (c) A linguistic message has the potential of reaching large audiences.
   (d) A linguistic message can be transmitted over great distances.
   (e) A linguistic message can rely on the context in which it is produced; the producer can refer to the time and place in which the message is produced without fearing misunderstanding.
   (f) A linguistic message relies on the senses of hearing, touching, and seeing.
   (g) The ability to produce linguistic messages is innate; it does not have to be learned consciously.
   (h) A linguistic message must be planned carefully before it is produced.
   (i) The production of a linguistic message can be accomplished simultaneously with another activity.

4. In this chapter we said that writing and gesture are visual modes of linguistic communication. What is the relationship between writing and Braille (the writing system used for the blind)? Is Braille a mode of linguistic communication? How many modes of linguistic communication are there?

5. Ask some acquaintances what they understand by the following terms: *sign, symbol, language, grammar, baby talk, sign language, gesture.* How similar are the notions of your friends to our discussion in this chapter? Do your friends tend to equate the single mode of writing with all forms of language?

6. List some of the circumstances in which each mode of linguistic communication would be preferred over the others. When there is a choice between linguistic modes, as in telephoning a faraway friend or sending a letter, what are the advantages and disadvantages of each mode?

SUGGESTIONS FOR FURTHER READING

Many of the topics covered in this chapter are treated clearly and concisely in Clark and Clark (1977), Ellis and Beattie (1986), and Slobin (1979). For sources on particular aspects of language as a system of rules and as a communicative tool, consult the "Suggestions for Further Reading" in subsequent chapters.

Several of the topics covered in this chapter will not be discussed in much detail anywhere in the book. For a discussion of the relationship between signs and symbols, consult Part I of de Saussure (1959) (originally published early in this century, it is considered to be the first book on modern linguistics). The papers in Haiman (1985) all touch on the still little understood iconic elements in syntax and intonation.

Sources on animal communication abound, ranging from the very popular to the very technical. A good survey of research can be found in Premack (1985), in which research on chimp Sarah is discussed in detail. Von Frisch (1967) reports the original findings on the "language" of bees. Research on Washoe's language-acquisition feats is compared to the language acquisition of children in Gardner and Gardner (1971; 1974; 1978). Vicki's attempts to speak are described in Hayes and Hayes (1952). Terrace (1979) is an account of the Nim Chimpsky project. Relevant to the study of animal language are Lieberman (1975; 1984), which present some fascinating hypotheses on how the ability to speak evolved in humans; in the 1984 work, Chapter 10 (entitled "Apes and Children") provides a good summary of the research on the language of chimpanzees.

Child language acquisition is treated at great length in Part 4 of Clark and Clark (1977), in Elliot (1981), in Chapter 4 of Slobin (1979), and in de Villiers and de Villiers (1978). For a more concise and less technical version of the latter, see de Villiers and de Villiers (1979). Miller (1977) is another concise overview of research on the topic. The quotation from Bloomfield about language acquisition is taken from his 1933 book entitled *Language*. Curtiss (1977) is a thorough account of the case of Genie, the child who received virtually no childhood language input. On the role of input in language acquisition, see Ferguson and Snow (1977) and Ochs and Schieffelin (1986). Berko-Gleason (1980) reports her observations of adults teaching children politeness rules while trick-or-treating, an example of consciously prescriptive input. The two volumes edited by Slobin (1986) contain a wealth of information on children acquiring language in different cultures of the world. Peters (1983) investigates the strategies that children use to analyze linguistic input.

Egocentric speech was originally discussed by Swiss psychologist Jean Piaget and Russian psychologist Lev Vygotsky; English translations of their accounts of egocentric speech can be found in Piaget (1955) and Vygotsky (1978). Sapir (1921) and Whorf (1956) laid the foundations of the Sapir-Whorf hypothesis, which is nicely summarized in Chapter 3 of Cole and Scribner (1974) and in Chapter 4 of Sampson (1980).

Finally, for sources on speaking and writing, refer to Chapters 10 and 11 of this book. For additional information on American Sign Language and other sign languages, see Stokoe (1970), and for a survey of sign languages among American Indians and Australian Aborigines, see Umiker-Sebeok and Sebeok (1978).

REFERENCES

Berko-Gleason, Jean. 1980. "The Acquisition of Social Speech: Routines and Politeness Formulas," in Howard Giles, W. Peter Robinson, and Philip M. Smith (eds.), *Language: Social Psychological Perspectives* (New York: Academic Press), pp. 159–167.

Bloomfield, Leonard. 1933. *Language* (New York: Holt, Rinehart and Winston; reprinted, Chicago: University of Chicago Press, 1984).

Clark, Herbert, and Eve Clark. 1977. *Psychology and Language: An Introduction to Psycholinguistics* (New York: Harcourt Brace Jovanovich).

Cole, Michael, and Sylvia Scribner. 1974. *Culture and Thought: A Psychological Perspective* (New York: John Wiley).

Curtiss, Susan. 1977. *Genie: A Psycholinguistic Study of a Modern-day "Wild Child"* (New York: Academic Press).

De Saussure, Ferdinand. 1959. *Course in General Linguistics*, translated from the 1917 French edition by Wade Baskin (New York: Philosophic Library).

De Villiers, Jill G., and Peter A. de Villiers. 1978. *Language Acquisition* (Cambridge: Harvard University Press).

De Villiers, Peter A., and Jill G. de Villiers. 1979. *Early Language* (Cambridge: Harvard University Press).

Elliot, Alison J. 1981. *Child Language* (Cambridge: Cambridge University Press).

Ellis, Andrew, and Geoffrey Beattie. 1986. *The Psychology of Language and Communication* (New York: Guilford Press).

Ferguson, Charles A., and Catherine Snow (eds.). 1977. *Talking to Children: Language Input and Acquisition* (Cambridge: Cambridge University Press).

Gardner, Beatrice T., and R. Allan Gardner. 1971. "Two-Way Communication with an Infant Chimpanzee," in A. M. Schrier and F. Stollnitz (eds.), *Behavior of Non-human Primates*, vol. 4 (New York: Academic Press), pp. 118–184.

———. 1974. "Comparing the Early Utterances of Child and Chimpanzee," in Anne D. Pick (ed.), *Minnesota Symposia on Child Language* (Minneapolis: University of Minnesota Press), vol. 8, pp. 3–23.

Gardner, R. Allan, and Beatrice T. Gardner. 1978. "Comparative Psychology and Language Acquisition," *Annals of the New York Academy of Science*, vol. 309, pp. 37–76.

Haiman, John (ed.). 1985. *Iconicity in Syntax* (Amsterdam: John Benjamins).

Hayes, Keith, and Catherine Hayes. 1952. "Imitation in a Home-Raised Chimpanzee," *Journal of Comparative and Physiological Psychology*, vol. 45, pp. 450–459.

Lieberman, Philip. 1975. *On the Origins of Language: An Introduction to the Evolution of Human Speech* (New York: Macmillan).

———. 1984. *The Biology and Evolution of Language* (Cambridge: Harvard University Press).

Miller, George A. 1977. *Spontaneous Apprentices: Children and Language* (New York: Seabury Press).

Ochs, Elinor, and Bambi Schieffelin. 1986. "Language Acquisition and Socialization: Three Developmental Stories and Their Implications," in Richard A. Shweder and

Robert A. LeVine (eds.), *Culture Theory: Essays on Mind, Self, and Emotion* (Cambridge: Cambridge University Press), pp. 276–320.

Peters, Ann M. 1983. *The Units of Language Acquisition* (Cambridge: Cambridge University Press).

Piaget, Jean. 1955. *The Language and Thought of the Child*, translated from the 1926 French edition by M. Gabain (New York: Meridian).

Premack, David. 1985. *Gavagai! On the Future History of the Animal Language Controversy* (Cambridge: MIT Press).

Sampson, Geoffrey. 1980. *Schools of Linguistics* (Stanford: Stanford University Press).

Sapir, Edward. 1921. *Language: An Introduction to the Study of Speech* (New York: Harcourt, Brace & World).

Slobin, Dan I. 1979. *Psycholinguistics*, 2nd ed. (Glenview, Ill.: Scott Foresman).

Stokoe, William C., Jr. 1970. *Semiotics and Human Sign Languages* (The Hague: Mouton).

Terrace, Herbert S. 1979. *Nim: A Chimpanzee Who Learned Sign Language* (New York: Knopf).

Umiker-Sebeok, Jean D., and Thomas A. Sebeok (eds.). 1978. *Aboriginal Sign Languages of the Americas and Australia*, 2 vols. (New York: Plenum Press).

Von Frisch, Karl. 1967. *The Dance Language and Orientation of Bees*, translated from the German edition by Leigh E. Chadwick (Cambridge: Harvard University Press).

Vygotsky, Lev S. 1978. *Mind in Society: The Development of Higher Psychological Processes*, ed. Michael Cole et al. (Cambridge: Harvard University Press).

Whorf, Benjamin L. 1956. *Language, Thought, and Reality: Selected Writings of Benjamin L. Whorf*, ed. John B. Carroll (Cambridge: MIT Press).

PART

I

LANGUAGE STRUCTURE

PHONETICS: THE SOUNDS OF LANGUAGE

2

SOUNDS AND SPELLINGS

Readers of English are accustomed to seeing language written down as a series of words set off by spaces, with each word consisting of a sequence of separate letters also separated by spaces. Thus we recognize that words exist as separate entities made up of a relatively small number of discrete sounds. The words *banana* and *cement*, for example, are readily judged by English speakers to have six sounds each, while *adult* has five, *post* four, and *set* three. Somewhat less obvious perhaps is the number of sounds that occur in the words *speakers, series, letters*, and *sequence*; these words do not have an exact correspondence between numbers of sounds and numbers of letters. This lack of correspondence is common in English. *Cough*, for instance, has three sounds, though it is spelled with five letters; *thorough* has only four sounds despite its eight letters. *Through* with seven letters and *thru* with four are alternative spellings for a word with three sounds.

Because of the close association between writing and speaking in the minds of most literate people, it is important to stress that in this chapter we are interested in the *sounds* of spoken language (particularly the English language), not in the letters of the alphabet that are used to represent those sounds. It is for this reason that we begin with a discussion of English spelling, hoping to clarify the differences between the sound system of a language and its representation in the ordinary writing system.

Same Spelling, Different Pronunciations

Observe the variety of pronunciations represented by the same letter or series of letters in different words. Consider the pronunciations of the following words, all of which are represented in part by the letters *ough*:

cough	"koff"
tough	"tuff"
bough	"bow"
through	"thru"
though	"tho"
thoroughfare	"thurafare"

Though the precise sounds of the words *cough, tough, bough, through, though*, and *thoroughfare* may vary somewhat among English speakers, still the lesson of the distant relationship between sounds and letters will not be lost on any of them. Orthographic *ough* represents at least six different sounds in English, as indicated in Figure 2-1.

Same Pronunciation, Different Spellings

Other sets of English words are pronounced alike but spelled differently, as school children learn when they are taught sets of homonyms like *led/lead, bear/bare*, and *to/two/too*.

Consider the set of words in Figure 2-2, where nine different spellings represent a single sound, as in the word *see*. Still other spellings for the sound of the word *see* could be cited, including some relatively common ones like *cease, seize*, and *siege* and some relatively rare ones like *situ* and *cee* (the name of the letter). Notice that the single letter *x*, as in *sexy*, actually represents the two sounds [k] and [s]; thus the phenomenon of identical pronunciations represented by different spellings applies not only to groups of letters but to single letters as well.

If you compare the sound and spelling of the words *woman* and *women*, you will note that the difference in the written vowels *a* and *e* does *not*

FIGURE 2-1
Same Spelling, Different Sounds

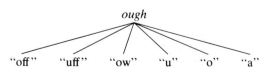

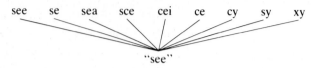

FIGURE 2-2
Different Spellings, Same Sound

represent a difference in pronunciation: the second syllables of these words are pronounced alike. On the other hand, the vowel letter that does not change (the *o*) represents two different sounds (the vowel sound of *wood* in *woman* and of *win* in *women*). The pair *Satan* and *satin* illustrates the same point: the constant written vowel (*a*) represents different sounds, while the varying written vowels (*a* and *i*) represent the same vowel sound.

Playwright George Bernard Shaw, a keen advocate of spelling reform, pointed up the problems in establishing correspondences between sounds and spelling in English when he alleged that *ghoti* could be pronounced "fish": the *gh* as in *cough*, the *o* as in *women*, and the *ti* as in *nation* (see exercise 8). Despite the efforts of Shaw and other reformers, English spelling has remained relatively fixed. One can see some very modest success at simplification in such isolated spellings as *thru, nite*, and *foto*—though not even these few examples have been widely adopted to replace the more traditional *through, night*, and *photo*.

The Whys and Wherefores of Sound/Spelling Discrepancies   There are five principal reasons for the discrepancy between the written representations of many English words and their actual pronunciation:

1. English orthography had several diverse origins with different spelling conventions:

(a)   The system that had evolved in Wessex before the Norman Invasion of 1066 gave us such spellings as *ee* for the sound in words like *deed* and *seen*.

(b)   The system that was overlaid on the Old English system by the Normans, with their French orthographic customs, gave us such spellings as *queen* (for the earlier *cween*) and *thief* (for earlier *theef*).

(c)   A Dutch influence from Caxton, the first English printer, who was born in England but lived in Holland for thirty years, gave us such spellings as *ghost* (which replaced *gost*) and *ghastly* (which replaced *gastlic*).

(d)   During the Renaissance, an attempt to reform spelling along etymological (that is, historically earlier) lines gave us *debt* for earlier *det* or *dette* and *salmon* for earlier *samon*.

2. A spelling system established several hundred years ago is still used for a language that continues to change and develop its spoken form. Thus the initial *k* in *knock, knot, know, knee,* and certain other words was once pronounced, as was the *gh* in *knight* and *thought*, among others. As to vowels, change in progress when the system was developing and continuing change in pronunciation have led to such matched spellings for mismatched pronunciations as *beat/great* and *food/foot*.

3. English is spoken differently in different countries throughout the world (and in different regions within a single country), despite a relatively uniform standard for the written orthography. Though this orthographic uniformity certainly facilitates international communication, it also increases the disparity between the way English is written and spoken in any given place.

4. Words (and their meaningful subparts) alter their pronunciation depending on the adjacent sounds and stress patterns. For example, in *electric* the second *c* represents the sound [k] as in *kiss*, but in *electricity* it represents the sound [s] as in *silly*. Compare also the pronunciation of *i* in *senile* (pronounced like the *i* of *I'll*) with its pronunciation in *senility* (in which it has the *i* of *ill*).

5. Spoken forms differ from one set of circumstances to another—for example, in formal and informal situations. While some degree of such variation is incorporated into the written system (*do not/don't*; *it was/'twas*), there is relatively little tolerance for such spelling variation as *gonna* ('going to'), *wanna* ('want to'), *gotcha* ('got you'), and *jeat yet?* ('did you eat yet?'). Such variable spelling of variable speech would force readers to determine the pronunciation of the represented speech before arriving at meaning, instead of reading directly for meaning, as adult readers normally do, without the necessity of silent pronunciation.

Some Advantages of Fixed Spellings While the disadvantages of an irregular set of sound/spelling correspondences are obvious, there are also certain advantages. Consider Chinese, in which many written characters have no reference to sounds but instead symbolize meanings directly—much as numerals such as "7" and "3" and miscellaneous other symbols like "+" and "%" do for European languages. With such characters, groups of people whose spoken languages are so dissimilar that mutual intelligibility is difficult can nevertheless communicate well in writing, as is the case between speakers of Cantonese and Mandarin Chinese. Thus the symbol "7" has a uniform meaning across the various European languages, even though the word for the concept for which it stands is pronounced and spelled differently in different speech communities: *seven* in English, *sept* in French, *sette* in Italian, *sieben* in German, and so on. Similarly, then, the fact that English orthography is somewhat removed from pronunciation is not altogether unfavorable for a language that has such exceptionally varied dialects, from New Zealand to Jamaica to India—to say nothing of pronunciations in hundreds of places where it is used in official capacities alongside indigenous native tongues or as a second language for scientific and other international enterprises. Despite various pronunciations around the globe, in the English language a uniform written symbol is associated with a single meaning. Moreover, in a language with different pronunciations for the same element of meaning, stable spellings can contribute to reading comprehensibility—as in *musical/ musician*, *electrical/electricity*, and even *judges/cats*.

The Independence of Script and Speech   The untidy relationship between sound and spelling is not limited to English; it is found in other languages (including French) whose orthographic systems are centuries old but whose spoken languages continuously renew themselves in the everyday usage of speakers. It is therefore important to distinguish between the sounds of a language and the way those sounds are customarily represented in the orthography.

To underscore the independence of sounds and orthographies, bear in mind that some languages are represented by two different writing systems. For instance, Hindi-Urdu is written by Hindus living in India in Devanāgarī, an Indic script that derives from Sanskrit. The same language is written with Arabic script by Moslems living in Pakistan and parts of India. Sometimes, too, people adopt a different orthography from one previously used. In the early part of this century, the government of Turkey switched from Arabic script to the Roman alphabet to represent Turkish.

Sometimes languages have different scripts for different purposes. Imagine how an international telegram is sent in a language that uses a script other than the Roman alphabet—in Japanese, Korean, Greek, Russian, Persian, Thai, or Arabic, for example. Rather than using their customary orthographies, speakers of these languages use the Roman alphabet for sending telegrams internationally. Even within a country, an alternative to the customary orthography may be needed: In China, a numeric system is used for sending telegrams; each character has a four-digit numeral assigned to it, and it is these numerals that are sent telegraphically and then "translated" back into Chinese characters. Sometimes a language uses more than one orthography for different aspects. Japanese, for example, has three different kinds of orthography: *kanji*, based on the Chinese character system, in which a symbol represents a word independent of its pronunciation; and two syllabaries, orthographic systems in which each symbol represents a syllable. Thus, throughout the world, wherever languages are written down, there are disparities between sounds as they are spoken and sounds as they are represented in writing.

In Chapter 11 we will return to the question of the relationship between sound and orthographic representation. Now, however, the focus of our attention is on the sounds of spoken language and not the letters of the alphabet. The rest of this chapter examines the human vocal apparatus and the sounds it can produce; Chapter 3 will examine the nature of the sound systems of human language.

PHONETICS

Phonetics, the study of the sounds made in the production of human languages, has three principal branches. *Articulatory phonetics* focuses on the human vocal apparatus and describes sounds in terms of their articulation in the vocal tract; it has been central to the discipline of linguistics. *Acoustic phonetics* uses the tools of physics to study the nature of sound waves produced in human language; it is playing an increasingly larger role in linguistics as attempts are made to use machines for interpreting speech patterns in voice identification and automatic voice-initiated mechanical operations. The third branch of phonetics studies the perception of sounds by the brain through the human ear; *auditory phonetics*, as this branch is called, has played only a minor role in linguistics to date, but it too can be expected to play a larger role in the future. Our discussion will be limited almost exclusively to *articulatory phonetics*—to the nature of human sounds as produced by the vocal apparatus.

Phonetic Alphabets

In discussing the sounds of human language from the point of view of their articulation, phoneticians have evolved descriptive techniques to allow comparison across languages and to avoid the difficulties inherent in describing sounds in terms of standard orthographic practices. We have seen that it is not possible to use customary orthographic representations to analyze sound structure: even within one language, some sounds correspond to more than one letter while some letters correspond to more than one sound. And, of course, a single letter can be used to represent different sounds in different languages. As a result, we need a completely separate system to represent the actual sounds of human languages.

In scientific discussion, the requisite characteristics of symbols to represent sounds are clarity and consistency. The best tool is a phonetic alphabet, and the one most widely used is the International Phonetic Alphabet (IPA). The IPA is an attempt to provide a unique written representation of each sound in the languages of the world independent of the orthographies of particular languages. Most dictionaries do not use the IPA, preferring systems of their own devising. Linguists, too, mix and match from different systems to suit their specific purposes. In keeping with customary practice in American books, we shall use a modified version of the IPA, substituting more traditional and more transparent orthographic symbols (sometimes with diacritics such as ˇ) for a few of the IPA symbols.

A list of the symbols used to represent the consonant sounds of English is given in Table 2-1. The table shows the phonetic symbol for each sound, alongside representative words that have the relevant parts emphasized. In the few instances in which our symbols differ from those of the IPA, the IPA symbol is shown in parentheses. The words illustrate word-initial, word-medial, and word-final occurrences of the sounds.

TABLE 2-1

English Consonants Arranged by Position in Word
(Alternative phonetic symbols in parentheses)

Phonetic Symbol	Initial	Medial	Final
p	pill	caper	tap
b	bill	labor	tab
t	till	petunia	bat
d	dill	seduce	pad
k	kill	sicker	lick
g	gill	dagger	bag
f	fill	beefy	chief
v	villa	saving	grave
θ	thin	author	breath
ð	then	leather	breathe
s	silly	mason	kiss
z	zebra	deposit	bruise
š (ʃ)	shell	rashes	rush
ž (ʒ)	———	measure	rouge
č (tʃ)	chill	kitchen	pitch
ǰ (dʒ)	jelly	bludgeon	fudge
m	mill	dummy	broom
n	nil	sunny	spoon
ŋ	———	singer	sing
h	hill	ahoy	———
y (j)	yes	beyond	toy
r	rent	berry	deer
l	lily	silly	mill
w	will	away	cow

The Vocal Tract

Human beings have no organs that are used only for speech. The organs that we use for producing speech sounds have evolved principally to serve the life-sustaining processes of breathing and eating. Speech is a secondary function of the human "vocal apparatus," and in that sense it is sometimes said to be parasitic on the organs used for these other functions.

Each consonant sound is produced in a different way by our vocal apparatus. Each consonant sounds different from every other consonant because of some unique combination of features in the way that we shape our mouth and tongue and move parts of the vocal apparatus when we make that consonant sound. Figure 2-3 is a simplified drawing of the vocal tract. In this

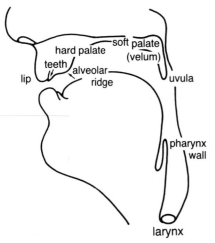 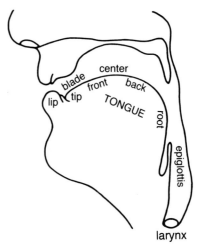

Upper surface of vocal tract   Lower surface of vocal tract

FIGURE 2-3
The Vocal Tract

SOURCE: Adapted from Ladefoged 1982

section we will look at the different parts of the human vocal tract and show how these parts work together to produce different sounds.

How are speech sounds made? First, air coming from the lungs passes through the vocal tract, which shapes it into different vowel and consonant sounds. The air then exits the vocal tract through the mouth or nose or both. The processes that the vocal tract uses in creating a multitude of sounds are very similar to those of wind instruments and organ pipes, which produce different musical sounds by varying the shape, size, and acoustic character of the cavities through which air passes.

No language takes advantage of all the possibilities for forming different sounds, and there are striking differences in the sounds that occur in different languages. For example, Japanese and Thai lack the *v* sound of the English *vat*, and Japanese lacks the *f* sound of *fat*. Thai lacks the sounds represented by *sh* as in *shine, g* as in *rouge, s* as in *pleasure, j* (and *dg*) as in *judge*, and *z* as in *zebra*. French, Japanese, and Thai lack both of the (quite different) *th* sounds in *either* and *ether*. Just as these languages lack sounds that English has, many languages possess sounds that English does not have. Most English speakers are aware that English lacks the rolled *r* that exists in Spanish and Italian and that Arabic has several sounds that do not occur in English. We recognize that German has a sound at the end of words like *Bach* 'stream' and *hoch* 'high' that does not occur among the inventory of English sounds. Arabic has a sound similar to the German *ch* in *Bach*, except that in Arabic it can occur word initially. A similar but different sound occurring finally in the German word *ich* does occur (for those dialects of English that pronounce the *h*) in the initial sound of *human* and *huge*. Still, it can be tough for English speakers learning German to pronounce the sound in a word like *ich* because in English it doesn't occur word finally as in German.

Describing Sounds

As we explore the inventory of sounds, produce with your vocal tract the sounds that are described. Pronounce the sounds aloud, noting the shape of your mouth and the position of your tongue as each sound is produced. Such first-hand experience will familiarize you with the reference points of phonetics and make the discussion easier to follow.

In our early discussion, we will continue to use square brackets to enclose the symbols representing sounds. Thus [t] will symbolize the initial sound of *tickle*, the initial and final sounds in *tot*, and the final sound of *bet* and *boat*; [d] will symbolize the initial and final sounds in *did*; [z] will symbolize the initial sound in *zebra*, the medial consonant in *busy*, and the final sound of *buzz*.

Different speech sounds can be identified in terms of their articulatory properties—that is, by *where* (in the mouth) and *how* they are produced. Some of the sounds that we have mentioned so far would be described as follows:

[f]	voiceless	labio-dental	fricative
[v]	voiced	labio-dental	fricative
[t]	voiceless	alveolar	stop
[d]	voiced	alveolar	stop
[z]	voiced	alveolar	fricative

Notice that each description includes reference to three features of articulatory phonetics—**voicing** (voiced or voiceless); **place of articulation** (for example, labio-dental or alveolar); and **manner of articulation** (such as fricative or stop). This kind of descriptive analysis can be extended to all the consonants of any language.

Voicing   Begin by distinguishing between [s] (as in *bus* or *sip*) and [z] (as in *buzz* or *zip*). When you pronounce a long, continuous [zzzzz] and alternate it with a long, continuous [sssss], you will notice that the position of your lips and the position of your tongue within your mouth remain the same for [s] and [z], even though these sounds are noticeably different.[1] Some English

---

[1] You can perceive the difference between voiced and voiceless consonants by alternating between the pronunciations of [f] and [v] or [s] and [z] while holding your hands clapped over your ears. You may also find it helpful to see whether you can tell from pronouncing the words *tall, tilt, talent, bid, dead*, and *dilemma* whether [t] or [d] is voiced; take care not to confuse the voicing that is part of the pronunciation of the vowels that follow the consonants in question—in English, vowels are always voiced. Check your conclusions against Table 2-7.

words (like *peace* and *peas, bus* and *buzz, sip* and *zip, sane* and *Zane*) are distinguished solely on the basis of the contrast between [s] and [z]. If you touch your **larynx** (Adam's apple) while alternately saying [zzzzz sssss zzzzz], you will *feel* the difference between [s] and [z]. The vibration that you feel from your larynx when you utter [zzzzz] but not [sssss] is called *voicing*; it is the result of air being forced through a narrow aperture (called the **glottis**) between two folds of muscle (the vocal cords) in the larynx, much like the leaf with a slit in it that children use to make a vibrating noise by blowing air through it. When the vocal cords are held together, the air forced through them from the lungs causes them to vibrate. It is precisely this vibration, or "voicing," that distinguishes [s] from [z] and enables speakers to differentiate between two otherwise identical sounds.[2] Using these very similar but distinct sounds enables us to create words that differ by only a single feature of voicing on a single sound but carry quite different meanings, as in *bus* and *buzz* or *sip* and *zip*.

Not only [s] and [z] but many other consonants—in English and many other languages—are characterized by a voiced versus voiceless contrast. Consider [f] and [v], as in *fine* and *vine*: Both sounds are produced with air being forced through a narrow aperture between the upper teeth and the lower lip; they are therefore labio-dental fricatives, [f] being voiceless, [v] voiced. Other voiceless/voiced pairs include [p] and [b] as in *pet* and *bet* and [t] and [d] as in *ten* and *den*. Most, perhaps all, languages have some pairs of consonants that are phonetically different only in that one is voiced and the other voiceless—though this difference is not necessarily significant in all languages, as we shall see in the case of Korean.

Manner of Articulation   Besides having a voicing feature, [s] and [z] can be further characterized as to their manner of articulation. In pronouncing them, air is continuously forced through a narrow opening at a place behind the upper teeth known as the *alveolar ridge* (see Figure 2-3). Compare the pronunciation of [s] and [z] with the sounds [t] and [d]. Unlike [s] and [z], [t] and [d] do not permit a continuous stream of air to pass through the mouth. Rather the air is completely stopped behind and above the upper teeth at the alveolar ridge and then released (or exploded) in a small burst of air. For this reason, [t] and [d] are called **stops**; because the air is released through the mouth (and not the nose), they can also be called oral stops. Sounds like [s] and [z] that are made by a continuous stream of air passing through a narrowed passage in the vocal tract are called **fricatives**. It may be helpful for you to check the sounds [p], [b], [f], and [v] to see which are stops and which are fricatives.

Place of Articulation   Of the consonant sounds we have analyzed so far, [s] and [t] are voiceless, while [z] and [d] are voiced. All four of them are

---

[2] The vocal cords offer a perfect illustration of the "parasitic" nature of speech: The primary function of these two muscle flaps is to keep food from going down the wrong tube and entering the lungs.

pronounced with the point of greatest closure right behind the upper teeth at the *alveolar ridge*. Pronounce *ten* and *den* aloud; feel where the tip of your tongue touches the top of your mouth for the consonants. Both words start (and finish) at the alveolar ridge. Because the three consonants [t], [d], and [n] are all articulated at the alveolar ridge, they are called **alveolars**. [s] and [z] are also articulated at the alveolar ridge, as you will notice by pronouncing the words *sin* and *zen*. (Of course, as to *manner* of articulation, [s] and [z] are fricatives, whereas [t] and [d] are stops.)

There are three major places of articulation for English stop consonants. One is the alveolar ridge. The others are the lips and the soft palate (or *velum*). If you say the words *pin* and *bin*, you will notice that for the initial sound in each word air is built up behind the two lips and then released. Thus the point of greatest closure is at the lips; [p] and [b] are therefore called **bilabial** stops. If you compare your pronunciations of [p] and [t], you will see that both are voiceless and that the sole difference between them is in the place of articulation.

Now attend to the pronunciation of the first sound of *kin*. Like [p] and [t], [k] is a voiceless stop, but it differs from them in its place of articulation: [k] is pronounced with the tongue touching the roof of the mouth at the velum and is therefore called a **velar**; [k] is thus a voiceless velar stop.

Corresponding to the three voiceless stops [p], [t], and [k], English has three parallel voiced stops: [b] as in *bib* is a voiced bilabial stop; [d] as in *did* is a voiced alveolar stop; and [g] as in *gig* is a voiced velar stop. Thus English has six stops, three pairs containing one voiceless and one voiced sound each— one pair pronounced at the lips, one at the alveolar ridge, and one at the velum.

Besides these three articulators, English takes advantage of other places of articulation for other sounds. The *th* of *thin* (the Greek letter theta [θ] serves as the phonetic symbol) is a fricative pronounced with the tongue between the teeth; it is described as a voiceless **interdental** fricative. [š] (represented by *sh* in *shoot* and *wish*) and [ž] (the final sound in *beige* and the medial consonant in *measure*) are pronounced with near closure at a place in the mouth between the alveolar ridge and the velum (or palate); sounds produced there are called **palato-alveolars**. [š] is a voiceless palato-alveolar fricative; [ž] is a voiced palato-alveolar fricative.

SOUNDS

Consonants

Consonants are sounds produced by partially or completely blocking air in its passage from the lungs through the vocal tract. If you review the inventory of English consonants given in Table 2-1 and pronounce the sounds aloud while concentrating on the place and manner of articulation, you will perceive how the rest of the table represents the distribution of English consonants according to their voicing, their place of articulation, and their manner of articulation. We will now describe these consonants, grouped here according to their manner of articulation and described in terms of their voicing and their place of articulation. While concentrating on the consonant sounds of English, we shall also mention selected consonants from other languages as a help to understanding.

Stops The stops of English are [p b t d k g]. By pronouncing words with these sounds in them (see Table 2-1), you can recognize that [p] and [b] are bilabial stops, [t] and [d] are alveolar stops, and [k] and [g] are velar stops.

	Place of Articulation		
Voicing	Bilabial	Alveolar	Velar
voiceless	p	t	k
voiced	b	d	g

In addition, many languages have a glottal stop, which is pronounced by briefly blocking air from passing in the throat with the glottis. The glottal stop is represented phonetically as [ʔ]. In English, the glottal stop occurs only as a marginal sound—between the two parts of the exclamation *Oh oh!* in American English and in Cockney English as the medial consonant of words like *butter*. In languages like Hawaiian, the glottal stop is a full-fledged consonant that can distinguish two different words; compare Hawaiian *paʔu* 'smudge' and *pau* 'finished.' There is no voiced equivalent of the unvoiced glottal stop [ʔ].

Nasals **Nasal** consonants are pronounced by lowering the velum, thus allowing the stream of air to pass out through the nasal cavity instead of through the oral cavity. English has three nasal stops: [m] as in *mad, Spam, drummer*; [n] as in *new, ten, sinner*; and a third, symbolized by [ŋ] and pronounced as in the words *sing* and *singer*.

Place of Articulation		
Bilabial	Alveolar	Velar
m	n	ŋ

[ŋ] does not occur word initially in English. Because of the way we spell it, English speakers sometimes think of [ŋ] as a combination of [n] and [g], but it is actually a single sound, as you can see by comparing your pronunciation of the words *singer* and *finger*. Leaving aside the initial sounds [s] and [f], if your pronunciation of these words differs (for some speakers of English it does not), then you have [ŋ] in *singer* and [ŋg] (not [ng]) in *finger*. Most American English speakers have a three-way contrast among *simmer, sinner*, and *singer* solely according to whether the medial consonant is [m], [n], or [ŋ]. By noticing where the tongue touches the upper part of the mouth in the articulation of these nasal consonants (and by comparing their place of articulation with other sounds identified above), you will be able to see that [m] is a bilabial nasal, [n] an alveolar nasal, and [ŋ] a velar nasal. If, while you are saying [mmmmm], you cut off the air stream passing through the nose by pinching it closed (as a clothespin would), the sound stops abruptly; this demonstrates that nasal stops are produced by passing air through the nose. Compare cutting off the air passing through your nose while saying [nnnnn] and [sssss], and you will get a clear sense of the use of the nasal and oral cavities in sound production. You will see that when you cut off the air passing through the nose for oral consonants there is virtually no difference in the quality of the sound, but when you cut off the air passing through the nose for a nasal consonant no sound is made at all.

If you have successfully identified the places of articulation for the nasals and understood why they fit in their particular slots in the consonant table, you will have noticed that English has three sets of consonants articulated in the same places though differing in their manner of articulation: the oral stops [p] and [b] and the nasal stop [m] are articulated at the two lips and are known as bilabials; the oral stops [t] and [d] and the nasal stop [n] are articulated at the alveolar ridge and are called alveolars; while [k], [g], and [ŋ] are articulated at the velum and are called velars.

The nasal consonants of English are: [m n ŋ]. Other languages have other nasals. French, Spanish, and Italian, for instance, all have a palatal nasal [ɲ]; examples include the French word *mignon* 'cute' (which English has borrowed in the set phrase *filet mignon*), the Spanish words *señor* and *cañón* (the latter borrowed into English as *canyon*), and the Italian *bagno* 'bath' and *lasagna* (also borrowed into English).

Fricatives To pronounce the alveolar fricatives [s] and [z], air is forced through a narrow opening between the tip of the tongue and the alveolar ridge. English has a large inventory of fricatives, some of them articulated in front of [s] and [z] in the mouth, others behind them. All are characterized by a similar forcing of air in a continuous stream through a narrow opening. In pronouncing the first sound in the words *thin, three*, and *theta* and the final sound in *teeth* and *bath*, notice that the tongue tip is placed between the upper and lower teeth, where the air stream is most constrained and makes its articulation. Represented by the phonetic symbol [θ], the sound in these words is a voiceless interdental fricative. The voiced counterpart is the initial sound in the words *there* and *then* and the medial consonant in *either*. Notice that in English the spelling *th* is used for two distinct sounds: [θ] as in *ether* and [ð] as in *either* or *feather*.

If you pronounce the following words, you will discover other fricatives and become aware of their common properties as well as their different places of articulation:

fine/vine [f v]: labio-dental fricatives

thigh/thy; ether/either [θ ð]: interdental fricatives

sink/zinc [s z]: alveolar fricatives

rush/rouge; fishin'/vision [š ž]: palato-alveolar fricatives

The complete set of English fricatives is: [f v θ ð s z š ž].

	Place of Articulation			
Voicing	Labio-dental	Interdental	Alveolar	Palato-alveolar
voiceless	f	θ	s	š
voiced	v	ð	z	ž

Some languages have other fricatives articulated in different parts of the vocal tract. Spanish, for example, has a voiced bilabial fricative (represented by the phonetic symbol [β]), as in *la vaca* 'the cow.' Japanese has a voiceless bilabial fricative represented by the phonetic symbol [Φ], which is pronounced like [f], but by bringing together both lips instead of the lower lip and the upper front teeth. The West African language Ewe has both a voiced [β] and an unvoiced [Φ]. Spanish has a voiceless velar fricative [x], which also exists in many other languages, and a voiced velar fricative [ɣ], which is less common. Pronounce [x] as if you were gently clearing your throat. The sound occurs in the Spanish word *joya* 'jewel' and in the personal name *José* (which, when they are borrowed into English, are pronounced with an [h], the closest sound to [x] that English has). [ɣ] occurs as *g* in Spanish *lago* 'lake.' German and Chinese have a voiceless palatal fricative [ç], as in the German word *Reich* 'empire.'

Notice that in English the physical distance in the mouth between the places of articulation for the fricatives is not as great as the distance for the different stops. The bilabial, alveolar, and velar places of articulation for the stop consonants are spaced farther apart than are the labio-dental, interdental, alveolar, and palato-alveolar articulations of the fricatives. The tighter packing of the fricatives in the mouth can cause difficulty in perceiving them as distinct, especially when any interference is present. If you ask a friend to identify the fricative sounds either over the telephone or when you pronounce them while facing away, you'll discover that they're tougher to distinguish from one another than you might have thought. The acoustic differences may be especially difficult to perceive for speakers of languages that have fewer fricatives than English does or have them better spaced. Because French does not have the interdental fricatives [θ] and [ð], some French speakers tend to perceive (and pronounce) English words like *thin* and *this* as though they were *sin* and *zis*.

Affricates   Two consonant sounds in English are a little more complex to describe than stops and fricatives but are closely related to them. These are the sounds that occur initially in the words *chin* and *gin* and finally in the words *batch* and *badge*. If you pronounce these sounds slowly enough, you can recognize that they are stop-fricatives. We shall refer to stop-fricatives as **affricates**. In the pronunciation of an affricate, air is built up by a complete closure of the oral tract at some place of articulation, then released (something like a stop) and continued (like a fricative). The sound in *chin*, for example, is a combination of the stop [t] and the fricative [š]; we represent it as [č]. The sound at the beginning and end of *judge* is a combination of the stop [d] and the fricative [ž]; we represent it as [j]. English has just two affricates: the voiceless [č] and the voiced [j], both of which are palato-alveolar affricates.

Other affricates occur in other languages. The most common are the alveolar affricates [ts] and [dz], which occur at the beginning of the Italian words *zucchero* 'sugar' and *zona* 'zone' respectively.

Approximants   There are five sounds in English that are known as **approximants**: [h y r l w]. [h] is simply the voiceless counterpart to the vowel that follows it, as in *history* or *here*. [y] is a palatal approximant as in *you*; the word *cute* begins with the consonant cluster [ky]. As to [r] and [l], among the languages of the world it is not so common as English speakers might expect to have them as distinctive sounds by which words can be contrasted, as in English *rid/lid* or *wear/wail*. The difference between [r] and [l] is that [r] is pronounced by channeling air through the central part of the mouth and [l] is pronounced by channeling it on each side of the tongue. ([r] is therefore called a central approximant, [l] a lateral approximant.) The difference between the two is not always easy to master, and even some native English speakers have difficulty with them. As we'll see, in some Asian languages, including Japanese and Korean, [r] and [l] are not distinctive sounds, so speakers of these languages sometimes have difficulty distinguishing them in English.

In the pronunciation of the approximant [w], the lips are rounded, as in *wild*. For some dialects, in some words [h] precedes [w] as in *which* or *whether*. When [w] is the second element of a cluster (as in *twine* or *quiet*) the initial sound ([t] or [k]) is rounded in anticipation of the [w].

One foreign approximant that is familiar to many English speakers is the French voiced uvular *r* (as in words like *Paris* or *rue* 'street'), which is made farther back in the mouth and is represented by the phonetic symbol [ʁ].

Other Sounds   Some consonant sounds are not stops, nasals, fricatives, affricates, or approximants. The medial consonant of the word *butter* is commonly pronounced in American English as an alveolar **flap**, produced by throwing the tongue against the alveolar ridge. We will represent this flap (which will be discussed in Chapter 3) with the symbol [D]. Spanish, Italian, and Fijian have an alveolar **trill** *r*, which occurs in the Spanish *correr* 'to run' and is represented by the symbol [r̃].

Some languages have consonants that belong to the same classes we have discussed but are strikingly different from those in European languages. Several languages of southern Africa, for instance, have among their stop consonants certain click sounds that are an integral part of their sound system. One example is the lateral click made on the side of the tongue; it occurs in English when we urge a horse to move on, for example, but it is not part of the inventory of English sounds. Another click sound that occurs in some of these languages can be represented in English writing by the reproach *tsk-tsk*. This last click is not a lateral but an alveolar, made with the tip of the tongue at the alveolar ridge.

Vowels

Vowel sounds differ from consonant sounds in that they are produced not by blocking air in its passage from the lungs but by passing air through different shapes of the mouth and different positions of the tongue and lips unobstructed by narrow passages (except at the glottis). Some languages have as few as three distinct vowels in their sound systems; others have more than a dozen. English has more than a dozen distinctive vowels, depending on dialect. Many people think of English as having only five vowels; but this is a reflection of the orthography rather than the spoken language (and is a clear example of the influence of writing on our thinking about language). In pronouncing the following words, you will realize that English has many more than five vowels: *peat, pit, pet, pate, pat, put, putt, poke, pot, part,* and *port.* Still other vowels can be identified in the words *boy, bout,* and *bite.*

Vowel Height and Frontness   Unlike consonants, which are described by place and manner of articulation, vowels are characterized by the position of the tongue and the lips, in particular by the relative height and relative frontness or backness of the tongue and the relative rounding of the lips. We refer to vowels as being high or low and front or back; we also consider whether the lips are rounded (as for *pool*) or nonrounded (as for *pill*). You can get a feel for these descriptors by alternately saying *feed* and *food*, the first of which contains a front vowel, the second a back vowel. To get a feel for tongue height, alternate saying *feet* and *fat*. If you fail to feel the difference between high and low vowels with this pair of sounds, look at yourself in the mirror (or at a classmate saying them); you'll see that because the tongue is lower, the mouth is open much wider for the vowel of *fat* than for the vowel of *feet*.

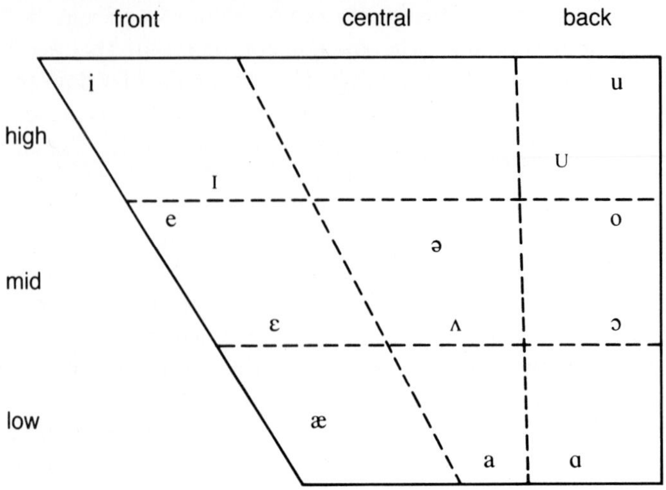

front   central   back

FIGURE 2-4
The Vowels of English

SOURCE: Adapted from Ladefoged 1982

Figure 2-4 indicates the relationship of the English vowels to one another and the approximate positions of the tongue during their articulation.

Here are English words for each of the vowel symbols shown in the figure:

i	Pete, beat			u	pool, boot
ɪ	pit, bit			ʊ	put, foot
e	late, bait	ə	about, sofa	o	poke, boat
ɛ	pet, bet	ʌ	putt, but	ɔ	port, bought
æ	pat, bat	a	park (in Boston)	ɑ	pot, father

[ə], called *schwa*, and the inverted v [ʌ], called *caret*, stand for sounds that are very much alike. They both occur in the word *above* [əbʌv]. In this book we use [ə] to represent a mid central vowel in unstressed syllables, as in *buses* [bʌsəz] and *capable* [kepəbəl], and before [r] in the same syllable whether stressed, as in *person* [pərsən] and *sir* [sər], or unstressed, as in *pertain* [pərten] and *tender* [tɛndər]. We use [ʌ] to represent mid central vowels in other stressed syllables, such as *flooded* [flʌdəd] and *suds* [sʌdz].

There are also three **diphthongs** in English, represented by pairs of symbols to capture the fact that a diphthong is a vowel sound for which the tongue starts in one place in the mouth and moves to another: /ay/ (as in *bite*); /aw/ (as in *pout, bout*); /ɔy/ (as in *boy, toy*). Thus American English generally has up to thirteen distinctive vowel sounds (plus three diphthongs), not the five vowels that are commonly assumed to exist by people who forget to distinguish between sounds and letters. In England and certain parts of the United States, including metropolitan New York City, sixteen distinct vowels and diphthongs exist; in some parts of the United States, including Pittsburgh and surrounding areas, fewer distinct vowel and diphthong sounds exist, because no distinction is made between the vowels of *caught* and *cot*.

Other Articulatory Features of Vowels   Languages have other possibilities besides tongue height and backness for creating differences among vowels. We will briefly discuss five features of vowel quality that languages can exploit to add to their inventory of distinctive vowels—tenseness, rounding, lengthening, nasalization, and tone.

In many languages a distinction is made between tense and lax vowels. Tense vowels are produced with greater overall muscular tension in the mouth; lax vowels are pronounced with less tension and tend to be shorter. In English the contrast between [i] of *peat* and [ɪ] of *pit* is in part a tense/lax contrast; likewise for *bait/bet* and *cooed/could*.

Whereas in English a high front vowel tends automatically to be unrounded (and a high back vowel to be rounded), some languages have both rounded and unrounded front vowels. To cite two familiar examples, French and German have high front and mid front rounded vowels as well as unrounded ones. French has a high front unrounded [i] in words such as *dire* 'to say' and *dix* 'ten' and a high front rounded vowel [ü], as in *rue* 'street'; it also has a contrast between upper mid front unrounded [e] (as in *fée* 'fairy') and upper mid front rounded [ø] (*feu* 'fire'); and between lower mid front unrounded [ɛ] (*serre* 'hothouse') and lower mid front rounded [œ] (*sœur* 'sister'). German has similar contrasts (see Table 2-4).

In fact, German has two of each vowel type—one long, the other short. The pronunciation of long vowels is held longer than that of short vowels. Long vowels are commonly represented with a macron (⁻) above the vowel symbol (sometimes a colon is used after the symbol instead). Thus, in addition to the short vowels [i] and [ü], as in *bitten* 'to request' and *müssen* 'must,' German has words with high front long vowels, such as unrounded [ī] in *bieten* 'to wish' and rounded [ǖ] in *Mühle* 'mill.' From these German examples, we see that languages can multiply differences among vowels by exploiting long and short varieties of the same vowel. English has vowels of differing length but does not exploit this difference to create different words (see Chapter 3).

All vowel types can also be nasalized. This is done by pronouncing the vowel while passing air through the nose (as for nasal stops) as well as through the mouth. Nasal vowels are symbolized by adding a tilde (˜) above the vowel symbol. One well-known example of a language with nasal vowels is French, which has several nasal vowels paralleling the oral vowels. Thus French has a contrast between *lin* [lɛ̃] 'flax' and *lait* [lɛ] 'milk,' between *ment* [mã] '(he) is lying' and *ma* [ma] 'my' (feminine), and between *honte* [ɔt] 'shame' and *hotte* [ɔt] 'hutch.' Other languages with nasal vowels include Irish, Hindi, and many American Indian languages, such as Delaware. English also has some nasal vowels, but they are not significant (see Chapter 3).

The last important feature of vowels is *tone*. In many languages of Asia, Africa, and North America, a vowel may be pronounced on several pitches and be perceived by the native speakers of these languages as different sounds. Typically, a vowel pronounced on a low pitch contrasts with the same vowel pronounced on a higher pitch. An example of such a two-tone language is Hausa, spoken in West Africa. In Hausa, the word *górà* 'bamboo,' in which the first vowel is pronounced with a high tone and the second vowel with a low tone (as symbolized by the accents ´ and `), contrasts with the word *gòrá* 'large gourd,' in which the tones are reversed. Other tone languages have more complex systems. The Běijīng (Peking) dialect of Chinese has four tones: a high level tone (symbolized with ¯); a rising tone (´); a falling-rising tone (ˇ), in which the pitch begins to fall and then rises sharply; and a falling tone (`), in which the pitch falls sharply. Thus there is a four-way contrast between the following four vowels pronounced on different tones; these vowels happen to be words by themselves, with separate meanings.[3]

ī	'one'
í	'proper'
ǐ	'already'
ì	'thought'

Some languages have even more complex tone systems: Thai has five tones; the standard dialect of Vietnamese has six tones; and the Guǎngzhōu (Canton) dialect of Chinese has nine different tones. Tone is thus not only a widespread phenomenon, but also a diverse one.

Tables 2-2 through 2-5 are vowel charts illustrating the sound patterns of four of the world's major languages—French, Spanish, German, and Japanese.

SUMMARY

Sounds must be distinguished from letters and other visual representations of language. Phonetic alphabets represent sounds in a way that is consistent and comparable across different languages; each sound is assigned a distinct

---

[3] Note that a given accent mark can be used to represent different tones in different languages. Thus, ´ represents a high tone in Hausa but a rising tone in Chinese; ` represents a low tone in Hausa but a falling tone in Chinese.

TABLE 2-2
French Vowels with Illustrative Words

	Front Unrounded	Front Rounded	Central Unrounded	Back Rounded
Oral Vowels				
high	i	ü		u
upper mid	e	ø		o
mid			ə	
lower mid	ɛ	œ		ɔ
low			a	
Nasal Vowels				
lower mid	ɛ̃	œ̃		ɔ̃
low				ɑ̃

Examples

i	gris 'grey'	ü	mûr 'ripe'	u	fou 'crazy'
e	fermé 'shut'	ø	jeûne 'fasts'	o	mot 'word'
ɛ	frais 'fresh'	œ	jeune 'young'	ɔ	fort 'strong'
		ə	chemin 'path'		
		a	par 'by'		
ɛ̃	brin 'sprig'	œ̃	brun 'brown'	ɔ̃	fond 'bottom'
				ɑ̃	faon 'fawn'

TABLE 2-3
Spanish Vowels with Illustrative Words

	Front Unrounded	Central Unrounded	Back Rounded
high	i		u
mid	e		o
low		a	

Examples

i	chiste 'joke'	a	mar 'sea'	o	boca 'mouth'
e	fe 'faith'			u	sur 'south'

TABLE 2-4
German Vowels with Illustrative Words

	Front Unrounded	Front Rounded	Central Unrounded	Back Rounded
high				
long	ɪ̄	ǖ		ū
short	i	ü		u
upper mid				
long	ē	ø̄		ō
short	e			o
mid				
short			ə	
lower mid				
long	ɛ̄			
short		œ		
low				
long			ā	
short			a	

Examples

ī	bieten 'to wish'	ǖ	Mühle 'mill'	ū	Huhn 'hen'
i	bitten 'to request'	ü	müssen 'must'	u	Mutter 'mother'
ē	wen 'whom'	ø̄	ölig 'oily'	ō	Ofen 'oven'
e	wenn 'when'	œ	röntgen 'X-ray'	o	Ochs 'ox'
ɛ̄	Käse 'cheese'			ə	liebe 'dear'
				ā	Rabe 'crow'
				a	Ratte 'rat'

TABLE 2-5
Japanese Vowels with Illustrative Words

	Front Unrounded	Central Unrounded	Back Unrounded	Back Rounded
high	i		ɯ	
mid	ɛ			ɔ
low		a		

Examples

i	ima 'now'			ɯ	buji 'safe'
ɛ	sensei 'teacher'			ɔ	yoru 'to approach'
		a	aki 'autumn'		

representation, independently of the customary orthography used to represent the language in which the sound occurs. The phonetic alphabet used in this book is very similar to the International Phonetic Alphabet (IPA).

All languages contain two basic kinds of sounds: consonants and vowels. Consonants are produced by obstructing the flow of air as it passes from the lungs through the vocal tract and out through the mouth or nose. In the production of fricative consonants, air is forced through a narrow opening in the passage to form a continuous noise, as in the initial and final sounds of the words *says* and *five*. For stop consonants the air passage is completely blocked and then released, as in the initial and final sounds of the words *tap* and *cat*. Affricates are produced by combining a stop and a fricative, as in the final sound of the word *peach* or the initial and final sounds of *judge*. Vowels are produced by positioning the tongue and mouth to form differently shaped passages. Oral vowels are released through the mouth, and nasal vowels are released through the nose, along with the mouth.

Consonant sounds can be characterized by specifying a combination of articulatory features: voicing, place of articulation, and manner of articulation. For example, [t] is a voiceless alveolar stop; [v] is a voiced labio-dental fricative. Vowels are described by citing the relative height and frontness of the tongue: thus [æ] is a low front vowel; [u] is a high back vowel. Sometimes secondary features of vowel production—such as tenseness, nasality, lengthening, or rounding—are specified. Finally, in many languages vowels can be pronounced on different pitches, or tones.

Different languages have different numbers of sounds in their inventories and draw on the inventory of possible human speech sounds in different ways. Tables 2-6 and 2-7 summarize all the vowels and consonants introduced in Chapter 2.

TABLE 2-6
Vowels Discussed in Chapter 2
(All vowels can be nasalized and either short or long.)

	Front Unrounded	Front Rounded	Central Unrounded	Back Unrounded	Back Rounded
high					
tense	i	ü		ɯ	u
lax	ɪ				ʊ
upper mid	e	ø			o
mid			ə		
lower mid	ɛ	œ	ʌ		ɔ
low	æ		a		ɑ

TABLE 2-7 Consonants Discussed in Chapter 2

Manner of Articulation and Voicing	Place of Articulation								
	Bilabial	Labio-dental	Inter-dental	Alveolar	Palato-alveolar	Palatal	Velar	Uvular	Glottal
Stops									
voiceless	p			t			k		ʔ
voiced	b			d			g		
Nasals	m			n		ɲ	ŋ		
Fricatives									
voiceless	Φ	f	θ	s	š	ç	x		h
voiced	β	v	ð	z	ž		ɣ		
Affricates									
voiceless				ts	č				
voiced				dz	ǰ				
Approximants									
voiceless									
voiced central	w			r		y		ʁ	
voiced lateral				l					
voiced trill				r̃					
voiced flap				D					

EXERCISES

1. Give a phonetic description of the following sounds. For consonants, include voicing and place and manner of articulation; for vowels, include height and a frontness/backness dimension. *Examples*: [s] voiceless alveolar fricative; [æ] low front vowel.

   Consonants: [z] [t] [b] [n̩] [ŋ] [r] [ĵ] [š]

   Vowels: [ɛ] [ɔ] [ɪ] [u] [o] [ə]

2. A minimal pair is a set of two words that have the same sounds in the same order, except that one sound differs: *pit* [pɪt]/*bit* [bɪt]; *bell* [bɛl]/*bill* [bɪl]; and *either* [iðər]/*ether* [iθər].

   (a) For each of the following pairs of English consonants, provide minimal pairs that illustrate their occurrence in initial, medial, and final position. (Examples are given for the first two pairs.)

		Initial	Medial	Final
[s]	[z]	sue/zoo	buses/buzzes	peace/peas
[k]	[b]	kit/bit	rocker/robber	tuck/tub
[t]	[b]			
[s]	[t]			
[r]	[l]			
[m]	[n]			

   (b) For each of these pairs of vowels, cite a minimal pair of words illustrating the contrast. *Example*: [u] [æ] boot/bat.

   [i] [ɪ]; [ɔy] [ay]; [u] [ʊ]; [æ] [ɛ]

3. Write out in standard orthography the words represented by the following transcriptions. *Examples*: [pɛn] pen; [smok] smoke; [bənænə] banana

[læŋgwəĵ]	[træpt]	[spawt]
[θwɔrt]	[ðiz]	[ðɪs]
[lʌvd]	[plɛžər]	[kwɪklɪ]
[mənatənəs]	[ɛntərprayzɪŋ]	[frənɛtək]

4. Transcribe each of the following words as you say them in casual speech. (Do not be misled by the orthography.) *Examples*: bed [bɛd]; rancid [rænsəd]; shnook [šnʊk]

friend	more	very	attitude	change
semantics	system	ready	more	teacher
crackers	peanuts	palm	music	musician
pneumonia	photograph	psalm	fuel	photographer

5. The following transcription represents one person's reading of a passage about love potions (adapted from *The Encyclopedia of Things That Never Were*, p. 159). Write out the passage using standard English orthography.

   [æz ðə nem ɪndəkets ðiz pošənz ar kampawndəd spəsɪfəklɪ tu ətrækt ə sʌbĵɛkt hu ɪz rilʌktənt tu sərɛndər tə wʊnz karnəl dəzayərz ðə pošən me bi hæd æt ə prays frəm ɛnɪ ælkəmɪst ɔr ʌðər pərsən skɪld ɪn ðə prɛpərešən əv mayn čenĵɪŋ

kɑmpawnz wɪčəz wɪzərdz ən sɔrsərərz hu ɑr jɛnrəlɪ nɑt ɪntərɛstəd ɪn lʌv ɑr
sʌmtaymz ənwɪlɪŋ tə mænyəfækšər ðə pošənz ðə pərčəsərz onlɪ prɑbləm me bi ðæt
əv pərswedɪŋ ðɪ ɑbjɛkt əv hɪz ɔr hər dəzayər tu swɑlo ɛnɪ əv ðə pošən ə risənt
rɛsəpɪ fɔr ə lʌv pošən ɪnkludəd jɪnjər sɪnəmən simən yurən drayd ən grawnd
tɛstɪz frəm ə mel ænəməl ɛkstrækt əv hyumən hɑrts ənd ɛnɪ sutəbəl ɑbjɛkt frəm ðə
pərsən sʌč æz hɛr blʌd ɔr nel klɪpɪŋz]

6. Examine the following list of consonants as they are represented in three popular
   desk dictionaries, and compare the dictionary symbols with the phonetic symbols
   used in this book. (WNNCD stands for *Webster's Ninth New Collegiate Dictionary*; WNWD stands for *Webster's New World Dictionary*, 2nd college ed.; AHD
   stands for *The American Heritage Dictionary*, 2nd college ed.)

Phonetic Symbol	WNNCD	WNWD	AHD
p	p	p	p
b	b	b	b
t	t	t	t
d	d	d	d
k	k	k	k
g	g	g	g
f	f	f	f
v	v	v	v
θ	th	th	th
ð	<u>th</u>	*th*	*th*
s	s	s	s
z	z	z	z
š	sh	sh	sh
ž	zh	zh	zh
č	ch	ch	ch
ǰ	j	j	j
m	m	m	m
n	n	n	n
ŋ	ŋ	ŋ	ŋ
h	h	h	h
y	y	y	y
r	r	r	r
l	l	l	l
w	w	w	w

Note that most of the symbols used by these dictionaries are the same as those
used in this book, but not all are the same. Choose three sounds for which one or
more of the dictionaries use a different symbol than the one used in this book, and
discuss why that different symbol might have been chosen.

7. Examine the following list of vowels as they are represented in three dictionaries;
   compare the dictionary symbols with the phonetic symbols used in this book. (See
   exercise 6 for identification of the dictionaries.)

Phonetic Symbol		WNNCD	WNWD	AHD
i	peat, feet	e	ē	ē
ɪ	pit, bit	i	i	ĭ
e	wait, late	ā	ā	ā
ɛ	pet, bet	e	e	ĕ
æ	pat, bat	a	a	ă
ə	above, soda	ə	ə	ə
ʌ	but, love	ə	u	ŭ
u	pool, boot	ü	o͞o	o͞o
ʊ	push, put	u̇	oo	o͝o
o	boat, sold	ō	ō	ō
ɔ	port, or	ȯ	ô	ô
ɑ	pot, bottle	ä	ä	ŏ
aw	cow, pout	au̇	ou	ou
ay	buy, tight	ī	ī	ī
ɔy	boy, toil	ȯi	oi	oi

In contrast to their practice with consonants, the desk dictionaries differ from one another and from our representation in their transcription of vowels. Cite three instances of a difference from our transcription; discuss the advantages and disadvantages of the dictionary's representation as compared to ours.

8. George Bernard Shaw's claim that English spelling is so chaotic that *ghoti* could be pronounced [fɪš] "fish" has been called unfortunate and misleading. Those judgments are based on observations like the following: *gh* can occur word initially in only a few words (for example, *ghost* and *ghastly*), and then it is always pronounced [g]; only following a vowel in the same syllable (as in *cough* and *tough*) can *gh* be pronounced as [f]; thus, *ghoti* could not be pronounced with an initial [f]. What other generalizations about the English spelling patterns of *gh*, *o*, and *ti* can be used to argue that Shaw's claim is at least exaggerated?

SUGGESTIONS FOR FURTHER READING

MacKay (1987) is the most complete elementary treatment of all aspects of phonetics; it is accessible and has excellent illustrations. Ladefoged (1982) is an excellent introduction to the production mechanisms of speech and to the variety of sounds in the languages of the world. Pullum and Ladusaw (1986) is a convenient discussion of the various symbols used in the International Phonetic Alphabet (IPA) and by various scholars in their treatments of phonetics and phonology; the book is arranged like a dictionary, with each symbol treated separately and clearly illustrated. Maddieson (1984) is a valuable report of the inventories of sounds for a representative sample of the languages of the world; the inventories it provides vary greatly—from a low of 11 sounds to a high of 141. Crystal (1985) is an excellent source of information about the meanings of terms used in phonetics and all other fields of linguistics. Stubbs (1980) has an excellent discussion of the relationship between sounds and spelling in English and other languages and offers insights into the problems facing spelling reform. Denes and Pinson (1973) is an accessible account of the physics of language sounds and acoustic phonetics.

REFERENCES

Crystal, David. 1985. *A Dictionary of Linguistics and Phonetics*. (Oxford: Basil Blackwell).

Denes, Peter, and E. N. Pinson. 1973. *The Speech Chain*. (Garden City, N.Y.: Anchor Books).

Ladefoged, Peter. 1982. *A Course in Phonetics*, 2nd ed. (New York: Harcourt Brace Jovanovich).

MacKay, Ian R. A. 1987. *Phonetics: The Science of Speech Production*, 2nd ed. (Boston: Little Brown).

Maddieson, Ian. 1984. *Patterns of Sound*. (Cambridge: Cambridge University Press).

Pullum, Geoffrey K., and William A. Ladusaw. 1986. *Phonetic Symbol Guide*. (Chicago: University of Chicago Press).

Stubbs, Michael. 1980. *Language and Literacy: The Sociolinguistics of Reading and Writing* (London: Routledge & Kegan Paul).

PHONOLOGY: THE SOUND SYSTEMS OF LANGUAGE

3

INTRODUCTION

This chapter focuses on the systematic structuring of sounds in languages—on which phonetic distinctions are significant in the sense that they can signal differences in meaning; on the relationship between how sounds are pronounced and how they are stored in the brain; and on the ways sounds are organized within words irrespective of meaning.

It may be useful to approach our task from the point of view of children acquiring their native language. Children acquire different parts of their language at different stages, but all of them learn a great deal about speaking before they learn even the most rudimentary things about the visual representation of speech in writing. To repeat a point we have stressed before, we are interested in sound systems as such—independently of their representation in writing.

Try to imagine the task of an infant listening to utterances made by its parents, siblings, and others. From the barrage of utterances that it faces in early life, a child must decipher the code of a language and learn to speak its mother tongue. Although caretakers sometimes use the slow and careful speech of baby talk in addressing children, they do not do so consistently; and the utterances that children hear are often incomplete, interrupted, or flawed in other ways.

In Chapter 2 you learned to distinguish the number of letters in a written word from the number of sounds in its pronunciation. You know, for example, that *set* has an equal number of sounds and letters, while *write* does not. In our discussion, we have taken for granted that words have a specific number of sounds. Children hearing language in their earliest months, however, have no ready access to that simple fact. It would be instructive to listen to a conversation in a language you do not know; if you attempt to gauge the number of words in a small sample of even a few seconds, you will discover that most words are run together with no separation—no silences—between them. This is true of all languages and all dialects.

Itisasifthesentencesonthispagewereprintedwithoutspacesbetween wordsitwouldbeverydifficulttofigureoutwouldntit?

As you can see, it would be tough to sort out the individual words. Compare those run-together words with the following:

It is as if the sentences on this page were printed without spaces between words; it would be very difficult to figure out, wouldn't it?

The task of sorting out the continuous noise of utterances into separate words is part of the challenge that every child faces in acquiring a language.

Actually, the task is even more difficult than is suggested by the run-together words in the sentence above. The reason is simple: Whereas the letters in the run-together sentence are distinct and separated from one another, the individual sounds in a spoken word are not separated; instead, they blend together into a continuous noise stream. To take our writing analogy a step further, imagine attempting to analyze the beginning and end points of each letter in a handwritten sample: this would more closely capture the challenge that infants face in deciphering the code of distinct sounds in their language. Consider the following:

In writing, the letters of each word are joined.

Although anyone who knows English and is able to decipher this handwriting can count the letters in each word, there is no clear separation in their visual representation. Each word is written continuously, with the letters blending into one another. No beginning or end spot can be pinpointed (except for the beginning of the first letter and the end of the last letter in each word). The same is true of the speech that infants hear; there is no separation between the individual sounds of a word, no beginning or end for each sound in the speech stream. Children nevertheless learn the words of their language in a short time, a feat all the more remarkable considering how much else they have to learn in their earliest years.

If you examine a physical "picture" of a word as is made by a sound spectrogram, you will see that there is no separation between the sounds. One

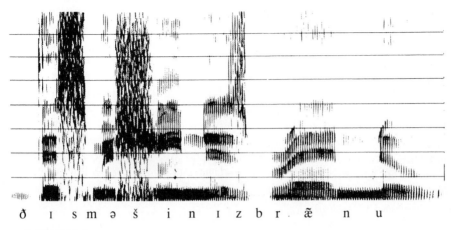

ð ɪ s m ə š i n ɪ z b r . æ̃   n   u

FIGURE 3-1
Sound Spectrogram of a Casual Utterance

reason for this is that a particular sound's various phonetic features—voicing, nasalization, and so on—do not all begin or end at the same time. For example, the voicing of a particular sound may be discontinued in anticipation of a following voiceless sound—as in *imp*, in which the tail end of [m] is devoiced preceding [p], which is voiceless. Figure 3-1 is a spectrogram that illustrates how the simple utterance *This machine is brand new* appears acoustically. There is not only no separation between one sound and another within a word but no physical separation between one word and the next. In the same way, the acoustic signal that an infant's ears pick up is continuous, and part of the task of acquiring a language is to sort out words within sentences and sounds within words. It simplifies only slightly to say that the language system that every child acquires must eventually contain words as separate units and sounds as separate units within a word.

We may ask, then: What must a child know in order to know a word of its language? It is obvious that to know a word is to know both its meaning and its sounds—that is, both content and expression.

Children pass through several stages in learning the words of their language, and there is some disagreement about how they succeed at this task. Some children appear to take up the phrases and clauses of utterances as whole units and later to dissect them into their word parts (a gestalt approach). Others seem to manage a more analytic approach from the start, taking up words directly and constructing phrases and clauses from them as necessary. All speakers eventually sort utterances into distinct units of meaning that are stored in the brain. It is in this internalized dictionary, called the **lexicon** (whose characteristics and structure remain under investigation by linguists and psychologists), that units of meaning are stored as they are acquired.

Focusing our attention on one crucial ingredient in the acquisition of words, we can ask what kind of information a child must learn about the sounds of a word. What is required to be able simply to recognize a word? One not terribly obvious thing is that we must recognize pronunciations of a given word by different people as the same word, whether it is uttered by a woman or a man, a teenager or an octogenarian, a sniffler with a cold, a tired person, or anyone else. To identify words—to understand language—it is essential to disregard certain voice characteristics and certain particularities of volume, speed, and pitch.

A child must observe a word's sounds and the order in which they occur. When learning the word *lip*, for example, a child must eventually know that the word contains the three sounds [l], [ɪ], and [p] and that it contains them in exactly that order. After all, *lip* and *pill* share the same sounds but not in the same order.

Phonemes and Allophones

Eventually every child also learns that certain sounds are pronounced one way in a given context and another way in a different context; thus the "same sound" can have more than one pronunciation.

An example will help reconcile this seeming contradiction. Although English speakers aren't generally aware of the fact, the words *cop* [kɑp] and *keep* [kip] begin with somewhat different [k] sounds, as you will notice if you alternately pronounce the two words. Do not just *listen* for the difference, which is very difficult for English speakers to hear; instead, notice where the tongue touches the roof of your mouth for each sound. You will discover that the tongue touches the velum farther back for *cop* than for *keep*. The reason for this difference is easy enough to understand: in anticipation of pronouncing the back vowel [ɑ], we pronounce the [k] in *cop* farther back in the mouth than the [k] that precedes the front vowel [i] of *keep*.

If pronouncing these words aloud while attending to the position of the back of your tongue as it touches the top of the mouth does not reveal the difference, try this: Position your tongue as if you were about to say *keep*. Then, when your tongue is in position for the initial sound of *keep*, say *cop* instead. You will discover that you have to reposition your tongue in order to pronounce *cop*; if you say *cop* from the *keep* position, it will sound "different," "peculiar," "foreign." The need to reposition the back of your tongue to achieve a natural pronunciation demonstrates that the two [k]-like sounds are not physically identical, though speakers of English think of them as the same.[1]

To cite one more example, you should readily be able to identify differences in the sounds represented by *p* in the first and second words of the word pairs *pot/spot* and *pour/spore*. If you hold the back of your hand (or a

---

[1] In some languages—Basque and Vietnamese, for example—the two [k]-like sounds function as distinct sounds. In fact, the IPA assigns different symbols to them. The voiceless velar stop of *cop* is represented by IPA [k], and the voiceless stop of *keep*, pronounced in the palatal region, is represented by IPA [c].

small piece of paper) up to your mouth when saying these word pairs, you should feel (or see) a considerable difference in the puff of air that accompanies the sounds represented orthographically by *p*. The sound that *p* represents in initial position in *pot* and *pour* is strong enough to blow out a lighted match held in front of the mouth; it is an **aspirated** stop, and we represent it as [pʰ]. The sound following *s* in *spot* and *spore* is not aspirated (and will not blow out a match); we represent it as [p].

In discussing these two *p* sounds, we have specified their respective positions within a word and noted that the different *p* sounds occur in different positions within words. Examine the following list of words and identify the positions in which the two *p* sounds occur.

pill	[pʰɪl]
poker	[pʰokər]
plate	[pʰlet]
sprint	[sprɪnt]
spine	[spayn]

You'll notice that aspirated [pʰ] occurs at the beginning of words (as in *pill*, *poker*, and *plate*), whereas unaspirated [p] occurs after [s] (as in *sprint* and *spine*). When different sounds do not occur in the same position in words but only in different positions, they cannot contrast; we therefore say they occur in **complementary distribution**. Complementary distribution simply means that where one sound occurs, the other does not occur.

In the words just listed, aspirated [pʰ] occurs only word initially, while unaspirated [p] occurs only after [s]; by definition, [pʰ] and [p] occur in complementary distribution and cannot serve to distinguish words from one another. Hence they are not distinctive sounds. Nondistinctive sounds such as [pʰ] and [p] are called allophones of a phoneme. **Allophones** are variants of a single abstract element, or **phoneme**, in the sound system of a language. They cannot serve to create different words, and thus we say they are noncontrastive; to native speakers they seem to be the same sound despite their physical difference. Given that aspirated [pʰ] and unaspirated [p] are allophones of the phoneme /p/ in English, there can be no pair of contrasting words such as [pʰɪt]/[pɪt]. Likewise the two [k] sounds of *cop* and *keep* are allophones of the phoneme /k/ in English and cannot serve to make contrasting words.[2]

Besides the aspirated and unaspirated allophones of /p/, there is a third voiceless bilabial stop in English, also represented orthographically by *p*, as in

---

[2] We have now started using slanted lines / / to enclose phonemes and square brackets [ ] to enclose allophones (that is, sounds). We will continue this practice from now on, though sometimes we will have to choose one representation or the other when either would serve as well.

the word *top*. This allophone of /p/ occurs sometimes at the end of a word that is pronounced at the end of an utterance: *Where's the mop*? In this utterance position, the lips can stay closed so that the sound represented by *p* is unreleased; we represent this allophone as [p˺]. In this case, however, we do not have complementary distribution because both unaspirated [p] and unreleased [p˺] can occur word finally. When two sounds can occur in the same position in a word without contrasting—that is, without creating different words—those sounds are said to occur in **free variation**. At the end of an utterance, English speakers can pronounce the word *lip* as [lɪp] or as [lɪp˺]. Thus, both the unaspirated and unreleased voiceless bilabial stops are allophones of /p/, and the phoneme /p/ therefore has three allophones: aspirated [pʰ], unaspirated [p], and unreleased [p˺]. To repeat, the allophones of a phoneme occur in complementary distribution or in free variation; in neither case can a change of meaning be signaled by the different allophones.

Distribution of Allophones

One way to differentiate phonemes from allophones is to view a phoneme as an abstract element in the sound system of a language—a unit of sound that lacks a fully specified pronunciation but can be pronounced in different ways depending on where in a word it occurs. For example, while all allophones of the phoneme /p/ are voiceless bilabial stops, one is aspirated, another is unaspirated, and a third is unreleased. The pronunciation of the phoneme /p/ cannot be fully specified unless its position in a word (or utterance) is known; only then can its characteristic aspiration and release be determined.

We have just seen that particular allophones are determined by where they occur in a word. If you examine the sets of words in Table 3-1, you will see that the picture is a bit more complicated than that. In these words the mark ˈ is used to indicate primary stress on the following syllable (as in ˈridicule versus riˈdiculous).

All the words have /p/ in syllable-initial position. The words in column A have stress on the first syllable, with [pʰ] as the initial sound. The words in column B also have aspirated [pʰ] word initially, though stress occurs on the

TABLE 3-1

A [pʰ]	B [pʰ]	C [pʰ]	D [p]
ˈpedigree	peˈtunia	emˈporium	ˈempathy
ˈpersonal	paˈternal	comˈputer	compuˈtational
ˈpersecute	peˈninsula	raˈpidograph	ˈrapid
ˈpilgrimage	peˈculiar	comˈpetitive	compeˈtition

TABLE 3-2

Phoneme	Allophones	Distribution
/p/ → [pʰ]	[pʰ]	in syllable-initial position in a stressed syllable and in word-initial position
→ [p]	[p]	elsewhere (as in a consonant cluster following /s/ and in word-final position)

second syllable. The words in columns A and B demonstrate that /p/ is aspirated word initially in stressed and unstressed syllables. In column C aspirated [pʰ] introduces the second syllable, which carries primary stress in each of these words. Thus aspirated [pʰ] occurs not only word initially but word internally, introducing a stressed syllable. The words in column D demonstrate that unaspirated [p] occurs word internally introducing unstressed syllables. We can summarize by saying that the phoneme /p/ is aspirated word initially in stressed and unstressed syllables but is aspirated word internally only initiating stressed syllables.

We must therefore refine our description of the distribution of the allophones of /p/ to take into consideration the stress patterns of a word. An accurate description of the distribution of these allophones of /p/ is shown in Table 3-2.

Keep in mind that certain differences between sounds in a particular language are significant, while other differences are not significant, in that they cannot signal a difference in meaning. The different allophones of /p/ cannot signal differences in meaning because they either occur in different positions within a word or occur in free variation.

Contrast these facts about [pʰ] and [p] with the facts about /s/ and /p/. If a child attempting to learn the word *sat* said *pat* instead, the child would have failed to make one of the significant differences in English: /s/ and /p/ are members of separate phonemes and can serve to distinguish words, as in the following pairs.

A		B		C		D	
[sɪt]	sit	[sʌn]	sun	[læst]	last	[sis]	cease
[pɪt]	pit	[pʌn]	pun	[læpt]	lapped	[sip]	seep

The words in each pair have different meanings and differ by only a single sound. In columns A and B, both words have three sounds, and the only difference between them is the first sound. Two words that differ by only a single sound constitute a **minimal pair**. (Note that the distinction depends on sounds, not on spelling.) Minimal pairs are valuable in identifying the significant sounds—the phonemes—of a language. Each minimal pair above demonstrates that /s/ and /p/ are distinct phonemes of English and not allophones of the same phoneme. Articulatory descriptions of /s/ and /p/ show that these two phonemes differ in both place and manner of articulation.

	/s/	/p/
Voicing	voiceless	voiceless
Place of articulation	alveolar	bilabial
Manner of articulation	fricative	stop

To take another example, /s/ and /b/ differ from one another not only in place and manner of articulation but also in voicing.

	/s/	/b/
Voicing	voiceless	voiced
Place of articulation	alveolar	bilabial
Manner of articulation	fricative	stop

/s/ is a voiceless alveolar fricative, /b/ a voiced bilabial stop. The fact that /s/ and /b/ contrast (as in the minimal pair *sat/bat*) provides definitive evidence that they are significantly different sounds—that they belong to distinct phonemes.

Sounds (allophones) that belong to a single phoneme share certain phonetic features but differ in one or more other features—such as voiced/voiceless, stop/fricative, or dental/alveolar. Therefore, when analyzing the sound system of a language, it is important to take particular note of the distributions of sounds that have similar phonetic descriptions. Consider this list of English words.

[pʰæt]	pat
[bæt]	bat
[tʰæp]	tap
[tʰæb]	tab
[spæt]	spat

[pʰ] and [b] are both bilabial stops; they share those two features. On the other hand, [pʰ] is voiceless and aspirated, while [b] is voiced and unaspirated. Are they distinct phonemes or allophones of a single phoneme? We cannot answer that question by examining the phonetic descriptions alone. Since there is at least one minimal pair above, we know that [pʰ] and [b] contrast. That is, *pat/bat* demonstrates that [pʰ] and [b] are members of different phonemes. Since there are no examples in English in which aspirated [pʰ] and unaspirated [p] contrast (in fact, they occur in complementary distribution), [pʰ] and [p] are allophones of a single phoneme. From the minimal pair *tap/tab* above, we know that unaspirated [p] contrasts with [b]; thus aspirated [pʰ] and unaspirated [p]—both voiceless bilabial stops—contrast with the voiced bilabial stop [b].

The phonemes /p/ and /b/ contrast in both word-initial and word-final position, as we saw above. Sometimes, however, two sounds contrast in some positions but not all. Nevertheless, two sounds remain distinctive if they contrast in *any* position. Consider, for example, the position following /s/ as in the word *s_at*: there are no two words of English like *sbat* and *spat* that carry different meanings. Thus, even though /p/ and /b/ are different phonemes in English, the contrast between them is not exploited in the position following /s/.

Now consider the very different situation in Korean. Like English, Korean has the three sounds [pʰ], [p], and [b], all of which are bilabial stops. The following list of words illustrates their typical occurrence.

[pʰul]	'grass'
[pul]	'fire'
[pəp]	'law'
[mubəp]	'lawlessness'

The minimal pair [pʰul] and [pul] demonstrates that in Korean [p] and [pʰ] contrast. On the other hand, even with a much larger sample of words no minimal pair could be found in which [p] contrasts with [b]; Korean [p] and [b] are in complementary distribution, with [b] occurring only between vowels or other voiced segments, as in [mubəp], and [p] never occurring in that environment. This demonstrates that while [p] and [pʰ] are distinct phonemes in Korean, [p] and [b] are allophones of a single phoneme.

The diagram in Table 3-3 represents the difference in the phonological systems of English and Korean with respect to these three sounds. It is important to underscore that although the same three sounds occur in both languages, their systematic role in those languages is altogether different. In English, [pʰ] and [p] are not functionally different; they are noncontrastive allophones of a single phoneme and cannot differentiate meanings. In Korean, [pʰ] and [p] are significantly different sounds; that is, they are

TABLE 3-3

English Phonemes	Sounds English and Korean	Korean Phonemes
/p/ ⟶	[pʰ] ⟵	/pʰ/
	[p] ⟵	/p/
/b/ ⟶	[b] ⟵	

separate phonemes and can distinguish one word from another (as in [pʰul] and [pul]). In terms of articulatory properties, voicing is phonemic in English; the voiced bilabial stop [b] is distinct from the voiceless bilabial stop [p]. Aspiration, however, is not phonemic: no two phonemes in English are different solely because one is aspirated and the other is not. In Korean, on the other hand, the voiced bilabial stop [b] is an allophone of /p/ occurring between voiced sounds; hence [b] and [p] cannot be used to distinguish Korean words. We can summarize by saying that in Korean voicing is not contrastive but aspiration is, while in English aspiration is not contrastive but voicing is.

Now consider the words of Japanese in Table 3-4, noting the distributional patterns of the sounds [l] and [r].

From these examples, we can hypothesize that [l] and [r] occur in complementary distribution and therefore cannot contrast in Japanese. The fact is that even with a good many additional examples we would find no instances of a minimal [l]/[r] pair: no pair of words such as *lan*/"*ran*" or "*ilo*"/*iro* exists. Instead, [l] occurs only word initially, as in the examples in column A, while [r] occurs only between vowels, as in column B. (Contrast this with English *lent*/*rent* or *miller*/*mirror*.) Thus [l] and [r] are allophones of a single Japanese phoneme, and their distribution can be specified as in Table 3-5.

TABLE 3-4

A		B	
lan	(a kind of flower)	nara	'if'
lika	'science'	amari	'extra'
lusu	'absence'	sore	'that'
lekishi	'history'	naru	'to ring'
loku	'six'	iro	'color'

TABLE 3-5

Phoneme	Allophones	Distribution
/r/ $\longrightarrow$ [l] [r]		word initially between vowels

Given the fact that [l] and [r] do not contrast in Japanese but occur in complementary distribution, it is interesting to ask whether a Japanese child who hears the words listed (and many others with similar patterns of distribution) will create distinct representations for [l] and [r] in its internalized lexicon. Before answering this question, it will be helpful first to examine a similar process that is more familiar to English speakers.

PHONOLOGICAL RULES AND THEIR STRUCTURE

Consider the process by which vowels become nasalized preceding nasal consonants in English words. In the following list, the words in column B have nasalized vowels (vowels pronounced through the nose, in addition to the mouth), while those in column A have oral vowels (vowels pronounced through the mouth).[3]

A	B
sit	sin
pet	pen
light	lime
brute	broom
sitter	singer

If you examine nasal vowels in English words, you will discover that all of them precede one of the nasal consonants /m n ŋ/. The distribution of nasal vowels in English is perfectly regular and predictable: before a nasal consonant a vowel is nasalized. Since the distribution is predictable, the occurrence of nasal vowels cannot signal a meaning distinction (as it can in

---

[3] To discover that the vowels in column B are nasalized, pinch your nose closed while saying the words in each column. For the words in column A, it will make no perceptible difference in the pronunciation; for those in column B, it will make a noticeable difference. This demonstrates that when you pronounce the words of column B, air from the lungs exits through the nasal passage; hence when that passage is blocked the sound of the vowel changes perceptibly.

French and some other languages). Two sounds whose distribution with respect to one another is predictable constitute allophones of a single phoneme; their distribution is describable by a general rule.

Regular **phonological rules** have this general form:

$$A \longrightarrow B \; / \; C \underline{\hspace{2cm}} D$$

Such a rule can be expressed as "A becomes B in the environment following C and preceding D." Often the phrase "in the environment" is omitted; thus "A becomes B following C and preceding D." A, B, C, and D are generally specified in terms of phonetic features, although in this book most rules will be presented in somewhat more informal terms. In cases where it is unnecessary to specify both C and D, one of them will be missing. For example, the phonological process of nasalization can be represented by the following rule statement:

$$\text{vowel} \longrightarrow \text{nasal} \; / \; \underline{\hspace{2cm}} \text{nasal}$$

(vowels become nasalized preceding nasal sounds)

As noted in the introduction to this chapter, in acquiring a word a child must learn the number of phonemes in the word, what those phonemes are, and in what order they occur. As the English *cop/keep* alternation shows for the allophones of /k/ and the *pour/spore* alternation shows for the allophones of /p/ (and as the [l]/[r] alternation shows for the allophones of /r/ in Japanese), a child must also learn to pronounce particular allophones of a phoneme depending on the phoneme's position in a word and the character of nearby sounds. This is done not by memorizing the sounds in each individual word but by acquiring rules that apply to all words, as in the nasalization rule above.

The situation for a child acquiring Japanese [l] and [r] is similar to that of an English-speaking child acquiring the process of forming nasal vowels. Since [l] and [r] never contrast, they are allophones of a single phoneme; thus only one form is needed to represent them in the lexicon (along with a phonological rule that specifies the distribution of [l] in word-initial position and [r] between vowels). The alternative to having a single representation in the lexicon for [l] and [r] in Japanese would involve considerable inefficiency. It would require a specific differentiation between these sounds in every word that contains either of them. For example, *loku* 'six' and *aruku* 'walk' would have different specifications for [l] and [r]. To a speaker of English (which does not have a predictable distribution of [l] and [r]), this differentiation seems quite natural and necessary. But to have different forms for [l] and [r] in the lexicon of a Japanese speaker would be equivalent to an English speaker's having different representations in the lexicon for the different /k/ sounds of *cop* and *keep*, for the different /p/ sounds of *pot* and *spot*, or for the different /ɪ/ sounds of *sit* and *sin*. Moreover, unless there were consistent different spellings assigned to each allophone, a reader coming across the preceding word pairs for the first time would be unable to know their pronunciations. However, each phoneme is in fact represented in the lexicon by only one underlying form. Native speakers internalize the phonological rules specifying the distribution of allophones and automatically apply these rules whenever the phoneme appears.[4]

Since the distribution of the allophones of every phoneme is regular, a great deal of memory in the mental dictionary is saved by specifying only the phonemes in a word; a few general phonological rules can then specify the correct allophone for each occurrence of the phoneme. To see how this process works, picture the brain as a computer with a very large but finite memory. Every redundant piece of information that is stored in a computer makes valuable memory space unavailable for other uses. Linguists think that a significant degree of "space" in the brain is saved by specifying only the distinctive features of each phoneme (thus, "voiceless bilabial stop" for /p/) and leaving the specification of allophonic features (such as "aspiration" or "release") to a few general rules that apply to thousands of words and to all new words as they enter a person's lexicon.

Generalizing Phonological Rules

Until now we have been considering phonological rules as though they were formulated to apply to particular sounds; in fact, they are more general. Consider the aspiration that accompanies the production of initial /p/ in English words like *pillow* and *pot*; it can be represented by the following rule:

(a) voiceless
     bilabial ———→ aspirated / word initially and initially
     stop   in stressed syllables

This representation says that a voiceless bilabial stop is aspirated when it initiates a stressed syllable and when it is word initial.

If you examine other English words with stop consonants, you will notice that it is not only /p/ that has aspiration when syllable initial but also /t/ and /k/. Since /p t k/ have parallel distributions of these allophones, English would appear to need two additional rules like the one in (a). These are given

---

[4] One indication, incidentally, that such information as the differences between allophones is not in fact stored in the lexicon can be found in pronunciations of a nonnative language. Consider a native speaker of English who knows no French and has been introduced by a native speaker of French to a friend named Pierre. Unlike English, French does not aspirate initial /p/, so the French speaker introducing Pierre will pronounce his name without aspiration. English speakers—despite the fact that they have *not* heard aspiration in the pronunciation of *Pierre*—will nevertheless tend to pronounce *Pierre* with an aspirated [pʰ]. This reformulation of Pierre's name to conform to the phonological rules of English indicates that English speakers have a general rule that aspirates initial /p/, even when speaking French. The subconscious application of the phonological rules of one's native tongue to a foreign language contributes to a foreign accent and marks one as a nonnative speaker.

as (b) and (c):

(b) For /t/:

> voiceless
> alveolar ⟶ aspirated / word initially and initially
> stop   in stressed syllables

(c) For /k/:

> voiceless
> velar ⟶ aspirated / word initially and initially
> stop   in stressed syllables

Because these three rules exhaust the list of voiceless stops in English, they can be collapsed into a single rule of greater generality as follows:

(d) For /p/, /t/, and /k/:

> voiceless ⟶ aspirated / word initially and initially
> stop   in stressed syllables

Notice in (d) that the combination of the phonetic features "voiceless" and "stop" leaves the place of articulation unspecified. In the absence of any specification, a phonological rule like (d) will apply to all voiceless stops irrespective of place of articulation; it will apply to bilabial, alveolar, and velar voiceless stops.

The more general a rule is, the easier it is to state using phonetic feature notation. Moreover, there is considerable evidence that the brain's lexicon seeks similar simplicity. It appears that internalized phonological rules are specified not in terms of allophones such as [p] and [pʰ], or in terms of phonemes such as /p/, /t/, and /k/, but in terms of *classes* of sounds specified by sets of phonetic features such as "voiceless" and "stop."

Natural Classes of Sounds

A set of phonemes such as /p t k/ that can be described using fewer features than would be necessary to describe each sound individually is called a **natural class of sounds**. A natural class of sounds contains all the sounds that share one or more features. Thus /p t k/ constitute the natural class of "voiceless stops" in English. /p t k/ share the two features "voiceless" and "stop," and there are no other sounds in English that have both of those features.

Now consider the set /p t k b d g/. This is the natural class of "stops." There are no other stops in English, and all the sounds in the set share the feature "stop."

The set of sounds /p t k b d/ would *not* constitute a natural class. To be sure, the five sounds share the feature "stop"—but so does /g/, which is not included. Whatever feature we use to describe this set would also describe /g/. Notice too that the set /p t k m/ does not constitute a natural class,

TABLE 3-6

Underlying Form	Surface Form	Written Form
/kʌlər/	[kʰʌlər]	color (aspiration)
/bʊk/	[bʊk]	book
/bit/	[bit]	beat
/ʌp/	[ʌp]	up
/spɪn/	[spɪ̃n]	spin (nasalization)
/pɪn/	[pʰɪ̃n]	pin (aspiration/nasalization)

because any feature we introduce to specify /m/ also belongs to other sounds. Adding the feature "nasal" to the description in order to accommodate /m/ would entail including /n/ and /ŋ/, because these too are nasals. Notice, however, that in order to specify the set /p t k m n ŋ/ we would need an either/or description: either "voiceless stop" or "nasal." There is no combination of features that uniquely specifies just those six sounds; hence /p t k m n ŋ/ is not a natural class.

Underlying Forms

Thanks to internalized rules that yield the correct allophones for every phoneme in a given word, children eventually can produce entries in their lexicons like those in Table 3-6. Such forms are called **underlying forms**; we will represent them between slanted lines, using the same notation we have used for phonemes. The **surface form**, which characterizes a word's actual pronunciation, results from the application of the phonological rules of English to the underlying forms. In some cases the surface form is the same as the underlying form simply because there are no applicable phonological rules.

Rule Ordering

One additional phonological rule will illustrate a point about the organization of phonological rules in the mind. Consider the following words:

A	B
write	ride
neat	need
rope	robe
lop	lob
lock	log
tap	tab
pick	pig

If you listen carefully while pronouncing these words, you may notice that the vowels in column B have a longer duration than those in the corresponding words of column A. We represent long vowels with a macron over them, as in ā. Since in English there is no minimal pair such as [pɪt]/[pīt] or [bɛt]/[bēt], we know that vowel length is noncontrastive, nonphonemic (see pp. 65–66). In English, vowel length is predictable and can be specified by a general phonological rule. What environment in the words in the list causes vowel lengthening? If you look past the spelling, you will see that the words of column A end with a voiceless consonant, while the words of column B end in a voiced consonant. In fact, there is a general process of English phonology that lengthens vowels preceding voiced consonants. We can state that rule as follows (V stands for vowel, C for consonant):

$$V \longrightarrow \text{long} \ / \ \underline{\hspace{1cm}} \ \begin{array}{c} C \\ \text{voiced} \end{array}$$

(vowels become long preceding voiced consonants)

As a result of this rule, the following processes take place in English:

$$\varepsilon \longrightarrow \bar{\varepsilon} \ / \ \underline{\hspace{1cm}} \ /d/ \quad \text{(as in } bed \text{ versus } bet\text{)}$$

$$\text{ɪ} \longrightarrow \bar{\text{ɪ}} \ / \ \underline{\hspace{1cm}}, \ /g/ \quad \text{(as in } pig \text{ versus } pick\text{)}$$

$$\text{ay} \longrightarrow \bar{\text{a}}\text{y} \ / \ \underline{\hspace{1cm}} \ /d/ \quad \text{(as in } slide \text{ versus } slight\text{)}$$

(Note that this rule applies to diphthongs like /ay/.) Because vowel length is predictable in English, it can be specified by rule and need not be learned for every word individually. In many other languages, vowel length is not predictable, not specifiable by a rule. In Fijian, for example, there is a minimal pair *oya* 'he, she' and *oyā* 'that [thing].' *Dredre* means 'to laugh'; *drēdrē* means 'difficult.' *Vakariri* means 'to boil'; *vakarirī* means 'speedily.' Thus in Fijian vowel length cannot be assigned by a phonological rule and is therefore contrastive, significant, phonemic in that language.

Now consider the following pairs of words, paying particular attention to how the pronunciation of each word in column A differs from that of the corresponding word in column B. Notice that the difference is not the one represented by the spelling difference of *t* and *d*; instead, it is a difference of vowel length. For most dialects of American English, the first vowels in the words of column B are longer than those of column A.

A	B
writer	rider
liter	leader
seater	seeder
sighter	cider
rooter	ruder

The reason the medial consonants do not differ in pronunciation is that Americans tend to "flap" /t/ and /d/ between vowels in these words. A flap is a sound produced when one articulator rapidly touches another articulator a single time (see Chapter 2). In the pronunciation of /t/ or /d/ in the words above, the tip of the tongue rapidly flaps against the alveolar ridge. Because the flap allophones of /t/ and /d/ are identical (represented by the symbol [D]), the difference of pronunciation that might have resulted from the t/d distinction is lost, or **neutralized**. Notice that the distinction is not lost in the words *write* [rayt]/*ride* [rāyd]. The flapping rule for American English is specified as follows, with V an abbreviation for vowel:

alveolar   ⟶   flap   /   V   _____   V
stop   voiced   stress   unstressed

(/t d/ become [D] between a stressed and an unstressed vowel)

Even though the t/d distinction is lost in this environment by the flapping rule, many Americans pronounce the words in column B above differently from those in column A. By combining the flapping rule and the lengthening rule, they pronounce the words in column B with a vowel of longer duration, despite the fact that there is no difference in the pronunciation of the medial consonant. Let's see why.

We have now specified two rules of English that can operate on the same words, and we want to see how they interact in producing a pronounceable surface form. Consider, for example, the pair of words *writer* and *rider*. Assume that the underlying forms in the lexicon are /raytər/ for *writer* and /raydər/ for *rider*. We can then represent the derivation of the surface forms as illustrated in Table 3-7. (When the form of a word does not meet the requirements of a rule, that rule does not apply, and we write DNA.) From the underlying forms and the application of the two rules in the order shown (lengthening first, flapping second), the surface forms [rayDər] and [rāyDər] are produced. This is in fact the correct output—the correct pronunciations

TABLE 3-7

	Dialect A	
Underlying form	/raytər/	/raydər/
Lengthening rule	DNA	
Derived form	[raytər]	[rāydər]
Flapping rule		
Surface form	[rayDər]	[rāyDər]

TABLE 3-8

	Dialect B	
Underlying form	/raytər/	/raydər/
Flapping rule	↓	↓
Derived form	[rayDər]	[rayDər]
Lengthening rule	↓	↓
Surface form	[rāyDər]	[rāyDər]

of these words for some speakers of English, whom we'll call speakers of dialect A.

If we apply the same two rules in the reverse order (flapping first, lengthening second), the results will be different because the flapped sound is voiced; therefore the vowel preceding it would be lengthened in both words. As Table 3-8 shows, this is precisely what happens for speakers of another variety of English, which we'll call dialect B.

The two identical surface forms [rāyDər] and [rāyDər] that are derived by applying the flapping rule preceding the lengthening rule would not be correct for dialect A. In that dialect (the more common one), *writer* and *rider* are not pronounced alike; instead, *rider* has a longer vowel than *writer*. Thus, given the same underlying forms, we see that the same pair of phonological rules if applied in one order produces surface forms that are correct in a given dialect; if applied in the other order, however, the rules produce incorrect forms. We conclude that rule ordering is an essential part of the organization of phonological rules.

It is important to recognize that the forms resulting from the second derivation, though incorrect in dialect A, are correct in dialect B. This illustrates how speakers of different dialects can share the same rules but apply them in different sequences. Dialects that apply the lengthening rule before the flapping rule will have distinct forms of *writer* and *rider*. Dialects that apply flapping before lengthening will produce identical forms, both with a long vowel. Different orderings of the same rules are thus one mechanism to explain pronunciation differences among dialects.

SYLLABLE STRUCTURE

We have said little so far about how sounds are organized sequentially within words. It may seem obvious that sounds occur in words simply as a sequence *abcdef*, but that is not entirely correct. Instead, sounds are organized into syllables using strictly limited vowel and consonant combina-

TABLE 3-9

One Syllable	Two Syllables	Three Syllables	Four Syllables
ton /tʌn/	even /i–vən/	loveliest /lʌv–li–əst/	anybody /ɛ–ni–bɑ–di/
spin /spɪn/	although /ɔl–ðo/	anyone /ɛ–ni–wən/	respectively /ri–spɛk–təv–li/
through /θru/	consists /kən–sɪsts/	syllable /sɪl–ə–bəl/	definition /dɛf–ə–nɪ–šən/
sail /sel/	writer /ray–tər/	computer /kəm–pyu–tər/	algebraic /æl–jə̌–bre–ək/

tions that differ from language to language. Syllables, in turn, are organized into words. Each word consists of one or more syllables, and each syllable consists of one or more sounds.

Syllable is generally an easy notion for native speakers of a language to understand, although technical definitions are not straightforward. Table 3-9 gives some English words with one, two, three, and four syllables. In general, a **syllable** is a phonological unit consisting of one or more sounds. Each syllable has a nucleus, which is usually a vowel (but it can be certain consonants such as [r] and [n]). Syllables are usually smaller than a word and bigger than a single sound, but some single sounds can be syllables and some single syllables are words. The English sound [ə] is a syllable and a word (as in *a book*).

The kinds of sounds that can make up a syllable differ from language to language and are strictly limited within each language. If you examine the four words of the following phrase, you will notice that English syllables allow several patterns of consonants and vowels. (We use the abbreviations C for consonant and V for vowel; as in the transcriptions above, we have separated the words into syllables with dashes – .)

in a pre–vi–ous chap–ter
/ɪn ə pri–vɪ–əs čæp–tər/
VC V CCV–CV–VC CVC–CVC

From this example, we see that English allows the following syllable types: VC, V, CCV, CV, and CVC. Other syllable structures can be seen in words like *past* (CVCC), *square* (CCCVC), *churned* (CVCCC), *squirts* (CCCVCCC); and there are still other possible syllable structures in English.

Not every language allows as wide a variety of syllable types as English does. In fact, the preferred syllable type among the world's languages is a simple CV—a single consonant followed by a single vowel. Another very common syllable is CVC, and a third is simply V. (All three of these occur in the illustrative phrase.) Polynesian languages such as Samoan, Tahitian, and Hawaiian have CV and V syllables only. Similarly, Japanese allows syllables only of the forms CV, V, and (if the last consonant is /n/) CVC. Korean permits V, CV, and CVC syllables.

It is not very common in the languages of the world to have initial consonant clusters—CC—as in the English words *try, twin*, and *pray*; and it is very uncommon to have initial consonant clusters of more than two consonants—CCC—as in *scream, sprint*, and *stress*. In fact, even in English there is a limited range of consonants that can occur in each of the positions C_1C_2 of a two-consonant cluster and an extremely narrow range of consonants in each of the positions $C_1C_2C_3$ of a three-consonant cluster. (It is no coincidence that our three illustrations of initial CCC all begin with /s/.) Likewise, English three-consonant clusters initiating a syllable have different constraints from those clusters that are syllable final.

The rules that describe possible syllable structures in a language are called **phonotactic constraints**. As a result of such constraints, there are—besides the words that exist in a language—thousands of words that do not exist but *could* and thousands upon thousands more that cannot exist because their syllable structures are not permissible sequences of vowels and consonants in that language. The following are impossible words of Hawaiian and Japanese: "pat" (CVC), "pleat" (CCVC), and "stew" (CCV).

Comedian Rich Hall has compiled books of "sniglets"—words that do not appear in the dictionary but should. Here are some of Hall's "sniglets," along with their proposed definitions.

charp 'the green mutant potato chip found in every bag'

elbonics 'the actions of two people maneuvering for one arm rest in a movie theater'

glarpo 'the juncture of the ear and skull where pencils are stored'

hozone 'the place where one sock in every laundry disappears to'

spibble 'the metal barrier on a rotary telephone that prevents you from dialing past 0'

Notice that these English "sniglets"—like all English words—conform to the phonotactic constraints of the language. The following are not possible English words; they cannot serve as "sniglets": "ptlin," "brkow," "tsmtot."

Facing foreign languages whose syllable structures differ from those of their native tongue, speakers often impose the constraints of their native syllable structures on the foreign words. Thus, because neither Spanish nor Persian permits initial consonant clusters such as /st/ and /sp/, native speakers of Spanish and Persian pronounce the English words *study* and *speech* as "e–study" /ɛstʌdɪ/ and "e–speech" /ɛspič/.

SUMMARY

Chapter 3 examines phonological systems. A *phoneme* is a unit in the phonological system of a language; it is an abstract element, a set of phonetic features having several possible manifestations, called *allophones*, in speech. Two words can differ minimally by virtue of having a single pair of different phonemes (as in *pin/bin*).

Each phoneme comprises a set of allophones—each allophone being the particular realization of the phoneme in a particular linguistic environment. The allophones of a phoneme occur in complementary distribution or in free variation; they never contrast. Allophones of a single phoneme cannot be the sole difference in a minimal pair of words with different meanings.

Different languages can have the same sounds and yet organize them differently in their sound systems. Both Korean and English have the three sounds [p], [pʰ], and [b] in their inventories. In English, unaspirated [p] and aspirated [pʰ] are allophones of one phoneme, while [b] belongs to a different phoneme. In Korean, on the other hand, aspirated [pʰ] and unaspirated [p] contrast, while [b] is merely the allophone of the phoneme /p/ that occurs between voiced sounds.

Each simple word in a speaker's internalized lexicon consists of a sequence of phonemes that constitutes the abstract underlying phonological representation of the word. *Underlying forms* differ from pronunciations; they are more abstract and must be inferred, and they cannot be directly observed in speech. From the underlying form of a word, the phonological rules of a language specify the allophonic features of its phonemes in accordance with the linguistic environment of the particular allophones.

One fundamental task of children in acquiring language is to uncover the phonological rules of their language and to infer the most efficient, economical, abstract underlying forms for word units. From these abstract underlying forms, the phonological rules of a language will specify the rule-governed features of the *surface form*.

Phonological rules are ordered with respect to one another, the first applicable rule applying to the underlying form to produce a derived form, the subsequent rules applying in turn to successive derived forms until the last applicable rule produces a surface form. The surface form is the basis of a word's pronunciation. Two dialects of a language could contain the same rules but apply them in a different order, thereby producing different surface forms for different pronunciations.

Words are made up of groups of sounds called *syllables*, not of sounds themselves. Various languages of the world have different limits on the structure of possible syllable types and the occurrence of particular consonants and vowels within syllable types. CV is the most common syllable type in the world's languages. English has an unusually large range of syllable types, including consonant clusters of two or three consonants.

EXERCISES

1.   Consider the following words of English with respect to how the sound represented by *t* is pronounced. Specify for each column what the phonetic character of the allophone is. Then, as was done in this chapter for the allophones of /p/, describe the allophones of /t/ in English and specify their distribution.

A	B	C	D
tougher	standing	matter	petunia
talker	still	data	potato
teller	story	petal	return

2.   Fijian is an example of a language with prenasalized stops in its phonological inventory. The prenasalized stop [^{n}d] consists of a nasal pronounced immediately before the stop, with which it forms a single sound unit. Consider the following Fijian words as they are pronounced in fast speech:

vi^{n}di	'to spring up'	dina	'true'
ke^{n}da	'we'	dalo	'taro plant'
tiko	'to stay'	vu^{n}di	'plantain banana'
tutu	'grandfather'	ma^{n}da	'first'
viti	'Fiji'	tina	'mother'
dovu	'sugarcane'	mata	'eye'
do^{n}do	'to stretch out one's hand'	mokiti	'round'
		veve^{n}du	(a type of plant)

On the basis of these data, determine whether in Fijian [d], [^{n}d], and [t] are allophones of a single phoneme or are two or three distinct phonemes. If you find that two of them (or all of them) are allophones of a single phoneme, state the rule that describes the distribution of each allophone. If they are all different phonemes, justify your answer. (Note that in Fijian all syllables must end in a vowel.)

3.   Examine the following words of Tongan, a Polynesian language:

tauhi	'to take care'	sino	'body'
sisi	'garland'	totonu	'correct'
motu	'island'	pasi	'to clap'
mosimosi	'to drizzle'	fata	'shelf'
motomoto	'unripe'	movete	'to come apart'
fesi	'to break'	misi	'to dream'

(a)   On the basis of these data, determine whether in Tongan [s] and [t] are allophones of a single phoneme or are two separate phonemes. If you find that they are allophones of the same phoneme, state the rule that describes the distribution of each allophone. If they are different phonemes, justify your answer. (In Tongan all syllables must end in a vowel.)

(b)   In each of the following Tongan words, one sound has been replaced by a blank. This sound is either [s] or [t]. Without more knowledge of Tongan than you were able to figure out from (a), is it possible to make an educated guess as to which of these two sounds fits in the blank? If so, provide the sound; if not, explain why.

___ili	'fishing net'	fe___e	'lump'
___uku	'to place'	lama___i	'to ambush'

(c) In the course of this century, Tongan has borrowed many words from English and has adapted them to fit the phonological structure of its words. Here are a few examples:

kāsete	'gazette'	sū	'shoe'
tisi	'dish'	koniseti	'concert'
sosaieti	'society'	pata	'butter'
salati	'salad'	suka	'sugar'
māsolo	'marshall'	sikā	'cigar'
sekoni	'second'	taimani	'diamond'

How does the phonemic status of [s] and [t] differ in borrowed words and in native Tongan words? Write an integrated statement about the status of [s] and [t] in Tongan. (Your statement will have to include information about which area of the Tongan vocabulary each part of the rule applies to.)

4. The distribution of the sounds [s] and [z] in colloquial Spanish is represented by the following examples in phonetic transcription:

izla	'island'	čiste	'joke'
fuersa	'force'	eski	'ski'
peskado	'fish'	riezgo	'risk'
muskulo	'muscle'	fiskal	'fiscal'
sin	'without'	rezvalar	'to slip'
rasko	'I scratch'	dezde	'since'
resto	'remainder'	razgo	'feature'
mizmo	'same'	beizbɔl	'baseball'
espalda	'back'		

Are [s] and [z] separate phonemes of Spanish or allophones of a single phoneme? If they are different phonemes, support your answer; if they are allophones of the same phoneme, state the rule that specifies their distribution.

5. Consider the following Russian words. On the basis of this limited list, where does Russian appear to have a contrast between [t] and [d] and where does it appear not to have one?

paroxot	'steamboat'	tyelo	'body'
gazyeta	'newspaper'	pot	'perspiration'
zapat	'west'	dorogiy	'dear'
rat	'glad'	dyelo	'business'
zdaniye	'building'	štat	'state'
most	'bridge'	pot	'under'

6. In Samoan, words may have two forms: a casual form used when addressing peers or kin and a formal form for use with chiefs or strangers. The difference between the two forms can be described by phonological rules.

Casual	Formal	
tātou	kākou	'us all'
teine	keiŋe	'girl'
taŋata	kaŋaka	'man'
ŋaŋana	ŋaŋaŋa	'language'
totoŋi	kokoŋi	'price'
nofo	ŋofo	'to stay'
ŋālue	ŋālue	'to work'
fono	foŋo	'meeting'

(a) Describe the phonological difference between the casual and formal forms. Which form is more basic—the formal form or the casual form (in other words, which form can serve as the underlying form for both forms)?

(b) Wherever possible, fill in the blanks in the following table. If it is impossible to know the form of a missing word, say why.

Casual	Formal	
manu		'bird'
mate		'dead'
	maŋō	'shark'
	kili	'fishing net'
tonu		'correct'
	kaŋi	'to cry'

7. In German, the sequence of letters *ch* can represent (among other things) either of two sounds: [ç] (a voiceless palatal fricative) or [x] (a voiceless velar fricative). On the basis of the following data, determine whether these two sounds are distinct phonemes in German or allophones of a single phoneme.

kɛlç	*Kelch*	'cup'
fıçtə	*Fichte*	'fir tree'
çarısma	*Charisma*	'charisma'
knœçl	*Knöchel*	'knuckle'
kɔx	*Koch*	'cook'
tsurɛçt	*zurecht*	'in good order'
vʊxt	*Wucht*	'weight'
çırʊrk	*Chirurg*	'surgeon'
nüçtən	*nüchtern*	'sober'
bʊx	*Buch*	'book'
bɛrayç	*Bereich*	'scope'
hɛkçən	*Häkchen*	'apostrophe'

If [ç] and [x] are distinct phonemes, justify your answer; if they are allophones of the same phoneme, provide the rule that determines which will appear in which context.

8. We do not think that any of the following words exist in English. Some of them are candidates for "sniglets" (that is, they *could* exist), while others violate the phonotactic constraints of English. Which are potential sniglets, and why are the others not permitted? For the words that are potential sniglets, provide an appropriate spelling in the standard orthography.

pɛtribɑr	twɪnč	rizənənt
læktomæŋgyulešən	pʌpkəss	blɪbyulə
pæŋgəkd	spret	spwent
čiDəl	ltrayk	

9. In light of our discussions in this chapter and your experience with the preceding exercises, discuss the following quote from Halle and Clements (1983).

> The perception of intelligible speech is . . . determined only in part by the physical signal that strikes our ears. Of equal significance . . . is the contribution made by the perceiver's knowledge of the language in which the utterance is framed. Acts of perception that heavily depend on active contributions from the perceiver's mind are often described as illusions, and the perception of intelligible speech seems . . . to qualify for this description. A central problem of phonetics and phonology is . . . to provide a scientific characterization of this illusion which is at the heart of all human existence.

SUGGESTIONS FOR FURTHER READING

Wolfram and Johnson (1982) is an excellent introduction to the phonological analysis of English, with many illustrations and examples. Sloat et al. (1978) is unusually clear and accessible in both phonetics and phonology and treats a range of languages. The "problem book" by Halle and Clements (1983) also has a broader coverage of languages than Wolfram and Johnson; besides an excellent introductory chapter that goes beyond what we have covered, there are separate chapters on complementary distribution, natural classes, phonological rules, and systems of rules. Anderson (1974) and Hyman (1975) pay attention to the development of phonological theory. Dell (1980) was first published in 1973 and is a valuable treatment—with a bias toward French—of the kind of phonology made popular in Chomsky and Halle's classic book (1968). More recent treatments of phonology include Kenstowicz and Kisseberth (1979), Lass (1984), and Hawkins (1984). Schane (1973) is very basic and clear.

REFERENCES

Anderson, Stephen. 1974. *The Organization of Phonology* (New York: Seminar Press).

Chomsky, Noam, and Morris Halle. 1968. *The Sound Pattern of English* (New York: Harper & Row).

Dell, François. 1980. *Generative Phonology*, translated from the 1973 French edition by Catherine Cullen (Cambridge: Cambridge University Press; Paris: Hermann).

Hall, Rich, and friends. 1984. *Sniglets* (New York: Collier Books).

Halle, Morris, and G. N. Clements. 1983. *Problem Book in Phonology* (Cambridge: MIT Press).

Hawkins, Peter. 1984. *Introducing Phonology* (London: Hutchinson).

Hyman, Larry M. 1975. *Phonology: Theory and Analysis* (New York: Holt, Rinehart and Winston).

Kenstowicz, Michael, and Charles Kisseberth. 1979. *Generative Phonology: Description and Theory* (New York: Academic Press).

Lass, Roger. 1984. *Phonology* (Cambridge: Cambridge University Press).

Schane, Sanford A. 1973. *Generative Phonology* (Englewood Cliffs, N.J.: Prentice-Hall).

Sloat, Clarence, Sharon Henderson Taylor, and James E. Hoard. 1978. *Introduction to Phonology* (Englewood Cliffs, N.J.: Prentice-Hall).

Wolfram, Walt, and Robert Johnson. 1982. *Phonological Analysis: Focus on American English* (Washington, D.C.: Center for Applied Linguistics and Harcourt Brace Jovanovich).

MORPHOLOGY: STRUCTURED MEANING IN WORDS

4

WORDS AND THEIR PARTS

For most people, the most basic and most tangible elements of a language are probably its words. "There's no such word," people occasionally say. Or, "What does the word *futharc* mean?" Or, from someone doing a crossword puzzle, "What's a three-letter word for 'excessively'?" We say that one person always uses "two-bit" words, while someone else exhibits a preference for "four-letter" words. Intuitively, people seem to have clear notions of what a word is.

When it comes to identifying meaningful units smaller than a word, our intuitions are not so clear. Though we readily intuit that *car, walk, sing*, and *tall* each have one single meaningful element and that *bookstore, gameshow*, and *sidestep* have two each, our intuitions are less certain about the number of meaningful elements in words such as *bookkeeper, sneakers, women's, impracticality, fenced, resumed*, and *presumption*. This chapter examines the segmentation of words into their meaningful elements, the principles that govern the construction of words from meaningful elements, and the functions of words and word parts in sentences. We will describe what it means to know a word, and we will discuss the ways in which a language can expand its stock of words.

Words

Let's examine a sentence of English with respect to its words:

> Not too proud to ask their wives for help in baking the apples, the men gave up hoping to surprise them with a homemade dessert.

As almost anybody who speaks English can tell you, that sentence has twenty-five words in it. But how does someone come up with that number? Probably with a simple procedure: counting the number of letter groups separated by spaces. Backing away from the printed version, however, if we say the sentence aloud it is possible that only one "space," or silence, will occur—the one between *apples* and *the men*. Of course, speakers are nevertheless correct in saying that the sentence has twenty-five words, not two. English speakers hearing the sentence said aloud could also determine that it has twenty-five words (presumably by matching items in their lexicons with parts of the utterance), even though the utterance has no "spaces" between words to parallel the written version.

Notice that in claiming twenty-five words, we count *the* twice (once each in *the apples* and *the men*) and *to* twice (once each in *to ask* and *to surprise*). In answer to the question "How many *different* words are there in the sentence?" we would say twenty-three. More technically, we could say that there are twenty-three distinct words and that two of these word types (*the* and *to*) have two occurrences each. (Notice, too, that *homemade* is counted as a single word.)

What about *too* in *too proud*? Is it the same word as the *to* of *to ask*? Judging by the customary spelling, *too* and *to* are different words. But, someone might ask, aren't they pronounced alike? In fact, they are not. *Too* is pronounced [tu], whereas *to* is normally [tə]. That observation argues for establishing *to* and *too* as distinct words. Other arguments could be based on their different meanings and different functions in the sentence. As to meaning, *Not too proud* could be paraphrased something like *not so proud* or *not excessively proud*. Functionally, *too* qualifies (or modifies) the adjective *proud*, and as such it is an adverb. The *to* of *to ask* and *to surprise* cannot be paraphrased in the same way; in fact, *to* does not have any easily paraphrased meaning. It seems counterintuitive to say *to* qualifies or modifies *ask* and *surprise*; it certainly does not modify them in the same way that *too* specifies a degree of *proud*. *To* is part of the verbs *ask* and *surprise*, but it does not alter or affect their meanings in any discernible way; instead, it serves to mark the infinitive form of these verbs (and in so doing is also different from the preposition *to* in a phrase like *to school*).

We have given three arguments (aside from spelling) in support of the view that *too* and *to* are different words: an argument from pronunciation, an argument from meaning, and an argument from function. Similar kinds of arguments could be advanced to demonstrate that *to* in *to ask* and *to surprise* are merely different occurrences of the same word. What about the two occurrences of *the* in *the apples* and *the men*? Are they occurrences of a single word, or are they different words? For most speakers of English, they are pronounced differently—as [ði] in *the apple* and as [ðə] in *the men*. We argued above that the different pronunciations of *too* and *to* pointed to their being different words. Do different pronunciations in the case of *the* argue for the existence of two words? Speakers of English will generally agree that the two pronunciations of *the* do not represent distinct words because they function in exactly parallel ways and "mean" the same thing. As you may have recognized, *the* is pronounced [ði] before vowels and [ðə] elsewhere. This distribution of pronunciations of the same word in accordance with different linguistic environments is predictable by a general rule. As we saw in Chapter 3, what is predictable by rule in pronunciation cannot be the principal bearer of a meaning distinction.

What It Means to Know a Word

Consider what a child must know when it knows a word in its language. A child able to utter a sentence like *My new dolls can cry* knows much more about the word *doll* than the kind of toy it refers to. The child knows what sounds make up *doll* and in what sequence they occur, as well as how to use *doll* in a sentence. The child also knows that *doll* is a common noun (and hence can be preceded by the possessive pronoun *my*, as here, or by an article like *a* plus an adjective); that *doll* is a count noun (that is, it can be followed by a plural marker -*s*, in contrast to mass nouns like *milk* and *sugar*, which do not take -*s*); and that the plural of *doll* is formed regularly and is not an irregular plural like *teeth* or *deer*. Children cannot, of course, articulate what we have just said, but it is clear from the sentences they utter that they have learned some version of the information we have just specified.

Thus, knowing a word requires having at least four kinds of information:

1. what sounds the word contains and their sequencing—this is *phonological* information (see Chapter 3)

2. the meanings of the word—this is *semantic* information (see Chapter 6)

3. how related words like plurals (for nouns) and past tenses (for verbs) are formed—this is *morphological* information (the topic of this chapter)

4. what category the word belongs to and how to use it in a sentence—this is *syntactic* information (see Chapter 5)

Knowing even the simplest word requires that phonological, morphological, syntactic, and semantic information be stored in the brain's dictionary (or *lexicon*) as part of that word's structure.

There are certain parallels between the kinds of information stored in the lexicon and the information that can be found in an ordinary desk dictionary. In a dictionary, basic phonological, semantic, morphological, and syntactic information is found along with information that neither children nor adult speakers need to possess in order to speak a language—information, for example, about a word's orthographic representation in writing or about its etymology (the history of its phonological development and the semantic path it followed in getting to its current meaning). In addition, dictionaries sometimes provide sample sentences for words or actual citations from well-known sources. Obviously a child will not normally have any orthographic, etymological, or illustrative information in its lexicon.

Word-Class Categories (Parts of Speech)

We have stated that small children implicitly know the syntactic category—that is, the part of speech—of every word in their lexicon, though of course they are unable to name categories like "noun" or "verb" or to articulate their knowledge in other ways. Still, the ability to use a word in a sentence requires knowledge of its syntactic category, and children use words correctly from a very early age. In this section we shall briefly describe four syntactic categories: verbs, nouns, adjectives, and adpositions. The first three are familiar; the last is the category to which the familiar prepositions of English belong.

Verbs   English-speaking children know that words that function as verbs can have, for example, past tense forms (*looked*), forms in *-ing* (*looking*), and third person singular forms (the *-s* of *she looks*). The articulation of this knowledge does not come easily when it is taught in elementary (or "grammar") school, but all of us know it implicitly, and we know it at an early age.

Another important kind of information that we must learn for each verb is what kind of sentence structure it allows. (We shall return to the subject of sentence structure in Chapter 5, but it is useful to introduce it briefly here.) Consider the following sentences:

(a)   Sarah purchased a book.

(b)   Sarah laughed at Fred.

(c)   *Sarah purchased.

(d)   Sarah laughed.

(e)   *Sarah laughed Fred.

(f)   *Sarah laughed a book.

The asterisks in front of sentences (c), (e), and (f) indicate that these are ill formed—that is, they are not permissible English sentences. If you examine sentences (a) through (f), you will notice that the verbs *purchased* and *laughed* require different sentence structures. The verb *purchase* requires a noun or noun phrase after it (*a book* is a noun phrase) and will result in an ill-formed sentence if it lacks either, as (c) demonstrates. But not all verbs require a noun to follow, as (d) illustrates. The verb *laugh* does not need a noun; in fact, it doesn't permit one, as (e) and (f) illustrate. *Laugh* does permit other structures to follow it, such as a prepositional phrase (*at Fred*), but never a noun or noun phrase. Other verbs like *eat* permit a following noun but don't require one, as the sentences below demonstrate:

(g)   The elephants ate.

(h)   The elephants ate the peanuts.

The examples in (a) through (h) illustrate an important point about words like *purchase, laugh,* and *eat*. All belong to the *category* verb, but each can be subcategorized according to the different sentence structures that they permit. In traditional grammatical terminology for English, verbs that take nouns (or noun phrases) after them are called **transitive** verbs, while verbs that do not require nouns are called **intransitive** verbs. Sentences (a) and (h) above contain transitive verbs; sentences (b), (d), and (g) contain intransitive verbs.

The kinds of structures that different verbs permit differ considerably from one another. As the following sentences illustrate, the verb *proclaim* permits a sentence to come after it, but it cannot be used intransitively, as in the ungrammatical (c) below, or with a simple noun, as in (b), though it does permit two nouns after it, as in (d).

(a)   Sarah proclaimed that Fred is funny.

(b)   *Sarah proclaimed Fred.

(c)   *Sarah proclaimed.

(d)   Sarah proclaimed Fred the winner.

Thus, besides being marked as a verb in a speaker's lexicon, each verb has certain sentence structures that it permits; in technical terms, it is *subcategorized* in the lexicon as transitive or intransitive. (A verb like *proclaim* will be marked as ditransitive because it permits two nouns, but not one.)

Nouns   Nouns constitute another category of words that share certain characteristics. In English, nouns usually have distinct **number** forms for singular and plural, like *cat/cats* or *child/children*, although a few exceptions like *deer/deer* have identical singular and plural forms. Only nouns can take determiners like *a/an/the/this/that: a book, an orchestra, the players, this problem, that guy;* **a tall, *the went, *an us.* (Of course, we can say *a blue book* or *the tall teacher*, but here the determiner is allowed because of the noun *book* or *teacher*, not the adjective *blue* or *tall*.) Finally, nouns can be preceded by modifying words like *old, blue,* and *enjoyable: old books, a blue stove, an enjoyable film.*

English nouns have, besides singular and plural forms, a form for the possessive case, as in *the dog's food* or *the runner's shoes.* In many other languages, there are several forms of the noun depending on its **case** in the sentence. Cases correspond to, or mark, such functions as subject, direct object, indirect object, and object of a preposition. Languages have several ways of marking case, one of which is variant forms of the noun. Although English has the ability to mark nouns only for possessive case, we can observe other case distinctions in pronouns such as *I/me* and *she/her*.

In many languages, nouns occur in several classes called **genders**. These grammatical genders are distinct from natural (biological) gender and have nothing to do with the sex of the object referred to.[1] In French, for example, the word *mur* 'wall' is masculine and the word *mer* 'sea' is feminine. When referring to 'a wall' with a pronoun, speakers of French use the masculine pronoun *il* 'he,' and when referring to 'the sea,' the feminine pronoun *elle* 'she' is used, whereas English speakers use *it* for both. In German, nouns can be masculine, feminine, or neuter; that is, they require masculine, feminine, or neuter pronouns and take articles and adjectives that "agree" in gender (see below). In some languages, notably the Bantu languages of Africa, noun classes are numerous—far more than the two or three genders found in European languages.

Adjectives   Modifying words like *blue* and *beautiful* are members of the category adjective. In English, they can occur preceding nouns in what is called **attributive** position (*the tall athlete, the blue stove*) or after certain kinds of verbs in **predicative** position (*The athlete looks tall, The stove is blue*).

Adjectives can be marked for two **degrees**: comparative (*older, grungier*) and superlative (*oldest, grungiest*). These comparative and superlative markers in English are not entirely productive, in that some adjectives require *more* and *most* instead of *-er* and *-est* to mark comparative and superlative degrees: *more/most beautiful* are grammatical; **beautifuller* and **beautifullest* are not grammatical. Some adjectives can indicate comparative and superlative degrees in both ways; they can add *-er* and *-est* (*cleverer, cleverest*) or be marked by *more* and *most* (*more clever, most clever*).

In some languages, adjectives agree with the nouns they modify. In languages that have **agreement**, the adjective that modifies a noun will have a marker—usually an affix—that agrees with the modified noun in such features as gender, number, and case. Thus an adjective modifying a masculine singular noun in the objective case will also carry a marker for masculine, singular, and objective; we say such an adjective *agrees* with the noun it modifies in number, gender, and case. In a language that has adjective-noun agreement, feminine and masculine nouns may require a modifying adjective to be marked differently. For example, in German one marks the adjectives *gut* 'good,' *schwer* 'hard,' and *kalt* 'cold' differently depending on the gender of the nouns they modify: *guter Wein* 'good wine' (*gut* carries an *-er* affix because *Wein* is a masculine noun), *schwere Arbeit*

---

[1] In the fifth century B.C., Protagoras first recognized three genders for Greek: masculine, feminine, and "things." Seeing that many "things" were grammatically masculine or feminine, Aristotle proposed "intermediate" as the third gender. Later the genders were called masculine, feminine, and "neither." *Neuter* is English for Latin 'neither.'

'hard work' (*schwer* carries an *-e* affix because *Arbeit* is feminine), and *kaltes Wasser* 'cold water' (*kalt* carries an *-es* affix because *Wasser* is neuter). In French one says *le petit garçon* 'the little boy' but *la petite maison* 'the little house.' Because *maison* is *grammatically* feminine (irrespective of its biological neutrality), the adjective modifying it must be marked as feminine (orthographically by the affix *-e*, in speech by pronouncing the second /t/), whereas the same adjective modifying the masculine singular noun *garçon* carries no such marker. Similarly, *petits garçons* (whose pronunciation happens to be identical to the singular despite the orthographic difference) means 'little boys.' Notice that the French definite article also varies, being *le* [lə] with the masculine class of nouns and *la* [la] with the feminine class of nouns (again, independently of biological gender).

Adpositions   **Prepositions** are words like *on, to, for,* and *before* that usually indicate a semantic relationship between two other entities. *The book is on/under/near the table* indicates location of one thing with respect to another. *Sarah rode to/from/through Athens* (indicates direction) *with/without Fred* (indicates accompaniment) *at/near/by her side* (indicates location of Fred with respect to Sarah). Words such as these are called *prepositions* in English because they precede the nouns that complement them (*to Athens*). In many other languages, "prepositions" *follow* the nouns that complement them and are therefore more accurately called **postpositions**. Japanese has postpositions, not prepositions; as the following Japanese-English pairs illustrate, prepositions and postpositions have similar functions:

Japanese Postpositions	English Prepositions
Tarō <u>no</u>	<u>of</u> Taro
hasi <u>de</u>	<u>with</u> chopsticks
Tōkyō <u>e</u>	<u>to</u> Tokyo

The term *adposition* is sometimes used as a cover term for both prepositions and postpositions. It is useful for English speakers to recognize that the position of our "pre"positions, which seems so natural to us, would seem unnatural to speakers of Japanese, Turkish, Hindi, and the many other languages that use postpositions instead of prepositions.

MORPHEMES: THE MEANING-BEARING CONSTITUENTS OF WORDS

We now turn to the smallest units of language that can be associated with meaning. Contrary to popular belief, those units need not be words.

English speakers are aware that words like *cat, girl, ask, tall, father, uncle,* and *orange* cannot be divided into smaller meaningful units. *Orange,* for example, is not made up of *o* + *range* or *or* + *ange* or *ora* + *nge*. Nor is *father* made up of, say, *fath* and *er*. But many words *do* have more than one meaningful part. Consider *oranges, fathers, grandmother, asks, asked, asking, homemade, taller,* and *tallest,* all of which have two meaningful elements. Other words having more than one element that contributes to their overall meaning include *beautiful, churches, supermarkets, bookshelves,* and *television.* A set of words can be built up by adding certain meaningful elements to a core element. For example, built up around the single element *true* is the following set of words:

truer	untrue	truthfully
truest	truth	untruthfully
truly	truthful	untruthfulness

Speakers of English recognize that these words share a core element whose meaning or grammatical function has been modified by the addition of other elements. The *meaningful* elements of a word are called **morphemes**. Thus, *true* is a single morpheme; *untrue* and *truly* contain two morphemes each; and *untruthfulness* contains five (UN + TRUE + TH + FUL + NESS). *Truer*, with the two elements TRUE and -ER ('more'), means 'more true.' The morphemes in *truest* are TRUE and -EST ('most'); in *truly*, TRUE and -LY; in *untrue*, TRUE preceded by UN-; in *truthful*, TRUE + -TH + -FUL.

Morphemes cannot be equated with syllables. On the one hand, a single morpheme can have two or more syllables, as in *harvest, grammar, river, gorilla, hippopotamus, America,* and *Connecticut.* On the other hand, there are sometimes two or more morphemes in a single syllable, as in *judged* (JUDGE + 'PAST TENSE'), *dogs* (DOG + 'PLURAL'), and *men* (MAN + 'PLURAL'), with two morphemes each, and *men's*, with three morphemes (MAN + 'PLURAL' + 'POSSESSIVE').

Free and Bound Morphemes

Some morphemes like TRUE, MOTHER, and ORANGE can stand alone as words. Others cannot stand alone; UN-, TELE-, -NESS, and -ER, for example, function only as parts of words. Morphemes that can stand alone as words are called **free morphemes**; those that function only as parts of words are called **bound morphemes**.

Derivational Morphemes

Certain bound morphemes (like the underscored parts of the following words) have the effect of changing the part of speech of the word to which they are affixed: *truthful, establishment, darken, frighten,* and *teacher.* When added to the noun *truth,* -FUL yields the adjective *truthful;* -MENT added to the verb *establish* yields the noun *establishment;* *dark* is an adjective, *darken* a verb; *fright* a noun, *frighten* a verb; *teach* a verb, *teacher* a noun. In English (though not in all languages) such morphemes tend to be added to the end of words. We can represent these processes as in the following rules:

Noun + *-ful*   ——————→ Adjective (doubtful, beautiful)

Adjective + *-ly* ——————→ Adverb (beautifully, truly)

Verb + *-ment*   ——————→ Noun (establishment, amazement)

Verb + *-er*   ——————→ Noun (teacher, rider, thriller)

Adjective + *-en* ——————→ Verb (sweeten, brighten, harden)

Noun + *-en*   ——————→ Verb (frighten, hasten)

Similar processes of derivation—that is, processes whereby one word is transformed into another word with a similar meaning but belonging to a different word class—are common in the languages of the world. We illustrate with these Persian words and their English glosses:

dana	'wise'	danai	'wisdom'
xub	'good'	xubi	'goodness'
darosht	'thick'	daroshti	'thickness'
mard	'man'	mardi	'manliness'

Notice that the suffix *-i* can be added to adjectives (as in *dana*) and to nouns (as in *mard*). Thus Persian has the following rules of derivational morphology:

Adjective A + *-i* ——————→ Noun 'the quality of being A'

Noun B + *-i*   ——————→ Noun 'like B'

Another derivational suffix of Persian is illustrated in these words:

garm	'warm'	garma	'heat'
sarm	'cold'	sarma	'cold'

Thus Persian has still another process of derivational morphology that can be expressed in this rule:

Adjective + *-a* ——————→ Noun

To cite another language, Fijian *vaka-*, meaning 'in the manner of,' is a derivational morpheme that can be prefixed to adjectives and nouns to derive adverbs according to these two rules:

$$vaka\text{-} + \text{Adjective} \longrightarrow \text{Adverb}$$

$$vaka\text{-} + \text{Noun} \longrightarrow \text{Adverb}$$

The following adverbs exhibit the morpheme VAKA-: *vaka-Viti* 'in the Fijian fashion' (from *Viti* 'Fijian'), *vakatotolo* 'in a rapid manner, rapidly' (from *totolo* 'fast, rapid'); to illustrate the derivation from a noun, consider *vakamārama* 'ladylike' (formed by prefixing *vaka-* to *mārama* 'lady').

Not all bound morphemes serve to change the word class of words. Adding other bound morphemes like English *dis-*, *re-*, and *un-* (*disappear*, *repaint*, *unfavorable*) to a word changes its meaning without altering its syntactic function—that is, its word class or part of speech remains the same. For example, *appear* and *disappear* are both verbs, as are *paint* and *repaint;* *favorable* and *unfavorable* both function as adjectives. There is a notable tendency in English for morphemes that change meaning without altering the part of speech to be added to the front of words as prefixes, though this is not universal across all languages (and in fact some languages, such as Turkish, lack prefixes altogether).

The two types of morpheme we have just examined are called **derivational morphemes**. To recapitulate, derivational morphemes can produce new words from existing words in two ways. First, they can change the meaning of a word: *true* and *untrue* have opposite meanings; *paint* and *repaint* have different meanings. Second, they can change the part of speech of a word, thereby permitting it to function differently in a sentence: *true* is an adjective, *truly* an adverb, *truth* a noun.

Inflectional Morphemes

Another type of bound morpheme is illustrated in the underscored parts of the words *cats*, *collected*, *sleeps*, and *louder*. These morphemes behave differently from derivational morphemes: they alter the form of a word without changing either its part of speech or its meaning (generally speaking). These **inflectional morphemes** create variant forms of a word to conform to different functional roles in a sentence or in discourse. On nouns and pronouns, for example, inflectional morphemes serve to mark grammatical functions like case or semantic notions like number. On verbs, they can mark such things as tense, while on adjectives they serve to indicate degree.

Sometimes inflectional morphemes serve merely to integrate a word into its sentence, redundantly indicating on a verb, for example, that the subject of the verb is third person, as in *She sleeps to dream.* Only in a very limited sense do inflectional morphemes change meaning. To be sure, *cigar* and *cigars* don't mean exactly the same thing, but *cigars* means simply 'more than one cigar.' With *collect* and *collected*, it would be accurate to think of them as meaning the same thing but orienting listeners (or readers) to different time frames. Like Old English (predecessor of Modern English), many languages to-

TABLE 4-1

Word Class	Category	Examples
Noun	Plural	cars, churches
	Possessive	car's, children's
Verb	Third Person	(she) swims, (it) seems
	Past Tense	wanted, showed
	Past Participle	wanted, shown
	Present Participle	wanting, showing
Adjective	Comparative	taller, sweeter
	Superlative	tallest, sweetest

day have large inventories of inflectional morphemes. Russian and German and Latin maintained fairly elaborate inflectional systems over the centuries, while their "cousin" English shed inflections, until today it has only eight remaining inflectional morphemes, two on nouns, four on verbs, and two on adjectives, as shown in Table 4-1.

Compare this inflectional system of English with the examples from the Russian noun *žena* 'wife' and verb *pisat'* 'to write' in Table 4-2.

The eight inflectional morphemes of English are fully productive. That is, when new nouns, verbs, and adjectives are added to the language they are extremely likely to be inflected like the examples just listed. A child hearing a

TABLE 4-2

	Singular	Plural
Noun		
Nominative	žena	ženy
Accusative	ženu	žen
Genitive	ženu	žen
Dative	žene	ženam
Instrumental	ženoy	ženami
After some prepositions	žene	ženax
Verb (present tense)		
First Person	pišu	pišem
Second Person	pišeš	pišete
Third Person	pišet	pišut

noun (like *pool* or *tooth*) or verb (like *talk* or *speak*) for the first time will automatically inflect it for plural and past tense in the regular rule-governed way. In fact, these inflectional rules of English are so productive, so automatic, that children produce not only the correct *pools* and *talked* but the incorrect "*tooths*" and "*speaked*"; at first they overgeneralize the rules and must learn item by item which words are exceptions to the rules governing inflectional morphemes.

Certain inflections that are no longer productive in English—that is, they do not affect new words—have nevertheless left traces and remain part of isolated words as relics of an earlier, more varied inflectional system. Word sets like *child/children, ox/oxen,* and *who/whom/whose* reflect earlier productive inflectional morphemes. The system of English pronouns gives some hint of an earlier inflectional morphology that also affected nouns. Except for *you,* English pronouns, like English nouns, have distinct singular and plural forms (*I* and *we; he, she, it,* and *they*). Unlike nouns, however, pronouns exhibit distinct forms for use in other than subject functions (*I* and *me; we* and *us; he* and *him; she* and *her; they* and *them*); *you* and *it* are exceptions. In Old English, nouns had inflected forms not only for number as they do today, but for several cases besides subject and object (see Chapter 14). In addition, Old English pronouns had three numbers, not just singular and plural. It had singular and plural pronouns for first, second, and third persons, but it also had a special form in the first and second persons to refer to just two people: 'we two' and 'you two.' We have mentioned the category of person in incidental ways earlier in this chapter; it may be helpful here to specify that **person** refers simply to the speaker (the first person: *I* or *we*), the person spoken to (the second person: *you*), or the person spoken about (the third person: *he, she, it, they*).

LINEAR AND HIERARCHICAL ORGANIZATION OF MORPHEMES IN WORDS

Linear Ordering of Morphemes

The morphemes in a word are not arranged randomly, as all readers of this book know implicitly. Rather, they have a strict linear sequence, a fact that can be easily overlooked when thinking about the task children face in acquiring language.

Some morphemes, called **suffixes,** always follow the stems they attach to, like 'PLURAL' in *boys* and -MENT in *commitment*: both "*sboy*" and "*mentcommit*" are non-English. Languages can also have **prefixes,** which attach to the front of another morpheme, as in the words <u>un</u>*true*, <u>dis</u>*appear*, and <u>re</u>*paint*. (Compare *true+un, *appear+dis, and *paint+re; and, of course, English does not permit *ness+ful+truth+un or any arrangement other than *untruthfulness.*)

In English, all inflectional morphemes are suffixes. Derivational morphemes, on the other hand, can be either prefixes (<u>un</u>*happy*, <u>dis</u>*appear*) or suffixes (*happi<u>ness</u>, appear<u>ance</u>*). Generally, inflectional morphemes are added to the outermost parts of words: they precede derivational prefixes or follow derivational suffixes.

Taken together, prefixes and suffixes are called **affixes**. Besides affixes, some languages have *infixes*. An **infix** is a morpheme that is inserted within another morpheme instead of being affixed to it. If English had morphemes TTH meaning 'tooth' and GSE meaning 'goose,' then we could say that -*oo*- was an infix meaning 'singular' and -*ee*- an infix meaning 'plural.' English speakers find any interpretation calling for singular and plural infixes in words like *tooth/teeth* and *goose/geese* to be counterintuitive, but other languages do exploit this morphological possibility. In Tagalog (the most widely spoken language of the Philippines), infixing does exist. The word *gulay* meaning 'greenish vegetables' can take the infix -*in*-, creating the word *ginulay*, meaning 'greenish blue.' Compared to prefixes and suffixes, infixes are relatively rare in the languages of the world. Some languages also have what may be called **circumfixes**—morphemes that occur in two parts, on both sides of another morpheme. In Samoan, for example, the morpheme FE-/-AʔI, meaning 'reciprocal,' exists. Thus the verb 'to quarrel' is *finau*; the verb meaning 'to quarrel with each other' is *fefinauaʔi*.

One interesting morphological phenomenon can be found in the system of marking of grammatical and derivational categories in Arabic and other Semitic languages like Hebrew. Arabic nouns and verbs generally have a root consisting of three consonants. One very commonly cited example is KTB/k-t-b/. Traditionally called a "triliteral root," /k-t-b/ has as its semantic content a wide range of things having to do with writing and books. (For example, the Arabic word for 'book' is *kitāb*.) By combining the root /k-t-b/ and various patterns of vowels and other consonants placed before, between, and following the elements of the root, Arabic is able to create a great many words—nouns, verbs, and adjectives—with this single root. The nouns and verbs in Table 4-3 all contain the same KTB root.

Besides the great power of such a derivational system, Arabic is able to signal many of the grammatical categories such as case, number, and

TABLE 4-3

Nouns		Verbs	
kitāba	'writing'	kataba	'he wrote'
kātib	'writer'	kātaba	'he corresponded with'
maktab	'office'	ʔaktaba	'he dictated'
maktaba	'library'	ʔiktataba	'he was registered'
maktūb	'letter'	takātaba	'to correspond with each other'
miktāb	'typewriter'	ʔinkataba	'to subscribe'
kutubī	'bookseller'	ʔiktataba	'to copy'

definiteness on nouns and person, number, and tense on verbs. Some of the inflected nouns built from the root KTB are listed below. Notice that each word contains the root /k-t-b/, with various vowel patterns that are systematic in ways that we will not describe here; suffice it to say that just as the root KTB has a fixed core meaning, so the various combinations of vowels and other consonants are patterned and have a grammatical or derivational meaning that can be transferred systematically among various roots.

kitāb	'book'
kutub	'books'
kitābun	'a book (nominative)'
kitābin	'a book (genitive)'
kitāban	'a book (accusative)'
ʔalkitābu	'the book (nominative)'
ʔalkitābi	'the book (genitive)'
ʔalkitāba	'the book (accusative)'

(See page 102 on nominative, genitive, and accusative cases.) We might mention that the English words *Moslem, Islam,* and *salaam,* which have been borrowed from Arabic, all contain the root SLM /s-l-m/, with its core meaning of 'peace, submission.'

Hierarchical Ordering of Morphemes

As with all other aspects of language, morphemes are organized within words in strictly rule-governed ways; as a speaker of a language, you know these rules implicitly, even if you would find it difficult to articulate them at this stage.

Besides being arranged in a linear order, the morphemes in words also have a hierarchical (or layered) structure. *Untrue,* for example, is *true* with *un-* prefixed to it (not *un* with *true* added). *Truthful* is composed of a stem *truth* with *-ful* suffixed to it (and *truth* is itself *true* with *-th* added). Examining more complex words, it is easy to see that *untruthful* would be incorrectly analyzed if we claimed that it was composed of *untrue* with *-thful* suffixed.

How is the word *uncontrollably* organized? Is it *controllably* with *un-* prefixed? Or *uncontrol* with *-ably* suffixed? It may be helpful to picture the sequence of morpheme structuring as follows:

control (Verb)	Verb + *-able* ⟶ Adjective
controllable (Adjective)	*un-* + Adjective ⟶ Adjective
uncontrollable (Adjective)	Adjective + *-ly* ⟶ Adverb
uncontrollably (Adverb)	

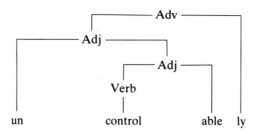

FIGURE 4-1

In looking at a sequence like this, it is clear that the root of *uncontrollably* is *control*. We say that *control* functions as the stem for *-able*, that *controllable* functions as the stem for *uncontrollable*, and that *uncontrollable* functions as the stem for *uncontrollably*. A representation using labeled brackets would be as follows:

$$[[un \ [[control \quad] + [able] \quad] \quad] \ ly \quad]$$
$$\text{Verb} \qquad\qquad \text{Adj} \ \text{Adj} \qquad \text{Adv}$$

It could also be represented using a tree diagram like the one in Figure 4-1.

THE ROLE OF MORPHOLOGY IN LANGUAGE

Grammatical Functions of Inflectional Morphology

Recall that the principal task of language is to express and communicate thoughts (not ideas principally, but wishes, greetings, warnings, requests, and other "thoughts"). To accomplish this work, languages have evolved a wealth of lexical, morphological, and grammatical structures. Different languages reveal different preferences for expressing equivalent "thoughts." Consider the following English sentences:

(a) The two nurses expressed their views about his health yesterday.

(b) Did the nurse talk to you about her fear concerning your father's health yesterday?

With respect to the inflectional morphology in these sentences, *nurses, views,* and *father's* are inflected nouns, each with two morphemes, while *expressed* is an inflected verb. Note that in the phrase *the two nurses*, the plural suffix *-s* is redundant, given the unambiguously plural word *two*. In the same vein, one could say that the past tense markings of *expressed* and *did* are redundant, given the adverb *yesterday*.

Though the conventional rules of English sentence formation would not allow it, if the sentences were expressed as follows no information would be lost:

(c)   *The two nurse express their view about his health yesterday.

(d)   *Do the nurse talk to you about her fear concerning your father's health yesterday?

As you can see, certain words in these sentences exhibit idiosyncratic characteristics that are required neither for clear communication nor by any general principles of language.

A meaning much the same as that conveyed by sentence (e) below is conveyed by the slightly altered version (f):

(e)   Did the nurse tell you her fear concerning your father's health yesterday?

(f)   *Did the nurse tell to you about her fear concerning your father's health yesterday?

This last sentence, of course, is not grammatical; it sounds odd (though one might not be surprised to hear it spoken by someone whose native language was not English).

This comparison shows that the verb *talk* requires the preposition *to* for the indirect object (the person told), while the equivalent verb *tell* does not require a preposition except when a direct object intervenes (as in *She told the story <u>to</u> John*). These, then, are facts about the verbs *tell* and *talk*.

A comparison of sentences (b) and (e) indicates that there are alternative ways of saying basically the same thing. Sentences (c) and (d) illustrate that there is considerable redundancy in English, that some of what English requires to be expressed is not necessary for full communication.

The conventional rules of a given language may or may not require such redundant expression. Consider this Indonesian sentence:

harimau makan kambing
tiger   eat   goat

Unlike English, Indonesian does not require the marking of definiteness or plurality on nouns, so the word *harimau* can be interpreted as 'tigers,' 'the tiger(s),' or 'a tiger'; the word *kambing* can mean 'a goat,' 'the goat(s),' or 'goats.' Indonesian does not require the marking of verbs for tense; hence the verb *makan* can be glossed as 'eats,' 'is eating,' 'ate,' 'was eating,' 'will eat,' and so on. Thus there are a great many possible interpretations for this three-word sentence, and a good many ways to translate it into English. Needless to say, not all the interpretations would be appropriate in all circumstances. It should also be pointed out that Indonesian does have ways of expressing these differences when it is important to do so. The point is that they need not always be expressed in Indonesian, though they must be expressed in English.

Now consider the following English sentences. It is obvious that despite the fact that they contain exactly the same words, they do not express the same content.

(a) The farmer saw the wolf.

(b) The wolf saw the farmer.

These two sentences illustrate how English exploits word order as a device to express meaning; different word orders can communicate different stories about *who* did *what* to *whom*.

A comparison with Latin may be enlightening. Compared to English, Latin had relatively free word order. If we let X represent "the farmer" and Y "the wolf," speakers of Latin could have arranged sentence (a) in either of these ways (among others):

X vidit Y.

Y vidit X.

Interestingly, sentence (b) (which has what we might regard as an opposite meaning) could be expressed in Latin using the same two word orders. This is possible because Latin distinguished who did what to whom not by word order but by inflections on nouns, a device not available in English. The following permissible Latin word orders all mean the same thing:

(a) Agrico<u>la</u> vidit lup<u>um</u>. ⎫

(b) Lup<u>um</u> vidit agrico<u>la</u>. ⎬ 'The farmer saw the wolf.'

(c) Agrico<u>la</u> lup<u>um</u> vidit. ⎭

To express the quite different meaning 'The wolf saw the farmer,' the same word orders could occur, but the words would be inflected differently:

(a) Agrico<u>lam</u> vidit lup<u>us</u>. ⎫

(b) Lup<u>us</u> vidit agrico<u>lam</u>. ⎬ 'The wolf saw the farmer.'

(c) Agrico<u>lam</u> lup<u>us</u> vidit. ⎭

From the inflectional suffixes *-a* on *agricola* and *-us* on *lupus*, speakers of Latin would understand these words to be the subjects of their sentences; *agricolam* and *lupum*, with their *-am* and *-um* inflections, would be identified as direct objects. Because English cannot mark case by inflecting the noun, it must rely on other devices, principally word order, to signal these functions.

A parallel to Latin noun inflections can be seen in English in certain pronominal uses, in which the form of the pronouns and the word order reinforce one another:

(a) She praised him.
     (*She* is the subject; *him* is the object.)

(b) He praised her.
     (*He* is the subject; *her* is the object.)

Nouns in both English and Latin have inflections for number (singular or plural) and case. English nouns exhibit only two cases, referred to as possessive and common. The *common case* is used for all grammatical functions except possession; it can serve as subject of a sentence, direct and indirect object, and object of a preposition. The *possessive case* is also called the *genitive case*, a word traditionally associated with the grammatical descriptions of languages like Latin, Old English, German, and Russian. In English it occurs in phrases like *the teacher's desk* and *a woman's purse*.

Besides a genitive case, Latin exhibited inflections for several other cases, notably *nominative* (used principally to mark subjects), *dative* (for indirect objects and the objects of certain prepositions), *accusative* (for direct objects and the objects of other prepositions), and *ablative* (for the objects of still other prepositions). Latin generally had five (or six) case inflections in the singular and a similar number in the plural, although in practice some inflectional forms came to be pronounced alike, as can be seen in Table 4-4. The set of forms constituting the inflectional variants of a particular word is

TABLE 4-4

	'farmer'	'garden'
Singular		
Nominative	agricola	hortus
Accusative	agricolam	hortum
Genitive	agricolae	hortı
Dative	agricolae	hortō
Ablative	agricolā	hortō
Plural		
Nominative	agricolae	hortī
Accusative	agricolās	hortōs
Genitive	agricolārum	hortōrum
Dative	agricolīs	hortīs
Ablative	agricolīs	hortīs

known as its inflectional **paradigm**, or **declension**. There were several noun declensions such as the two given for *agricola* and *hortus*.

Here are the paradigms for the equivalent English words *farmer* and *garden*:

Singular		
Common	farmer	garden
Possessive	farmer's	garden's
Plural		
Common	farmers	gardens
Possessive	farmers'	gardens'

Notice that the four orthographic forms in the English paradigms represent only two distinct forms of speech: [farmər] versus [farmərz] and [gardən] versus [gardənz]. The orthographically distinct forms for possessive singular and for common and possessive plurals do not represent distinct spoken forms. In spoken English, there are generally only two forms of a noun, except that when a plural noun is irregular there are four spoken forms as well as four orthographic forms (as in *man, man's, men, men's; child, child's, children, children's*).

For some English pronouns a third case form exists. Known as the objective case form, it is roughly comparable to the dative, accusative, and ablative cases of Latin. In Table 4-5, compare the paradigms for first and third person pronouns in English. First person pronouns exhibit distinct forms for three cases in the singular and three cases in the plural. Third person pronouns have distinct masculine, feminine, and neuter forms in the singular,

TABLE 4-5

	First Person	Third Person		
		Masc.	Fem.	Neuter
Singular				
Common	I	he	she	it
Possessive	mine	his	hers	its
Objective	me	him	her	it
Plural				
Common	we		they	
Possessive	ours		theirs	
Objective	us		them	

TABLE 4-6

	Pronouns		Nouns
Singular	Second	Third	
Common	you	it	farmer
Possessive	yours	its	farmer's
Plural			
Common	you		farmers
Possessive	yours		farmers'

although no distinction for gender is made in the plural. The neuter singular *it* does not distinguish subjective and objective case forms.

Second person pronouns and third person singular neuter pronouns do not have distinct objective forms, as can be seen in Table 4-6; like regular nouns, they have only two forms.

In English, gender distinctions in pronouns are based on natural sex. Males are referred to by the masculine pronoun, females by the feminine pronoun. Things that are neither male nor female are referred to by the neuter pronoun *it*.

In many languages, including Latin, German, and Old English, nouns have grammatical gender; they are masculine, feminine, or neuter independently of the sex (or natural gender) of the object to which they refer. The gender of nouns is important because certain classes of words such as articles and adjectives are inflected to agree with the nouns in gender, number, and case.

In contrast to the English definite article *the* (with a single orthographic form representing the two phonological variants /ðə/ and /ði/), the German

TABLE 4-7

	Masculine	Feminine	Neuter
Singular			
Nominative	der	die	das
Accusative	den	die	das
Genitive	des	der	des
Dative	dem	der	dem
Plural		Masc./Fem./Neuter	
Nominative		die	
Accusative		die	
Genitive		der	
Dative		den	

TABLE 4-8

	French		Spanish	
Masculine				
	le chat	'the cat'	el gato	'the cat'
	les chats	'the cats'	los gatos	'the cats'
Feminine				
	la maison	'the house'	la casa	'the house'
	les maisons	'the houses'	las casas	'the houses'

definite article has forms for three genders and four cases in the singular, though it does not distinguish genders in the plural, as Table 4-7 illustrates.

French and Spanish also exhibit variant forms of the definite article, though neither is as varied as German. French distinguishes only two genders in nouns and marks masculine nouns with the definite article *le* (indefinite *un*) and feminine *la* (indefinite *une*); *les* is the common plural form for both genders. Spanish is similar except that the gender distinctions are marked in the plural as well as the singular. Table 4-8 gives examples from both languages.

Some languages have far more complex word-class systems; Swahili is a frequently cited example of a language with a large number of noun categories.[2]

We have now examined a number of ways in which languages exploit inflectional morphology to mark grammatical relations like subject and direct object and certain categorical information like number, gender, and case on nouns and pronouns and to signal tense and person on verbs.

Derivational Morphology and Extension of the Vocabulary

Open and Closed Classes of Morphemes and Words   Languages have different word classes like noun, verb, and preposition. Some word classes

---

[2] Some languages, on the other hand, have little or no inflectional morphology (and some languages have very little morphology at all, either derivational or inflectional). Chinese is an oft-cited example of an *isolating* language—so called because each word tends to have just a single (that is, isolated) morpheme. By the use of separate words, Chinese signals certain content that an inflecting language can signal by using inflectional affixes. For example, whereas English permits both an inflectional possessive (*the boy's hat*) and an analytical possessive (*hat of the boy*), Chinese permits only the equivalent of *hat of the boy*. Vietnamese, even more than Chinese, approximates the one-morpheme-per-word model that is characteristic of isolating languages. While isolating languages commonly tend not to utilize inflectional morphology, some do exploit derivational morphology to extend their word stocks in economical ways. Indonesian has only two inflectional affixes but exploits about two dozen derivational morphemes.

increase their membership with ease. The need for new nouns, adjectives, and verbs arises frequently in daily life, and additions to these categories occur freely; for this reason, noun, adjective, and verb are called *open classes*. Other word classes are relatively closed, and additions are made rarely. Prepositions and conjunctions tend to be *closed classes*; new words are very seldom added to a language in either of these categories.

In almost every century, English has added thousands (and sometimes tens of thousands) of new words, many borrowed from other languages, many more constructed from existing elements already in the English word stock. A book called *12,000 Words* was published in 1987, listing new items that were added to English after 1961. The vast majority of the recent additions are nouns, verbs, and adjectives. Very few words have been added in any other word class, and none are thought to have been added in the categories of pronouns, adverbs, prepositions, or conjunctions.

Functions of Derivational Morphology Derivational morphemes serve functions very different from those of inflectional morphemes. A derivational affix can change the part of speech of a word (as *-ment* changes *commit* from a verb to a noun), or it can alter the meaning of a word (as *re-* changes the meaning of *paint* to 'paint again'). Languages frequently need new words, and they have basically three ways of extending their word stock: they can borrow words that already exist in other languages—and this they often do, especially if the cultural item or concept for which the new word is needed is also borrowed; or they can create entirely new words; or they can form new words from existing resources within their own word stocks. To produce new words from existing morphemes and words requires application of the processes of derivational morphology.

Let's look at the rarest kind of word addition first. Occasionally languages create new words from scratch. This process has swelled the English lexicon with words like *Kleenex, granola, zap,* and *quark.*

More commonly, languages form new words from existing words and morphemes. It is much easier for speakers to extend the meaning of a word to cover new but usually related referents than to invent an entirely new word, and it is easier to understand the meaning of a word whose scope of reference has been extended in some way than to imagine the meaning of a newly coined word that lacks previous associations. Several morphological processes can be exploited for the creation of new words from existing morphemes and words, and we shall examine some of these in detail. After looking at these derivational processes, we shall conclude with a brief discussion of word borrowing.

Functional Shift, or Conversion *Functional shift* is the simple transfer of a word existing in one word class for use in another without altering its form by derivation. We direct a computer to *print out* (verb) a report and then refer to the report as a *printout* (noun). Conversion of this type commonly leads to noun/verb and noun/adjective pairs; as Table 4-9 illustrates, sometimes the same form can be used for all three functions—as noun, verb, and adjective.

TABLE 4-9

Noun	Verb	Adjective
printout	print out	
bust	bust	
outrage	outrage	
homer	homer	
delay	delay	
plot	plot	
play	play	
prime		prime
inaugural		inaugural
advance	advance	advance
average	average	average
model	model	model
surprise	surprise	surprise
ghost	ghost	ghost

Semantic Shift   Words can take on new meanings, shrinking or (more commonly) extending the domain of their reference. During the Vietnam War, the word *hawk* came to be used in reference to supporters of the war while *dove* referred to supporters of peace, extending the meaning of these words from the combative nature of hawks and the symbolically peaceful role assigned to doves. The new meanings did not replace the earlier ones but gave us, in effect, new words by extending the domain of reference for old words. This phenomenon, called *semantic shift* or *metaphorical extension*, creates *metaphors* (see Chapter 6). The metaphorical use of words often leads to new meanings that come to seem perfectly natural and whose metaphorical content is all but lost. Consider the meanings of the underscored parts of the following phrases: *to derail congressional legislation, a buoyant spokesman, an abrasive chief of staff, to sweeten the farm bill with several billion dollars to skirt a veto fight.* Such originally metaphorical uses have become an integral part of the language.

Compounding   English speakers have long shown a strong preference for putting existing words together to create new words. This process is called *compounding.* Recent compounds include *moonshot, waterbed, upfront, color-code, computerlike,* and *radiopharmaceutical.* Notice that the popular compounds *convenience food* and *natural food* are not structured alike. *Convenience food* 'food that is convenient to buy, cook, or eat' is a noun-noun compound. *Natural food* 'food made with natural ingredients, free of chemical preservatives and pesticides' is an adjective-noun compound. Both compounds function as nouns. Notice, too, that the relationship of *natural* to *food* in *natural food* differs from that of *natural* to its mates in *natural scientist* 'a scientist engaged in the study of the processes of nature' and *natural language* 'a language not designed primarily for use with computers,' each of which also differs from the other.

To gauge the popularity (both current and historical) of compounding in English, consider that one relatively short piece in the *Los Angeles Times* recently provided the following compounds (among others): the adjectives *whistle-blowing, baby-faced, highranking, overzealous*, and *born-again*; the nouns *whistle-blower, pay phone, phone call, government documents, government witness, training course, debt ceiling, subcommittee hearing, petroleum engineer, aircraft carrier* (with *aircraft* also a compound), *school records, supply schemes, reserve account, brain cancer, cover-up, kickbacks, sea power, breakup, storerooms*, and *troublemaker*. In the same piece, there were also several rather complex noun compounds such as *beneficial suggestion program* and *House government operations subcommittee*. The newsweeklies are filled with such complex phrases as *four-page options paper, let's-make-a-deal philosophy, House Ways and Means Committee Chairman Dan Rostenkowski, legislative scheduling session*, and *podium-pounding hardliner*.

Compounding occurs in many languages. Chinese, for example, has numerous compounds in its lexicon. Compounds such as *fàn-wǎn* 'rice bowl,' *diàn-nǎo* ('electric' + 'brain') 'computer,' *tái-bù* 'tablecloth,' *fēi-jī* ('fly' + 'machine') 'airplane,' and *hē-bǎn* ('black' + 'board') 'blackboard' can be found in the Běijīng dialect. Another language famous for its compounding tendencies is German: the word *Fernsprecher* (literally 'far speaker') was for a long time the preferred word for what is today usually called *Telefon* in the German-speaking world. A ballpoint pen is called *Kugelschreiber* ('ball' + 'writer'); a glove is *Handschuh* ('hand' + 'shoe'); a mayor is *Bürgermeister* ('citizen' + 'master'). Indonesian has exploited compounding in a word made familiar to westerners from its use as the assumed name of a well-known World War I socialite and spy: *matahari*, meaning 'sun,' comes from *mata* 'eye' and *hari* 'day.' The element *mata* can also be found in the word for 'eyeglasses,' which is *kacamata*, a compound of *kaca* 'glass' and *mata*; this Indonesian compound is similar to the English compound *eyeglasses* but with a different order of the compounded elements.

Reduplication   *Reduplication* is the morphological process by which a morpheme is repeated, thereby creating a word with a different meaning or a different word class. For example, the Mandarin Chinese word *sànsànbu* 'to take a leisurely walk' is formed by reduplicating the first syllable of *sànbu* 'to walk' (itself a compound of *sàn* 'to tread' and *bù* 'a step'); and *hónghóng* 'bright red' is formed by reduplicating *hóng* 'red.' There are two types of reduplication: *partial reduplication*, which reduplicates only part of the morpheme, and *full reduplication*, in which the entire morpheme is reduplicated. In Motu, a language of Papua New Guinea, *mahuta* 'to sleep' reduplicates fully as *mahutamahuta* 'to sleep constantly' and partially as *mamahuta* 'to sleep' (when agreeing with a plural subject). Reduplication is not to be confused with repetition, which does not create new words. In English, *very* can be repeated in *She's very, very tired* and *night* in *night-night*, but the result is not a new word, simply two words. English does not have a productive process similar to Chinese and Motu reduplication.

Reduplication can have a variety of functions in the languages in which it is found. It can have a moderating or intensifying effect on the meaning of the word, as illustrated by the Chinese and Motu examples just given. It can be used to mark grammatical categories. In Indonesian, the plural of a noun is formed by reduplicating it: *babibabi* 'pigs' is the reduplicated form of *babi* 'pig.'

Affixation   Adding affixes to an existing word is another very common way of creating new words. English has exploited this possibility by adding the agentive suffix *-er* to the prepositions *up* and *down* to create the nouns *upper* and *downer*, which were invented in connection with drugs but have extended their meaning to anything that lifts or dampens one's spirits. More commonly, *-er* is suffixed to verbs (V) and means 'one who V's' as in *runner, campaigner*, and *designer*.[3]

English takes advantage of both principal kinds of affixation: prefixing and suffixing. Prefixes like *un-, pre-*, and *dis-* serve to change the meaning of words, though not usually their part of speech. Thus the prefix *un-* added to an adjective creates a new adjective with the opposite meaning, as in *unpopular, unsuccessful, untrue*, and *unfavorable*. The prefix *dis-* added to a verb derives a verb with the opposite meaning, as in *disobey, disappear, dishonor*, and *displace*. *Pre-* serves as a prefix to several classes of words. It can be prefixed to verbs, as in *preaffirm, preallot, preplan, prewash*, and *premix*. It can also be prefixed to adjectives (*pre-Copernican, precollegiate, precultural, presurgical*) and to nouns (*preantiquity, preaffirmation, preplacement*). The prefix *pre-* means roughly the same thing in each of these words; in each of them it creates from an existing word a new word in the same part of speech.

Suffixes in English usually operate differently from prefixes. More often than not, they change the part of speech of a word. The suffix *-ment*, for example, when added to a verb, makes a noun of it, as in *displacement, arrangement, agreement*, and *consignment*. The suffix *-ation* does the same thing: *resignation, organization, implementation, observation*, and *reformation*. *Discrimination* and *alienation*, which may look like the result of the same affix, are more accurately analyzed as coming from the verbs *discriminate* and *alienate*, the latter itself derived from the suffix *-ate* being added to the noun *alien*.

---

[3] Note that *-er* in *campaigner* has been suffixed to the verb *campaign*, which is itself a functional shift of the noun *campaign*. Note, too, that the noun *designer* enters into noun-noun compounds like *designer jeans, designer drugs*, and *designer clothes*, none of which yet appears in many dictionaries. *Computerese, computerite*, and *computernik*, along with *computerize, computerizable*, and *computerization*, are all derived by affixation from *computer* and its derivatives. Even the word *computer* itself is derived by affixing the agentive suffix *-er* to the verb *compute*.

Suffixes are widely exploited in the other languages of the world as well as in English. The Indonesian suffix *-kan* changes a noun to a verb; among the various meanings it can produce are these two: 'to cause to become X' (as in *budakkan* 'to enslave' from *budak* 'slave' + *-kan*, or *rajakan* 'to crown' from *raja* 'king') and 'to put in X' (as in *penjarakan* 'imprison' from *penjara* 'prison' + *-kan*).

Back Formation   The derived forms of *computer* suggest a less common kind of word formation process known as *back formation*. From the word *computer* (which was originally formed by affixing the agentive suffix *-er* to *compute* in the mathematical sense), a new verb *compute* has been "back formed" to mean 'to use a computer' (for computation or any other task). Other back formations are the verbs *typewrite* and *baby-sit*, which were invented historically after their noun forms *typewriter* and *baby-sitter*. The verb *lase* has been back formed from the noun *laser*, presumably on the mistaken notion that *laser* contained the agentive suffix *-er*.

Blends   English speakers are fond of *blending*, creating new words by combining parts of existing words. Among the better-known blends are *smog* (from *smoke* and *fog*) and *motel* (*motor* and *hotel*); others like *glasphalt* (*glass* and *asphalt*) and *modem* (*modulator* and *demodulator*) crop up from time to time. There are even blends to describe the degree to which modern languages borrow from each other: *Spanglish, Franglais, Yinglish* (Yiddish and English).

Shortenings   Besides the special shortening called back formation, shortenings of various other sorts are a popular means of increasing the word stock of a language. Regular shortenings like *radial* (from *radial tire*), *jet* (from *jet airplane*), *narc* (from *narcotics agent*), and *obits* (from *obituaries*) are common enough. There are also *acronyms*, in which the initials of a phrase are joined together and pronounced as a word, as in *UNESCO, NATO, wasp, radar* (from <u>*ra*</u>*dio* <u>*d*</u>*etecting* <u>*a*</u>*nd* <u>*r*</u>*anging*), and *yuppy* (<u>*y*</u>*oung* <u>*u*</u>*rban* <u>*p*</u>*rofessional* + *-y*). There are also, of course, plain old workaday abbreviations like *BYOB, poly sci, chem,* and *demo*.

Borrowings   "Neither a borrower nor a lender be," Shakespeare advises, but languages pay no heed. They borrow and lend to one another like the busiest banks and loan sharks. In fact, it is only by a loose interpretation of the notion *borrowing* that we can regard languages as engaging in this practice, for languages take words from one another with no commitment or obligation to repay them.

Over the course of its history, English has proved to be an extraordinary host to tens of thousands of words from scores of languages. In a later chapter we will examine the borrowings of earlier generations. Here, suffice it to mention that nearly a hundred languages have contributed words to English during this century alone. As has been true for most of its history, English has borrowed more from French during this century than from any other language, followed at some distance by Japanese and Spanish, Italian and

Latin, and Greek, German, and Yiddish. In smaller numbers, English has borrowed words from Russian, Chinese, Arabic, Portuguese, and Hindi, as well as from numerous African languages.

In turn, many languages have welcomed borrowings from English, while others have been rather guarded in their openness to words from other languages. The Japanese have drafted the words *bēsubōru* 'baseball,' *futtobōru* 'football,' and *bōringu* 'bowling' along with the sports they name, trading them (in sports terminology) for *judo, jujitsu,* and *karate,* which have joined the English-speaking team. Officially, at least, the French are not open to borrowings, especially those from English, and have banned the use of such English and American compound nouns as *weekend, drugstore, brainstorming,* and *countdown,* as well as the very popular international term of English origin *jumbo jet* (for the use of which Air France was fined by the French government, which had ordered that the term *gros porteur* be used instead). The Americanism *OK* is now in use virtually everywhere, as are terms such as *jeans* and *discos,* which accompanied the items that they name as they spread among adolescents around the globe.[4]

The overwhelming majority of borrowings into English have been nouns (and this is true of borrowings into languages in general), but some adjectives have been borrowed, as have a few verbs and interjections. Among the borrowed nouns having to do with food and drink are *hummus* (from Arabic), *aioli* (from Provençal), *mai tai* (from Tahitian), and *frijoles refritos* (from Spanish for 'beans refried'). Yiddish has given us the more general term *nosh.* Other popular recent borrowings include Italian *ciao,* Spanish *macho,* Chinese (Cantonese) *wok,* German *glitch,* and Yiddish *chutzpah, klutz,* and *nebbish.*

Despite their somewhat unusual spellings, these words, like borrowed words in general, come sooner or later to conform to the rules of English phonology, morphology, and syntax. In time, borrowed words undergo the same morphological processes that affect other words. *Nosh,* for example, was borrowed as an intransitive verb (*I feel like noshing*) but has since taken on new use as a transitive verb (*Let's nosh some hot dogs*). It has also added the agentive suffix *-er,* as in *nosher* 'one who noshes.' By a functional shift, the verb *nosh* has come to be used as a noun meaning 'a snack.' In British usage, *nosh* has been compounded into the noun *nosh-up* 'a large or elaborate meal.'

---

[4] *Jean* is a Middle English form of the word *Genoa; jeans* is the plural of a shortening of *jean fustian* 'Genoa fustian.'. (Denim, also named after a city, is a shortening of *serge de Nîmes,* French for 'serge of Nîmes.') The word *disco* also has a fascinating history: it is an abbreviation of the French compound *discothèque* 'record library,' which is made up of two other French morphemes, the word *disque* meaning 'disk' or 'record' and the suffix *-thèque* as in *bibliothèque* 'library.' *Discotheque* is first recorded in English in the year 1954; it was later abbreviated to *disco,* which was first recorded in print ten years later. First recorded in 1979 is the use of the word *disco* as a verb meaning to 'dance to disco music.' Thus the English verb *disco* has undergone functional shift from the English noun *disco,* which is a shortening of the word *discotheque,* which was borrowed from French, where it was formed by affixation of *-thèque* to *disc* + *o.* It has now spread around the world and can be found in many major cities whose inhabitants speak neither English nor French.

ENGLISH MORPHOPHONOLOGY

Before leaving the subject of morphology, let's examine the pronunciation of some of the most productive inflectional suffixes of English: we will discuss the phonological processes that affect plural and possessive morphemes on nouns and the third person singular and past tense morphemes on verbs. Then we will analyze variation in the surface forms of free morphemes in different lexical environments.

English Plural, Possessive, and Third Person Singular Morphemes

For regular nouns, there are several pronunciations of the plural morpheme, as in *lips* [lɪp + s], *seeds* [sid + z], and *fuses* [fyuz + əz]. The various surface forms underlying different pronunciations of a morpheme are called **allomorphs** of that morpheme. As the words in the following lists demonstrate, the allomorphs of the plural morpheme are determined by the last sound of the singular noun to which the morpheme is attached.

[əz]	[s]	[z]
bushes	cats	pens
judges	tips	seeds
peaches	books	dogs
buses	whiffs	cars
fuses	paths	rays

These lists, though far from complete, indicate the pattern of distribution for the plural allomorphs of English.

1. [əz] occurs on nouns that end in /s, z, š, ž, č, ǰ/ (sounds constituting the natural class of *sibilants*)
2. [s] occurs following all other voiceless sounds
3. [z] occurs following all other voiced sounds

You may want to think of arguments for positing one of the three allomorphs as the abstract underlying form of the plural morpheme. We will assume that it is /z/. From this underlying form, all three allomorphs must be derivable by general rules that apply to all regular nouns (that is, nouns other than those that are specially marked as taking an irregular plural marker).

From an underlying /z/, a rule of the following sort would be needed in order to derive the [əz] allomorph following sibilants; note that + marks a morpheme boundary and # marks a word boundary.

Schwa Insertion Rule

/z/ ———→ [əz] / sibilant + _____ #

(schwa is inserted before a word-final /z/ that follows a morpheme ending in a sibilant)

In order to derive the allomorph [s] from the underlying morpheme /z/ following voiceless sounds, a rule that partially assimilates the voiced /z/ to the unvoiced sound of the stem morpheme would be needed.

Assimilation Rule

/z/ ———→ voiceless / voiceless + _____ #

(word-final /z/ is devoiced following a morpheme ending in a voiceless sound)

These two rules must have considerable generality because they must derive the correct forms of all regular plural nouns. Table 4-10 illustrates this for the nouns *coops, judges,* and *weeds,* which exemplify the three different allomorphs. (Recall that DNA means that a rule does not apply because the conditions necessary for its application are not present; slanted lines / / represent underlying forms; and square brackets [ ] represent forms derived from application of a phonological rule.)

Our rules for deriving the plural forms of regular nouns have much wider applicability. If we examine two other inflectional morphemes of English— namely, the possessive of nouns (*judge's, cat's,* and *dog's*) and the third person singular marker on verbs (*teaches, laughs,* and *swims*)—we discover that the distribution of the allomorphs of these morphemes is parallel to the distribution for the plural morpheme.

TABLE 4-10

	coops	judges	weeds
Underlying form	/kup+z/	/jʌǰ+z/	/wid+z/
Schwa insertion	DNA		DNA
Derived form	[kup+z]	[jʌǰ+əz]	[wid+z]
Assimilation		DNA	DNA
Surface form	[kup+s]	[jʌǰ+əz]	[wid+z]

Possessive Morpheme on Nouns

---

[s]   ship, cat, Jack
[z]   John, arm, dog
[əz] church, judge, fish

Third Person Singular Morpheme on Verbs

---

[s]   leap, eat, kick, laugh
[z]   hurry, seem, lean, crave, see
[əz] preach, tease, judge, buzz, rush

If we posit /z/ as the underlying phonological form of these morphemes, then the very same rules that derive the correct allomorphs of the plural morpheme will also derive the correct allomorphs of the possessive morpheme of nouns and the third person singular morpheme of verbs. (Unlike plurals, many of which are irregular, all nouns are regular with respect to the possessive morpheme, and all verbs are regular with respect to the third person singular morpheme except for *is, has, says,* and *does.*)

English Past Tense Morpheme

The inflectional morpheme that marks the past tense of regular verbs in English has three allomorphs:

---

[t]   wish, kiss, talk, strip, preach
[d]   wave, bathe, play, lie, stir, tease, roam, ruin
[əd] want, wade, wait, hoot, plant, seed

If we posit /d/ as the underlying phonological form of the past tense morpheme, then we need just two simple rules to derive the past-tense forms of all regular verbs.

Schwa Insertion Rule

/d/ ——→ [əd] / alveolar stop + _____ #

(schwa is inserted preceding a word-final /d/ that follows a morpheme ending in an alveolar stop)

Assimilation Rule

/d/ ——→ voiceless / voiceless + _____ #

(word-final /d/ becomes [t] following a morpheme that ends in a voiceless sound)

TABLE 4-11

	wished	wanted	waved
Underlying form	/wɪš+d/	/wɑnt+d/	/wev+d/
Schwa insertion	DNA	↓	DNA
Derived form	[wɪš+d]	[wɑnt+əd]	[wev+d]
Assimilation	↓	DNA	DNA
Surface form	[wɪš+t]	[wɑnt+əd]	[wev+d]

Derivations of the past tense forms of the verbs *wish*, *want*, and *wave* are provided in Table 4-11 as examples.

Inspection of the last two sets of rules reveals striking similarities in both the schwa insertion processes and the assimilation processes required to generate the correct forms of four inflectional morphemes: the plural and possessive forms of nouns, the third person singular forms of verbs, and the past tense forms of verbs.

Underlying Phonological Form of Morphemes in the Lexicon

Consonants The same kinds of phonological processes that operate between a stem and an inflectional suffix also operate between a stem and a derivational morpheme. Imagine, for example, that you are a child who knows the words *metal* and *medal*. For a speaker of North American English, the sound that occurs in the middle of both words is an alveolar flap, neither [t] nor [d] but [D].[5]

As a child hearing *metal* and *medal*, you would have entered exactly what you heard into your lexicon—/mɛDəl/ in both cases. But consider what must happen after you have internalized /mɛDəl/ for both and then subsequently hear someone say that her new car is painted *metallic* [mətʰæl+ək] red. If you failed to recognize that *metallic* and *metal* share an element of meaning, you would simply enter a new morpheme into your lexicon. That new morpheme would have the meaning 'metallike' but would not be related to the morpheme METAL; the two entries would be completely independent of one

---

[5] An alveolar flap, as you recall from Chapters 2 and 3, is the sound created when the tip of the tongue flaps quickly against the alveolar ridge (as in *metal* and *medal*). [D], which is phonetically different from both [t] and [d], is the way most Americans usually say the middle consonant of *metal* and *medal*, so that if the words are differentiated in pronunciation it is usually not by virtue of there being a [t] in one, a [d] in the other.

another. However, once you recognize that *metallic* is made up of METAL with the derivational suffix -*ic* added, then the two pronunciations [mɛDəl] and [mətʰæl+ək] must be reconciled. (This recognition will accompany the knowledge that -IC is a morpheme that also appears in such words as *atomic, Germanic, alcoholic*, and *demonic*.) The task of a language learner is to posit the simplest underlying form from which, given the phonological rules of English, all surface forms for pronunciation can be correctly derived.

Now consider the task you face when you subsequently hear someone report that the car's *medallion* is missing from the hood. For *medal* and *medallion*, you hear [mɛDəl] and [mədælyən]. What underlying form must be posited in the lexicon once the morpheme MEDAL is recognized as occurring in both words?

Assume you recognized that METAL was a common element in both *metal* and *metallic* and that MEDAL was a common element in *medal* and *medallion*. The following pronunciations can be observed:

metal		medal	
[mɛDəl]	[mətʰæl + ək]	[mɛDəl]	[mədæl + yən]
metal	metallic	medal	medallion

You can account for the different pronunciations of the morpheme METAL by positing the form /mɛtæl/ in the lexicon and postulating phonological rules that change this abstract underlying form into the various surface forms that do occur. Ignoring the vowels for a moment, the underlying form /mɛtæl/ will require a process that changes /t/ into [D] in the word *metal* [mɛDəl]. This same process will be needed to change /d/ into [D] in the word *medal* [mɛDəl]. The flapping rule changes underlying /t/ and /d/ to [D] when they occur between a stressed vowel and an unstressed one (see Chapter 3). Using a more formal notation, the rule would be:

$$\begin{matrix} \text{alveolar} \\ \text{stop} \end{matrix} \longrightarrow \text{flap} \ / \ \begin{matrix} \text{vowel} \\ \text{stress} \end{matrix} \underline{\hspace{2cm}} \begin{matrix} \text{vowel} \\ \text{unstressed} \end{matrix}$$

Thus we see that phonological rules that must be postulated to account for one set of facts sometimes account for other facts. Phonological rules, after all, apply to all morphemes and words indifferently unless there is a specific marking in the lexical entry of a particular morpheme to block the application of some process. For instance, irregular plurals like *tooth/teeth* are marked in the lexicon as not taking the regular plural morpheme. If the morpheme TOOTH were not so marked, then speakers would say *tooths* instead of *teeth*, exactly as children do before they learn to exempt TOOTH from these regular morphological and morphophonemic processes.

Thus the relationship between the phonological representation of morphemes in the lexicon and their actual pronunciation in speech is mediated by a set of phonological processes that can be represented in rules of significant generality. It is not only *metal* and *medal* that will be affected by the flapping rule but every word that meets the conditions specified in the rule. This includes single-morpheme words like *butter*, *bitter*, and *meter*, two-morpheme words like *writer*, *rider*, *raider*, *rooter*, and thousands of others.

Vowels   Consider a youngster who knows the words *photograph* [foDəgrÃf] and *photographer* [fətʰɑgrəf + ər]. At some point every speaker of English posits a single entry in the lexicon to represent the core of these two words—that is, PHOTOGRAPH. When you think sufficiently about what the underlying form must be, you will see that /fotɑgrÃf/ best represents the knowledge needed to produce the two pronunciations above. Given the underlying representation /fotɑgrÃf/ and the surface forms [foDəgrÃf] and [fətʰɑgrəf + ər], a rule that changes unstressed vowels into [ə] will produce the correct vowels.

If instead we postulated /ə/ in the underlying form, it would be impossible to formulate a rule that would produce the correct surface forms. In order to produce the [ɑ] in [fətʰɑgrəf + ər] from an underlying form with schwas /fətəgrəf + ər/, we would need a rule that produced [ɑ] from underlying /ə/. For the word *photograph*, on the other hand, we would need a rule that produced [o] from underlying /ə/ in the first syllable and [Ã] from underlying /ə/ in the third syllable. This would amount to knowing which vowels exist in the surface pronunciation and encoding that knowledge in the underlying form along with the /ə/, but that is exactly what we assume does *not* happen. Instead, we postulate different vowels in the underlying forms and a single rule that derives [ə] from any underlying vowel in unstressed position; we can now derive the customary pronunciations for these words. We formulate the rule as follows:

$$\begin{matrix} \text{vowel} \\ \text{unstressed} \end{matrix} \longrightarrow [\text{ə}]$$

(unstressed vowels become schwa)

This rule will not affect stressed vowels; underlying vowels that are unstressed become schwa [ə]. Of course, a rule that relies on information about stress requires prior assignment of stress. The rules for assigning stress in English are more complex than we can discuss in this chapter. For those who wish to pursue the topic further, some of the references at the end of Chapter 3 contain treatments of the stress placement rules of English.

SUMMARY

A morpheme is a minimal unit of meaning in language. Although some words (like *house*, *swim*, and *tall*) contain a single morpheme each, many words comprise several smaller units of meaning. As an entry in the lexicon, each morpheme has abstract phonological, morphological, grammatical, and semantic information as part of its structure.

Morphemes can be realized in various phonological shapes depending on their environment in words. The allomorphs of the morpheme 'PLURAL' occur in three principal shapes in English: [əz] after sibilants, [s] after other voiceless sounds, and [z] after other voiced sounds. The plural morpheme in English is an example of a *bound* morpheme—it cannot occur as an independent word but must be attached to another morpheme. Other morphemes are free: CAR, HOUSE, FOR.

Bound morphemes serve two principal functions. They can mark nouns for information like number (as with 'PLURAL') and case (as with 'POSSESSIVE), or they can mark verbs for information like tense (as with 'PAST') and person (as with 'THIRD PERSON SINGULAR'). Bound morphemes can also serve to derive different words from existing morphemes, as in <u>un</u>true (an adjective with the opposite meaning derived from an adjective), <u>dis</u>please (a verb with the opposite meaning derived from a verb), and commit<u>ment</u> (a noun with a related meaning derived from a verb). Bound morphemes can occur as prefixes or suffixes (together called affixes) or as infixes or circumfixes. Morphemes are arranged in words with a significant linear and hierarchical structure.

The phonological information that is entered into the internalized lexicon cannot be directly observed in the pronunciation of a word; instead, morphemes have an abstract underlying form from which all the allomorphs can be derived by regular phonological processes of a language.

Every language has a wide range of morphological devices for extending vocabulary, including compounding, reduplication, affixation, and abbreviation. Languages also borrow words from one another, each language eventually submitting most borrowings to its own phonological constraints and regular morphological processes, both inflectional and derivational.

EXERCISES

1. Argue for (or against) the claim that the following sets of English homonyms contain different words:

ail ale	flour flower
air heir	holy wholly
altar alter	it's its
boarder border	metal mettle medal meddle
buy by bye	nose knows
cell sell	pare pear pair
clause claws	reign rain rein
complement compliment	seize seas sees

2. The vitality of English suffixation is illustrated by the following sentence from a book review. *The author acknowledges his debt to Marxists, Freudians, structuralists, and McLuhanites.* Do the suffixes *-ist*, *-ian*, and *-ite* have different meanings?

If not, what accounts for their differential use in this sentence? Check a good desk dictionary to see what differences in the use of these suffixes are recorded.

3. Compare a one-page piece in a newsweekly like *Time* or *Newsweek* with a piece of equivalent length in a newspaper. Make a list of all the compound nouns in each. What parts of speech are the constituents of the compounds? Choose five of the compounds and explain the relationship between the parts of speech of the elements and the meaning of the compound. Write rules for the formation of these five compounds.

4. Consider the following two analyses of *untruthful*. What arguments could be given for preferring one analysis over the other?

[[[un + [true]   ] + th] + ful]   [un[[[true] + th] + ful]   ]
    Adj Adj   N   Adj   Adj   N   Adj Adj

5. Consider the following pairs of singular and plural words in Persian. How are plural nouns formed in Persian? What are the underlying forms of each noun?

zan	'woman'	zanān	'women'
barādar	'brother'	barādarān	'brothers'
bačče	'child'	baččegān	'children'
gorbe	'cat'	gorbegān	'cats'
bande	'slave'	bandegān	'slaves'

6. Consider the following Persian word pairs with their English glosses and propose an analysis of the derivational process that forms the abstract nouns of column B from the nouns and adjectives of column A.

A		B	
zende	'alive'	zendegi	'life'
šāyeste	'worthy'	šāyestegi	'worthiness'
xaste	'tired'	xastegi	'fatigue'
mard	'man'	mardi	'manliness'
bačče	'child'	baččegi	'childhood'

7. For each of these English words, provide an additional word that will aid a speaker to internalize the correct adult underlying form as compared to the form that would be posited on the basis of the pronunciation of the given word alone.

Example: Given *photograph* [foDəgræf] (with stress on the first and third syllables), the word *photographer* [fətʰɑgrəfər] (with stress on the second syllable) will help arrive at the correct adult form because it will provide the pronunciation for the second underlying vowel, which cannot be a schwa if *photographer* is to be pronounced.

solemn	compute	bomb
history	record (noun)	prosper
professor	sulphur	music

8. Provide phonetic transcriptions for the pronunciations of *rhetoric* and *rhetorical*. What abstract underlying form would best explain the two pronunciations? Explain how the underlying form you have posted would generate the correct surface forms.

9. Consider the following verb forms in the Tailevu dialect of Fijian:

rai	'see'	ki^{n}do	'startle'
raiði au	'see me'	ki^{n}dori au	'startle me'
raiði iko	'see you'	ki^{n}dori iko	'startle you'
raiðia	'see him'	ki^{n}doria	'startle him'

^{m}biu	'abandon'	^{m}bese	'be tired of'
^{m}biuti au	'abandon me'	^{m}beseki au	'be tired of me'
^{m}biuti iko	'abandon you'	^{m}beseki iko	'be tired of you'
^{m}biutia	'abandon him'	^{m}besekia	'be tired of him'

(a) What underlying form do we need to posit for the root of each of these four verbs? Remember that the underlying form of the root must contain enough phonological information for all forms of the verb to be derived, and bear in mind that morpheme boundaries are not necessarily the same thing as word boundaries.

(b) Consider the following short sentences, in which the verbs are the same as in (a). List all the different morphemes that you can identify in these six sentences, and provide an accurate gloss for each.

au a ^{m}biuti iko	'I abandoned you'
e a raiðia	'he saw him'
e a ^{m}biuti au	'he abandoned me'
o a ki^{n}dori au	'you startled me'
au a raiðia	'I saw him'
o a ^{m}besekia	'you were tired of him'

(c) If *levaðia* means 'be angry at him,' how are the following sentences said in the Tailevu dialect?

You were angry at him.
I was angry at you.
He was angry at me.

10. In the Niutao dialect of Tuvaluan, a Polynesian language, some verbs and adjectives have different forms with singular and plural subjects, as in these examples:

Singular	*Plural*	
kai	kakai	'eat'
mafuli	mafufuli	'turned around'
fepaki	fepapaki	'collide'
apulu	apupulu	'capsize'
nofo	nonofo	'stay'
maasei	maasesei	'bad'
takato	takakato	'lie down'
valea	valelea	'stupid'

(a) Describe the rule of morphology that derives the plural forms of these verbs and adjectives from the singular forms.

(b) In the Funaafuti dialect of the same language the process is slightly different, as the following plural forms of the same verbs and adjectives show. (Double consonants indicate that the phoneme is held for a longer period of time.) How are plural forms formed from singular forms in this dialect? How does that process differ from the process of plural formation in the Niutao dialect described in part (a)?

kkai   nnofo
maffuli   maassei
feppaki   takkato
appulu   vallea

11. Column A lists Russian words, and column B lists a number of Russian prefixes. (The apostrophe in this instance indicates that the previous consonant is palatalized—that is, followed by a very short /y/.)

A		B	
davno	'a long time ago'	ne-	'non-'
zvezdniy	'starry'	so-	'together'
avtor	'author'	pred-	'before, pre-'
sčast'e	'happiness'	polu-	'half'
son	'sleep'		
kul'turniy	'cultured'		
znanie	'knowledge'		
oxranenie	'protection'		

On the basis of these lists, determine the English translation of the following Russian words. *Example*: If *oxota* means 'wish,' *neoxota* means 'nonwish' (that is, 'reluctance').

soavtor   sozvezdniy   predoxranenie
poluson   nedavno   neznanie
nekul'turniy nesčast'e   sooxranenie

12. The following are different forms of the same Russian words. The left-hand column contains simple roots; the right-hand column contains forms that are derived from the corresponding form in the left-hand column by processes of inflectional or derivational morphology.

paroxot	'steamboat'	paroxody	'steamboats'
zapat	'west'	zapada	'of the west'
rat	'glad'	radnost'	'gladness'
most	'bridge'	mostom	'to the bridges'
pot	'perspiration'	poty	'perspirations'
štat	'state'	štatu	'to the state'
pot	'under'	podo	'under' (alternative form)

On the basis of this list, how can we describe the distribution of [t] and [d] in Russian? (*Hint*: we want to be able to derive the word in the left-hand column from the same underlying form as the corresponding morpheme in the right-hand column.)

13. Traditionally, linguists have distinguished three types of morphological structures that are found among the world's languages. In a language that has an *isolating* morphology, each unit of meaning is represented by a different word, as

in the following Chinese sentence:

wǒ gāng yào gěi nǐ nà yì bēi chá
I just want for you bring one cup tea
'I am about to bring you a cup of tea.'

A second type of language has an *inflectional* morphology, in which words change their shape according to their function in the sentence. Russian is an example of a language with an inflectional morphology. (*Sing.* stands for 'singular.')

Oni   kupili   synu   igrusky
they-Subject buy-Past-Plural for-son-Sing. toy-Object-Sing.
'They bought a toy for their son.'

A third type of language (which was not discussed in this chapter) has an *agglutinative* morphology. Such a system has many prefixes and suffixes that can be attached to words. Greenlandic Eskimo is an example of such a language, as illustrated by the following sentence, in which dashes represent morpheme boundaries within the same word:

Qajar–taa–va asirur–sima–vuq
kayak–new–his break–done–it
'His new kayak has been destroyed.'

   Although many languages are difficult to classify strictly according to these distinctions, the distinctions are still useful in describing morphological systems. On the basis of the examples given, determine whether the following languages have an isolating, inflectional, or agglutinative morphology, and justify your answer.

Samoan:
   Ɂua   mālamalama aɁu i   le matāɁupu
   Present understand I   Object the lesson
   'I understand the lesson.'

Turkish:
   Herkes   ben üniversite–ye bašla–yacağ–im san–iyor
   everyone I   university–to start–Future–I believe–Present
   'Everyone believes that I will start university.'

Finnish:
   Tyttö   silitti   paidat
   girl–Subject–Sing. iron–Past–Sing. shirt–Object–Plural
   'The girl ironed the shirts.'

Japanese:
   Akiko wa   Haruko ni mainiti   tegami o   kaku
   Akiko Subject Haruko to every day letter   Object write
   'Akiko writes a letter to Haruko every day.'

Mohawk:
   t–en–s–hon–te–rist–a–wenrat–eɁ
   Dual–Future–Repetitive–Plural–Reflexive–metal–cross–Punctual
   'They will cross over the railroad track.'

Thai:

Khruu hây sàmùt   nákrian săam lêm
teacher give notebook student three Article
'The teacher gave the students three notebooks.'

14. The following are sentences from Tok Pisin (New Guinea Pidgin English):

Manmeri ol   wokabaut long rot
people   they stroll   on   road
'People are strolling on the road.'

Mi harim toktok bilong yupela
I   listen speech of   you–Plural
'I listen to your (plural) speech.'

Mi harim toktok bilong yu
I   listen speech of   you–Sing.
'I listen to your (sing.) speech.'

Em no brata   bilong em ol   harim toktok bilong mi
he   and brother of   he they listen speech of   me
'He and his brother listen to my speech.'

Mi laikim dispela manmeri long rot
I   like   these people   on   road
'I like these people (who are) on the road.'

Dispela man no prend bilong mi ol   laikim dispela toktok
this   man and friend of   me they like   this   speech
'This man and my friend like this speech.'

Relying on the meaning of the morphemes that you can identify in the above sentences, translate the following sentences into Tok Pisin:

These people like my speech.
I am strolling on the road.
I like my friend's speech.
I like my brother and these people.
These people on the road and my friend like his speech.
You and my brother like the speech of these people.
These people listen to my friend's and my brother's speech.

SUGGESTIONS FOR FURTHER READING

Two valuable introductions to English word formation are Adams (1973) and Bauer (1983). Marchand (1969) is a reference book on the same subject. More general treatments of morphological processes can be found in Matthews (1974) and Lyons (1968); the latter has useful discussions of morphology in Chapter 5 and of grammatical categories in Chapter 7. Matthews (1972) treats inflectional morphology, principally in Latin. Chapter 2 of Langacker (1972) is a good general discussion of morphology with illustrations from many languages, including several American Indian languages. The principal structural grammarians of the early part of this century gave considerable attention to morphology; useful discussions and interesting examples can be found in Sapir (1921) and Bloomfield (1933). Nida (1949) is a traditional descriptive text with more than two hundred problems from a variety of languages. Recent treatments of morphology can be found in Shopen (1985), especially the chapters by Stephen R. Anderson on "Typological Distinctions in Word Formation" and "Inflectional Morphology," by Bernard Comrie on "Causative Verb Formation and Other Verb-Deriving Morphology," and by Comrie and Sandra A. Thompson on "Lexical Nominalization." Comrie (1987), from which a few of the examples in this chapter are taken, provides valuable descriptions of more than forty major languages usually including extensive discussion of morphology. The latest words to be added to English are listed in *12,000 Words* (1987).

REFERENCES

Adams, Valerie. 1973. *An Introduction to Modern English Word-Formation* (London: Longman).

Bauer, Laurie. 1983. *English Word-Formation* (Cambridge: Cambridge University Press).

Bloomfield, Leonard. 1933. *Language* (New York: Holt, Rinehart and Winston).

Comrie, Bernard (ed.). 1987. *The World's Major Languages* (New York: Oxford University Press).

Langacker, Ronald W. 1972. *Fundamentals of Linguistic Analysis* (New York: Harcourt Brace Jovanovich).

Lyons, John. 1968. *Theoretical Linguistics* (Cambridge: Cambridge University Press).

Marchand, Hans. 1969. *The Categories and Types of Present-Day English Word-Formation*, 2nd ed. (Munich: C. H. Beck).

Matthews, Peter H. 1972. *Inflectional Morphology* (Cambridge: Cambridge University Press).

Matthews, Peter H. 1974. *Morphology* (Cambridge: Cambridge University Press).

Nida, Eugene A. 1949. *Morphology: The Descriptive Analysis of Words*, 2nd ed. (Ann Arbor: University of Michigan Press).

Sapir, Edward. 1921. *Language* (New York: Harcourt Brace Jovanovich).

Shopen, Timothy (ed.). 1985. *Grammatical Categories and the Lexicon*, vol. 3 of *Language Typology and Syntactic Description* (Cambridge: Cambridge University Press).

12,000 Words: A Supplement to Webster's Third New International Dictionary. 1987. (Springfield, Mass.: G. & C. Merriam).

SYNTAX: SENTENCES AND THEIR STRUCTURE

5

INTRODUCTION

This chapter explores how morphemes and words are organized within sentences. It examines the parts of a sentence, the relationships among them, and the relationships among various kinds of sentences such as statements and questions. The structure of a sentence, as well as its study, is called **syntax**.

The first observation to be made in studying sentence structure is that all languages have ways of referring to entities—to people, places, things, ideas, events, and so on. **Referring expressions** are nouns or noun phrases. There are simple ones like the proper nouns *Lauren, Paris,* and *Labor Day,* the common nouns *books* and *justice,* and the personal pronouns *you* and *it.* There are also more complicated expressions like these noun phrases: *a magical book, the ghost, his mother, the star of the film, a judge he had known forty years earlier,* and *the strict-constructionist way that Wapner settled another dispute over the ownership of a dog.*

The second observation to be made about syntax is that all languages have ways of saying something about the entities they make reference to. In other words, all languages can make **predications** about the things referred to by the referring expressions. All languages have ways of making statements, both affirmative and negative. They can also ask questions, issue directives, and so on.

Let's illustrate with affirmative statements. In the following sentences, reference is made to an entity and then a predication is made about it.

Referring Expression	Predication
Judge Wapner	uses an answering machine.
She	has a daughter.
The ghost	reappeared last night.

In the first example, reference is made to "Judge Wapner"; something is then predicated of him—namely, that he "uses an answering machine." Likewise for the second and third examples.

Sentences often consist of more elaborate referring expressions and more elaborate predications than these. The two sentences below illustrate more elaborate predications. In the first example, reference is made to "the dog" and then a predication about the dog is made. In the second example, reference is made to "the bride" and then a predication is made about her. In these examples, the predication is underlined.

The dog bit the man who had agreed to care for it.

The bride swore that her father had promised to foot the bill.

The processes that a language uses to refer to things and make predications about them are part of its syntax. Syntax governs the way a language makes statements, asks questions, gives directives, and so on. In other words, the study of syntax treats the structure of sentences and their structural relationships to one another. To repeat: A typical sentence consists of two parts, one a referring expression and the other a predication about the entity referred to. In syntactic terms, referring expressions are noun phrases, and predicates are verb phrases. All languages, however much they differ from one another in the other categories or parts of speech, have nouns (and noun phrases) and verbs (and verb phrases).

SENTENCE TYPES

In many traditional grammars three major sentence types are distinguished. A **simple sentence** consists of a single clause that stands alone as its own sentence. In a **coordinate sentence** (called "compound" in traditional grammars), two or more clauses are joined by a conjunction in a coordinate relationship. A **complex sentence** combines two (or more) clauses in such a way that one clause functions as a grammatical part of the other one.

Simple Sentences

Simple sentences are those that contain one clause; a **clause** contains a single verb (or predicate). The following are examples of simple sentences:

(a)   Dan <u>washed</u> the dishes.

(b)   Karim <u>assembled</u> the new grill.

(c)   Joe <u>cooked</u> the hot dogs.

(d)   A runner from Ohio <u>won</u> the marathon last year.

(e)   Denise <u>will buy</u> a new raincoat this fall.

(f)   Her uncle <u>had put</u> the gifts in the car.

(g)   The psychiatrist <u>should have believed</u> in banshees.

Each of these sentences contains only one verb, but you can see that a verb itself can consist of a single word (as in *washed, assembled, cooked,* and *won*) or of more than one word (as in *will buy, had put,* and *should have believed*). The clauses just cited are called sentences because they stand independently as sentences; if they were incorporated into other sentences, they would be called clauses. In English and many other languages, the central element in a clause is the verb; each clause—and therefore each simple sentence—contains just one verb.

Coordinate Sentences

Two clauses can be joined to make a coordinate sentence, as in these examples:

(a)   Karim assembled the new grill, <u>and</u> Joe cooked the hot dogs.

(b)   Denise bought a new coat, <u>but</u> she didn't wear it often.

A coordinate sentence consists of two clauses joined by a word such as *and, but,* or *or,* which are called *coordinating conjunctions,* or simply *conjunctions.* Conjunctions can be used to join sentences (as we have just seen), but they can also join other constructions; for example, nouns in *trick <u>or</u> treat* and *dungeons <u>and</u> dragons;* verbs in *trip <u>and</u> fall* and *break <u>and</u> enter;* adjectives in *slow <u>and</u> painful* and *tried <u>and</u> true.* To repeat a point made in the preceding section, when clauses are combined to form a single sentence we generally reserve the word *sentence* for the larger structure and refer to the structures that make it up as *clauses.*

The clauses in a coordinate sentence hold equal status as parts of the sentence: neither is part of the other one, and each could stand by itself as an

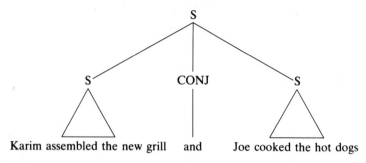

Karim assembled the new grill   and   Joe cooked the hot dogs

FIGURE 5-1

independent sentence. Figure 5-1 represents the structure of a coordinate sentence and illustrates the equivalent status of the clauses (called *coordinate clauses*). We use the label S for both the whole sentence and for each coordinate clause in it; CONJ stands for conjunction.

Complex Sentences

Embedded Clauses   One clause can be incorporated into another clause. The clause *Dan washed the dishes* can be incorporated into another clause to produce the sentence *Sue said Dan washed the dishes*. In each of the following examples, the underlined portion is a clause that is incorporated (or *embedded*) into another clause.

   (a)   Sue said <u>Dan washed the dishes</u>.

   (b)   <u>That the runner from Ohio won the marathon</u> surprised us.

   (c)   She is wondering <u>whether Denise will buy a new raincoat</u>.

   (d)   She didn't suspect a party <u>until her uncle put the gifts in the car</u>.

   (e)   It was clear <u>that the patient should have received a refund</u>.

In sentence (a), the clause *Dan washed the dishes* is embedded into the clausal structure *Sue said ——*. The clause *Dan washed the dishes* functions as the direct object of the verb *said*. It is thus functionally equivalent (though not semantically equivalent) to the word *something* in the sentence *Sue said something*; both are direct objects. In (b), the clause *That the runner from Ohio won the marathon* is embedded into the clausal structure *—— surprised us*. In this case, the embedded clause functions as the subject of the verb *surprised*. The embedded clause in (b) (*That the runner from Ohio won the marathon*) is grammatically equivalent to *It* in *It surprised us* or to *The news* in *The news surprised us*. In (c), the clause *whether Denise will buy a new raincoat* is embedded into the clause *She is wondering ——*; it serves as a complement to the verb *is wondering*.

Subordinators   In most of the examples just given, the embedded clause is introduced by a word that would not occur there if the clause were standing as an independent sentence: words like *that* in (b) and (e), *whether* in (c), and *until* in (d). When a clause is embedded into another clause, it is often introduced by such a **subordinator**. Subordinators serve to mark the beginning of an embedded clause and to help identify its function in the sentence. Not all embedded clauses must be introduced by a subordinator, although in English they usually can be. Compare these sentence pairs:

(a) Sue said that Dan washed the dishes.
(b) Sue said Dan washed the dishes.

(c) That she won surprised us.
(d) *She won surprised us.

Notice that (a) and (b) are well formed with or without the subordinator. But of the pair (c) and (d), only (c) is well formed. (The asterisk preceding (d) indicates a structure that is not well formed.)

The Form of Embedded Clauses   When a clause is embedded within certain other clauses, its form may differ from the form it would have if it stood independently as a simple sentence. In these pairs, compare sentence (a) with (b) and (c) with (d):

(a) Sue said Dan washed the dishes.
(b) Sue wanted Dan to wash the dishes.

(c) That the runner from Ohio won the marathon surprised us.
(d) For the runner from Ohio to win the marathon surprised us.

The clause *Dan to wash the dishes* is not a well-formed English sentence; yet when it is embedded into the clausal structure *Sue wanted ——*, it is perfectly well formed. As a matter of fact, any other form would be unacceptable, as illustrated:

(a) *Sue wanted Dan washed the dishes.
(b) *Sue wanted that Dan will wash the dishes.
(c) *Sue wanted Dan washes the dishes.

The form of an embedded clause can depend on the particular verb of the clause in which it is embedded. Compare the sentences in each of these pairs:

(a) Sue wanted Dan to wash the dishes.
(b) *Sue wanted Dan washed the dishes.

(c) Sue said Dan washed the dishes.
(d) *Sue said Dan to wash the dishes.

These sentences suggest that the verb *want* requires a clause form with *to*, as in *wanted Dan to wash the dishes*; whereas the verb *say* does not permit an embedded clause to take the form *Dan to wash the dishes* but does permit the independent sentence form *Dan washed the dishes*.

Unlike coordinate sentences, which contain clauses of equal status, *complex* sentences contain clauses of unequal status. In the complex sentences we have been examining, one clause is subordinate to another clause and functions as a grammatical part of that clause. We call the subordinate clause an *embedded clause* and the clause into which it is embedded a *matrix clause*. Every subordinate clause is by definition embedded in a matrix clause, in which it serves in a grammatical function such as subject, direct object, or adverbial. For example, in the next sentences, in which brackets set off the embedded clauses, each embedded clause functions as a grammatical unit in its matrix clause. Each embedded clause has the same grammatical function in its matrix clause as the underlined word has in the sentence directly below it:

(a) Sally said [she saw a ghost].
(b) Sally said <u>it</u>. (<u>it</u> is the direct object of the verb *said*)

(c) [That Jack feared witches] upset his wife.
(d) <u>It</u> upset his wife. (<u>it</u> is the subject of the sentence)

(e) Joe cooked the hot dogs [after Karim assembled the grill].
(f) Joe cooked the hot dogs <u>then</u>. (<u>then</u> is an adverbial modifier)

In (a), the embedded clause *she saw a ghost* functions as the direct object of the verb *said*, just as the word *it* does in (b). In (c), the embedded clause *That Jack feared witches* functions as the subject of the verb *upset*, just as *it* does in sentence (d). In (e), *after Karim assembled the grill* functions as an adverbial modifying the verb phrase *cooked the hot dogs*, just as *then* does in (f).

TREE DIAGRAMS AND CONSTITUENCY

Tree Diagrams

We can represent some of the things we have been exploring in *tree diagrams* like those on the following pages. The tree in Figure 5-2 represents the fact that the sentence *Sue liked Casper* consists of two parts: the referring

FIGURE 5-2

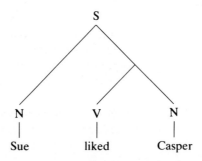

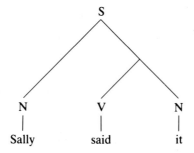

FIGURE 5-3

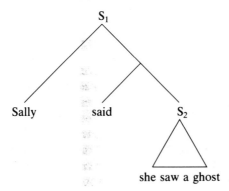

FIGURE 5-4

expression *Sue* and the predicate expression *liked Casper*. In each diagram, S stands for sentence (or clause), N stands for noun or pronoun, and V stands for verb.

This tree diagram can also represent other clauses such as *Sally said it*, as illustrated in Figure 5-3. These trees somewhat oversimplify the structures represented, as we shall see.

Tree diagrams can also illustrate the relationship among the clauses of a sentence like *Sally said she saw a ghost*. In representing a complex sentence, we can substitute the clause *she saw a ghost* for the word *it*, as in Figure 5-4. This diagram captures the fact that the embedded clause S_2 (*she saw a ghost*) functions structurally as part of the matrix clause S_1 (*Sally said* ——). The embedded clause fills the same slot in the matrix clause as the word *it* fills in the clause *Sally said it*.

We saw earlier that coordinate sentences are made up of coordinate clauses. The next examples illustrate that a subordinate clause can be embedded within a coordinate clause of a coordinate sentence.

The tree diagram in Figure 5-5 represents the fact that S_2 and S_3 are coordinate clauses of S_1 and that S_4 is embedded in the matrix clause S_2.

The diagram in Figure 5-6 captures the fact that S_2 and S_3 are coordinate clauses and that S_4 is embedded in the matrix clause S_3.

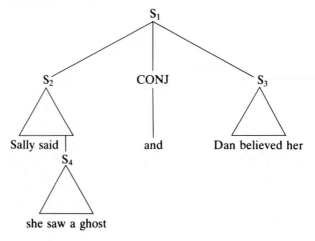

FIGURE 5-5

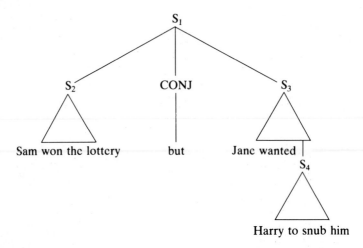

FIGURE 5-6

In the remainder of this chapter, we shall focus principally on clauses that are embedded in other clauses, and we shall make only incidental reference to sentences containing coordinate clauses.

Constituency

In analyzing the structure of sentences, one pivotal tool is the simple notion that sentences consist of smaller structural units called **constituents**. For example, the sentence *Sally said she saw a ghost* can be viewed in several ways. Obviously, it is made up of words, each of which contains at least one morpheme. Since these morphemes have sounds associated with them, we could say that the sentence is made up of sounds (such as /g/, /o/, /s/, /t/ in

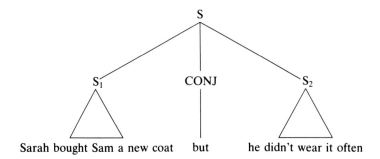

FIGURE 5-7

ghost and /s/, /ɛ/, /d/ in *said*), or of morphemes (SAY and 'PAST TENSE'), or of words (*Sally* and *said*). Such an approach would be like describing a shopping center as made up of cement and electrical wires—accurate, but beside the point. We want to say that a shopping center has shops, restaurants, parking areas, recreational facilities, and so on. We could then go further and describe the composition and relationship of these units; the point is to identify structural units that are relevant to some purpose or some level of organization.

Linguists find it useful to treat sentences as consisting, first, of the largest grammatical units. These largest units in turn can be analyzed as consisting of smaller units, which in turn can be analyzed. From this point of view, the immediate constituents of a coordinate sentence are the clauses constituting it and the conjunction joining them, as in this example:

$$\underline{\text{Sarah bought Sam a new coat}} \text{ but } \underline{\text{he didn't wear it often}}.$$
$$\text{clause 1 (S}_1\text{)} \qquad\qquad \text{clause 2 (S}_2\text{)}$$

This structure can be represented schematically as in Figure 5-7.

The immediate constituents of a complex sentence are its clauses, as in the next example:

$$\underline{\text{That Jack feared witches}} \quad \underline{\text{upset his wife}}.$$
$$\text{clause 2 (S}_2\text{)} \qquad \text{clause 1 (S}_1\text{)}$$

This structure can be represented as in Figure 5-8.

Linear Ordering of Constituents It is obvious that in every language the words of a sentence must occur in some order. It follows that constituents, too, have their elements in some order. In speaking the order is chronological. In writing the order can be from left to right (as in English), right to left (as in Arabic and Persian), top to bottom (as in Japanese), and so on. Sentences are thus expressed with an ordered sequence of morphemes and words. *The little old lady from Pasadena sits in the park, Jill touched the*

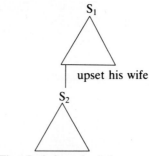

upset his wife

That Jack feared witches

FIGURE 5-8

harpie, Helen claims to be from Xanadu, and all other clauses and sentences in every language necessarily express words in a sequential, or linear, order.

Now we ask the question: Is the order in which words are arranged fixed or not? If it is fixed, is it equally fixed across different languages? We begin by examining the following sentences:

The farmer saw the ghost.

The ghost saw the farmer.

Both are well-formed sentences of English, and both contain exactly the same words. Clearly, however, they do not mean the same thing. Since the words themselves are the same, the only thing that could signal the difference in meaning is the word order. It is the word order in the sentence that signals who is doing what to whom. Now consider the following:

The farmer saw the ghost.

*Farmer the ghost the saw.

The first is well formed; the second is not. Word order is clearly an essential part of English sentence structure. If we rearrange the words in an English sentence, we sometimes get other well-formed sentences that have a different meaning, but we can also produce sentences that are not well formed. Sometimes, too, a change of word order can produce a different well-formed sentence with the same meaning, as here:

Yesterday I heard a poltergeist in the attic.

I heard a poltergeist in the attic yesterday.

Thus word order is not absolutely fixed. However, since rearranging the order of words can sometimes change meaning and sometimes produce an ill-formed sentence, the order of words in an English sentence *is* significant.

Not all languages exploit word order to the same extent that English does. As we saw in Chapter 4, Latin could express 'The farmer saw the ghost' by using any of the following word orders:

Agricola	vidit	umbram.
farmer	saw	ghost
Agricola	umbram	vidit.
Umbram	agricola	vidit.

'The farmer saw the ghost.'

Grammatical relations like subject and direct object are indicated in Latin not by word order, as they are in English, but by inflectional suffixes; the same is true of Russian, German, and many other languages. Thus, with constant inflections on the nouns, each of the following Latin sentences has the same meaning:

Umbra	vidit	agricolam.
ghost	saw	farmer
Umbra	agricolam	vidit.
Agricolam	umbra	vidit.

'The ghost saw the farmer.'

There are other possible orders for arranging these three words in sequence, and all would indicate the same content. (Though all are well formed, not all are equally likely to occur in Latin speech; some would seem more natural than others.) Word order is a potential marker of meaning in all the world's languages, but not all languages exploit this potentiality, and very many languages do not exploit it to the same extent as English does.

Hierarchical Ordering of Constituents   Is there any other structure to a sentence besides linear order? To answer this question, consider the phrase *gullible boys and girls*. It can mean either 'gullible boys and gullible girls' or 'gullible boys and (all) girls.' This ambiguity of interpretation reflects the fact that the phrase *gullible boys and girls* has two possible internal organizations for the same linear sequence of words. These internal organizations differ as to whether the adjective *gullible* modifies *boys and girls* or just *boys*. We call the internal organization of a linear string of words its **constituent structure**. Constituent structure refers to the grouping of words (and morphemes) into grammatical units; we represent constituent structure using brackets or tree diagrams. The following illustrates both ways of representing the phrase *gullible boys and girls*. In the tree diagrams of Figure 5-9, notice that at the highest level there are two constituents in the left-hand tree but three in the tree on the right; at the lowest level, there are the same number of constituents in each. Below each tree is an equivalent representation using brackets.

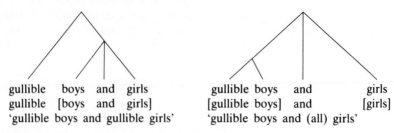

gullible	boys	and	girls
gullible	[boys	and	girls]

'gullible boys and gullible girls'

gullible boys	and	girls
[gullible boys]	and	[girls]

'gullible boys and (all) girls'

FIGURE 5-9

Notice, then, that a string of words with a specified linear order can have more than one constituent structure. Both of these tree diagrams represent the same four words in the same linear order. But the constituent structures are different. In the first tree diagram, the phrase *gullible boys and girls* consists of two constituents: (1) *gullible*; (2) *boys and girls*. In the second tree, there are three constituents: (1) *gullible boys*; (2) *and*; (3) *girls*. The difference in meaning between these two identical sequences of words is the result of their having different constituent structures at the highest level of analysis.[1]

Structural ambiguity of the sort we have just examined is not limited to phrases. It can occur in larger units as well. Consider sentence (a):

(a)   He sold the car to his brother in New York.

This string of words is *ambiguous*; it has more than one possible interpretation. Sometimes ambiguity results from the fact that a word has two meanings, as in *He ate near the bank* (in which *bank* can be a financial institution or the bank of a river) or *He gave her his chair* (in which *chair* can be a physical object or a place to sit). In sentence (a) the ambiguity arises not from the individual words (which are all unambiguous) but from the fact that the string of words has more than one possible constituent structure. We can bracket (a) in different ways to indicate the different constituent structures, as shown here:

(b)   He sold the car   [to   [his brother in New York]   ].
(c)   He sold the car   [to his brother]   [in New York].

Sentence (b) can be paraphrased as (d) below but not as (e) or (f); sentence (c) can be paraphrased as (e) or (f) but not as (d):

(d)   It was to his brother in New York that he sold the car.

---

[1] To refer without ambiguity to the meaning shown in the second tree, you could alter the word order and say *girls and gullible boys*.

(e)   It was in New York that he sold the car to his brother.

(f)   In New York he sold the car to his brother.

These examples illustrate that the words of a sentence are organized into units called constituents and that such constituents are not available to inspection—they cannot be identified from the string of words itself. The linear order of words in a written English sentence—which word is first, which second, and so on—is available to inspection (it is obvious), but it takes a speaker of English to recognize constituent structure and to recognize that a given string of words may have two possible constituent structures.

MAJOR CONSTITUENTS OF SENTENCES: NOUN PHRASES AND VERB PHRASES

Sentences have a linear order that is obvious and a constituent structure that is not obvious but is nevertheless understood by native speakers. The linear order of speech is automatically represented when we write down a sentence, with each word located sequentially with respect to other words in the sentence. Consider the sentences in Figure 5-10, which have two simple constituents each.

Even more elaborate sentences can be analyzed similarly, as in Figure 5-11.

FIGURE 5-10

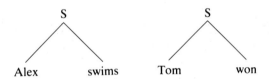

FIGURE 5-11

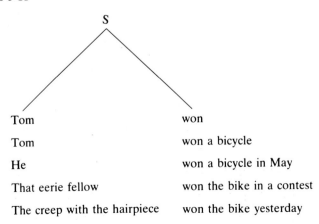

An alternative tool in representing constituent structure is bracketing, as illustrated here:

(a) [Alex] [swims].

(b) [The dog] [is barking].

(c) [Jennifer] [said something].

(d) [Ruth] [spilled the potion].

(e) [The creep with the hairpiece] [won the bike yesterday].

(f) [The witch] [said Ruth spilled the potion].

In general, simple sentences (and therefore clauses) consist of two principal constituents. In each of the preceding examples, the constituent on the left is called an NP (for Noun Phrase), and the one on the right is called a VP (for Verb Phrase). Each NP contains a noun (or pronoun). Each VP contains a verb. Each NP is a referring expression; each VP makes a predication. We identify NPs and VPs sometimes by the slots they fill in a sentence and sometimes from their functions in the sentence. Thus *Alex* in sentence (a) and *The creep with the hairpiece* in (e) function in the same way: they are referring expressions about which the predication in the sentence is made. Similarly, *swims* in (a) and *said Ruth spilled the potion* in (f) function alike in their sentences; they are predications made of an NP.

NPs can also be identified by substitution procedures such as those implied in the list of alternatives to the basic two-part structure in Figure 5-11. Thus, for *Tom* we could substitute forms varying from *He* to *The creep with the hairpiece*. Both the short *He* and the longer phrase are NPs because they can occur in the slot —— *won a bicycle.*

Other slots in a sentence can also be filled by an NP. In sentence (d), the VP is *spilled the potion*. Unlike the VP of (a), which consists of the single word *swims*, the VP of (d) contains two parts: the verb *spilled* and the NP *the potion*. Thus a VP can contain an NP. In fact, several of our sentences have an NP within the VP, as the underlining shows:

	NP	VP
(a)	[Alex]	[swims].
(b)	[The dog]	[is barking].
(c)	[Jennifer]	[said something].
(d)	[Ruth]	[spilled the potion].
(e)	[The creep with the hairpiece]	[won the bike yesterday].
(f)	[The witch]	[said Ruth spilled the potion].

Something, the potion, the bike, Ruth, and *the potion* are NPs. To repeat two points made earlier, an NP contains a noun (or a pronoun) and in some respects functions like a noun within a sentence. Thus anything that you could insert in the slots here would be an NP:

She enjoyed talking about —— incessantly.

Invariably, —— upset her.

The following words and phrases could be inserted in either slot and are therefore NPs; we have underlined the *head noun* in each. (Sometimes an NP contains more than one noun, a topic to which we will return later in this chapter.)

<u>animals</u>   the little old <u>lady</u> from Pasadena
the <u>weather</u>   his <u>return</u> to his first wife
her aged <u>instructor</u>   the <u>fact</u> that her family is so poor
the <u>thief</u> who stole her purse   Peter's <u>winning</u> the race
<u>it</u>   the <u>creep</u> with the hairpiece

Notice that instead of containing a head noun, an NP can be a pronoun like *it*. Pronouns are a variety of NP in that they have the same distribution in clauses; they occur where NPs can occur.

Verb Phrases, or VPs, can be identified using similar substitution procedures. Consider the frame *Tom* ——. The following strings fit this frame and are thus VPs (the head verb in each VP is underlined):

<u>won</u>
<u>won</u> the race
<u>claimed</u> he won a prize
<u>claimed</u> he won a prize for his efforts in the tournament
<u>admitted</u> that he would not enter the contest in any case

To this point, we have seen two major constituents in a sentence: NP and VP. The NP usually refers to a person or a thing; the VP makes a predication about the NP. What we have uncovered about the structure of simple sentences applies equally to subordinate clauses that are embedded within other clauses: clauses have two principal constituents—NP and VP.

Active/Passive Sentences   An NP functions as a single unified constituent in a sentence, regardless of how big or small the NP is and regardless of how simple or complex. Even elaborate NPs like *the fellow with the silly hairpiece* or *what she wanted to receive for her twenty-fifth birthday* function in a sentence exactly like the simple NPs *lions, she*, and *Ruth*. In this section we will investigate the formation of passive sentences in English to illustrate the unity of NPs.

Consider these active/passive sentence pairs:

(a)   Zelda auctioned the famous wooden spoon.
(b)   The famous wooden spoon was auctioned by Zelda.

(c)   The judge fined an old lady from Pasadena.
(d)   An old lady from Pasadena was fined by the judge.

(e)   The mail truck crushed the bike I gave Karim.
(f)   The bike I gave Karim was crushed by the mail truck.

Even schoolchildren who have never heard of active and passive sentences can usually provide the passive version of an active sentence when given a few model pairs. They implicitly know the rule by which passive sentences can be formed from active ones. Let's attempt to make explicit what that rule must be.

On the basis of sentences (a) and (b) above, one might hypothesize the following rule: "To make an active sentence passive, interchange the first word with the last four." (For our present purposes, we ignore the verb *be* and the preposition *by*, but in a complete statement of the rule those aspects of passivization would also have to be addressed.) Our tentative hypothesis produces a well-formed string when applied to sentence (a); but if it is applied to (c) or (e), it produces the ill-formed structures of (g) and (h):

(c)   The judge fined an old lady from Pasadena.
(g)   *Old lady from Pasadena judge was fined an by the.

(e)   The mail truck crushed the bike I gave Karim.
(h)   *Bike I gave Karim mail truck was crushed the by the.

Check for yourself to see that (g) and (h) are indeed the structures that would result from interchanging the first word and the last four words of the active sentences (c) and (e) (and introducing *by* and an appropriate form of *be*). Clearly, what speakers of English know about the relationship between active and passive sentences depends not on counting words, but on knowledge about constituent structure.

Refer again to the constituents that are interchanged in the active/passive pairs of sentences (a) through (f). The strings of words in each of the following sets share a structural property in that they function similarly:

A.   <u>Zelda</u>/The <u>judge</u>/The <u>mail truck</u>

B.   the famous wooden <u>spoon</u>/an old <u>lady</u> from Pasadena/the <u>bike</u> I gave Karim

Each NP in sets A and B contains at least one noun, a head noun, which is underlined. They share an ability to function alike in sentences, that is, to fill certain frames and to be movable *as units* in syntactic processes such as passivization. In the process of forming passives, NPs thus function as syntactic *units* no matter how long they are.

PHRASE-STRUCTURE RULES

Rules for Rewriting Noun Phrases

We can now characterize and exemplify certain types of NP:

Noun (N):
Karim, oracles, elixir, justice, swimming

Determiner (DET) + Noun (N):
the amulet, a potion, some gnomes, a saucer

Determiner (DET) + Adjective (ADJ) + Noun (N):
an ancient oracle, these hellish precincts, the first omen, a lasting peace, a flying saucer

One way of representing these various NP patterns is by the use of **phrase-structure rules** (also called **rewrite rules**) like the following:

(a) NP ⟶ N   (that is, NP consists of an N)

(b) NP ⟶ DET N   (NP consists of DET and N)

(c) NP ⟶ DET ADJ N   (NP consists of DET and ADJ and N)

These three rules can be collapsed into a single rule if we adopt the convention of placing parentheses around optional elements (that is, around elements that can be present but need not be present). Notice that DET is not required in all three rules, so it can be placed in parentheses. ADJ is also optional, so it appears in parentheses. The collapsed, or abbreviated, rule will look like this:

(d) NP ⟶ (DET) (ADJ) N

This rule can be expanded into the three separate rules that we intended to represent in the collapsed version. Notice that the collapsed rule has one expansion that we did not anticipate: because DET and ADJ are each optional, we can rewrite NP not only as in (a), (b), and (c) above but also as follows:

(e) NP ⟶ ADJ N

Our collapsed rule thus suggests an expansion that we did not set out to capture. If there are well-formed NP structures that consist of an adjective and a noun, then our rule is valid; otherwise, we would have to revise it to exclude structures that are not well formed. Of course, English does indeed permit NPs that consist of ADJ and N, as in examples like *supernatural beings, extraterrestrial life,* and *great imagination.* (One advantage of using formalisms such as the collapsed rewrite rule in (d) is that they sometimes entail claims that can be checked against other data; they thus provide a test of their own validity.)

Rules for Rewriting Sentences and Verb Phrases

To capture the fact that sentences and clauses have two basic constituent parts, we formulate the following phrase-structure rule:

$$S \longrightarrow NP \quad VP$$

Every rewrite rule can generate a tree diagram, and this phrase-structure rule (rewrite S as NP and VP) would generate the following tree:

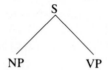

Having seen various expansions of NP, we turn now to the internal structure of VP to explore its expansions and the rewrite rules necessary to accommodate them. The following expansions of our frame for identifying VPs reveal that the structures on the right are VPs; the labels under parts of the VPs indicate the categories of constituents of those structures.

$$\underline{\quad VP \quad}$$
Tom   jogged
      V

$$\underline{\qquad VP \qquad}$$
Tom   won a bicycle
      V   NP

$$\underline{\qquad\quad VP \qquad\quad}$$
Tom   won the bike in May
      V   NP   PP

The notation PP stands for prepositional phrase. (Other examples of PP from previous sentences in this chapter include *in the car, from Xanadu, in New York, to his brother, with the hairpiece,* and *by the judge.*) Every PP consists of a preposition (PREP) and a noun phrase (NP). The rewrite rule for PP is this:

$$PP \longrightarrow PREP \quad NP$$

The sentences about Tom indicate that there are at least three ways to expand VP:

$$VP \longrightarrow \begin{array}{l} V \\ V \quad NP \\ V \quad NP \quad PP \end{array}$$

Using parentheses to enclose optional elements, these rewrite rules can be collapsed into a single rule, which says that a VP must have a V and may have an NP and a PP:

$$VP \longrightarrow V \quad (NP) \quad (PP)$$

Just as we discovered an option that we had not previously considered when we collapsed three rules for NP into one, so the collapsed rule for VP will generate the structure V PP, which was not represented among the sentences above that formed the basis of the three VP rewrite rules. The expansion V PP is needed for VP in order to generate sentences such as these:

_____VP_____

Jane   swam in the pool.
      V   PP

_____VP_____

Alex   ran around the track.
      V   PP

_____VP_____

She   flew to Balnibarbi.
      V   PP

Phrase-Structure Rules and Tree Diagrams

We have now formulated four phrase-structure rules:

$$S \longrightarrow NP \quad VP$$
$$NP \longrightarrow (DET) \quad (ADJ) \quad N$$
$$VP \longrightarrow V \quad (NP) \quad (PP)$$
$$PP \longrightarrow PREP \quad NP$$

These rules represent the fact that every sentence has an NP and a VP; that every NP has an N; that every VP has a V; and that every PP has a PREP and an NP. According to these rules, other possibilities are optional.

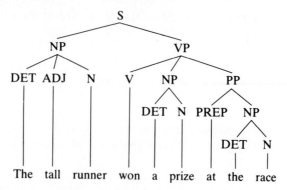

The   tall   runner   won   a   prize   at   the   race

FIGURE 5-12

The following tree diagram can be generated by our rules:

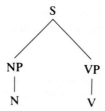

It would represent sentences like *Tom jogged, He fell, Mary swims*. Now consider another structure generated by our rewrite rules; in the example shown in Figure 5-12, we have supplied one sample sentence for the structure.

Refining the Phrase-Structure Rules

Now we examine certain other sentences to see whether they can be generated by the four rewrite rules above. Consider the following:

```
_NP_  _____VP_____
Tom   claimed   [he won a prize].
 N       V           S
```

This sentence cannot be generated by our four phrase-structure rules, and it thus indicates that the following is needed as a rewrite for VP:

$$VP \longrightarrow V \ S$$

Other well-formed English sentences indicate that a VP can also consist of V NP S, as here:

```
_NP_  _____VP_____
Julia   advised   [the cook]   [that he should wash the celery].
          V          NP                    S
```

From these examples, it is clear that a more adequate rewrite rule for VP would be the following:

$$VP \longrightarrow V \quad (NP) \quad (S) \quad (PP)$$

This rule can be expanded into all the following:

$$VP \longrightarrow
\begin{array}{llll}
V & & & \\
V & NP & & \\
V & NP & S & \\
V & NP & S & PP \\
V & & S & \\
V & & & PP \\
V & NP & & PP \\
V & & S & PP
\end{array}$$

In addition, PP can be repeated, a fact that we do not take account of here. We have now arrived at the following phrase-structure rules for English:

$$S \longrightarrow NP \quad VP$$

$$NP \longrightarrow (DET) \quad (ADJ) \quad N$$

$$VP \longrightarrow V \quad (NP) \quad (S) \quad (PP)$$

$$PP \longrightarrow PREP \quad NP$$

In these phrase-structure rules, we begin with an initial symbol S. S is expanded by a rewrite rule into NP and VP. In turn, both NP and VP can be rewritten. NP can be rewritten as DET and N, for example. Some symbols (NP, VP, and PP) can be rewritten as a sequence of symbols. Other symbols (N or PREP, for example) cannot be expanded further. Finally one arrives at a string in which no symbol can be rewritten or expanded further except by attaching individual morphemes or words. This is called a **terminal string**.

GRAMMATICAL RELATIONS: SUBJECT, DIRECT OBJECT, AND OTHERS

We have had occasion in the course of discussing English clauses and sentences to use the terms *subject* and *direct object*. Until now we have used these notions only incidentally, relying on readers' past acquaintance with them. Using phrase-structure rules, it is now possible to define subject and direct object precisely for English. In defining them, two rules are important:

$$S \longrightarrow NP \quad VP$$

$$VP \longrightarrow V \quad (NP) \quad (S) \quad (PP)$$

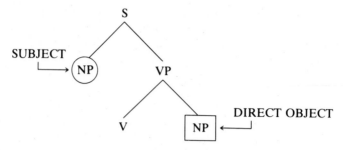

FIGURE 5-13

The first rule says that S consists of NP and VP. The second rule says that VP must contain V and may contain NP (it also says that VP may contain other constituents, which are not relevant to the present discussion). We can represent the relevant parts of these phrase-structure rules in a tree diagram that they would generate. Looking at the diagram in Figure 5-13, we see that the circled NP is directly under the S node, that the boxed NP is directly under the VP node, and that the VP node is directly under the S node. When one node is directly under another node, we say that it is *immediately dominated* by that node. Thus V is immediately dominated by VP; the circled NP is immediately dominated by S; the boxed NP is immediately dominated by VP; further, VP and the circled NP are immediately dominated by S.

We can now define subject and direct object in terms of phrase-structure rules and the tree diagrams they generate. In English and some other languages (but not all languages), **subject** is defined as the NP that is immediately dominated by S. In our diagram, the circled NP is the subject of sentence S. Subject NPs appear in tree diagrams as follows:

Direct object (again, in English and some other languages) is defined as an NP that is immediately dominated by VP. In Figure 5-13 it is the boxed NP. Direct object NPs appear in tree diagrams as follows:

Since NP is an optional element in the expansion of VP, it follows that not every sentence will have an NP immediately dominated by VP; that is, not every sentence will have a direct object. A sentence that does not contain a direct object has what traditional grammars call an *intransitive verb* (see

Chapter 4). Intransitive verbs such as *die, hurry*, and *talk* do not take direct objects. A verb that takes a direct object is called a *transitive verb*. Typical examples are *make, buy*, and *find*, as in *make a potion, buy a pestle*, and *find a penny*.

Verbs are specified in the lexicon as being either transitive or intransitive. In a sentence, a transitive verb has (at least) two NPs, which are called **arguments** of the verb.

The ghost frightened the child.
The king summoned Beowulf.

Intransitive verbs have only one argument, as illustrated here:

The child screamed.
Grendel died.

Sometimes the same verb can be used transitively or intransitively, as shown in the following sentences:

Intransitive	Transitive
Casper won.	Casper won a prize.
Marguerite sings.	Marguerite sings lullabies.
Ed studied at Oxford.	Ed studied physics at Oxford.

Subject and direct object are functions known as grammatical relations. **Grammatical relation** is a term usually used to capture the syntactic relationship that exists in a clause between an NP and its predicate—to indicate, in other words, the *syntactic role* that an NP plays in its clause. Certain structural characteristics of subjects and direct objects cannot be altogether equated with anything else, including meaning; hence the term *grammatical* relation (or *syntactic* role). Besides subject and direct object, languages can have grammatical relations such as **indirect object**, **oblique** (in English, object of a preposition), and **possessor**. English has the grammatical relations oblique (*The ghost spoke about a toothache*) and possessor (*Joan's car*). There is disagreement about the status of indirect object as a grammatical relation in English.[2]

---

[2] It is debatable whether English has indirect object as a distinct *grammatical* relation and, if so, whether it occurs in sentences like *The witch offered the child a potion* or *The witch offered a potion to the child*. The syntactic properties of *the child* differ in the two sentences (for example, it can be passivized in the first but not in the second), thus demonstrating that they have different grammatical relations. Of course, *the child* has the same *semantic* role in both sentences—namely, recipient, which has traditionally been associated with indirect objects (see Chapter 6 for semantic roles). The point is to distinguish semantic and syntactic roles.

Passive Construction Having defined subject and direct object in structural terms, we can now return to a syntactic process examined earlier (see page 140). The notions subject and direct object allow us to reformulate the passive rule as follows: "To form a passive, interchange the subject NP and the direct object NP." (As earlier, provision must be made for the preposition *by* and a form of the verb *be*, aspects of passivization not addressed in this book.) The following sentence will serve as an example:

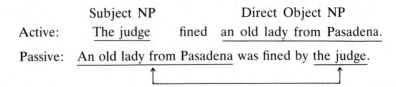

From these sentences, it is clear that passivization involves two movements: the direct object NP is moved into the position of the subject NP (that is, into the NP position dominated by S), and the subject NP moves into the direct object NP position (dominated by VP), now preceded by the preposition *by*.

SURFACE STRUCTURES AND UNDERLYING STRUCTURES

We have seen that speakers understand more about the structure of a sentence than is apparent in the linear sequence of its words; for one thing, they have implicit knowledge of constituent structure. In addition, speakers sometimes understand more elements in a sentence than are actually expressed. For example, knowledge of English syntactic rules is essential to understand the meaning of sentences such as the following:

Alex won a prize but Mary . . .

- (a) didn't.
- (b) didn't care.
- (c) didn't know about it.
- (d) didn't tell Sarah.
- (e) didn't celebrate with him.
- (f) didn't visit Paris to buy a dress.
- (g) didn't train tigers.
- (h) didn't win a prize.

Although the list of possible sentences following this pattern is endless, the only legitimate interpretation of (a) is the one represented by (h). Sentences (b) through (g), though well formed, do not represent possible interpretations of (a). Sentence (a) is understood as having the implicit completion "win a prize." How can this fact about our understanding of unexpressed constituents of a sentence be explained?

Earlier we postulated abstract underlying forms of sounds in our discussion of phonology and abstract underlying forms of morphemes in our discussion of words. It will therefore not be surprising to learn that we can accommodate implicit knowledge of sentence structure by positing *underlying forms* of syntactic structures. For instance, we can represent the meaning of sentence (a) by positing an underlying form something like:

Alex won a prize but Mary didn't win a prize.

If we were to assume such an abstract underlying form, certain *syntactic processes* (or *operations*) of English would have to be postulated in order to delete the second occurrence of *win a prize* and generate the sentence *Alex won a prize but Mary didn't*. (We call such syntactic processes *transformations*; we will discuss various transformations of English shortly.)

Consider the following sentences with an eye to spotting an element in (b) that is not expressed but is nevertheless understood as part of its meaning:

(a) Fred wanted Sarah to win.

(b) Fred wanted to win.

Given the ordinary interpretation of sentence (b), it would be reasonable to suppose that it has an underlying structure parallel to that of (a), something like the following:

(c) Fred wanted Fred to win.

We could represent this sentence by Figure 5-14, in which the subscript $_i$ is an index indicating that *Fred* refers to the same person in both instances. If this structure is taken as a rough approximation of the underlying structure of *Fred wanted to win*, then a syntactic process must be postulated that deletes *Fred* from the embedded clause S_2. Known as the *equi-NP deletion transformation*, this syntactic operation deletes the subject NP of an embedded clause when that NP is the same as the subject NP of the matrix clause and has the same index. If such a process were not postulated, then *Fred* would not be deleted from the underlying structure and this ill-formed string would result: *$Fred_i$ wanted $Fred_i$ to win*.

From these and other examples, we can conclude that the underlying structures of sentences can differ from their surface structures in systematic

FIGURE 5-14

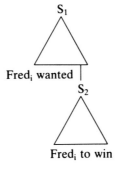

S_1

$Fred_i$ wanted

S_2

$Fred_i$ to win

ways. From the underlying structure of a sentence, the syntactic rules of a language generate surface structures. To capture the facts just examined in sentences like *Fred wanted to win*, we postulate two levels of sentence structure. The level that is represented by the linear string of morphemes and words as uttered or written is called a **surface structure**. Surface structure encompasses both the linear order (which is obvious from inspection) and the hierarchical order of the constituents (which is not expressed explicitly but is understood). The other level of structure is an abstract level underlying the surface structure. Structures at this level are called **underlying structures** (or **deep structures**).

From an underlying structure, a surface structure is generated by application of a series of syntactic processes called **transformational rules**, or **transformations**, that change an underlying constituent structure into a surface constituent structure. We can represent the situation schematically as follows:

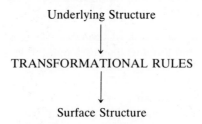

Underlying Structure

TRANSFORMATIONAL RULES

Surface Structure

In a widely adopted model of this type, the phrase-structure rules that we proposed earlier would actually generate underlying structures. Then the syntactic processes—the transformations—would operate on the underlying structure generated by the phrase-structure rules to produce a surface structure. It is this surface structure, in turn, that the phonological rules of the language operate upon to produce a pronounceable sentence. The expanded schema would look like this:

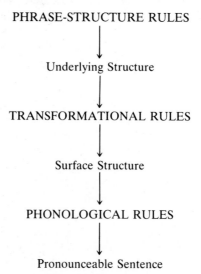

PHRASE-STRUCTURE RULES

Underlying Structure

TRANSFORMATIONAL RULES

Surface Structure

PHONOLOGICAL RULES

Pronounceable Sentence

TRANSFORMATIONS

We have already seen several transformational rules of English including passivization and equi-NP deletion. Now we will analyze several other transformational rules that have been proposed by researchers.

Reflexive Transformation

Examine the following sentences. (As before, identical subscripts are used to index NPs with the same referent; different subscripts index different referents.)

(a) Sarah hurt Jane.
(b) Sarah$_i$ hurt her$_j$.
(c) Sarah$_i$ hurt herself$_i$.

(d) Bill praised Sam.
(e) Bill$_i$ praised him$_j$.
(f) Bill$_i$ praised himself$_i$.

We say that *Bill$_i$* and *himself$_i$* are *coreferential* NPs because they refer to the same entity, as indicated by their identical indexes. In contrast, *Bill* and *Sam* are not coreferential. On the basis of sentences (a) through (f), we might hypothesize the following rule: "English requires a reflexive pronoun (like *herself* or *himself*) for the second of two coreferential NPs." Some further examples follow:

(g) Sarah$_i$ praised herself$_i$.

(h) The postman$_i$ wrote himself$_i$ a letter.

(i) Santa$_i$ doesn't give himself$_i$ anything for Christmas.

The situation seems more complex, however, when we look at these next sentences, in which parentheses surround optional words:

(j) Sarah said (that) Fred$_i$ praised himself$_i$.

(k) Sarah$_i$ said (that) Fred praised her$_i$.

(l) *Sarah$_i$ said (that) Fred praised herself$_i$.

In (j), the reflexive NP *himself$_i$* follows *Fred$_i$*, an NP with the same index. In (k), however, the nonreflexive NP *her$_i$* follows Sarah$_i$, an NP with the same referent; yet, as (l) illustrates, an ill-formed sentence results if *her$_i$* is made reflexive.

It is challenging to explain these facts of English without reference to meaning. Reference to meaning in explaining which sentences are well formed would beg the question, for it is *how* the particular structures of (j), (k), and (l) convey their meaning that we are attempting to explain. The meanings are conveyed by a string of linearly and hierarchically organized words; it would be circular to explain the meaning of a string by its structure and explain the structure by its meaning.

Let's look again at sentence (g), repeated here as (a), and at several related structures:

(a) $Sarah_i$ praised $herself_i$.

(b) $Sarah_i$ praised her_j.

(c) $Sarah_i$ wanted to praise $herself_i$.

On the basis of sentences like these, we have hypothesized that the second of two coreferential NPs is reflexivized. This hypothesis will account for these particular sentences: in (a), *Sarah* and *herself* are coreferential. In (b), *Sarah* and *her* are not coreferential (as the different indexes indicate), so reflexivization is blocked; in (c), *Sarah* and *herself* are coreferential, and the reflexivized pronoun is predicted by our hypothesis.

Unfortunately, our hypothesis does *not* account for the well-formedness of (d) in the next example or the ill-formedness of (e):

(d) $Sarah_i$ wanted Fred to praise her_i.

(e)   *$Sarah_i$ wanted Fred to praise $herself_i$.

In (d), *Sarah* and *her* are coreferential; by our hypothesis, either *her* should be a reflexive or the structure should be ill formed; as it happens, *her* is not a reflexive and the structure is nevertheless well formed. In (e), *Sarah* and *herself* are coreferential; our hypothesis predicts that this sentence should be well formed, but it isn't. Clearly, the hypothesis is inadequate.

To refine the hypothesis, let's consider how we would explain that in the following group (b) is an acceptable interpretation of (a) but (c) is not.

(a)   Sarah didn't want $Jane_i$ to hurt $herself_i$.

(b)   Sarah didn't want $Jane_i$ to hurt $Jane_i$.

(c) $Sarah_i$ didn't want Jane to hurt $Sarah_i$.

Sentence (a) means the same as (b); (a) cannot mean the same as (c). Both (b) and (c) are somewhat awkward structures. They are likely to occur only in situations calling for contrast, clarification, or emphasis, with the final word receiving extra stress. The preferred ordinary structure corresponding to (b) would be (a), and the preferred ordinary structure corresponding to (c) is given in (d):

(d)   Sarah didn't want Jane to hurt her.

Notice that (d) is actually ambiguous; besides meaning 'Sarah didn't want Jane to hurt Sarah' (as proposed), it can also mean '$Sarah_i$ didn't want $Jane_j$

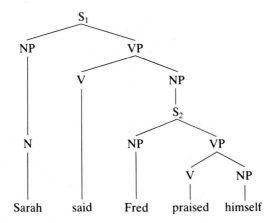

FIGURE 5-15

to hurt her$_k$,' in which *Sarah, Jane,* and *her* refer to three different persons. One thing that (d) *cannot* mean is 'Sarah didn't want Jane$_i$ to hurt Jane$_i$.'

If you carefully examine well-formed sentences containing reflexive pronouns, you will see that a reflexive pronoun can appear only as the second of two coreferential NPs *within the same clause.* Consider the following sentences from earlier in this chapter:

(a) Sarah$_i$ hurt herself$_i$.

(b) Bill$_i$ praised himself$_i$.

(c) Sarah said (that) Fred$_i$ praised himself$_i$.

(d) Sarah didn't want Jane$_i$ to hurt herself$_i$.

It may help to visualize the relationship among sentence, clause, and co-referential NPs with an illustrative tree diagram of sentence (c) (without the optional subordinator *that*), as shown in Figure 5-15.

Of the well-formed sentences with reflexive pronouns that we have examined, only one does not appear to meet the criterion of having coreferential NPs within the same *clause*; it is this sentence:

(a) Sarah$_i$ wanted to praise herself$_i$.

This sentence has a reflexive pronoun in the embedded clause *to praise herself.* Figure 5-16 is a rough tree diagram of it. Although *Sarah* and *herself* are coreferential, *herself* in S$_2$ cannot be made reflexive as a result of being preceded by *Sarah* in the matrix clause S$_1$. The reason is that, if a co-referential NP in the matrix clause could trigger reflexivization in the embedded clause, then we would also expect to find the reflexive form *herself* in the following sentence (b). But a reflexive form in this case would be ill formed, as (c) illustrates.

FIGURE 5-16   FIGURE 5-17

(b)   Sarah$_i$ wanted Fred to praise her$_i$.

(c)   *Sarah$_i$ wanted Fred to praise herself$_i$.

Let's examine a reduced tree diagram of (b), shown in Figure 5-17. Even though *Sarah* and *her* are coreferential, *her* cannot be made reflexive without producing the ill-formed sentence (c).

Now notice that in *Sarah wanted to praise herself* the embedded clause has no expressed subject. Compare Figure 5-17 with Figure 5-19. In the latter, *Sarah*, the subject NP of the embedded clause in the underlying structure (Figure 5-18), has been deleted by the equi-NP deletion transformation. The underlying structure for *Sarah wanted to praise herself* is given in the tree diagram in Figure 5-18.

The effect of equi-NP deletion on the constituent structure of Figure 5-18 is shown in Figure 5-19. *Her$_i$* in the embedded clause of Figure 5-18 is reflexivized because it is the second of two coreferential NPs in the same clause (namely S$_2$). Only after reflexivization is *Sarah$_i$* deleted from S$_2$ by equi-NP deletion. Thus in Figure 5-18 the result of applying these two transformations in the order "first reflexive, then equi-NP deletion" is to generate the surface structure *Sarah wanted to praise herself*.

FIGURE 5-18   FIGURE 5-19

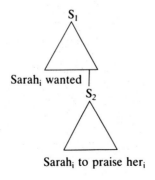

An examination of all the illustrative sentences analyzed so far leads to the following revised hypothesis about English reflexives: "The second of two coreferential NPs *within the same clause* is a reflexive." Given our revised hypothesis that a reflexive pronoun occurs in English only when two coreferential NPs occur *in the same clause*, we can now understand why *Sarah wanted Fred to praise herself* is ill formed: the coreferential NPs *Sarah* and *herself*, though they are in the same sentence, do not occur within the same clause.

It should be noted that the reflexive transformation must precede the equi-NP deletion transformation. If equi-NP deletion applied first, then the two coreferential NPs within a single clause that are necessary for reflexivizing would no longer be there. Instead of a structure like Figure 5-18, we would have Figure 5-19, and the reflexive transformation would not apply because the **structural description** necessary for the transformation to apply would not be met. The ill-formed structure *Sarah_i wanted to praise her_i* would result.

Imperative Transformation

We have now seen three transformations: *passive*, which moves NPs from one place in the constituent structure to another place; *reflexive*, which makes reflexive an NP that is the second of two coreferential NPs in the same clause; and *equi-NP deletion*, which deletes the second of two coreferential NPs under specific conditions. Another relatively straightforward deletion transformation accounts for the relationship between imperative sentences like those in column B and the sentences in column A:

A	B
You wash the dog.	Wash the dog.
You take out the garbage.	Take out the garbage.
You study hard.	Study hard.
You have a good time.	Have a good time.
You wash yourself.	Wash yourself.

Traditional grammars discuss imperative sentences as having an "understood" *you* as subject. In some transformational analyses of grammar, this understood subject is accounted for by postulating *you* in the underlying structure and deleting it by a transformational rule. By the imperative transformation, a sentence like *Wash the dog* is derived from the structure underlying a sentence like *You wash the dog* by deleting the subject NP *You*. The imperative transformation would transform an underlying constituent

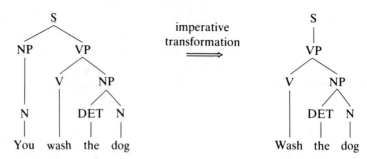

FIGURE 5-20

structure like the one on the left in Figure 5-20 into the constituent structure on the right. The imperative transformation deletes the subject NP *you* from an underlying structure, thus generating a surface structure without an expressed subject.

By examining two transformations whose effects on a constituent structure interact with one another, we can explore further how transformational operations are ordered with respect to one another. Recall from Chapter 3 that certain phonological processes are ordered with respect to one another in order to generate correct pronunciations. Earlier in this chapter we briefly touched on the ordering of the reflexive and equi-NP deletion transformations. Here we examine the interaction of the imperative and reflexive transformations.

The reflexive transformation requires the presence of the subject NP *You* of *You wash you* in order to "trigger" reflexivization of the second NP, as in *(You) wash yourself*. If the imperative transformation (which deletes the subject NP) were to apply first, it would delete the subject NP *You*, thus depriving the constituent structure of the necessary triggering element for the reflexive transformation. The string resulting from application of the imperative transformation would thus be: *Wash you*. Since this string would not meet the structural description needed for the reflexive transformation to apply, the reflexive transformation would not apply, and the ill-formed string *Wash you* would be generated. We conclude that transformations are ordered and that the reflexive transformation must precede the imperative transformation.

Subject-Auxiliary Inversion and WH-Fronting Transformations

We have now examined the operation of two deletion transformations (equi-NP deletion and imperative) and one movement transformation (passive) as well as the reflexive transformation, which changes constituents. In this section we want to explore two other movement transformations, involved in asking questions; we will then note the implications of these transformations for the underlying structure of every English sentence.

Information Questions   Two principal kinds of questions exist in English. They are known as yes/no questions and information questions. Information questions require more than a simple yes-or-no answer. Because information questions contain a WH-word (like *who, why, when, what,* or *how*), they are sometimes called WH-questions. In an information question, the information that is sought—the questioned constituent—is identified by a WH-word.

Information questions occur in two forms. One is called an echo question because it "echoes" the form of a statement, as in the following examples:

(a)   (She was looking for Sigmund Freud today.)
      She was looking for <u>who</u> today?[3]

(b)   (He is boiling horsefeathers.)
      He is boiling <u>what</u>?

In echo questions, the form of the question is identical to the form of the statement, except that a WH-word occurs in place of the questioned constituent. Echo questions are used when you cannot believe what you have heard or you have failed to hear something completely.

A more common type of information question than echo questions is the ordinary type illustrated here:

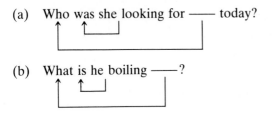

(a)   Who was she looking for —— today?

(b)   What is he boiling ——?

If we compare these information questions with echo questions, we can see that two movement transformations have occurred:

1.   The WH-word (the questioned constituent) is moved to the front of its clause (by a movement transformation called WH-fronting).

2.   The subject NP and the auxiliary verb are inverted.

Notice that information questions of this type (but not echo questions) leave a "gap" in the structure at the place vacated by the fronted WH-word (as indicated by the dash ——).

---

[3] In the example sentences in the remainder of this chapter, we use what seem to us the most common forms of *who* and *whom* in the context of a particular sentence; in so doing, we sometimes ignore the distinction drawn between these forms in traditional grammar and in much careful writing and speaking.

Yes/No Questions   Now examine the following statements and questions; these questions are called yes/no questions because they can be answered with a simple *yes* or *no* reply.

(a) John was winning the race when he fell.

Was John winning the race when he fell?

(b) Sue will earn a fair wage.

Will Sue earn a fair wage?

Like information questions, yes/no questions invert the subject NP and the auxiliary verb. But unlike information questions, yes/no questions do not contain a WH-word. Yes/no questions are syntactically marked as questions solely by inversion of the subject NP and the auxiliary verb. (Verbs such as *was* in the preceding (a) and *will* in (b), and *did* and *does* in the following (c) and (d), are called auxiliary verbs; **auxiliary verbs** are those that can be inverted with the subject NP in questions and that carry the negative element in contractions such as *can't, shouldn't*, and *wasn't*.) In fact, a yes/no question *must* express an auxiliary verb, even when the corresponding statement form does not:

(c) Alice studied alchemy in college.
     Did Alice study alchemy in college?

(d) Inflation always hurts the poor.
     Does inflation always hurt the poor?

Sentence pairs like these provide one argument for positing an auxiliary verb in the underlying structure of every sentence, even though not every sentence expresses an auxiliary in the surface form. For sentences in which the underlying auxiliary verb has no manifestation in the surface structure, the auxiliary verb would have to be deleted by a syntactic operation (about which we will have nothing further to say in this book). Notice, however, that an auxiliary verb does appear on the surface of a sentence for stress, in yes/no questions, and in negatives (*Alice didn't study alchemy in college*).

On the basis of the fact that an auxiliary verb does often appear in the surface structure of a sentence (and for other reasons that we cannot discuss here), an auxiliary constituent is postulated in the underlying structure of every sentence. The auxiliary (abbreviated AUX) is generated in the underlying structure by a rewrite rule. Instead of the earlier phrase-structure rule that expanded S as NP VP, the following rule is used:

$$S \longrightarrow NP \ AUX \ VP$$

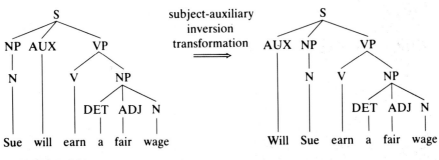

FIGURE 5-21

We can represent the structure generated by this rule in a tree diagram:

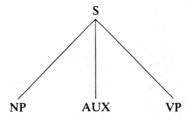

We would thus represent the underlying form of the sentences of (b) on page 158 as in the tree on the left in Figure 5-21. The tree on the right is the constituent structure that results from application of the subject-auxiliary inversion transformation, which inverts the subject NP and the AUX.

Relative Clause Transformation

Another major movement transformation in English generates relative clause structures. A **relative clause** is formed when one clause is embedded into an NP of another clause to produce structures like the following, in which the relative clauses are underlined:

(a)   The board promoted the teacher <u>who flunked me</u>.

(b)   The jewels <u>which he bought</u> were fakes.

(c)   This is the officer <u>that I talked to last night</u>.

(d)   Sally saw a new film by the director <u>that she raves about</u>.

(e)   Sally saw a new film by the director <u>she raves about</u>.

When two clauses share a pair of coreferential NPs, a relative clause is formed by embedding one clause into the other, as in this illustration, in which identical indexes indicate coreferential NPs:

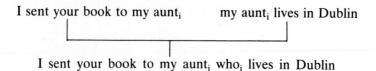

I sent your book to my aunt$_i$ who$_i$ lives in Dublin

In English, relative clauses contain (and are usually introduced by) a relative pronoun such as *who* (or *whom*), *which*, or *that*. As in (e) above, the pronoun can be omitted in certain structures. Relative clauses modify nouns, and the noun that the relative clause modifies is called the *head noun*. In English, the head noun is repeated in the embedded clause, where it is relativized. A relative clause becomes part of the same noun phrase as its head noun. The structure of the resulting noun phrase can be represented as in Figure 5-22, in which the head noun *aunt* is labeled N. Notice that the relativized NP functions as the subject of its clause. In other clauses, the relativized NP may be another grammatical relation like direct object, as in this illustration:

The jewels which he bought were fakes.

Here the relative clause *which he bought* derives from the underlying clause *he bought the jewels*.

A relativized NP can also be an oblique, as in

This is the officer that I talked about.

Or it can be a possessor, as in

This is the officer whose car was vandalized.

Thus in English a relativized NP can be subject, direct object, oblique, or possessor.

FIGURE 5-22

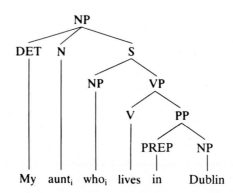

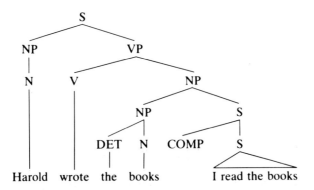

FIGURE 5-23

Now let's analyze the syntactic processes associated with relative clause formation in English. Examine the following sentences, noting the "gap" in the structure (indicated as before by the dash ——):

(a)   She is the teacher that I told you about ——.

(b)   Harold wrote the books which I read ——.

(c)   He's the musician who —— won the prize.

We can represent the underlying constituent structure of these sentences in a tree diagram, as Figure 5-23 illustrates for sentence (b).

In order to produce the relative clause structure given in (b), the relativized NP *the books* must be pronominalized and moved to the front of its clause by the WH-fronting transformation that we described for information questions. In Figure 5-23 there is a node labeled COMP (for 'complementizer'), which we have not previously identified. It is possible to discuss the WH-fronting transformation for relative clauses without utilizing the COMP node (as we did for information questions), but there is evidence that such a node exists and serves as a kind of target or magnet for the movement of WH-constituents. Thus the COMP node attracts WH-constituents such as *which, who, that* (illustrated above), and the other relative pronouns, as well as the WH-constituents of information questions. As transformations change one constituent structure into another, we can represent the result of the WH-fronting transformation applied to the preceding structure by the tree in Figure 5-24. Thus, by the WH-fronting transformation, a WH-constituent is extracted from S and attached to the COMP node. We have examined this movement transformation with respect to relative clauses, but it should be clear that the same transformation could move any WH-constituent to the COMP node, including question words in the formation of information questions.

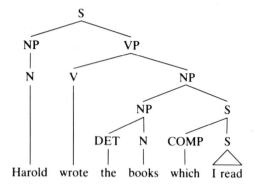

FIGURE 5-24

TYPES OF TRANSFORMATIONS

We have now examined three types of syntactic processes in English. The equi-NP deletion transformation deletes an NP in an embedded clause under specified conditions, and the imperative transformation deletes the subject NP *you* from an underlying imperative structure. Another kind of operation introduces new elements into a constituent structure or alters existing elements, as with reflexivization. Most transformations are movement rules: they move a constituent from one slot in the constituent structure to another slot, thus rearranging the linear or hierarchical ordering of constituents. Subject-auxiliary inversion in question formation and the WH-fronting transformation are both movement rules.

While it is not known for certain how many types of syntactic processes exist in human languages, there is increasing evidence that there may be fewer types and fewer instances of transformations than was previously thought. In fact, transformations may be of a considerably more general nature than our somewhat detailed descriptions of specific transformations have suggested. Movement rules are extremely common in the languages of the world, and they are the area of study that has received the most attention from linguists in recent years. In one theoretical model of syntax, all transformations are forms of movement rules.

CONSTRAINTS ON TRANSFORMATIONS

One question that continues to challenge linguists is whether and to what extent limitations exist on the kinds of transformational rules that can operate in human language. We can illustrate the kinds of constraints that may exist by analyzing a constraint on movement transformations. In each of the following sets of four sentences, the first sentence is an echo question, the second the corresponding information question, the third an echo question in which the WH-word is contained in a coordinate noun phrase of the type "NP *and* NP," and the fourth the ill-formed structure that would result if the

WH-word were moved to the front of its clause. It is clear from examples (a-iv), (b-iv), and (c-iv) that WH-movement cannot occur when the WH-word is part of a coordinate NP structure.

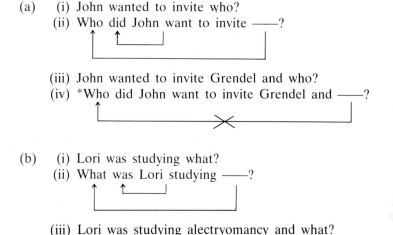

(a)   (i) John wanted to invite who?
      (ii) Who did John want to invite ——?

      (iii) John wanted to invite Grendel and who?
      (iv) *Who did John want to invite Grendel and ——?

(b)   (i) Lori was studying what?
      (ii) What was Lori studying ——?

      (iii) Lori was studying alectryomancy and what?
      (iv) *What was Lori studying alectryomancy and ——?

(c)   (i) The wizard is mixing what?
      (ii) What is the wizard mixing ——?

      (iii) The wizard is mixing what and fingernails?
      (iv) *What is the wizard mixing —— and fingernails?

These sentences illustrate that the WH-movement transformation is blocked from moving a WH-constituent out of a coordinate noun phrase. This constraint is called the *coordinate NP constraint.*

The coordinate NP constraint applies not only to WH-movement but to other transformations as well. For example, in each of the following sets of sentences, the first is a **basic sentence**—one that has not undergone transformations[4]—while the second and third are derived passive structures in which one NP of the coordinate NP object ("NP *and* NP") has been moved into subject position. As with WH-movement out of a coordinate NP, so with

---

[4] In practice, we use the term "basic" to refer to sentences that have not undergone the major transformations discussed in this chapter.

passivization—ungrammatical sentences are produced (or sentences that are ungrammatical in the intended meaning).

(d)   The police captured the criminals and their loot.
      *The criminals were captured by the police —— and their loot.

      *Their loot was captured by the police the criminals and ——.

(e)   John and his mother saw the robbery.
      *The robbery and his mother were seen by John.

      *John and the robbery were seen by his mother.

These examples demonstrate that the passive transformation is blocked from moving an NP out of a coordinate noun phrase in forming passive sentences. Thus the coordinate NP constraint restricts the operation of two transformations, as we have seen. In fact, the coordinate NP constraint appears to be a general constraint: it blocks extraction of an NP out of a coordinate noun phrase for all transformations.

There are other restrictions on transformations as well. To the extent that such general constraints exist, the detailed specification of how particular transformations operate becomes unnecessary, not only in writing descriptive grammars but, more importantly, in the process of language acquisition by children. The more such constraints as the coordinate NP constraint control the operation of transformations, the easier it must be for a child to acquire its language, having less to learn about the operation of syntactic rules.

SUMMARY

Languages have referring expressions and predication expressions; in syntactic terms, a referring expression is called NP (for noun phrase) and the predication expression VP (for verb phrase). Sentences consist of one or more clauses. An English clause consists of a verb with the necessary set of NP arguments. Simple sentences have a single clause and can be coordinated with another clause to form a coordinate sentence or embedded into another clause to form a complex sentence. The rules that govern the formation of clauses and the joining of clauses into coordinate and complex sentences constitute the syntax of a language. Speakers of a language can generate an unlimited number of sentences from relatively few rules for combining words and morphemes. The syntactic rules of a language are of two types. Phrase-structure rules generate underlying constituent structures, which are then altered by various transformational operations that change one constituent structure into another constituent structure until a surface structure is generated.

Underlying structures are posited to capture the striking regularity of certain relationships between sentences. Underlying structures are constructs that help explain certain elements of meaning and certain syntactic and semantic relationships that we understand between sentences. In order to explain how speakers relate two structures to one another (such as *Martha doesn't believe in poltergeists* and *Doesn't Martha believe in poltergeists?*), linguists posit a rule of English that transforms the structure underlying the first, or basic, sentence into the structure underlying the second, or derived, sentence. A rule that changes a constituent structure into another constituent structure is called a transformational rule.

Increasingly, it appears that the most important and most general transformations are movement transformations such as WH-movement and subject-auxiliary inversion. The former applies in the formation of relative clauses, and both apply in the formation of information questions. Certain constraints on transformations limit the ways in which they can operate. In limiting the range of possible grammars of human languages, such constraints may facilitate the process of language acquisition in children.

EXERCISES

1. For each of the expansions of VP given on page 145, provide an illustrative English example; thus, for V PP, you might give (Sarah) *swims in the pond*.

2. Draw a labeled tree diagram for each of the English phrases given below.

   (a) ancient inscriptions
   (b) in the dark night
   (c) concocted a potion
   (d) bought the book that the teacher recommended
   (e) the monstrous members of the reptile kingdom

3. (A) Provide a tree diagram for each of the English sentences given below. (B) For each of the underlined groups of words, determine whether it is a constituent or not, and give the name of the constituent for those that are.

   (a) Witches frighten her.
   (b) The skies deluged the earth with water.
   (c) A ghost is the spirit of a dead person.
   (d) Do ghosts exist in the physical world?
   (e) Does she believe that ghosts exist?
   (f) The dream that I described to you came true.

4. Consider the following sentences. What is the difference in the relationship between Harry and the verb *see* in (a) and (b)? Draw tree diagrams of the

underlying structure of the two sentences that will reveal the difference in the structures.

(a)   John advised Harry to see the doctor.
(b)   John promised Harry to see the doctor.

5.   Provide a pair of sentences for each of the following transformations: reflexive; passive; equi-NP deletion; imperative; subject-auxiliary inversion; WH-movement. The first string should illustrate what results when the transformation has not applied, and the second should illustrate the sentence that results when the transformation has applied. *Example:* reflexive: (a) *Jack bit Jack. (b) Jack bit himself.

6.   Consider the following tree diagram for this Fijian sentence:

ea-biuta   na ŋone vakaloloma na tamata ðā e   na basi
Past-abandon the child poor   the man   bad on the bus
'The bad man abandoned the poor child on the bus.'

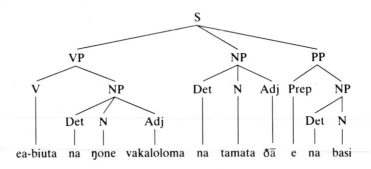

(A) Notice that the order of certain constituents in the Fijian sentence differs from that of English. What are the major differences between Fijian and English with respect to constituent order?
(B) On the basis of the tree structure, determine which of the following sequences of words are constituents and which are not; give the name of each constituent.

biuta na   na basi
vakaloloma na tamata   e na basi
na tamata ðā   na tamata ðā e na basi
ea-biuta   ea-biuta na ŋone vakaloloma
e   ŋone
                                  na ŋone vakaloloma na tamata ðā

7.   English has a movement transformation called *dative movement* that derives sentence (b) from the structure underlying basic sentence (a):

(a)   I sent a letter to Hilda.
(b)   I sent Hilda a letter.

The following are also examples of sentences in which dative movement has applied:

He told <u>his brother</u> a tall tale.
Harold won't give <u>me</u> Hilda's new phone number.
I'm taking <u>my little sister</u> a new pair of pajamas.

(A) Give the three basic sentences that correspond to the three derived sentences.

(B) Dative movement applies to prepositional phrases that begin with the preposition *to* and cannot apply to prepositional phrases that begin with most other prepositions:

*I will finish you the homework. (*from* I will finish the homework with you.)
*My neighbor heard the radio the news. (*from* My neighbor heard the news on the radio.)

But dative movement does not apply to *all* phrases that begin with the preposition *to*. The sentences in (a) below cannot undergo dative movement, as witnessed by the ungrammaticality of the corresponding sentences in (b).

(a) He's driving a truck to New Orleans.
     He'll take his complaint to the main office.

(b) *He's driving New Orleans a truck.
     *He'll take the main office his complaint.

Describe in detail the dative movement transformation.

(C) Now observe the ungrammatical sentences in (a) below, which are derived through dative movement from the sentences underlying the corresponding basic sentences in (b). How must your description of the transformation be modified so that it does not generate the ungrammatical sentences of (a)?

(a) *I gave my new neighbor it.
     *I'm taking my little sister them.
     *They will probably send him me.

(b) I gave it to my new neighbor.
     I'm taking them to my little sister.
     They will probably send me to him.

8. Although we have ignored the difference between *who* and *whom* in the examples in this chapter, speakers of English who regularly distinguish these two words in relative clauses do so as follows:

(a) That's the ghost who visits me each year.
(b) That's the goblin whom I was talking about.
(c) That's the wizard from whom I bought the potion.
(d) That's the witch whom I stole the bread crumbs from.
(e) That's the witch who married the wizard.
(f) That's the demon whom he sold his soul to.
(g) That's the ghost of the man whom Grendel slew.

After examining these sentences, formulate a statement that will capture the facts about when speakers of this variety of English use *who* and *whom* in relative clauses. (*Hint*: examine the grammatical relation of the relative pronoun in its clause.)

9.   English has two types of relative clauses. Type 1, which was described in this chapter, leaves prepositions where they are in the original clause.

> This is the man [who I talked *to* last night] (*original clause*: I talked to the man last night)

In Type 2, the preposition moves to the beginning of the clause with the WH-word.

> This is the man [*to* whom I talked last night]

Describe the relative-clause transformation that forms Type 2 relative clauses, focusing on how it differs from the transformation that forms Type 1 relative clauses. Discuss which relative pronouns can occur in which type of relative clause, and in which cases the two types differ. Base your discussion on the following data:

> This is the man [that left].   (Types 1 and 2)
> *This is the man [left].   (Types 1 and 2)

> This is the man [that I saw].   (Types 1 and 2)
> This is the man [who I saw].   (Types 1 and 2)
> This is the man [whom I saw].   (Types 1 and 2)
> This is the man [I saw].   (Types 1 and 2)

> This is the man [who I gave the book to].   (Type 1)
> This is the man [whom I gave the book to].   (Type 1)
> This is the man [that I gave the book to].   (Type 1)
> This is the man [I gave the book to].   (Type 1)
> *This is the man [to who I gave the book].   (Type 2)
> This is the man [to whom I gave the book].   (Type 2)
> *This is the man [to that I gave the book].   (Type 2)
> *This is the man [to I gave the book].   (Type 2)

> This is the woman [who Harry left his wife for].   (Type 1)
> This is the woman [whom Harry left his wife for].   (Type 1)
> This is the woman [that Harry left his wife for].   (Type 1)
> This is the woman [Harry left his wife for].   (Type 1)
> *This is the woman [for who Harry left his wife].   (Type 2)
> This is the woman [for whom Harry left his wife].   (Type 2)
> *This is the woman [for that Harry left his wife].   (Type 2)
> *This is the woman [for Harry left his wife].   (Type 2)

10. There are two types of relative clauses in English: *restrictive* relative clauses provide essential information about the head noun as in (a); *nonrestrictive* relative clauses provide incidental information about the head noun as in (b). In (a), the hearer must have the information provided in the relative clause in order to understand which potion the speaker is referring to; in (b), this is not the case.

(a)   The potion that I mixed yesterday is in the pestle.
(b)   The potion, which I mixed yesterday, is in the pestle.

Compare the following sets of restrictive and nonrestrictive relative clauses, and describe in detail the structural differences between the two types of relative clauses.

The man <u>who had been standing outside</u> suddenly dashed away.
The man, <u>who had been standing outside</u>, suddenly dashed away.

The detective movie <u>that I saw yesterday</u> was terrible.
The detective movie, <u>which I saw yesterday</u>, was terrible.
*The detective movie, <u>that I saw yesterday</u>, was terrible.

The book <u>which I had not opened in years</u> was all dusty.
The book, <u>which I had not opened in years</u>, was all dusty.

The jacket <u>I wore at the reception</u> cost me $250.
*The jacket, <u>I wore at the reception</u>, cost me $250.

SUGGESTIONS FOR FURTHER READING

There have been many exciting developments in the study of syntax in the last thirty years. The major works in this line of development are Chomsky (1957), (1965), and (1981); except for the first, these works require considerable background, though Chomsky (1965) can probably be read with this chapter as background. Chomsky (1981) should not be attempted before Radford (1981) and van Riemsdijk and Williams (1986). Even these last two, however, may be too advanced for those whose only background in syntax is this chapter. The last three all focus on syntactic theory and syntactic argumentation, neither of which has been stressed here. Lightfoot (1982) is a useful introduction to Chomsky's work. A clear and useful but lengthy treatment of the nature of syntactic argumentation, with English examples, can be found in Perlmutter and Soames (1979), whose premise is that the best way to learn syntax is to "do" syntax, not merely read about it. Much can nevertheless be learned from reading the book; it has many problems with solutions provided, often with helpful discussion. The model of syntax presented there (as in much of our discussion) is the generative-transformational model of the early 1970s. Given the nature of syntactic argument today, a thorough grounding in the syntax of the late 1960s and the 1970s seems necessary in grasping current views on constraints.

A more basic and more accessible presentation of syntax than those in the preceding references can be found in Smith and Wilson (1979) (which covers more than syntax). Newmeyer (1980) provides an interesting account of the development of syntactic theory during the past three decades. Given the enormous impact that the so-called Chomskyan revolution has had on linguistics and other fields, Newmeyer's book is interesting for the sociology of knowledge that it reveals in its discussion of how Chomsky's ideas were spread. Comrie (1981), a clear and accessible discussion of syntactic universals across a wide range of languages, expresses reservations about the generative-transformational approach to syntax; as a follow-up to this chapter, we particularly recommend Comrie's chapters on "Word Order," "Subject," "Case Marking," and "Relative Clauses."

The volumes edited by Shopen (1985) contain a wealth of useful material; volume I, *Clause Structure*, and volume II, *Complex Constructions*, are relevant to this chapter. Going beyond what we have covered here but probably accessible to most interested readers who have mastered the material in this chapter are two excellent chapters of volume I: "Parts of Speech Systems" (written by Paul Schachter) and "Passive in the World's Languages" (written by Edward L. Keenan). Volume II contains valuable discussions of "Complex Phrases and Complex Sentences" (by John R. Payne), "Complementation" (by Michael Noonan), and "Relative Clauses" (by Edward L. Keenan).

REFERENCES

Baker, C. L. 1978. *Introduction to Generative-Transformational Syntax* (Englewood Cliffs, N.J.: Prentice-Hall).

Chomsky, Noam. 1957. *Syntactic Structures* (The Hague: Mouton).

———. 1965. *Aspects of the Theory of Syntax* (Cambridge: MIT Press).

———. 1981. *Lectures on Government and Binding: The Pisa Lectures* (Dordrecht, Holland: Foris).

Comrie, Bernard. 1981. *Language Universals and Linguistic Typology: Syntax and Morphology* (Chicago: University of Chicago Press).

Lightfoot, David. 1982. *The Language Lottery* (Cambridge: MIT Press).

Newmeyer, Frederick J. 1980. *Linguistic Theory in America: The First Quarter-Century of Transformational Generative Grammar* (New York: Academic Press).

Perlmutter, David, and Scott Soames. 1979. *Syntactic Argumentation and the Structure of English* (Berkeley: University of California Press).

Radford, Andrew. 1981. *Transformational Syntax: A Student's Guide to Chomsky's Extended Standard Theory* (Cambridge: Cambridge University Press).

Shopen, Timothy (ed.). 1985. *Language Typology and Syntactic Description.* Vol. I (*Clause Structure*); Vol. II (*Complex Constructions*) (Cambridge: Cambridge University Press).

Smith, Neil, and Deirdre Wilson. 1979. *Modern Linguistics: The Results of Chomsky's Revolution* (New York: Penguin Books).

van Riemsdijk, Henk, and Edwin Williams. 1986. *Introduction to the Theory of Grammar* (Cambridge: MIT Press).

SEMANTICS: WORD MEANING AND SENTENCE MEANING

6

THE STUDY OF MEANING

Introduction

Of the various parts of grammar that people may have occasion to refer to, "semantics" is one of the most familiar; certainly it is a far more familiar term than phonology, morphology, or syntax. "That's just semantics" is a frequent claim in arguments and debates. Even the proverbial person in the street knows that semantics has something to do with meaning. Linguistic semantics is the study of the systematic ways in which languages structure meaning, especially in words and sentences. This chapter focuses on the study of meaning in words and in sentences. Eventually the meaning of whole texts, not just words and sentences, must be studied, but we will not do so in this chapter.

In defining linguistic semantics (which we will refer to as **semantics** from now on), we must invoke the word *meaning*. Just as we have many everyday notions of what semantics is, we use the words *to mean* and *meaning* in many contexts and for different purposes. For example:

(a)   The word *perplexity* <u>means</u> 'the state of being puzzled.'

(b)   The word *rash* has two <u>meanings</u>: 'impetuous' and 'skin irritation.'

(c)   In Spanish, *espejo* <u>means</u> 'mirror.'

(d)   I did not <u>mean</u> that he is incompetent, just inefficient.

(e)   The <u>meaning</u> of the cross as a symbol is complex.

(f)   I <u>meant</u> to bring you my paper, but left it at home.

What Is Meaning?

Linguists also attach different interpretations to the word *meaning*. Because the purpose of linguistics is to explain precisely how languages are structured and used, it is important to distinguish among the different ways of interpreting the word *meaning*.

A few examples will illustrate why we need to develop a precise way of talking about meaning. Consider these sentences:

(a)   I went to the store this morning.

(b)   All dogs are animals.

The sentences make sense—that is, have meaning—for quite different reasons. Whether sentence (a) is true depends on whether or not the speaker is in fact telling the truth; nothing about the words of the sentence makes the sentence inherently true. Sentence (b), in contrast, is true because we know that the word *dogs* describes entities that are also described by the word *animals*. The truth of sentence (b) does not depend on whether or not the speaker is telling the truth; it has solely to do with the meanings of the words *dogs* and *animals*.

Now compare the following pairs of sentences:

(c)   You are too young to drink.
      You are not old enough to drink.

(d)   Harold spent several years in northern Tibet.
      Harold was once in northern Tibet.

The sentences of (c) basically "say the same thing" in that the first describes exactly what the second describes—no more, no less. We say that they are *synonymous* sentences, or that they paraphrase each other. Of the two sentences in (d), the first sentence *implies* the second but not vice versa. If indeed Harold spent several years in northern Tibet, then he must have set foot in that area of the world at some stage in his life; but if he was once in northern Tibet, it is not necessarily the case that he spent several years there.

Next, consider the following sentences:

(e)   The unmarried woman is married to a bachelor.

(f)   My toothbrush is pregnant.

Sentences (e) and (f) are well formed syntactically, but there is something wrong with the meaning of both sentences. The meanings of the words that make up sentence (e) contradict each other: an unmarried woman cannot be married, and certainly not to a bachelor. Sentence (e) thus presents a *contradiction*. Sentence (f) is different: given that toothbrushes are not capable of being pregnant, its meaning is *anomalous*. To diagnose precisely what is wrong with both sentences, we need to distinguish between contradictory and anomalous sentences.

Finally, examine sentences (g) and (h):

(g)   I saw her duck.

(h)   She ate the pie.

Sentence (g) may be interpreted in two ways: *duck* may be a verb referring to the act of bending over slightly (while walking through a low doorway, for example), or it may be a noun referring to a domesticated bird. These two word meanings give the whole sentence different meanings. Because there are two possible readings for (g), it is an **ambiguous** sentence. While sentence (h) is not ambiguous, taken out of context there is an imprecise quality to it. While we know that the subject is a female, we cannot know who *she* refers to, or what particular pie was eaten, though the structure of the phrase *the pie* indicates that the speaker has a particular one in mind. Taken out of context, (h) is thus *vague* in that certain details are left unspecified; but it is not ambiguous.

These observations illustrate that meaning is a multifaceted notion. A sentence may be meaningful and true because it states a fact about the world or because the speaker is telling the truth. Two sentences may be related to each other because they mean exactly the same thing or because one implies the other. Finally, when we feel that there is something wrong with the meaning of a sentence, it may be because the sentence is contradictory, anomalous, ambiguous, or merely vague. One purpose of semantics is to distinguish among these different ways in which language "means."

REFERENTIAL, SOCIAL, AND AFFECTIVE MEANING

There are three types of meaning: referential meaning, social meaning, and affective meaning. Very loosely, **referential meaning** is the object, notion, or state of affairs described by a word or sentence. **Social meaning** is the level of meaning that we rely on when we identify certain social characteristics of speakers and situations from the character of the language used. **Affective**

meaning is the emotional connotation that is attached to words and utterances. We will discuss and illustrate each component of meaning in turn.

Referential Meaning

One way of defining meaning is to say that the meaning of a word or sentence is the person, object, abstract notion, event, or state to which the word or sentence makes reference. The meaning of *John Smith*, for example, is the person who goes by that name. The phrase *Fred's dog* refers to the particular domesticated canine that belongs to Fred. That particular animal can be said to be the meaning of the linguistic expression *Fred's dog*. This type of meaning is *referential* meaning. The canine described by the expression *Fred's dog* is the **referent** of the *referring expression Fred's dog*. Speakers of English know what the referents of referring expressions like *father, book,* and *truth* are, although they may be hard put to explain exactly what these referents look like and may have slightly different notions of what these referents are, particularly in the case of abstract referring expressions like *truth*.

Words, of course, are not the only linguistic units to carry referential meaning. Sentences also have meaning because, like words and phrases, they *refer* to actions, states, and events in the world around us. *John is sleeping on the sofa* refers to the fact that a man known as John is currently lying down (or sitting) on an elongated piece of furniture generally meant to be sat upon. The referent of the sentence *John is sleeping on the sofa* is thus the action (or, in this case, state of being) of John on the piece of furniture in question.

Social Meaning

Referential meaning is not the only type of meaning that language users communicate to each other. Consider the following sentences:

(a)   Then I says to her she can't talk to me like that.

(b)   Is it a doctor in here?

(c)   Y'all come visit over the Christmas vacation.

(d)   I adore your lavender shawl; it's absolutely gorgeous!

(e)   Great chow!

In addition to representing actions, states, and mental processes, these sentences convey information about the identity of the person who has uttered them. In (a), the use of the verb *says* with the first person singular pronoun reveals something about the speaker's social class. In (b), the form *it* where other varieties use *there* indicates a speaker of an ethnically marked nonstandard variety of English. In (c), the pronoun *y'all* identifies a particular regional dialect of American English. The choice of words in (d) suggests a female speaker; it is thus marked with respect to gender. Finally, the choice of words in (e) indicates that the comment was made in an informal context.

Social class, ethnicity, regional origin, gender, and context are all *social* factors. In addition to referential meaning, therefore, language also conveys *social* meaning.

It is not only examples like (a) through (e) that are easily recognized as socially marked. Every utterance carries social meaning, not only in the sentence as a whole but in word choice (such as *y'all* and *chow*) and pronunciation (as in *gonna* or *nothin'*).

Affective Meaning

Besides referential and social meaning, there is a third kind of meaning. Compare the following examples:

(a) Harold, who always boasts about his two Ph.D.s, lectured me the entire evening on Warhol's art.

(b) Harold, who has two Ph.D.s., gave me a fascinating overview of Warhol's art last night.

These two sentences can be used to describe exactly the same event: they have similar referential meaning. At another level, however, the information they convey is different. Sentence (a) gives the impression that the speaker considers Harold a pretentious bore. Sentence (b), in contrast, indicates that the speaker finds Harold interesting. The "feeling" of the utterances is thus quite different.

Word choice is not the only means of communicating feelings and attitudes toward utterances and contexts. A striking contrast is provided by sentences that differ only in terms of stress or intonation. This string of words can be interpreted in several ways depending on its intonation:

Harold is really smart.

The sentence can be uttered in a matter-of-fact way, without emphasizing any word in particular, in which case it will be interpreted literally as a remark acknowledging Harold's intelligence. But if the words *really* and *smart* are stressed in an exaggerated manner, the sentence may be interpreted sarcastically to mean exactly the opposite. Intonation (often accompanied by appropriate facial expressions) is used frequently as a device to communicate attitudes and feelings; it can completely override the literal meaning of a sentence.

Consider a final example. Suppose that Mary Smith, happily married to John Smith, addresses her husband as follows:

John Smith, how many times have I asked you not to flip through the TV channels?

There would be reason to look beyond the words for the "meaning" of this unusual form of address. Mrs. Smith may address her husband as *John Smith* to show her exasperation, as in this example. What she conveys by choosing to address her husband as *John Smith* instead of the usual *John* is frustration and annoyance. Her choice of name thus "means" that she is exasperated. Contrast the tone of that sentence with a similar one in which Mrs. Smith addresses Mr. Smith as *dear*.

The level of meaning that conveys the language user's feelings, attitudes, and opinions about a particular piece of information or about the ongoing context is called *affective* meaning. Affective meaning is not an exclusive property of sentences: words like *alas!* and *hurray!* obviously have affective meaning, as do words like *funny, sweet*, and *obnoxious*. In fact, even the most common words—like *father, democracy*, and *old*—evoke in us particular emotions and feelings. The difference between synonymous or near-synonymous pairs of words like *vagrant* and *homeless* is essentially a difference at the affective level; in this particular pair, the first word carries a rather negative affective meaning, while the second is neutral or positive. Little is known yet about how affective meaning works, but it is of great importance to all verbal communication.

From our discussion so far, we can see that meaning is not a simple notion but a complex combination of several aspects: referential meaning (the real-word object or concept described by language); social meaning (the information about the social nature of the language user or of the context of utterance); and affective meaning (what the language user feels about the topic under discussion or about the ongoing context). The referential meaning of a word or sentence is frequently called its *denotation*, in contrast to the *connotation*, which includes both its social and affective meaning.

Traditionally, semantics has dealt only with referential meaning. Accordingly, this chapter focuses primarily on referential meaning, though we will occasionally refer to the three-way distinction. Social meaning will be investigated in detail in Chapters 12 and 13, and certain aspects of affective meaning will be discussed in Chapter 15.

WORD MEANING, SENTENCE MEANING, AND UTTERANCE MEANING
Meaning of Words and Sentences

We have talked about words and sentences as the two units of language that carry meaning. **Content words**—principally nouns, verbs, adjectives, and adverbs—have meaning in that they refer to concrete objects and abstract concepts; are marked as being characteristic of particular social, ethnic, and regional dialects and of particular contexts; and convey information about the feelings and attitudes of language users. **Function words** such as prepositions and articles also carry meaning, though in a different way from content words, as we will discuss later in this chapter. Like individual words, sentences also have social and affective connotations. The study of word meaning, however, differs from the study of sentence meaning because the units are different in kind.

In order for a sentence to have meaning, we must rely on the meaning of individual words that make it up. How we accomplish the task of retrieving sentence meaning from word meaning is a complex question. One obvious hypothesis is that the meaning of a sentence could simply be the sum of the meanings of its words. To see that this is *not* the case, consider the following sentences, in which the individual words (and therefore their *sum* meanings) are the same:

The hunter bit the lion.

The lion bit the hunter.

Clearly, the sentences refer to different events and hence have distinct referential meanings. This is conveyed by the fact that the words of the sentences are ordered differently. In English, the order in which words are arranged in a sentence can be crucial to meaning (see Chapter 5). Thus we cannot simply say that in order to retrieve the meaning of a sentence, all we need to do is add up the meanings of its components. What we must take into consideration, in addition to the meaning of individual words, is the **semantic role** assigned to each word. By semantic role we mean such things as *who* did *what* to *whom*, with *whom*, or for *whom*. In other words, the semantic role of a word is the role that its referent plays in the action or state of being described by the sentence. Sentence semantics is concerned with the relationship between words and their semantic roles.

While it is important to distinguish between word meaning and sentence meaning, the two interact on many levels. A clear example of this mutual interaction is provided by the following sentence:

He may leave tomorrow if he finishes his term paper.

In this sentence, the words *may*, *tomorrow*, and *if* have meanings as individual function words: *may* denotes permission or possibility; *tomorrow* indicates a future time unit that begins the following midnight; and *if* indicates a condition. But the impact of these words goes beyond the phrases in which they occur and affects the meaning of the entire sentence. Indeed, if we replace *may* with *will*, the sentence takes on a completely different meaning:

He will leave tomorrow if he finishes his term paper.

The sentence with *may* denotes a permission or possibility, while the sentence with *will* is simply the description of a future event. Thus *may* affects the meaning of the entire sentence.

The *scope* of the meaning of the function word *may* is the entire sentence. This is also true of *tomorrow* and of *if*. Many function words (and grammatical morphemes, for that matter) have sentence scope. What this example illustrates is that word meaning and sentence meaning are intimately related.

Meaning of Utterances

In addition to words and sentences, there is a third unit that also carries meaning, though we may not notice it as clearly because we often take it for granted in day-to-day interactions. Consider the following utterance:

I now pronounce you husband and wife.

This sentence may be uttered in at least two different sets of circumstances: (a) by a pastor presiding at a ceremony to a young couple getting married in the presence of their assembled families; or (b) by an actor dressed as a pastor to two actors before a congregation of Hollywood extras assembled in the same church by a director giving instructions for the filming of a television soap opera. In the first instance, *I now pronounce you husband and wife* will effect a marriage between the couple intending to get married. But that same utterance will have no effect on the marital status of any party on the movie location. Thus the circumstances of utterance create different meanings, although we could not say that the referential meaning of the sentence changes. It is therefore necessary to know the circumstances of utterance in order to appreciate and understand the effect or force of the utterance. We say that the sentence uttered in the wedding context and the sentence uttered in the film context have the same referential meaning but are different **utterances**, each with its own *utterance meaning*.

The difference between sentence meaning and utterance meaning can be further illustrated by the question *Can you shut the window?* There are at least two ways in which the addressee might react to this question. One possible response would be to say *Yes* (meaning 'Yes, I am physically capable of shutting the window') and to do nothing about it. We will call this the "smart-aleck interpretation"; it is of course not the way such a question is meant in most cases. Another way in which the addressee might react would be to get up and shut the window. Obviously, these interpretations of the same question are different: the smart-aleck interpretation treats the question as a request for information; the second interpretation treats it as a request for action, which is the way it is most likely to have been meant. To describe the difference between these interpretations, we can say that they are distinct utterances.

Sentence semantics is not concerned with utterance meaning. (Utterances are the subject of investigation of another branch of linguistics called *pragmatics*, which is the topic of Chapters 7 and 10.) One of the basic premises of sentence semantics is that sentences must be divorced from the context in which they are uttered. To experienced language users, this stance may appear strange and counterintuitive, since so much of a sentence's meaning depends on context. The point is not to discard context as unimportant or uninteresting but to recognize that, in a fundamental sense, sentence meaning is independent of context, while utterance meaning depends on the circumstances of the utterance. The branch of linguistics called semantics examines word meaning and sentence meaning while generally ignoring context; pragmatics, in contrast, pays less attention to the relationship of word meaning to sentence meaning and more attention to the relationship of an utterance to its context.

LEXICAL SEMANTICS

The *lexicon* can be viewed as a compendium of all the words of a language. Words are sometimes called **lexical items**, or *lexemes* (the *-eme* ending is the same as in *phoneme* and *morpheme*). The branch of semantics that deals with word meaning is called **lexical semantics**.

Lexical semantics is primarily concerned with relationships between word meanings. What, for example, is the relationship between the words *man* and *woman* on the one hand and *human being* on the other hand? How are the adjectives *large* and *small* in the same relationship to each other as the pair *dark* and *light*? What is the difference between the meaning of words like *always* and *never* and the meaning of words like *often* and *seldom*? What do language users actually mean when they say that a dog is "a type of" mammal? Lexical semantics is concerned with such questions: it is the study of how the lexicon is organized and of how the meanings of lexemes are interrelated. The principal aim of lexical semantics is building a model for the structure of the lexicon by categorizing the types of relationships between words.

Lexical Fields

Consider the following sets of words:

(a) cup, mug, wineglass, tumbler, plastic cup, goblet
(b) hammer, cloud, tractor, eyeglasses, dead leaf, justice

The words of set (a) all refer to concepts that can be described as 'vessels from which one drinks,' while the words of set (b) denote concepts that have nothing in common with each other. We say that the words of set (a) constitute a **lexical field**—that is, a set of words with identifiable semantic affinities. The following set of words is also a lexical field, because all the words in the set refer to emotional states:

angry, sad, happy, exuberant, depressed, afraid

Thus we see that words can be classified into sets according to their meaning.

In a lexical field, not all lexical items necessarily have the same status. Consider the following sets, which together form the lexical field of color terms (of course there are other terms in the same field):

(a) blue, red, yellow, green, black, purple
(b) indigo, saffron, royal blue, aquamarine, bisque

The colors referred to by the words of set (a) are more "usual" than those described in set (b). These colors are said to be less **marked** than the second set; therefore the words in set (a) are less marked members of the lexical field than the words in set (b). The less marked members of a lexical field will usually be easier to learn and remember than more marked members; children learn the term *blue* before they learn the terms *indigo, royal blue*, or *aquamarine*. Typically, a less marked word consists of only one morpheme, in contrast to more marked words (contrast *blue* and *royal blue*). The less marked member of a lexical field cannot be described by using the name of another member of the same field, while more marked members can be thus described (indigo is a kind of purple). Less marked terms also tend to be used more frequently than more marked terms; *blue*, for example, occurs considerably more frequently in conversation and writing than either *indigo* or *aquamarine*. (A survey of a million words of written English found 126 occurrences of *blue* but only one of *indigo* and none of *aquamarine*.) Less marked terms also are often broader in meaning than more marked terms; *blue* describes a broader range of colors than *indigo* or *aquamarine*. Finally, less marked words are not the result of the metaphorical usage of the name of another object or concept, whereas more marked words often are (for example, saffron is the color of a spice that gave its name to the color).

Using our definitions of lexical field and markedness, we now turn to the identification of types of relationships between words. We will see how the words of a lexical field can have different types of relationships to each other and to other words in the lexicon, and we will classify these relationships.

Hyponymy

Consider again the following set of unmarked color terms:

blue, red, yellow, green, black, purple

Any speaker of English can identify these words as referring to different colors. The description that these terms have in common is that they refer to (unmarked) colors. The terms *blue, red, yellow, green, black*, and *purple* are hyponyms of the term *color*, whose referent includes the referents of all the terms in the set. A **hyponym** is the term whose referent is included in the referent of another term (the prefix *hypo-* in *hyponym* means "below"). The relationship may be illustrated by the following diagram, in which the lower terms are the hyponyms (the higher term—*color* in this case—is sometimes called the *hypernym*).

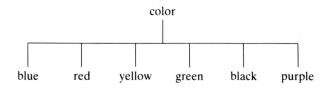

Another example is the term *mammal*, whose referent includes the referents of many other terms.

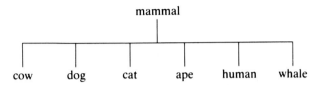

The relationship between each of the "lower" terms and the "higher" term is called *hyponymy*.

Hyponymy is not restricted to objects like mammal and abstract concepts like color—or even to nouns, for that matter. Hyponymy can be identified in many other areas of the lexicon. The verb *to cook*, for example, has many hyponyms.

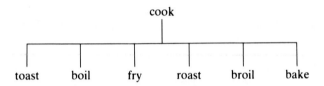

Not every set of hyponyms has a term that includes them all. Consider the terms *uncle* and *aunt*; they obviously form a lexical field because we can easily identify a property that their referents share. Yet in English we do not have a term that refers specifically to both uncles and aunts (that is, to 'siblings of parents and their spouses').

Other languages, in contrast, have a hypernym for the equivalent field. In Spanish, the plural term *tíos* can include both aunts and uncles, and the Spanish equivalent of the terms *uncle* and *aunt* are its hyponyms.

While hyponymy is found in all languages of the world, which concepts will have words in hyponymic relationships may vary from one language to the next. In Tuvaluan (a Polynesian language of the central Pacific), the higher term *ika* (roughly translated as 'fish') has as hyponyms not only all terms that refer to the animals that English speakers would recognize as fish but also terms for whales and dolphins (which speakers of English recognize as mammals) and for sea turtles (which are reptiles). Of course, we are dealing with folk classifications here, not scientific classifications.

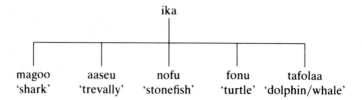

magoo 'shark'	aaseu 'trevally'	nofu 'stonefish'	fonu 'turtle'	tafolaa 'dolphin/whale'

Thus there is variability across languages as to the exact nature of particular hyponymic relationships.

In a lexical field, hyponymy often exists at more than one level. A term may at the same time have a hyponym and a hypernym, as *blue* does in Figure 6-1. The terms *turquoise, aquamarine,* and *royal blue* are hyponyms of *blue,* since they refer to different "types" or "shades" of blue. The term *blue* in turn is, along with many other color terms, a hyponym of the term *color.* We thus obtain a hierarchy of terms related to each other through hyponymic relationships. Similar hierarchies can be established for many lexical fields almost without limit. In the "cooking" field, *fry* has hyponyms in the terms *stir-fry, sauté,* and *deep-fry* and is itself a hyponym of *cook.* The "lower" we get in a hierarchy of hyponyms, the more marked the terms: *cook* is relatively unmarked; *stir-fry* is considerably more marked. The intermediate term *fry* is less marked than its hyponym *stir-fry* but more marked than *cook.*

Examples of multiple layers of hyponymic relationships abound in the area of folk biological classification, as illustrated by the tree in Figure 6-2. Note that the term *animal* appears on two different levels. English speakers indeed use the word to refer to at least two different referents: animals as distinct from plants and rocks, and animals (generally mammals other than humans) as distinct from humans, birds, and bugs. Cases in which a word has different meanings at different levels of a hyponymic hierarchy are not uncommon.

Hyponymy is one of several relationship types with which language users organize the lexicon. It is based on the notion of reference *inclusion*: if the referent of term A includes the referent of term B, then term B is a hyponym of term A. Note that hyponymy is important to everyday conversation—we use it whenever we say "B is a kind of A"—and to such tasks as using a thesaurus, which is organized according to hyponymic relationships.

FIGURE 6-1

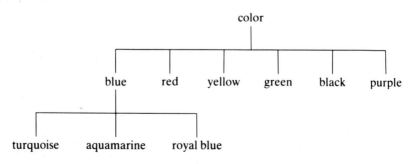

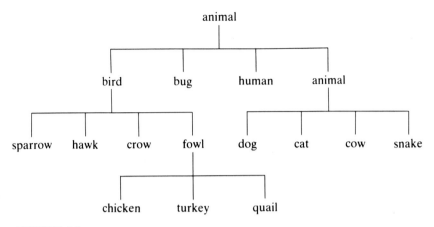

FIGURE 6-2

Part/Whole Relationships

A second important hierarchical relationship between words is that found in pairs of words like *hand* and *arm* or *room* and *house*. Here the referent of the first term in each pair is included in the referent of the second term. A hand, however, is not "a kind of" arm, and thus the relationship between *hand* and *arm* is not hyponymic. We need to establish a distinct relationship type to describe what the term *hand* is to the term *arm*. We call this a *part/whole relationship*. Part/whole relationships are not a property of pairs of words only: *hand, elbow, forearm, wrist*, and several other words are all in a part/whole relationship with *arm*. Other important examples of part/whole relationships include words like *second* and *minute, minute* and *hour, hour* and *day, day* and *week*, none of which could be described without reference to the fact that it is a subdivision of another.

Synonymy

We say that two words are **synonymous** if they "mean the same thing." The terms *movie, film, flick*, and *motion picture* all refer to the same set of referents in the real world and are usually taken to be synonymous terms. To address the notion of synonymy more formally, term A is synonymous with term B if every referent of term A is described by term B and vice versa. The "vice versa" is important: if it were not there, we would be defining hyponymy.

Why would the speakers of a language bother to keep synonyms at all, since they only add redundancy to the lexicon? One way in which a language acquires synonyms is through borrowings from other languages (see Chapter 4). Borrowed terms often come to coexist with native terms rather than replace them. So, in English, we have many pairs of synonymous words like *cloudy* and *nebulous, help* and *assist, skewed* and *oblique* that result from English having borrowed the second term of each pair from French or Latin.

When we assert that two terms are synonymous, we usually base our conclusion on referential meaning only. For example, even though *movie, film, flick,* and *motion picture* all have the same referential meaning, the terms differ in social and affective meaning. *Film* strikes us as a British word or as a word that applies more to movie classics or art movies. *Flick* is recognized as a term that can be used only in the most informal contexts. The term *motion picture* is quaintly outdated; if someone were to use it in a conversation, it would be for its connotation as a term from the thirties or forties. Thus we can consider the terms to be synonymous if we specify that we are taking only referential meaning into consideration. At the social and affective levels, the terms are not synonymous.

In fact, there are very few true synonyms in the lexicon. More often than not, terms that appear to be synonymous have different social and affective connotations. Even if we restrict the definition of meaning to referential meaning, we often find that words which appear synonymous at first glance are used to refer to slightly different sets of concepts or occur in different situations of use. The adjectives *fast, quick,* and *rapid* may be used interchangeably in reference to someone's running speed, for example. But only *fast* can be used to describe someone's talking speed (as in *a fast talker*—which is different from a "quick talker") or in the expression *life in the fast lane*; *quick* is the most appropriate term to describe a mind or a glance; and *rapid* is more usual than the other two terms if reference is made to a person's strides. Can we say that the three adjectives are synonymous?

The fact that there are few true synonyms in the lexicon of a language reflects the general tendency of language users to make the most of what is available to them. If two terms have the same referent, why not modify the meaning of one of them to express subtle shades of meaning or differences in social or affective meaning?

Because words with similar meanings are commonly distinguished by subtle shades of meaning at the referential level and frequently have different social and affective connotations, true synonymy is rare. But the notion is useful because it helps describe similarities between the meanings of different terms in the lexicon.

Antonymy

The word **antonymy** derives from the Greek root *anti-* (meaning 'opposite') and denotes opposition in meaning. In contrast to synonymy and hyponymy, antonymy is a *binary* relationship in that it can characterize the relationship between only two words at a time.

The prototypical pairs of antonyms are pairs of adjectives that describe opposite notions: *large* and *small, wide* and *narrow, hot* and *cold, open* and *closed, married* and *single, alive* and *dead*. Terms A and B are antonyms if, when A describes a referent, B cannot describe the same referent, and vice versa. Antonymy is not restricted to adjectives. The nouns *male* and *female* are also antonyms because an individual cannot be described by both terms at once. *Always* and *never* form an antonymous pair of adverbs because they have mutually exclusive referents. The verbs *love* and *hate* can also be viewed as antonyms because they refer to mutually exclusive emotions. Antonymy is thus a binary relationship between terms with *complementary* meanings.

Intuitively, we see a difference between the antonymous pair *large* and *small* and the antonymous pair *open* and *closed*. The adjectives of the first pair denote notions that are relatively subjective. Most of us would agree that humpback whales are large mammals and that mice are small mammals, but whether German shepherds are small or large dogs depends on one's perspective. The owner of a Chihuahua will say that German shepherds are large, but the owner of a Great Dane may find them on the small side. Futhermore, adjectives like *large* and *small* have superlative and comparative forms: humpback whales are the *largest* of all mammals; German shepherds are *larger* than Chihuahuas but *smaller* than Great Danes. Antonymous pairs that have these characteristics are called *gradable* pairs.

In contrast to *large* and *small*, *open* and *closed* are mutually exclusive and complementary. A door must be open or closed; it cannot be both at once. Hence *open* and *closed* are mutually exclusive terms. The status of a door cannot be described with a term that does not have either *open* or *closed* as a hyponym (*ajar* means 'slightly open' and therefore is a hyponym of *open*); thus *open* and *closed* are complementary. Furthermore, *open* and *closed* generally cannot be used in a comparative or superlative sense (something being physically "more open" than something else is a little strange). The pair is an example of *nongradable* antonymy (also sometimes called *complementarity*).

There are thus two types of antonymy: gradable and nongradable antonymy. If terms A and B are gradable antonyms and if A can be used to describe a particular referent, then B cannot be used to describe the same referent, and vice versa. If A and B are nongradable antonyms, the same condition applies along with an additional condition: if A cannot describe a referent, then that referent must be described by B, and vice versa. So *male* and *female, married* and *single, alive* and *dead* can be viewed as nongradable antonyms: *hot* and *cold, love* and *hate, always* and *never* are all gradable antonyms. Typically, for gradable antonyms, there will be words to describe intermediate stages: *sometimes, seldom, occasionally, often* are all gradations between *always* and *never*.

The distinction between gradable and nongradable antonymy is sometimes violated by language users. In English, for example, it is reasonable to assume that whatever is alive is not dead and that whatever is dead is not alive, and thus that the adjectives *dead* and *alive* form a nongradable pair. However, we do have expressions like *half-dead, barely alive*, and *more dead than alive* which seem to imply that, in some contexts, we see *alive* and *dead* as a gradable antonymous pair. The distinction between the two types of antonymy is thus not always observed by native speakers; but it is nevertheless useful in that it describes an important distinction between two types of word relationships.

Finally, words that are in an antonymous relationship often do not have equal status with respect to markedness. When we inquire about the weight of an object, for example, we say *How heavy is it?* and not *How light is it?* unless we already know that the object is light. Notice also that the noun *weight*, which describes both relative heaviness and relative lightness, is associated with *heavy* rather than with *light* (as in the expressions *to carry a lot of weight* and *to throw one's weight around*). Of the antonymous pair *heavy* and *light*, *heavy* is more neutral than *light* and is thus less *marked*. In the same fashion, *tall* is less marked than *short, hot* is less marked than *cold*, and *married* is less marked than *single* (we say *marital status*, not *singleness status*). Although there are some variations across languages as to which word of a pair is considered less marked, there is a great deal of agreement in this respect from language to language.

Converseness

Another important relationship type invokes the notion of opposition, although it does so in a different way from antonymy. Consider the relationship between the word *wife* and the word *husband*. If A is the husband of B, then B is the wife of A. Thus *wife* is the *converse* of *husband*. **Converseness** characterizes the relationship between pairs of words and is thus a binary relationship. Other examples of converse pairs include terms denoting many other kinship relations like *grandchild* and *grandparent* or *child* and *parent*, terms describing professional relationships like *employer* and *employee* or *doctor* and *patient*, and terms denoting relative positions in space or time such as *above* and *below, north of* and *south of*, or *before* and *after*. Pairs of words that consist of an active verb and its passive equivalent are also in a converse relationship: if A kisses B, then B is kissed by A, and *to kiss* is the converse of *to be kissed*.

Converse pairs can combine with other types of opposition to form complex relationships. The antonymous pair *father : mother* is in a converse relationship with the antonymous pair *son : daughter*. Generally, converse pairs denote relationships between objects or between people.

Some converse relationships are a little more complex. The verb *to give*, for example, is usually ditransitive, which means that it requires a subject and two objects. The converse of *to give* is *to receive*, except that the relationship is not a "reversal" of the subject and the direct object as in the pair *to kiss* and *to be kissed* or a mutual subject/possessor relation like *husband* and *wife*; rather, it is a relationship between the subject and the indirect object.

John gave a present to Harold.

Harold received a present from John.

Pairs of words with a similar relationship include *lend* and *borrow*, and *buy* and *sell*. Note that *rent* is its own converse in American English.

John rents an apartment to Harold.

Harold rents an apartment from John.

When there is any possibility of confusion, the preposition *out* is attached to *rent* in the meaning of 'lending out for money.' In British English, this sense of *rent* is described by the verb *let*. In some languages, the same word is used for 'buy' and 'sell.' In Samoan, for example, the word *faʔatau* carries both meanings (sometimes an adverb that indicates direction is attached when there is potential ambiguity); and the Mandarin Chinese words *mǎi* 'sell' and *mài* 'buy' are etymologically related. These facts suggest that converseness is an intuitively recognizable relationship.

Polysemy and Homonymy

Two additional notions that are closely related to the basic relationship types are **polysemy** and **homonymy**. In contrast to the notions discussed earlier in this section, these two notions refer to the similarities rather than the differences between words and their meanings. A word is *polysemic* when it has more than one meaning. The word *plain*, for example, can have several meanings, among which figure (a) 'easy, clear'; (b) 'undecorated'; (c) 'not good-looking'; and (d) 'a level area of land.' *Plain* is thus polysemic. Two or more words are *homonymic* when they sound the same but have different meanings. The words *I, eye*, and *aye* are homonymic: they have different meanings but are identical in spoken form. These two notions are useful when dealing with relationships between words and meanings. Languages exhibit polysemy and homonymy in their lexicons to varying degrees. A language like Hawaiian, for example, which has a restricted set of possible words because of its phonological structure, has a great deal more homonymy than English.

An inherent difficulty arises in distinguishing between polysemy and homonymy: When do we know that we have separate lexical items rather than a single word with different meanings? Because *plain* 'a level area of land' is a noun, it is a distinct word from *plain* in the first three meanings, all of which are adjectives. How would we know whether or not the other three meanings of *plain* are different words that happen to sound the same? Using spelling as a criterion is misleading: many sets of words are obviously distinct but have the same spelling—as, for example, the noun *sound* 'noise' and the adjective *sound* 'healthy' or *bank* 'financial institution' and *bank* 'shore of a river.' Yet the problem is an important one, especially for anyone who wants to arrange or use the entries of a dictionary (in which different meanings of the same word are grouped under a single entry but each homonymous form has a distinct entry).

There is no simple solution to the problem. If there is a clear distinction between polysemy and homonymy, it must involve several criteria, none of which is sufficient by itself and each of which may yield different results. We have already excluded spelling as an unreliable criterion. One modestly reliable criterion is the word's *etymology*, or historical origin. We can consider that there are two words of the form *sound* corresponding to the two meanings given earlier because they derive from different Anglo-Saxon roots. The word *bank* with the meaning 'financial institution' is an early borrowing from French, while *bank* in the 'shore of a river' sense has a Scandinavian origin. The various antonyms and synonyms of a word provide a second criterion that we may use to distinguish between polysemy and homonymy. The word *plain* in its meaning of 'easy, clear' and in its meaning 'undecorated' both have a synonym in *simple* and an antonym in *complex*. This fact suggests that they are indeed two meanings of the same polysemic word. No such common synonym or antonym can be found for the two meanings of *sound*. Finally, we may ask whether there is any commonality between the different meanings of what appears to be the same word. The first two meanings of *plain* can be characterized as 'devoid of complexity,' which suggests that they are related; we can find no such hypernymic description for *bank* and *bank*. Thus *plain* in these two meanings is polysemic, while the two meanings of *bank* reflect homonymous lexical items. (Of course, other meanings of *plain* may or may not belong to separate words.)

While the criteria just outlined help distinguish between polysemy and homonymy, they are not always foolproof. It is often difficult to decide whether a particular pair of look-alike and sound-alike word forms are separate homonymous words or simply the same polysemic word with different meanings. Though homonymy and polysemy can be distinguished as different notions, the boundary between them is not clear-cut.

Metaphorical Extension

The difficulties in defining the distinction between polysemy and homonymy partly arise from the fact that language users often extend the primary meaning of words to form metaphors. A **metaphor** is an extension of the use of a word beyond its primary meaning to describe referents that bear similarities to the word's primary referent. The word *eye*, for example, can be used to describe the hole at the dull end of a needle, the bud on a potato, or the center of a storm. The similarities between these referents and the primary referent of the word *eye* are their roundish shape and their more or less central location on a larger shape. Language users constantly create new metaphors. Once a metaphor becomes accepted, speakers tend to view the metaphorical meaning as separate from its primary meaning—as in *booking* a flight, *tabling* a motion, *understanding* a concept, *seeing* the *point, stealing* the *head*lines, *buying time*, studying a foreign *tongue*. Hence difficulty exists in determining whether we still have one word with two meanings or two words with different but metaphorically related meanings.

All languages appear to have metaphors. Metaphors are so fundamental to human communication that small children can be observed creating them in the process of acquiring language. Very early, children extend the meaning of the words that they know to cover objects and concepts for which they do not yet know the adult word. Linguist Eve Clark reports the example of a child who first said the word *mooi* (*moon*) while looking at the moon; before long, the child was using the word *mooi* to describe cakes, circles drawn on foggy windows, postmarks, and the letter *O*. Clearly, the child noticed that all these objects had the same general round shape and used the word *mooi* to refer to round objects. This early process of applying a particular word to meanings that resemble the primary meaning of the word is called *overgeneralization* and can be thought of as a primitive kind of metaphor. As adults, we use metaphors not because we are unaware of the names of objects and concepts but because we find in metaphors a tool to describe things vividly and creatively.

Metaphors occur constantly in day-to-day speaking and writing. The following examples were gleaned from the front page of a typical newspaper:

Tennis star Martina Navratilova *breezed* through the championship match.

The dollar is *falling sharply*.

His speech was the *catalyst* that gave the *signal* for a new popular upheaval.

In the first example, the verb *to breeze* is of course not meant literally; it is used to give the impression that Navratilova won the championship effortlessly, as a breeze would blow over a tennis court. Similarly, the italicized words in the other two sentences are clearly meant to be interpreted as metaphors. The use of metaphors relies on our ability to see that in some contexts words are not to be interpreted literally. (The mechanisms that we use in figuring out when a word must be interpreted metaphorically will be discussed in Chapter 10.)

Metaphors are not formed haphazardly. Observe, for example, the following metaphors that refer to the notion of time:

I look *forward* to seeing you again this weekend.

Experts do not *foresee* an increase in inflation in the near future.

He *drags up* old grudges from his youth.

Once in a while, we need to *look back over our shoulders* at the lessons that history has taught us.

A pattern becomes apparent in these examples: in English, we construct time metaphors as if we physically moved through time in the direction of the future. Thus the future is forward in the first two examples. Metaphors that refer to the past use words that refer to what is left behind, as in the latter two examples. Metaphors that violated this pattern would sound very strange:

*I look *back* to seeing you again this weekend.

*He *drags down* old grudges from his youth.

Another principle that governs the creation of metaphors is the following: "Ideas are objects that can be sensed." Thus ideas can be smelled, felt, and heard.

Your proposal *smells* fishy.

I failed to *grasp* what she was trying to prove.

I'd like your opinion as to whether my plan *sounds* reasonable.

Writers and critics often talk about the writing process as "cooking."

I let my manuscript *simmer* for six months.

Who knows what kind of a story he is *brewing*!

Her last book was little more than a *half-baked concoction* of earlier work.

"The heart is where emotions are experienced" is a common principle on which we base our metaphors for emotions.

It is with a *heavy heart* that I tell you of her death.

One should not speak *lightheartedly* about this tragedy.

The rescuers received the survivors' *heartfelt* thanks.

The construction of metaphors thus follows preset patterns.

Most of the metaphors discussed so far are relatively conventionalized; that is, they are found in the speech and writing of many language users. Not much creativity goes into the use of conventionalized metaphors, because they are preset. But language lends itself to creative activities, and language users do not hesitate to create metaphors of their own. Here are a few examples on the theme of grief from losing a friend:

The loss of a friend is *a heavy weight to carry*.

The loss of a friend is *a dark cloud over one's life*.

The loss of a friend is *a severe blow*.

The loss of a friend *reaches into the depths of one's soul*.

The loss of a friend can *trigger serious thinking about one's own mortality*.

Even when speakers and writers create their own metaphors, however, they must follow the principles that regulate conventionalized metaphors. In English, for example, metaphors that refer to time must obey the convention of "moving through time in the direction of the future."

Life is a carpet that *unrolls before us.*

If these principles are violated, the result is likely to sound strange.

*The afternoon was slowly *regressing* toward a hot, moist, tropical dusk.

To what extent do the principles of metaphorical extension vary from language to language? There is strong evidence that some metaphorical patterns are frequent across the world's languages. For example, in many languages the word for "eye" is used metaphorically to refer to roundish objects like protuberances on a potato or to the centrally located portion of an object like the center of a storm.

But other principles of metaphorical extension vary from language to language. Mandarin Chinese metaphors for time, for example, move in the direction of the *past.* Similarly, "the heart is the seat of emotions" does not apply to metaphors in many languages. Polynesian languages like Samoan and Tahitian, for example, treat the *stomach* as the metaphorical seat of emotions. It is likely that some of these principles reflect different cultures' views of the world. The exact workings of this link between culture and language are still poorly understood. Increased knowledge about metaphors in different languages should help us determine which principles are shared by most or all languages, which are specific to some languages, and to what extent metaphors reflect cultural perspectives.

Lexical Semantics: Discovering Relationships in the Lexicon

Hyponymy, part/whole relationships, synonymy, gradable and nongradable antonymy, converseness, polysemy, homonymy, and metaphorical extension—lexical semantics is primarily concerned with discovering relationships in the lexicon of languages. The semantic relationships in which a word is involved are, in a sense, part of its meaning: the word *cold* can be defined as a gradable antonym of *hot,* as having the expression *sensation of heat* as hypernym, and as being more marked than *hot* but less marked than terms like *chilly* and *freezing.* By investigating how the meaning of a particular word interacts with the meaning of other words, we can begin to understand the meaning of that word.

Lexical semantics, of course, cannot explain the difference in meaning between word pairs like *gorilla* and *doubtful.* For lexical semantics to be useful, it must be applied to particular areas of the lexicon where the meanings of words have common characteristics. Thus the notion of lexical field becomes useful. If the word *gorilla* is placed in its appropriate lexical field, its relationship to words like *chimpanzee* and *great ape* can be investigated. Similarly, the word *doubtful* can be contrasted with other words that express likelihood or certainty.

The different types of relationships we have been describing are the most basic tools of lexical semantics. They are basic because one type cannot be characterized in terms of another type. For example, an antonymous relationship between two words cannot be explained in terms of hyponymy, part/whole relationships, synonymy, converseness, or metaphorical extension. Whether additional basic types are needed to account for relationships between words is not clear. Even now lexical semantics can explain a great deal using just these types.

FUNCTION WORDS AND CATEGORIES OF MEANING

The lexicon is not made up exclusively of content words like *father, pigeon, stir-fry*, and *democracy*, which refer to objects, actions, or abstract concepts. It also contains function words (or "grammatical" words) like the prepositions *to, from*, and *about*; the conjunctions *if, however*, and *or*; the determiners *a, the,* and *some*; and the auxiliaries *may, should*, and *will*. The role of these lexical items is to signal grammatical relationships.

Tense and Modality

Many categories of meaning are associated with function words and morphemes. Bound morphemes can denote several categories of meaning in English, including number, tense, and person. In other languages, the same categories are expressed not by means of bound morphemes but by separate words. In Tongan, the function word *ʔoku*, which precedes the verb, denotes present tense, while the word *naʔe* denotes past tense.

ʔoku   ʔalu e   fineʔeiki ki kolo.
Present go   the lady   to town
'The lady is going to town.'

Naʔe ʔalu e   fineʔeiki ki kolo.
Past go   the lady   to town
'The lady was going to town.'

Whether tense is expressed through bound morphemes or separate lexical items is not important for semantics. What is important is that there is a semantic category *tense* that affects the meaning of sentences in both Tongan and English.

Semantic categories like tense are conveyed by function words and function morphemes, but their scope goes beyond the noun phrase or verb phrase in which they occur. The meaning of tense morphemes affects the whole sentence, since the **tense** of the verb determines the time reference of the entire clause. The category *tense* (and other semantic categories like it) thus refers to both word meaning and sentence meaning.

Modality, or *mood*, is the category through which speakers convey their attitude toward the truth of their assertions (*epistemic modality*) or express obligation, permission, or suggestion (*deontic modality*). The sentences in the following pairs differ as to their epistemic modality:

(a) She has <u>probably</u> left town by now.   (probability)
She has <u>left</u> town by now.   (assertion)

(b) Harry <u>must</u>'ve been very tall when he was young.   (conjecture)
Harry was very tall when he was young.   (assertion)

(c) They <u>may</u> come to the party.   (possibility)
They are coming to the party.   (assertion)

And the sentences in the following pairs differ as to their deontic modality:

(d) He <u>must</u> come tomorrow.   (command)
He is coming tomorrow.   (statement)

(e) They <u>may</u> take the dishes away.   (permission)
They <u>are</u> taking the dishes away.   (statement)

The two types of modality are obviously interrelated, as witnessed by the fact that the same words (*must* and *may*, among others) can denote either type, depending on the context. Modality may be expressed through auxiliary verbs such as *may, should,* or *must,* which are called *modal* auxiliaries; through *modal* verbs like *order, assume,* and *allow;* through *modal* adverbs like *possibly* or *certainly;* and, in some languages, through affixes attached to verbs or nouns. The latter type is common in American Indian languages, some of which have extremely complex systems of modal affixes and particles.

Reference

Another important semantic category is **reference**, through which we provide information about the relationship between noun phrases and their referents. For example, there is a semantic difference between the following sentences:

(a) <u>The</u> woman came to see you.

(b) <u>A</u> woman came to see you.

In (a), the speaker assumes that the hearer is able to identify which woman is in question, while no such assumption is made in (b). (Reference is investigated in depth in Chapter 7.)

Deixis

The word *deixis* comes from the Greek verb *deiktikós* meaning 'to point.' **Deixis** is the marking of the orientation or position of objects and events with respect to certain *points of reference.* Take, for example, the following sentence addressed by a restaurant customer to a waiter and uttered while the speaker points to items on a menu:

I want this dish, this dish, and this dish.

In order to interpret the sentence, the waiter needs to have information about who *I* refers to, about the time at which the utterance is produced, and about what the three noun phrases *this dish* refer to. We say that *I*, the present tense form of the verb, and the three noun phrases *this dish* are *deictic expressions*. Our ability to interpret them enables us to decipher the meaning of the sentence.

Deixis consists of three semantic notions, all of which are related to the orientation or position of events or objects in the real world. *Personal deixis* is most commonly conveyed through personal pronouns: *I* versus *you* versus *he* or *she*. *Spatial deixis* refers to orientation in space: for example, *this* versus *that*. *Temporal deixis* refers to orientation in time: present versus past, for example.

Personal Deixis   Many of the utterances that we produce daily are comments and questions about ourselves or our interlocutors.

I really should be going now.

Did you pick up a carton of milk as I asked you?

In this family, we rarely smoke or drink.

The pronouns *I, you,* and *we*—along with *she, he, it*, and *they* (and alternative forms)—are markers of personal deixis. When we use these pronouns, we orient or place our utterances with respect to ourselves, our interlocutors, and third parties.

Personal pronouns are of course not the only tool we use to mark personal deixis. The phrase *this person* in the sentence *You may enjoy scary roller-coaster rides, but this person doesn't care for them at all* may be used to refer to the speaker if the speaker wishes to express annoyance or disdain. Similarly, if we are entertaining royalty etiquette requires that the noun phrase *Her Majesty* be used to refer to the addressee: *Would Her Majesty like some more fried oysters?*

Personal deixis is thus not associated exclusively with pronouns, although pronouns are the most common way to express personal deixis. In this discussion, we will concentrate primarily on pronouns as markers of personal deixis.

The most basic opposition of personal deictic systems is the opposition between speaker (*I* or *me*) and addressee (*you*). This opposition in *person* is so basic that it is reflected in the pronominal systems of all languages of the world. Pronouns that refer to the speaker (or to a group of people that includes the speaker) are called *first person* pronouns, and pronouns that refer to the addressee (or to a group of people that includes the addressee) are called *second person* pronouns.

Besides the opposition between first person and second person, pronoun systems often have separate forms for the *third person*—namely, an entity other than the speaker and the interlocutor. In English, *he, she,* and *it* denote third person entities. But special third person pronouns are not found in all languages. Many languages simply do not have a special form to refer to third person entities; in these languages, such entities are referred to with the help of a demonstrative like *this* or *that* or are simply not stated. In Tongan, a verb without an expressed subject must be understood as having a third person subject.

> Naʔe aʔu.
> Past arrive
> '(He/She/It) arrived.'

Tongan does have a third person pronoun form, but it is used only when the third person entity is emphasized.

> Naʔe aʔu   ia.
> Past arrive he/she
> 'He/She is the one that arrived.'

The fact that many languages do not have separate third person pronouns is a reflection of the fact that the third person is less important than the first and second persons in personal deixis. In fact, the third person can be defined as an entity other than the first person and other than the second person. Because it can be described in terms of the other two persons, it is a less basic distinction in language in general. The singular pronoun system of English can thus be described as follows:

speaker only	I
hearer only	you
neither speaker nor hearer	he/she/it

Some languages make finer distinctions than English does in their pronominal systems, while others make fewer distinctions (see Chapter 8). In all languages, though, there is a separate first person pronoun and second person pronoun.

Besides person, personal-deixis systems may mark distinctions in gender and number. The gender distinction is made in English in the third person only: *he* is used for masculine referents and *she* for feminine referents. In other languages, gender may be marked in the other persons as well. In Hebrew, the second person singular pronoun is *atah* for masculine referents but *at* for feminine referents. Number is marked on English pronouns in the first person (*I* versus *we*) and in the third person (*he/she/it* versus *they*); the second person pronoun *you* can refer to both singular and plural entities. In many other languages, including French, there are separate second person singular and plural pronouns. Singular and plural are not the only number categories that must be distinguished: some languages have distinct *dual* pronoun forms to refer to exactly two people, and a few languages even mark a distinction between "a few" and "many" referents (see Chapter 8).

Finally, personal deixis frequently reflects the social status of referents. In French and many other languages, the choice of a pronoun form in the second person depends on the nature of the speaker's relationship to the addressee. If the speaker and addressee are of roughly equal social status, the pronoun *tu* is used; to mark or create social distance or social inequality, a speaker uses the plural pronoun *vous* instead of *tu*, even when addressing one person. Considerably more complex systems are found in languages like Japanese, Thai, and Korean. Strictly speaking, the use of deictic devices to reflect facts about the social relationship of the participants is a distinct type of deixis, commonly referred to as *social deixis*.

Thus personal deixis can mark a number of overlapping distinctions: person, gender, number, and social status. Different languages combine these distinctions in different combinations, marking some and not marking others. The basic distinction between first person and second person, however, is found in all languages and appears to be a basic semantic category in all deictic systems.

Spatial Deixis   *Spatial deixis* is the marking in language of the orientation or position in space of the referent of a linguistic expression. The following sentences differ in terms of spatial deixis:

I will be going to Australia next year.

I will be coming to Australia next year.

The first sentence is used when the point of reference is that of the speaker; the second sentence implies that the point of reference is that of the addressee. An example of a context in which it is appropriate to shift the point of reference to the addressee is a letter to someone in Australia. The English verbs *come* and *go* are thus marked for spatial deixis.

The categories of words that are most commonly used to express spatial deixis are demonstratives (*this* versus *that*) and adverbs like *here* and *there*. Demonstratives and adverbs of place are by no means the only categories that have spatial deictic meaning; as just illustrated, the directional verbs *go* and *come* also carry deictic information, as do verbs like *bring* and *take*.

Languages differ in terms of the number and meaning of demonstratives and adverbs of place. The demonstrative system of English distinguishes only between *this* (proximate—close to the speaker) and *that* (remote—away from the speaker). It is one of the simplest systems found among the world's languages. At the other extreme are languages like Eskimo, which has thirty demonstrative forms. In all languages, however, the demonstrative system treats the speaker as a point of reference. Thus the speaker is a basic point of reference for spatial deixis.

Many spatial deixis systems have three terms. Three-term systems fall into two categories. In one type, the meanings of the three terms are 'near the speaker,' 'a little distant from the speaker,' and 'far from the speaker.' The three Spanish demonstratives *este, ese, aquel* have these three respective meanings. In another type of three-term demonstrative system, the three terms have the meaning of 'near the speaker,' 'near the hearer,' and 'away from both speaker and hearer.' Fijian is an example of such a system.

na ŋone oⁿgō
the child this (near me)
'this child (near me)

na ŋone oⁿgori
the child this (near you)
'that child (near you)'

na ŋone oyā
the child that (away from you and me)
'that child (away from you and me)'

In both systems, however, the speaker is taken as either the sole point of reference or as one of two points of reference.

Spatial deixis thus represents the orientation of actions and states in space. It is most commonly conveyed by demonstratives and adverbs of place. Languages may have anywhere from two to thirty distinct demonstrative forms, but all demonstrative systems take the speaker as a basic point of reference.

Temporal Deixis   A third type of deixis is *temporal deixis*—the orientation or position of the referent of actions and events in time. All languages have words and phrases that are inherently marked for temporal deixis, like the English terms *before, last year, tomorrow, now*, and *this evening*. In many languages (but not all), temporal deixis can be marked through tense, which is encoded on the verb with affixes or expressed in an independent morpheme. In English, we must make an obligatory choice between the past tense and the non-past tense form of verbs.

I walk to school every day.   (non-past tense)

I walked to school every day.   (past tense)

To express a future *time*, English cannot inflect a verb (it lacks a future *tense*) but must use a phrasal verb in the non-past tense.

I will walk to school every day.   (non-past tense for future time)

Tuvaluan is like English: *e* denotes non-past, while *ne* is a past tense marker.

Au e   fano ki te fakaala.
I   Non-past go   to the feast
'I am going/will go to the feast.'

Au ne   fano ki te fakaala.
I   Past go   to the feast
'I went to the feast.'

In some languages, the choice is between future and non-future (with undifferentiated present and past).

In a number of languages, temporal deixis can be marked only with optional adverbs. The following Chinese sentence can be interpreted as past, present, or future, depending on the context:

xià   yǔ.
down rain
'It was/is/will be raining.'

When there is the possibility of ambiguity, an adverb of time ('last night,' 'right now,' 'next week') is added to the sentence.

In languages that do not mark tense on verbs, another semantic category not directly related to temporal deixis—**aspect**—is frequently obligatory. Aspect refers to the ways in which actions and states are viewed: as continuous (*I was walking*), repetitive (*I walked (every day)*), instantaneous (*I walked*), and so on.

Tense is thus not the only marker of temporal deixis, although it is very frequently exploited by languages as the primary means of marking temporal deixis.

The most basic point of reference for tense is the moment at which the sentence is uttered. Any event that occurs before that moment is marked as past, and any event that occurs after that moment is marked as future.

The train arrived.   (any time before this moment)

The train is arriving.   (right now)

The train will arrive.   (any time after this moment)

When the point of reference for tense is some point in time other than the moment of utterance, we say that tense is *relative*. Relative tense is used in many languages when speakers wish to compare the time of occurrence of two different events.

After I had left home, I went to the public library.

Before I saw you yesterday, I had run into a lamppost.

Languages may have complex rules of *tense concord* that dictate the form of verbs in relative contexts.

Deixis as a Semantic Notion   The three types of deixis illustrate how semantic categories permeate language beyond the simple meaning of words. The deictic orientation of a sentence or of part of a sentence can be conveyed through bound morphemes such as tense endings, through free morphemes and function words such as pronouns and demonstratives, or through content words such as *come* and *bring*. Deictic meaning is independent of the means that are employed to convey it.

One of the purposes of semantics is to describe which parameters are important or essential to characterize deixis (as well as other semantic categories) in language in general. We noted, for example, that distinguishing between the speaker and the addressee is an essential function of the personal deixis system of all languages. Similarly, we found that every spatial deixis system has at least one point of reference, a location near the speaker. Besides this point of reference, a spatial deixis system may have a secondary point of reference, a location near the hearer. Uncovering which parameters are important to deictic systems is the purpose of the semantic investigation of deixis.

There is a great deal of overlap between the different types of deixis. Note, for example, that personal, spatial, and temporal deixis all share a basic point of reference: the speaker's identity and location in space and time. Many linguistic devices can also be used to mark more than one type of deixis. In English, for example, the demonstrative *this* can be used for personal deixis (*this person*), spatial deixis (*this object*), and temporal deixis (*this morning*). Clearly, personal, spatial, and temporal deixis are closely related notions.

There is one type of deixis that we have not yet discussed in this section. *Textual deixis* is the orientation of utterances with respect to other utterances in the string of utterances in which it occurs. Consider for example the following pair of sentences:

He started to swear at me and curse me. *This* made me very angry.

The demonstrative *this* at the beginning of the second sentence refers not to a direction in space but rather to something previously mentioned. This demonstrative marks textual deixis. Textual deixis is thus a tool that enables language users to "package" utterances together and indicate relationships across utterances. Because textual deixis is primarily concerned with utterances and their context, it goes beyond the scope of semantics as traditionally defined, although its importance is not to be underestimated.

SEMANTIC ROLES AND SENTENCE SEMANTICS

We have noted that, like words, sentences must "carry" meaning for language speakers to understand each other at all, but that the meaning of sentences cannot be obtained merely by adding up the meaning of each content word of the sentence. This fact was illustrated in the last section, where we saw that bound morphemes and function words may also carry meaning that has implication for the meaning of the entire sentence. We also noted earlier that the following sentences have very different meanings, even though they contain exactly the same words:

(a) The hunter bit the lion.

(b) The lion bit the hunter.

Clearly, summing up the meaning of each word will not retrieve the full meaning of sentences. Such a process will not even distinguish between these two sentences. In defining what the meaning of a sentence consists of, we need to take more than just the meaning of the individual content words into consideration. What notion must we turn to?

Consider the following active/passive counterparts, which, at the level of referential meaning at least, describe the same situation:

(c) The hunter bit the lion.

(d) The lion was bitten by the hunter.

These sentences have the same deep structure, but they differ in that the derivation of sentence (d) involves passivization, whereas (c) does not (see Chapter 5). Since our concern here is with meaning, we must ask how to account for the synonymy between the two sentences.

Furthermore, consider the following sentences:

(e) Seymour sliced the salami with a knife.

(f) Seymour used a knife to slice the salami.

Here is a situation not unlike the active/passive counterparts of (c) and (d), in that the sentences have the same referential meaning. But (e) and (f) do not have the same deep structure; we have no transformation that would explain how (e) differs from (f). Nevertheless, we need to describe how sentences (e) and (f) mean "the same thing."

A slightly different situation is presented by the contrast between the following examples:

(g) Harold was injured by a stone.

(h) Harold was injured with a stone.

These sentences share some properties (for example, both describe someone being injured and a stone being involved), but they are not completely synonymous: if the stone was part of a natural rockfall, only sentence (g) applies, because (h) implies that someone threw a stone at Harold with intent to do harm. How can we describe such meaning differences?

The three situations just presented all suggest that the crucial factor in the way sentence meaning is constructed is the *role* played by each noun phrase in relation to the verb. We thus need to introduce a new notion—the **semantic**

role of a noun phrase—which refers to the way in which the referent of the noun phrase contributes to the state, action, or situation described by the sentence. The semantic role of a noun phrase differs from its syntactic role (subject, object, and so on), as illustrated by the contrast between sentences (c) and (d): in both sentences, the way in which the lion and the hunter are involved in the action is the same, even though (for example) the lion is the direct object of sentence (c) and the grammatical subject of sentence (d).

Semantic role, furthermore, is not an inherent property of a noun phrase, since a given noun phrase can have different semantic roles in different sentences, as in the following contrast:

Harold was injured by *a friend*.

Harold was injured with *a friend*.

Rather, semantic role is a way of characterizing the meaning relationship between a noun phrase and the verb of a sentence.

The first semantic roles we need to identify are the role of *agent* (the responsible initiator of an action) and of *patient* (the entity that undergoes a certain change of state). In both (c) and (d) above, the agent is *the hunter*, and the patient is *the lion*. That the sentences describe the same situation (and hence have the same referential meaning) can thus be explained by the fact that in both sentences each noun phrase has the same semantic role.

The role of the subject noun phrases in the following sentences is not that of agent, because Hilda is not really the responsible initiator of the actions denoted by the verbs:

Hilda likes blueberry pancakes.

Hilda felt threatened by the lion.

In both sentences, Hilda is experiencing a physical or mental sensation. The semantic role of *Hilda* is *experiencer*, defined as that which receives a sensory input. In English, experiencers can be either subjects or direct objects, depending on the verb. Compare these sentences, in which the experiencer is the subject, with the following sentence, in which the experiencer is the direct object:

Harold sometimes astounds *me* with his stupidity.

So far, we have identified the semantic roles of agent, patient, and experiencer. Now consider again the semantic roles of the noun phrases in the following sentences:

(g)   Harold was injured by a stone.

(h)   Harold was injured with a stone.

Recall that the difference between the sentences is that (h) implies that someone used a stone to attack Harold, while (g) does not require this implication. In sentence (h), we say that *a stone* is the *instrument*—the intermediary through which the agent performs the action; note that the definition requires that there be an agent, which is consistent with our interpretation of sentence (h). In sentence (g), *a stone* could be assigned the role of an instrument only if there was an agent doing the injuring; if the stone that injured Harold were part of a rockfall, *a stone* would be assigned the semantic role of *cause*—defined as any natural force that brings about a change of state. Instruments and causes can be expressed as prepositional phrases (as in the previous examples) or as subjects.

The bigger key opens the door to the cellar.   (instrument)

The snow caved in the roof.   (cause)

That the noun phrase *the bigger key* is indeed an instrument and not an agent is supported by the fact that it cannot be conjoined (linked by *and*) with an agent, as the following anomalous example shows:

*The bigger key and John open the door to the cellar.

However, an instrument *can* be conjoined with another instrument, and an agent can be conjoined with another agent.

A push and a shove opened the door to the cellar.

Harold and Hilda opened the door to the cellar.

In addition to an agent, a patient, an experiencer, an instrument, and a cause, a noun phrase can be a *recipient* (that which receives a physical object), a *benefactive* (that for which an action is performed), a *locative* (the location of an action or state), or a *temporal* (the time at which the action or state occurred).

I gave *Hilda* a puppy.   (recipient)

Harold passed the message to me for *Hilda*.   (benefactive)

The Midwest is cold in winter.   (locative)

She left home *the day before yesterday*.   (temporal)

The point of this enterprise is to characterize all possible semantic roles that noun phrases can fill in a sentence. Every noun phrase in a clause is assigned a semantic role, and, aside from coordinate NPs, the same semantic role cannot be assigned to two different noun phrases within the same clause. So, for example, a sentence like the following is ruled out as being semantically anomalous because it contains two different instrumental noun phrases, namely the two underlined noun phrases:

> *This key opens the door with a hammer.

In addition, in most cases a single noun phrase can be assigned only one semantic role. In rare instances, a noun phrase can be assigned two different roles; in the sentence *Harold rolled down the hill*, if Harold rolls down the hill deliberately, he is both agent and patient, because he is at once the responsible initiator of the action and the entity that undergoes the change of state.

Semantic Roles and Grammatical Relations

It is important to understand the relationship between semantic roles and grammatical relations. We noted earlier that the two notions are different. In English, for example, the subject of a sentence can be an agent (as in the underlined noun phrase in sentence (a)), a patient (b), an instrument (c), a cause (d), an experiencer (e), a benefactive (f), a locative (g), or a temporal (h), depending on the verb.

(a)   The janitor opened the door.

(b)   The door opened easily.

(c)   His first record greatly expanded his audience.

(d)   Bad weather ruined the corn crop.

(e)   Serge heard his father whispering.

(f)   The young artist won the prize.

(g)   Arizona attracts asthmatics.

(h)   The next day found us on the road to Alice Springs.

Furthermore, in certain English constructions the subject does not have any semantic role; such is the case of the so-called "dummy *it*" construction, in which the pronoun *it* fills a semantically empty subject slot.

> It became clear that the government had jailed him there.

So the notion of subject is independent of the notion of semantic role; and we could show the same thing for direct objects and other grammatical relations. Conversely, semantic roles do not appear to be constrained by grammatical relations. A locative, for example, may be expressed as a subject (as in sentence (a)), a direct object (b), an indirect object (c), or the object of a preposition (d).

(a)   The garden will look great in the spring.

(b)   Harold planted the garden with cucumbers and tomatoes.

(c)   The begonias give a cheerful look to <u>the garden</u>.

(d)   The gate opens on <u>a garden</u>.

Nevertheless, there is a clear relationship between grammatical relations and semantic roles. Consider the following sentences, all of which have *to open* as a verb:

Harold opened the door with this key.

The door opens easily.

This key will open the door.

The storm opened the door.

The grammatical subjects of these examples are an agent (*Harold*), a patient (*the door*), an instrument (*this key*), and a cause (*the storm*). Such extreme variety is not found with all verbs. The verb *to soothe* can take an instrument or a cause as subject.

This ointment will soothe your sunburn.

The cold stream soothed my sore feet.

To have an experiencer as the grammatical subject of the verb *to soothe*, we must use a passive construction.

I was soothed by the herbal tea.

Clearly, the range of variation allowed in each case is controlled by the verb. Language users know the semantic roles that each verb allows as subject, direct object, and so on. Attached to the verb *to soothe* is a "tag" indicating that only instruments and causes are allowed in subject position, whereas the "tag" attached to the verb *to open* permits the subject to be agent, patient, instrument, or cause.

Semantic roles are universal features of the semantic structure of all languages, but how they interact with grammatical relations like subject and direct object differs from language to language. The first evidence of this variation is the fact that equivalent verbs in different languages do not carry similar tags. The tag attached to the English verb *to like*, for example, permits only experiencers as subjects.

I like French fries.

But only patients can be the subjects of the equivalent Spanish verb *gustar*.

Las papas fritas me   gustan.
the French-fries to-me like
'I like French fries.'
(literally: 'French fries to me like.')

A similar situation is found for verbs of "liking" and "pleasing" in many other languages including Russian. In some languages, the verb 'to understand' carries a tag that allows its subjects to be either experiencers or patients, as in Samoan. The choice depends on emphasis and the focus of discussion.

?ua   mālamalama a?u i   le   matā?upu.
Present-tense understand   I   Object-marker the lesson
'I understand the lesson.'

?ua   mālamalama le   matā?upu iāte a?u.
Present-tense understand   the lesson   to   me
'I understand the lesson.'
(literally: 'The lesson understands to me.')

Some languages distinguish between agent and experiencer much more carefully than English does. For example, the verb might take a subject when the action described is intentional but take a direct object when the action is unintentional.

In addition to cross-linguistic variation with respect to specific verbs, we find a great deal of variation among languages in the degree to which different semantic roles can fit into different grammatical slots in a sentence. In English, the subject slot can be occupied by noun phrases of any semantic role—depending, of course, on the verb. Many English verbs allow different semantic roles for subject, direct object, and so on. But the situation is different in many other languages. In a language like Russian, verbs do not allow nearly as much variation as English verbs do. There is a much tighter bond between semantic roles and grammatical relations, so that the subjects of most Russian sentences are agents, while direct objects are mostly patients. In English, the relationship between semantic roles and grammatical relations is considerably looser. Between the extremes illustrated by English and Russian, we find many degrees of relative looseness and tightness between the syntax and the semantics.

SUMMARY

Semantics is the study of meaning in language. While semantics has traditionally focused on referential meaning, language also conveys social meaning (information about the social characteristics of the context of production) and affective meaning (information about the emotional characteristics of the context of production). Referential meaning is often called *denotation*, while social and affective meanings are covered by the term *connotation*. Words, sentences, and utterances can all carry meaning. We must distinguish between sentence meaning and utterance meaning. While the study of sentence meaning is primarily the responsibility of semantics, pragmatics is the branch of linguistics that concerns itself with utterance meaning.

Lexical semantics is the study of meaning relationships in the lexicon. The types of relationships must be universal, though the word sets to which they apply will vary from language to language. Lexical fields are sets of words whose referents belong together on the basis of one or more fundamental characteristics. The words in a lexical field are often arranged in terms of the following relationships: hyponymy (a kind of), part/whole (subdivision), synonymy (similar meaning), gradable and nongradable antonymy (opposite meaning), converseness (reciprocal meaning), polysemy (many meanings), homonymy (same phonological shape), and metaphorical extension (derived meaning).

Content words are not the only units of language that carry meaning. Semantic notions like deixis, for example, can be conveyed through bound morphemes and function words as well as content words. Several types of deixis can be identified: personal deixis, spatial deixis, and temporal deixis. All necessitate that a point of reference be identified. The here-and-now (in relation to the speaker and the moment of utterance) is highly privileged as a point of reference for all three types of deixis, although it is not the only possible reference point.

The meaning of a sentence is not simply the sum of the meaning of its words. Rather, sentence semantics aims to discover the basic relationships that exist between noun phrases and the verb of the sentence. These semantic roles are relational notions and not inherent properties of noun phrases. They are also independent of the grammatical function of the noun phrase in the sentence; the verb determines which semantic role may be used in particular grammatical slots of the sentence. We have described the following semantic roles: agent, patient, experiencer, instrument, cause, benefactive, locative, and temporal. While these categories must be universal, different languages may have different rules as to how semantic role is encoded in syntax.

EXERCISES

1. In the first section of the chapter we introduced the terms *synonymy, implication, contradiction, anomaly, ambiguity*, and *vagueness* to describe various sentences and sentence pairs. Determine which of these notions applies to each of the following sentences and sentence pairs:

   Harry's cat called me on the phone.
   Visiting relatives can be boring.
   His daughter is her brother's grandmother.
   My wife just returned from the store. I am a married man.
   I don't like locking my car. My car's doors can be locked.
   The basil I will plant next weekend is growing well.
   She swims.
   I was fatally ill last year.
   It is still too warm to start a fire. It is not cold enough to start a fire.
   The wine I didn't drink tasted sour to me.

> My dog wants out. The canine creature that belongs to me is experiencing
> the desire to proceed outdoors.
> Hilda kissed Harold, and Jerry too.

2. The following sentences are ambiguous. Based on the discussion in this chapter
   and Chapter 5, describe the ambiguity in detail:

> They found the peasants revolting.
> The car I'm getting ready to drive is a Lamborghini.
> There is nothing more alarming than developing nuclear power plants.
> Hilda does not like her husband, and neither does Gertrude.
> They said that they told her to come to them.
> Challenging wrestlers will be avoided at all costs.
> He met his challenger at his house.

3. Identify the differences in referential, social, and affective meaning between the
   words in each of the following lists:

   (a) hoax, trickery, swindle, rip-off, ruse, stratagem
   (b) delightful, pleasant, great, far-out, nice, pleasurable, bad, cool
   (c) man, guy, dude, jock, imp, lad, gentleman, hunk, boy
   (d) eat, wolf down, nourish oneself, devour, peck, ingest, chow down, graze,
        fill one's tummy
   (e) tired, fatigued, pooped, weary, languorous, zonked out, exhausted, for-
        done, spent
   (f) stupid person, idiot, nerd, ass, jerk, turkey, wimp, punk, airhead, bastard

4. Among the following lists of terms, some form lexical fields. For each list:
   (A) Identify the words that do not belong to the same lexical field as the others
   in the list.
   (B) Identify the hypernym of the remaining lexical field, if there is one (it may
   be a word in the list).
   (C) Determine whether some terms are less marked than others, and justify
   your claim.

   (a) affected, prissy, interesting, sociable, well-mannered, elegant, friendly,
        personable, vain
   (b) acquire, buy, collect, hoard, win, inherit, steal
   (c) whisper, talk, narrate, report, tell, harangue, scribble, instruct, brief
   (d) road, path, barn, way, street, freeway, avenue, thoroughfare, Interstate,
        method
   (e) stench, smell, reek, aroma, bouquet, odoriferous, perfume, fragrance,
        scent, olfactory

5. Traditionally, a thesaurus is used to find the synonyms of a word. The following
   is a typical entry from *Roget's Thesaurus* (Harmondsworth, England: Penguin
   Books, 1962):

> **710.** Concord—N. *concord*, harmony, unison, unity, duet   24 n. *agree-*
> *ment*; unanimity, bi-partisanship   488 n. *consensus*; understanding, rapport;
> solidarity, team-spirit   706 n. *cooperation*; reciprocity, sympathy, fellow-
> feeling; compatibility, coexistence, league, amity   880 n. *friendship*; rap-
> prochement, reunion, reconciliation   719 n. *pacification*; entente cordiale,
> happy family   717 n. *peace*; goodwill, honeymoon.

Adj. *concordant*, harmonious; en rapport, eye to eye, unanimous, of one mind, bi-partisan   24 adj. *agreeing*; co-existent, compatible, united; amicable, on good terms   880 adj. *friendly*; frictionless, happy   717 adj. *peaceful*; agreeable, congenial   826 adj. *pleasurable*.

Vb. *concord*, harmonize; agree   24 vb. *accord*; see eye to eye   706 vb. *cooperate*; reciprocate, respond, run parallel; fraternize   880 vb. *be friendly*; keep the peace, work for peace.

(A)   Using the terms introduced in our discussion of lexical semantics, describe how this entry is organized. Include information on how punctuation is used in the entry.

(B)   To what extent are the words in the entry synonymous? Provide specific examples to support your point.

(C)   What are the advantages and limitations of using a thesaurus? In particular, what kinds of information does a thesaurus entry offer and not offer?

(D)   On the basis of your answer to (C), describe in detail some of the difficulties that (i) children and (ii) nonnative speakers of English might encounter in using a thesaurus.

6.   Consider the following three sequences of dictionary entries, taken (and slightly abbreviated) from the *American Heritage Dictionary of the English Language* (Boston: American Heritage and Houghton Mifflin, 1975):

Sequence 1

husk·y[1] *adj.* **-ier, -iest.**   **1.** Hoarse, as from overuse or emotion.   **2.** Like or resembling a husk.   **3.** Full of or containing husks. [Originally, "dry as a husk."] **—husk'i.ly** *adv.* **—husk'i.ness** *n.*

husk.y[2] *adj.* **-ier, -iest.** *Informal.* Rugged and strong; burly. **—***n., pl.* **huskies.** A husky person. [From HUSKY (hoarse).]**—husk'i.ness** *n.*

husk.y[3] *n., pl.***-kies.**   **1.** *Sometimes capital H.* A dog of a breed developed in Siberia for pulling sleds, having a dense, furry, variously colored coat. Also called "Siberian husky."   **2.** A dog of any of several breeds of Arctic origin. [Probably a shortened variant of ESKIMO.]

Sequence 2

junior *adj.*   **1.** *Abbr.* **Jr., Jun.** Younger. Used to distinguish the son from the father of the same name, and written after the full name: *William Jones, Jr.*   **2.** Designated for or including youthful persons: *a junior tennis match*; *junior dress sizes.*   **3.** Lower in rank or shorter in length of tenure: *the junior senator.*   **4.** Designating the third or penultimate year of a U.S. high school or college.   **5.** Lesser in scale than the usual. **—***n. Abbr.* **Jr., jr., Jun., jun.**   **1.** A younger person or individual.   **2.** A person lesser in rank or time of participation or service; subordinate.   **3.** An undergraduate in his third or penultimate year of a U.S. high school or college.

Sequence 3

bay[1] *n.*   **1.** *Abbr.* **b., B.** A body of water partly enclosed by land, but having a wide outlet to the sea.   **2.** A broad stretch of low land between hills.   **3.** An arm of prairie partly enclosed by woodland. [Middle English *baye*, from Old French *baie*, from Old Spanish *bahia*, perhaps from Iberian.]

bay[2] *n.*   **1.** *Architecture.* A part of a building or other structure marked off by vertical elements.   **2.a.** A **bay window** (*see*).   **b.** Any opening or recess in a wall.   **3.** An extension of a building; wing.   **4.** A compartment in a barn, used for storing hay or grain.   **5.** A ship's sickbay.   **6.** A compartment in an aircraft: *the bomb bay*. [Middle English, from Old French *baee*, an opening, from *baer*, to gape, from Vulgar Latin *batāre*, to yawn, gape.]

bay³ *adj.* Reddish-brown: *a bay colt.* —*n.* **1.** A reddish brown.   **2.** An animal, especially a horse, of this color. [Middle English, from Old French *bai*, from Latin *badius*.]

bay⁴ *n.* **1.** A deep, prolonged barking, especially of hounds closing in on prey.   **2.** The position of one cornered by pursuers and forced to turn and fight at close quarters.   **3.** The position of one checked or kept at a safe distance. —*v.* **bayed, baying, bays.** —*intr.* To utter a deep, prolonged bark or howl. —*tr.* **1.** To pursue or challenge with barking: "*I had rather be a dog, and bay the moon*" (Shakespeare).   **2.** To express by barking. [Middle English *baien*, short for *abaien*, from Old French *abaiier*, *abayer*, from Vulgar Latin *abbaiāre*.]

bay⁵ *n.* **1.** A laurel, *Laurus nobilis*, native to the Mediterranean area, having stiff, glossy, aromatic leaves. Also called "bay laurel," "bay tree."   **2.** Any of several similar trees or shrubs.   **3.** *Usually plural.* A crown or wreath made of the leaves and branches of the bay or similar plants, given in classical times as a sign of honor.   **4.** *Plural.* Reknown; honor. [Middle English *baye*, laurel berry, from Old French *baie*, from Latin *bāca*, berry.]

Using the terms introduced in our discussion of lexical semantics, describe in detail how these dictionary entries are organized. Include a discussion of the criteria that are used to create different entries or subentries for homonymous words.

7. Following are sets of sentences in which one or more words are used metaphorically. Provide a general statement describing the principle that underlies these sets of metaphors; then add to the set one metaphor that follows the principle.

Example:
   I let my manuscript *simmer* for six months.
   She *concocted* a retort that readers will appreciate.
   There is no *easy recipe* for writing effective business letters.

General statement: "The writing process is viewed as cooking."
Additional example: He is the kind of writer that *whips up* another trashy novel every six months.

(a)   Members of the audience *besieged* him with counterarguments.
      His opponents *tore* all of his arguments *to pieces.*
      My reasoning left them *with no ammunition.*
      The others will never be able to *destroy* this argument.
      His question betrayed a *defensive stance.*

(b)   This heat is *crushing.*
      The sun is *beating down* on these poor laborers.
      The clouds seem to be *lifting.*
      The northern part of the state is *under* a heavy snowstorm.
      The fresh breeze *cleared up* the *oppressive* heat.

(c)   She has *an eye* for handsome men.
      He has *a palate* for good Indian curry.
      My neighbor has *an ear* for gossip.
      I used to have *an eye* for good etchings.
      French people commonly have *a nose* for cheese.

8. Determine whether the words in each of the following sets are polysemic, homonymous, or metaphorically related. In each case, state the criteria used to arrive at your conclusion. You may use a dictionary.

(a) to run down (the stairs); to run down (an enemy); to run down (a list of names)

(b) the seat (of one's pants); the seat (of the government); the (driver's) seat (of a car)

(c) an ear (for music); an ear (of corn); an ear (as auditory organ)

(d) to pitch (a baseball); pitch (black); the pitch (of one's voice)

(e) to spell (a word); (under) a spell; a (dry) spell

(f) vision (the ability to see); (a man of) vision; vision (during a hallucination)

(g) the butt (of a rifle); the butt (of a joke); to butt (as a ram)

9. Identify the semantic role of each noun phrase in the following sentences:

Last October, I looked off the wooden bridge into the small river behind our home.
I have forgotten everything that I learned in grade school.
The Grand Tetons tower majestically over the valley.
The snow completely buried my car during the last storm.
Fifty kilos of cocaine were seized by the drug enforcement authorities.
Kathy was awarded one thousand dollars' worth of damages.
The hurricane destroyed half of the island.
His ingenuity never ceases to amaze me.

10. In this chapter we said that a "tag" is attached to every verb in the lexicon indicating which semantic role can be assigned to each noun argument. The verb *to bake*, for example, can have as its subject an agent (as in sentence (a)), a patient (b), a cause (c), or an instrument (d). But it does not allow locatives (e) or temporals (f) in subject position, among other things.

(a) Harold baked scones.
(b) The cake is baking.
(c) The sun baked my lilies to a crisp.
(d) This oven bakes wonderful cakes.
(e) *The kitchen bakes nicely.
(f) *Tomorrow will bake nicely.

(A) Determine which semantic roles the following verbs allow in subject position on the basis of the sentences provided: *feel, provide, absorb, thaw, taste.*

His hands felt limp and moist.
I could feel the presence of an intruder in the apartment.
This room feels damp.
They all felt under the blanket to see what was there.
This semester feels very different from last year to me.

Gas lamps provided light for the outdoor picnic.
These fields provide enough wheat to feed a city.
Who provided these scones?
The Middle Ages provided few famous mathematicians.
The accident provided me plenty to worry about.
Your textbooks provide many illustrations of this phenomenon.
The bylaws provide for the dissolution of the board in cases like these.

The students have absorbed so much material that they can't make head
or tail of it anymore.
This kind of sponge does not absorb water well.
The United States absorbed the Texas Republic in 1845.
My work hours are absorbing all my free time.
The soil is absorbing the rain.

If Antartica suddenly thawed, the sea level would rise dramatically.
Chicken does not thaw well in just two hours.
The crowd thawed after Kent arrived.
Kent's arrival thawed the party.
The heat of the sun will thaw the ice in the ice chest.
Ice thaws at 0 degrees Celsius.
The peace treaty will thaw relations between the United States and the
Soviet Union.

This wine tastes like vinegar.
He's tasted every single hors d'oeuvre at the party.
I can taste the capers in the sauce.

(B) Languages may differ with respect to the semantic roles that particular
verbs may take. The following are semantically well-formed French sentences
with the verb *goûter* 'to taste':

Il n'a   jamais goûté au caviare.
he not-have ever   tasted the caviar
'He's never tasted caviar.'

Je goûte un goût amer dans ce   café.
I taste a taste bitter in   this coffee
'I taste a bitter taste in this coffee.'

The following sentence, in contrast, is not well constructed:

*Les cuisses de grenouille goûtent bon.
 the thighs of frog   taste   good
'Frog's legs taste good.'

What is the difference between *to taste* and *goûter* in terms of the range of
semantic roles that they may take?

SUGGESTIONS FOR FURTHER READING

The major reference work on semantics is Lyons (1977), which (in two volumes) is
thorough and provides a wealth of information and critical discussion. Palmer (1981)
and Leech (1974) provide concise overviews of the field. Bierwisch (1970) is a clear
and concise summary of lexical semantics, though it is a little outdated. More detailed
and up-to-date discussions of lexical semantics are provided in Lehrer (1974), which
focuses on semantic universals (discussed in Chapter 8 of this text), and in Wierzbicka
(1985), in which the main concern is the meaning of the notion 'kind of.' Cruse (1986)
is a good overview of lexical semantics. Several of the papers in Holland and Quinn
(1987) investigate connotation and the cultural elements in the organization of
semantic fields. A basic work on metaphors is Lakoff and Johnson (1980); some of the

ideas presented in that earlier work are developed further in Lakoff (1987). Deixis is discussed in detail in Anderson and Keenan (1985) and in Chapter 2 of Levinson (1983). For a concise discussion of tense and related notions, consult Chung and Timberlake (1985); further details on aspect can be found in Comrie (1985), further details on mood and modality in Palmer (1986). Sentence semantics and semantic roles were originally discussed in Fillmore (1968) and refined in Fillmore (1977); good critical overviews of the brand of sentence semantics presented in this chapter can be found in the general works on semantics mentioned above. For a textbook on the areas of semantics not covered in this chapter, see Kempson (1977). The example of semantic overgeneralization in child language quoted here is from Clark (1975).

REFERENCES

Anderson, Stephen R., and Edward L. Keenan. 1985. "Deixis," in Timothy Shopen (ed.), *Language Typology and Syntactic Description* (Cambridge: Cambridge University Press), vol. 3, pp. 259–308.

Bierwisch, Manfred. 1970. "Semantics," in John Lyons (ed.), *New Horizons in Linguistics* (Harmondsworth, England: Penguin Books), pp. 166–184.

Chung, Sandra, and Alan Timberlake. 1985. "Tense, Aspect, and Mood," in Timothy Shopen (ed.), *Language Typology and Syntactic Description* (Cambridge: Cambridge University Press), vol. 3, pp. 202–258.

Clark, Eve V. 1975. "Knowledge, Context, and Strategy in the Acquisition of Meaning," in D. P. Dato (ed.), *Georgetown University Roundtable in Language and Linguistics 1975* (Washington, D.C.: Georgetown University Press), pp. 77–98.

Comrie, Bernard. 1985. *Tense* (Cambridge: Cambridge University Press).

Cruse, D. A. 1986. *Lexical Semantics* (Cambridge: Cambridge University Press).

Fillmore, Charles J. 1968. "The Case for Case," in Emmon Bach and Robert T. Harms (eds.), *Universals in Linguistic Theory* (New York: Holt, Rinehart and Winston), pp. 1–88.

———. 1977. "The Case for Case Reopened," in Peter Cole and Jerold M. Saddock (eds.), *Syntax and Semantics 8: Grammatical Relations* (New York: Academic Press), pp. 59–82.

Holland, Dorothy, and Naomi Quinn (eds.). 1987. *Cultural Models in Language and Thought* (Cambridge: Cambridge University Press).

Kempson, Ruth M. 1977. *Semantic Theory* (Cambridge: Cambridge University Press).

Lakoff, George. 1987. *Women, Fire, and Dangerous Things: What Categories Reveal about the Mind* (Chicago: University of Chicago Press).

Lakoff, George, and Mark Johnson. 1980. *Metaphors We Live By* (Chicago: University of Chicago Press).

Leech, Geoffrey. 1974. *Semantics* (Harmondsworth, England: Penguin).

Lehrer, Adrienne. 1974. *Semantic Fields and Lexical Structure* (Amsterdam: North-Holland).

Levinson, Stephen C. 1983. *Pragmatics* (Cambridge: Cambridge University Press).

Lyons, John. 1977. *Semantics*, 2 vols. (Cambridge: Cambridge University Press).

Palmer, F. R. 1981. *Semantics*, 2nd ed. (Cambridge: Cambridge University Press).

———. 1986. *Mood and Modality* (Cambridge: Cambridge University Press).

Wierzbicka, Anna. 1985. *Lexicography and Conceptual Analysis* (Ann Arbor, Mich.: Karoma).

PRAGMATICS: INFORMATION STRUCTURE

7

THE ENCODING OF INFORMATION STRUCTURE

Syntax and semantics are not the only regulators of sentence structure. A sentence may be grammatically and semantically well formed but still exhibit problems when used in a particular context. Examine the sentences that make up the following two versions of a typical local news report.

Version 1

At 3 a.m. last Sunday, the Santa Clara Fire Department evacuated two apartment buildings at the corner of Country Club Drive and 5th Avenue. Oil had been discovered leaking from a furnace in the basement of one of the buildings. Firemen sprayed chemical foam over the oil for several hours. By 8 a.m., the situation was under control. Any danger of explosion or fire had been averted, and the leaky furnace was sealed. Residents of the two apartment buildings were given temporary shelter in the Country Club High School gymnasium. They regained possession of their apartments at 5 p.m.

Version 2

As for the Santa Clara Fire Department, it evacuated two apartment buildings at the corner of Country Club Drive and 5th Avenue at 3 a.m. last Sunday. There was someone who had discovered a furnace in the basement of one of the buildings from which oil was leaking. What was sprayed by firemen over the oil for several hours was chemical foam. It was by 8 a.m. that the situation was under control. What someone had averted was any danger of explosion or fire, and as for the leaky furnace, it was sealed. What the residents of the two apartment buildings were given in the Country Club High School gymnasium was temporary shelter. Possession of their apartments was regained by them at 5 p.m.

Virtually the same words are used in the two versions, and every sentence in both versions is grammatically and semantically well formed. Still, there is something fundamentally odd about version 2: it runs counter to expectations of how information should be presented in a text. Somehow, the second version emphasizes the wrong elements at the wrong time.

The problem with version 2 is the way in which different pieces of information are marked for relative significance. In any sequence of sentences, it is essential to mark elements as being more or less important or essential. Speakers and writers are responsible for highlighting certain elements and backgrounding other elements, exactly as a painter highlights particular details and deemphasizes others with a judicious use of color, shape, and position.

In language texts, this highlighting and deemphasizing are called **information structure**. Unlike syntax and semantics, which are sentence-based aspects of language, information structure requires consideration of whole texts—of sequences of sentences rather than isolated ones. Out of context, there is nothing wrong with the first sentence of version 2:

As for the Santa Clara Fire Department, it evacuated two apartment buildings at the corner of Country Club Drive and 5th Avenue at 3 a.m. last Sunday.

It is only when this sentence serves to open a news report that it is inappropriate. Thus, when we talk about information structure we must take into account the *discourse context* of a sentence—that is, the environment in which it is produced, especially what comes before it. We can describe a **discourse** as a sequence of sentences that "go together": a conversation over the family dinner table, a newspaper column, a personal letter, a radio interview, or a subpoena to appear in court. We may also say that *Oh, look!* (uttered, for example, to draw attention to a beautiful sunset) is discourse, even though it is not a sequence of utterances, because the utterance is produced within an extralinguistic environment that helps determine an appropriate information structure.

In marking (or encoding) information structure in a sentence, speakers rely on the fact that the rules of syntax permit alternative ways of shaping sentences. The following is an incomplete list of alternative sentences that "say the same thing." It illustrates how broad a choice we have in expressing even simple predications.

The fireman discovered a leak in the basement.

A leak was discovered by the fireman in the basement.

A leak in the basement was discovered by the fireman.

It was the fireman who discovered a leak in the basement.

What the fireman discovered in the basement was a leak.

What the fireman discovered was a leak in the basement.

It was a leak that the fireman discovered in the basement.

What was discovered by the fireman was a leak in the basement.

The fireman, he discovered a leak in the basement.

In the basement, the fireman discovered a leak.

It is such a choice of alternatives that we exploit to mark information structure; this chapter will describe how that is done.

The term **pragmatics** is often used as an alternative to the term *information structure*. Pragmatics is the branch of linguistics that studies information structure. (Chapter 10 will discuss another aspect of language that is also sometimes referred to as "pragmatics.")

One of the first tasks that pragmatics must tackle is identifying the categories needed to talk about information structure. The fact that there are so many different ways to express the same thought demonstrates the need to make more subtle distinctions to describe the differences between these alternatives. A set of basic constructs must be developed to describe pragmatic differences in English and other languages.

CATEGORIES OF INFORMATION STRUCTURE

In order to describe the differences between alternative ways of "saying the same thing," we must identify the basic categories of information structure. These categories must be applicable to all languages (though the ways they are used may differ). With these categories, we want to explain how discourse is constructed in any language. Ultimately, these explanations may suggest hypotheses about how the different components of the human mind (such as memory, attention, and logic) work and interact with each other. Thus categories of information structure, like other aspects of linguistics, should be as independent of particular languages as possible.

There is an important difference between the types of syntactic constructions found in particular languages and the categories of information structure. The range of syntactic constructions available in different languages differs considerably; for example, some languages have a passive construction, while others do not. Since the categories of information structure are not language dependent, they cannot be defined in terms of particular structures.

Nevertheless, there is a close kinship between pragmatics and syntax. In all languages, one principal function of syntax is to encode pragmatic information. What differs from language to language is the way in which pragmatic structure maps onto syntax.

Given and New Information

One major category of information structure is the distinction between given and new information. **Given information** is information currently in the forefront of the hearer's mind; **new information** is information being introduced into the discourse. Consider the following two-turn interaction:

Alice: Who ate the custard?

Tom: Mary ate the custard.

The noun phrase *Mary* represents new information in Tom's answer because it is just being introduced into the discourse there; *the custard*, in contrast, is given information in the reply because it can be presumed to be in the mind of Alice, who has just introduced it into the discourse in the previous turn. (Because it is given information in Tom's reply, *the custard* would normally be expressed simply by the pronoun *it: Mary ate it.*)

Given information need not be introduced into a discourse by a second speaker. In the following sequence of sentences, uttered by a single speaker, the underlined element represents given information because it has just been introduced in the previous sentence and can thus be assumed to be in the hearer's mind.

A man called while you were on your break. He said he'd call back later.

A piece of information is sometimes taken as given because of its close association with something that has been introduced into the discourse. For example, when a noun phrase is introduced into a discourse all the subparts of the referent can be treated as given information.

Kent returned my car last night after borrowing it for the day. One of the wheels was about to fall off and the dashboard was missing.

My mother went on a Caribbean cruise last year. She loved the food.

Because face-to-face conversation and most other kinds of discourse have at least implicit speakers and addressees, interactors always take first person (speaker) and second person (addressee) pronouns to be given information. These noun phrases thus do not need to be introduced into the discourse as new information.

Noun phrases carrying new information usually receive more stress than those carrying given information, and they are commonly expressed in a more elaborate fashion—for example, with a full noun phrase instead of a pronoun, and sometimes with a relative clause or adjectival modifiers. The following is typical of how new information is introduced into a discourse.

When I entered the room, there was <u>a tall man with an old-fashioned hat on, quite elegantly dressed</u>.

In contrast, given information is commonly expressed in more attenuated ways—ways that are abbreviated or reduced. Typical attenuating devices used to encode given information include pronouns and unstressed noun phrases. Sometimes given information is simply left out of a sentence altogether. In the following interaction, the given information *is at the door* is omitted entirely from B's answer, which expresses only new information.

A: Who's at the door?

B: The mailman.

The contrast between given and new information is important in characterizing the function of several constructions in English and other languages, as we will show in the next section.

Topic

The **topic** of a sentence is its center of attention—what the sentence is about, its point of departure. The notion of topic is opposed to the notion of *comment*, the element of the sentence that says something about the topic.

Often, given information is the sentence element about which we say something; in other words, given information is the topic. New information, on the other hand, represents what we want to say about the topic; it is the comment. Thus, if *Mary ate the custard* is offered in answer to the question *What did Mary do?*, the topic would be *Mary* (the given information) and the comment would be *ate the custard* (the new information). The topic of a sentence can often be phrased as in this example:

<u>Speaking of Mary</u>, she ate the custard.

Given information is not always the topic. In the second sentence of the following sequence, the noun phrase *her little sister* is both new information and the topic.

Mary ate the custard. As for <u>her little sister</u>, she drank the cod-liver oil.

Similarly, given information can serve as comment, as the underlined element in the following sequence illustrates:

Harold didn't believe anything the charlatan said. As for Hilda, she <u>believed everything he said</u>.

So the given/new contrast differs from the topic/comment contrast.

It is difficult to define precisely what a topic is. While the topic is the element of a sentence that functions as the center of attention, a sentence like *Oh, look!*, uttered to draw attention to a beautiful sunset, has an unexpressed topic ("the setting sun" or "the sky"). Thus topic is not necessarily a property of the sentence; it may be a property of the discourse context.

Topics are less central to the grammar of English than to the grammar of certain other languages. Indeed, the one construction of English that unequivocally marks topics is the relatively rare *as for* construction. In English, marking the topic of a sentence is far less important than marking the subject.

Marking topic is considerably more important in certain other languages. Languages such as Japanese and Korean have function words whose sole purpose is to mark a noun phrase as topic. In Chinese and other languages, no special function words attach to topic noun phrases, but they are marked by word order. In these three languages, noun phrases marked in one way or another as the topic occur very frequently. Thus, despite the difficulty in defining it, the notion of topic is important and needs to be distinguished from other categories of information structure.

Contrast

A noun phrase is **contrastive** if it occurs in opposition to another noun phrase in the discourse. Here, for example, the noun phrase *Hilda* in B's answer is contrasted with the noun phrase *Matt*.

A: Did Matt see the ghost?

B: No, <u>Hilda</u> saw the ghost.

Contrast that answer by B with the following one, in which *Matt* is not contrastive.

B: Yes, Matt saw the ghost.

Contrast is also marked in sentences that express the narrowing down of a choice from several candidates to one. In such sentences, the noun phrase that refers to the candidate thus chosen is marked contrastively.

Of all present, only <u>Hilda</u> knew what was going on.

Compare that sentence with the following one, in which *Hilda* is not contrastive.

Gerard knew what was going on, and Hilda knew what was going on.

A simple test exists for contrast: if a noun phrase can be followed by *rather than*, it is contrastive.

A: Did Matt see the ghost?

B: No, <u>Hilda</u>, rather than Matt, saw the ghost.

A single sentence can have several contrastive noun phrases; in B's answer in the following exchange, *Hilda* contrasts with *Matt*, and *an entire cast of spirits* contrasts with *a ghost*.

A: Did Matt see a ghost?

B: Yes, Matt saw a ghost, but <u>Hilda</u> saw <u>an entire cast of spirits</u>.

The entity with which a noun phrase is contrasted is understood sometimes from the discourse context and sometimes from the nonlinguistic context. In the following example, *Hilda* could be marked contrastively if the sentence were part of a conversation about how the interlocutors dislike going to Maine during the winter.

<u>Hilda</u> likes going to Maine during the winter.

In the next exchange, between an employee and one of several managers, the noun phrase *I* in the manager's reply can be made to contrast with "other managers," which is understood from the context.

Employee: Can I leave early today?

Manager: <u>I</u> don't mind.

The implication of the manager's answer is "It's fine with me, but I don't know about the other managers." The employee can readily understand the implication from knowledge of the context.

In English, contrastive noun phrases can be marked in a variety of ways, the most common of which is by pronouncing the contrastive noun phrase with strong stress.

You may be smart, but <u>he</u> is good-looking.

Other ways of marking contrastiveness will be investigated in the next section.

Definiteness

Speakers mark a noun phrase as **definite** when they assume that the listener can identify the referent of the noun phrase; otherwise, the noun phrase is marked as **indefinite**. In this example, the definite noun phrase *the neighbor* in B's answer presupposes that A can determine which neighbor B is talking about.

A: Who's at the door?

B: It's the neighbor.

B's answer is appropriate if A and B have only one neighbor or have reason to expect a particular neighbor. If they have several neighbors, none of whom they know particularly well, B cannot assume that A will be able to identify which neighbor is at the door, and the answer to A's question must be indefinite.

B: It's a neighbor.

Pronouns and proper nouns are generally definite. Pronouns like *you* and *we* usually refer to particular individuals, who are identifiable in the context of the discourse. And a speaker who refers to someone by the name *Hilda* or *Harry* assumes that a listener will be able to determine the referents of these names. Still, there are exceptions. Clerks in a government office may say to each other:

I have a Susie Schmidt here who hasn't paid her taxes since 1947.

And they can do this irrespective of whether the speaker or hearer knows which particular individual goes by the name of Susie Schmidt.

Definiteness in English and many other languages is marked by the choice of articles (definite *the* versus indefinite *a*) or by demonstratives (*this* and *that*, both definite). But article choice is not always a way to mark definiteness. Some languages have only one article. In Fijian, *na*, the only article, is definite, while indefiniteness is marked with the help of the expression *e dua* 'there is one.'

na   tūraŋa   (definite)
Article gentleman
'the gentleman'

e dua   na   tūraŋa   (indefinite)
there is one Article gentleman
'a gentleman'

Hindi, in contrast, has only an indefinite article *ek*; a noun phrase with no article is interpreted as definite.

Maĩ kitaab D^hūūR^h rahii t^hii.   (definite)
I   book   search -ing Past-tense
'I was looking for the book.'

Maĩ ek kitaab D^hūūR^h rahii t^hii.   (indefinite)
I   a book   search   -ing Past-tense
'I was looking for a book.'

Many languages do not have articles and must rely on other means to mark definiteness, if they mark it at all. In Mandarin Chinese, word order is used to mark definiteness. When the subject comes before the verb, as in (a), it must be interpreted as definite; if it follows the verb, as in (b), it is indefinite.

(a) Huǒ che lái   le.
    train   arrive New-situation
    'The train has arrived.'

(b) Lái   huǒ che le.
    arrive train   New-situation
    'A train has arrived.'

More exotic systems also exist; in Rotuman, spoken in the South Pacific, most words have two forms, one definite and one indefinite.

Definite		Indefinite	
futi	'the banana'	füt	'a banana'
vaka	'the canoe'	vak	'a canoe'
rito	'the young shoot'	ryot	'a young shoot'

The indefinite form can be derived from the definite form through a series of phonological rules.

Definiteness must be distinguished from givenness because a noun phrase can be definite and given, indefinite and given, definite and new, or indefinite and new. The first and the last combinations are the most common: here, the underlined noun phrase in the first sentence is indefinite and new, and the one in the second sentence is definite and given.

Once upon a time, there was a young woman who lived on a remote farm in the country. The young woman was named Mary.

But a noun phrase that refers to new information can also be definite. The following sentence, in which *the plumber* is definite, is acceptable whether or not the speaker has introduced a particular identifiable plumber into the previous discourse.

The kitchen faucet is leaking; we have to call the plumber.

In certain circumstances, a noun phrase can be both indefinite and given, as with the underlined noun phrase in this example:

I ate a hamburger for breakfast—a hamburger, I might add, that was one of the worst I've ever eaten.

Clearly, definiteness and givenness are distinct categories of information structure.

Referentiality

A noun phrase is **referential** when it refers to a particular entity. In the first example, the noun phrase *an Italian with dark eyes* does not refer to anyone in particular and is therefore nonreferential. In the second example, in contrast, the same noun phrase does have a referent and is referential.

Katie wants to marry <u>an Italian with dark eyes</u>, but she hasn't found one yet.

Katie wants to marry <u>an Italian with dark eyes</u>; his name is Mario.

Out of context, *Katie wants to marry an Italian with dark eyes* is ambiguous because nothing in the sentence indicates whether or not a particular man is intended. In real-life natural discourse, sentences of this type are rarely ambiguous because of the power of context to clarify.

Referentiality and definiteness must be distinguished because a noun phrase can be:

Referential and Definite

I'm looking for <u>the dog</u>.   (that is, the family dog)

Referential and Indefinite

I'm looking for <u>a dog</u>. It's a fawn-colored boxer with a white chest and floppy ears.

Nonreferential and Definite

I'm looking for <u>the most intelligent dog</u>. But I haven't found it yet.

Nonreferential and Indefinite

I'm looking for <u>a dog</u>. Do you have any for sale?

While pronouns and proper nouns are usually referential, certain pronouns such as *you, it, they*, and *one* are often nonreferential.

If <u>you</u> can't stand the heat, get out of the kitchen.

<u>It</u> is widely suspected that linguistics is fun to study.

They have just changed the tax laws.

One just doesn't know what to do in these circumstances.

None of these pronouns refers to a particular entity: they are nonreferential.

Categories of Information Structure

You have now seen five categories of information structure: givenness, topic, contrast, definiteness, and referentiality. Other categories could be distinguished, although we will not cover them in detail here. For example, a noun phrase may be *generic* or *specific* depending on whether it refers to a category or to a particular member of a category. In the first of the following sentences, *the giraffe* is generic because it refers to the set of all giraffes; but *the giraffe* in the second sentence, which could have been uttered during a visit to the zoo, must refer to a particular animal, and is thus specific.

The giraffe has a long neck.

The giraffe has a sore foot.

The generic/specific contrast thus differs from definiteness and specificity, and must be considered a separate category.

Of the categories discussed in this section, givenness, topic, and contrast are not inherent properties of particular noun phrases. Like semantic roles, these categories can be defined only in relation to the context in which the noun phrase occurs. For example, we can identify whether a noun phrase is contrastive or not only if we know the sentence or even the discourse in which it occurs. Givenness, topic, and contrast are thus *relational* categories of information structure.

Definiteness, referentiality, and the generic/specific contrast are *inherent* properties of the noun phrase. Given a particular noun phrase (and some information about what it refers to), we can usually decide whether it is definite or indefinite, referential or nonreferential, and generic or specific without knowing the sentence in which it occurs.

Information structure is not marked solely on noun phrases. Other parts of speech, verbs in particular, can be given or new information and can also be contrastive. In the following exchange, the underlined verb represents contrastively marked new information.

Jerry comes to visit occasionally, but Hilda moves in every holiday.

Similarly, function words like prepositions can sometimes be marked for information structure. It is not difficult to come up with examples of contrastively marked prepositions.

I said the phone book was on the table, not under it!

In this chapter, we concentrate almost exclusively on the marking of information structure on noun phrases, in part because the role of other constituents in the structure of discourse is still poorly understood.

PRAGMATIC CATEGORIES AND SYNTAX

The categories of information structure can now be used to describe the functions of transformations and other phenomena found in different languages. As noted earlier, every language can express a given "thought" in a variety of ways. The difference between these various ways of expressing the same thing is most frequently a pragmatic one. In this section we will analyze a number of constructions, many of which are found in English, and illustrate how information structure is an important determiner of the choices that we make in expressing ourselves verbally.

Languages differ in the extent to which and the way in which pragmatic information is encoded in morphology and syntax. Some languages like Japanese have function words whose sole purpose is to indicate pragmatic categories. Other languages like English depend on syntactic transformations like passivization to convey pragmatic information. Intonation is also used in many languages to mark contrast, for example. In English, intonation is an important tool in marking information structure; it is less important in languages like French and unimportant in Chinese. Thus different languages use different strategies to encode pragmatic information. What follows is a sampling of some of these strategies.

Fronting

The first strategy that may be used to mark information structure is fronting. *Fronting* is a movement transformation that operates in many languages, although its exact function varies from language to language. In English, it creates sentence (a) from the structure underlying sentence (b), which has the same meaning.

(a)   Hilda I cannot stand.

(b)   I cannot stand Hilda.

In English, the main function of fronting is to mark givenness. The fronted noun phrase must represent given information.

A: I heard that you really like mushrooms.

B: <u>Mushrooms</u> I'd kill for.

A noun phrase can be fronted if its referent is part of a set that has been mentioned previously in the discourse, even though it may not represent given information itself. In the following, *mushrooms* is a hyponym of *vegetable*, which is mentioned in the question that immediately precedes the fronted noun phrase; the result is pragmatically acceptable.

A: What's your favorite vegetable?

B: Mushrooms I find delicious.

Fronted noun phrases are often contrastive in English.

A: Do you eat cauliflower?

B: I hate cauliflower, but <u>mushrooms</u> I find delicious.

The fronted noun phrase must be the more salient element of the sentence. If this requirement is violated, the result is pragmatically ill formed. In B's answer in the following interaction, *mushrooms* is not the most salient element in the sentence, because the hearer's attention is distracted by the phrase *with butter and parsley*.

A: What's your favorite vegetable?

B: *Mushrooms I love to eat with butter and parsley.

(In this chapter, asterisks * are used to mark not ungrammatical sentences but sentences that are pragmatically ill formed—that is, sentences that do not fit well into the discourse context in which they occur.)

In other languages, fronted noun phrases do not necessarily have the same function as in English. In Mandarin Chinese, fronted noun phrases are commonly used to represent the topic of the sentence.

Zhèi běn   shū pí zi hěn hǎo kàn.
this Classifier book cover very good-looking
'This book, the cover is nice looking.'

Zhèi ge   zhǎn lǎn huì, wǒ kàn dào hěn duō   yóu huàr.
this Classifier exhibition   I   see   very many painting
'(At) this exhibition, I saw many paintings.'

What is interesting about Chinese fronted noun phrases is that they do not necessarily have a semantic role in the rest of the sentence. In the following sentence, for example, *mó gu* 'mushrooms' cannot be a patient because the sentence already has a patient: *zhèi ge dōng xi* 'that sort of thing.' Yet the sentence is both grammatical and pragmatically acceptable.

Mó gu   wǒ hěn xǐ huan chī zhèi ge   dōng xi.
mushroom I   very like   eat this Classifier thing
'Mushrooms, I like to eat that sort of thing.'

Furthermore, fronted noun phrases do not need to be contrastive in Chinese, though they frequently are in English.

The comparison of English and Chinese fronting illustrates an important point: a grammatical process such as a movement transformation may have comparable syntactic properties in two languages, but its pragmatic functions may differ considerably.

Left-Dislocation

Left-dislocation is a transformation that derives sentences like the following (a) from the same underlying structures as basic sentences like (b).

(a)   Margaret, I can't stand her.

(b)   I can't stand Margaret.

Though left-dislocation is syntactically similar to fronting, there are several differences between the two. In particular, a fronted noun phrase does not leave a pronoun in the sentence, whereas a left-dislocated noun phrase does.

Margaret I can't stand.   (fronting)

Margaret, I can't stand her.   (left-dislocation)

Unlike fronted noun phrases, a left-dislocated noun phrase is also set off from the rest of the sentence by a very short pause, represented in writing by a comma. Left-dislocation is similar in nature and function to *right-dislocation*, which moves the noun phrases to the right of a sentence.

I can't stand her, Margaret.

In this discussion, we will concentrate on left-dislocation.

Left-dislocation is primarily used to reintroduce given information that has not been talked about for a while. In the following long example, the speaker lists a number of people and comments on them. Harold, one of the people mentioned earlier in the discourse, is reintroduced in the last sentence. Because nothing has been said about Harold in the previous two sentences, the speaker reintroduces *Harold* as a left-dislocated noun phrase.

I've kept in touch with many people from my school days. I still see Harold, who was my best friend in high school. And then there's Jim, who was my college roommate, and Stan and Hilda, who I met in my sophomore year at State. I really like Jim and Stan and Hilda. But Harold, I can't stand him now.

In addition to reintroducing given information, left-dislocation is contrastive. In this example, *Harold* clearly contrasts with *Jim, Stan,* and *Hilda*. As a result of its double function, left-dislocation is typically used when speakers go through lists and make comments about each individual element in the list.

Some languages exploit left-dislocation considerably more frequently than English does. In spoken colloquial French, left-dislocated noun phrases are frequent, considerably more so than the equivalent basic sentences.

<u>Mon frère</u>,   il s'en va en Mongolie.
my   brother he is-going to Mongolia
'My brother, he is leaving for Mongolia.'

Right-dislocation, illustrated by the following sentence, is equally common.

J' sais   pas, <u>moi</u>, c'qu'il   veux.
I know not me   what-he wants
'Me, I don't know what he wants.'

Left-dislocation in colloquial French has a different function from the equivalent transformation in English. In French, a left-dislocated noun phrase represents a topic. Left-dislocated noun phrases are particularly frequent when a new topic is introduced into the discourse (as in the first of the following examples) or when the speaker wishes to shift the topic of the discourse (as in the second example).

[Asking directions of a stranger in the street]
Pardon,   <u>la gare</u>,   où   elle est?
excuse-me the station where it   is
'Excuse me, where is the station?'

Pierre: Moi, j'aime bien les croissants.
me   I like   the croissants
'Me, I like croissants.'

Marie: Oui, mais <u>le   pain   frais</u>, c'est bon   aussi.
yes   but the bread fresh it-is good too
'Yes, but fresh bread is also good.'

The pragmatic function of left-dislocation in French is thus considerably broader than its function in English.

Clefting and Pseudoclefting

Clefting and *pseudoclefting* are transformations that are commonly used in English and many other languages to mark information structure in the sentence. In the next examples, sentence (a) is a cleft sentence, sentence (b) is a pseudocleft sentence, and sentence (c) is the basic sentence that corre-sponds to (a) and (b)—that is, the sentence that is derived from the same underlying structure but to which no transformation has applied.

(a)   It was Harold that Stan saw at the party.

(b)   What Stan saw at the party was Harold.

(c)   Stan saw Harold at the party.

Cleft sentences are of the form *It* BE ... *that*, in which BE stands for some form of the verb *to be* (such as *is*, *was*, or *will be*) and what comes between the first part and the second part of the construction is the clefted noun phrase or prepositional phrase. Pseudocleft constructions can be of the form WH-word ... BE, in which the WH-word is usually *what*. In pseudocleft constructions, the pseudoclefted noun phrase or prepositional phrase is placed after the verb *to be*, and the rest of the clause is placed between the two parts of the construction. Other variants of pseudocleft sentences also exist.

> *the one that/who* ... BE
> The one who saw Harold at the party was Stan.
>
> ... BE *what/who* ...
> Harold is who John saw at the party.

Both cleft and pseudocleft constructions are used to mark givenness. In a cleft construction, the clefted noun phrase presents new information, and the rest of the sentence is given information. Thus the information question in (a) can be answered with (b), in which the answer to the question is clefted, but not with (c) because the clefted element is not the requested new information.

(a)   Who did Stan see at the party?

(b)   It was Harold that Stan saw at the party.

(c)   *It was Stan who saw Harold at the party.

That the part of the sentence following *that* in a cleft sentence presents given information is illustrated by the fact that it can refer to something just mentioned in the previous sentence. In the following example, the second sentence is a cleft construction in which the elements following *that* are simply repeated from the previous sentence in the discourse.

> Alice told me that Stan saw someone at the party that he knew from his high school days. It turns out that it was Harold <u>that Stan saw at the party</u>.

Clearly, the element following *that* in a cleft sentence represents given information.

Pseudocleft constructions are similar to cleft constructions. In pseudocleft sentences, the new information comes after the verb *to be*, and the rest of the clause is placed between the WH-word and the *be* verb.

(a)   What did Stan see at the party?

(b)   What Stan saw at the party was Harold dancing the rhumba.

Question (a) could not be answered with either of the following pseudoclefted sentences (c) or (d) because in neither of these sentences is the pseudoclefted noun phrase the new information.

(c)   *The one who saw Harold dancing the rhumba was Stan.

(d)   *Where Stan saw Harold was at the party.

The rest of a pseudoclefted sentence marks given information, as in clefted sentences. The following sentence pair, in which given information is underlined, illustrates this fact.

I liked her latest novel very much. In particular, what <u>I liked about it</u> was the way the characters' personalities are developed.

The effect of both clefting and pseudoclefting is to highlight which element is new information and which element is given information.

In addition, both constructions can mark contrast. Consider the following two sequences. In the first sequence (in which the second sentence is a cleft construction) and the second (whose second sentence is a pseudocleft), the new information can easily be understood as being contrastive. Possible implied information is provided in square brackets after each example.

Alice said that Stan saw someone at the party that he knew from his high school days. It turns out it was Harold <u>that Stan saw at the party</u>. [. . . not Larry, as you might have thought.]

I liked her latest novel very much. In particular, what <u>I liked about it</u> was the way the characters' personalities are developed. [. . . I liked the character development more than the style of writing.]

You might wonder why English should have two constructions with the same function. Languages usually exploit different structures for different purposes—and, indeed, there is a subtle difference in the uses for these two constructions. A cleft construction can be used to mark given information that the listener or reader is not necessarily thinking about; in a pseudocleft construction, though, the listener or reader *must* be thinking about the given information. Thus it is possible to begin a narrative with a cleft construction but not with a pseudocleft construction. This first sentence, a cleft construction, would be an acceptable opening sentence for a written historical narrative; but the second sentence, a pseudocleft construction, would not normally make a good beginning.

It was to gain their independence from Britain that the colonists started the Revolution.

*What the colonists started the Revolution to gain was their independence from Britain.

The first sentence is an acceptable opening because it does not necessarily assume that the reader has in mind the given information ("the colonists started the Revolution") when the narrative begins. The second sentence does assume that the given information is in the reader's mind and thus does not make a good opening sentence.

The difference between cleft and pseudocleft constructions shows that given information is not an absolute notion. There may be different types of givenness: information that the listener knows but is not necessarily thinking about at the moment versus information that the listener both knows and is thinking about.

Clearly, the contrast between given information and new information is important for explaining the functional differences between many constructions in many languages. But language users are also capable of more subtle distinctions: they can know a piece of information without necessarily thinking about it, or they can know a piece of information and be thinking about it. It is not surprising that these different capacities of our memory should be reflected in language.

Sentence Stress

In English and some other languages, intonation is an important information-marking device. Generally, noun phrases representing new information receive stronger stress than noun phrases representing given information, and they are uttered on a slightly higher pitch than the rest of the sentence. This is called *new-information stress*.

A: Whose foot marks are these on the sofa?

B: They're <u>Hilda's</u> foot marks.

English speakers also exploit stress to mark contrast.

A: Are these your foot marks on the sofa?

B: No, they're not mine, they're <u>Hilda's</u>.

They told Harold he had to put in two more years to graduate, but they gave <u>Hilda</u> an <u>honorary doctorate</u>.

Phonetically new-information stress and contrastive stress are very similar, but functionally they are different. English uses stress in very complex ways, much more so than such languages as French and Chinese.

Information-Structure Morphemes

Some languages have grammatical morphemes whose sole function is to mark categories of information structure. In Japanese, the function word *wa*, which is placed after noun phrases, marks either givenness or contrastiveness. When a noun phrase is neither given nor contrastive, it is marked with a different function word (usually *ga* for subjects and *o* for direct objects). That *wa* is a marker of given information is illustrated by the following exchange:

A: Basu ga   imasuka?
bus   Subject come-Question
'Is the bus coming?'

B: <u>Basu wa</u>   imasu.
bus   Given coming-is
'The bus is coming.'

In A's question, *basu* could not be marked with *wa* unless A and B had been talking about it in the previous discourse. But in B's answer, *basu* is given information and must be marked with *wa*. Here is another example:

Basu ga   imasu.   <u>Basu wa</u>   konde imasu.
bus   Subject coming-is bus   Given crowded-is
'The bus is coming. The bus is crowded.'

Japanese *wa* also marks contrastive information, as in the following sentence:

<u>Basu wa</u>   imasu,   demo <u>takushī wa</u>   kimasen.
bus   Contrast coming-is but   taxi   Contrast coming-isn't
'The bus is coming, but the taxi isn't (coming).'

Here, *basu wa* need not represent given information, for *wa* can simply mark the fact that the noun phrase to which it is attached is in contrast with another noun phrase also marked with *wa* (*takushī* 'taxi').

Like Japanese, many languages use function words to mark different categories of information structure. This device is the most transparent way of marking information structure. Unlike movement transformations, such grammatical morphemes as Japanese *wa* do not affect the overall shape of a sentence; rather, in a straightforward fashion, they point out which element of a sentence is given, which is contrastive, and so on.

Passives

As with other languages that have a passive construction, the choice between an active sentence and its passive equivalent can be exploited in

English to mark information structure. Compare the following sentences:

(a)   The old man was scolding the mermaid.

(b)   The mermaid was being scolded by the old man.

(c)   The mermaid was being scolded.

Of these three sentences, all of which can describe essentially the same situation, (a) is active, while the other two are passive structures. In (b), the agent is expressed (*by the old man*), whereas there is no expressed agent in (c). We call a passive construction like (b) an *agent passive* construction; (c) is an example of an *agentless passive*.

In general, speakers and writers of English prefer active to passive sentences. What makes a sentence like *A good time was had by all* humorous is the fact that it is passive without a reason. Such unmotivated passives occur frequently among beginning writers, who appear to labor under the mis-apprehension that passive structures are more literary than active ones. (On the stylistic distribution of active and passive structures, see Chapter 13.)

Agentless and agent passives are used in English for specific purposes. First of all, a sentence is expressed as an agentless passive if the agent is particularly unimportant in the action or state that the sentence describes. Such a situation may arise, for example, when the agent is a generic entity whose identity is irrelevant to the point of the sentence.

A new shopping mall is being built near the Interstate.

New Christmas stamps are issued every year.

Linguistics 100 has been canceled today.

In the first sentence, the agent is likely to be some real-estate developer; in the second sentence, the postal authorities; in the third sentence, the linguistics department or the professor. In each case, the exact identity of the agent is either known or irrelevant to the situation described by the sentence. In spoken language, agentless passives are often equivalent to active sentences with an indefinite and nonreferential pronoun *they*.

They're building a new shopping mall near the Interstate.

They issue new Christmas stamps every year.

They've canceled Linguistics 100 today.

An agent passive construction is used if a noun phrase other than the agent is given information. Suppose that a news report begins as follows:

The World Health Organization held its annual meeting last week in Geneva.

This sentence establishes the *meeting* as given information for the rest of the report. If the next sentence uses the noun phrase *the meeting*, it is likely that the phrase will occur in subject position because it is given information. If the noun phrase *the meeting* does not have the semantic role of agent in the next sentence, the sentence is likely to be expressed as a passive construction in order to allow *the meeting* to be the grammatical subject.

The meeting was organized by health administrators from fifty countries.

This rule is of course not absolute, and indeed there is nothing fundamentally wrong with the following sequence, in which the second sentence is active rather than the passive predicted by the rule.

The World Health Organization held its annual meeting last week in Geneva. Health administrators from fifty countries organized the meeting.

But the equivalent sequence with a passive second sentence seems to flow better and may be easier to understand:

The World Health Organization held its annual meeting last week in Geneva. The meeting was organized by health administrators from fifty countries.

Clearly, in English the choice of a passive sentence over its active counterpart is regulated by information structure. Specifically, agentless passives are used when the agent is either known or is not significant; agent passives are used when a noun phrase other than the agent of the sentence is more prominent as given information than the agent itself.

Not all languages have a passive construction. Chinese and Samoan, for example, do not. Such languages have other ways of saying what English speakers express with the passive. In Samoan, for example, when the agent of a sentence is not important, it is simply not expressed; the sentence remains an active structure.

ʔua   ʔoteŋia le keiŋe.
Present-tense scold   the young-woman
'The young woman is being scolded.'
(Literally: 'Is scolding the young woman.')

Word Order

Many languages use the sequential order of noun phrases to mark differences in information structure. English cannot use the full resources of word order for this purpose because it uses word order to mark subjects and direct objects (see Chapter 5). In the following English sentence, the word order indicates who is doing the chasing and who is being chased.

The cat is chasing the dog.

If we invert the two noun phrases, the semantics of the sentence (who is agent and who is patient) changes.

The dog is chasing the cat.

In a language like Russian, however, we can scramble the noun phrases without changing the semantics. All the following sentences mean the same thing.

Koška presleduet sobaku.
cat   is chasing dog

Sobaku presleduet koška.
Presleduet koška sobaku.
Presleduet sobaku koška.   'The cat is chasing the dog.'
Koška sobaku presleduet.
Sobaku koška presleduet.

In each of these sentences we know who is doing what to whom because the inflections on the noun vary with its grammatical function. The -*u* ending of *sobaku* 'dog' marks it as the direct object (if it were the subject, it would be *sobaka*), and the -*a* ending of *koška* 'cat' marks it as the subject (as direct object, it would be *košku*).

The differences among these versions of the same sentence reside in their information structure. More precisely, in Russian word order marks givenness. The information question *Što koška presleduet?* 'What is the cat chasing?' can only be answered as follows:

Koška presleduet sobaku.
cat   is chasing dog
'The cat is chasing the dog.'

On the other hand, the question *Što presleduet sobaku?* 'What is chasing the dog?' must be answered as follows:

Sobaku presleduet koška.
dog   is chasing cat
'The cat is chasing the dog.'

Thus what comes first in the Russian sentence is not the subject but the given information, and what comes last is the new information. In answer to the question *What is the cat chasing?*, *the dog* is new information and comes at the end of the Russian sentence. In contrast, *the cat* is new information in answer to the question *What is chasing the dog?*, and it therefore comes last in the sentence. Word order in Russian, as in many other languages, is thus used to mark givenness. Similar explanations could be offered for the other four variants of the Russian sentence we have cited, but we will not develop them here.

Typically, in languages that exploit word order to encode pragmatic information, syntactic constructions like passives, clefts, and pseudoclefts do not exist (or are rare). Russian has a grammatical construction that resembles the English passive, but it is rarely used. The reason is simple: given the rich inflectional system that marks grammatical relations, word order can be used to mark information structure, and there is really no need to use complex structures like passives to mark givenness. Passives are useful only in languages in which word order is exploited for other purposes and thus cannot be manipulated to indicate pragmatic structure.

Restrictive and Nonrestrictive Relative Clauses

In English and many other languages, there are two types of relative clauses. Here, sentence (a) contains a noun phrase modified by a *restrictive relative clause*, and sentence (b) includes a noun phrase modified by a *nonrestrictive relative clause*.

(a)   The tree that had been blocking the view was struck by lightning.

(b)   The tree, which had been blocking the view, was struck by lightning.

A restrictive relative clause enables the hearer to identify the particular referent of the head of the relative clause (*the tree* in example (a)). A nonrestrictive relative clause provides additional information (description, modification, or explanation) about the referent of the head noun, information that is not essential for the hearer to identify the referent of the head noun. Thus (b) could be paraphrased by the following (c), but (a) could not because the relative clause in (a) represents a piece of information essential to identifying the tree in question.

(c)   The tree was struck by lightning.

Nonrestrictive relative clauses are usually set off from the rest of the sentence by short pauses, represented in writing with commas.

There is no definiteness restriction on noun phrases modified by either type of relative clause. Modified noun phrases can be indefinite or definite, as in these examples:

(a)   A man who had been standing around suddenly darted inside the store.   (indefinite, restrictive)

(b)   A man, who had been standing around, suddenly darted inside the store.   (indefinite, nonrestrictive)

(c)   John objected to the report that Sheila wrote at his suggestion. (definite, restrictive)

(d)   John objected to the report, which Sheila wrote at his suggestion. (definite, nonrestrictive)

But restrictive and nonrestrictive relative clauses differ with respect to referentiality. The head of a restrictive relative clause may be either referential, as in (a), or nonreferential, as in (b).

(a)   I'm looking for a dog that has a fawn coat and a good disposition. It's my dog and it ran away.   (referential head, restrictive)

(b)   I'm looking for a dog that has a fawn coat and a good disposition. Any dog that meets that description will do.   (nonreferential head, restrictive)

The head of a nonrestrictive relative clause, on the other hand, must be referential.

(c)   I am looking for a dog, which has a fawn coat and a good disposition. It's the family dog and it ran away.   (referential head, nonrestrictive)

(d)   *I am looking for a dog, which has a fawn coat and a good disposition. Any dog that meets that description will do.   (nonreferential head, nonrestrictive)

Restrictive and nonrestrictive relative clauses thus impose different restrictions on the referentiality of the head noun that they modify.

If we now take the entire noun phrase composed of the head noun with its relative clause, we find that noun phrases modified by both types of relative clauses must be referential. Thus we cannot interpret the noun phrase *a dog that has a fawn coat and a good disposition* as a nonreferential noun phrase later in the discourse.

(e)   *I am looking for a dog that has a fawn coat and a good disposition. Any dog will do.   (nonreferential phrase, restrictive)

In (e), the sentence *Any dog will do* contradicts the previous sentence, because it implies that the speaker does not want to refer to any dog in particular. In fact, the speaker has already narrowed down the choice of a dog by modifying the noun phrase with a restrictive relative clause in the first sentence.

The function of a restrictive relative clause is thus clear: it may modify either a referential or a nonreferential head noun, but it turns a nonreferential head noun into a referring noun phrase. Restrictive relative clauses that modify already referential head nouns and nonrestrictive relative clauses, which can modify only referential head nouns, do not affect the referentiality of an expression.

Relative clauses are thus sensitive to referentiality. Modifying a nonref-erential noun phrase with a restrictive relative clause is one strategy available to turn that nonreferential expression into a referential expression.

PRAGMATICS: THE RELATIONSHIP OF SENTENCES TO DISCOURSE

We have outlined some of the basic notions needed to describe how information is structured in discourse and have analyzed a number of constructions in terms of information structure. From the discussion in this and the previous chapter, it should be clear that the syntactic structure of any language is driven by two factors. On the one hand, syntax must encode semantic structure: the syntactic structure of a sentence must enable language users to identify who does what to whom—the agent of a sentence, the patient, and other semantic roles. On the other hand, syntax must encode information structure: which element of a noun phrase is given information, which is new information, which can be easily identified by the hearer, which cannot, and so on. Schematically, the relationship is as follows:

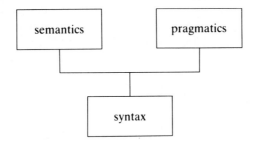

Syntax thus is used to convey two types of information: semantic information and pragmatic information.

Different syntactic constructions may have very similar pragmatic func-tions. For example, at first glance cleft and pseudocleft constructions are similar in terms of information structure. But such similarities may be deceiving; indeed, when we investigated the pragmatic functions of cleft and pseudocleft constructions, we found a difference between the two structures (see p. 229).

The differences between various syntactic constructions need not be purely pragmatic in nature. Some constructions simply have a different syntactic distribution: while left-dislocation may apply to any noun phrase of a clause, for example, fronting can apply to all noun phrases other than subjects. Such restrictions affect the choice of syntactic construction used to encode pragma-tic information. Finally, stylistic factors are also important. Left-dislocation and fronting are characteristic of informal spoken language and seldom occur in writing. The pragmatic information that is encoded with the help of left-dislocation in informal spoken language is encoded in writing with the help of other constructions such as passives.

Two languages may have the same transformation in their grammar—fronting, for example—but use it for different pragmatic purposes. A particular transformation may be used to mark given information in one language and new information in another. Although there appears to be a general tendency for certain transformations to mark particular categories (passive constructions almost always mark given information), there is no absolute cross-linguistic association between particular syntactic operations and particular information-structure categories.

It is unclear how many basic categories of information structure we need to identify, or what they are. As we have seen, categories sometimes must be refined; to describe the functional difference between cleft and pseudocleft construction, we had to distinguish between different types of given information. It is also possible that other categories like contrast need to be subdivided into different types. Pragmatics is still in its infancy as an area of linguistic investigation, and there is relatively little known about the pragmatic structure of non-Western languages.

There are at least two ways to find out how a particular language encodes pragmatic structure. First of all, we can rely (as we have generally done in this chapter) on native speakers' intuitions about particular sentences or sequences of sentences. Secondly, we can turn to spoken or written texts and observe how native speakers and writers use their own language. Such texts may consist of newspaper columns, letters, conversations between family members over dinner, political speeches, television commercials, or any type of discourse produced in any natural setting. These two research strategies complement each other.

SUMMARY

Pragmatics is concerned with the encoding of information structure—the relative significance of different elements in a clause, principally noun phrases. Pragmatics treats the relationship of sentences to their discourse environment.

Several categories of information structure must be distinguished. Relational categories include *givenness* (whether a piece of information is new or already exists in the discourse context), *topic* (the center of attention), and *contrast* (whether or not a piece of information is contrasted with another piece). Nonrelational notions include *definiteness* (whether or not the referent of a noun phrase is identifiable) and *referentiality* (whether or not a noun phrase has a referent).

The function of many syntactic transformations is to mark certain elements of sentences for these different pragmatic categories. In English, transformations like fronting, left-dislocation, cleft, pseudocleft, and passivization have the effect of singling out particular noun phrases as sentence topics or as given or new information. The marking of contrast is achieved through sentence stress and is a secondary function of certain transformations like fronting. A restrictive relative clause may be used to turn a nonreferential noun phrase into a referential noun phrase. Many languages exploit word order and grammatical morphemes to mark information structure. The functions of a particular transformation or information-structure device may differ from one language to another: each language favors particular strategies over others.

Syntax is thus used to encode two types of information: *semantic* information (the semantic role of a noun phrase) and *pragmatic* information (the relative significance of noun phrases in a discourse).

EXERCISES

1. Describe in detail why the following text is poorly constructed. Analyze each of the seven sentences in its context and state what is wrong with it in terms of information structure.

   (1) As for the Fire Department, it evacuated two apartment buildings at the corner of Country Club Drive and 5th Avenue at 3 a.m. last Sunday. (2) There was someone who had discovered a furnace in the basement of one of the buildings from which oil was leaking. (3) What was sprayed by firemen over the oil for several hours was chemical foam. (4) It was by 8 a.m. that the situation was under control. (5) What someone had averted was any danger of explosion or fire, and as for the leaky furnace, it was sealed. (6) What the residents of the two apartment buildings were given in the Country Club High School gymnasium was temporary shelter. (7) Possession of their apartments was regained by them at 5 p.m.

2. Choose a short article (approximately one newspaper column) or an excerpt of an article from the front page of a newspaper. Identify all the sentences in the article that have undergone a transformation of some kind (such as passivization or clefting). In each case, explain carefully the most likely reason for using a transformed sentence instead of the equivalent basic sentence.

3. In certain dialects of English there is a rule that moves a noun phrase to the beginning of its clause. This transformation derives sentence (a) from the same underlying structure as the basic sentence (b):

   (a) A bottle of champagne and caviar he wants.
   (b) He wants a bottle of champagne and caviar.

   The transformation is called *Yiddish movement* because it is characteristic of the English dialect spoken by native speakers of Yiddish. Yiddish movement is syntactically similar to fronting but differs in terms of its pragmatic function. Here are three pragmatic contexts in which Yiddish movement is appropriate. On the basis of these data, describe succinctly the pragmatic function of Yiddish movement.

   A: What does he want?
   B: A bottle of champagne and caviar he wants!

   A: How's your daughter?
   B: So many worries she causes me to have!

A: Are you willing to help me?
B: A finger I would not lift for you!

Compare in particular the following interactions; in the first, the answer can undergo Yiddish movement; in the second, it cannot.

A: Who is Hilda going to marry?
B: A scoundrel Hilda is going to marry!

A: Who is going to marry Hilda?
B: *Hilda a scoundrel is going to marry!

4. In English, *presentational constructions* are sentences in which a noun phrase is preceded by *there is/was* (or any other tense variant) and followed by a relative clause. Here are two typical examples:

Once upon a time there was a poor peasant who had three sons.
There's a man who wants to talk to you; he's been waiting for more than an hour.

Presentational constructions must be distinguished from constructions with *there* that indicate location, as in: *There's my lavender shawl.* Describe succinctly the pragmatic function of presentational constructions. In your discussion, you may refer to the following additional examples:

(a) There is a dog I've been looking for. It's a fawn boxer with a white chest and cropped ears.
(b) *There's a dog I've been looking for. Any dog will do.
(c) There's the new Fellini movie that's playing at the Arts Theater.
(d) There's that weird guy who called yesterday that's waiting for you in your office.

5. A noun phrase modified by a restrictive or a nonrestrictive relative clause can be marked for contrast or topic (see pp. 217–18). Provide one example of each of the following:

(a) a contrastive noun phrase modified by a restrictive relative clause, with the head noun contrastive
(b) a contrastive noun phrase modified by a restrictive relative clause, with the relative clause contrastive
(c) a contrastive noun phrase modified by a nonrestrictive relative clause, with the head noun contrastive
(d) a contrastive noun phrase modified by a nonrestrictive relative clause, with the relative clause contrastive
(e) a noun phrase modified by a restrictive relative clause that represents a topic
(f) a contrastive noun phrase modified by a nonrestrictive relative clause that represents a topic

6. As in Russian, word order in Spanish is used to encode information structure. The constituents of a sentence may be ordered in a variety of ways, as shown by the following examples from Castilian Spanish, all of which can describe the same

event. (S = subject; V = verb; O = direct object)

Consuelo envió el paquete. (SVO)
Consuelo sent the package

Envió Consuelo el paquete. (VSO)
sent Consuelo the package

'Consuelo sent the package.'

Envió el paquete Consuelo. (VOS)
sent the package Consuelo.

El paquete lo envió Consuelo. (OVS)
the package it sent Consuelo

Consider the following conversational exchanges, focusing on the order of constituents in the answers.

(a) Q: ¿Qué hizo Consuelo?
     what did Consuelo
     'What did Consuelo do?'

    A: Consuelo preparó la sangría.
       Consuelo prepared the sangria
       'Consuelo made the sangria.'

(b) Q: ¿Quién comió mi bocadillo?
     who ate my sandwich
     'Who ate my sandwich?'

    A: Tu bocadillo lo comió Consuelo.
       your sandwich it ate Consuelo
       'Consuelo ate your sandwich.'

(c) Q: ¿A quién dió Consuelo este regalo?
     to whom gave Consuelo this present
     'Who did Consuelo give this present to?'

    A: Este regalo lo dió Consuelo a su madre.
       this present it gave Consuelo to her mother
       'Consuelo gave this present to her mother.'

(d) Q: ¿Qué pasó?
     what occurred
     'What happened?'

    A: Se murió Consuelo.
       died Consuelo
       'Consuelo died.'

(e) Q: ¿Recibió Consuelo el premio?
     received Consuelo the prize
     'Did Consuelo get the prize?'

    A: No, el premio lo recibió Paquita.
       no the prize it received Paquita
       'No, *Paquita* got the prize.'

(f) Q: ¿Recibió Consuelo esta carta?
  received Consuelo this letter
  'Did Consuelo get this letter?'

  A: No, Consuelo recibió   este paquete.
  no Consuelo received this package
  'No, Consuelo got this *package*.'

(g) Q: ¿Recibió Consuelo el premio?
  received Consuelo the prize
  'Did Consuelo get the prize?'

  A: Sí, el premio lo recibió   Consuelo.
  yes the prize   it received Consuelo
  'Yes, Consuelo got the prize.'

(A) On the basis of these data, describe how word order is used to mark information structure in statements (but not in questions). In particular, state which categories of information structure are marked through which word order possibility. Make the statement of your rules as general as possible.

(B) Notice that in certain sentences the pronoun *lo* 'it' appears before the verb. What is the syntactic rule that dictates when it should and should not appear? Which rule of English does the presence of the pronoun in these sentences remind you of?

7. In Tongan, a transformation called *noun-incorporation* incorporates the direct object into the verb, forming a verb-noun compound. It generates a sentence like (a) from the same underlying structure as the basic sentence (b):

(a) Na?a   ku inu   pia.
   Past-tense I   drink beer
   'I drank beer.'   (literally: 'I beer-drank.')

(b) Na?a   ku inu   ?a   e   pia.
   Past-tense I   drink Object the beer
   'I drank the/a beer.'

Following are a few more examples of object-incorporated constructions in Tongan (translated in loose English to highlight the meaning of the Tongan sentence):

?oku   nau fie kai   ika.
Present-tense they hungry-for fish
'They are fish-hungry.'

Na?a   ma sio faiva.
Past-tense we see movie
'We (went) movie-watching.'

?oku   ne fa?u   hiva kakala.
Present-tense she compose love-song
'She is love-song composing.'

An incorporated direct object cannot be followed by a restrictive relative clause, while a direct object that has not been incorporated can be. Compare:

*Na?a   ku inu pia [na?a   nau omai].
Past-tense I drink beer Past-tense they give-me
'I drank beer [that they gave me].'

Na?a   ku inu ?a   e pia [na?a   nau omai].
Past-tense I drink Object the beer Past-tense they give-me
'I drank the/a beer [that they gave me].'

Assuming that restrictive relative clauses have the same function in Tongan and English, describe the pragmatic function of Tongan object-incorporation.

SUGGESTIONS FOR FURTHER READING

Overviews of the issues addressed in this chapter can be found in Leech (1983), Brown and Yule (1983), Foley and Van Valin (1985), Givón (1979a), and Chafe (1976). The papers in Givón (1979b) and Li (1976) investigate the interaction of syntax and pragmatics in various languages. Chafe (1970) is an important study of this interaction in English. Givenness and related topics are discussed in Gundel (1977) and Prince (1979), definiteness in Hawkins (1979). Japanese *wa* and other particles are discussed in Kuno (1973). Our discussion of English cleft and pseudocleft constructions is based on Prince (1978) and that of fronting and Yiddish movement on Prince (1981). Lambrecht (1981) is an analysis of left- and right-dislocation in spoken French; left-dislocation in Italian is discussed in Duranti and Ochs (1979).

English passive constructions are investigated in Thompson (1987) and in Weiner and Labov (1983). There is a concise discussion of the function of Russian word order in Comrie (1979), with which Thompson's (1978) study of English word order can be usefully contrasted. For an overview of research on intonation and sentence stress and their pragmatic functions, see Bolinger (1986). Other means of marking pragmatic structure in English are discussed in Halliday and Hasan (1976). Quirk et al. (1985), an extensive description of English grammar, discusses the pragmatic functions of particular constructions.

REFERENCES

Bolinger, Dwight L. 1986. *Intonation and Its Parts: Melody in Spoken English* (Stanford: Stanford University Press).

Brown, Gillian, and George Yule. 1983. *Discourse Analysis* (Cambridge: Cambridge University Press).

Chafe, Wallace L. 1970. *Meaning and the Structure of Language* (Chicago: University of Chicago Press).

———. 1976. "Givenness, Contrastiveness, Definiteness, Subjects, Topics, and Point of View," in Li (1976), pp. 25–55.

Comrie, Bernard. 1979. "Russian," in Timothy Shopen (ed.), *Languages and Their Status* (Cambridge, Mass.: Winthrop), pp. 91–151.

Duranti, Alessandro, and Elinor Ochs. 1979. "Left-dislocation in Italian Conversation," in Givón (1979b), pp. 377–416.

Foley, William, and Robert Van Valin, Jr. 1985. "Information Packaging in the Clause," in Timothy Shopen (ed.), *Language Typology and Syntactic Description* (Cambridge: Cambridge University Press), vol. 1, pp. 282–384.

Givón, Talmy. 1979a. *On Understanding Grammar* (New York: Academic Press).

Givón, Talmy (ed.). 1979b. *Syntax and Semantics 12: Discourse and Syntax* (New York: Academic Press).

Gundel, Jeannette K. 1977. *Role of Topic and Comment in Linguistic Theory* (Bloomington: Indiana University Linguistics Club).

Halliday, M. A. K., and Ruqaiya Hasan. 1976. *Cohesion in English* (London: Longman).

Hawkins, John A. 1979. *Definiteness and Indefiniteness* (London: Croom Helm).

Kuno, Susumu. 1973. *The Structure of the Japanese Language* (Cambridge: MIT Press).

Lambrecht, Knud. 1981. *Topic, Antitopic, and Verb Agreement in Non-standard French* (Amsterdam: Benjamins).

Leech, Geoffrey N. 1983. *Principles of Pragmatics* (London: Longman).

Li, Charles N. (ed.). 1976. *Subject and Topic* (New York: Academic Press).

Prince, Ellen F. 1978. "A Comparison of WH-clefts and *It*-clefts in Discourse," *Language*, vol. 54, pp. 883–906.

———. 1979. "On the Given/New Distinction," *Papers from the Fifteenth Regional Meeting of the Chicago Linguistic Society*, pp. 267–278.

———. 1981. "Topicalization, Focus Movement, and Yiddish Movement: A Pragmatic Differentiation," *Proceedings of the Seventh Annual Meeting of the Berkeley Linguistics Society*, pp. 249–264.

Quirk, Randolph, Sidney Greenbaum, Geoffrey Leech, and Jan Svartvik. 1985. *A Comprehensive Grammar of the English Language* (London: Longman).

Thompson, Sandra A. 1978. "Modern English from a Typological Point of View: Some Implications of the Function of Word Order," *Linguistische Berichte*, vol. 54, pp. 19–35.

———. 1987. "The Passive in English: A Discourse Perspective," in Robert Channon and Linda Shockey (eds.), *In Honor of Ilse Lehiste* (Dordrecht, Netherlands: Foris), pp. 497–511.

Weiner, Judith E., and William Labov. 1983. "Constraints on the Agentless Passive," *Journal of Linguistics*, vol. 19, pp. 29–58.

LANGUAGE UNIVERSALS AND LANGUAGE TYPOLOGY

8

SIMILARITY AND DIVERSITY ACROSS THE LANGUAGES OF THE WORLD

The various languages of the world are structured according to many different patterns at the level of phonology, morphology, syntax, and semantics. For example, some languages have very large inventories of phonemes, while others have very few phonemes. In some languages such as English, French, and Italian, the basic structure of the clause is SVO: subject first, then verb, then direct object; other languages like Japanese place both the subject and the direct object before the verb in a pattern of SOV. One might legitimately wonder whether the world's languages have any characteristics in common.

As it happens, there are basic principles that govern the structure of *all* languages. These language **universals** regulate what is possible and what is impossible in the structure of a language. For example, some languages have both voiceless stops and voiced stops in their phonemic inventory. Other languages have only voiceless stops among their phonemes. No language has yet been encountered, however, that has voiced stops but lacks voiceless stops. This observation can be translated into a rule expressing what is possible in the structure of a language (that is, a language can have both voiced and unvoiced stops or only voiceless stops in its phonemic inventory) and into a law that excludes a combination of phonemes that is not known to occur in any of the world's languages (that is, voiced stops without voiceless stops).

The Value of Uncovering Universals

The study of language universals is valuable for several reasons. First of all, language universals are statements of what is possible and impossible in language. Viewed from a purely practical perspective, such principles are useful in that, if we can assume them to apply to all languages, they need not be repeated in the description of each language. Thus the study of language universals underscores the unity underlying the enormous variety of languages found in the world.

Language universals are also important to our understanding of the brain and of the principles that govern interpersonal communication in all cultures. In the course of evolution, the ability to speak is something that the human species alone has developed, thus distinguishing itself from other higher mammals. However, the human species has developed not a single language spoken and understood by every human being but, rather, nearly five thousand different languages, many of which are completely unrelated and each of which is as complex and sophisticated as the next. If basic principles exist that govern all languages, they are likely to be the direct result of whatever cognitive and social skills enabled human beings to develop the ability to speak in the first place. By studying language universals and by trying to explain why they exist, we begin to understand what in the human brain and the social organization of everyday life enables people to communicate through language. The study of language universals offers a glimpse of the cognitive and social foundations of human language, about which so little is known.

When postulating language universals, researchers must exercise caution. First of all, universals are statements to the effect that some characteristics are found in all the world's languages while others are not found in any. When we make such statements, it is sobering to bear in mind that, of the thousands of languages spoken in the world, only a relatively few have been adequately described. Furthermore, a great deal more is known about European languages and the major non-Western languages (such as Chinese, Japanese, Hindi, and Arabic) than about the far more numerous other languages of Africa, Asia, the Americas, and Oceania. In Papua New Guinea alone, over seven hundred languages are spoken, although grammatical descriptions of only a few dozen are available; very little—and sometimes nothing at all—is known about the rest. Linguists proposing language universals must be very cautious that the proposed principles are not applicable only to European languages. Language universals must be valid for all (or nearly all) languages of the world, whether those languages are spoken by only a few dozen people in a small highlands village of Papua New Guinea or by millions of people in

Europe, Africa, or Asia. Since little or nothing is known about the structure of hundreds of languages, universal principles can be proposed only as tentative hypotheses based on the languages for which descriptions are available. Fortunately, many linguists are studying lesser-known languages and those about which nothing is yet known; more often than not, as first-time grammars become available they confirm rather than disprove the language universals that have been proposed.

Caution must also be exercised in drawing inferences from language universals. As mentioned earlier, these universal principles help explain why language is species specific; but there is a big step between uncovering a language universal and explaining it as a symptom of the cognitive or social abilities that humans have developed in the course of evolution. More often than not, explanations for language universals as symptoms of cognitive or social factors rely on logical arguments rather than solid empirical proof. Of course, the fact that explanations can be only tentative does not mean they should not be proposed. Rather, it means that linguists must be cautious and keep in mind that languages fulfill many roles at once.

Language Types

A prerequisite to the study of universals is a thorough understanding of the variety found among the world's languages. Language **typology** is a field of inquiry that focuses on classifying languages according to their structural characteristics. (*Typology* means the study of types or the classification of objects into types.) An example of a typological classification would be languages that have both voiced and voiceless stops in their phonemic inventories (like English, French, and Japanese) and languages that have only voiceless stops (like Mandarin Chinese, Korean, and Tahitian). Remember, there is no language in the world that has voiced stops but no voiceless stops, so that type does not exist. Of course, if we look at other criteria of classification, the composition of each category will be different. For instance, if we establish a typology of languages according to whether or not they have nasal vowels in their phonemic inventory, English, Japanese, Mandarin Chinese, Korean, and Tahitian will fall into the category of languages that lack nasal vowels. In contrast, Standard French has four nasal vowels (some French dialects have only three): /ɛ̃/ as in *faim* /fɛ̃/ 'hunger'; /œ̃/ as in *brun* /bʁœ̃/ 'brown'; /ɑ̃/ as in *manger* /mɑ̃že/ 'to eat'; and /ɔ̃/ as in *maison* /mɛzɔ̃/ 'house.' Standard French thus falls into the category of languages that have nasal vowels, along with Hindi, Tibetan, and Yoruba (a language widely spoken in Nigeria). Clearly, linguists can establish categories only according to specific criteria; the world's languages are so diverse in so many different ways that no overall typological classification of languages exists, even within a single level of linguistic structure such as phonology.

Typological categories have no necessary correspondence with groups of genetically related languages. Typological categories cut across language families. In the last example just given, English, Japanese, and Tahitian are not related languages; yet they fall into the same language type with respect to the presence or absence of nasal vowels. On the other hand, French and English *are* related, but they fall into two different types. Though language types are in principle independent of language families, it is not uncommon for members of the same family to share certain typological characteristics as a result of a common heritage. Therefore linguists are always careful to include as many unrelated languages as possible in their proposed language types, so as to make certain that the similarities between languages of any category are not the result of genetic relationships.

This chapter explores both the variety found among the world's languages and the unity that underlies this variety. Uncovering language universals and classifying languages into different types are related but complementary tasks. In order to uncover universal principles, we first need to know the extent to which languages differ from one another in terms of their structure. We would not want to posit a language universal on the basis of a limited sample of languages, only to discover that our putative universal did not work for a type of language that we had failed to consider. A universal must work for all language types and all languages.

Similarly, the way in which we go about classifying languages and describing the different types of structures is determined in large part by the search for universals. It would be possible, for example, to set up a typological category grouping all languages that have the sound /o/ in their phonemic inventory. But such a typology would tell us nothing about any universal principle underlying the structure of these languages; indeed, their structures might have little in common other than the fact that /o/ is an element of their phonemic inventory. In contrast, a typology of languages based on the presence or absence of nasal vowels reveals interesting patterns. It turns out that no language in the world has only nasal vowels. All languages must have oral vowels, whether they have nasal vowels or not. This suggests that oral vowels are in some sense more "basic" or more indispensable than nasal vowels, a fact that could be of great interest to our understanding of language structure. So this typology is a useful one in that it has helped uncover a language universal. Whether a particular typological classification is interesting or useful depends on whether it helps uncover universal principles in the structure of languages.

EXAMPLES OF LANGUAGE UNIVERSALS AND LANGUAGE TYPES

This section presents examples of language universals and of language types from semantics, phonology, syntax, and morphology. For each example, observe carefully the interaction of language typologies with linguistic universals, and note how different types of language universals are stated. A number of the examples will be taken up again in the last section of this chapter, which will examine some cognitive and social explanations that linguists have proposed to account for language universals and language types.

Semantic Universals

Semantic universals are rules that govern the composition of the vocabulary of all the world's languages. That semantic universals should exist at all may seem surprising at first. Anyone who has studied a foreign language knows how greatly the vocabularies of two languages can differ. Some ideas that are conveniently expressed with a single word in one language may require an entire sentence in another language. The English word *privacy*, for example, does not have a simple equivalent in French (which does not mean that the French do not have the notion that the word denotes!). Similarly, English lacks an equivalent for the Hawaiian word *aloha*, which can be roughly translated as 'love,' 'compassion,' 'pity,' 'hospitality,' or 'friendliness' and is also used as a general greeting and farewell. Despite these cross-linguistic differences, however, there are some fundamental areas of the vocabulary of every language that are subject to universal rules. These areas include color terms, body part terms, animal names, and verbs of sensory perception.

Semantic universals typically deal with the less marked members of lexical fields (see Chapter 6), which are called *basic terms* in this context. Consider, for example, the following terms, all of which refer to shades of blue: *turquoise, royal blue*, and *blue*. Intuitively, *blue* is a more basic term than the others. *Turquoise* derives from the name of a precious stone of the same color, while *royal blue* refers to a shade of blue. The word *blue* is thus more basic than each of the other words, though for different reasons: unlike *turquoise*, *blue* refers primarily to a color, not an object; unlike *royal blue*, it is a simple, unmodified term. The combination of these characteristics makes *blue* a less marked (more basic) color term than the others. Basic terms are morphologically simple, are less specialized in meaning, and have not been recently borrowed from another language. Semantic universals deal with terms like *blue* and not with terms like *turquoise* and *royal blue*.

Basic Color Terms   Basic color terms are one of the most striking lexical fields in which universal rules operate. Languages differ greatly in how many basic color terms are included in their vocabularies. Some languages have as few as two. In Dugum Dani, which is spoken in Irian Jaya (the western half of New Guinea), the terms *modla* and *mili*, which may be roughly translated as 'light, bright' and 'dark, dull' respectively, are the only words that can be identified as color terms. Like several other languages, English has eleven basic color terms: *black, white, red, yellow, blue, green, orange, brown, purple, pink*, and *gray*. Between these two extremes are languages with many different color term systems of different sizes.

How can universal principles be found amid such diversity? Before seeking universals in color terminology, we need to recognize that in every language there is a prototype associated with every basic term. The word *blue*, for example, can be applied to all types and shades of blue; but there is a prototypical blue, which most native speakers of English will recognize as the most typical or the best example of a blue. This shade is called the *focus* of the term. It turns out that the focus of basic color terms is essentially the same across languages. Thus, even though two languages may have very different color term systems, the foci of the color terms of one language will be the same as the foci of the color terms of the other language. The focus of the Dugum Dani word that speakers of that language apply to all dark colors, for example, is the same as the focus of the English word *black*. Research on the color terminology of many languages indicates that there are eleven basic color foci. Some languages have words for all of them, other languages for only a subset of these eleven foci.

Perhaps the most interesting observation about color term systems is that, if the speakers of a language have fewer than eleven color terms in their vocabulary, which colors they will have terms for is determined by a set of universal principles. These universal principles can be discovered by establishing a typology of languages based on their color terms. All languages that have only two basic color terms like Dugum Dani have one term whose focus is black and one term whose focus is white. (Of course, the two terms will commonly be used to refer to all dark colors and all light colors respectively; remember that we are solely concerned with color foci.) In languages that have three basic color terms, the focus of one term is black, the focus of the second term is white, and the focus of the third term is red. Languages with three basic color terms include Pomo (an American Indian language spoken in California), Swahili, and several Australian Aboriginal languages. There is no language in the world with three basic color terms whose foci are, for example, red, yellow, and white.

All languages with four basic color terms (including Tongan and Somali) have a term whose focus is black, another whose focus is white, a third whose focus is red, and a fourth whose focus is yellow, green, or blue (some of these languages have a single term with two foci, one of which is green, the other blue). Somali, for example, has basic terms for black, white, red, and green, while Tongan and Ancient Greek have a term for yellow but no term for either blue or green. Typically, in languages like Somali, the term for green also applies to all shades of blue (although a term that applies specifically to a shade of blue may have been borrowed into the language, as happened in Somali). Languages that have five basic color terms have terms for *both* yellow and green/blue in addition to terms for black, white, and red. Such languages include Hopi, Shona (the principal language of Zimbabwe), and Greenlandic Eskimo.

The pattern should now be clear: the basic color terms in all languages of the first type—namely, languages with two color terms—have foci on black and white; languages of the second type (with three color terms) have terms with foci on black, white, and red; the third language type has four basic color terms, which must have foci on black, white, red, and either yellow or green/blue; and the fourth language type has five basic color terms with foci on black, white, red, yellow, and green/blue. Thus the basic color vocabulary in languages of type 4 includes all the terms found in the basic color vocabulary of languages of type 3, the basic color vocabulary in languages of type 3 includes all the terms found in the basic color vocabulary of languages

TABLE 8-1

	Language Type			
	1	2	3	4
Basic color terms	white black	< red <	green/blue yellow <	yellow green/blue
Example	Dugum Dani	Pomo	Somali	Hopi

of type 2, and the basic color vocabulary in languages of type 2 includes all the terms found in the basic color vocabulary of languages of type 1. We can represent these patterns schematically as in Table 8-1.

The progression goes on following similar patterns. Any language with six basic color terms will have all the terms found in languages with five terms as well as a term whose focus is blue to distinguish between green and blue. Mandarin Chinese is such a language. Languages with seven basic terms will also have a term for brown (Javanese is an example). Finally, languages with more than seven terms will have terms for all the colors named in the seven-term languages, plus one or more terms from this list: purple, pink, orange, and gray. The full progression thus reads as in Table 8-2.

This universal progression can be interpreted in a variety of ways. One way to interpret it is by identifying a language typology based on color term systems, as we have done. Type 1 languages, for example, have two basic color terms, which must be focused on black and white. Type 2 languages have three color terms, which must be focused on black, white, and red. With all the possible combinations, we have seven possible language types, all of

TABLE 8-2

	Language Type						
	1	2	3	4	5	6	7
Basic color terms	white black	< red <	green/blue yellow	<	yellow green/blue	<	green blue	< brown <	purple pink orange gray
Number of color terms	2	3	4		5	6	7	8–11

which are manifest in the languages of the world. Furthermore, all languages for which we have linguistic descriptions fall into one of these seven categories. From this we can reasonably assume that all languages, including those about which we know nothing or very little, fall into one of the seven categories.

The progression can also be interpreted in terms of a series of universal rules. Several such rules were established earlier; for example, since all languages with two color terms have terms for black and white, we established a rule stating that if a language has two basic color terms they must be 'black' and 'white.' In a similar vein, we can establish a rule that describes the color term system of all language types. For example, languages of type 6 (seven basic color terms) always include in their inventory all the terms included in the inventory of type 5 languages (black, white, red, yellow, green, and blue). Since this is true for all language types, we can derive the following universal principle: languages of type n must include in their color inventory all the color terms of languages of type n − 1.

Color term systems can thus be described either by establishing a set of language types, which are defined in terms of the number and nature of the basic color terms present in the inventories, or in terms of universal rules. These rules dictate the compositions of color term inventories.

Pronouns   Many areas of the lexicon other than color terms are governed by sets of universal rules, and it is not only content words that are subject to universal principles, but also function words. Pronoun systems, for example, can differ greatly from language to language; yet the pronoun system of every language follows the same set of universal principles.

First, all known languages, without any exception, have pronouns for at least the speaker and the addressee: the first person (*I, me*) and the second person (*you*). But as with colors, there is great variability among the world's languages in the number of distinctions that are made by pronouns. The following chart presents the English pronominal system (we shall limit ourselves to subject pronouns).

	Singular	Plural
First person	I	we
Second person	you	you
Third person	he, she, it	they

In this chart, the first column represents "singular," the second column "plural"; the first row lists first person pronouns, the second row second person pronouns, and the third row third person pronouns. In standard American English the same form is used for second person singular and plural.

Turning to the pronoun systems of other languages, we encounter different patterns. Spoken Castilian Spanish has separate forms for the singular and plural in each person; in this example, the two forms of the plural are the masculine and feminine forms (the "polite" pronoun forms have been ignored).

	Singular	Plural
First person	yo	nosotros, nosotras
Second person	tú	vosotros, vosotras
Third person	él, ella	ellos, ellas

Some languages make finer distinctions in number. For example, speakers of ancient Sanskrit made a distinction between two people and more than two people in the first and second persons; the form for two people is called the *dual*, and the form for more than two people is referred to as the *plural* (the three forms of the third person singular are the masculine, feminine, and neuter forms).

	Singular	Dual	Plural
First person	aham	āvām	vayam
Second person	tvam	yūvām	yūyam
Third person	sas, tat, sā	tau, te, te	te, tāni, tās

Other languages have a single pronoun to refer to the speaker and the addressee together (and perhaps other people) and a separate pronoun to refer to the speaker along with other people but not the addressee; the first of these is called a first-person *inclusive* pronoun, and the second is called a first-person *exclusive* pronoun. In English, both notions are encoded with the pronoun *we*. In contrast, Tok Pisin (also known as Neo-Melanesian or New Guinea Pidgin) has separate inclusive and exclusive pronouns.

	Singular	Plural
First person exclusive	mi	mipela
First person inclusive		yumi
Second person	yu	yupela
Third person	em	ol

Tok Pisin is an English-based creole (see Chapter 9), and thus most of its vocabulary comes from English. The English pronouns and other words that were taken by Tok Pisin speakers to form the Tok Pisin pronoun system are easily recognizable: *mi* is from *me, yu* from *you, em* probably from *him, yumi* from *you-me, ol* from *all*, and the plural suffix *-pela* probably from the English *fellow*.

Fijian has one of the largest pronoun systems of any language. It has a singular form for each pronoun, a dual form for two people, a trial form that refers to about three people, and a plural form that refers only to more than three people (in actual usage, trial pronouns refer to a few people and the plural refers to a multitude). In addition, in the first person dual, trial, and plural, Fijian has separate inclusive and exclusive forms, like Tok Pisin. Here is the Fijian pronoun system.

	Singular	Dual	Trial	Plural
First person exclusive	au	keirau	keitou	keimami
First person inclusive		kedaru	kedatou	keda
Second person	iko	kemudrau	kemudou	kemunī
Third person	koya	irau	iratou	ira

Between the extremes represented by English and Fijian are many variations. Some languages have separate dual pronouns, others do not; some pronoun systems make a distinction between inclusive and exclusive reference, others do not.

All of the world's languages, however, have distinct first and second person pronouns; and most languages have third person pronouns, inclusive first person pronouns, and exclusive first person pronouns. A four-person system (inclusive first and exclusive first, second, and third person) is by far the most common. The four-person type of pronoun system is thus somehow more basic than a two- or three-person type. English, in this respect, is atypical.

Furthermore, variations in pronoun systems are governed by a set of universal rules. To discover these universals, we need to establish a typology of pronoun systems. Here are some of the types:

(a) systems with singular and plural forms (like English and Spanish)

(b) systems with singular, dual, and plural forms (like Sanskrit)

(c) systems with singular, dual, trial, and plural forms (like Fijian)

(d) systems that do not make an inclusive/exclusive distinction in the first person plural (like English, Spanish, and Sanskrit)

(e) systems that make an inclusive/exclusive distinction in the first person plural (like Tok Pisin and Fijian)

Types that we will *not* find include:

(f) systems with no pronouns for the first and second persons

(g) systems with singular and dual forms but no plural forms

(h) systems with singular, dual, and trial forms but no plural forms

(i) systems that make an inclusive/exclusive distinction, but not in the first person

Based on what we do and do not find in our typology, we can derive the following universal rules:

1. All languages have pronouns for at least two persons: the first and the second person.

2. If a language has separate singular and dual forms, then it must have separate plural forms.

3. If a language has separate singular, dual, and trial forms, then it must have separate plural forms.

4. If a language makes an inclusive/exclusive distinction in its pronoun system, it must make it in the first person.

Note that the converse of these rules is not true. The converse of universal rule 2, for instance, would state that if a language had separate plural forms then it must have separate dual forms; English has separate plural forms, but no dual. The implications thus go in only one direction.

It is important to note that semantic typologies and universals do not represent a measure of complexity in language or culture. The fact that the Papuan language Dugum Dani has only two basic color terms while English has eleven does not in itself demonstrate that English is generally spoken in technologically complex societies, while Dugum Dani is not. Many languages spoken in technologically simple societies have complex color term systems: Zuñi, an Amerindian language of the American Southwest, has the same number of basic color terms as English; yet it is and was spoken in a society that was considerably less complex, from a technological perspective, than most Euro-American societies. The most we can infer from these differences is that color categories are more salient in some cultures than in others. Cultures in which color categories are not salient may emphasize other areas of sensory perception, which will be described more fully in the lexicon. Polynesian languages, most of which have only three basic color terms, make complex distinctions in basic types of smells and odors, many of which do not have equivalents in English. Comparing the two examples of semantic universals discussed in this section, we also see that, while English has a rich color lexicon, its pronoun system is one of the most restricted in the world. Thus different areas of the lexicon exhibit different degrees of elaboration in different languages. This fact does not mean that some languages are "richer" or "better" or "more developed" than others.

Phonological Universals

Vowel Systems   Another area of linguistic structure in which we can identify universal rules and classify languages into useful typological categories is phonology. In Chapter 2 we discussed the fact that languages could have very different inventories of sounds. Figure 8-1 represents the vowel system of Standard American English, classified according to place of articulation. Compare this with Figure 8-2, which represents the vowel system of Standard Parisian French (a conservative dialect retaining a few oppositions that have been lost in many other French dialects). The symbol /ü/ represents a high front rounded vowel as in the word /ʁü/ *rue* 'street'; /ø/ is an upper mid rounded vowel as in /fø/ *feu* 'fire'; /œ/ is a lower mid rounded vowel as in /bœʁ/ *beurre* 'butter'; and /ɛ̃/, /œ̃/, /ɔ̃/, and /ɑ̃/ are nasal vowels.

Finally, in Figure 8-3, compare the vowel systems of two other languages, Quechua (spoken in Peru and Ecuador) and Hawaiian.

The first thing these four examples demonstrate is that different languages may have very different sets of vowels. The vowels found in French and English differ considerably: English has several vowels in its inventory that French does not have and vice versa. Second, the number of vowels in a language can also vary considerably. Quechua has only three distinct vowels;

FIGURE 8-1
Vowels of American English

FIGURE 8-2
Oral and Nasal Vowels of Parisian French

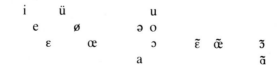

FIGURE 8-3
Vowels of Quechua and Hawaiian

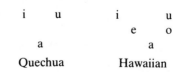

along with the vowel systems of Greenlandic Eskimo and Moroccan Arabic, the Quechua vowel system is one of the smallest found among the languages of the world. (One language, Kabardian, which is spoken in the Caucasus, may have only a two-vowel system that consists of /a/ and /ə/, with many allophones, but the facts are still not clear.) Hawaiian has five vowels, which is a very common number. At the other end of the spectrum, English has thirteen vowels and French has fifteen.

Underlying such diversity, however, we find universal patterns. The first task in discovering these is to identify vowel system types. If we charted the vowel inventories of all known languages, we would first confirm that all languages have vowel systems that fall between the two extremes represented by Quechua and French. Thus every language has at least three vowel phonemes. Some have four vowels, like Malagasy, the language of Madagascar (whose vowels are /i, ɛ, a, ʊ/), and the American Indian language Kwakiutl (which has /i, a, ə, u/). Some, like Hawaiian and Mandarin Chinese, have five vowels; others, such as Persian and Malay, have six; and so on up to fifteen.

Comparing all the charts, we find that all languages include in their vowel inventory a high front unrounded vowel (/i/ or /ɪ/), a low vowel (/a/), and a high back rounded vowel (/u/ or /ʊ/). These vowels may have allophones in some languages, particularly in languages with few vowels. In Greenlandic Eskimo, for example, /i/ has the allophones [i], [e], [ɛ], and [ə], depending on the consonants that surround it; but there are no minimal pairs that distinguish between these variants. Small variations also exist: a language may have a phoneme /ʊ/ instead of /u/, as in Malagasy. But these variations do not really contradict the universal rule, which can be stated as follows: All languages have a high front unrounded vowel, a low vowel, and a high back rounded vowel in their phoneme inventory. Note that this first universal rule is analogous to the first rule of color vocabularies ("all languages have terms for black and white"). Both are statements that describe what constitutes the minimal type in a typology of languages, and what is included in all other types.

Of the languages that have four or more vowels in their inventories, all have vowels similar to /i, a, u/ (as indicated by the first universal rule) plus either a high central vowel /ɨ/ (as in Russian vɨ 'you') or a mid front unrounded vowel (either /e/ or /ɛ/). Languages with five-vowel systems must include a mid front unrounded vowel /e/ or /ɛ/; this is the third universal rule that we can uncover from our vowel charts. In the five-vowel system of Hawaiian, for example, /e/ has allophones [e] and [ɛ]. Other languages with five-vowel inventories include Japanese (whose inventory is /i, ɛ, a, ɔ, ɯ/), Zulu (/i, ɛ, a, ɔ, u/), and Mandarin Chinese (/i, ü, a, ë, u/; the vowel ë is a lower mid back unrounded vowel, like /ɔ/ but unrounded). The majority of languages with five vowels have a mid back rounded vowel (either /o/ or /ɔ/) in their inventory, like Japanese, Hawaiian, and Zulu. In a small number of languages we find a five-vowel system that lacks such a vowel, Mandarin Chinese being an example.

	Language Type			
	1	2	3	4
i a < u		ɨ < ɛ	ɛ < ɔ	ɔ e
Number of vowels	3	4	5	6
Example	Quechua	Malagasy	Hawaiian	Malayalam

FIGURE 8-4
Summary of Universal Vowel Rules

We can thus state that languages with five-vowel inventories *generally* (but not always) have a mid back rounded vowel. This observation is applicable to languages with more than five vowels as well. The fourth universal rule thus reads: Languages with five or more vowels in their inventories *generally* have a mid back rounded vowel phoneme. This rule is stated in a different way from the first three rules in that it is not absolute. But it still is an interesting observation because it does describe a significant tendency across languages.

Languages with six-vowel inventories like Malayalam (spoken in southwestern India) include /ɔ/ in their inventory and either /ɨ/ or /e/. Malayalam has in its inventory the three "obligatory" vowels /i, a, u/; the vowels /e/ and /ɔ/, as predicted by the second and third universal rules; and /ɨ/, as predicted by the fourth rule.

All these universal rules can be summarized in Figure 8-4, a diagram that resembles the one established for color terms.

Nasal and Oral Vowels   Many more universal rules that regulate the vowel inventories of the world's languages can be uncovered, but we will mention only two more. The first states that when a language has nasal vowels, the number of nasal vowels never exceeds the number of oral vowels. Thus we can find examples of languages with fewer nasal vowels than oral vowels; Standard French, for example, has four nasal vowels and eleven oral vowels. We can also find examples of languages with an equal number of oral and nasal vowels, like Punjabi (a language of northern India), which has ten of each. But there are no languages with a greater number of nasal vowels than oral vowels.

The second universal rule of interest is not a rule in the usual sense but a description of the most common vowel system: a five-vowel system consisting of a high front unrounded vowel (/i/ or /ɪ/), a mid front unrounded vowel (/e/ or /ɛ/), a low vowel (/a/), a mid back rounded vowel (/o/ or /ɔ/), and a high back rounded vowel (/u/ or /ʊ/). Hawaiian is an example of such a language. There is something very balanced about such a system. This "balance" should be obvious if you look at the symmetry in the chart for Hawaiian vowels (see page 256). Each vowel is maximally distant from the others, thus minimizing the possibility of two vowels being confused. There is thus an ideal quality to such a five-vowel system, to which we will return later in this chapter.

Consonants Vowel systems are obviously not the only area of phonology in which universal rules can operate. The consonant inventories of the languages of the world exhibit as many universal properties as the vowel inventories, if not more. A few examples of such universals are presented here, though not in great detail since they do not differ in nature from universals of vowel systems.

You will recall (from Chapter 2) that the sounds /p, t, k/ are voiceless stops. Every language has at least one of these voiceless stops as a phoneme. We may find languages that lack affricates or trills, but voiceless stops are found in all languages. In fact, most languages have all three of these sounds, even languages with small consonant inventories. For example, Niuean (a Polynesian language) has only three stops, three nasals, three fricatives, and an approximant, totaling ten consonants (in contrast to the twenty-four of American English). Yet the three stops are /p, t, k/. When we put this generalization in the form of a universal, it reads as follows: Most languages have the three stops /p, t, k/ in their consonant inventory. This universal suggests that these three consonants are in some sense more basic than others.

It is clear, given our discussion, that this universal is not an absolute rule. Hawaiian (a language related to Niuean) has only /p/ and /k/. (That is why English words with the sound /t/ are borrowed into Hawaiian with a /k/, like *kikiki* 'ticket'). This universal is thus a *tendency*, rather than a statement of what is and is not found among the world's languages.

Another important universal referring to stops has already been mentioned. Recall that the difference between the two sets of stops /p, t, k/ and /b, d, g/ is that the first are voiceless stops and the second are voiced. All six sounds have phonemic status in English, and the same is true in French, Spanish, Quechua, and many other languages. In some languages, however, we find only voiceless stops; such is the case of Hawaiian (and all other Polynesian languages), Korean, and Mandarin Chinese. Thus far, we have identified two types of languages: (a) languages with both voiced and voiceless stops; and (b) languages with only voiceless stops. As noted, every language has at least one voiceless stop in its inventory; consequently, there are no languages that have (c) voiced stops but no voiceless stops; or (d) neither voiced stops nor voiceless stops. This typology allows us to derive the following universal rule: No language has voiced stops without voiceless stops.

Note that of the universals of stop inventories explored thus far, only one rule (and it is really only a tendency) says anything about *which* stops are included in the inventories of languages. But there are other universals that deal with this question. We will give only one example here: If a language lacks a stop, there is a strong tendency for that language to include in its inventory a fricative sound with the same place of articulation as the missing stop. For instance, Standard Fijian, Amharic (the principal language of Ethiopia), and Standard Arabic all lack the phoneme /p/, which is a labial stop. As predicted by the universal rule, all these languages have a fricative whose place of articulation is similar to that of /p/—namely, either /f/ or /v/. The fricative thus "fills in" for the missing stop. This rule, again, is only a tendency, as there are languages that violate it. Hawaiian, which lacks a /t/, has none of the corresponding fricatives /ð/, /θ/, /z/, or /s/. But most languages do follow the rule.

Syntactic and Morphological Universals

Word Order   Speakers of English and other European languages commonly assume that the normal way of constructing a sentence is to place the subject of the sentence first, then the verb, and then the direct object (if there is one). Indeed, in English, the sentence *Mary hit John*, which follows this order, is grammatical, while variations like *John Mary hit* and *hit Mary John* are not grammatical.

However, the normal order of words in a sentence differs considerably from language to language. Consider the following Japanese sentence, in which the subject is a girl called *Akiko*, the verb is *butta* 'hit' (past tense), and the direct object is a boy called *Taro*.

    Akiko ga   Tarō o   butta.
    Akiko Subject Taro Object hit
    'Akiko hit Taro.'

In Japanese, the normal word order is thus subject first, direct object second, and verb last. If we changed this order (in an effort to make Japanese syntax conform to English syntax, for example), the result would be ungrammatical.

Now consider Tongan, in which the verb must come first, the subject second, and the direct object last. In the following sentence, the verb is *taaʔi* 'to hit,' the subject is a person named *Hina*, and the direct object is a person called *Vaka*.

    Naʔe taaʔi ʔe   Hina ʔa   Vaka.
    Past hit   Subject Hina Object Vaka
    'Hina hit Vaka.'

Of course, not all English sentences follow the order subject–verb–direct object. To emphasize particular noun phrases, English speakers sometimes place direct objects in clause-initial position (*It was John that Mary hit*); such constructions are called cleft sentences. In questions like *Who did John hit?*, the direct object is placed in first position. Similar word order variants are found in most languages of the world. But cleft sentences and questions are not basic constructions, in that they are derived from active sentences with the help of a transformation (see Chapter 5). Cleft sentences and questions are also less common than sentences that follow the order subject–verb–direct object. Thus, even though some English constructions do not follow this order, we say that the order subject–verb–direct object is "basic" in English, and that English is an SVO language. Examples of SVO languages include Romance languages (such as French, Spanish, and Italian), Thai, Vietnamese, and Indonesian. Japanese is an SOV language, as are Turkish, Burmese, Hindi, and the American Indian languages Navajo, Hopi, and Luiseño. Tongan is a VSO language, as are most other Polynesian languages, some dialects of Arabic, Welsh, and a number of American Indian languages like Salish, Squamish, and Chinook.

There are, of course, three other logical possibilities for combining verbs, subjects, and direct objects besides the orders VSO, SVO, and SOV. Remarkably, however, very few languages in the world have VOS, OVS, or OSV as basic word order. There are only a handful of VOS languages, the best-known being Malagasy and Fijian; following is a basic sentence in Fijian showing that the direct object precedes the subject.

Ea   taya na ŋone na yalewa.
Past hit   the child the girl
'The girl hit the child.'

OVS and OSV are confirmed as the basic word order of only a handful of languages of the Amazon Basin including Hixkaryana (OVS) and Nadëb (OSV). By far the most common word orders found among the world's languages are SVO, SOV, and, to a lesser extent, VSO.

What is the difference between VSO, SVO, and SOV, on the one hand, and VOS, OVS, and OSV, on the other hand? In the first three configurations, the subject *precedes* the direct object, while it *follows* the direct object in the last three configurations. We can thus make the following generalized statement: In the basic word orders of the languages of the world there is an overwhelming tendency for the subject of a sentence to precede the direct object.

There is a great deal more to universals of syntax. Let us focus on the two extreme cases: languages in which the verb comes first in the clause (called verb-initial languages and illustrated by Tongan) and languages in which the verb comes last (called verb-final languages and illustrated by Japanese). For the sake of simplicity, we will exclude VOS and OSV languages from our discussion, though they follow basically the same rules as VSO and SOV languages respectively.

Possessor Noun Phrases   If we look at the order of other syntactic constituents in these two types of languages, we find extremely regular and interesting patterns. First of all, in most verb-final languages like Japanese, possessor noun phrases precede possessed noun phrases.

Tarō no imōto
Taro of sister
'Taro's sister'

In verb-initial languages the opposite order is most commonly found; in the following example from Tongan, the possessed entity is expressed first, the possessor last.

ko e tuonga?ane ?o Vaka
the   sister   of Vaka
'Vaka's sister'

We have thus established the following rule: There is a strong tendency for possessor noun phrases to *precede* possessed noun phrases in verb-final languages and to *follow* possessed noun phrases in verb-initial languages.

Adpositions   To express position or direction, many languages use prepositions. As the word indicates, *pre*positions come *before* modified nouns. In Tongan, for example, the prepositions *ki*, which indicates direction, and *?i*, which denotes location, both precede the noun they modify.

ki Tonga   ?i Tonga
to Tonga   in Tonga
'to Tonga'   'in Tonga'

Other languages have postpositions instead of prepositions. Postpositions fulfill exactly the same functions as prepositions, but they follow nouns, as in this Japanese example.

Tōkyō ni
Tokyo to
'to Tokyo'

Overwhelmingly, verb-initial languages have prepositions and verb-final languages have postpositions. The third rule can be stated as follows: There is a strong tendency for verb-initial languages to have prepositions and for verb-final languages to have postpositions.

Relative Clauses   In different languages, relative clauses either precede or follow head nouns. In English relative clause constructions (*the book that Mary wrote*), the relative clause (*that Mary wrote*) follows its head (*the book*). The same is true in Tongan.

ko e tohi [na?e fa?u ?e   Hina]
the book Past write Subject Hina
'the book that Hina wrote'

In Japanese, however, the relative clause precedes its head.

[Hirō ga   kaita] hon
 Hiro Subject wrote book
'the book that Hiro wrote'

The great majority of verb-initial languages place relative clauses after the head noun, and the great majority of verb-final languages place relative clauses before the head noun. We can therefore note the following universal: There is a strong tendency for verb-initial languages to place relative clauses after the head noun and for verb-final languages to place relative clauses before the head noun.

Overall Patterns of Ordering   We have established that verb-initial languages (VSO) place possessors after possessed nouns, place relative clauses after head nouns, and have prepositions. Verb-final languages (SOV), on the other hand, place possessors before possessed nouns, place relative clauses before head nouns, and have postpositions.

In all these correlations a pattern emerges. Notice that possessors and relative clauses modify nouns; the noun is a more essential element to a noun phrase than any of the modifiers. In a similar sense, noun phrases modify prepositions or postpositions; likewise, though it is not intuitively obvious, the most important element of a prepositional phrase is the preposition itself, not the noun phrase—it is the preposition that makes it a prepositional phrase. Finally, in a verb phrase, the direct object modifies the verb. In light of these remarks, we can draw a generalization about the order of constituents in different language types: In verb-initial languages the modifying element follows the modified element, while in verb-final languages the modifying element precedes the modified element. This pattern is illustrated in Table 8-3.

This generalization is of course based on tendencies rather than absolute rules. At each level of the table some languages violate the correlations. Persian, for example, is an SOV language like Japanese and thus should have

TABLE 8-3

Verb-initial Languages (Example: Tongan)	Verb-final Languages (Example: Japanese)
Modified–Modifier	Modifier–Modified
verb–direct object	direct object–verb
possessed–possessor	possessor–possessed
preposition–noun phrase	noun phrase–postposition
head noun–relative clause	relative clause–head noun

the properties listed in the right-hand column of the chart. But in Persian possessors follow possessed nouns, prepositions are used, and relative clauses follow head nouns—all of which are properties of verb-initial languages. Such counterexamples to the correlations are rare, however.

Notice that our discussion has mentioned nothing about verb-medial (SVO) languages like English. These languages appear to follow no consistent pattern. English, for example, places relative clauses after head nouns and has prepositions (both properties of verb-initial languages). With respect to the order of possessors and possessed nouns, English has both patterns (*the man's arm* and *the arm of the man*). In contrast, Mandarin Chinese, another verb-medial language, has characteristics of verb-final languages.

Word order universals are an excellent illustration of the level that linguists attempt to reach in their description of the universal properties of language. The table implies that in the structure of virtually all verb-initial and verb-final languages, the same ordering principle is at play at the level of the noun phrase, the prepositional phrase, and the whole sentence. This fact is remarkable in that it applies to a great many languages whose speakers have never come in contact with each other. It is thus likely that underlying this ordering principle there may be some cognitive process shared by all human beings.

Relativization Hierarchy   Another area of syntactic structure in which striking universal principles are found is the structure of relative clauses. English can relativize the subject of a relative clause, the direct object, the indirect object, obliques, and possessor noun phrases (see Chapter 5). The following set of English examples illustrates these different possibilities.

the man [that talked at the meeting]   (subject)

the man [that I mentioned to you]   (direct object)

the man [that I told the story to]   (indirect object).

the man [that I heard the story from]   (oblique)

the man [whose book I read]   (possessor)

Other languages might not allow all these possibilities. Some languages allow relativization on only some of these categories but not others. For example, a relative clause in Malagasy is grammatical only if the relativized noun phrase is the subject of the relative clause.

ny mpianatra [izay nahita ny vehivavy]
the student   who saw   the woman
'the student who saw the woman'

In Malagasy there is no way of directly translating a relative clause whose direct object has been relativized ('the student that the woman saw'), or the indirect object ('the student that the woman gave a book to'), or an oblique ('the student that the woman heard the news from'), or a possessor ('the student whose book the woman read'). If speakers of Malagasy need to convey what is represented by these English relative constructions, they must apply a transformation like passivization to the sentence before constructing the relative clause, so that the head noun phrase becomes the grammatical subject ('the student who was seen by the woman'). Alternatively, they can express their idea in two clauses—that is, instead of 'the woman saw the student who failed his exam,' they might say that 'the woman saw the student, and that same student failed his exam.'

Some languages have relative clauses in which either the subject or the direct object can be relativized, but not the indirect object, an oblique, or a possessor. An example of such a language is Kinyarwanda, spoken in East Africa. Other languages like Basque have relative clauses in which the subject, the direct object, and the indirect object can be relativized, but not an oblique or a possessor. Yet another type of language adds obliques to the list of categories that can be relativized; such is the case in Catalan, spoken in northeastern Spain. Finally, languages like English and French allow all possibilities.

In Table 8-4, which recapitulates the types of relative clause systems found among the world's languages, the plus sign (+) indicates a grammatical category that can be relativized, while a minus sign (−) indicates one that cannot be relativized.

Remarkably, there are no languages in which, for example, an oblique can be relativized ('the man [that I heard the story from]') but not subjects, direct objects, and indirect objects as well. Indeed, relative clause formation in all languages is sensitive to the following *hierarchy* of grammatical relations:

subject < direct object < indirect object < oblique < possessor

The hierarchy predicts that if a language allows a particular category on the hierarchy to be relativized, then the grammar of that language will also allow all positions to the left to be relativized. For example, in English possessors can be relativized ('the woman [whose book I read]'); the hierarchy predicts that English would allow all positions to the left of possessor— oblique, indirect object, direct object, and subject—to be relativized. The hierarchy also predicts that Basque, which permits indirect objects to be

TABLE 8-4

Language Type	Subject	Direct Object	Indirect Object	Oblique	Possessor	Example
1	+	−	−	−	−	Malagasy
2	+	+	−	−	−	Kinyarwanda
3	+	+	+	−	−	Basque
4	+	+	+	+	−	Catalan
5	+	+	+	+	+	English

relativized, will also allow direct objects and subjects to be relativized; it does *not* allow categories to the right of indirect object on the hierarchy (obliques or possessors) to be relativized. The hierarchy is thus a succinct description of the types of relative clause formation patterns found in the languages of the world.

TYPES OF LANGUAGE UNIVERSALS

In this section we will draw on the universals covered in the last section in order to classify the different types of universals. It should be clear by now that language universals are not all alike. Some do not have any exceptions; others hold for most languages but are violated by a handful of languages. It is important to distinguish between these two types of universals because the first type appears to be the result of an absolute constraint on language in general, while the other is the result of a tendency.

Absolute Universals and Universal Tendencies

The first two types of universals are distinguished by whether or not they may be stated as absolute rules. The typology of vowel systems established earlier indicated that the minimum number of vowels a language can have is three; these three vowels are /i, a, u/. The two universal rules that are suggested by the typology read as follows: (1) all languages have at least three vowels; and (2) if a language has only three vowels, these vowels must be /i, a, u/. From the descriptions of all languages studied to date, it appears that these two rules have no exceptions. The two rules are thus examples of **absolute universals**—universal rules that have no exceptions. Other examples of absolute universals include: all languages have terms for black and white; if a language has a set of dual pronouns, it must have a set of plural pronouns; if a language has voiced stops, it must have voiceless stops.

In contrast to absolute universals, we have seen a number of universal rules that had some exceptions. A good example is the rule stating that if a language has a gap in its inventory of stops, it is likely to have a fricative with the same place of articulation as the missing stop. This rule holds for most languages that have gaps in their inventory, but not all. Such rules are called **universal tendencies** (or *relative universals*). They are not less interesting than absolute universals: the fact that they describe strong tendencies across languages is significant. But they are different in nature from absolute universals.

Naturally, we must be careful when deciding that a particular rule is absolute. Until a few years ago, it would have been easy to assume that no language existed with OVS or OSV as basic word order (since none had been described) and that there was an absolute universal stating that "no language has OVS or OSV for basic word order." However, we now know of a few OVS and OSV languages, all spoken in the Amazon Basin. Thus the rule that had been stated as an absolute universal seemed absolute only because no one had come across a language that violated it. Obviously we must exert caution when stating that a particular rule is an absolute universal.

Implicational and Nonimplicational Universals

Independently of the contrast between absolute universals and tendencies, we can draw another important distinction, between implicational universals and nonimplicational universals. Some universal rules are in the form of a conditional implication, as in the following examples: if a language has three color terms, it has to have terms for black, white, and red; if a language has five vowels, it generally has the vowel /o/ or /ɔ/; if a language is verb-final, then in that language possessors are likely to precede possessed noun phrases. All these rules are of the form "if condition P is satisfied, then conclusion Q holds"; they are called **implicational universals**. Other universals can be stated without the help of a condition: all languages have at least three vowels. Such universals are called **nonimplicational universals**.

There are thus four types of universals: implicational absolute universals; implicational tendencies; nonimplicational absolute universals; and nonimplicational tendencies. Examples of each type can be identified in the discussion of the previous section.

EXPLANATIONS FOR LANGUAGE UNIVERSALS

By any standard, it is remarkable that all languages of the world should fall into clearly defined types and be subject to universal rules, given the extreme structural diversity they otherwise exhibit. It is thus reasonable to ask why universal rules exist at all. The question is extremely complex, and no one can claim to have come up with a definitive explanation for any universal. However, for many universals, we can make empirically based hypotheses at best, and educated guesses at worst, about the reasons for their existence.

Original Language Hypothesis

The first explanation for language universals that may come to mind is that all languages of the world derive historically from the same original language. This hypothesis is difficult to support, however. First of all, archaeological evidence strongly suggests that the ability to speak developed in our ancestors in several parts of the globe at about the same time; it is difficult to imagine that different groups of speakers not in contact with one another would have developed exactly the same language. Secondly, even if we ignore the archaeological evidence, the existence of an original language is impossible to prove or disprove because we have no evidence for or against the hypothesis at our disposal. Finally, if the "original" language had been a verb-final language with all the characteristics of SOV languages, for example, how would VSO languages have acquired the regularities that they exhibit today? Conversely, if it had been a verb-initial language with typical characteristics, how did verb-final languages develop? Thus the original language hypothesis is not a very good explanation; at best, it is so hypothetical that it does not adequately fulfill the function of an explanation.

Universals and Perception

A more likely explanation for language universals is the hypothesis that they are symptoms of how all humans perceive the world and conduct verbal interactions. In what follows, several such explanations will be applied to the universals established earlier in this chapter.

Perception of Colors   Remember that the color term systems of all languages are organized according to a set of specific universal rules. These rules single out two colors, black and white, as being more basic than other colors: they are the two colors that all languages have terms for, including languages with only two color terms. The physiological mechanisms through which humans perceive colors are based on three fundamental factors: the relative brightness of colors and two color/hue gradations. The two poles of the brightness gradation are the colors black and white. The poles of one hue are red and green, and the poles of the other hue are yellow and blue. These six colors are the first six colors of the color term hierarchy. Other colors are perceived as gradations along these three dimensions.

It is clear that the most fundamental distinction made in all color term systems is the distinction between maximally bright (white) and minimally bright (black)—that is, between the two poles of the brightness gradation. The four next most fundamental color types (in the sense that they are the next most frequent across the world's languages) are red, yellow, green, and blue—that is, the poles of the two hue gradations.

To summarize, the fact that all languages have terms for black and white and that many languages also have terms for red, yellow, green, and blue appears to be a direct consequence of the special perceptual salience of these colors. The colors are the poles of three gradations through which we perceive all visible light. Color term universals thus have a perceptual explanation: they reflect how we sense colors.

Perception of Vowels   A similar explanation may be proposed to explain universals of vowel inventories. In the discussion of vowel systems, you may have noticed that the three vowels found in all languages—/i, a, u/—are the most mutually distant vowels in a vowel chart. The two vowels /i/ and /u/ differ in terms of both frontness and rounding, and /a/ differs from the other two in terms of frontness, rounding, and height. There is no other set of three vowels that differ from each other more dramatically. From these observations, it is not difficult to hypothesize why these three vowels would be the most fundamental vowels across languages.

Acquisition and Processing Explanations

Some language universals have psychological explanations that have no physiological basis. The explanations for word order universals that have been proposed, for example, are based on the notion that the more regular the structure of a language, the easier it is for children to acquire that language. Thus the fact that verb-initial languages have prepositions and place adjectives after nouns, possessors after possessed nouns, and relative clauses after head nouns can be summarized by the following rule: in verb-initial languages, the modifier follows the modified element. Languages that strictly follow this rule exhibit a great deal of regularity from one construction to the other; a single ordering principle regulates the order of verbs and direct objects, adpositions and noun phrases, nouns and adjectives, possessors and possessed nouns, and relative clauses and head nouns. Such a language would be easier to acquire as a native tongue than a language with two or more ordering principles underlying different areas of the syntax. The fact that so many languages in the world follow one overall ordering pattern (modified-modifier) or the other (modifier-modified) with such regularity thus reflects the general tendency for the structure of language to be as regular as possible so as to make it as easy as possible to acquire.

Psychological explanations have also been proposed to explain the relative clause formation hierarchy. Relative clauses in which the head functions as the subject of the relative clause ('the woman [that left]') are easier to learn and to understand than relative clauses in which the head functions as the direct object of the relative clause ('the man [that I saw]'). Small children generally acquire the ability to use the first type before they begin using the second type. Finally, people take less time to understand the meaning of relative clauses on subjects than on direct objects. Relative clauses on direct objects, in turn, are easier to understand than those on indirect objects, and so on down the hierarchy:

subject < direct object < indirect object < oblique < possessor

There is thus a psychological explanation for the cross-linguistic patterns in the typology of relative clause formation: a language allows a "difficult" relative clause type only if all the "easier" types are also allowed in the language.

Social Explanations

Finally, recall that language is both a cognitive and a social phenomenon (see Chapter 1). While some language universals have a basis in cognition, others reflect the fact that language is a social tool.

Universals of pronoun systems must be explained in terms of the uses of language. Why, for example, do all languages have first person and second person singular pronouns? The most basic type of verbal interaction that humans engage in is face-to-face conversation. Other contexts in which language is used to communicate (through writing, over the telephone, on the radio, and so on) are relatively recent inventions compared to the development of the ability to carry on a conversation; they occur less frequently and perhaps less naturally than face-to-face interactions. In a face-to-face interaction, it is essential to be able to refer to the speaker and the addressee, the two most important entities involved in the interaction, in an efficient and concise manner. Imagine an argument between two individuals who were unable to refer to *I* and *you*, or who had to refer to themselves and each other by name! Obviously, the first person and second person singular pronouns are essential for ordinary efficiency of social interaction. It is thus not surprising that every language has a first person and second person singular pronoun form, even though it may have a gap elsewhere in its pronoun system. The universal that all languages have first and second person pronoun forms thus has a social motivation.

Furthermore, as noted earlier, the most frequent pronoun system has separate first, second, and third person forms, and separate first person inclusive ('you and me and perhaps other people') and exclusive ('other people and me, but not you') forms. Why would this system be so frequent and in some way more basic than other systems? Pronoun systems can be characterized as a matrix, each slot of the matrix being characterized by whether or not the speaker and the addressee are included in the reference of the pronoun.

	Speaker included	Speaker excluded
Addressee included	——— first person inclusive plural	second person singular second person plural
Addressee excluded	first person singular first person exclusive plural	third person singular third person plural

That speaker and addressee inclusion or exclusion should be the crucial factor in defining each slot of the matrix should come as no surprise in light of the fact that speaker and addressee are the more important elements of face-to-face interactions. The more basic (and most common) type of pronoun system is thus the most balanced matrix, one in which each slot is filled with a separate form.

Language universals may thus stem from the way in which humans perceive the world around them, learn and process language, and organize their social interactions. Underlying the search for universals is the linguist's desire to learn more about each of these areas of cognition and social life.

SUMMARY

The languages of the world offer a diverse panorama of structures. Some languages have many vowels in their phonemic inventory, others have few; some are verb-final languages, others are verb-initial; some languages have extensive pronoun systems, others have only a restricted number of pronoun forms. Underlying this diversity, however, universal principles are at play in many areas of language structure. The study of language typology aims to catalog languages according to types, while the study of language universals aims to formulate the universal principles themselves.

Universals are found at all levels of language. In lexical semantics, the vocabulary of basic color terms of the world's languages, which at first glance exhibits much diversity, is structured by a hierarchy that predicts which color terms are named in each type of color term system. The composition of pronoun systems, in which cross-linguistic variation is also found, is dictated by several universal rules that regulate distinctions in number and person. Vowel systems and inventories of stops are two examples of universals at play in phonology. In syntax and morphology, universals are found regulating the basic order of constituents in sentences and phrases. The relativization hierarchy is another striking example of a universal principle at the level of syntax. The salient characteristic of all universals is that the most common patterns at all levels of linguistic structure are also the most regular and harmonious.

Four types of universal rules can be distinguished, according to whether or not they have exceptions (absolute universal versus universal tendency) and according to their logical form (implicational versus nonimplicational universal).

The ultimate goal of the study of language universals is to provide explanations for such universal principles. Language universals are often symptoms of how humans perceive the world around them. For example, languages tend to highlight categories that are physiologically and perceptually salient for humans, as with basic colors. Secondly, structural simplicity and consistency make language easier to acquire and process; thus many universals predict that the simplest and most consistent systems will be preferred. Finally, distinctions drawn in the expression side of language reflect important social distinctions on the content side. Universals thus may have physiological, psychological, or social explanations.

EXERCISES

1. Determine whether each of the following is an absolute implicational universal, an absolute nonimplicational universal, an implicational universal tendency, or a nonimplicational universal tendency.

   (a) The consonant inventories of all languages include at least two different stops that differ in terms of place of articulation.
   (b) Languages always have fewer nasal consonants than oral stops.
   (c) In all languages, the number of front vowels of different height is greater than or equal to the number of back vowels of different height.
   (d) Most VSO languages have prepositions, not postpositions.
   (e) Diminutive particles and affixes tend to exhibit high front vowels.
   (f) If a language has separate terms for 'foot' and 'leg,' then it must also have different terms for 'hand' and 'arm.'
   (g) The future tense is used to express hypothetical events in many languages, and the past tense is often used to express nonhypothetical events.

(h)   Languages that have a relatively free word order tend to have inflections for case.

(i)   Many verb-initial languages place relative clauses after the head of the relative clause.

2.   In English, conditions can be expressed in two ways: by placing the conditioning clause first and the conditioned clause second, as in (a), or by placing the conditioning clause second and the conditioned clause first, as in (b). In numerous languages, however, only the first pattern is grammatical. In Mandarin Chinese, the conditioning clause must come first, as in (c); if it is placed second, as in (d), the resulting sentence is ungrammatical. No language allows only pattern (b)—conditioning clause second, conditioned clause first.

(a)   If you cry, I'll turn off the TV.
(b)   I'll turn off the TV if you cry.
(c)   Rú guǒ wǒ dì di   hē   jiǔ,   wǒ jiù   hěn shēng qì.
         if   my younger-brother drink wine I   then very angry
         'If my younger brother drinks wine, I'll be very angry.'
(d)   *Wǒ hěn shēng qì rú guǒ wǒ dì di   hē   jiǔ.
         I   very angry   if   my younger-brother drink wine

(A) From this information, formulate descriptions of (i) an absolute implicational universal, (ii) an absolute nonimplicational universal, and (iii) a universal tendency, all of which refer to conditional clauses.
(B) Propose an explanation for the universal ordering patterns that you formulated in (A). (*Hint*: think of the order in which the actions denoted by the conditioning and the conditioned clauses must take place.)

3.   The composition of vowel inventories of the world's languages is predicted by the hierarchy given in Figure 8-4 (p. 258). The hierarchy predicts the composition of a vowel inventory that consists of six phonemes. Complete the next step in the hierarchy by determining the composition of seven-vowel inventories; use the following information on the composition of the seven-vowel inventories of four languages, which you should assume are representative of possible seven-vowel inventories.

Burmese	i	e	ε	a	ɔ	o	u
Sundanese	i	ɨ	ε	a	o	u	ə
Washkuk	i	ɨ	e	ε	a	ɔ	u
Tunica	i	e	ε	a	ɔ	o	u

4.   Consider the following typology of pronoun systems found among the world's languages. The first column of each set represents singular pronouns, the second column dual pronouns, and the third column plural pronouns; and an example of a language also is given for each type (incl. = inclusive, excl. = exclusive).

Eight-pronoun systems
(a)   I   we-2   we   Greenlandic Eskimo
        thou   you-2   you   (Greenland)
        s/he   they

(b)   I   we   Arabic
        thou   you-2   you
        s/he   they-2   they

(c) | I | we-2-incl. | we-incl. | Southern Paiute
| | | we-excl. | (North America)
| thou | | you |
| s/he | | they |

Nine-pronoun systems

(a) | I | we-2 | we | Lapp
| thou | you-2 | you | (Arctic Scandinavia)
| s/he | they-2 | they |

(b) | I | we-2-incl. | we-incl. | Maya
| | we-2-excl. | we-excl. | (Central America)
| thou | | you |
| s/he | | they |

(c) | I | we-2-incl. | we | Lower Kanauri
| | we-2-excl. | | (India)
| thou | you-2 | you |
| s/he | | they |

Ten-pronoun systems

(a) | I | we-2-incl. | we | Coos
| | we-2-excl. | | (North America)
| thou | you-2 | you |
| s/he | they-2 | they |

(b) | I | we-2-incl. | we-incl. | Kanauri
| | we-2-excl. | we-excl. | (India)
| thou | you-2 | you |
| s/he | | they |

Eleven-pronoun systems

(a) | I | we-2-incl. | we-incl. | Hawaiian
	we-2-excl.	we-excl.
thou	you-2	you
s/he	they-2	they

(b) | I | we-2-incl. | we-incl. | Ewe
| | we-2-excl. | we-excl. | (West Africa)
thou	you-2	you
s/he		they
		he and they

(A) On the basis of these data, which you may assume to be representative, formulate a set of absolute universal principles that describe the composition of eight-, nine-, ten-, and eleven-pronoun systems. State your principles as generally as possible.

(B) Of these systems, the most commonly found is the eleven-pronoun system of type (a), exemplified by Hawaiian, followed by the nine-pronoun system of type (a), exemplified by Lapp. Formulate a set of universal tendencies that describe the preponderance of examples of these two systems.

5. Words for basic life forms like *animal, tree*, and *bug* refer to broad categories of living things. Languages could conceivably have very different inventories of such

terms, but when we compare these inventories among the world's languages we find that their composition is predicted by a universal hierarchical principle similar to the hierarchy for color terms. On the basis of the following inventories of basic plant form words, establish a typology of basic plant form vocabularies and formulate the hierarchy that predicts their composition. You may assume that the examples are representative of basic plant form vocabularies and that no type other than those represented here is found.

Language	Plant-form word inventory
American English	*tree, grass, vine, shrub, plant* (for small herbs)
Eskimo	*qiyuk* 'tree,' *ivit* 'grass'
Hmong (Southeast Asia)	*ntoo* 'tree,' *nroj* 'herb,' *hmab* 'vine'
Shuswap (American Indian)	*tsegap* 'tree'
Delaware	*hɪtukw* 'tree,' *skihw* 'herb'
Hindi	*per* 'tree,' *latā* 'vine,' *jhārī* 'bush,' *ghās* 'grass'
Japanese	*ki* 'tree,' *kusa* 'herb,' *shiba* 'grass'
Kalam (Papua New Guinea)	*mon* 'tree,' *mn* 'vine,' *bd* 'bush,' *mjkas* 'herb'
Zuñi (American Indian)	*tattaawe* 'tree,' *haʔtaawe* 'herb,' *peʔtaawe* 'bush'
Navajo (American Indian)	*tshin* 'tree,' *tɬoh* 'grass,' *tcilnaaskhaatíin* 'vine'
Nez Perce (American Indian)	*tewlííkt* 'tree,' *ćíxćix* 'grass,' *pátan* 'vine'

6. From a logical standpoint, the possible basic ordering combinations of subject, verb, and direct object are SOV, SVO, VSO, VOS, OVS, and OSV. We have seen that there is great variation in the number of languages exhibiting each combination as a basic word order. Linguists have recognized this fact for several decades, but there has been little agreement on the exact distribution of these basic word order variations across the world's languages. Here are results from five researchers who conducted cross-linguistic analyses of the distribution of basic word order possibilities. (The figures are cited from Tomlin 1986.)

Researcher	Languages sampled	Percentage of sampled languages that are						
		SOV	SVO	VSO	VOS	OVS	OSV	unclassified
Greenberg	30	37	43	20	0	0	0	0
Ultan	75	44	34.6	18.6	2.6	0	0	0
Ruhlen	427	51.5	35.6	10.5	2.1	0	0.2	0
Mallinson, Blake	100	41	35	9	2	1	1	11
Tomlin	402	44.8	41.8	9.2	3.0	1.2	0	0

(A) In what ways do these researchers agree, and where do they disagree? Describe in detail.

(B) What are the possible causes of the discrepancies in the results?

(C) What lesson can typologists learn from this comparison?

7. Relative clauses in the world's languages can be formed in a variety of ways. In English, we "replace" the relativized element by a relative pronoun that links the relative clause to its head (type 3). Other languages do not have relative pronouns

but replace the relativized element with a personal pronoun (type 1). For example, in Gilbertese (spoken in the central Pacific), the position of the relativized element in the relative clause is marked with a personal pronoun.

te ben   [e bwaka iaon te auti]   te anene   [i nori-a]
the coconut it fall   on   the house   the coconut I saw-it
'the coconut [that fell on the house]'   'the coconut [that I saw]'

In other languages like Finnish, relative clauses are formed simply by deleting the relativized element from the relative clause; no relative pronoun or personal pronoun is added to the relative construction (type 2).

[tanssinut]   poika   [nakemani] poika
had-danced boy   I-had-seen boy
'the boy [that had danced]'   'the boy [that I had seen]'

Some languages have several types of relative clauses. Mandarin Chinese has types 1 and 2. (In Chinese, the relative clause is ordered before its head and is separated from the head by particle *de*).

Type 1   *Type 2*
[mǎi píng guǒ de]   rén   [tā jiè jie zài Měi Guó de]   rén
buy apples   Particle man   his sister is-in America Particle man
'the man [who bought apples]'   'the man [whose sister is in America]'

Type 1 is used only when relativizing a subject or direct object, while type 2 can be used when relativizing a direct object, an indirect object, an oblique, or a possessor, as indicated in the table below. Whenever two types of relative clauses are found in a language, the pattern is the same: as we go down the relativization hierarchy (from subject to direct object to indirect object to oblique to possessor), one type can end but the other type takes over. Here are the patterns for some languages:

			Grammatical Relation Relativized			
		subject	direct object	indirect object	oblique	possessor
Aoban (South Pacific)	Type 1	+	−	−	−	−
	Type 2	−	+	+	+	+
Dutch	Type 1	+	+	−	−	−
	Type 2	−	−	+	+	+
Japanese	Type 1	+	+	+	+	+
	Type 2	−	−	−	−	+
Kera (Central Africa)	Type 1	+	−	−	−	−
	Type 2	−	+	+	+	+
Mandarin Chinese	Type 1	+	+	−	−	−
	Type 2	−	+	+	+	+
Roviana (South Pacific)	Type 1	+	+	+	−	−
	Type 2	−	−	−	+	+
Tagalog (Philippines)	Type 1	+	−	−	−	−
	Type 2	+	−	−	−	−
Catalan (Spain)	Type 1	+	+	+	−	−
	Type 2	−	−	−	+	−

What cross-linguistic generalizations can you draw from these data on the distribution of relative clause types in each language? How can we expand the universal rules associated with the hierarchy to describe these patterns?

SUGGESTIONS FOR FURTHER READING

The most readable introductory book on the study of language universals and linguistic typology is Comrie (1981), which focuses principally on syntax and morphology. Mallinson and Blake (1981) is another good introduction to language typology. Shopen (1985) is a collection of excellent essays by different authors on selected areas of syntactic typology; it is also a useful reference on the range of variation found among the world's languages in morphology and syntax. Volume 1 treats *Clause Structure*, volume 2 *Complex Constructions*, and volume 3 *Grammatical Categories and the Lexicon*. Some of the most seminal work on language universals was conducted by Greenberg, who has edited a four-volume compendium of very detailed studies of universals on specific areas of linguistic structure (1978); several papers from these volumes provided data for the exercises of this chapter. Volume 1 treats *Method and Theory*, volume 2 *Phonology*, volume 3 *Word Structure*, and volume 4 *Syntax*. Semantic universals of color terms were first proposed in Berlin and Kay (1969). Brown (1984) is an interesting investigation of universals of words for plants and animals. Lehrer (1974) is a good summary of research on semantic universals. The most comprehensive theoretical analysis of word order universals is Hawkins (1983). Tomlin (1986) is a good survey work on the basic word order of the world's languages. The relativization hierarchy was first proposed in Keenan and Comrie (1977). For a less technical discussion of relative clause universals, refer to Chapter 7 of Comrie (1981). Butterworth et al. (1984) is a collection of papers on theoretical explanations for language universals.

REFERENCES

Berlin, Brent, and Paul Kay. 1969. *Basic Color Terms: Their Universality and Evolution* (Berkeley: University of California Press).

Brown, Cecil H. 1984. *Language and Living Things: Uniformities in Folk Classification and Naming* (New Brunswick, N.J.: Rutgers University Press).

Butterworth, Brian, Bernard Comrie, and Östen Dahl (eds.). 1984. *Explanations for Language Universals* (Berlin: Mouton).

Comrie, Bernard. 1981. *Language Universals and Linguistic Typology: Syntax and Morphology* (Chicago: University of Chicago Press).

Greenberg, Joseph H. (ed.). 1978. *Universals of Human Language*, 4 vols. (Stanford: Stanford University Press).

Hawkins, John A. 1983. *Word Order Universals* (New York: Academic Press).

Keenan, Edward L., and Bernard Comrie. 1977. "Noun Phrase Accessibility and Universal Grammar," *Linguistic Inquiry*, vol. 8, pp. 63–99.

Lehrer, Adrienne. 1974. *Semantic Fields and Lexical Structure* (Amsterdam: North-Holland).

Mallinson, George, and Barry J. Blake. 1981. *Language Typology* (Amsterdam: North-Holland).

Shopen, Timothy (ed.). 1985. *Language Typology and Syntactic Description*, 3 vols. (Cambridge: Cambridge University Press).

Tomlin, Russell S. 1986. *Basic Word Order: Functional Principles* (London: Croom Helm).

THE
HISTORICAL
DEVELOPMENT
OF LANGUAGES

9

LANGUAGES: ALWAYS CHANGING

It's no secret that languages change over the years. Sometimes, especially in times of social and political upheaval, they may change dramatically. Usually, though, the changes are virtually imperceptible. Not all aspects of a language change at the same rate. There is no reason to expect that vocabulary, pronunciation, morphology, syntax, and semantics will all change at the same pace, and in fact they usually do not.

All of us can recognize different speech patterns between one generation and the next. There are probably notable differences between the speech patterns of your parents and your friends, and even greater ones between your grandparents and your friends. The most noticeable differences between one generation and another are in vocabulary. What one generation calls *icebox, record player* (or *hi-fi*), *car phone*, and *studious young man*, a younger generation calls *fridge, stereo, cellular phone*, and (in some instances) *nerd*. Our grandparents certainly didn't hear of *doublespeak, tank tops, six-packs,* or *sitcoms* in their youth; nor could they refer to some of their verbal actions as *bad-mouthing* or *dumping on* someone.

Pronunciation changes too, of course. A change is currently underway for the word *nuclear*, which a couple of decades ago was more commonly pronounced /nukliər/ but today is increasingly pronounced /nukyələr/. In the same vein, the word *realtor*, formerly pronounced /riəltər/, is increasingly pronounced /rilətər/. Regional accents and dialects change: the /r/ in words like *tar* and *beard*, which is of course pronounced in most of the United States, is now coming to be pronounced more and more in New York City, where it has been missing for a couple of centuries. Southerners raised in the age of national television programming sound more like Yankees than their parents do. And throughout the United States there seems to be an increasing tendency not to differentiate the vowel sounds in word pairs like *knot* and *nought* and *cot* and *caught*.

The meaning of a term can also change. About a thousand years ago, the English verb *starve* (Old English *steorfan*) meant simply 'die (by any cause)'; today, *starve* refers principally to deprivation and death by hunger (or, by metaphorical extension, 'deprive of affection'). Similarly, the Old English verb *berēafian* meant 'to deprive of, take away, rob'; today, the much narrower principal meaning of *bereave* is 'to deprive of life or hope.' Until relatively recently, the seven-hundred-year-old adjective *natural* did not have the meaning 'without chemical preservatives' that it now commonly has, as in *all natural ice cream*. And the meanings of *joint*, *bust*, and many other words have been extended by their use in the underground world of drugs. Finally, think of the special meanings that the words *dove* and *hawk* acquired during the Vietnam War.

There can also be morphological and syntactic differences in the speech of different generations. *Goes the king hence today?*, Shakespeare wrote in Macbeth. Today, the same sentiment would have a form more like *Is the king going out today?* simply because certain syntactic and morphological characteristics of seventeenth-century English are no longer available to the modern speaker.

Linguistic alterations very often prompt comment, especially from people who feel that language change reflects corruption and is invariably for the worse; for many, the best language forms are those that have stood the test of time. (On attitudes toward language change, see Chapter 15.) Though generalizing from one's own linguistic experience can sometimes be risky, it is safe to say that the common experience of noticing linguistic differences between one generation and another reflects the simple fact that languages are always in the process of changing, that languages do not stand still.

In this chapter, we shall explore language change itself: what kinds of change occur, how languages are related to one another historically, and how language families are established. We shall also describe the linguistic and cultural prehistory of one representative group, the Polynesians, as a way of illustrating how some challenges of historical linguistics are met.

LANGUAGE FAMILIES

One result of the ongoing changes that affect a language is that a single language can develop into several languages. The early stages of such development are apparent in the differences among Australian, American, Canadian, and Indian English dialects, all of which have sprung from the English spoken in the United Kingdom. In order for different dialects to develop into separate languages, groups of speakers must remain relatively isolated from one another, separated either by such physical barriers as geographical distance, impassable mountains, and bodies of water, or by such social and political barriers as those drawn along tribal, religious, racial, and national boundaries.

You have probably heard it said that French, Spanish, and Italian "come from" Latin. This statement is true, provided that by "Latin" one understands the many different dialects spoken throughout the Roman Empire, not the written variety of classical Latin still studied in school. The "Vulgar Latin" spoken throughout the Roman Empire lives on in today's French, Italian, Spanish, and Portuguese as well as in Rumanian, Catalan, and Provençal, all of which are its direct descendants. On the other hand, the classical Latin of Cicero, Virgil, Caesar, and other Roman writers is "dead": the written varieties of French, Spanish, and Italian are more or less closely based on the modern spoken languages, not the classical written language.

You may also have heard it claimed that English comes from Latin. That claim is false. English and Latin are indeed related languages, but Latin is not an ancestor of English. The truth of the matter is that both English and Latin come from a common ancestor, but they traveled along different genealogical paths. During the Renaissance, English borrowed thousands of words from Latin and thereby created striking lexical parallels especially in the sciences and humanities. But by no stretch of the imagination is English a daughter of Latin in the sense that Spanish, French, Italian, and Portuguese are. English is descended from Proto-Germanic, a language that was spoken about the time of classical Latin and a few centuries earlier and that ultimately also gave rise not only to English but to German, Dutch, Norwegian, Danish, and Swedish (among others). Thus, as Latin is the parent language of French and Spanish, so Proto-Germanic is the parent language of English and German.

Except for a few carved runic inscriptions from the third century A.D., Proto-Germanic (unlike Latin) has left no written records. Modern knowledge of Proto-Germanic—and it is considerable—has been inferred from its daughter languages through *comparative reconstruction*, a technique explained in this chapter. Proto-Germanic and Latin are themselves daughters of Proto-Indo-European, another *unattested* (unrecorded) language. In a very oversimplified manner, we can represent the situation by the language tree in Figure 9-1, which has two *branches*.

While the notion that languages change and give rise to new languages is not strange to modern readers, it is a notion that was postulated clearly only two hundred years ago. In 1786, while serving as a judge in Calcutta, Sir

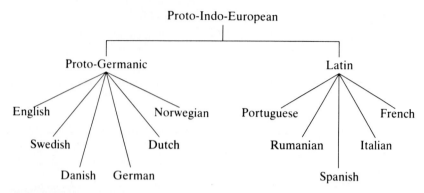

FIGURE 9-1
Germanic and Romance Branches of the Indo-European Family

William Jones addressed the Royal Asiatick Society of Bengal about his experience.

> The Sanskrit language, whatever be its antiquity, is of a wonderful structure; more perfect than the Greek, more copious than the Latin, and more exquisitely refined than either, yet bearing to both of them a stronger affinity, both in the roots of verbs and in the forms of grammar, than could possibly have been produced by accident; so strong indeed, that no philologer could examine them all three, without believing them to have sprung from some common source, which, perhaps, no longer exists: there is a similar reason, though not quite so forcible, for supposing that both the Gothic and the Celtic, though blended with a very different idiom, had the same origin with the Sanskrit; and the old Persian might be added to the same family. . . .

Today linguists would shy away from making such comparative statements as Sanskrit having a "more perfect" structure than Greek and being "more exquisitely refined" than Latin, but we must credit Jones with a clear recognition that languages give rise to other languages. Indeed, we now know that Sanskrit, Latin, Greek, Celtic, Gothic, and Persian did spring from a "common source" that "no longer exists." Jones had made an important discovery, and his formulation has proved to be a most influential hypothesis.

The common source of Latin, Greek, Sanskrit, Celtic, Gothic, Persian, and many other languages (including English and its Germanic relatives, and French and Spanish and their Romance relatives) is Proto-Indo-European. A parent language and the daughter languages that have developed from it are collectively referred to as a **language family**. The family that Jones discovered is called the **Indo-European** family. While there are no written records of Proto-Indo-European itself, a rich vein of information about its words and structures can be deciphered from the linguistic characteristics of its daughter languages. Exercising certain well-defined precautions, scholars can confidently reconstruct a parent language from the shared characteristics of its daughters. The working assumption of historical linguists is this: a feature that occurs widely in daughter languages and whose presence cannot be explained by reference to language typology, language universals, or borrowing from another tongue is likely to have been inherited from the parent language.

RECONSTRUCTING THE LINGUISTIC PAST

People have always been on the move. The past century has witnessed great migrations from one end of the globe to another—from Europe to the Americas and Australia, from the Far East to North America and Southeast Asia, and so on. This drive to migrate is nothing new; there is evidence of massive migrations from Central Asia to Europe in about 4000 B.C. by a people who probably spoke Proto-Indo-European. That far back into prehistory, there are no written records to document these migrations, but archaeologists have found buried remains from the daily life of people who inhabited particular parts of the globe. Combined with what we can reconstruct of ancestral languages, these archaeological records enable researchers to make educated guesses about where our ancestors came from, where they migrated, and how they lived and died.

When scholars reconstruct an ancestral language, they also implicitly reconstruct an ancestral society and an ancestral culture. Every language lives on the lips of its speakers; words that are ascribed to a prehistoric group represent artifacts in their culture and facets of the social and physical activities of their daily life. In this chapter, we will concentrate not on Indo-European culture and the Indo-European homeland (which are thoroughly discussed in accessible sources) but on the Polynesians, whose linguistic development presents another interesting case of reconstruction of a protolanguage and the culture of its speakers.

Polynesian and Pacific Background

On land, the only obstacles to sustained contacts between people are insurmountable mountains and wide rivers, which are in fact not very common. As a result, boundaries between different languages and cultures are often blurred. In contrast, once people settle on an isolated island, contact with inhabitants of other islands is difficult, and languages and cultures develop in relative isolation. Islands thus offer an opportunity to study what happens when a protolanguage evolves into distinct daughter languages. Because the South Pacific region consists of small islands and island groups quite isolated from one another, it provides an almost ideal "laboratory" for researchers interested in the past.

The South Pacific is home to three different cultural areas—Polynesia ('many islands'), Melanesia ('black islands'), and Micronesia ('small islands')—whose approximate boundaries are shown in Figure 9-2. Among other things, each area is distinguished by the physical appearance of its inhabitants: Polynesians are generally large, with olive complexions and

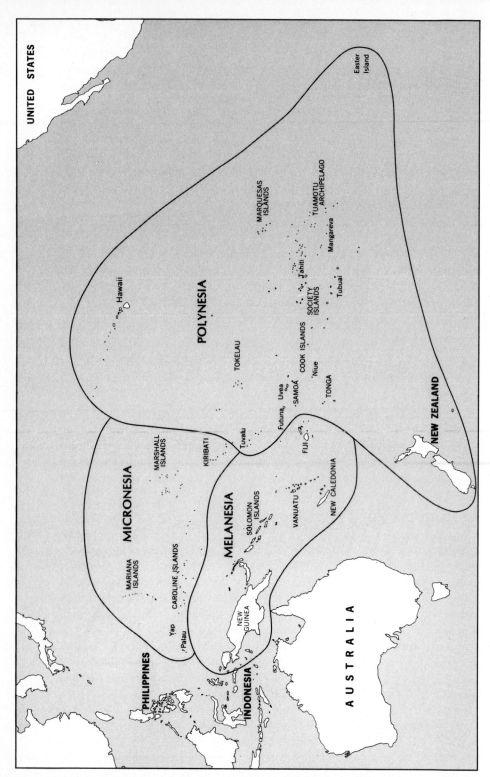

FIGURE 9-2
Cultural Areas in the Pacific

straight or wavy hair; Melanesians typically are dark skinned, with smaller frames and curlier hair; and Micronesians are slight of frame, with light brown complexions and straight hair. We will concentrate on Polynesians and ask what we can learn about their origins and their early life in Polynesia from the languages they speak today.

The islands of Polynesia vary greatly in size and structure. The main island of Hawaii and the islands of Samoa and Tahiti are comparatively large land masses formed through volcanic eruptions. Other islands are tiny atolls, little more than sand banks and coral reefs that barely reach the surface of the ocean; typically, one can walk (or wade) around an atoll in a few hours. Atolls are found in Tuvalu, the Tuamotu Archipelago, and the northern Cook Islands. Some coral islands in Tonga and elsewhere have been raised by underground volcanic activities and are medium sized and often hilly—in contrast to atolls, which are utterly flat.

There are no written records to aid in tracing the Polynesians' cultural and linguistic development because they had no system of writing before literacy was introduced by Westerners. But the modern languages and the archaeological record provide useful tools for reconstruction.

There is every indication that all the islands of Polynesia were settled by a people who shared a common language, a common culture, and a common way of dealing with the environment. That they traveled by sea from west to east, settling islands on their way, we know because the languages of Polynesia are clearly related to languages spoken to the west in Melanesia but have no connection with languages spoken to the east in South America. In addition, Polynesian cultures have many affinities with Melanesian cultures but virtually none with those of South America. Finally, the human bones, artifacts, and other archaeological remains found on the western islands of Polynesia are older than those found on the eastern islands. The obvious conclusion that western Polynesia was settled prior to eastern Polynesia contradicts the theory, popularized by Norwegian explorer Thor Heyerdahl, that the Polynesians originated in South America.[1]

The oldest archaeological records in Polynesia were found in western Polynesia: in Tonga, Samoa, Uvea, and Futuna. Consisting mostly of pottery fragments similar to those found in Melanesia, these records date to between 1500 and 1200 B.C. This implies that people moved from somewhere outside Polynesia and settled on these western islands about thirty-five hundred years ago. No pottery has been found in eastern Polynesia (the Cook Islands, Tahiti and the Society Islands, the Marquesas Islands, and the Tuamotu Archipelago), but other remains indicate that these eastern islands were settled around the first century A.D. The most recent archaeological remains are found in Hawaii and New Zealand. That these two island groups were settled

---

[1] By sailing from South America to eastern Polynesia in a reed vessel named *Kon-Tiki*, Heyerdahl proved that such a crossing could have been made, but he did not demonstrate that the original Polynesians did in fact make it. Today, while generally agreeing that eastern Polynesians and early South American Indians may have been in contact at some stage, most scientists do not think that the Polynesians originated in the Americas.

last is not surprising, given that they are the most remote from other islands of the region. The earliest artifacts found on these islands suggest that the ancient Hawaiians and the ancestors of the New Zealand Maoris first arrived on their respective island homes between the seventh and eleventh centuries A.D.

Polynesian Languages and Their History

We said earlier that all of Polynesia was settled by the same people or by groups of closely related people from a single region. Linguistic evidence can help us determine the original homeland of the Polynesians. Table 9-1 illustrates some typically striking similarities among words in five Polynesian languages. These and other widespread similarities of expression for equivalent content demonstrate that the languages of Polynesia are manifestly related. Not finding similar close correspondences in vocabulary between the languages of Polynesia and any other language, we can safely say that Polynesian languages form a language family. In other words, all the Polynesian languages are daughter languages of a single parent language, the ancestor of the thirty or so Polynesian languages and of no other existing language. Known as Proto-Polynesian, the parent language was spoken by the people who first settled western Polynesia between 1500 and 1200 B.C.

In Table 9-1, the word *manu* 'bird' is exactly the same—in form and content—in all five languages. The other words have the same vowel correspondences (where one has /a/, all have /a/) and differ slightly from one another in some of the consonants. The Polynesian words in each line of the table are **cognates**—words that have developed from a single, historically earlier word.

In examining other words, we find the consonant correspondences between the different languages to be strikingly regular. On the basis of many words

TABLE 9-1
Common Words in Five Polynesian Languages

Tongan	Samoan	Tahitian	Maori	Hawaiian	
manu	manu	manu	manu	manu	'bird'
ika	iʔa	iʔa	ika	iʔa	'fish'
kai	ʔai	ʔai	kai	ʔai	'to eat'
tapu	tapu	tapu	tapu	kapu	'forbidden'
vaka	vaʔa	vaʔa	waka	waʔa	'canoe'
fohe	foe	hoe	hoe	hoe	'oar'
mata	mata	mata	mata	maka	'face'
ʔuta	uta	uta	uta	uka	'bush'
toto	toto	toto	toto	koko	'blood'

such as those in Table 9-1, it can be seen that in words in which the phonemes /m/ and /n/ (as in *manu*) occur in one Polynesian language, they tend to occur in all. On the other hand, Tongan, Samoan, Tahitian, and Maori /t/ correspond to /k/ in Hawaiian (as in the words for 'forbidden' and 'face'). We can represent these *sound correspondences* as in this chart.

Tongan	Samoan	Tahitian	Maori	Hawaiian
m	m	m	m	m
n	n	n	n	n
t	t	t	t	k

If we examine still other words, these sound correspondences are maintained, and additional *correspondence sets* can be established. As the words in Table 9-2 reveal, Tongan and Maori /k/ corresponds to a glottal stop /ʔ/ in Samoan, Tahitian, and Hawaiian, while Tongan, Samoan, and Maori /ŋ/ corresponds to Tahitian /ʔ/ and Hawaiian /n/.

We can thus establish regular sound correspondences among modern-day Polynesian languages. Table 9-3 presents the consonant correspondences exhibited in the words presented so far.

In comparative reconstruction, it is important to exclude all borrowed words. The only words that can profitably provide sounds for use in a correspondence set are those that have descended directly from the ancestor language. For example, because Proto-Polynesian *s became /h/ in Tongan (but remained /s/ in other daughter languages), Tongan has very few words with /s/—among them *sikaleti*, meaning 'cigarette.' While *sikaleti* was obviously borrowed from a language outside the Polynesian family, words

TABLE 9-2
Cognates in Five Polynesian Languages I

Tongan	Samoan	Tahitian	Maori	Hawaiian	
toki	toʔi	toʔi	toki	koʔi	'axe'
taŋi	taŋi	taʔi	taŋi	kani	'to cry'
taŋata	taŋata	taʔata	taŋata	kanaka	'man'
kafa	ʔafa	ʔaha	kaha	ʔaha	'rope'
kutu	ʔutu	ʔutu	kutu	ʔuku	'louse'
kata	ʔata	ʔata	kata	ʔaka	'to laugh'
moko	moʔo	moʔo	moko	moʔo	'lizard'

TABLE 9-3
Sound Correspondences in Five Polynesian Languages

Tongan	Samoan	Tahitian	Maori	Hawaiian
m	m	m	m	m
n	n	n	n	n
ŋ	ŋ	ʔ	ŋ	n
p	p	p	p	p
t	t	t	t	k
k	ʔ	ʔ	k	ʔ

borrowed from other languages within the same family may not be nearly so easy to spot.

Comparative Reconstruction   The method of reconstruction that we have just illustrated is known as the method of **comparative reconstruction**. It aims to reconstruct an ancestor language from the evidence that remains in daughter languages. Its premise is that, borrowing aside, similar forms with similar meanings across related languages are reflexes of a similar form with a related meaning in the parent language. This commonsense approach is at the foundation of the comparative method and, indeed, of historical linguistics.

When we examine *correspondence sets* such as m-m-m-m-m and t-t-t-t-k in Table 9-3, it seems an easy and obvious step to assume that *m and *t existed in the parent language and that /m/ was retained in each of the daughter languages, while /t/ was retained except in Hawaiian, in which it became /k/. Such assumptions are the everyday fare of historical linguistics. When we assume the existence of a sound (or other structure) in a language for which we have no evidence except what can be inferred from daughter languages, that sound (or structure) is said to be *reconstructed*. Reconstructed forms are "starred" to indicate that they are unattested. We can represent the reconstructions from correspondence sets this way:

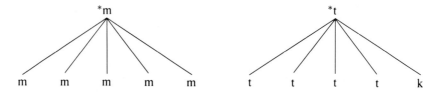

In describing the development of Hawaiian from Proto-Polynesian, we would postulate a historical rule of the form: *t > k. (Note that a shaftless arrow is used to indicate that one form developed into another form over time.) Instead of *t, we could have reconstructed a *k in Proto-Polynesian that was retained in Hawaiian and became /t/ in *all* the other languages, but cautious reconstruction and experience with many languages have led historical linguists to prefer reconstructions that assume the least change consistent with the facts, unless there is reason to do otherwise.

Let's inspect the reconstruction of *m more closely. That *m existed in the protolanguage and was retained in all the daughter languages is the simplest but not the only logical hypothesis. For example, we could hypothesize some other sound in the protolanguage that independently became /m/ in each daughter language. Both the *bilabial* *b and the *nasal* *n would be likely candidates for this reconstruction in that they share phonetic features with /m/, a *bilabial nasal*. However, since Polynesian languages generally lack the phoneme /b/, it seems more reasonable to assume that the parent language also lacked *b. Alternatively, we could reconstruct an *n that changed to /m/ in all the daughters independently of one another. This hypothesis must be rejected for two reasons: first, it is not a minimal assumption; second, the daughter languages have an /n/ that also must have a source in the parent language. We thus postulate reconstructed Proto-Polynesian *m and *n, which were retained unchanged in all the daughter languages.

Let's examine one other correspondence set: ŋ-ŋ-ʔ-ŋ-n. We have just postulated Proto-Polynesian *n as the reconstructed **etymon**, or earlier form, of the correspondence set n-n-n-n-n. It is interesting to compare this reconstruction with one for the correspondence set ŋ-ŋ-ʔ-ŋ-n, for which the most likely reconstruction is *ŋ.

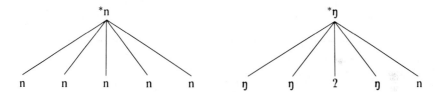

Thus *ŋ was retained in Tongan, Samoan, and Maori but became /ʔ/ in Tahitian and /n/ in Hawaiian. As a result, the distinction between *n and *ŋ that existed in Proto-Polynesian and is maintained in Tongan, Samoan, and Maori does not exist in Hawaiian, in which *n and *ŋ have merged in /n/. Hawaiian /n/ therefore has two historical sources. We can represent the historical merger in rules (*n > n; *ŋ > n) or schematically.

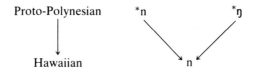

Subgroups   On the basis of lexical and structural characteristics, it is apparent that some Polynesian languages are more closely linked than others. As shown in Table 9-4, Tongan differs from other Polynesian languages in at least two respects: it has initial /h/ where other languages do not have anything; and it has nothing where other languages have either /l/ or /r/.

TABLE 9-4
Cognates in Five Polynesian Languages II

Tongan	Samoan	Tahitian	Maori	Hawaiian	
hama	ama	ama	ama	ama	'outrigger'
hiŋoa	iŋoa	iʔoa	iŋoa	inoa	'name'
mohe	moe	moe	moe	moe	'to sleep'
hake	aʔe	aʔe	ake	aʔe	'up'
ua	lua	rua	rua	lua	'two'
ama	lama	rama	rama	lama	'torch'
tui	tuli	turi	turi	kuli	'knee'

Niuean, another Polynesian language, shares these and certain other characteristics with Tongan. On the basis of such evidence, Tongan and Niuean can be seen to form a **subgroup**, or *branch*, of Polynesian. This implies that Tongan and Niuean were at one time a single language distinct from Proto-Polynesian and that Proto-Tongic, as it is called, developed certain features before splitting into Tongan and Niuean. The retention in both languages of these features (those that developed after Proto-Tongic split from Proto-Polynesian but before Tongan and Niuean split into separate languages) constitutes the characteristic shared features of the Proto-Tongic branch of the Polynesian family.

In the meantime, the other branch of Proto-Polynesian also evolved independently after its speakers lost contact with speakers of Proto-Tongic. As this second branch, called Proto-Nuclear-Polynesian, developed its distinctive characteristics, it emerged as a separate language that gave rise to others. Except for Tongan and Niuean, all modern Polynesian languages share certain features inherited from Proto-Nuclear-Polynesian. In turn,

FIGURE 9-3
Polynesian Languages

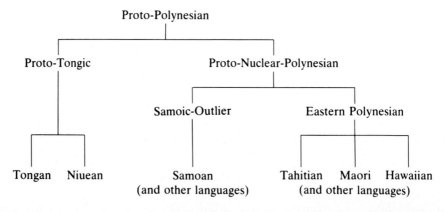

Proto-Nuclear-Polynesian has two main subgroups: Samoic-Outlier and Eastern Polynesian. The evolution of Polynesian languages can be represented in the genetic tree, or *family tree*, shown in Figure 9-3. Family trees such as these are useful in representing the general genetic relationships in a family of languages, but they inevitably oversimplify the complex facts of history, especially by excluding borrowing and other influences that languages from within and without the family can exert on one another.

Reconstructing the Proto-Polynesian Vocabulary

On the basis of the evidence provided by modern-day Polynesian languages, we can reconstruct the phonology and lexicon of Proto-Polynesian (and make educated guesses about its grammatical structure). In turn, reconstructed linguistic information can tell us a good deal about the people who first settled Polynesia more than three thousand years ago.

A word can be reconstructed for Proto-Polynesian if we find *reflexes* of it—that is, cognates—in at least one language of each major subgroup, Tongic, Samoic-Outlier, and Eastern Polynesian, and are confident that the cognates are not borrowed words.[2] For example, since cognate words for 'bird,' 'fish,' and 'man' are found in all major subgroups of the Polynesian family (as shown in Tables 9-1 and 9-2), we can reconstruct a Proto-Polynesian form for each. According to regular sound correspondences and the most plausible reconstructed sounds, these words are: *manu, *taŋata, and *ika. In contrast, the word for a 'night of full moon,' which in Maori and Tahitian is *hotu* and in Hawaiian *hoku*, cannot be reconstructed for Proto-Polynesian because there is no cognate in any Tongic or Samoic-Outlier language. Similarly, an etymon for the Tongan and Niuean word *kōkō* 'windpipe' cannot be reconstructed for Proto-Polynesian because there is no reflex in any Samoic-Outlier or Eastern Polynesian language.

Using the comparative method of historical reconstruction just outlined, the following lexical items, all referring to the physical environment, can be reconstructed for Proto-Polynesian.

*awa	'channel'	*hafu	'waterfall'
*hakau	'coral reef'	*lanu	'fresh water'
*kilikili	'gravel'	*lolo	'flood'
*peau	'wave'	*mato	'precipice'
*sou	'rough ocean'	*maʔuŋa	'mountain'
*tahi	'sea'	*rano	'lake'
*ʔone	'sand'	*waitafe	'stream'

---

[2] If we reconstructed a lexical item for Proto-Polynesian based simply on evidence from Tongan and, say, Samoan, we would run the risk of having found a word that existed originally only in Tongan (after Tongan became a separate language) and was borrowed by the early Samoans. (You can see from Figure 9-2 that Tonga and Samoa are close enough to have had contacts in prehistoric times.)

From this list, we see that the Proto-Polynesian people had words for ocean-related notions (the left-hand column) and for topographic features typically found on large volcanic islands (the right-hand column). As it happens, there are no waterfalls, mountains, precipices, or lakes on coral atolls, and only rarely are they found on raised coral islands.

In interpreting such results, linguists make the commonsense assumption that the presence of a word for a particular object in a language usually indicates the presence of that object in the speakers' environment. (There are exceptions to this rule, as we will see, but they are few and far between.) In particular, complete landlubbers will not normally have an elaborate native vocabulary for the sea and for seafaring activities (barring the possibility of a recent move inland from a coastal area). We thus surmise that the early Polynesians inhabited a high island or a chain of high islands but lived close enough to the ocean to be familiar with the landscape and phenomena of the sea.

We can also reconstruct the following Proto-Polynesian names for animals and make the assumption that the ancient Polynesians were familiar with them.

*maŋō	'shark'	*kulī	'dog'
*kanahe	'mullet'	*puaka	'pig'
*sakulā	'swordfish'	*moko	'lizard'
*ʔatu	'bonito'	*kumā	'rat'
*ʔono	'barracuda'	*ŋata	'snake'
*ʔume	'leatherjacket'	*fonu	'turtle'
*manini	'sturgeon'	*peka	'bat'
*nofu	'stonefish'	*namu	'mosquito'
*fai	'stingray'	*lulu	'owl'
*kaloama	'goatfish'	*matuku	'reef heron'
*palani	'surgeonfish'	*akiaki	'tern'
*toke	'eel'	*moa	'chicken'

Names of many other reef and deepwater fish and other sea creatures can be reconstructed besides those listed in the left-hand column. In contrast, we can reconstruct only a handful of names for land animals: a few domesticated animals (dog, pig, chicken) and a few birds and reptiles. We surmise that the Polynesians' original habitat was rich in sea life and probably relatively poor in land fauna—that the Polynesians originally inhabited coastal regions and not island interiors.

The character of the land fauna offers pointed information about the Proto-Polynesian homeland. Since the Proto-Polynesian terms *peka* 'bat' and *lulu* 'owl' can be reconstructed, we can exclude as possible homelands Tahiti, Easter Island, and the Marquesas, where these animals are not found.

Furthermore, snakes are found only east of Samoa. Though we find reflexes of Proto-Polynesian *ŋata* 'snake' in many languages, we find no snakes east of Samoa. Had the Proto-Polynesians inhabited an island west of Samoa, they would very likely have lost the term *ŋata over the centuries. Similarly, we know that pigs (for which the word *puaka can be reconstructed) are not native to Polynesia, but Europeans first arriving between the sixteenth and nineteenth centuries found them everywhere except on Niue, Easter Island, and New Zealand. These three regions are thus unlikely homelands.

Words for some animals have undergone interesting changes in certain Polynesian languages. For example, New Zealand is much colder than the rest of Polynesia, and its native animals are very different from those found on the tropical islands to the north. Upon arrival in New Zealand, the ancient Maoris encountered many new species to which they gave the names of animals they had left behind in tropical Polynesia; thus the following correspondences exist.

Proto-Polynesian		Maori	
*pule	'cowrie shell'	pure	'bivalve mollusk'
*ŋata	'snake'	ŋata	'snail'
*ali	'flounder'	ari	'small shark'

Other animal names were dropped from the Maori vocabulary or applied to things commonly associated with the animal.

Proto-Polynesian		Maori	
*ane	'termite'	ane	'rotten'
*lupe	'pigeon'	rupe	'mythical bird'

Other changes are more complex. The word *lulu* (or *ruru*) refers to owls in languages (such as Tongan, Samoan, and Maori) that are spoken in areas where owls are found. On some islands like the Marquesas and Tahiti, owls do not exist, and the reflex of Proto-Polynesian *lulu 'owl' has either disappeared from the language, as in Marquesan, or has been applied to another species, as in Tahitian. Owls inhabit Hawaii, but the Proto-Polynesian term *lulu has been replaced by the word *pueo* there.

Why would the early Hawaiians replace one word with the other? In the Marquesas, as we have said, there are no owls, and the language spoken there has no reflex of *lulu. Apparently the ancient Polynesians settled the Marquesas and stayed there for several centuries, during which they lost the word *lulu* for lack of anything to apply it to. When they subsequently traveled north and settled Hawaii, they encountered owls, but by that time the word *lulu* had long been forgotten, and a new word had to be found.

The linguistic evidence testifies that the ancestors of the Polynesians were fishermen and cultivators. Here are a few of the many terms that refer to fishing and horticulture.

*mata?u	'fishhook'	*tō	'to plant'
*rama	'to torch-fish'	*faki	'to pick'
*pā	'fish lure'	*lohu	'picking pole'
*kupeŋa	'fishnet'	*hua	'spade'
*afo	'fishing line'	*ma?ala	'garden'
*fāŋota	'to fish'	*pulapula	'seedling'

In contrast to this rich vocabulary, hunting terms are limited, with three words apparently exhausting all possible reconstructions for verbs related to hunting: *fana* 'to shoot with a bow,' *welo* 'to spear,' and *seu* 'to snare with a net.' It is probably safe to infer that the major source of food for the ancient Polynesians was not the bush but sea and garden.

One field with a notable array of vocabulary is canoe navigation, with the following reconstructions: *folau* 'to travel by sea,' *?uli* 'to steer,' *fohe* 'paddle,' *fana* 'mast,' *lā* 'sail,' *kiato* 'outrigger boom,' *hama* 'outrigger.' That the speakers of Proto-Polynesian were expert seafarers comes as no surprise, given that they traveled enormous distances between islands (two thousand miles stretch between Hawaii and the closest inhabited island).

Historical Linguistics and Prehistory

The linguistic evidence combined with evidence from archaeology leads to the following hypotheses:

1. The speakers of Proto-Polynesian inhabited the coastal region of a high island or group of high islands.

2. This homeland is likely to have been in the region between Samoa and Fiji, including the islands of Tonga, Uvea, and Futuna.

3. The ancient Polynesians were fishermen, cultivators, and seafarers.

4. Around the first century A.D., the ancient Polynesians traveled eastward from their homeland, settling eastern Polynesia: Tahiti, the Cook Islands, the Marquesas, the Tuamotu, and the neighboring island groups.

5. Then, between the fourth and sixth centuries, Easter Island, Hawaii, and New Zealand were settled from eastern Polynesia.

The history of Polynesian settlement and migrations is summarized in Figure 9-4.

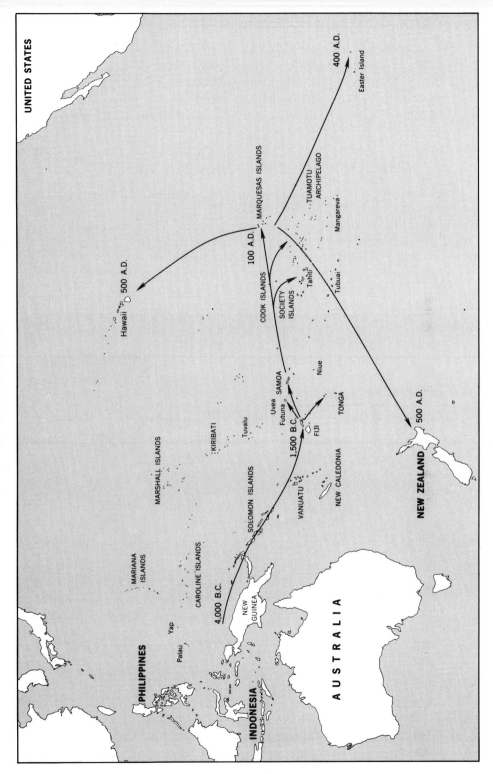

FIGURE 9-4
The Settlement of Polynesia

This discussion has focused on Polynesian origins and migrations. By judiciously combining linguistic evidence with evidence from other disciplines, we constructed a probable picture of an ancient people, the environment they lived in, and the skills they developed for survival. Linguists have applied the same methods to other peoples, including the Indo-Europeans and the Algonquian Indians.

THE LANGUAGE FAMILIES OF THE WORLD

The same comparative method used to trace the historical development of languages can be applied to determine which languages are related within families. In this section we survey the major language families of the world, paying particular attention to those families with the greatest number of speakers and those that include most languages.

Counting Speakers and Languages

It is not easy to determine with certainty how many people speak languages like English, Chinese, and Arabic. Nevertheless, these and a few others stand out for the sheer number of people that claim them as a native language. Of the world's several thousand languages, about a dozen are spoken natively by 100 million individuals or more. In the following table, numbers have been rounded off to the nearest 50 million.

Chinese	1 billion
English	350 million
Spanish	300 million
Hindi-Urdu	150 million
Portuguese	150 million
Indonesian-Malay	150 million
Russian	150 million
Arabic	150 million
Bengali	150 million
French	100 million
German	100 million
Japanese	100 million

Six of these languages—Chinese, English, Spanish, Russian, Arabic, and French—are the working languages of the United Nations.

Equally difficult to estimate is the number of languages currently spoken in the world. The figure commonly cited is four thousand to five thousand, while a more conservative estimate would be about two thousand. It is indeed difficult to decide, in many cases, whether particular communities speak different dialects of the same language or different languages. Furthermore,

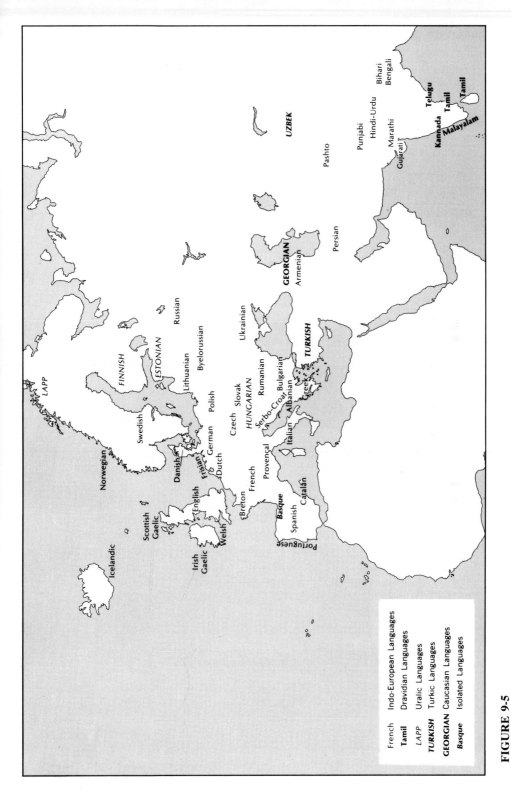

FIGURE 9-5
Location of the Major Indo-European, Dravidian, Caucasian, Uralic, and Turkic Languages

French	Indo-European Languages
Tamil	Dravidian Languages
LAPP	Uralic Languages
TURKISH	Turkic Languages
GEORGIAN	Caucasian Languages
Basque	Isolated Languages

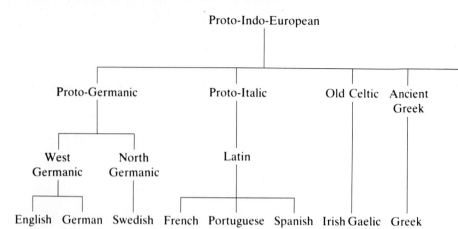

FIGURE 9-6
Partial Tree of the Indo-European Language Family

little is known about many of the world's languages. In Papua New Guinea, a nation of only 3 million, it is estimated that as many as eight hundred languages (about a fifth of the world's total) are spoken, but we have descriptions of only a handful. Many Papuan languages are spoken in remote communities by only a few hundred speakers, or even a few dozen.

The distribution of speakers among the languages in the world is extremely top heavy: the dozen languages with more than 100 million speakers account for a large portion of the world's population, while the rest is linguistically very fragmented. In this section we will investigate some of this fragmentation.

The following discussion is arranged by language family, beginning with the Indo-European family, the Sino-Tibetan family, the Austronesian family, and the Afroasiatic family, which together are the four most important families in terms of both numbers of speakers and numbers of languages. The three major language families of sub-Saharan Africa are then discussed together, followed by other language families of Europe and Asia, including important isolated languages like Japanese. Finally, we discuss the native languages of the Americas, Australia, and central Papua New Guinea. Pidgins and creoles will be discussed at the end.

The Indo-European Family

To the Indo-European language family belong most languages of Europe (which are now spoken natively in the Americas and Oceania and play prominent roles in Africa and Asia) as well as most languages of Iran, Afghanistan, Pakistan, Bangladesh, and most of India. Of the twelve languages with more than 100 million native speakers, eight belong to the Indo-European family. Yet Indo-European languages number only about 150, a small fraction of the world's languages. The extensive spread of Indo-European languages is shown in Figure 9-5.

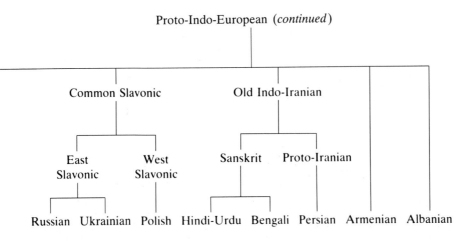

Proto-Indo-European (*continued*)

The Indo-European family is divided into several groups, which we discuss briefly. Figure 9-6 is a family tree showing a few languages for each group.

Germanic Group   Modern-day Germanic languages include English, German (and its derivative Yiddish), Norwegian, Swedish, Danish, Dutch (and its modern derivative Afrikaans), and a few other languages like Icelandic, Faroese, and Frisian. Frisian, spoken in the northern Netherlands, is the closest relative to English. As Table 9-5 illustrates, Germanic languages bear striking similarities to one another in vocabulary; similarities in phonology and syntax also are numerous. Some Germanic languages are mutually intelligible, and all bear the imprint of their common ancestor, Proto-Germanic.

Swedish, Danish, Norwegian, Icelandic, and Faroese—the North Germanic group—are more closely related to each other than to the other languages of the Germanic group. They descended from Proto-North-Germanic,

TABLE 9-5
Common Words in Seven Germanic Languages

English	German	Dutch	Swedish	Danish	Norwegian	Icelandic
mother	Mutter	moeder	moder	moder	moder	móðir
father	Vater	vader	fader	fader	fader	faðir
eye	Auge	oog	óga	øje	øye	auga
foot	Fuss	voet	fot	fod	fot	fótur
one	ein	een	en	en	en	einn
three	drei	drie	tre	tre	tre	þrír
month	Monat	maand	månad	maaned	måned	mánaður

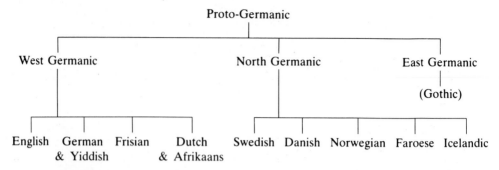

FIGURE 9-7
Germanic Languages

which evolved as a single language for a longer period of time than the West Germanic subgroup that includes English, Frisian, Dutch, and German. We also have written records of Gothic, which was spoken in central Europe and which disappeared around the eighth century. Gothic alone forms the East Germanic subgroup. Figure 9-7 is the family tree for the Germanic group (Gothic is in parentheses because it is extinct).

The number of native speakers of English is about 350 million. English is native to the inhabitants of the British Isles, the United States, most of Canada, the Caribbean, Australia, New Zealand, and South Africa. In addition, there are numerous bilinguals of English and another language on the Indian subcontinent, in eastern and southern Africa, and in Oceania. To these we must add the countless speakers of English as a second language scattered around the globe. English is the second most popular spoken language in the world after Chinese, but it is unrivaled in terms of its geographical spread and popularity as a second language. German, which has not spread as much as English, is still one of the world's most widely spoken languages. It claims about 100 million native speakers, mostly in central Europe.

Italic Group and Romance Subgroup   The Romance languages include French, Spanish, Italian, Portuguese, and Rumanian, as well as Provencal (spoken in the south of France) and Catalan (spoken in northern Spain). The Romance languages are closely related to each other, as witnessed by the sample of vocabulary correspondences in Table 9-6. The Rumanian words for 'mother,' 'father,' 'foot,' and 'moon' are not derived from the same roots as those in the other Romance languages; they illustrate the type of historical change that hinders communication between speakers of closely related languages. Such examples are particularly common in Rumanian, which is geographically isolated from the other Romance languages.

The languages of the Romance family are descendants of Vulgar Latin. Because the Romance languages have remained in close contact over the centuries, subgroups are more difficult to identify than for Germanic languages. Latin is one descendant of Proto-Italic. Oscan and Umbrian, the

TABLE 9-6
Common Words in Six Romance Languages

	French	Italian	Spanish	Rumanian	Catalan	Portuguese
'mother'	mère	madre	madre	mamă	mare	mãe
'father'	père	padre	padre	tată	pare	pai
'eye'	œil	occhio	ojo	ochiu	ull	ôlho
'foot'	pied	piede	pie	picior	peu	pé
'one'	un	uno	uno	un	un	um
'three'	trois	tre	tres	trei	tres	três
'month'	mois	mese	mes	lŭna	mes	mês

other principal descendants, were once spoken in southern Italy but are now extinct. While written records abound for Latin, little is known about Oscan and Umbrian. The tree for Italic and Romance languages is shown in Figure 9-8.

Spanish, with approximately 300 million native speakers in Spain and the Americas, is the third most popular language in the world. Portuguese is spoken by 150 million people, principally in Portugal and Brazil. French has about 100 million native speakers in France, Canada, and the United States, as well as many second-language speakers, particularly in North Africa and West Africa. As with English, the spread of these three languages is linked to European colonialism of the fifteenth to nineteenth centuries.

Slavonic Group   Slavonic languages are spoken in eastern Europe and the Soviet Union. The Slavonic group can be divided into three subgroups: East Slavonic, which includes Russian, Ukrainian, and Byelorussian (spoken in the westernmost part of the USSR); South Slavonic, which includes Bulgarian and Serbo-Croat (spoken in Yugoslavia); and West Slavonic, which groups together Polish, Czech, Slovak, and a few minor languages. All are derived from Common Slavonic (see Figure 9-9).

FIGURE 9-8
Italic Languages

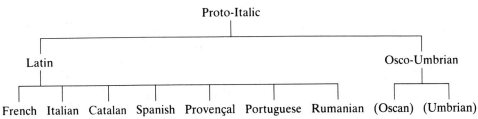

FIGURE 9-9
Slavonic Languages

Even more so than the Germanic and the Romance languages, Slavonic languages are remarkably similar to each other, especially in their vocabulary (see Table 9-7).

By far the most widely spoken Slavonic language is Russian, the official language of the Soviet Union; it is spoken natively by more than 150 million people and as a foreign language by an additional 65 million. Ukrainian has 50 million speakers, Polish 35 million, Serbo-Croat 17 million, Czech 10 million, and Byelorussian 10 million.

Indo-Iranian Group   At the other geographical extreme of the Indo-European family we find the Indo-Iranian group, which is subdivided into Iranian and Indic (see Figure 9-10). The two most important Iranian languages are Persian (also called Farsi), with 35 million speakers in Iran, and Pashto, with 15 million speakers in Afghanistan and northern Pakistan. Indic languages include Hindi-Urdu, spoken by about 150 million people in India (where it is called Hindi and is written in Devanāgarī script) and Pakistan (where it is called Urdu and uses the Arabic script); Bengali, spoken in India and Bangladesh by 150 million people; Bihari, spoken in northeastern India by 25 million; Punjabi, with 20 million speakers in northern India and

TABLE 9-7
Common Words in Six Slavonic Languages

	Russian	Ukrainian	Polish	Czech	Serbo-Croat	Bulgarian
'mother'	mat'	mati	matka	matka	mati	mayka
'father'	otec	otec'	ojciec	otec	otac	bašča
'eye'	oko*	oko	oko	oko	oko	oko
'foot'	noga	noga	noga	noha	noga	krak
'one'	odin	odin	jeden	jeden	jedan	edin
'three'	tri	tri	trzy	tři	tri	tri
'month'	mesyac	misyac'	miesiac	měsíc	mjesec	mesec

* Russian *oko* 'eye' is archaic; the more modern word is *glaz*.

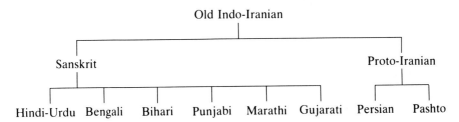

FIGURE 9-10
Indo-Iranian Languages

Pakistan; Marathi, spoken in central India by 15 million people; and Gujarati, spoken in western India by 15 million. Many of these languages are also spoken by ethnic Indian populations in Southeast Asia, Africa, the Americas, Great Britain, and Oceania. The parent language of the modern Indic languages is Sanskrit, the ancient language of India immortalized in the Vedas and other classical texts.

Table 9-8 presents sample vocabulary correspondences between a few Indo-Iranian languages. Not all the words with one meaning are cognates. Some have sources other than a common parent language and are thus not all reflexes of a single etymon.

Hellenic Group   The sole member of the Hellenic group is Greek. Certain languages, while belonging to a major language family, were isolated early enough that they do not bear any particularly close affiliations to other languages of the family. Such is the case with Greek, which evolved through the centuries in relative isolation. Greek stands out from other isolated Indo-European languages because of its relatively large number of speakers (10 million) and its historical importance in Indo-European linguistics because early written records of Ancient Greek have survived.

Other Indo-European Language Groups   The Germanic, Italic, Slavonic, Indo-Iranian, and Hellenic groups of Indo-European do not include all the

TABLE 9-8
Common Words in Six Indic Languages

	Hindi	Bengali	Marathi	Gujarati	Persian	Pashto
'mother'	mātā	ma	mā	mā	mādar	mōr
'father'	bāp	bāp	baba	bāp	pedar	plār
'eye'	ākh	cókh	dola	ānkh	čašm	starga
'foot'	pāw	pā	pā	pāg	pā	xpa
'one'	ek	ak	ek	ēk	yek	yau
'three'	tīn	tīn	tīn	trān	si	drē
'month'	mahīnā	mas	mahīnā	mahīno	māh	miāsht

descendants of Proto-Indo-European. Of the remaining groups, Celtic includes Irish Gaelic, Scottish Gaelic, Breton, and Welsh, which together are spoken by no more than 1 million people today; Baltic includes Lithuanian, with 3 million speakers; and Tocharian and Anatolian (including Hittite) are now extinct. Armenian and Albanian, each with 4 million speakers, form two additional language groups.

The Sino-Tibetan Family

Included in the Sino-Tibetan family are about three hundred East Asian languages, many of which remain relatively unexplored. This family is divided into a Sinitic group and a Tibeto-Burman group.

The Sinitic group includes a dozen languages, most of which are so similar structurally that they can be considered dialects of a single language. This language, with more than 1 billion speakers the most popular language in the world, is of course Chinese. Five dialect groups can be identified. The Mandarin group includes the Běijīng (Peking) dialect, which serves as the official language of the People's Republic of China; the Yuè dialects include the dialect of Guǎng Zhōu (Canton), which is spoken by the greatest number of overseas Chinese scattered throughout the world.

By comparison, the Tibeto-Burman group includes many different languages, each with relatively few speakers. The only members of this group that have more than a million speakers are Burmese (15 million) and Tibetan (3 million). Figure 9-11 maps the location of the major Sino-Tibetan languages.

The Austronesian Family

The Austronesian family has up to one thousand different languages scattered over one third of the Southern Hemisphere. It includes Indonesian-Malay, spoken by about 150 million people in Indonesia and Malaysia; Javanese, with 60 million speakers on the island of Java in Indonesia; Tagalog or Pilipino, the official language of the Philippines, with 12 million native speakers; Cebuano, another language of the Philippines (10 million speakers); and Malagasy, the principal language of Madagascar (10 million speakers). Most other Austronesian languages have fewer than 1 million speakers each, and many of them are spoken by only a few hundred people.

The Austronesian family contains several groups. The most ancient division is between three groups of minor Formosan languages spoken in the hills of Taiwan and all other Austronesian languages; the latter group is called Malayo-Polynesian. The most important split divides Western Malayo-Polynesian, which groups together languages spoken in Indonesia, Malaysia, Madagascar, the Philippines, and Guam, and Oceanic (or Eastern Malayo-Polynesian), which extends from the coastal areas of Papua New Guinea into the islands of the Pacific. Fijian and the Polynesian languages are Oceanic languages. Table 9-9 gives a sample of vocabulary correspondences between

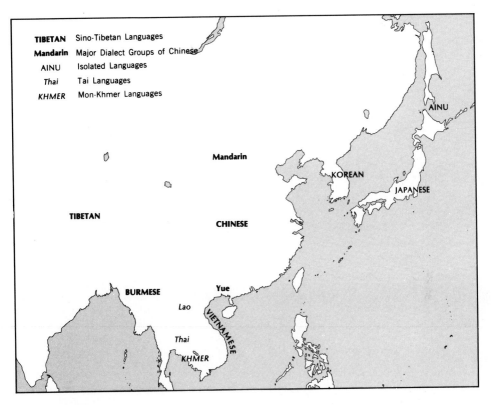

TIBETAN   Sino-Tibetan Languages
Mandarin   Major Dialect Groups of Chinese
AINU   Isolated Languages
Thai   Tai Languages
KHMER   Mon-Khmer Languages

FIGURE 9-11
Location of the Major Sino-Tibetan, Mon-Khmer, and Tai Languages and of the Major Isolated Languages of Asia

TABLE 9-9
Common Words in Six Austronesian Languages

	Malay	Malagasy	Tagalog	Motu	Fijian	Samoan
'mother'	ibu	ineny	inâ	sina	tina	tinā
'father'	bapak	ikaky	amá	tama	tama	tamā
'eye'	mata	maso	mata	mata	mata	mata
'one'	satu	isa	isa	ta	dua	tasi
'three'	tiga	telo	tatló	toi	tolu	tolu
'stone'	batu	vato	bato	nadi	vatu	fatu*
'louse'	kutu	hao	kuto	utu	kutu	ʔutu

* Samoan *fatu* actually means 'fruit pit,' a meaning closely related to 'stone.'

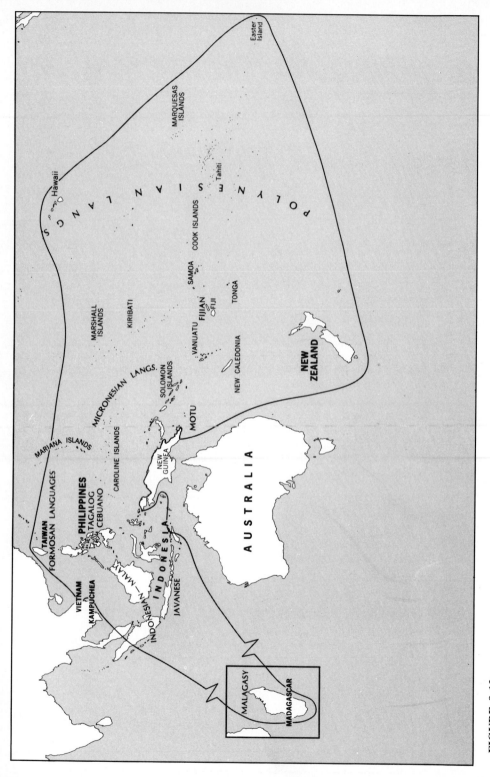

FIGURE 9-12
Austronesian Languages

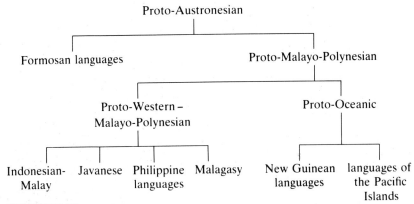

FIGURE 9-13
Austronesian Languages

representative Austronesian languages. Figure 9-13 is a simplified tree of the family, and the distribution of Austronesian languages is illustrated in Figure 9-12.

The Afroasiatic Family

The Afroasiatic family comprises about 250 languages scattered across the northern part of Africa and western Asia. It includes Arabic, one of the world's major languages, dialects of which are spoken across the entire northern part of Africa and the Middle East; Hebrew, the traditional language of the Jewish nation, which has been revived in this century as the national language of Israel; Egyptian, the now extinct language of the ancient Egyptian civilization; and Hausa, one of Africa's major languages, spoken by about 25 million people in Chad, Nigeria, and neighboring nations (see Figure 9-14).

Hebrew and Arabic form the Semitic group within the Afroasiatic family. To this group also belong Amharic, the official language of Ethiopia, and Akkadian, a language of ancient Mesopotamia, now extinct. Akkadian is important in that it appears to have been the first language to be written. One of the distinctive properties of Semitic languages is their morphological system; Semitic nouns and verbs consist of a series of consonants, between which vowels are inserted to represent inflection (see Chapter 4).

Ancient Egyptian forms a separate Afroasiatic group. Somali, the principal language of Somalia, is one of forty languages of the Cushitic group. Kabyl and other languages that belong to the Berber group (with 10 million speakers) are scattered across North Africa. Hausa (with 15 million speakers) and about 130 other languages form the Chadic group, all of which have developed tone systems. Table 9-10 is a comparative vocabulary for representative members of the Afroasiatic family. (ħ is the symbol for a voiceless pharyngeal fricative and ʕ for its voiced counterpart.)

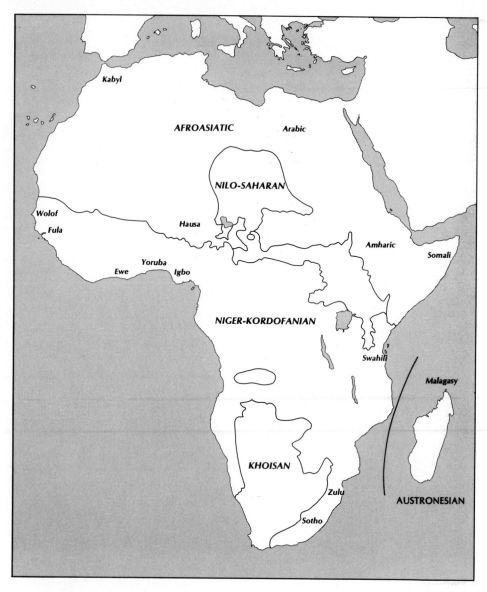

FIGURE 9-14
The Language Families of Africa
SOURCE: Adapted from Gregersen 1977

The Three Major Language Families of Sub-Saharan Africa

Besides the Afroasiatic family spoken north of the Sahara Desert, Africa contains three large language families: the Niger-Kordofanian family, with several hundred languages spoken by about 150 million people in a region that stretches from Senegal to Kenya to South Africa; the Nilo-Saharan

TABLE 9-10
Common Words in Six Afroasiatic Languages

	Arabic (colloquial)	Hebrew (modern)	Amharic	Kabyl	Hausa	Somali
'mother'	um	em	annat	yemma	inna	hooyyo
'father'	ab	av	abbat	baba	baba	aabe
'eye'	ʕaīn	ayin	ayn	allen	ido	il
'foot'	ʔežer	rɛgɛl	agar	aḍaṛ	k'afa	ʕag
'one'	waḥad	ɛxad	and	waḥed	'daya	hal
'three'	ṭalaṭa	šloša	sost	tlata	uku	saddeħ
'month'	šaher	xodɛš	wár	eccher	wata	bil

family, with about a hundred languages spoken by 10 million people in and around Chad and the Sudan; and the Khoisan family in southern Africa, with fifty languages spoken by fewer than 75,000 people altogether. The Khoisan family, traditionally associated with the Bushmen of the Kalahari Desert, is the only language family in the world that has click sounds (discussed in Chapter 2). The boundaries between these language families are shown in Figure 9-14.

Most of the better-known languages of sub-Saharan Africa belong to the Niger-Kordofanian family. These include Fula, spoken by 6 million speakers in Senegal; Wolof, with 2 million speakers in Senegal, Gambia, Mali, and Guinea; Yoruba, spoken in Nigeria by more than 15 million; Ewe, spoken by 1 million in Togo, Benin, and Ghana; Igbo, with 5 million speakers in Nigeria; Swahili, with approximately 20 million in East Africa; and other Bantu languages of southern Africa like Zulu (5 million speakers) and Sotho (4 million).

Other Language Families of Asia and Europe

Scattered throughout Asia and Europe are a number of smaller language families and isolates—languages that are not genetically related to any other language family, as far as linguists can determine. These isolated languages are not negligible; some, like Japanese and Korean, are spoken by large populations.

Some of these languages are grouped into smaller families of a few dozen languages. Others, like Japanese, do not have any relatives. The genetic isolation of these languages has been the subject of much speculation by fertile imaginations that have tried to link them to just about every language family. Many hypotheses, most unfounded, have been advanced linking Korean or Japanese to Austronesian, Dravidian, Hungarian, Basque, and Ancient Egyptian, as well as to certain combinations of these.

We will first survey briefly the Dravidian, Mon-Khmer, Tai, Caucasian, Turkic, and Uralic language families before turning to the major isolated languages of Eurasia.

The Dravidian Family Languages of the Dravidian family are spoken principally in southern India (see Figure 9-5). The four major Dravidian languages are Tamil (30 million speakers), Malayalam (20 million speakers), Kannada (20 million speakers), and Telugu (40 million speakers), all of which have been written for many centuries. All Dravidian languages have been somewhat influenced by the Indic languages spoken to their north. In Table 9-11, the Indic influence is evident in the Tamil word for 'foot' and the Tamil and Kannada words for 'month,' which are of Indo-European origin and were borrowed into these languages.

The Mon-Khmer Family The Mon-Khmer family includes about a hundred languages spoken in Southeast Asia (Vietnam, Laos, Kampuchea, Thailand, and Burma). The most important of these is Cambodian or Khmer, the official language of Kampuchea (formerly Cambodia), spoken by nearly 8 million people (see Figure 9-11). The Mon-Khmer languages may be related to other minor families of the same region.

The Tai Family The best known languages of the Tai family are Thai (40 million speakers) and Lao (10 million speakers), the official languages of Thailand and Laos respectively (shown in Figure 9-11). There are about fifty other members of the Tai family scattered throughout Thailand, Laos, Vietnam, Burma, eastern India, and southern China, where they intertwine with Sino-Tibetan languages, Mon-Khmer languages, and Vietnamese. Tai languages may be related to a number of languages spoken in Vietnam, with which they may form a Kam-Tai family. It has also been suggested that Tai languages may be related to Austronesian, but the evidence supporting that hypothesis is scanty.

The Caucasian Family With about thirty languages, the Caucasian family is confined to the mountainous region between the Black Sea and the

TABLE 9-11
Common Words in Four Dravidian Languages

	Tamil	Malayalam	Kannada	Telugu
'mother'	ammal	amma	amma	amma
'father'	appan	āchchan	appa	nānna
'eye'	kaṇ	kaṇṇu	kaṇṇu	kannu
'foot'	pādam	kāl	kālu	kālu
'one'	ondru	oru	ondu	okaṭi
'three'	mūndru	mūnnu	mūru	mūdu
'month'	mātam	nela	māsam	tinglu

Caspian Sea, which today is part of the Soviet Union, Turkey, and Iran. Spoken by about 5 million people altogether, Caucasian languages typically have complex phonological and morphological systems. The best known Caucasian language is Georgian (see Figure 9-5).

The Turkic Family   This family comprises about sixty languages, all of which are quite similar. The better known members are Turkish, spoken by 25 million people, and Uzbek, with 10 million speakers in the southern Soviet Union. Most Turkic languages are spoken in Turkey and central Asia (see Figure 9-5).

The Uralic Family   With about thirty members, the Uralic family is thought by some to be related to the Turkic family, though this link is tenuous. The better-known Uralic languages are Finnish (5 million speakers) and Hungarian (15 million speakers); also included are Estonian and Lapp (see Figure 9-5).

Japanese   Japanese, whose more than 100 million speakers make it one of the world's major languages, does not have any known relatives, although two distant cousins have been hypothesized in Ainu (spoken by 15,000 people in the north of Japan) and Korean. Japanese has received considerable influence from Chinese, to which it is not related (see Figure 9-11).

Korean   Korean is spoken by 35 million people. Although it may be a distant relative of Japanese, it has no established genetic relationship with any language. Like Japanese, it has been greatly influenced by Chinese over the centuries (see Figure 9-11).

Vietnamese   Vietnamese, the language of the 60 million inhabitants of Vietnam and neighboring areas, does not have any clear genetic relationships, although it may be a distant relative of Mon-Khmer languages (see Figure 9-11).

Other Isolated Languages of Asia and Europe   Of the remaining isolated languages of Eurasia, Basque is probably the best known. It is spoken by about 1 million inhabitants of an area that straddles the Spanish-French border on the Atlantic coast (see Figure 9-5). Basque has no known relatives.

Native American Languages

Compared to the Old World, the linguistic situation in the Americas is bewildering, with numerous American Indian language families in North and South America. While proposals for the genetic integration of these languages have been made, solid evidence for a pan-American genetic link is lacking.

In North America, we must distinguish the Eskimo-Aleut family (whose speakers are not genetically related to Amerindians) from all other language families. There are many American Indian language families, most of which include ten to fifty languages. The better-known families are Athabaskan (including Navajo and Apache), Iroquoian (including Cherokee and

Mohawk), Siouan (including Dakota), Algonquian (including Arapaho, Blackfoot, Cheyenne, Cree, Menomini, and Ojibwa), Uto-Aztecan (including Hopi), and, in Central America, Mayan. The approximate location of illustrative languages is shown in Figure 9-15.

Indigenous South American languages are equally diversified. The genetic affiliation of Quechua, the most widely spoken native South American language (with 6 million speakers in the Andes), is unclear. Many languages

FIGURE 9-15
The Major Languages of the Native Americas

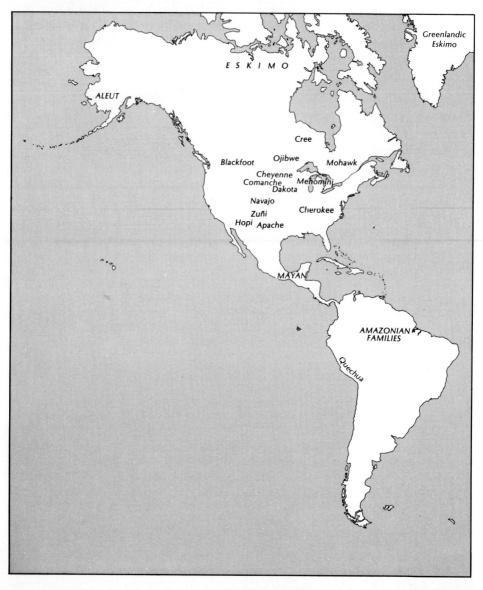

of the Americas have disappeared or are in grave danger of disappearing in the face of mounting pressure for their speakers to adopt English, Spanish, or Portuguese.

Languages of Aboriginal Australia

Before settlement by Europeans in the eighteenth century, Australia had been inhabited by Aborigines for up to fifty millennia. It is estimated that at the time of first contact with Europeans about two hundred to three hundred Aboriginal languages were spoken. Today many of these languages have disappeared completely along with their speakers, decimated by imported diseases and sometimes (as on the island of Tasmania) by genocide at the hands of whites. Today, only about a hundred Aboriginal languages survive, most spoken by tiny populations of older survivors.

Virtually all Australian languages fall into a single family with two groups: the large Pama-Nyungan group, which covers most of the continent and includes most Aboriginal languages, and the Non-Pama-Nyungan group, which includes about fifty languages in northern Australia (see Figure 9-16).

FIGURE 9-16

Australian Aboriginal Language Groups and Boundary Between Papuan and Austronesian Languages in Papua New Guinea

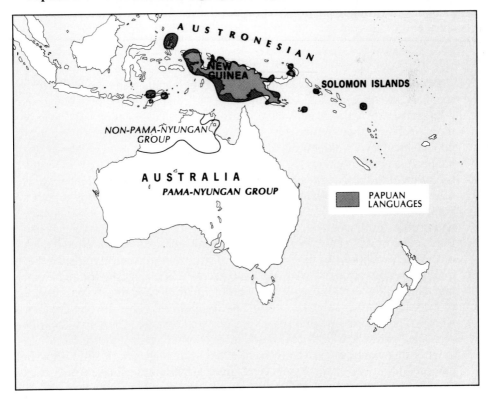

Papuan Languages

Papuan languages are spoken on the large island of New Guinea, which is today divided politically between the nation of Papua New Guinea and the Indonesian-controlled section called Irian Jaya (see Figure 9-16). While the inhabitants of coastal areas of the island speak Austronesian languages, about eight hundred of the languages are not Austronesian languages. Referred to as Papuan (or Non-Austronesian) languages, most are not in any danger of extinction, though many are spoken by very small populations. They fall into more than sixty different families, with no established genetic link among them. Little is known about most of these languages.

LANGUAGES IN CONTACT

Speakers of different languages have always been in contact with each other. But at no other time in history have there been such intensive contacts between language communities as in the last few centuries. As a result of the exploratory and colonizing enterprises of the English, French, Dutch, Spanish, and Portuguese, European languages have come into contact with languages of Africa, Native America, Asia, and the Pacific. These colonizing efforts, along with the somber endeavors that accompanied them, like slavery and other forms of exploitation, also had the consequence of putting members of different speech communities into contact with each other. For example, the importing of slaves from Africa to the Americas brought speakers of different African languages to live side by side.

Multilingualism

Bilingualism   Several language contact phenomena can take place when speakers of different languages interact. The first of these phenomena is **bilingualism** or multilingualism, in which members of a community acquire more than one language natively. In a multilingual community, children grow up speaking several languages and usually gain as much competence in one language as in the others. (In many multilingual communities, however, the use of the different languages is compartmentalized, as when one language is used at home and another at school or at work.) Multilingualism is such a natural solution to the problem of language contact that it is extremely widespread throughout the world. In this respect, industrialized societies like the United States and Japan, in which bilingualism is not widespread, stick out as the exception. In the United States bilingualism is mostly relegated to immigrant communities, who are expected to learn English, the dominant language, upon arrival. Frequently, these immigrants are also under pressure to lose their native language (witness the English-only laws of recent years), which often occurs within one or two generations. The adaptation is one-sided in contrast to what is found in most other areas of the globe, where neighboring communities learn each other's languages with little ado. In central Africa, India, and Papua New Guinea, it is commonplace to see small children grow up speaking four or five languages. In Papua New Guinea, multilingualism is a highly valued attribute that enhances a person's status in the community.

Nativization   A possible side effect of multilingualism is **nativization**, which takes place when a community adopts a new language as its own (in addition to its native language) and modifies the structure of that new language, thus developing a new dialect that becomes characteristic of the community. That is precisely what has happened with English in India since the nineteenth century. Indian English is now recognized as a separate dialect of English with its own structural characteristics. Indeed, it has become one of the two national languages (along with Hindi, the most widely spoken indigenous language) and is used in education, in government, and in communications within India and with the rest of the world. Nativization is a widespread phenomenon; one could even argue that the emergence of American English as a socially recognized variety of English was a nativization process.

Pidgins   Another process that may take place in language contact situations is pidginization. The origin of the word **pidgin** is unclear, but it is used to refer to a contact language that develops where individuals are in a dominant/subordinate situation, usually in the context of colonization. Pidgins appear to have begun arising around the seventeenth century with the intensification of European colonial ventures throughout the world. Pidgins arise when members of a politically or economically dominant group do not learn the native language of the people they interact with as political or economic subordinates. To communicate, members of the subordinate community create a variety of the language of the dominant group as their own second language; this created version is simplified and partly adapted to their own native languages. Pidgins then become the language of interaction between the colonizer and the colonized. Pidgins are thus defined in terms of sociological and linguistic characteristics: they are based on the language of the dominant group but are structurally simpler. They have no native speakers and are typically used for a restricted range of purposes.

Pidgins have arisen in many areas of the world, including West Africa, the Caribbean, the Far East, and the Pacific. Many pidgins have been based on English and French, the languages of the two most active colonial powers in the eighteenth and nineteenth centuries. Other languages that have served as a base for the development of pidgins include Portuguese, Spanish, Dutch, Swedish, German, Arabic, and Russian.

From Pidgin to Creole   Today, most pidgins have given way to creole languages. At some point, a pidgin may begin to fulfill a greater number of roles in social life; instead of using the pidgin language only in the workplace to communicate with the colonizers, speakers of the pidgin may begin to use the language at home or among themselves. Such situations frequently arise when the colonized population is linguistically diversified. Members of that community may find it convenient to adopt the new language as a **lingua franca**—a means to communicate across language boundaries. As a result, small children begin to grow up speaking the new language, and as greater demands are put onto that language its structure becomes more complex. We call this process *creolization*. A **creole** language is thus a former pidgin that has "acquired" native speakers. Creoles are structurally complex, often as complex as any other language, and they differ from pidgins in that they exhibit less variability from speaker to speaker.

The boundary between pidgin and creole is often difficult to establish. Creolization is a gradual process; we find many situations in which pidgins are undergoing creolization. In such situations, there will be much variability from speaker to speaker and from situation to situation. For some speakers and in some contexts, the language will clearly be at the pidgin stage; for speakers whose language is more advanced in the creolization process, or in contexts that call for a more elaborated variety, the language will be structurally more complex. Furthermore, as a creole gains wider usage and becomes structurally more complex, it often comes to resemble the language on which it is based. For example, in the Caribbean and in Hawaii, English-based creoles are so similar to standard English for many speakers that they can almost be considered nonstandard varieties of English. Typically, in such situations we find a continuum from speaker to speaker and from situation to situation—from a nonstandard dialect of the parent language to a very basic pidgin.

Figure 9-17 shows the location of the more important creoles in the world. Note that in common parlance many creoles are called pidgins. Such is the case with Hawaiian "Pidgin" and Papua New Guinea "Tok Pisin" (from *talk pidgin*), both of which are actually creoles.

Some creoles have low status where they are spoken. Such is the case with Hawaiian creole, or Da Kine Talk, which is often referred to derogatorily as a "bastardized" version of English or "local broken English." The fact is that Hawaiian creole has its own structure, which differs from that of English, and one cannot pretend to speak Da Kine Talk by speaking "broken" English.

In contrast, in many areas of the world creoles have become national languages used in government proceedings, education, and the media. In Papua New Guinea, Tok Pisin is one of the three national languages (along with English and Hiri Motu, also a creole) and has become a symbol of national identity. Some creoles have become the language of important bodies of literature, particularly in West Africa. Elsewhere, creoles are used in newspapers and on the radio for all types of purposes, including cartoons and commercials. Figure 9-18 is a publicity cartoon in Papua New Guinea Tok Pisin; the English translation of the captions is given underneath. Tok Pisin is even used to write about linguistics, as illustrated by the discussion of relative clause formation in Tok Pisin that starts at the top of page 316; it begins with three example sentences.

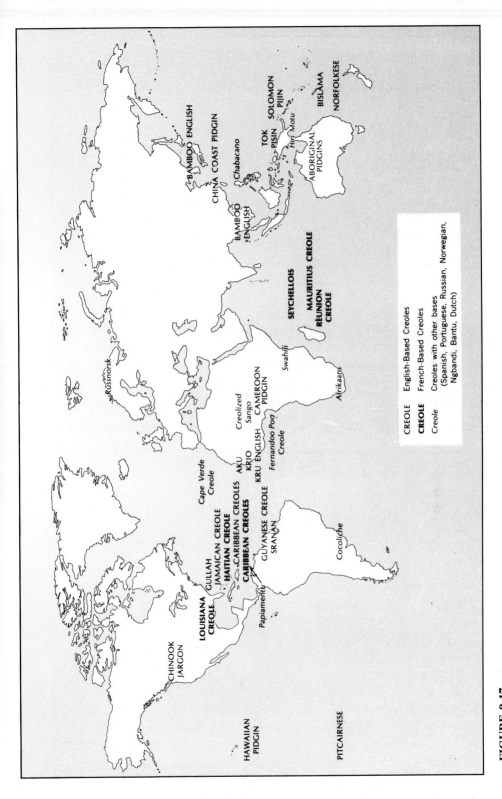

FIGURE 9-17
Location of Major Pidgin and Creole Languages in the World

(1) Ol ikilim pik bipo.
(2) Na pik bai ikamap olosem draipela ston.
(3) Na pik *ia* [ol ikilim bipo *ia*] bai ikamap olosem draipela ston.

Sapos yumi tingting gut long dispela tripela tok, yumi ken klia long tupela samting. Nambawan samting, sapos pik istap long (1) em inarapela pik, na pik istap long (2) em inarapela, orait, yumi no ken wokim (3). Tasol sapos wanpela pik tasol istap long (1) na (2), em orait long wokim (3). Na tu,

---

FIGURE 9-18

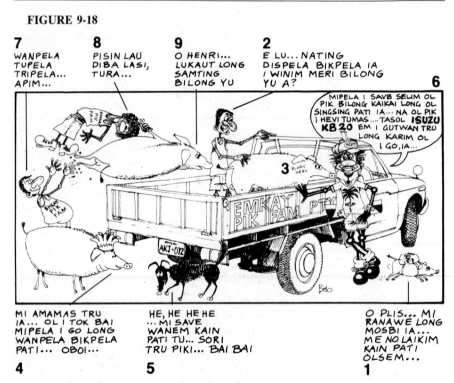

7 WANPELA TUPELA TRIPELA... APIM...

8 PISIN LAU DIBA LASI, TURA...

9 O HENRI... LUKAUT LONG SAMTING BILONG YU

2 E LU... NATING DISPELA BIKPELA IA I WINIM MERI BILONG YU A?

6 MIPELA I SAVE SELIM OL PIK BILONG KAIKAI LONG OL SINGSING PATI IA... NA OL PIK I HEVI TUMAS....TASOL ISUZU KB20 EM I GUTWAN TRU LONG KARIM OL I GO, IA...

3 BLARY NERV

EMKAY PIK FAM PTY

AKJ-072

4 MI AMAMAS TRU IA... OL I TOK BAI MIPELA I GO LONG WANPELA BIKPELA PATI... OBOI...

5 HE, HE HE HE ...MI SAVE WANEM KAIN PATI TU... SORI TRU PIKI... BAI BAI

1 O PLIS... MI RANAWE LONG MOSBI IA... ME NO LAIKIM KAIN PATI OLSEM...

① Oh, please. I'm running away to Port Moresby. I don't like this kind of party.
② Hey, Lu! It's not for nothing that this big fat one beats your wife (in size).
③ The bloody nerve!
④ I am so happy. They all say that we are going to a big party. Oh, boy.
⑤ Hee, hee, hee, hee. I know what kind of party too. Very sorry, Piggy. Bye bye.
⑥ We frequently sell pigs for eating at dance parties. But pigs are very heavy so Isuzu KB20s are excellent to carry them all away.
⑦ One, two, three, up . . .
⑧ (speaking in Hiri Motu) Friend, I don't speak Tok Pisin.
⑨ Hey, Henry! Watch out for your things.

tingting istap long (1) ia, mi bin banisim insait long tupela banis long (3), long wonem, em bilong kliaim yumi long women pik Elena itok en.

[Translation]

(1) They killed the pig.
(2) The pig looks like a big rock.
(3) The pig [that they killed] looks like a big rock.

If we think carefully about these three sentences, we can obtain three interpretations. First, if the pig of sentence (1) is one pig, and the pig of sentence (2) is another pig, then we cannot construct (3). However, if the pig in (1) and (2) is the same, then we can construct (3). Thus, I have bracketed in (3) the meaning corresponding to (1) with two brackets, because it has the purpose of identifying for us which pig Elena [the speaker who produced these sentences] is talking about.

In short, creoles can fulfill all the demands that are commonly imposed on a language.

The worldwide structural similarities among creoles are striking. Many creoles, for example, lack indefinite articles and a distinction between the future and other tenses, and many have preposition stranding (like the English *the house I live in*). These and other similarities have led some researchers to propose that the development of pidgins and creoles follows a "program" that is genetically innate in humans. There are, however, many differences among the world's creoles, in which we find the imprint of various native languages. In many South Pacific creoles, for example, a distinction is made in the pronoun system between dual and plural and between inclusive first person dual and plural and exclusive first person dual and plural (see Chapter 8, where the Tok Pisin pronoun system is given). These distinctions are not found in West African creoles, and their presence in South Pacific creoles reflects the fact that many languages spoken in the South Pacific make these distinctions. In Nigerian creole, on the other hand, we find honorific terms of address (*Mom* and *Dad*) that are used when addressing high-status individuals. These honorifics are not found in any other creole; again, they are transferred from local languages. Thus there is both homogeneity and heterogeneity among the creoles of the world.

Artificial Languages

From time to time since the end of the eighteenth century (and the beginning of the Romantic Era), idealists have proposed that the human race would be better served by a single language in place of the babel of tongues now spoken around the globe. Some intrepid souls have devised new languages that they hoped would be adopted by every nation. The best known and probably most successful artificial language is Esperanto.

Perhaps it is not surprising that artificial languages, despite claims that they have what it takes to become a language of universal use, often bear the imprint of the native language of their inventors. Esperanto resembles the

Romance and Germanic languages on which it is based. It has an accusative case, for example—hardly an essential feature of language but one that is found in Russian, Latin, and German.

Unfortunately, artificial language movements overlook many important factors about human languages, not least of which is the fact that language is a powerful symbol of cultural identity. The philosophy behind artificial language movements also overlooks the certainty that (at least if history is any guide to the future) regional variations would quickly crop up in any artificial language widely adopted. Before long they would become dialects and then separate languages, just as we have seen in the natural course of events for all languages in the past. For better or worse, linguistic diversity is a fundamental feature of the human race, as languages come to reflect the history and experience of their users.

One goal of the artificial language movement is to simplify language by making it more regular. In Esperanto, for example, noun declensions, verbal conjugations, and agreement rules have no exceptions. What the engineers of Esperanto overlook is that even if Esperanto were adopted as a universal language, it would begin changing, and the changes would introduce irregularities and exceptions as other languages have. Only languages that have no living speakers remain static. Even with universal adoption of Esperanto tomorrow, an introductory linguistics textbook written in the year 4000 would certainly contain a section on the languages of the world.

SUMMARY

Languages are ever-changing. All levels of the grammar change: phonology, morphology, syntax, and semantics. From one language many other languages can develop in the course of time if groups of speakers remain physically or socially separated from one another. The method of comparative reconstruction enables linguists to make educated guesses about the structure and vocabulary of prehistoric peoples and to infer a good deal about their cultures from the nature of the reconstructed lexicon. The thousands of languages in the world can be grouped for the most part into language families, whose branches represent languages that are genealogically closer to one another than other languages of the family. When speakers of different languages come into contact, bilingualism may develop, with speakers commanding two or more languages. In some circumstances—usually when a dominant and a subordinate group are in contact—a pidgin may spring up for very limited use, usually in trade. If in time the pidgin comes to be used for other purposes and children learn it at home as a first language, the process of creolization starts. Creolization is a process of expansion in terms of both uses and structures. Artificial languages have also been developed, although they are not in widespread use and would not yield the long-term benefits their designers promise, if the history of language change is any guide to the future.

EXERCISES[3]

1. The following is a comparative word list from seven languages spoken in the South Pacific. (β represents a voiced bilabial fricative and ɣ a voiced velar fricative.)

	Hiw	Waskia	Motu	Amara	Sowa	Mota	Raɣa
'wind'	yoŋ	utuwura	lai	akauliŋ	laiŋ	laŋ	laŋi
'sand'	en	laŋ	miri	olov	on	one	one
'stone'	βət	maŋa	nadi	epeiouŋo	βət	βət	fatu
'turtle'	yə	didu	matabudi	opon	tariβanaβi	uwə	afua
'fish'	eɣə	wal	gwarume	ouŋa	ek	iɣa	iɣe
'mosquito'	noɣa	kasim	namo	ovinkin	tapken	nam	namu
'name'	yo	nup	lada	serio	se	sasa	iha
'child'	moɣoye	kulak	natu	emim	dozo	natu	nitu
'pig'	suɣe	buruk	boroma	esnei	bo	kpwoe	poe
'sugarcane'	tø	kemak	tohu	elgo	ze	tou	toi

(A) Identify which languages are likely to be related and which are not, and justify your claims.

(B) Of the languages that appear to be part of the same family, which are more closely related? Justify your answer.

2. The following is a comparative word list from Lusi and Bariai, closely related languages spoken on the island of New Britain in Papua New Guinea.

Lusi	Bariai		Lusi	Bariai	
βaza	bada	'to fetch'	βua	bua	'Areca nut'
kalo	kalo	'frog'	niu	niu	'coconut'
ɣali	gal	'to spear'	uβu	ubu	'hip'
ahe	ae	'foot'	rai	rai	'trade wind'
zaŋa	daŋa	'thing'	oaɣa	oaga	'canoe'
tazi	tad	'sea'	mata	mata	'eye'
tupi	tup	'to peck'	zoɣi	dog	'type of plant'
tori	tol	'to dance'	hani	an	'food'
ŋiŋi	ŋiŋ	'to laugh'	aŋari	aŋal	'type of bird'

(A) List the consonant correspondences between Lusi and Bariai.

(B) Identify which vowel is lost in Bariai and give a rule that states where it is lost.

3. Table 9-3 (p. 286) provides some correspondence sets among five Polynesian languages. We noted that Tongan had lost a phoneme /r/ from its inventory, which was kept as /r/ or became /l/ in the other four languages. Furthermore, Tongan has kept a phoneme /h/ in certain words, which has been lost in all other Polynesian languages. The following cognates illustrate these two changes.

---

[3] The Amara data used here are taken from an unpublished Amara lexicon by Bil Thurston; the Hiw, Sowa, Mota, and Raɣa data, from Darrell Tryon, *New Hebrides Languages* (Pacific Linguistics, series C, vol. 50, 1976); the Waskia data, from Malcolm Ross and John Natu Paol, *A Waskia Grammar Sketch and Vocabulary* (Pacific Linguistics, series B, vol. 56, 1978); the Lusi and Bariai data, from Rick Goulden, "A Comparative Study of Lusi and Bariai" (McMaster University M.A. thesis, 1982).

Tongan	Samoan	Tahitian	Maori	Hawaiian	
hama	ama	ama	ama	ama	'outrigger'
ama	lama	rama	rama	lama	'torch'

(A) On the basis of this information and the following words, complete the table of consonant correspondences for Tongan, Samoan, Tahitian, Maori, and Hawaiian.

Tongan	Samoan	Tahitian	Maori	Hawaiian	
le?o	leo	reo	reo	leo	'voice'
?uha	ua	ua	ua	ua	'rain'
lili	lili	riri	riri	lili	'angry'
hae	sae	hae	hae	hae	'to tear'
hihi	isi	ihi	ihi	ihi	'strip'
huu	ulu	uru	uru	ulu	'to enter'
fue	fue	hue	hue	hue	'type of vine'
afo	afo	aho	aho	aho	'fishing line'
vela	vela	vera	wera	wela	'hot'
hiva	iva	iva	iwa	iwa	'nine'

(B) Using your table of consonant correspondences and assuming that vowels have not undergone any change in any Polynesian language, complete the following comparative table by filling in the missing words.

Tongan	Samoan	Tahitian	Maori	Hawaiian	
kaukau					'to bathe'
	mata				'eye'
		tafe	kahe		'to flow'
la?e					'forehead'
			wa?a		'canoe'
laŋo					'fly'

(C) Reconstruct the Proto-Polynesian consonant system, on the basis of the information you now have, and taking into account the genetic classification of Polynesian languages discussed in this chapter. (*Hint*: The proto system has to be full enough to account for all the possible correspondences found in the daughter languages. No daughter language has innovated new phonemes, but all have lost one or more from the proto system.)

(D) Reconstruct the Proto-Polynesian words for 'outrigger,' 'rain,' 'to enter,' 'strip,' and 'nine.'

4. Following is a list of Modern French words in phonetic transcription with the Vulgar Latin words from which they derive. (Notice that word-initial /k/ in Latin becomes /k/, /š/, or /s/ in Modern French, depending on where it occurs.)

Modern French	Vulgar Latin	
koʁd	korda	'rope'
šã	kampus	'field'
sɛdʁ	kedrus	'cedar'
kʁaše	krakkāre	'to spit'
šamo	kamēlus	'camel'
sɛʁkl	kirkulus	'circle'
kuʁiʁ	kurrere	'to run'
šaʁ	karrus	'carriage'

kle	klavis	'key'
siteʁn	kisterna	'tank'
kɔlɔ̃b	kolomba	'dove'
ša	kattus	'cat'
ku	kollum	'neck'

(A) Describe a rule that predicts which of the three French phonemes will appear where Latin had /k/. (Consider only the first phoneme of words.)

(B) Consider the additional data below.

Modern French	Vulgar Latin	
šov	kalvus	'bald'
šɛn	katena	'chain'
šo	kalidum	'hot'
šɛʁ	karo	'flesh'

At first glance, these forms are problematic for the rule that you stated in (A). Note, however, that these four words are spelled in Modern French *chauve*, *chaine*, *chaud*, and *chair*, respectively. Given the fact that French orthography often reflects an earlier pronunciation of the language, explain in detail what has happened to the four words in the history of the language.

5. Consider the following Proto-Indo-European reconstructions. Conspicuously, no word for 'sea' can be reconstructed for Proto-Indo-European.

*rtko	'bear'	*peisk	'fish'
*laks	'salmon'	*sper	'sparrow'
*er	'eagle'	*trozdo	'thrush'
*gwou	'cow/bull'	*sū	'pig'
*kwon	'dog'	*agwʰno	'lamb'
*mori	'lake'	*sneigwʰ	'snow'
*bʰerəg	'birch'	*grəno	'corn'
*yewo	'wheat'	*medʰu	'honey'
*weik	'village'	*sel	'fortification'
*sē̄	'to sow'	*kerp	'to collect (food)'
*yeug	'to yoke'	*webʰ	'to weave'
*snē̄	'to spin'	*arə	'to plow'
*ayes	'metal'	*agro	'field'

(A) Describe in detail what these reconstructions (or lack of reconstruction) tell us about the Proto-Indo-Europeans, the environment in which they lived, and their activities.

(B) Based on these reconstructions and on what you know about the current distribution of Indo-European languages, which area or areas of the world would be the best candidates as the homeland of the Proto-Indo-Europeans?

6. The following is a list of Proto-Indo-European reconstructions. Cite a Modern English word that contains a reflex for each one of them; ignore the question as to whether the Modern English word is itself a borrowing or not.

*akwā̄	'water'	*bʰugo	'ram, goat'
*agro	'field'	*bʰreu	'to boil'
*kwetwer	'four'	*carcer	'prison'

*pel	'skin'	*genə	'to give birth'
*reg	'to rule'	*gel	'to freeze'
*wen	'to strive for'	*gʰans	'goose'
*yeug	'to join together'	*macula	'blemish'
*ped	'foot'	*med	'to measure'

SUGGESTIONS FOR FURTHER READING

There are several good textbooks on historical linguistics, including Hock (1986), Lehmann (1973), Anttila (1972), and Jeffers and Lehiste (1979); Bynon (1977) and Aitchison (1981) combine traditional historical analysis with sociolinguistic insights. Lehmann (1967) provides many of the original documents of historical work from the nineteenth century, including the speech of Sir William Jones quoted on page 280. Bellwood (1979; 1987) and Jennings (1979) are surveys of research on Polynesian and Austronesian migrations; all include extensive discussions of language history. Pawley and Green (1971) discusses the linguistic evidence for the location of the Proto-Polynesian homeland.

An excellent reference work treating about a dozen language families and forty of the world's major languages is Comrie (1987); a useful list of references is appended for each family and language. For more detailed information, the encyclopedic fourteen-volume survey edited by Sebeok (1963–76), several volumes of which are dedicated to particular linguistics areas, can be consulted. In addition, there are two excellent book series on language areas and language families: the older Faber and Faber Language Series, which includes volumes on language families and groups like Romance and Germanic and on particular languages like Chinese; and the more up-to-date Cambridge Language Survey Series. The latter series includes volumes on lesser known areas and language families like Comrie (1981), Dixon (1980), Foley (1986), and Suárez (1983). Outside these series, African languages are succinctly surveyed in Gregersen (1977), North American Indian languages in Campbell and Mithun (1979), Amazonian languages in Derbyshire and Pullum (1986), and South American languages in Manelis Klein and Stark (1985). The proposal that all Amerindian languages can be classified into three families appears in Greenberg (1987). Esperanto and other artificial languages are discussed in Large (1985).

Conveniently appended to the 1969 College Edition of the *American Heritage Dictionary of the English Language*—revised and published separately as Watkins (1985)—is an interesting article titled "Indo-European and the Indo-Europeans" by Calvert Watkins, along with a list of Indo-European roots with cognates in several languages; the article contains a description of the Indo-European language and discusses the cultural inferences that can be drawn from the reconstructed lexicon. Buck (1949) is a compilation of Indo-European roots with their reflexes in various languages. Lockwood (1969; 1972) and Baldi (1983) are useful overviews of the Indo-European language family.

Nativization is discussed in Kachru (1982). Good recent surveys of the structure and use of pidgins and creoles include Mülhäusler (1986) and Romaine (1988). The papers in Hymes (1971) and Valdman (1977) also touch on aspects of pidgins and creoles worldwide. An interesting hypothesis about pidginization as an innate program is advanced by Bickerton (1981). On Hawaiian Da Kine Talk, see Carr (1972). The Tok Pisin excerpt on linguistics is taken from Gillian Sankoff's paper entitled "Sampela

Nupela lo Ikamap Long Tok Pisin" ('Some New Rules of Tok Pisin'), published in McElhanon (1975).

Two reference volumes list the languages of the world and their genetic affiliation: Voegelin and Voegelin (1977) and Ruhlen (1986); though generally reliable, there are some inaccuracies of detail. Additional problems of comparative reconstruction are provided in Cowan (1971) and, with some solutions, in Chapter 5 of Langacker (1972).

REFERENCES

Aitchison, Jean. 1981. *Language Change: Progress or Decay?* (New York: Universe Books).

Anttila, Raimo. 1972. *An Introduction to Historical and Comparative Linguistics* (New York: Macmillan).

Baldi, Philip. 1983. *An Introduction to the Indo-European Languages* (Carbondale: Southern Illinois University Press).

Bellwood, Peter. 1979. *Man's Conquest of the Pacific: The Prehistory of Southeast Asia and Oceania* (New York: Oxford University Press).

——. 1987. *The Polynesians: Prehistory of an Island People*, rev. ed. (London: Thames and Hudson).

Bickerton, Derek. 1981. *Roots of Language* (Ann Arbor: Karoma).

Buck, Carl D. 1949. *A Dictionary of Selected Synonyms in the Principal Indo-European Languages* (Chicago: University of Chicago Press).

Bynon, Theodora. 1977. *Historical Linguistics* (Cambridge: Cambridge University Press).

Campbell, Lyle, and Marianne Mithun (eds.). 1979. *The Languages of Native America: Historical and Comparative Assessment* (Austin: University of Texas Press).

Carr, Elizabeth Ball. 1972. *Da Kine Talk: From Pidgin to Standard English in Hawaii* (Honolulu: University Press of Hawaii).

Comrie, Bernard. 1981. *The Languages of the Soviet Union* (Cambridge: Cambridge University Press).

——(ed.). 1987. *The World's Major Languages* (New York: Oxford University Press).

Cowan, William. 1971. *Workbook in Comparative Reconstruction* (New York: Holt, Rinehart and Winston).

Derbyshire, Desmond C., and Geoffrey K. Pullum (eds.). 1986. *Handbook of Amazonian Languages* (New York: Mouton de Gruyter), vol. 1 (vols. 2 and 3 forthcoming).

Dixon, R. M. W. 1980. *The Languages of Australia* (Cambridge: Cambridge University Press).

Foley, William A. 1986. *The Papuan Languages of New Guinea* (Cambridge: Cambridge University Press).

Greenberg, Joseph H. 1987. *Language in the Americas* (Stanford, Calif.: Stanford University Press).

Gregersen, Edgar A. 1977. *Language in Africa: An Introductory Survey* (New York: Gordon & Breach).

Hock, Hans Henrich. 1986. *Principles of Historical Linguistics* (New York: Mouton de Gruyter).

Hymes, Dell (ed.). 1971. *Pidginization and Creolization of Languages* (Cambridge: Cambridge University Press).

Jeffers, Robert J., and Ilse Lehiste. 1979. *Principles and Methods for Historical Linguistics* (Cambridge: MIT Press).

Jennings, Jesse D. (ed.). 1979. *The Prehistory of Polynesia* (Cambridge: Harvard University Press).

Kachru, Braj (ed.). 1982. *The Other Tongue: English Across Cultures* (Urbana: University of Illinois Press).

Langacker, Ronald W. 1972. *Fundamentals of Linguistic Analysis* (New York: Harcourt Brace Jovanovich).

Large, Andrew. 1985. *The Artificial Language Movement* (Oxford: Basil Blackwell).

Lehmann, Winfred P. 1973. *Historical Linguistics: An Introduction*, 2nd ed. (New York: Holt, Rinehart and Winston).

———(ed.). 1967. *A Reader in Nineteenth-Century Historical Linguistics* (Bloomington: Indiana University Press).

Lockwood, W. B. 1969. *Indo-European Philology* (London: Hutchinson).

———.1972. *A Panorama of Indo-European Languages* (London: Hutchinson).

Manelis Klein, Harriet E., and Louisa R. Stark (eds.). 1985. *South American Indian Languages: Retrospect and Prospect* (Austin: University of Texas Press).

McElhanon, K. A. (ed.). 1975. *Tok Pisin i Go We?* (Ukarumpa: Linguistic Society of New Guinea).

Mülhäusler, Peter. 1986. *Pidgin and Creole Linguistics* (Oxford: Basil Blackwell).

Pawley, Andrew, and Kaye Green. 1971. "Lexical Evidence for the Proto-Polynesian Homeland," *Te Reo*, vol. 14, pp. 1–35.

Romaine, Suzanne. 1988. *Pidgin and Creole Languages* (London: Longman).

Ruhlen, Merritt. 1986. *A Guide to the World's Languages* (Stanford, Calif.: Stanford University Press).

Sebeok, Thomas A. (ed.). 1963–76. *Current Trends in Linguistics* (The Hague: Mouton).

Suárez, Jorge A. 1983. *The Mesoamerican Indian Languages* (Cambridge: Cambridge University Press).

Valdman, Albert. 1977. *Pidgin and Creole Linguistics* (Bloomington: Indiana University Press).

Voegelin, Charles F., and Florence M. Voegelin. 1977. *Classification and Index of the World's Languages* (Amsterdam: Elsevier).

Watkins, Calvert (ed.). 1985. *The American Heritage Dictionary of Indo-European Roots* (Boston: Houghton Mifflin).

PART
II

—

LANGUAGE USE

SPEECH ACTS
AND
CONVERSATION

10

LANGUAGE IN USE

As emphasized in the opening chapter of this book, language is principally a tool for doing things. People use language to ask questions, request favors, make comments, report news, give directions, offer greetings, and perform hundreds of other ordinary verbal actions in daily life. Through language, people occasionally *do* things as well: propose marriage, declare a mistrial, swear to tell the truth, fire an employee, and so on. These speech *acts* are part of speech *events* such as conversations, lectures, student-teacher conferences, news broadcasts, marriage ceremonies, and courtroom trials.

The early chapters of this book examined the structure of sentences. We now turn to the question of what people do with sentences and describe some of the ways in which sentences are used in verbal interactions. This chapter examines the nature of speech acts and how sentences are used in speech events to accomplish all that we achieve through language. Subsequent chapters will explore the functions of language variation and of the attitudes that people have toward language and language variation.

Knowing a language is not simply a matter of knowing how to encode messages and transmit them to a second party, who by decoding them understands what we intended to say. If language use were simply a question of encoding and decoding messages—in other words, of *grammatical* competence—every sentence would have a fixed interpretation irrespective of its context of use. That is not the case, of course, as the following scenarios illustrate.

1. You are stopped by a police officer, who surprises you by informing you that you have just driven through a stop sign. "I didn't see the stop sign," you say.

2. A friend has given you directions to her new house, including the instruction to turn left at the first stop sign after the intersection of First and Main. You arrive about thirty minutes late and say, "I didn't see the stop sign."

3. You are driving with an aunt, who is in a hurry to get to church. You slow down and glide through a stop sign, knowing that there is seldom traffic at that intersection on Sunday mornings. As you enter the intersection, you see a car approaching and you jam on the brakes, unsettling your aunt. "I didn't see the stop sign," you say.

To the police officer, "I didn't see the stop sign" is an *explanation* for failing to stop and a *plea* not to be cited for the violation. To the friend, the utterance is an *excuse* for your tardiness and an *explanation* that it was neither intended nor entirely your fault. To your aunt, the same sentence—an untruthful one—is uttered as an *apology* for having frightened her. She recognizes your intention to apologize and says, "It's all right. But please be careful." The meaning of the sentence *I didn't see the stop sign* is the same in all three cases, but its utterance in different contexts serves quite different purposes and conveys distinct messages.

SENTENCE STRUCTURE AND THE FUNCTION OF UTTERANCES

Traditional grammar books would lead us to assume that declarative sentences make statements (*It's raining*), imperative sentences issue directives (*Close the door*), and interrogative sentences ask questions (*What time is it?*). This analysis is oversimplified and misleading. Consider the sentence *Can you shut the window?* Taken literally, its interrogative structure (marked by the inversion of the subject and the auxiliary) asks about the addressee's *ability* to shut some particular window. If asked this question by a roommate trying to study while a marching band practiced nearby (or in many other ordinary uses), one would normally interpret it not as a yes/no question requiring a verbal response but as a request for a physical action—a request to shut the window.[1] Conversely, the imperative structure *Tell me your name again* would normally be taken not as a directive to do something but as a request for information.

---

[1] A request in question form is marked in speech by the absence of voice raising and sometimes in writing by the absence of a question mark (*Can you please respond promptly*).

Take another case: Suppose that a knock is heard at the door, and Mary says to Alice *I wonder who's at the door*. If Mary suspected that Alice knew the answer, this declarative sentence might be uttered as an information question. More often, though, it would actually be a polite request for Alice to open the door. Finally, interrogative sentences can sometimes be used to make statements, as in Sarah's reply to Fred's question.

Fred: Is Amy pretty easy to get along with?

Sarah: Do hens have teeth?

Sarah's yes/no question communicates an emphatically negative *answer* to Fred's inquiry.

Two things are clear, then: People often employ declarative, interrogative, and imperative sentences for purposes other than making statements, asking questions, and giving commands, respectively; and a very important element in the interpretation of an utterance is the *context* in which it is uttered.

Recall that a sentence is a structured string of words that carries a certain meaning. An utterance, in contrast, is a sentence that is *said, written,* or *signed* in a particular context by someone with a particular intention, by means of which the "speaker" intends to create an effect on the "hearer." Thus, as an interrogative sentence *Can you shut the window?* has the meaning of a request for *information* ('are you able to shut the window?'); but as a contextualized utterance it would more often than not be a request for *action* ('please shut the window'). Drawing the requisite inferences from conversation is an essential ingredient for interpreting utterances appropriately. To understand utterances, one must be highly skilled at "reading between the lines." The skills one employs in using the sentences that are shaped by grammatical competence are part of one's communicative competence.

SPEECH ACTS

Besides what we accomplish through physical acts such as cooking, eating, driving, bicycling, gardening, laying bricks, or getting on the bus, we accomplish a great deal each day by verbal acts. In face-to-face conversation, telephone calls, job application letters, notes scribbled to a roommate, and a multitude of other speech events, we perform verbal actions of different types. In fact, language is the principal means we have to greet, compliment, and insult one another, to plead or flirt, to seek and supply information, and to accomplish hundreds of other tasks in a typical day. Actions that are carried out through language are called **speech acts**.

Types of Speech Acts

Various kinds of speech acts have been identified, chiefly by philosophers taking a functional approach to sentences in use.

Speech acts that represent a state of affairs are called *representatives*: assertions, statements, claims, hypotheses, descriptions, and suggestions. Representatives can generally be characterized as being true or false.

Speech acts that commit a speaker to a course of action are called *commissives*: promises, pledges, threats, and vows.

Speech acts intended to get the addressee to carry out an action are *directives*: commands, requests, challenges, invitations, entreaties, and dares.

Speech acts that bring about the state of affairs they name are called *declarations*: blessings, firings, baptisms, arrests, marrying, declaring a mistrial.

Speech acts that indicate the speaker's psychological state or attitude are called *expressives*: greetings, apologies, congratulations, condolences, and thanksgivings.

Speech acts that make assessments or judgments are called *verdictives*: ranking, assessing, appraising, condoning. Because some verdictives (such as calling a baseball player "out") combine the characteristics of declarations and representatives, these are sometimes called *representational declarations*.

Locutions and Illocutions

Every speech act has two principal components: the utterance itself and the intention of the speaker in making it. First, every utterance is represented by a sentence with a grammatical structure and a meaning; this is variously called the **locution** or the utterance act. Second, speakers have some intention in making an utterance, something they intend to accomplish; that intention is called an **illocution**, and every utterance consists of performing one or more illocutionary acts. (A third component of a speech act—one we will not discuss at length—is the effect of the act on the hearer; this is called the *perlocution* of the utterance, or its "uptake.")

The utterance *Can you shut the window?*, for example, comprises a locution and an illocution. The locution is a yes/no question about the addressee's ability to close a particular window; as such, convention would require an answer of *yes* or *no*. The illocution, let us assume, is a request for the addressee to shut the window; as such, convention would enable the addressee to recognize the question as a request for action and to comply (or not). In discussions of speech acts, it is common for the illocutionary act itself to be called the speech act; thus promises, assertions, questions, directives, and so on would be speech acts.

Distinguishing Among Speech Acts

How do we distinguish among different types of speech acts? How do we know whether a locution such as *Do you have the time?* is a yes/no question

(*Do you have the time* [to help me]?) or a request for information about the time of day? To put the matter in more technical terms, given that a locution can serve many functions, how do we know the illocutionary force of a particular utterance? The answer of course is "context." But how do we interpret context accurately?

Let us begin by distinguishing between two broad types of speech act. Compare the following two utterances:

(a)   I now pronounce you husband and wife.

(b)   It is very windy today.

In an appropriate context, the first utterance creates a new relationship between two individuals; it is a declaration that effectuates a marriage. The second utterance is a simple statement or representation of a state of affairs. Certainly it has no effect on the state of the weather. As mentioned earlier, utterances such as (b) that make assertions or state opinions are called *representatives*. Utterances like (a) that change the state of things are called *declarations*; they provide a striking illustration of how language in use is a form of action. Children exposed to fantastical declarations like "Abracadabra, I change you into a frog!" eventually learn that real-life objects are more recalcitrant than fairy-tale objects, but all speakers come to recognize a verbal power over certain aspects of life, especially with respect to social relationships.

With the utterance *I now pronounce you husband and wife*, the nature of the social relationship between two people can be profoundly altered. Similarly, the utterance *You're under arrest!* can have consequences for one's social freedom, as can *Case dismissed.* An umpire can change a baseball game with such declarations as *Foul ball!* and *Safe!* Typically, to be effective, declarations of this type must be uttered by a specially designated person. If called by a nondesignated individual—a fan in the stands, for example—*Out!* would be a verdictive, not a declaration. Indeed, a declaration by a single designated umpire will override a contrary call by a whole team of players and an entire stadium of fans.

Appropriateness Conditions and Successful Declarations   The efficacy of any declaration depends on well-established conventions. *I now pronounce you husband and wife* can bind two individuals in marriage only if a number of conditions are satisfied: the setting must be a wedding ceremony and the utterance said at the appropriate moment; the speaker must be designated to marry others (a judge, minister, rabbi) and must intend to marry the two individuals; the two individuals must be legally qualified to marry each other (that is, of age and not closely related by blood); and they must intend to become spouses. And of course the words themselves must be uttered. If any of these conditions is not satisfied, the utterance of the words will be ineffectual as a performative. Made on a Hollywood movie set by an actor in the role of a pastor and addressed to two actors playing characters about to marry, the utterance will be vacuous (see Chapter 6).

The conventions that regulate the conditions under which an utterance serves as a particular speech act—as a question, marriage, promise, arrest, invitation—are called **appropriateness conditions**, which can be classified into four categories. The first condition, known as the *propositional content condition*, requires merely that the words of the sentence be conventionally associated with the speech act intended and convey the content of the act. The locution must exhibit conventionally acceptable words for effecting the particular speech act: *Is it raining out?; I now pronounce you husband and wife; You are under arrest; I promise to . . .; I swear . . . .*

The second condition requires a conventionally recognized context in which the speech act is embedded. In a marriage, the situation must be a genuine wedding ceremony (however informal) at which two people intend to exchange vows in the presence of a witness. This condition is called the *preparatory condition.*

The third condition requires the speaker to be sincere in uttering the declaration. At a wedding, the speaker must intend that the marriage words should effectuate a marriage; otherwise, the *sincerity condition* will be violated and the speech act will not be successful.

Finally, the fourth condition requires that the involved parties all intend by this ceremony and the utterance of the words *I now pronounce you husband and wife* to create a marriage bond; this is the *essential condition.*

Successful Promises   Now consider the commissive *I promise to help you with your math tonight.* In order for such an utterance to be successful, it must be recognizable as a promise; in addition, the preparatory, sincerity, and essential conditions must be met. In the propositional content condition, the speaker must state the intention of helping the addressee with math. The preparatory condition is that speaker and hearer are sane and responsible human beings and that the speaker believes she is able to help with the math and that the addressee would like to have help. The preparatory condition would be violated if, for example, the speaker knew that she could not be there or that she was incapable of doing the math herself, or if the participants were reading the script of a movie in which the utterance appears. If the speaker knew that the hearer did not *want* help, the promise would not succeed. For the sincerity condition to hold, the speaker must sincerely intend to help the addressee. This condition would be violated (and the promise formula abused) if the speaker had no such intention. Finally, the essential condition of a promise is that the speaker intend by the utterance to place herself under an obligation to provide some help to the hearer. These four appropriateness conditions define a successful promise.

Successful Requests and Other Speech Acts   Appropriateness conditions are useful in describing not only declarations and commissives but all other types of speech acts. In a typical request (*Please pass me the salt*), the content of the utterance must identify the act requested of the hearer (passing the salt), and its form must be a conventionally recognized one for making requests. The preparatory condition includes the speaker's belief that the addressee is capable of passing the salt and that had he not asked her to pass the salt, she would not have ventured to do so. The sincerity condition requires that the speaker genuinely desire the hearer to pass the salt. Finally, the essential condition is that the speaker intend by the utterance to get the hearer to pass the salt to him.

THE COOPERATIVE PRINCIPLE

The principles that govern the interpretation of utterances are diverse and complex—so much so that we may wonder how language succeeds at communication as well as it does. Despite occasional misinterpretations, people in most situations manage to understand utterances as they were intended. The reason is that, without cause to expect otherwise, communicators normally trust that their interlocutors will not deliberately mislead them, lie to them, or insult them. There is an unspoken pact that people will *cooperate* in communicating with each other. The explanation for the pact is simple: unless speakers cooperate in the endeavor to communicate reliably and efficiently, the communicative process will break down—to the detriment of everyone.

The **cooperative principle**, as enunciated by philosopher H. Paul Grice, is as follows: "Make your conversational contribution such as is required, at the stage at which it occurs, by the accepted purpose or direction of the talk exchange in which you are engaged." This pact of cooperation touches on four areas of communication. Each can be described in a *maxim*, or general principle.

Maxim of Quantity

First, speakers are expected to give as much information as is necessary for their interlocutors to understand their utterances but to give no more information than is necessary. If we ask someone whether she has any pets and she answers, "I have two cats," it is the *maxim of quantity* that permits us to assume that she has no other animals. If it turned out that she had three dogs and a llama as well, we would have every reason to feel deceived. While what she said was not false as far as it went, the unspoken commandment not to conceal relevant information would have been violated. Listeners expect speakers to abide by this rule, and speakers assume that their interlocutors believe they are abiding by it. Indeed, without such a belief lying would not be possible.

Suppose that you asked a man painting his house what color he had chosen for the living room, and he replied:

> The walls are off-white to contrast with the black sofa and the Regency armchairs that I inherited from my late great-aunt. (Bless her soul; she passed away last year after a long and sad marriage to a man who really wasn't able to support her in the manner to which she was accustomed.) Then the trimmings will be peach except for the ones near the door, which my wife said should be salmon because otherwise they will clash with the

yellow, black, and red Picasso print that I brought back from Spain—I was on vacation in Spain in August of, let's see, 1982, and I bought it then. Oh, and the stairway leading to the bedrooms will be pale yellow.

In providing too much information, far more than was asked for, the man is as uncooperative as the woman who withheld information about her dogs and llama.

The maxim of quantity provides that, in normal circumstances, speakers supply no more and no less information than is necessary for the purpose of the communication: "Be appropriately informative." Society stigmatizes individuals who habitually violate the maxim of quantity; those who give too much information are described as "never shutting up" or "always telling everyone their life story," while those who habitually fail to provide enough information are branded as sullen, secretive, or untrustworthy.

Maxim of Relevance

The second maxim directs speakers to organize their utterances in such a way that they are relevant to the ongoing context. The following interaction illustrates a violation of this maxim.

Speaker A: How's the weather outside?

Speaker B: There's a great movie on TV Thursday night.

Taken literally, B's utterance seems unrelated to what A has said immediately before; it therefore violates the *maxim of relevance*. Typically, when someone produces an apparently irrelevant utterance, hearers will try to understand how the utterance could possibly be relevant (as a joke, perhaps, or as an indication that the speaker is expressing displeasure with the way the conversation is going). Chronic violations of this maxim are characteristic of schizophrenics, whose sense of "context" differs radically from that of healthier people.

Maxim of Manner

Third, people follow a set of miscellaneous rules that are grouped under the *maxim of manner*. Summarized by the directive "Be orderly and clear," this maxim dictates that speakers and writers avoid ambiguity and obscurity and be orderly in their utterances. In the following example, the maxim of manner is violated with respect to orderliness.

A birthday cake should have icing; use unbleached flour and sugar in the cake; bake it for one hour; preheat the oven to 325 degrees, and beat in three fresh eggs.

This recipe is odd for the simple reason that speakers of English normally follow a chronological order of events in describing a process such as baking.

Orderliness is dictated not only by the order of events: in any language, there are rules that dictate the most natural order of details in a description. In American English, more general details usually precede more specific details, and when a speaker violates this rule the result appears odd.

My hometown has five shopping malls. It is the county seat. My father and my mother were both born there. My hometown is a midwestern town of 105,000 inhabitants situated at the center of the Corn Belt. I was brought up there until I was thirteen years old.

Maxim of Quality

The fourth general principle governing norms of language use is that speakers and writers are expected to say only what they believe to be true and to have evidence for what they say. This *maxim of quality* is central, of course: without it, the other maxims are of little value or interest. Brief and lengthy lies, relevant and irrelevant lies, and orderly and disorderly lies are all equally false. It might be pointed out that this maxim applies principally to assertions. Some other speech acts such as questions (*Is it raining out?*) can hardly be judged as true or false.

VIOLATIONS OF THE COOPERATIVE PRINCIPLE

People sometimes violate the maxims of the cooperative principle. For one thing, not all speakers are completely truthful on all occasions; others, though truthful, have not learned that efficiency is the desired norm in conversational interaction. Sometimes speakers are forced by cultural norms or other external factors to violate a maxim. Irrespective of our esthetic judgment, we may feel constrained to say *What a lovely painting!* to a host who is manifestly proud of his art work. The need to adhere to social conventions of politeness commonly invites people to violate maxims of the cooperative principle.

Indirect Speech Acts

As mentioned earlier, interrogative structures can be used to make polite requests for action, imperative structures can be used to ask for information, and so on. Such uses of an utterance with one meaning for a different purpose play a frequent role in ordinary interaction, as in this exchange between colleagues who have stayed at the office after dark.

Sue: Is the boss in?

Alan: The light's on in his office.

Sue: Oh, thanks.

Alan's answer makes no apparent reference to the information Sue is seeking. Thus in theory it would appear to violate the maxim of relevance. Yet Sue is satisfied with Alan's answer. Recognizing that the *literal* interpretation of

Alan's utterance violates the maxim of relevance and assuming that as a cooperative interlocutor Alan has some reason for saying what he says, Sue seeks a secondary, or *indirect*, interpretation. To help her, she knows certain facts about their boss's habits: that he does not work in the dark, that he works in his own office, and that he is not in the habit of leaving the light on when not in. Relying on this information, Sue assigns an interpretation to Alan's utterance: the boss is likely to be in.

Alan's reply is an example of an indirect speech act. **Indirect speech acts** involve an apparent violation of the cooperative principle but are in fact indirectly cooperative. For example, an indirect speech act can be based on an apparent violation of the maxim of quality. When we describe a friend as *someone who never parts with her Walkman*, we don't mean it literally; we are exaggerating. By overgeneralizing the information, we are seemingly flouting the maxim of quality. But most listeners will appreciate that the statement should not be interpreted literally and will make an appropriate adjustment in their interpretation. Similarly, we may exclaim in front of the World Trade Center *That's an awfully small building!* This utterance too appears to violate the maxim of quality in that we are expressing an evaluation that is manifestly false. But speakers readily spot the irony of utterances such as this and take them to be indirect speech acts intended to convey an opposite meaning to what the sentence means literally.

Characteristics of Indirect Speech Acts From these examples, we can identify four characteristics of indirect speech acts:

1. Indirect speech acts violate at least one maxim of the cooperative principle.

2. The literal meaning of the locution of an indirect speech act differs from its intended meaning.

3. Hearers and readers identify indirect speech acts by noticing that an utterance has characteristic 1 and by assuming that the interlocutor is following the cooperative principle.

4. As soon as they have identified an indirect speech act, hearers and readers identify its intended meaning with the help of knowledge of the context and of the world around them.

Thus, to interpret indirect speech acts, hearers use the maxims to sort out the discrepancy between the literal meaning of the utterance and an appropriate interpretation for the context in which it is uttered.

Indirect Speech Acts and Shared Knowledge One prerequisite for a successful indirect speech act is that interactors share sufficient background about the context of the interaction, about each other and the society in which they live, and about the world in general. If Fred asks Ellen *Are you done with your sociology paper?* and she replies *Is Rome in Spain?*, he will certainly recognize the answer as an indirect speech act. But whether or not he can interpret it will depend on his knowledge of geography.

Using and understanding indirect speech acts requires familiarity with both language and society. To cite a remote example, when speakers of the Polynesian language Tuvaluan want to comment on the fact that a particular person is in the habit of talking about himself, they may say *Koo tagi te tuli ki tena igoa* 'The plover bird is singing its own name.' The expression derives from the fact that the plover bird's cry sounds like a very sharp "tuuuuuliiiii," from which speakers of Tuvaluan have created the word *tuli* to refer to the bird itself. Thus the expression has become an indirect way of criticizing the trait of singing one's own praises. In order to interpret the utterance as an indirect speech act, one not only must be familiar with the plover bird's cry and the fact that it resembles the bird's name but also must know that Tuvaluans view people who talk about themselves as being similar to a bird "singing its own name." The amount of background information about language, culture, and environment needed to interpret indirect speech acts is thus considerable.

Politeness

Indirect speech acts appear to be a complicated way of communicating. Not only must we identify them, but we must then go through a complex reasoning process to interpret them. It would be more efficient to communicate directly, one might think. The fact is, though, that indirect speech acts have uses besides asking and answering questions, issuing directives, and so on. They are sometimes used humorously and often used to show politeness. Ellen's humor in reply to Fred's question suggests 'Don't be ridiculous; of course, I'm not done.' Questions such as *Can you shut the window?* are perceived as more polite and less confrontational and abrasive than commands. One message that indirect speech acts convey is 'I am being polite toward you.' Indirect speech acts are thus an efficient tool of communication: they can convey two or more messages simultaneously.

Metaphors

Metaphors can be viewed as a special type of indirect speech act. Taken literally, the utterance *The loss of a friend is a dark cloud over one's life* violates the maxim of quality, for the loss of a friend is not a cloud. This apparent violation signals that the literal meaning and the intended meaning of the utterance are distinct. A listener can then use knowledge about dark clouds (that most people find them unpleasant and undesirable, that they block the sun's light) and infer that it is some of these unpleasant characteristics that are shared by a dark cloud and the loss of a friend. Thus the mental processes used to interpret metaphors are the same as those used to arrive at the intended meaning of indirect speech acts.

SPEECH EVENTS

A political rally or debate, a public speech, a classroom lecture, a religious sermon, and a disk jockey's "Top 40 countdown" are all speech events—social activities in which language plays a particularly important role.

"Speech" events need not involve speaking: personal letters, short stories, shopping lists, office memos, and birthday cards are also speech events.

Conversation provides the matrix in which native languages are acquired, and it stands out as the most frequent, most natural, and most representative of verbal interactions. A person can spend a lifetime without writing a letter, composing a poem, or debating public policy, but only in rare circumstances does anyone *not* have frequent conversation with friends and companions. Conversation is an everyday speech event. We engage in it for entertainment (gossiping, passing the time, affirming social bonds) and for accomplishing work (getting help with studies, renting an apartment, ordering a meal at a restaurant). Whatever its purpose, conversation is our most basic verbal interaction.

Though movie-screen lovers can conduct heart-to-heart conversations with their backs to each other, conversation usually involves individuals facing each other and taking turns at speaking, neither talking simultaneously nor letting the conversation lag. Even with several conversationalists in a single conversation, there are only tenths of a second between turns and extremely little overlap in speaking. At the beginning of a conversation, people go through certain rituals, greeting one another or commenting about the weather. Likewise, at the end of a conversation people don't simply turn their backs and walk away; they make sure that all the participants have finished what they wanted to say and then utter something like *I have to run* or *Take care.* Throughout the entire interaction, conversationalists maintain a certain level of orderliness—taking turns, not interrupting one another too often, and following certain other highly structured but implicit guidelines for conversation.

These guidelines can be considered norms of conduct that govern how conversationalists comport themselves. Though it is tempting to think of relaxed conversation as essentially free of rules or constraints, the fact is that many rules are operating, and the unconscious recognition of these rules helps identify particular interactions as conversations.

THE ORGANIZATION OF CONVERSATION

If it seems surprising that casual conversation should be organized by rules, the reason is that, as in most speech events, more attention is paid to content than to organization; we take the organization of conversations for granted.

A conversation can be viewed as a series of speech acts—greetings, inquiries, congratulations, comments, invitations, requests, refusals, accusations, denials, promises, farewells. To accomplish the work of these speech acts, some organization is essential: we take turns at speaking, answer questions, mark the beginning and end of a conversation, and make corrections when they are needed. To accomplish such work expeditiously, interlocutors could give one another traffic directions.

Okay, now it's your turn to speak.

I just asked you a question; now you should answer it, and you should
do so right away.

If you have anything else to add before we close this conversation, do it
now because I am leaving in a minute.

Such instructions would be inefficient and would detract attention from the
content. In unusual circumstances, conversationalists do invoke the rules
(*Would you please stop interrupting?*; *Well, say something!*), but such cases
are avoided where possible because they underscore the fact that rules have
been violated and they can seem impolite. Conversations are usually organized covertly, and the organizational principles provide a discreet interactional framework.

The covert architecture of conversation must achieve the following:
organize turns so that more than one person has a chance to speak and the
turn taking is orderly; allow for interlocutors to expect what is going to
happen next and, where there is a choice, how the selection is to be decided;
provide a way to repair glitches and errors when they occur.

Turn Taking and Pausing

Participants must tacitly agree on who should speak when. Normally we
take turns at holding the floor and do so without negotiation. A useful way to
uncover the conventions of turn taking is to observe what happens when they
break down. When a participant fails to take the floor despite indications that
it is his turn, other speakers usually pause, and then someone else begins
speaking. In this example, Alice repeats her question, assuming that Bill
either did not hear or did not understand it the first time.

Alice: Is there something you're worried about?
        [pause]

Alice: Is there something you're worried about?

Bill: No, but I was wondering if you could help me with a problem I'm
        having with my brother.

Turn-taking conventions are also violated when two people attempt to
speak simultaneously. In the next example, the beginning and end of the
overlap are marked with brackets.

Speaker 1: After John's party we went to Fred's house.

Speaker 2: So you—   so you—   you—

                    [   ]

Speaker 3:   What—   what—   time did you get there?

When such competition arises in casual conversation, a speaker may either
quickly relinquish the floor or turn up the volume and continue speaking.

Both silence and simultaneous speaking are serious problems in conversation, which the turn-taking norms are designed to minimize.

Cultures have different degrees of tolerance for silence between turns, overlaps in speaking, and competition among speakers. In some cultures, including many Native American nations and the Eskimos, people sit comfortably together in silence. At the other extreme, in French and Argentinian cultures several conversationalists often talk at the same time, and people interrupt each other more frequently than most Americans feel comfortable doing.

However much tolerance they may have for silences and overlaps, people from all cultures appear to regulate turn taking in conversation in basically similar ways. There are two simple rules: Speakers signal when they wish to end their turn, selecting the next speaker or leaving the choice open. The next speaker takes the floor by beginning to talk. This very simple principle, which is second nature to us, regulates conversational turn taking very efficiently.

Turn-Taking Signals   Speakers signal that their turn is about to end with verbal and nonverbal cues. As most turns end in a complete sentence, the completion of a sentence may signal the end of a turn. A sentence ending in a tag question (*isn't it?*, *are you?*) explicitly invites an interlocutor to take the floor.

Speaker A: Pretty windy out today, isn't it?

Speaker B: Sure is!

The end of a turn may also be signaled by sharply raising or lowering the pitch of one's voice, or by drawling the last syllable of the final word of the turn. In very informal conversations, one common cue is the phrase *or something*.

Speaker 1: So he was behaving as if he had been hit full speed by a truck or something.

Speaker 2: Really?

Other expressions that can signal the completion of a turn are *y'know, kinda, I dunno*, and a trailing *uhm*. As with *y'know*, some of these can also function within a turn for the speaker to keep the floor while thinking about what to say next.

Another way to signal the completion of a turn is to pause and make no attempt to speak again.

Speaker A: I really don't think he should've said that at the meeting, particularly in front of the whole committee. It really was pretty insensitive.
[pause]

Speaker B: Yeah, I agree.

Speakers often pause in the middle of a turn to think about what to say next, to catch a breath, or to stress a point. To signal that a speaker has finished, the pause must be long enough, and "long enough" differs from culture to culture.

Nonverbal as well as verbal signals can indicate the end of turns. Though the principal role of gestures in speaking is to support and stress what we say, continuing to make hand gestures lets our interlocutors know that we have more to say. Once we put our hands to rest, our fellow conversationalists may conclude that we are yielding the floor.

In a more subtle vein, eye gaze can help control floor holding and turn taking. In mainstream American society, speakers do not usually stare continuously at their interlocutors; instead, their gaze goes back and forth between their listener and another point in space, alternating quickly and almost imperceptibly. Because listeners, on the other hand, usually fix their gaze on the speaker, a speaker reaching the end of a turn simply returns her gaze to an interlocutor, thereby signaling her own turn to listen and the interlocutor's to speak. In cultures in which listeners look away while speakers stare, a speaker who wishes to stop talking simply looks away. It is clear, however, that the role of eye gaze in allocating turns is not essential, since telephone conversations are as successful in their turn taking as face-to-face conversation is.

Getting the Floor   In multiparty conversations, the last speaker can select who will speak next, or the next speaker can select himself. In the first instance, the last speaker may signal the choice by addressing the speaker by name (*What have you been up to these days, Helen?*) or by turning toward the selected next speaker. If the last speaker does not select the next speaker, anyone may take the floor, often by beginning the turn at an accelerated pace so as to prevent other potential claims for the floor.

When the last speaker does not select who will talk next, competition can arise, as in the following example, in which overlaps are indicated with square brackets.

Speaker 1: I wonder who's gonna be at Jake's party Saturday night.

  [pause]

Speaker 2:   Todd to—

                           [   ]

Speaker 3: I don't kn—

  [pause]

Speaker 2: Todd   told me—

               [   ]

Speaker 3:   I don't   know who's—

  [short pause]

Speaker 2: [to speaker 3]   Go ahead!

Speaker 3: Todd told me a lotta people would be there.

Speaker 2: Yeah, that's what I was gonna say. I don't know who's gonna be there but I know it'll be pretty crowded.

Friendly participants strive to resolve such competition quickly and smoothly.

Social inequality between conversationalists (boss and employee, parent and child, doctor and patient) is often reflected in how often and when participants claim the floor. In American work settings, superiors commonly initiate conversations by asking a question and letting subordinates report. Thus subordinates hold the floor for longer periods of time than superiors; subordinates perform while superiors act as spectators. In some cultures, superiors talk while subordinates listen.

Adjacency Pairs

One useful mechanism in the covert organization of conversation is that certain turns have specific follow-up turns associated with them. Questions take answers. Greetings are returned by greetings, invitations by acceptances or refusals, and so on. Certain sequences of turns go together, as in these exchanges.

Question and Answer

Speaker 1: Where's the milk I bought this morning?

Speaker 2: On the counter.

Invitation and Acceptance

Speaker 1: I'm having some people to dinner Saturday, and I'd really like you to come.

Speaker 2: Sure!

Assessment and Disagreement

Speaker 1: I don't think Harold would play such a dirty trick on you.

Speaker 2: Well, you obviously don't know Harold very well.

Such **adjacency pairs** comprise two turns, one of which directly follows the other. In a question/answer adjacency pair, the question is the first part, the answer the second part. Here are other examples of adjacency pairs.

Request for a Favor and Granting

Speaker 1: Can I use your phone?

Speaker 2:   Sure.

Apology and Acceptance

Speaker 1: Sorry to bother you this late at night.

Speaker 2: No, that's all right. What can I do for you?

Summons and Acknowledgment

Mark: Bill!

Bill: Yeah?

The Structure of Adjacency Pairs   Three characteristics of adjacency pairs can be noted. First, the two parts are contiguous and are uttered by different speakers. An interaction in which a speaker makes a statement before answering a question that has been posed sounds strange (and can provoke anger) because the parts of the adjacency pair are not consecutive:

Speaker 1: Where's the milk I bought this morning?

Speaker 2: They said on the radio that the weather would clear up by noon. It's on the counter.

Second, the two parts are ordered. Except on certain TV game shows, the answer to a question cannot precede the question; in ordinary conversation, one cannot accept an invitation before it has been offered; and an apology cannot be accepted before uttered (except sarcastically).

Third, the first and second parts must be appropriately matched to avoid such odd exchanges as the following:

Speaker 1: Do you want more coffee?

Speaker 2: That's all right, you're not bothering me in the least!

Insertion Sequences   Occasionally, the requirement that both parts be adjacent is violated in a systematic and socially recognized way.

Speaker 1: Where's the milk I bought this morning?

Speaker 2: The skim milk?

Speaker 1: Yeah.

Speaker 2: On the counter.

In order to provide an accurate answer to speaker 1's question, speaker 2 must first know the answer to another question and thus initiates an insertion sequence—another adjacency pair that interrupts and puts the original adjacency pair "on hold." The interaction thus consists of one adjacency pair embedded in another one, as in the following telephone conversation.

main adjacency pair

Speaker 1: Can I speak to Mr. Higgins?

Speaker 2: May I ask who's calling?

Speaker 1: Arthur Wilcox.

Speaker 2: Please hold.

secondary adjacency pair (insertion sequence)

Preferred and Dispreferred Responses   Certain kinds of adjacency pairs are marked by a preference for a particular type of second part. For example, requests, questions, and invitations have preferred and dispreferred answers. Compare the following interactions, in which the first one has a preferred (positive) second part and the second one has a dispreferred (negative) second part.

Speaker 1: I really enjoyed the movie last night. Did you?

Speaker 2: Yeah, I thought it was pretty good.

Speaker A: I really enjoyed the movie last night. Did you?

Speaker B: No, I thought it was pretty crummy, though I can see how you could've liked certain parts of it.

To an assessment also, the preferred second part is agreement.

Speaker 1: I think Ralph's a pretty good writer.

Speaker 2: I think so too.

Speaker A: I think Ralph's a pretty good writer.

Speaker B: Well, I can see how you'd find his imagery interesting, but apart from that I don't really think he writes well at all.

Dispreferred second parts tend to be preceded by a pause and to begin with a hesitation particle such as *well* or *uh*. Preferred second parts tend to follow the first part without a pause and to consist of structurally simple utterances.

Speaker 1: Would you like to meet for lunch tomorrow?

Speaker 2: Sure!

Speaker A: Would you like to meet for lunch tomorrow?

Speaker B: Well, hmm, let's see .... Tomorrow's Tuesday, right? I told Harry I'd have lunch with him. And I told him so long ago that I'd feel bad canceling. Maybe another time, okay?

In addition, dispreferred second parts often begin with a token agreement or acceptance, or with an expression of appreciation or apology, and usually include an explanation.

Speaker 1: Can I use your phone?

Speaker 2: Oh, I'm sorry, but I'm expecting an important long-distance call any minute. Could you wait a bit?

Opening Sequences

Conversations are opened in socially recognized ways. Before beginning their first conversation of the day, conversationalists normally greet each other, as when two office workers meet in the morning.

Jeff: Mornin', Stan!

Stan: Hi. How's it goin'?

Jeff: Oh, can't complain, I guess. Ready for the meeting this afternoon?

Stan: Well, I don't have much choice!

Greetings exemplify opening sequences, utterances that ease people into a conversation. They convey the message "I want to talk to you."

Greetings are usually reserved for acquaintances who have not seen each other for a while, or as opening sequences for longer conversations between strangers. Some situations do not require a greeting, as with a stranger approaching in the street to ask for the time: *Excuse me, sir, do you know what time it is?* The expression *Excuse me, sir* serves as an opening sequence appropriate to the context. Thus greetings are not the only type of opening sequences.

Very few conversations do not begin with some type of opening sequence, even as commonplace as the following:

Speaker A: Guess what.

Speaker B: What?

Speaker A: I broke a tooth.

Conversationalists also use opening sequences to announce that they are about to invade the personal space of their interlocutors. Here, two friends are talking on a park bench next to a stranger; at a pause in their conversation, the stranger interjects:

Stranger: Excuse me, I didn't mean to eavesdrop, but I couldn't help hearing that you were talking about Dayton, Ohio. I'm from Dayton.

[Conversation then goes on among the three people.]

It is not surprising that opening sequences should take the form of an apology in such situations.

Finally, opening sequences may serve as a display of one's voice to enable the interlocutor to recognize who is speaking, especially at the beginning of telephone conversations. Here, the phone has just rung in Alfred's apartment.

Alfred: Hello?

Helen: Hi!

Alfred: Oh, hi, Helen! How ya doin'?

In the second turn, Helen displays her voice to enable Alfred to recognize her. In the third turn, Alfred indicates his recognition and simultaneously provides the second part of the greeting adjacency pair initiated in the previous turn.

Opening Sequences in Other Cultures   In many cultures, the opening sequence appropriate to a situation in which two people meet after not having met for a while is an inquiry about the person's health, as in the American greeting *How are you?* Such inquiries are essentially formulaic and not meant literally. Indeed, most speakers respond with a conventional upbeat formula (*I'm fine* or *Fine, thanks*) even when feeling terrible. In other cultures, the conventional greeting may take a different form. Traditionally, Mandarin Chinese conversationalists ask *Nǐ chī guo fàn le?* 'Have you eaten rice yet?' When two people meet on a road in Tonga, they ask *Ko hoʔo ʔalu ki fe?* 'Where is your going directed to?' These greetings are as formulaic as the American *How are you?*

In formal contexts, or when differences of social status exist between participants, many cultures require a lengthy and formulaic opening sequence. In Fiji, when an individual visits a village, a highly ceremonial introduction is conducted before any other interaction takes place. This event involves speeches that are regulated by a complex set of rules governing what must be said, and when, and by whom. This ceremony serves the same purpose as opening sequences in other cultures.

Functions of Opening Sequences   One last aspect of opening sequences in which cultural differences are found is the relative importance of their various functions. In American telephone conversations, opening sequences serve primarily to identify speakers and solicit the interlocutor's attention. In France, opening sequences normally apologize for invading someone's privacy.

Person called: Allo?

Caller: Allo? Je suis désolé de vous déranger. Est-ce que j'peux parler à Marie-France?   ('Hello? I'm terribly sorry for disturbing you. Can I speak to Marie-France?')

In an American telephone conversation, such an opening sequence is not customary. Thus, in two relatively similar cultures, the role played by the opening sequence in a telephone call is different. As a result, the French can find Americans intrusive and impolite on the telephone, while Americans are puzzled by French apologetic formulas, which they find pointless and exceedingly ceremonious.

Closing Sequences

Conversations must also be closed appropriately. A conversation can be closed only when the participants have said everything they wanted to say. Furthermore, a conversation must be closed before participants begin to feel uncomfortable about having nothing more to say. As a result, conversationalists carefully negotiate the timing of closings, seeking to give the impression of wanting neither to rush away nor to linger on.

These objectives are reflected in the characteristics of the closing sequence. First of all, a closing sequence includes a conclusion to the last topic covered in the conversation. In conclusions, conversationalists often make arrangements to meet at a later time or express the hope of so meeting. These arrangements may be genuine, as in the first example here, or formulaic, as in the second.

> Speaker 1: Okay, it's nice to see you again. I guess you'll be at Kathy's party tonight.
>
> Speaker 2: Yeah, I'll see you there.

> Speaker A: See you later!
>
> Speaker B: See ya!

The first step of a closing sequence helps ensure that no one has anything further to say. This is accomplished by a simple exchange of short turns such as *okay* or *well*. Typically, such preclosing sequences are accompanied by a series of pauses between and within turns that decelerate the exchange and prepare for closing down the interaction. In the following example, speaker 2 takes the opportunity to bring up one last topic, after which speaker 1 initiates another closing sequence.

> Speaker 1: Okay, it's nice to see you again. I guess you'll be at Kathy's party tonight.
>
> Speaker 2: Yeah, I'll see you there.
>
> Speaker 1: Okay.
>
> Speaker 2: I hear there's gonna be lotsa people there.
>
> Speaker 1: Apparently she invited half the town.

Speaker 2: Should be fun.

Speaker 1: Yeah.

Speaker 2: Okay.

Speaker 1: Okay. See ya there.

Speaker 2: Later!

Sometimes, after a preclosing exchange, speakers refer to the original motivation for the conversation. In a courtesy call to inquire about someone's health, the caller sometimes refers to this fact after the preclosing exchange.

Caller: Well, I just wanted to see how you were doing after your surgery.

Person called: Well, that was really nice of you.

If the purpose of a conversation was to seek a favor, this short exchange might take place:

Speaker 1: Well, listen, I really appreciate your doing this for me.

Speaker 2: Forget it. I'm glad to be of help.

Finally, conversations close with a parting expression: *goodbye, bye, see you, catch you later*.

The striking thing about closings is their deceptive simplicity. In fact, they are complex. Participants exercise great care not to give the impression that they are rushing away or that they want to linger on, and they try to ensure that everything on the unwritten agenda of any participant has been touched on. However informal and abbreviated, closing sequences are characterized by a great deal of negotiated activity.

Repairs

A **repair** takes place in conversation when a participant feels the need to correct herself or another speaker, to edit a previous utterance, or simply to restate something, as in these examples, in which a dash indicates an abrupt cutoff.

(a) Speaker: I was going to Mary's— uh, Sue's house.

(b) Speaker: And I went to the doctor's to get a new— uh— a new whatchamacallit, a new prescription, because my old one had expired.

(c) Speaker 1: Look at these daffodils, aren't they pretty?

Speaker 2: They're pretty, but they're narcissus.

(d)   Speaker 1: Todd came to visit us over the Christmas break.

Speaker 2: What?

Speaker 1: I said that Todd was here over the Christmas break.

In example (b), the trouble source is the fact that the speaker cannot find a word. In example (d), speaker 2 initiates a repair because he has not heard or has not understood speaker 1's utterance. Conversationalists thus make repairs for a variety of reasons.

To initiate a repair is to signal that one has not understood or has misheard an utterance, that a piece of information is incorrect, or that one is having trouble finding a word. To resolve a repair, someone must repeat the misunderstood or misheard utterance, correct the inaccurate information, or supply the word. To initiate a repair, we may ask a question, as in example (d); repeat part of the utterance to be repaired, as in the following example (e); abruptly stop speaking, as in example (f); or use particles and expressions like *uh*, *I mean*, or *that is*, as in example (a).

(e)   Speaker: I am sure—   I am absolutely sure it was him that I saw last night prowling around.

(f)   Speaker 1: And here you have what's called the—
              [pause]

Speaker 2: The carburetor?

Speaker 1: Yeah, that's right, the carburetor.

Repairs can be initiated and resolved by the person who uttered the words that need to be repaired or by another conversationalist. There are thus four possibilities: self-initiated, self-repaired; other-initiated, self-repaired; self-initiated, other-repaired; and other-initiated, other-repaired. Of these four possibilities, conversationalists show a clear preference for self-initiated self-repairs, which are least disruptive to the conversation and to the social relationship between the conversationalists. In general, conversationalists wait for clear signals of communicative distress before repairing an utterance made by someone else. The least preferred pattern is for other-initiated, other-repaired. Individuals in the habit of both initiating and repairing utterances for others are often branded as poor conversationalists or know-it-alls.

Found in many cultures, these preference patterns reflect an unspoken basic rule that all participants in a conversation among equals be given a chance to say what they want to say by themselves. Conversationalists provide assistance to others in initiating and resolving repairs only if no other option is available.

POLITENESS: AN ORGANIZATIONAL
FORCE IN CONVERSATION

Violations of the turn-taking principles by interrupting or by failing to take turns are considered impolite. Turning one's back on interlocutors at the end of a conversation without going through a closing sequence is also stigmatized by the conventions of politeness. Other aspects of politeness are more subtle but nevertheless play an important role in structuring conversation.

Positive and Negative Politeness

There are two basic aspects to being polite. The first rests on the fact that human beings respect one another's presence, privacy, and physical space. We *avoid* intruding on other people's lives, try *not* to be too inquisitive about their activities, and take care *not* to impose our presence on them. This is called *negative politeness*. On the other hand, when we let people know that we enjoy their company, feel comfortable with them, like something in their personality, or are interested in their well-being, we show *positive politeness*.

While everyone has need of both negative and positive politeness, the first requires us to leave people alone, while the second requires us to do the opposite. Fortunately the needs for negative and positive politeness usually arise in different contexts. When we shut ourselves in a room or take a solitary walk on the beach, we affirm our right to negative politeness. When we attend a party, invite someone to dinner, or call friends on the telephone to check up on them, we extend positive politeness.

In conversation, we give each other messages about our needs for negative and positive politeness and acknowledge our interlocutors' needs for both types as well. The expectation that others won't ask embarrassing questions about our personal lives results from a need for negative politeness. When we tell a friend about personal problems and expect sympathy, we are asking for positive politeness. Excusing ourselves before asking a stranger for the time is a recognition of the stranger's need for negative politeness. When we express the hope of meeting an interlocutor at a later date (*Let's get together some time!*), we acknowledge that person's need for positive politeness.

There are also covert ways in which we communicate negative and positive politeness. When we expect interlocutors to allow us to both initiate and resolve a repair ourselves, we are expecting them to respect our right to make a contribution to the conversation without intrusion from others; that is, we are asking them to show negative politeness. Similarly, we recognize another person's need for negative politeness when, instead of ending a conversation, we initiate a preclosing exchange, affording the interlocutor a chance to say something further before closing. In contrast, when we initiate a conversation with a greeting, we convey concern about the addressee's health and well-being, thereby acknowledging his need for positive politeness. Many of the principles of conversational architecture can be explained in terms of politeness and the recognition of the politeness needs of others.

CROSS-CULTURAL COMMUNICATION

When people of different cultures have different norms about what type of politeness is required in a particular context, trouble can easily arise. We have described how callers in France begin telephone conversations with an apology; such apologies rarely form part of the opening sequence of an American telephone conversation. Obviously, members of the two cultures view telephone conversations differently: Americans generally see the act of calling as a sign of positive politeness, while the French tend to view it as a potential intrusion.

When two cultures are in close contact with each other, such differences can have unfavorable consequences. In the United States, many social conflicts that arise between blacks and whites result from differences in the norms of communication in particular contexts. Take flirting, for example. White working-class men and women tend to be very attentive to each other's needs for negative politeness; generally speaking, they make relatively few overt references to sexual matters and allude to, rather than state, their interest in each other. In contrast, black working-class men and women may make sexual overtures more bluntly and do not shy away from making explicit complimentary remarks about physique; their patterns of flirting thus place greater emphasis on positive politeness needs than on negative politeness needs. As long as both parties share the same norms of flirting, no problems arise. But when a white man attempts to flirt with a black woman, or a black man with a white woman, misunderstanding can occur. Thomas Kochman's useful analysis of such situations is worth quoting:

> A white female will . . . be disturbed by what she perceives to be a mismatch in the situation. The black male presents his rap in a verbally skillful, assertive manner, accustomed as he is to interacting with black females who are also verbally skillful and assertive. But the white female has been brought up in a culture that teaches women to be passive and sexually receptive vis-à-vis men and to rely on them, rather than on themselves, for sexual protection. . . . Consequently, she believes herself unable to manage the kind of self-assertion or verbal skill that she feels is necessary to achieve parity in the situation. She may also be handicapped by norms of politeness that make her reluctant to assert herself when that might also hurt another person's feelings. Thus she will conclude that the only tactics available to her are to ignore the approach or, if that is not possible, to plead with the black man to let her alone.

As a consequence of cultural variability, people from different cultures often misinterpret each other's signals. In the conversations of Athabaskan Indians, a pause of up to about one and a half seconds does not necessarily indicate the end of a turn; Athabaskans often pause that long in the middle of a turn. Most European-Americans consider a pause of more than one second sufficiently long to signal the end of a turn (though there may be social variation). When Athabaskan Indians and European-Americans interact with each other, the latter often misinterpret the Athabaskans' mid-turn pauses as end-of-turn signals and feel free to claim the floor. From the Athabaskans' perspective, the European-Americans' claim of the floor at this point is an interruption. With the same situation occurring time and again in interactions between the two groups, negative stereotypes arise. Athabaskans find mainstream Americans rude, pushy, and uncontrollably talkative, while mainstream Americans find Athabaskans conversationally uncooperative, sullen, and incapable of carrying on a coherent conversation. Carrying those stereotypes unwittingly into a classroom, white teachers may judge Indian students unresponsive or unintelligent, for they expect students to speak up, interact, and be quick in their responses. While these tend to be the reactions of children in mainstream American culture, Athabaskan children, following the norms of their own culture, do not have these characteristics, at least not to the same degree. Though most people are totally unaware of such subtle cross-cultural differences, they can have profound social consequences.

SUMMARY

Utterances are used to accomplish things like asserting, promising, pleading, and greeting. Actions accomplished through language are called *speech acts*. That language is commonly used to perform actions is most clearly illustrated by declarations. All speech acts, whether declarations or not, can be described with a set of four appropriateness conditions, each of which describes one aspect of or prerequisite for a successful speech act: the content of the speech act, the preparatory condition, the sincerity condition, and the essential condition.

Language users are bound by an unspoken pact, which they adhere to in most normal circumstances and expect others to adhere to. This *cooperative principle* consists of four maxims—of quantity, quality, relevance, and manner. On occasion, a speaker or writer may flout a maxim to signal that the literal interpretation of the utterance is not the intended one. To encode and decode the intended meaning of such indirect speech acts, people use reasoning patterns based on knowledge of their language, their society, and the world around them. Indirect speech acts convey more than one message; they are commonly used for politeness and humor.

A *speech event* is a social activity in which spoken or written language plays an important role. Speech events are structured; appropriate verbal and nonverbal behavior characteristic of particular speech events can be described systematically. Conversations are organized according to a number of principles that regulate various aspects of conversational behavior. Turn taking is regulated by one set of norms. Adjacency pairs are structured by a local set of organizational principles; many have preferred and dispreferred second parts. Still other organizational principles shape conversational openings and closings. The organization of repairs can be described with a set of rules that rank different repair patterns in terms of preference; self-initiated self-repairs are favored. At the root of many organizational principles in conversation is the need for human beings to display both respect and sympathy for one another. Acknowledging other people's needs for respect expresses negative politeness, while displaying sympathy shows positive politeness. When and where negative and positive politeness behaviors are displayed is determined by culture-specified norms. As a result, cross-cultural variation is considerable in the organization of polite behavior in conversation, and miscommunication of intent is common.

EXERCISES

1. Make a list of the headlines on the first two pages of a daily newspaper. Indicate which of the headlines report physical actions and which speech acts.

2. Observe a typical lecture meeting of one of your courses and identify the characteristics that define it as a lecture (as distinct from an informal conversation, workshop, seminar, or lab meeting). Identify characterizing features in the areas listed. To what extent is there room for variability in how a lecture is conducted (depending, for example, on the personality of the participants)? When does a lecture stop being a lecture?

   (a) setting (physical setting, clothing, social identity of the participants, and so on)
   (b) nonverbal behavior of the participants (body movement, stance and position with respect to each other, and so on)
   (c) verbal behavior of the participants (turn taking, openings, closings, assignment of pair parts among participants, and so on)
   (d) topic (what is appropriate to talk about? to what extent can this be deviated from? and so on)

3. Make a tape recording of the first minute of a radio interview. Transcribe what is said during that first minute in as much detail as possible (indicating, for example, who talks, when pauses occur, and what hesitations occur). Label each turn as to its illocutionary force (greeting, inquiry, compliment, and so on). Then describe in detail the strategies used in opening the radio interview. Illustrate your description with specific examples taken from your transcript.

4. Make a tape recording of the first minute of a broadcast of the evening news on radio or television. Transcribe what is said during that minute in as much detail as possible. Then answer the following questions, citing specific illustrations from your transcript.

   (A) What effect do radio or television newscasters try to achieve initially?
   (B) How is this accomplished? Describe at least two strategies, using specific illustrations.
   (C) Suppose you played your tape recording to friends without identifying what was taped. Exactly what features would help them recognize it as a recording of the evening news? Cite three specific telltale characteristics other than content.
   (D) Which of the news items are reports of physical actions and which are reports of speech acts?

5. Observe the following interaction between two people who are working at nearby desks.

> Anne: Ed?
> Ed: Yeah?
> Anne: Do you have a ruler?

Anne's first turn is an opening sequence. What does it signal, and what does Ed's response indicate? Why did Anne not merely open with *Do you have a ruler?*

6. The next time you talk on the telephone to a friend, observe the distinctive characteristics of talk over the telephone, and take notes immediately after you hang up. Identify several ways in which a telephone conversation differs from a face-to-face conversation. Try to re-create specific linguistic examples from your telephone conversation to illustrate your points.

7. Consider the following excerpts, each of which contains a repair. For each excerpt, determine whether the repair is: (a) self-initiated and self-repaired; (b) self-initiated and other-repaired; (c) other-initiated and self-repaired; or (d) other-initiated and other-repaired.

(A) Pierre: What's sales tax in this state?
    James: Five cents on the dollar.
    Patricia: Five cents on the dollar? You mean six cents on the dollar.
    James: Oh, yeah, six cents on the dollar.

(B) Anne: There's a party at Rod's tonight. Wanna go?
    Sam: At Rod's? Rod's outta town!
    Anne: I mean Rick's.

(C) Peter: And then he comes along an' tells me that he's dropping his accounting— uh, his economics class.
    Frank: Yeah, he tole me the same thing the next mornin'.

(D) Rick: His dog's been sick since last month an' he won't be able to go to the wedding because he's gotta take care of him.
    Alice: Well, actually, his dog's been sick for at least two months now. So it's nothin' new.

(E) Samantha: Do you remember the names of all their kids? The oldest one is Daniel, the girl's Priscilla, then there's another girl— what's her name again?
    Reginald: Susie, I think.
    Samantha: Yeah, Susie, that's it.

(F) Ellie: What do they charge you for car insurance?
    Ted: Two hundred bucks a year, but then there's a three-hundred-dollar deductible. Three hundred or one hundred— I can't remember.
    Ellie: Probably's one hundred, right?
    Ted: Yeah, I think you're right. One hundred sounds right.

(G) Sarah: He's been cookin' all day for that dinner party.
    Anne: Actually he's been cooking for three days now.

(H) Will: There wasn't much I could do for her. She needed five thousand
              bucks to pay for tuition and I jus' didn't have it.
      David: I thought it was four thousand.
      Will: Yeah, four thousand, but still I didn't have that much.

8. Consider the following excerpts, all of which are prestructures initiating conversation. Describe in detail the structure and the function of each prestructure,
   using the terms *turn* (or *turn taking*), *signal*, *adjacency pair*, *first part*, *second
   part*, and *claiming the floor*.

   Larry: Guess what.
   Lauren: What?
   Larry: Pat's coming tomorrow.

   Tom: [reading the newspaper] I can't believe this!
   Fred: What?
   Tom: Congress passed that new immigration law.

   Ruth: [chuckles while reading a book]
   Anne: What're you chuckling about?
   Ruth: This story, it's so off the wall!

9. Consider the following excerpt from a conversation among three friends.

   (1) Cindy: Heard from Jill recently? She hasn't written or called in ages.
   (2) Larry: Yeah, she sent me a postcard from England.
   (3) Barb: From England?
   (4) Larry: Oh, maybe it was from France, I can't remember.
   (5) Cindy: What's she doin—
   (6) Barb: No, I know it must've been from France 'cuz she was gonna stay
                there all year.
   (7) Cindy: What's she doin' in France?
   (8) Larry: Why are you asking about her?
   (9) Cindy: I dunno, I've jus' been thinkin' about 'er.
   (10) Larry: She's on some sort of exchange program. Studyin' French or
                somethin'.
   (11) Cindy: Sounds pretty nice to me.
   (12) Larry: Yeah. Well, I dunno. She said she was tired of Europe and she
                wants to come home.

   Analyze this conversation turn by turn, using the following terms: *turn* (or *turn
   taking*), *signal*, *claiming the floor*, *adjacency pair*, *first part*, *second part*,
   preferred, *dispreferred*, *repair*, *trouble source*, *initiation*, and *resolution*.

10. Conversations quoted in writing and re-created in movies differ from real
    day-to-day conversations. The following is an excerpt of a conversation from
    Part III of Isak Dinesen's autobiographical novel *Out of Africa* (New York:
    Random House, 1937).

    "Do you know anything of book-keeping?" I asked him.
    "No. Nothing at all," he said, "I have always found it very difficult to add
    two figures together."
    "Do you know about cattle at all?" I went on. "Cows?" he asked. "No, no.
    I am afraid of cows."

"Can you drive a tractor, then?" I asked. Here a faint ray of hope appeared on his face. "No," he said, "but I think I could learn that."

"Not on my tractor though," I said, "but then tell me, Emmanuelson, what have you even been doing? What are you in life?"

Emmanuelson drew himself up straight. "What am I?" he exclaimed. "Why, I am an actor."

I thought: Thank God, it is altogether outside my capacity to assist this lost man in any practical way; the time has come for a general human conversation. "You are an actor?" I said, "that is a fine thing to be. And which were your favourite parts when you were on the stage?"

"Oh I am a tragic actor," said Emmanuelson, "my favourite parts were that of Armand in 'La Dame aux Camelias' and of Oswald in 'Ghosts'."

On the basis of this example, analyze the differences between the organization of conversations quoted in writing and the organization of actual conversations. Why do these differences exist?

SUGGESTIONS FOR FURTHER READING

The analysis of speech acts has been an enterprise chiefly of philosophers. Austin (1962) is a set of twelve readable lectures laying out the nature of locutionary acts, illocutionary acts, and perlocutionary acts. Grice (1975) formulates the cooperative principle and enumerates the conversational maxims discussed in this chapter. Searle (1976) discusses the classification of speech acts and their syntax, while Searle (1975) lays out the structure of indirect speech acts. Besides these primary sources, there are several good discussions of the work of Austin, Grice, and Searle in various chapters of Cole and Morgan (1975), Levinson (1983), and Wardhaugh (1986).

Profoundly differing from the philosophical traditions in their methodological approach, the inductive studies of the conversation analysts are technical and difficult to read: turn taking was first analyzed systematically by Sacks et al. (1974), closings by Schegloff and Sacks (1973), and repairs by Schegloff et al. (1977). Atkinson and Heritage (1984) and Schenkein (1978) are good collections of papers on various aspects of the organization of conversation. More accessible are these textbooks on conversation analysis and language use in various informal contexts: Levinson (1983), McLaughlin (1984), chapters 8 and 10 of Ellis and Beattie (1986), and chapters 10 and 12 of Wardhaugh (1986); Wardhaugh (1985) is very accessible.

The theoretical background to the study of speech events is presented in Goffman (1974). Goffman (1981) presents interesting and entertaining analyses of various speech events including lectures (chapter 4) and radio talk (chapter 5). Kendon et al. (1975) and Goodwin (1981) describe how talk and gestures are integrated in conversation. The organization of conversation in the workplace is investigated in Boden (1988), and verbal communication (and miscommunication) between doctors and patients is analyzed in West (1984). The characterization of communication between subordinates and superordinates as spectator/performer or performer/spectator was proposed in Bateson (1972), which lays out the philosophical foundation for the study of human communication. Cross-social and cross-cultural differences in the organization of conversation are analyzed in Gumperz (1982), Gumperz (ed., 1982), Kochman (1981), and Scollon and Scollon (1981). A few examples from the latter two books were used in this chapter. Gumperz et al. (1979), a one-hour video on miscommunication between East Indian immigrants and the British in institutional settings in

England, is a moving demonstration of the painful difficulties that can arise from differing conversational norms across cultural boundaries. Godard (1977) is an interesting study of Franco-American differences in behavior on the telephone. Brown and Levinson (1987) and various chapters of Levinson (1983) and Wardhaugh (1986) discuss politeness.

REFERENCES

Atkinson, J. Maxwell, and John Heritage (eds.). 1984. *Structures of Social Action: Studies in Conversation Analysis* (Cambridge: Cambridge University Press).

Austin, John. 1962. *How to Do Things with Words* (New York: Oxford University Press).

Bateson, Gregory. 1972. *Steps to an Ecology of Mind* (New York: Bantam).

Boden, Deirdre. 1988. *The Business of Talk: Organizations in Action* (Cambridge, England: Polity Press).

Brown, Penelope, and Stephen C. Levinson. 1987. *Politeness: Some Universals in Language Usage* (Cambridge: Cambridge University Press); reprinted from Esther Goody (ed.), *Questions and Politeness: Strategies in Social Interaction* (Cambridge: Cambridge University Press), pp. 56–311.

Cole, Peter, and Jerry L. Morgan (eds.). 1975. *Syntax and Semantics*, vol. 3 "Speech Acts" (New York: Academic Press).

Ellis, Andrew, and Geoffrey Beattie. 1986. *The Psychology of Language and Communication* (New York: Guilford Press).

Godard, Daniele. 1977. "Same Setting, Different Norms: Phone Call Beginnings in France and the United States," *Language in Society*, vol. 6, pp. 209–219.

Goffman, Erving. 1974. *Frame Analysis: An Essay on the Organization of Experience* (New York: Harper & Row).

———. 1981. *Forms of Talk* (Philadelphia: University of Pennsylvania Press).

Goodwin, Charles. 1981. *Conversational Organization: Interaction between Speakers and Hearers* (New York: Academic Press).

Grice, H. Paul. 1975. "Logic and Conversation," in Cole and Morgan (1975), pp. 41–58.

Gumperz, John J. 1982. *Discourse Strategies* (Cambridge: Cambridge University Press).

——— (ed.). 1982. *Language and Social Identity* (Cambridge: Cambridge University Press).

Gumperz, John J., T. C. Jupp, and C. Roberts. 1979. *Crosstalk: A Study of Cross-cultural Communication* (London: National Centre for Industrial Language Training and BBC).

Kendon, Adam, Richard M. Harris, and Mary Ritchie Key (eds.). 1975. *Organization of Behavior in Face-to-Face Interaction* (The Hague: Mouton).

Kochman, Thomas. 1981. *Black and White Styles in Conflict* (Chicago: University of Chicago Press).

Levinson, Stephen C. 1983. *Pragmatics* (Cambridge: Cambridge University Press).

McLaughlin, Margaret L. 1984. *Conversation: How Talk Is Organized* (Beverly Hills, Calif.: Sage).

Sacks, Harvey, Emanuel A. Schegloff, and Gail Jefferson. 1974. "A Simplest Systematics for the Organization of Turn-taking in Conversation," *Language*, vol. 50, pp. 696–735.

Schegloff, Emanuel A., Gail Jefferson, and Harvey Sacks. 1977. "The Preference for Self-correction in the Organization of Repair in Conversation," *Language*, vol. 53, pp. 361–382.

Schegloff, Emanuel A., and Harvey Sacks. 1973. "Opening Up Closings," *Semiotica*, vol. 7, pp. 289–327.

Schenkein, Jim (ed.). 1978. *Studies in the Organization of Conversational Interaction* (New York: Academic Press).

Scollon, Ron, and Suzanne B. K. Scollon. 1981. *Narrative, Literacy and Face in Interethnic Communication* (Norwood, N.J.: Ablex).

Searle, John R. 1975. "Indirect Speech Acts," in Cole and Morgan (1975), pp. 59–82.

———. 1976. "A Classification of Illocutionary Acts," *Language in Society*, vol. 5, pp. 1–23.

Wardhaugh, Ronald. 1985. *How Conversation Works* (New York: Basil Blackwell).

———. 1986. *An Introduction to Sociolinguistics* (New York: Basil Blackwell).

West, Candace. 1984. *Routine Complications: Troubles in Talk Between Doctors and Patients* (Bloomington: Indiana University Press).

WRITING

11

INTRODUCTION

Humans have possessed the ability to speak for hundreds of thousands of years. It arose as part of our intellectual developments during evolution and as a response to the need to communicate as efficiently as these intellectual developments allowed. In contrast, writing was invented only recently. Humans have been able to represent speech in written form for a mere five or six thousand years. Even today, many people go through life without ever learning to read and write. Though language is involved in both spoken and written communication, the two channels are fundamentally different in nature: speaking developed in us, but we had to invent writing; speaking has been with us for hundreds of millennia, writing for only a few; every physically and mentally healthy human being knows how to speak, but writing is an advanced technology, some might say a luxury.

Writing has become second nature to most members of literate societies, so much so, in fact, that it governs much of our thinking about language itself. If we ask elementary school graduates how many vowels there are, the most common answer will be five: *a, e, i, o, u* (and, some will add, sometimes *y*). Obviously this common reply misses the mark; the explanation lies in the fact that when most of us talk of sounds we usually think of letters of the alphabet. It is common in literate societies to find that people speaking about "language" say things appropriate only to written language, not to spoken language. This is perhaps not surprising in English-speaking societies, in which the first time language is discussed objectively is in school. The schools' primary language objective is to teach children to read and write—to master the written word. The spoken word does not commonly play a significant role in our formal education. Thus, at an early age, we come to think of writing as an essential part of our linguistic activities.

In this chapter we will examine the history of writing, the development of different types of writing, and the relationship between speech and writing. As will become apparent, our knowledge about the history and the nature of writing is uneven. While we have a reasonably good idea of how writing has evolved over the centuries, exactly how it was invented remains unclear. While we understand how spoken language differs from written language, exactly how these differences arose is open to discussion. But such un-answered questions do not prevent us from marveling at the extraordinary achievement that we call writing.

THE HISTORICAL EVOLUTION OF WRITING

Long before they developed writing, humans produced graphic representa-tions of the objects that surrounded them. The prehistoric records in the extraordinary cave paintings of Spain, France, and the Sahara Desert, which are between twelve thousand and forty thousand years old, bear witness to people's age-old fascination with animals, hunters, and deities. In that they represent concepts rather than words, these paintings are very different from writing. They are representations of real-life objects, not of the words that represent these objects. Writing, by contrast, is a system of visual symbols representing audible symbols.

Of course the drawings and paintings that prehistoric people produced contained the seeds of writing. At first, people would communicate by using drawings. In time, certain stylized representations of objects like the sun came to be associated with the words for those objects. Thus, to take a made-up example, the drawing ☼, which originally could have repre-sented the sun as an object or concept, could have come to be associated with the sound of the word *sun*—with [sʌn]. This association was the first symp-tom of the birth of a writing system, in which a drawn representation did not directly evoke a concept but evoked the spoken word for the concept. The stage was set for using such a visual symbol to represent other words that sounded the same. If we think of English, the symbol ☼ as a representa-tion of the sun could be extended to represent the word *son*, for example, or the first part of *Sunday*. From a picture of an object, a written symbol of a *sound* is born.

The Leap from Pictures to Writing

To use a *written* symbol to represent a sound is a great achievement (comparable to using a spoken symbol to represent a concept). To use one symbol to represent another, as writing does, required a staggering leap of the imagination. For all that is known, it was probably made only once in human history. Indeed, many of the world's greatest civilizations never made the leap. The Aztecs, for example, technological geniuses of pre-Columbian

FIGURE 11-1
Aztec Inscription

SOURCE: Gelb 1963 (from Eduard Seler, *Gesammelte Abhandlungen zur amerika-nischen Sprach- und Alterthumskunde*)

Central America, developed intricate systems of drawings and symbols for their calendars. An illustration of these **pictograms** (from the Latin root *pictus* 'painted' and the Greek root *graphein* 'to write') is provided in Figure 11-1. But the Aztecs never thought of using these pictograms to represent the sounds of spoken language, and the Aztec pictograms thus never evolved into writing.

The same impetus that gave rise to the first writing system recurs today so commonly that it is difficult to appreciate the magnitude of that original leap of the imagination that used a written symbol not to represent an object itself but to represent another symbol, an oral symbol of the object. Writing thus involved a leap from primary to secondary symbolization.

A modest modern example of creative secondary symbolization occurs when automobile owners are permitted to design their own license plates. The plates' space limitations invite such secondary symbolization as "GR8" and "GR8FUL," "SK8ING" and "4GET IT," along with the more inventive items "C-SIDE," "7T YRS," and "PLEN-T," some of which have arisen because the words' traditional spellings are too long or have been preempted by other license-plate holders. The tremendous human ingenuity now used on license plates or in advertising commercial products originally sparked what is arguably humanity's greatest invention, for once a symbol like "8" came to stand for the sound [et] and not for the notion 'eight,' an alphabetic writing system was birthing.

The extraordinary leap of imagination that gave rise to writing took place between the Tigris and Euphrates rivers in a region known as Mesopotamia ('between the rivers') sometime between 3500 and 2600 B.C. (Today, Meso-potamia is part of Iraq.) This region, sometimes referred to as "the cradle of Western civilization," was inhabited at the time by the Sumerians and the Akkadians. These peoples were city dwellers who had a sophisticated economic system based on agriculture, cattle, and commerce. Exactly how the Sumerians and Akkadians invented writing will never be known, but we surmise that its potential was discovered by accident as someone struggled to formulate a visible message for which no agreed-upon visual symbols had hitherto existed.

From Mesopotamia, writing appears to have spread both south and east. As early as 3000 B.C. the Egyptians had developed their own writing system, which was inspired by that of the Sumerians and Akkadians but used different symbols. Writing also appeared in the valley of the Indus (now in Pakistan and India) around 2500 B.C., presumably inspired by the writing system originally devised in Mesopotamia. Around 2000 B.C. the Chinese began using pictograms as symbols for words rather than concepts. By 1500 B.C. the world's most technologically complex civilizations had developed systems to commit spoken language to visual representation.

The most ancient inscribed stone tablets that have been found talk of cattle, sales, and exchanges. Thus the most extraordinary invention in human history may have arisen as an answer to the mundane task of recording commercial transactions. Gradually, over the centuries, our ancestors began exploring the world of possibilities opened by the invention of writing. Writing could be used to record important events in a way that was considerably more secure and less likely to be distorted than oral accounts. Dwellers of the ancient world also found that writing could be exploited to communicate across distances that would render oral communication impossible: one could write a letter and entrust it to a messenger, who would then deliver it to its addressee. Letters can be more confidential and more secure than oral messages sent by messenger; they often could not be read by the messenger, and they could be sealed. The uses of literacy as a recording tool and as a means to communicate at a distance could also be combined, as the Mesopotamians and the ancient Chinese discovered, to build and maintain large states ruled by a central government: laws could be recorded by those in command; orders could be transmitted to lower-echelon executives in faraway provinces; data on the citizenry could be stored and retrieved whenever needed. In short, a literate bureaucracy could function with an efficiency that could never have been attained in a preliterate culture.

Of course, it took centuries for early societies to explore the various avenues opened by the invention of writing. The ability to read and write does not automatically make a society more technologically developed, better equipped to become a bureaucratic state, or otherwise superior to a preliterate society. As recently as the Middle Ages, for example, the English had a basic suspicion of written land-sale contracts, which could be tampered with, and the courts gave more credence to oral testimony if a land dispute arose. It took centuries for Europeans to discover that sentence boundaries could be marked with punctuation to ease reading and that book pages could be numbered to ease the task of retrieving information. Obviously, the fact that a particular society is literate does not necessarily mean that its members will exploit all the possibilities literacy offers. Sometimes strong social pressures prohibit the writing down of certain materials. For example, the Warm Springs Indians of Oregon regard any attempt to make written records of their traditional religious songs and prayers as very offensive. For them, writing down these texts would violate their sacredness. Literacy opens novel ways of communicating and recording language, but whether or not these possibilities will be exploited depends in large part on a society's norms.

WRITING SYSTEMS

The writing systems developed in ancient Mesopotamia, India, and China were fundamentally different from the writing system now used in Western societies. Ours is an *alphabetic* system based on the premise that one graphic symbol—a letter—should correspond to one significant sound—a phoneme—in the language to be represented. The writing systems originally developed in the Middle East and Asia were based not on a relationship between graphs and individual sounds but on a relationship between graphs and words or syllables. Though they developed at different times in history, all three types of writing—alphabetic, syllabic, and word writing—are still in use today.

Syllabic Writing

When the dwellers of the ancient Middle East and Asia began developing their writing systems, they had at their disposal the earlier pictograms, which were symbols for objects and concepts. Rather than create an entirely new system of symbols, the inventors of writing modified these pictograms and used them to develop writing systems. The pictograms were not, of course, modified overnight; their shapes gradually became more and more stylized in the process of becoming written symbols. Table 11-1 illustrates the evolution of a number of symbols over time. The table's left-hand column shows the original pictograms, which become more like writing as we proceed to the right. After many centuries of gradual evolution, the symbols illustrated in the right-hand column had become so stylized that they no longer bore any resemblance to the pictograms from which they originated.

The written symbols that the Sumerians and Akkadians had developed at that stage are called **cuneiform** symbols. *Cuneiform* means literally 'in the shape of a wedge'; the term refers to the peculiar shape that the symbols had taken. There is a very practical explanation why the symbols were wedge-shaped: The ancient Mesopotamians were not familiar with paper, but clay from the Tigris-Euphrates river basin was readily available as a raw material. From the beginning, writing consisted of engraving marks pressed into soft clay tablets with a hard, sharp, pointed object called a *stylus*. Since it is difficult to draw curved strokes on clay with a stylus, the first written symbols consisted of different combinations of straight strokes.

Not only the shape but also the meaning of cuneiforms evolved from early pictograms. The pictogram that represented an arrow evolved into this cuneiform symbol for the Sumerian word /ši/ 'arrow':

TABLE 11-1
The Evolution of Cuneiform Writing from Pictograms

PICTOGRAMS		'CLASSICAL' SUMERIAN c.2400 BC		OLD-AKKADIAN c.2200 BC	OLD-ASSYRIAN c.1900 BC	OLD-BABYLONIAN c.1700 BC	NEO-ASSYRIAN c.700 BC	NEO-BABYLONIAN c.600 BC	Picture	Meaning
URUK c.3100 BC UPRIGHT	JEMDET NASR TURNED 90° TO LEFT c.2800 BC	LINEAR	CUNEIFORM							
									NECK + HEAD	HEAD FRONT
									NECK+HEAD + BEARD or TEETH	MOUTH NOSE TOOTH VOICE SPEAK WORD
									SHROUDED BODY (?)	MAN
									SITTING BIRD	BIRD
									BULL'S HEAD	OX
									STAR	SKY HEAVEN-GOD GOD
									STREAM or WATER	WATER SEED FATHER SON
									LAND-PLOT + TREES	ORCHARD GREENERY TO GROW TO WRITE

SOURCE: Gaur 1984

Sumerian scribes had difficulty finding appropriate symbols for more abstract notions. There was no modified pictogram for the word 'life,' for example. But the word for 'life' was homophonous with the word for 'arrow' (as the *bank* of a river and a financial *bank* are homonymous in English).[1] Since finding a symbol for the concept 'life' was not an easy task, why not use the symbol for 'arrow'—seeing that 'arrow' and 'life' are both pronounced /ši/? Notice that it was through this extension of a symbol from representing a thing to representing a sound that writing as we know it was invented.

Having solved that problem, the Sumerians recognized that the same symbol could also be used to represent the syllable /ši/ whenever it occurred in a word. For example, they started using it to represent the first syllable of the word /šibira/ 'blacksmith.' In due course, the cuneiform symbol lost its original association with the concept 'arrow' and became a symbol for the syllable /ši/ wherever that syllable occurred. Cuneiform writing is thus a **syllabic writing** system, in which graphic symbols represent whole syllables, not individual sounds as in our alphabet.

---

[1] *Homophonous* means 'having the same sound.' Thus we can speak of homophonous syllables, morphemes, and words (as well as letters and groups of letters). *Homonymous* means 'having the same name.' *Homophonous* and *homonymous* are often used interchangeably.

FIGURE 11-2
Egyptian Hieroglyphics*

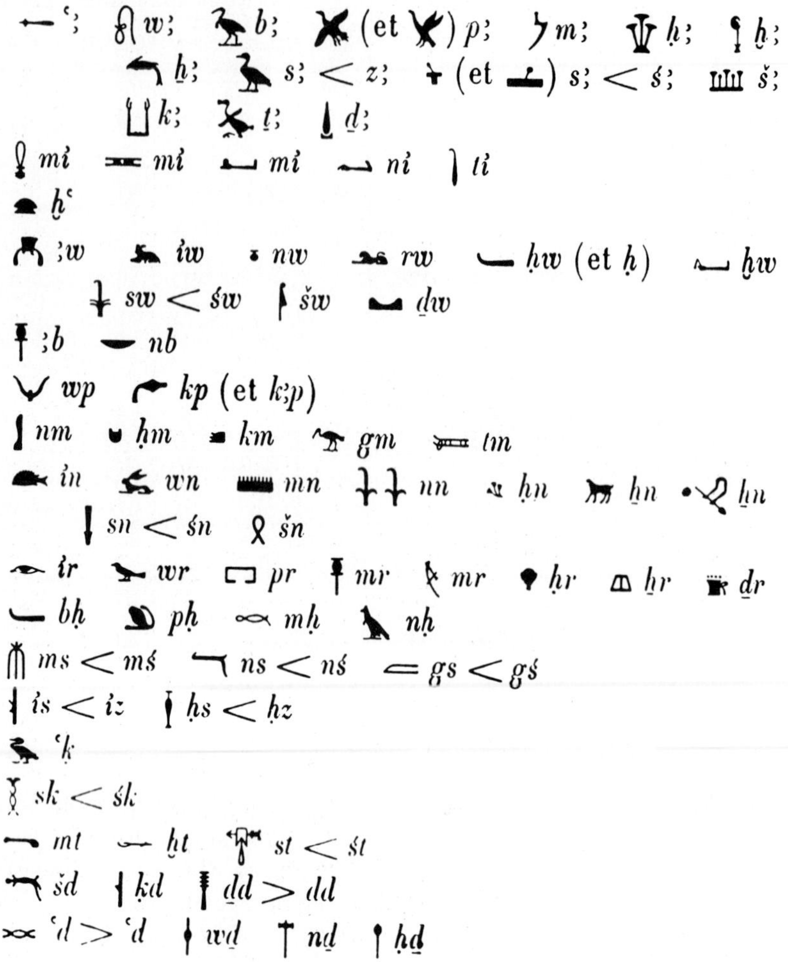

*Because this figure comes originally from a French language source, the French word *et* 'and' appears in several lines.

SOURCE: Gelb 1963

Needless to say, the process through which early pictograms evolved from being graphic symbols for concepts to being graphic symbols for syllables was a long and arduous one. Archaeological remains found in Mesopotamia indicate that for many centuries the Sumerians and the Akkadians used an extremely complex system in which some symbols were "ideograms" while others were true writing representing syllables. Even when all graphic symbols had come to represent syllables, the system was imperfect, because some graphs could represent different syllables depending on the word in which they were used. Despite its imperfections, this system appears to have been used for many centuries.

TABLE 11-2
The Vai Syllabary

	i	a	u	e	ɛ	ɔ	o
p							
b							
ɓ							
mɓ							
kp							
mgb							
gb							
f							
v							
t							
d							
l							
ɖ							
nɖ							
s							
z							
c							
j							
nj							
y							
k							
ŋg							
g							
h							
w							
–							

⟨⟩ Syllabic nasal

Nasal syllables

	ĩ	ã	ũ	ɛ̃	ɔ̃
ɦ					
m					
n					
ny					
ŋ					

SOURCE: Sylvia Scribner and Michael Cole. 1981. *The Psychology of Literacy* (Cambridge: Harvard University Press).

The Mesopotamian syllabic system became the model for several other systems. The ancient Egyptians, who had their own ideographic system, borrowed from the Sumerians and Akkadians the idea of representing spoken syllables with graphic symbols and began using their ideograms to represent different sound combinations around 3000 B.C. Egyptian written symbols are called *hieroglyphics* (see Figure 11-2). Like cuneiform writing, hieroglyphic writing was basically a syllabic system, and it had the same complexity and shortcomings as cuneiforms. Thus the hieroglyphic sign for 'house' (third sign from the left in thirteenth line of Figure 11-2) stood for several syllables with the consonants /p/ and /r/ coupled with any permitted vowels such as /per/ and /par/.

TABLE 11-3
The Tamil Syllabary*

		அ a	ஆ ā	இ i	ஈ ī	உ u	ஊ ū
க்	k	க ka	கா	கி	கீ	கு	கூ
ங்	ṅ	ங ṅa	ஙா	ஙி	ஙீ	ஙு	ஙூ
ச்	ç	ச ça	சா	சி	சீ	சு	சூ
ஞ்	ɲ	ஞ ɲa	ஞா	ஞி	ஞீ	ஞு	ஞூ
ட்	ḍ	ட ḍa	டா	டி	டீ	டு	டூ
ண்	ṇ	ண ṇa	ணா	ணி	ணீ	ணு	ணூ
த்	t	த ta	தா	தி	தீ	து	தூ
ந்	n	ந na	நா	நி	நீ	நு	நூ
ப்	p	ப pa	பா	பி	பீ	பு	பூ
ம்	m	ம ma	மா	மி	மீ	மு	மூ
ய்	y	ய ya	யா	யி	யீ	யு	யூ
ர்	r	ர ra	ரா	ரி	ரீ	ரு	ரூ
ல்	l	ல la	லா	லி	லீ	லு	லூ
வ்	v	வ va	வா	வி	வீ	வு	வூ
ழ்	ṛ	ழ ṛa	ழா	ழி	ழீ	ழு	ழூ
ள்	ḷ	ள ḷa	ளா	ளி	ளீ	ளு	ளூ
ற்	r	ற ra	றா	றி	றீ	று	றூ
ன்	n	ன na	னா	னி	னீ	னு	னூ

* A dot beneath the phonetic representation indicates a retroflex sound (one in which the tip of the tongue is curled up and back just behind the alveolar ridge). Note that there are two graphic symbols for /r/ and two for /n/.

There is nothing inherently cumbersome in syllabic systems of writing. The difficulties of the Mesopotamian and Egyptian systems can be attributed to the fact that they continued to bear traces of their ideographic origins. Syllabic systems have proved useful enough that they are still employed today in a number of cultures. The Vai, an ethnic group of about twelve thousand people in western Liberia, developed a syllabic writing system at the beginning of the nineteenth century. The Vai system has one graph for each of the approximately two hundred syllables in the language. This system is particularly well adapted to the Vai language, which has a relatively small number of possible syllables. The Vai syllabary is given in Table 11-2.

Syllabic writing is also used in various languages of India. Tamil, spoken in the southern tip of the subcontinent, is written with a syllabic system of 246 graphic symbols, given in Table 11-3. The Tamil syllabic system is highly regular. Each vowel has two graphic representations in the syllabary. One is

எ e	ஏ ē	ஐ ai	ஒ o	ஓ ō	ஒள au
கெ	கே	கை	கொ	கோ	கௌ
ஙெ	ஙே	ஙை	ஙொ	ஙோ	ஙௌ
செ	சே	சை	சொ	சோ	சௌ
ஞெ	ஞே	ஞை	ஞொ	ஞோ	ஞௌ
டெ	டே	டை	டொ	டோ	டௌ
ணெ	ணே	ணை	ணொ	ணோ	ணௌ
தெ	தே	தை	தொ	தோ	தௌ
நெ	நே	நை	நொ	நோ	நௌ
பெ	பே	பை	பொ	போ	பௌ
மெ	மே	மை	மொ	மோ	மௌ
யெ	யே	யை	யொ	யோ	யௌ
ரெ	ரே	ரை	ரொ	ரோ	ரௌ
லெ	லே	லை	லொ	லோ	லௌ
வெ	வே	வை	வொ	வோ	வௌ
ழெ	ழே	ழை	ழொ	ழோ	ழௌ
ளெ	ளே	ளை	ளொ	ளோ	ளௌ
றெ	றே	றை	றொ	றோ	றௌ
னெ	னே	னை	னொ	னோ	னௌ

an independent graph used at the beginning of a word; the other is used when the vowel combines with a consonant elsewhere in a word. Thus, in initial position, /ā/ is represented by ஐ but appears as ா when it combines with consonants as in /kā/ கா, /ḍā/ டா, /tā/ தா. To represent a consonant sound alone, the graph used to represent that consonant as it appears with /a/ is used, but a dot is placed above the symbol. Thus, except for the dot above each one, the graphs of the first column are identical to those of the second column. In the first row across the top of the syllabary are written the vowel symbols and their phonemic value; next to each graph of the first column is given its phonemic value. It is easy to recognize that part of the symbol represents the consonant, while the other part represents the vowel. Learning this system thus amounts to learning the different parts of symbols and the possible combinations between these different parts. One of the attractive features of the Tamil system is that its simplicity and regularity make it easy to learn.

Syllabic systems thus have the potential of being highly regular, with a one-to-one correspondence between syllables and graphs. Furthermore, the shape of the graphic symbols can be such that their pronunciation is retrievable from a decomposition of the graph into different parts. A regular syllabary like the Vai or Tamil systems is easily learned and simple to handle. Such a writing system is best adapted to languages that have a limited number of possible syllables. Syllabic systems can be economical, needing only as many symbols in a word as there are syllables.

Logographic Writing

Around four thousand years ago, a new writing system was developed in China that used symbols to represent *words*, not syllables. Such a **logographic writing** system differed fundamentally from the Sumerian-Akkadian syllabic system; partly for this reason, it is commonly believed that the Chinese did not borrow the idea of writing from the Mesopotamians but developed it on their own.

Like the ancient Middle Eastern syllabic writing, the Chinese logographic system originated in ideograms. From archaeological records, we know that ideograms like those in Figure 11-3 were used to represent objects and ideas such as 'cow,' 'river,' and 'below.'

Toward the end of the Bronze Age (around 1700–500 B.C.), these ideograms came to represent not concepts but words. Today, in the three

FIGURE 11-3

cow river below

cow river below

FIGURE 11-4

characters (or logographic symbols) that denote the Modern Chinese words *niú* 'cow,' *quān* 'river,' and *xià* 'below,' we can recognize in Figure 11-4 the ideograms that originally represented these three notions.

From a very early stage, ideograms were combined to represent abstract ideas and other notions that are difficult to represent graphically. Figure 11-5 (a), for example, is made up of two ideograms placed one on top of the other. The lower part represents a type of dish used in divination ceremonies; the upper part represents a tree, upon which the divination dish was suspended. This complex ideogram was modified over the centuries to become a character that in Modern Chinese represents the word *gào*, which means 'to announce, proclaim.' As Figure 11-5 (b) shows, the modern character with this meaning bears a striking resemblance to the ideogram from which it originates. Such similarities between modern-day characters and ancient ideograms are few and far between. The shapes of most modern Chinese characters have lost all traces of the original ideograms from which they originated some three or four thousand years ago.

Modern Chinese Characters In an ideal logographic system each word of the spoken language would be represented by a different graphic symbol. To a certain extent, the Modern Chinese system has this characteristic, in that a portion of its vocabulary is represented by individual characters, as illustrated by Figure 11-6.

FIGURE 11-5

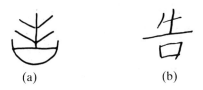

(a) (b)

FIGURE 11-6

guó wǒ fá
'country' 'I, me' 'way'

wéi	guó	tú	yuán	gù
'enclosure'	'country'	'map'	'garden'	'obstinate'

FIGURE 11-7

Most modern Chinese characters can be decomposed into two elements. The one is frequently called the *radical* (or *signific*) and can sometimes hint at meaning. The other element, of which there are many types, can sometimes give a clue to pronunciation and is known as the *phonetic*. Radicals can also be used alone as characters, and some dictionaries are organized according to radicals, of which there are 214. The signific that traditionally corresponds to the character for the word *wéi* 'enclosure' occurs as the radical of many characters, some of which have a meaning related to 'enclosure' and some of which have little to do with the meaning of the radical (see Figure 11-7). In Modern Chinese, the radical for 'enclosure' is in disuse as an independent character and has been replaced by the more complex character 圍—which has the same meaning and pronunciation.

It is difficult to know exactly how many different characters the Chinese logographic system contains, just as it is virtually impossible to know how many words are in the lexicon of any language. It is commonly believed that one must be able to recognize about five thousand characters (and have a good command of spoken Chinese) in order to read a Chinese newspaper. To read a learned piece of literature, a reader must be familiar with up to thirty thousand characters. Compared to the number of words needed for similar tasks in English, these numbers are relatively modest. The reason can be found in the morphological structure of Chinese. In Chinese, morphemes (which are always one syllable long) can combine with each other to form compounds that together denote a new idea whose meaning is more or less clearly related to the meaning of the parts. Of course, this is reflected by corresponding compounds in writing. The word for 'bicycle,' for example, is made up of three morphemes that together mean 'self-propelled vehicle'; the three characters corresponding to these three morphemes are used to represent 'bicycle' in writing. Similarly, the word for 'grammar' is a compound that means 'language rule' (see Figure 11-8).

Though compounding greatly reduces the number of characters needed in common use, learning to read and write the Chinese logographic system is still a formidable task, considerably more difficult and time consuming than learning the Vai or Tamil syllabary or the English alphabet. Bear in mind that since the modern characters provide a reader virtually no clue to the pronunciation or meaning of the words they represent, learning to read and

自行車

zì xíng chē
'bicycle'

語法

yǔ fǎ
'grammar'

FIGURE 11-8

write Chinese involves learning the shape of characters as well as their meaning and pronunciation. Though several transcription systems have been devised for Chinese (some of which use the Roman alphabet, some a type of syllabic system), the logographic system continues to survive after nearly four thousand years.

Why would such a seemingly impractical and complex system endure for so long? The Chinese logographic system has a number of important advantages. The first stems from the fact that though there are many homophonous words in Chinese, they usually have different written representations—as illustrated by the five characters in Figure 11-9, each of which represents a word that is pronounced [jɪn]. This list presents only a few of the characters that are pronounced [jīn]. Thus the Chinese character system provides a way of distinguishing in writing among different words that a syllabic system or an alphabet could not provide. (Compare the unusual distinction in English of a pair of homophones like *read* and *reed* with the more common orthographic confusion between a river *bank* and a savings *bank*). A logographic system enables writers to compensate for homophony. This feature is especially advantageous for a language with as many homophonous words as Chinese.

The second major advantage of the Chinese logographic system is peculiar to the Chinese situation. The language that is called Chinese is not a single variety but a set of numerous spoken dialects, some of which are mutually intelligible, some not. Fortunately for written communication, all these dialects use the same set of characters. A character may be pronounced one way in one region of China and another way in another region, but the *meaning* of the character remains the same throughout that vast country. For example, the character 我 is read [wǒ] in the Beijing (Peking) dialect, [gòa] in the Taiwanese dialect, [wà] in the Min Nan dialect (spoken in south

斤   金   津   筋   襟

'hatchet'   'gold'   'ford'   'tendon'   'lapel'

FIGURE 11-9

China), [ŋə] in the northwestern dialect of Shan Xi, [ŋō] in the southern dialect of Hu Nan, and [ŋú] in the Shanghai dialect. In all dialects, it means 'I' or 'me.' Furthermore, since the syntax of most Chinese dialects is similar, any dialect can be more or less understood *in writing* (though not in speech) by speakers of a wide variety of dialects. The character system thus has a unifying force for a nation that comprises so many ethnicities speaking so many different language varieties.

The Chinese logographic system thus meets two very important needs: the need to distinguish between homophones and the need to communicate across dialect boundaries. It is a system well equipped for the situation it serves, despite the difficulties involved in learning it and in managing the enormous variety of characters in arenas like computer processing and telegraphic communication.

In the course of history, many nations of the Far East have borrowed the Chinese logographic system. The Vietnamese modified certain Chinese characters to create their own writing system, which was essentially logographic as well. Today the Vietnamese no longer use this system. The Koreans and the Japanese borrowed the Chinese character system very early; in due time, each developed several subsidiary systems. Koreans now write their language with the help of both an alphabet and the original Chinese characters. Similarly, several systems are combined for use in modern Japan: two syllabic systems known as *hiragana* and *katakana*, as well as Chinese characters, called *kanji* (a word borrowed from the Chinese compound *hàn zì* 'character'). Both written Korean and written Japanese are curious in that symbols from different systems can appear in the same sentence and even in the same word. Today the Chinese remain the only people to make exclusive use of a logographic system.

Alphabetic Writing and Orthography

An **alphabet** is a set of written symbols that represent the distinctive sounds of a language. Alphabetic writing thus differs from syllabic writing (whose graphs represent syllables) and logographic writing (whose graphs represent words). The first alphabet was developed by the ancient Greeks from a Middle Eastern syllabic system that they had borrowed around 800 B.C. Around 600 B.C., the Romans developed the basics of the alphabet we use today. The Roman alphabet is not the only alphabet currently in use: the Greeks use an alphabet of their own, as do the Russians, Ukrainians, Bulgarians, and Serbs. These alphabets are based on the same principles as the Roman alphabet, differing only in the shape of some of the letters. The alphabet currently in use for Russian, called the Cyrillic alphabet in honor of Saint Cyril, who devised it in the ninth century, is given in Table 11-4. It contains thirty-three graphs, many of which resemble letters of the Roman alphabet.

An alphabet is matched as closely as possible to the sound system of the language. The system used to achieve this match is the spelling system, also known as the **orthography**. In an ideal orthography, each phoneme of the

TABLE 11-4
The Cyrillic Alphabet as Used in Modern Russian
Only printed lower-case letters are shown.

Cyrillic letter	Russian phoneme represented	Cyrillic letter	Russian phoneme represented
а	a	р	r
б	b	с	s
в	v	т	t
г	g	у	u
д	d	ф	f
е	yɛ	х	x
ё	yo	ц	ts
ж	ž	ч	č
з	z	ш	š
и	i	щ	šč
й	y	ъ	(apostrophe)
к	k	ы	i̇
л	l	ь	(y)
м	m	э	ɛ
н	n	ю	yu
о	o	я	ya
п	p		

spoken language would be represented by a different graph, and each graph would represent only one phoneme. Spanish orthography comes very close to this ideal. In Spanish, there is virtually a one-to-one correspondence between letters of the alphabet and phonemes of the language. This almost-perfect match between the Roman alphabet and the Spanish sound system is what students of Spanish mean when they say that in Spanish "every letter is pronounced." In contrast, when we turn to languages like English and French we do not find anything close to a perfect match. As we saw in Chapter 2, the number of distinctive sounds in English includes twenty-four consonants and between fourteen and sixteen vowels and diphthongs. With only twenty-six letters of the alphabet, English orthography falls far short of the ideal one-sound/one-graph model. Because there are not enough letters to provide a symbol for each phoneme, many phonemes must be represented by more than one letter (for example, the phoneme /i/ is represented by a double *e* in *meet*; the phoneme [θ] is represented by the two letters *th*). In addition, English pronunciation and English orthography have not kept pace with each other over time, so that some words contain letters that no longer represent any sounds (like the *k* and *gh* in *knight*). And a particular sequence of letters can represent a wide spectrum of sounds, as illustrated by the different pronunciations represented by *ough* in *cough, tough, through, trough, though, thorough, bough,* and *hiccough.*

One common response to the chaos of the English orthography is to cry out for spelling reform, as George Bernard Shaw did earlier in this century. But for an international language like English, an orthography that genuinely attempted to represent pronunciation would sacrifice the uniformity that exists across national and regional varieties. Spelling reform would raise other serious problems as well. As an example, consider the English word *photograph.* The pronunciations of this word in its normal phonological contexts have different stress patterns, which are automatically assigned by the stress rules of English phonology: ['fotəgræf] versus [fə'tɑgrəfər]. Compare the three vowels in *photograph* [o, ə, æ] with the first three in *photographer* [ə, ɑ, ə]. An orthography that attempted to represent actual sounds would be forced to represent the vowels of *photograph* and *photographer* differently, perhaps as "photəgræph" and "phətagrəphər."

Because English derivational morphology and morphophonemic alternations are complex, the differences in the pronunciation of related words like *photograph* and *photographer* can be considerable. If a writing system were devised in which sounds and symbols were closely matched, the task of reading would be greatly complicated. We would have many pairs, trios, and other sets of words like *wife/wives* in which the spelling system would have to represent many types of variation patterns. We would also be forced to spell the plural ending of *boys* and *cats* differently, though they represent the same morpheme. Similarly, the morpheme MUSIC would sometimes be spelled *muzək* (as in *musical*) and sometimes *muzɪš* (as in *musician*). By the same token, all homophonous words would be spelled alike, so that *wood/would, balm/bomb, sea/see,* and *to/too/two* could not be distinguished.

Advocates of English spelling reform thus tend to overlook the advantages of the spelling system currently in use. Just as the Chinese logographic system is well adapted to the situation in which it functions, the Roman alphabet and English orthography are remarkably well adapted to English.

Developing Writing Systems in Newly Literate Societies

Since the turn of the century, the world has witnessed an enormous increase in communications among regions, countries, and continents. Oceans and mountains, sometimes insurmountable obstacles a hundred years ago, are now easily overflown by airplanes. Today there is probably not a single inhabited area of the world that has had no contact with the outside. This is a remarkable fact, given that as recently as the 1950s large inhabited areas of Papua New Guinea, Amazonia, and the Philippines were still completely isolated from the rest of the world.

The consequence of this communications boom is that many people who had never seen writing a few decades ago are now literate. When a language is written down for the first time, a number of important questions arise: What kind of writing system should be used? How should the writing system be modified or adapted to fit the needs of the language and its speakers? Who makes these decisions?

Literacy is often introduced to a people along with a new religion. For example, literacy was first imported into Tibet from India in the seventh century, at the same time as the Tibetans converted to Buddhism. Today literacy is commonly introduced to preliterate societies by Christian missionaries. What links religion and literacy is the fact that the reading of religious texts is an important element of the doctrine of many religions. Because literacy is commonly introduced by foreign missionaries, the foreign writing system is usually adopted by the members of the incipiently literate society to write their own language. Today, newly literate societies commonly adopt the Roman alphabet because English-speaking missionaries are the most active promoters of literacy in many regions of the world.

At times a culture will change from one writing system to another. Vietnam, for example, was colonized by the Chinese around 200 B.C. and remained colonized for about twelve centuries. During that time, Chinese was used in writing, and Vietnamese remained unwritten. After the end of Chinese domination, the Vietnamese began to use a syllabic writing system adapted from Chinese logographic writing for their own language. Then, at the beginning of the seventeenth century, Jesuit missionaries devised an alphabetic system for Vietnamese. Though the Jesuits failed to convert much of Vietnam's population to Catholicism, the Vietnamese gradually adopted the Jesuits' alphabetic orthography, partly under pressure from the French colonial government. Today the system devised by the Jesuits is the only one in use for Vietnamese.

One thorny problem that newly literate societies face is developing a standard orthography that everyone will agree to use. Ideally, an orthography must be regular, so that native writers will be able to spell a word that they have never before seen in writing. The orthography must also be easy to learn and use. Finally, it must be well adapted to the phonological and morphological structure of the language. As we saw in our discussion of English orthography, satisfying all these requirements can be challenging. A system that looks complex at first blush might have hidden advantages. Devising a standard orthography can be such a difficult task that a few Western nations (including Norway) have not yet done so, even after centuries of literacy.

Language-related concerns are not the only factors involved in devising orthographies. One extremely important factor is social acceptance. An orthography that, for one reason or another, rubs users the wrong way will never be successful. If the orthography is imposed by an outside political or religious body, it may take on negative associations and never succeed. For several decades, the United States Bureau of Indian Affairs hired linguists and anthropologists to devise orthographies for American Indian languages, but because the Indians viewed the bureau and its activities with suspicion, the orthographies were never really accepted.

Likewise, on the South Pacific island of Rotuma, at the end of the last century Methodist and Catholic missionaries devised different orthographies to transcribe Rotuman. Since then, because relations between Methodist Rotumans and Catholic Rotumans have been strained, both orthographies have survived, and there is no prospect of one group's adopting the other's orthography. Similar situations can involve not only orthographies but writing systems. In Serbia and Croatia, two regions of Yugoslavia, a single language is used. However, the Serbs use a Cyrillic alphabet similar to that used for Russian, while Croats use the Roman alphabet. Both groups adamantly keep their alphabet as a symbol of social identity. Social acceptance is thus extremely important to the development of a standard orthography.

SPOKEN AND WRITTEN LANGUAGE: SIMILARITIES AND DIFFERENCES

Though it is commonly said that writing is speech written down or that writing is visual language as distinct from audible language, writing and speaking ordinarily serve different purposes and have somewhat different linguistic characteristics. Conversation, for example, does not usually take place in writing (except as represented in novels), nor are legal contracts ordinarily spoken (though one so drawn might be legally binding). Think of how the words and even the syntax of a written will would differ from one made by a testator using a videotape. Or consider the difference in language that would be necessary in leaving a note on the refrigerator as distinct from telling someone basically the same thing face to face.

Please take chicken out of fridge now and peel potatoes. Will cook dinner when I return!

When you get home from work, would you take the chicken out of the fridge and maybe peel a few potatoes?—'cause I need to start cooking dinner right away when I get back.

It isn't difficult to recognize which of these examples is the written note and which is part of a conversational exchange. They can be recognized by identifying the linguistic features that characterize each mode. Speaking and writing are thus not mirror images of one another.

How do writing and speaking differ as communicative activities? First of all, we have fewer resources to communicate information in writing than in speaking. Oral communication can exploit such devices as intonation and voice pitch to convey information; face-to-face oral communication can also utilize gestures, posture, and physical proximity between participants. In writing, by contrast, the only tools we have are the words and syntax of the language as well as certain conventions of punctuation. In speaking, we can communicate on different levels; we can describe someone's personality in a seemingly objective manner while expressing with intonation or body language how little we really think of the person. In writing, however, everything must be communicated overtly, though there are ways of achieving an ironic tone through syntax and lexicon, and readers can often read "between the lines."

A second important difference between speaking and writing is in the amount of planning generally available and the consequences for the linguistic form of each. In most writing activities, there is time to think before and to revise afterward. But, if speakers so much as hesitate in the middle of a sentence in a conversation, they run the risk of losing the floor. Because of this difference in the time available for planning, writing often contains characteristic syntactic patterns that do not readily occur in speech. More significantly, writers are much more likely to use a varied vocabulary, because they have time to think of which words best convey their intentions and can even interrupt their writing to look up words in a thesaurus.

Of course, writing is not always more planned than speaking. There are contexts in which we are expected to produce highly planned spoken language—for an academic lecture or a job interview, for example. Similarly, some types of written language are produced with relatively little planning; if we scribble a letter a few minutes before the mail pickup, the language may be more like speech and lack many of the characteristics of planned writing.

A third distinction between writing and speaking is that speakers can commonly interact with their addressees, whereas writers usually cannot. While spoken language is usually produced in a face-to-face situation (except when it is transmitted electronically over telephone wires or radio waves), written language is almost invariably produced when the interactors are not within sight or hearing range of one another. In many face-to-face verbal interactions, the immediacy of the interlocutors and the contexts of interaction allow them to refer to themselves (*I think, you see*) and their own opinions and to be more personal in their interaction. The contexts of writing, in contrast, impose limitations on the degree to which it can be personal. Again, however, we must be careful not to overgeneralize. Consider, for example, a personal letter and a personal conversation. Language users often feel that they have the right to be equally personal in both contexts. The impersonal characteristic of writing is thus a feature of some types of writing but not all.

Written communication tends to rely on the context of the interaction less than spoken discourse does. In spoken language, we can use demonstratives like *this* and *that* or expressions like *today* and *next year* in contexts in which, in writing, they would be either unclear (because we cannot point) or confusing (is *today* relative to the time of writing or of reading, and if to writing then how is one to know when an undated document was written?). But, again, this is not an absolute difference between speaking and writing. In telephone conversations, for example, we cannot say *this thing* and point to what we mean because our interlocutor cannot see what we are pointing at. In contrast, we can leave a written note on the kitchen table that reads *Please eat this for lunch* as long as the meaning of *this* is obvious from what is near the note.

There are many ways in which speaking and writing differ. But when we investigate the differences between them (as we have just done), we find no absolute dichotomy. It is difficult, for example, to think of any words that could occur *only* in speech or *only* in writing, even though certain words may occur more frequently in one mode or the other. Instead, we find tendencies: written language *tends* to be more formal, more informational, and less personal. Speech and writing differ along a series of continuous dimensions: Along the "personal/impersonal" continuum, for example, the type of writing found in legal documents will be at the impersonal end, while informal conversation will tend toward the personal end. But personal letters may be very close to conversations. Writing and speaking thus do not form a simple dichotomy. To describe the differences between the two activities, we must ask in each case what type of writing or what type of speaking is being considered.

SUMMARY

Writing is a relatively recent invention that developed from pictograms, which became writing when they began to refer to sounds rather than to objects and concepts. There are several types of writing systems in use today. In *syllabic* writing, symbols represent syllables; in *logographic* writing, symbols represent morphemes or words; and in *alphabetic* writing, symbols represent phonemes. The writing system for English uses the Roman alphabet. The system that dictates how the letters of the alphabet are used to represent the phonemes of English is called its *orthography*. Devising orthographies for hitherto unwritten languages is a difficult task, which must take into account both linguistic and social factors. Writing differs from speaking in a number of fundamental ways, but the linguistic differences between the two modes are not absolute. To describe the differences between spoken and written language, we need to invoke a series of continuous dimensions along which different styles of speaking and writing align themselves.

EXERCISES

1. Discuss the relative merits and disadvantages of logographic, syllabic, and alphabetic writing systems. In your discussion of each type of system, address the following questions:

    (A) How easy is it to learn the system?
    (B) How easy is it to write the individual graphs?
    (C) How efficiently can one read the graphs?
    (D) What kinds of problems does the system present for printing?
    (E) How adaptable is it to computer technology such as word processing?
    (F) How easy is it to represent foreign names and new borrowings from other languages?

(G) What sociological and historical factors might interact with the preceding questions in evaluating the appropriateness of each system to particular situations? (Be concrete by considering a particular situation you are familiar with.)

2. English is often said to have a phonemic orthography (approximating one graph for each distinct sound). To some extent this is true in that English orthography distinguishes between, say, *b* and *p* but not among [pʰ], [p], and [p˺]. In light of this claim, examine the following typical sets of words and compare their orthographic representation with their pronunciation: *cats/dogs/judges*; *history/historical*.

(A) Is English orthography phonemic? Explain.

(B) In what sense would it be more accurate to describe the English orthographic system as morphophonemic?

(C) To what extent would it be fair to say that English is logographic in representing such sets of homonyms as the following: *meet/meat/mete*; *leaf/lief*; *seize/sees/seas*?

(D) What is the nature of such graphic symbols as *3, 1001, &, $,* and *%*? Can they be called logographic? Explain.

3. Using the Tamil syllabic symbols given in Table 11-3 (pp. 366–67), transcribe the following Tamil words into Roman script. Briefly describe the general patterns that are used in forming syllabic characters in this script. For example, how is the symbol for /ke/ formed from the symbols for /k/ and /e/? How are word-final consonants and word-initial vowels represented?

தொழில்	'work'	எழு	'seven'
மூக்கு	'nose'	புலி	'tiger'
அவன்	'he'	ஆடு	'goat'
வாழைப்பழம்	'banana'	மரம்	'tree'

4. The following table (adapted from Sampson 1985) is a partial representation of the inventory of graphs used in writing Korean consonants. "Tense" means (in part) that the sound is held for a longer period of time than normal and "lax" that the sound is held for the normal duration. (The tenseness is represented in phonetic symbols with an apostrophe, as in p'.) What principles govern the shape of graphs in this system? What are the advantages of such a system over an alphabetic system like the Roman system, in which the shape of graphs is completely arbitrary?

	Bilabial	Dental	Palatal	Velar
Lax nasals	ㅁ m	ㄴ n		
Lax fricatives		ㅅ s		
Lax stops/affricate	ㅂ p	ㄷ t	ㅈ c	ㄱ k
Tense aspirated stops/affricate	ㅍ pʰ	ㅌ tʰ	ㅊ cʰ	ㅋ kʰ
Tense fricative		ㅆ s		
Tense unaspirated stops/affricate	ㅃ p'	ㄸ t'	ㅉ c'	ㄲ k'

5. Suppose that you were devising a syllabic writing system for English. How would you make such a system as simple to learn and use as possible? To what extent does the phonological and morphological structure of English present problems for syllabic writing? Illustrate your discussion with a concrete proposal for an English syllabic writing system, for which you may make up your own symbols.

6. Hebrew and Arabic are commonly written with a type of alphabetic writing called "consonantal" writing. Here is an example of a Classical Hebrew sentence from the Old Testament (adapted from Comrie (ed.), 1987).

וְאֵינָם מַכִּירִים לְדַבֵּר יְהוּדִית

Transliteration: W?YNM MKYR̄YM LDBR YHWDYT̄

Pronunciation: wə?ēʸn'ȧm makkīʸr'īʸm ləðabb'er yəhūʷð'īʸθ

[Note: ȧ represents a low round back vowel]

'And they do not know how to speak Judean.'

(A) On the basis of this sample, describe precisely how consonantal writing differs from straightforward alphabetic writing.

(B) Try to write an English sentence in Roman script using the principle of consonantal writing; then ask other people to figure out what you have written. Explain how practical such a system would be for English.

(C) Recall what we said about the morphological structure of Hebrew and Arabic in Chapter 4. What makes consonantal writing better adapted to these languages than to English?

7. In Chapter 10 we defined speech events as social activities in which spoken or written language plays an important role. We added that speech events are structured, in that they have characteristics that identify them as being of a particular type. Using two or three personal letters that have been addressed to you, describe in detail the linguistic and social characteristics of personal letters as a speech event. In your discussion, use examples from your letters to show who writes personal letters to whom and in what context; how personal letters begin and end; what they talk about; and what kind of language they characteristically use. As speech events and in terms of their linguistic characteristics, how do personal letters compare with other types of letters such as business letters, letters of application, and letters to the editor?

8. Repeat exercise 7, this time focusing on academic term papers. What characteristics of term papers distinguish them from other speech events?

SUGGESTIONS FOR FURTHER READING

Gelb (1963) is a classic study of the development of different writing systems in antiquity. A more linguistically oriented survey of writing systems can be found in Sampson (1985). Gaur (1984) is a most readable and lavishly illustrated history of writing. The history of the decipherment of ancient scripts is narrated in Gordon (1982). The discovery and development of alphabetic writing through the centuries are discussed in Diringer (1968). Comrie (1987) provides illustration and discussion of orthography for many of the world's major languages.

Interesting hypotheses about the influence of literacy on thinking and on culture are advanced in Goody (1977) and in Ong (1982). These hypotheses are constructively criticized by Street (1983). Biber (1988) is a study of the lexical and syntactic differences between speaking and writing in English; it also summarizes previous research on the subject. Smith (1983) examines writing from a pedagogical perspective; chapter 6, "The Uses of Language," and chapter 9, "Myths of Writing," treat the communicative functions of writing.

REFERENCES

Biber, Douglas. 1988. *Variation Across Speech and Writing* (Cambridge: Cambridge University Press).

Comrie, Bernard (ed.). 1987. *The World's Major Languages* (New York: Oxford University Press).

Diringer, D. 1968. *The Alphabet* (London: Hutchinson).

Gaur, Albertine. 1984. *A History of Writing* (London: The British Library).

Gelb, I. J. 1963. *A Study of Writing*, 2nd ed. (Chicago: University of Chicago Press).

Goody, Jack. 1977. *The Domestication of the Savage Mind* (Cambridge: Cambridge University Press).

Gordon, Cyrus H. 1982. *Forgotten Scripts: Their Ongoing Discovery and Evolution*, 2nd ed. (New York: Basic Books).

Ong, Walter. 1982. *Orality and Literacy* (London: Methuen).

Sampson, Geoffrey. 1985. *Writing Systems: A Linguistic Introduction* (Stanford, Calif.: Stanford University Press).

Smith, Frank. 1983. *Essays into Literacy* (Exeter, N.H.: Heinemann Educational Books).

Street, Brian V. 1983. *Literacy in Theory and Practice* (Cambridge: Cambridge University Press).

DIALECTS: LINGUISTIC VARIATION AMONG SOCIAL GROUPS

12

LANGUAGES AND DIALECTS

It is an obvious fact that people of different nations tend to use different languages. Along with physical appearance and cultural characteristics, language differences are part of what distinguishes one nation from another. Of course, it isn't only across national boundaries that people speak different languages. In Canada, inhabitants of the same cities and rural areas have spoken different languages for centuries. In Quebec province, ethnic French-Canadians maintain a strong allegiance to the French language, while ethnic Anglos maintain a loyalty to English. In India, literally dozens of languages are spoken, some confined to small areas, others spoken regionally or nationally. In some parts of India two or more languages are spoken by different ethnic groups.

Among speakers of a single language there is considerable international variation. Thus we distinguish Australian, American, British, and Indian English, among many others. Striking differences can be noticed between the varieties of French spoken in Montreal and in Paris, and marked distinctions exist among the varieties of Spanish in Spain, Mexico, and the South American countries. In basically monolingual countries like Germany, France, England, and the United States, there is also variation from one group to another: even casual observers know that residents of different parts of the country speak regional varieties of the national language. When Americans speak of a "Boston accent," a "Southern drawl," or "Brooklynese," they reveal that American English is perceived as varying from place to place and, in general, that languages have regional dialects. These linguistic markers of region serve to identify people as belonging to a particular social group, even though that group may be loosely bound together (as are most regional groups in the United States). In countries where regional affiliation may have other social correlates—of ethnicity or religion or social status—regional varieties are relatively more important markers of social affiliation. The existence of regional varieties of a language, like the existence of different languages themselves, demonstrates that people who speak *with* one another tend to speak *like* one another.

A language can be thought of as a collection of dialects that are usually similar to one another structurally and lexically and that are used by different social groups who *choose* to say that they are speakers of the same language. To take one example, the New York City dialect can be distinguished from the dialect of Texas (among many other ways) in the pronunciation of the word *car* as "cah." The Southern dialect of American English (really a group of dialects) is unique in that it has a second person pronoun form *y'all*. The New York City dialect and the Southern dialect are thus different regional dialects of American English. In many countries, the differences between regional dialects are much greater than in the United States.

Social Boundaries and Dialects

Language varies not only from region to region but also across ethnic, socioeconomic, and gender boundaries. Speakers of American English know that white Americans and black Americans tend to speak differently, even when they live in the same city. Similarly, middle-class speakers can often be distinguished from working-class speakers. We know too that women and men differ in how they use language. These variations across ethnic groups, socioeconomic classes, and gender groups also constitute dialects. Black and white Americans speak the same language, though slightly differently. The American middle class and working class share the same language, though the speech of each class has distinct characteristics. And though mainstream American women and men speak the same language, their speech patterns differ in recognizable ways. Throughout the world, in addition to regional dialects, there are ethnic, social, and gender dialects.

Dialects and Registers

The term **dialect** refers to the language varieties of different social groups. Partly through a dialect we recognize a person's regional, ethnic, social, and gender affiliation; thus dialect has to do with language *users*. In addition, however, all dialects vary according to the situation in which they are used: a northwestern American middle-class black woman, for example, will speak one way at a picnic with friends and another way in a job interview. Her language thus varies according to the situations of *use*. Sensitive to differences in situations, human beings habitually adapt their speech accordingly. The term *register* refers to language varieties looked at from the point of view of the uses to which they are put. Languages, dialects, and registers are all called language **varieties**. In this chapter we shall deal with dialects—language varieties viewed according to users. In Chapter 13 we shall examine registers—language varieties viewed according to the different uses to which they are put.

DIFFERENTIATION AND MERGER OF LANGUAGE VARIETIES

How is it that certain similar language varieties come to differ so greatly from one another, while other varieties remain very much alike? There is no simple answer to that question, but this much seems clear: The more people interact with one another, the more alike their language will become or remain. The less contact two social groups have, the more likely their languages are to become differentiated.

Geographical separation and social distance can give rise to notable differences in speechways. From the Proto-Indo-European spoken about six millennia ago have come most of today's European languages as well as many tongues of Central Asia and the Indian subcontinent. Not only the Romance languages but the Celtic, Greek, Baltic, Slavic, and Indo-Iranian tongues have all developed from Proto-Indo-European, as have the Germanic languages including English, Norwegian, Swedish, Danish, Dutch, and German. When we consider that only some two hundred generations have lived and died during that six-thousand-year period (and that each of us can witness speakers over a span of up to seven generations), we can appreciate how quickly a multitude of different tongues can develop from a single parent language. Scores of mutually unintelligible languages have developed from Proto-Indo-European, all within about six thousand years.

In the same vein, but more recently, the Spanish varieties of the New World are developing along lines somewhat different from the Spanish of the Iberian Peninsula. Similar contrasts can be observed between the French of Paris and Montreal and among British, American, Australian, Canadian, New Zealand, Irish, and Indian English. So physical distance can be a crucial factor in promoting dialects and keeping them distinct.

Similarly, social distance can contribute to creating and maintaining distinct dialects. Black English remains distinct from other varieties of American English partly because of the social distance between whites and blacks in the United States. Middle-class dialects differ from working-class dialects partly because of the relative lack of sustained contacts across class boundaries in American society. A dialect links its users through recognition of shared linguistic characteristics; speakers' ability to use and understand a dialect marks them as "insiders" and allows them to identify (and exclude) "outsiders."

All languages and language varieties change and develop continuously. When two groups of people speaking a common tongue stop having sufficient social interaction to keep their language developing along the same path, the changes in the speech patterns of each group can eventually produce mutual unintelligibility. That is what happened in the evolution of the many derivatives of Proto-Indo-European and Proto-Polynesian.

Dialects or Languages?

The Romance languages arose from the regional varieties of Latin spoken in different parts of the Roman Empire. Those dialects of Latin eventually gave rise to Italian, French, Spanish, Portuguese, and Rumanian, now the distinct languages of different countries. Though these tongues share many structural features of syntax, phonology, and lexicon, the nationalistic pride taken by the Italians, French, Spaniards, Portuguese, and Rumanians contributes to the varieties' being viewed as different languages rather than as dialects of a single language. The opposite situation characterizes the Chinese language, which comprises several distinct dialects. Though not all Chinese dialects are mutually intelligible, their speakers choose to regard themselves as sharing the same language.

Thus the difference between a language and a dialect is as much a social as a linguistic question; it is strongly influenced by psychological factors such as nationalistic and religious attitudes. The Hindus of northern India speak Hindi, while the Moslems there and in neighboring Pakistan speak Urdu. Opinions differ among them as to the extent to which they can understand one another. Until recently, these two varieties were a single linguistic unit called Hindustani. The fact that linguists write grammars of "Hindi-Urdu" reflects their professional judgment that these varieties require only a single grammatical description, despite the different language names assigned to them by their speakers. Naturally, with the passing years, these varieties—whose different names proclaim that their speakers belong to different social, political, and religious groups—will become increasingly differentiated, as French and Spanish have done over the centuries. Just as groups of people who speak to one another tend to speak increasingly alike, so groups that are not in close communication or wish to distance themselves from one another will speak ever more distinctly.

As physical and social distance enable speakers of particular varieties to distinguish themselves from speakers of other varieties, so close contact and frequent communication foster linguistic uniformity. As dialects spoken by people in close social contact tend to become alike, so different languages spoken in a community can become more similar and even tend to merge in some circumstances. The type and degree of merger are determined by the type and degree of social integration and shared values.

Language Merger in an Indian Village

One fascinating case of merger has occurred in Kupwar, a village in India on the border between two major language families: the Indo-European family (which includes the languages of North India) and the unrelated Dravidian family (comprising the languages of South India). In Kupwar, the three thousand villagers regularly use three languages in their daily activities. There are three principal groups: the Jains, who speak Kannada (a Dravidian language); the Moslems, who speak Urdu (an Indo-European language closely related to Hindi); and the Untouchables, who speak Marathi (the regional Indo-European language surrounding Kupwar and the principal literary language of the area). The three groups have lived in the village for centuries, and most men are bilingual or multilingual. Over the course of time, with the various groups switching back and forth among at least two of the village varieties, these varieties have come to be more and more alike. In fact, the grammatical structures of the village varieties are now so similar that a word-for-word translation is possible among the languages. This means that the word order and other structural characteristics of the three languages are virtually identical. This merging is all the more remarkable because the varieties of these same languages that are used elsewhere are very different from one another. Indeed, they belong to two unrelated language families and cannot be translated word for word into one another.

Even in Kupwar, however, where the grammars of the different languages have been merging, the vocabulary of each variety has remained quite distinct. On the one hand, the need for communication among the different groups has fostered a convergence of grammars; on the other hand, the social separation needed to maintain religious and caste differences has supported the continuation of separate vocabularies. The needs of intercommunication among the groups have had the effect of making it easy to communicate across the languages; and the fact that the groups remain distinct from one another has kept their languages from becoming so much alike that it would prove difficult to tell linguistically what group an individual belonged to. As things now stand, communication is relatively easy (certainly easier than speaking across different languages), while affiliation and group identification remain clear.[1] This is the linguistic equivalent of having your cake and eating it too.

In the following example sentence from the three Kupwar varieties, the word order and morphology are relatively uniform across the languages, but it is clear from the vocabulary which language is being spoken in each case.

Urdu	pala	jəra	kāt	ke	le	ke	a		ya
Marathi	pala	jəra	kap	un	gʰe	un	a	l	o
Kannada	tapla	jəra	kʰod	i	təgond	i	bə		yn
	greens	a little	cut		having	taken	having	come	Past I

'I cut some greens and brought them.'

[1] We do a similar thing in the United States with very similar grammars across regional boundaries but distinct regional pronunciations. As a result, we have no difficulty communicating, but there is little doubt about regional affiliation.

Thus, while the three grammars have merged to some extent, combining elements from the grammars of each language, social distinctions remain marked (and are partly maintained) by clear differences in vocabulary.

Language/Dialect Continua

In contrast to the situation in Kupwar, Spanish, French, Italian, Portuguese, and the other Romance languages have evolved distinct national varieties from the relatively uniform colloquial Latin that was spoken throughout their regions in Roman times. While language varieties have converged and become more similar in Kupwar, the language varieties spoken in the area where Latin was formerly used have diverged over the centuries. The reasons in both cases are the same. First, people use language to mark their social identity. Second, people who talk *with* one another tend to talk *like* one another. A corollary of the second principle is that people not talking with one another tend to become linguistically differentiated.

Today the languages of Europe (in the Romance-speaking area and elsewhere) look separate and tidily compartmentalized on a map. In reality they are not so neatly distinguishable. Instead, there is a continuum of variation, and languages "blend" into one another. Near language-area borders the change is slightly more abrupt. The national border between France and Italy, for example, also serves as a dividing line between the French-speaking and the Italian-speaking area. But in fact the French spoken just over the French border shares features with the Italian spoken by Italians on the Italian side. From Paris to the Italian border, there is a continuum along which the local French varieties become more and more "Italian-like." Likewise, from Rome to the French border, Italian varieties can be viewed as becoming more "French-like."

Similar situations exist all over Europe. As a result, Swedes of the far south using their local dialects can communicate better with Danish speakers in nearby Denmark than with fellow countrymen in distant northern Sweden. The same situation exists with residents along the border between Germany and Holland. Using their own local varieties, speakers of German can communicate better with speakers of Dutch who live near them than with speakers of southern German dialects. Examples of geographical dialect continua are found throughout Europe. In fact, while the standard varieties of Italian, French, Spanish, Catalan, and Portuguese are not mutually intelligible, the local varieties form a continuum from Portugal through Spain and halfway through Belgium and then through France and down to the southern tip of Italy. There is also a Scandinavian dialect continuum, a West Germanic dialect continuum, and South Slavonic and North Slavonic dialect continua. Just as different languages may form a dialect continuum, so can different dialects of a single language constitute a continuum. This is the case in China, where several mutually unintelligible varieties constitute a single language. In the case of Kupwar, if there were no outside reference varieties against which to compare the varieties spoken in the village, we might be inclined to say that the varieties spoken there were dialects of one language;

they do, after all, have basically one grammar. The residents of Kupwar, however, have found it socially valuable to continue speaking what they regard as different languages, despite increasing grammatical and lexical similarity. It is the view of native speakers that matters in deciding on designations for varieties and on whether these represent dialects of a single language or separate languages.

REGIONAL VARIETIES OF ENGLISH

British and American Varieties

The principal varieties of English throughout the world are customarily divided into British and American types, with subdivisions in each. British English is the basis for the varieties spoken in England, Ireland, Wales, Scotland, Australia, New Zealand, India, Pakistan, Malaysia, Singapore, and South Africa. American (or North American) includes chiefly the English of Canada and the United States.

This division inevitably oversimplifies the facts. For example, despite the groupings just suggested, certain characteristics of Canadian English are closer to British English, while certain characteristics of Irish English are closer to North American English. And there are many differences between, say, Standard British English and Standard Indian English. But we can still make a number of generalizations about British-based varieties and American-based varieties as long as we keep in mind that neither group is completely homogeneous.

There are well-known spelling differences between British and American English. Red, white, and blue are *colours* in Britain and *colors* in America. The British put *tyres* on their cars and drive to the *theatre*, where they park near the *kerb*. Interestingly, Canadians usually follow British spelling rather than American spelling, a reflection of the close historical association between Canada and Britain. But these minor spelling differences do not reflect spoken differences. On the other hand, in the phonology, morphology, syntax, and lexicon of the two sets of varieties we do find a number of marked differences.

Speakers of most American varieties, for example, consistently pronounce the vowel of words like *can't* as [æ], while speakers of British varieties usually have the sound [ɑ̄] in such words. Between two vowels the first of which is stressed, Americans and Canadians usually pronounce the stop /t/ as a flap [D] so that the word *sitter* is pronounced [sɪDər]. Speakers of British varieties, in contrast, do not readily change /t/ to [D] between vowels. Finally, most American varieties have a retroflex /r/ in word-final position in words like *car, sir*, and *near*, whereas in many British varieties /r/ is dropped in these words. With respect to the last feature, speakers of Irish and Scottish English follow the American pattern rather than the British pattern—while residents of New York City and Boston, among others, follow the British pattern. This patterning illustrates the fact that British varieties can differ widely from one another, and so can American varieties.

There are also a number of morphological and syntactic differences between British and American varieties. Many noun phrases that denote locations in time or space take an article in American English but not in British English.

American	British
in the hospital	in hospital
to the university	to university
the next day	next day

Another grammatical difference is that collective nouns (those that refer to groups of people or institutions) are plural in British varieties but usually singular in American varieties. An American watching a college soccer game would say *Cornell is ahead by two*, while a British observer would say *Cornell are ahead by two*. A final illustration of the grammatical differences between the two varieties is the use of the verb *do* with the auxiliaries *do, can*, and *have*. If asked *Did he find the book?*, an American may answer *Yes, he did*, while a speaker of a British variety can also answer *Yes, he did do*. If asked *Have you finished the assignment?*, an American may say *Yes, I have*, while British English also allows *Yes, I have done*. Asked whether flying time to Los Angeles varies, a British flight attendant might reply *It can do* as well as *It can*.

Finally, there are differences between the word stocks of American and British varieties of English, many of which are well known.

American	British
elevator	lift
second floor	first floor
TV	telly
flashlight	torch
hood (of a car)	bonnet
trunk	boot
cookies	biscuits
gas/gasoline	petrol
truck	lorry
can	tin
intermission	interval
line	queue
exit	way out

In general, the structural differences between British varieties and American varieties are not great. But combined with social and political factors, the structural differences are sufficient to make speakers of English everywhere intensely aware of the dialect boundary that the Atlantic Ocean constitutes.

Regional Varieties of American English

Most Americans are keenly aware of regional variation in their speech. Although regional differences have always been greater in Great Britain than in the United States, the last few American presidents have highlighted regional differences in American speech. John F. Kennedy and his successor, Lyndon B. Johnson, spoke markedly different dialects. Likewise Jimmy Carter and Ronald Reagan, also successive occupants of the White House, spoke of strikingly different policies with strikingly different speechways, the latter a reflection of their different regional origins.

Although one can still hear it said that the principal kinds of American English are Northern, Southern, and General American, the findings of dialect geographers working on the Linguistic Atlas of the United States and Canada suggest a refined scheme. In the late 1940s, scholars examining vocabulary patterns in the eastern United States threw out the notion of General American and began distinguishing chiefly among Northern, Midland, and Southern dialects. Each dialect has subdivisions. Midland is divided into North Midland and South Midland varieties. Boston is a distinct variety of the Northern dialect and metropolitan New York of the Mid-Atlantic dialect. Midwestern states such as Illinois, Indiana, and Ohio, which were formerly thought of as exhibiting General American, are actually situated principally in the North Midland region, with a narrow strip of Northern variety across their northernmost counties and a larger strip of South Midland across their southern counties. Figure 12-1 gives a rough approximation of the various dialect regions of the United States as they were understood several decades ago.

Mapping Dialects   In order to propose a map like the one in Figure 12-1, dialectologists traveled through various parts of the United States examining word usage and pronunciation as well as certain characteristic patterns of morphology and syntax. A dialectologist would come to a small town and, using a lengthy questionnaire, would inquire of residents what they called certain things or how they expressed certain meanings. To take an example, when researchers in different locations asked what word was used for a child born out of wedlock (for which the standard nonregional word is *bastard*), they uncovered surprising variety. The term *woods colt* was said throughout Virginia and North Carolina; *come-by-chance* was said in most of Pennsylvania and parts of New York State. In other parts of New York State, the preferred expression was *ketch-colt*. In coastal Virginia, *old-field colt* occurred commonly. The locations of the respondents to the survey for the eastern United States and the various responses they gave are identified by markers on Figure 12-2.

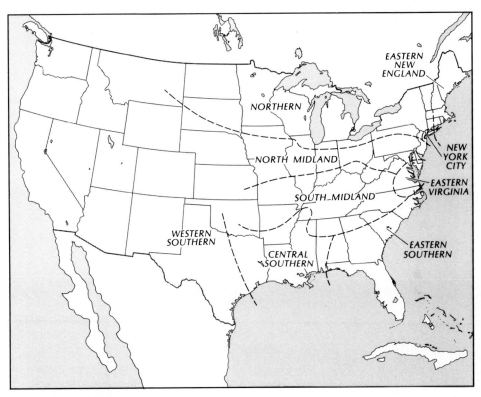

FIGURE 12-1
Regional Dialects in the United States as Viewed in 1967
SOURCE: Shuy 1967

As a further example, consider Figure 12-3, which demonstrates the distribution of various words for the dragonfly. *Darning needle* was most common in upstate New York, the metropolitan area of New York (including northern and eastern New Jersey and Long Island), and northern Pennsylvania. *Mosquito hawk* predominated in coastal North Carolina and Virginia, *snake doctor* occurred widely in inland Virginia, and *snake feeder* predominated along the northern Ohio River in West Virginia, Ohio, western Pennsylvania, and the entire upper Ohio Valley toward Pittsburgh. *Snake feeder* seems to have been concentrated in the northeastern Virginia Piedmont. Notice that not all the words were tidily limited to an area in which no other word was used. Instead, a mixture of two or more forms occurred in many areas. In other areas a single form occurred exclusively. The Os on the map in New England and New York indicate that *darning needle* was the only term found among respondents there.[2]

---

[2] If you are from one of these areas and find the terms on the maps unfamiliar, bear in mind that the data were often gathered in rural areas and represent not only "cultivated" speech but "folk" speech as well. Moreover, the data are now more than fifty years old, and a preference was given to older respondents in the survey.

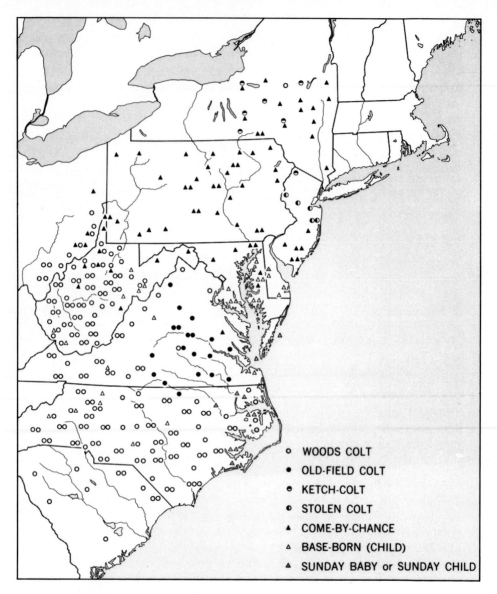

FIGURE 12-2
Words for 'bastard' in the Eastern States
SOURCE: Kurath 1949

As an illustration of a syntactic feature, Figure 12-4 indicates the areas in which *I want off* was commonly heard. Elsewhere, people said *I want to get off*, and these responses are not marked on the map.

Determining Isoglosses   Once a map has been marked with symbols for variant usages, lines can be drawn at the boundary between regions that use

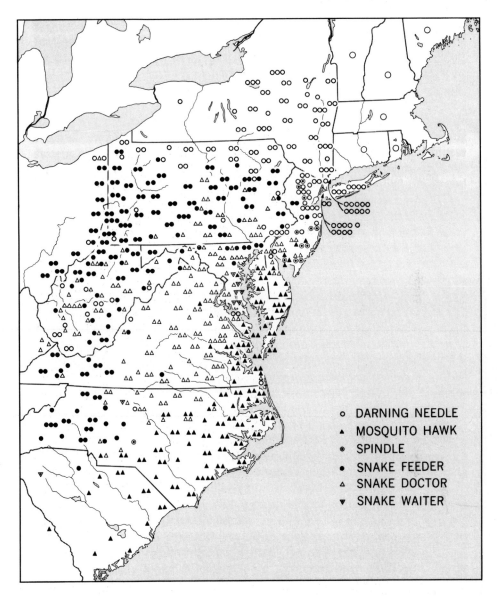

FIGURE 12-3
Words for 'dragonfly' in the Eastern States
SOURCE: Kurath 1949

different forms. From Figure 12-3, showing the distribution of regional words for the dragonfly, and from Figure 12-4, showing the distribution of *I want off*, as well as from a third map that we have not provided (one for *Sook!* as a call to cows), we can derive Figure 12-5, on which boundaries between different areas have been marked on the basis of the data recorded on Figures 12-3 and 12-4.

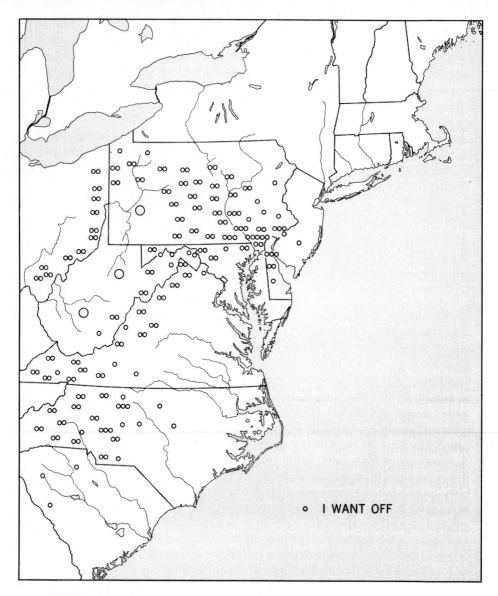

FIGURE 12-4
Distribution of *I want off* in the Eastern States
SOURCE: Kurath 1949

A boundary line that indicates the limit of the distribution of a particular usage is called an **isogloss**. Isoglosses can be drawn to mark the distribution of phonological, morphological, and syntactic features as well as the distribution of words. The isoglosses for *snake feeder* and *I want off* illustrated in Figure 12-5 are reasonably neat; for some words, however, the isogloss may be more difficult to draw because boundaries between different word regions are

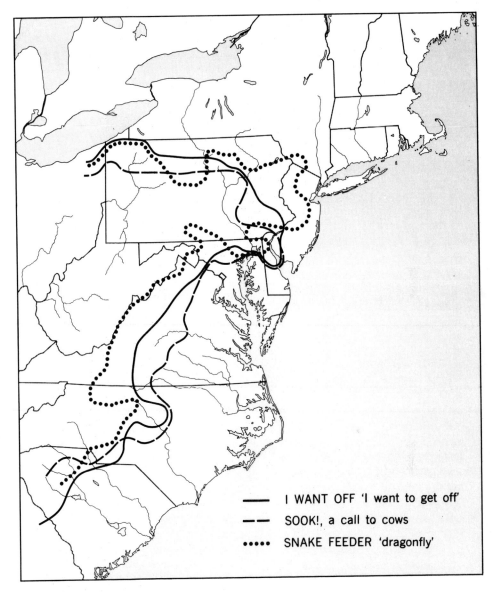

——	I WANT OFF 'I want to get off'
– – –	SOOK!, a call to cows
•••••	SNAKE FEEDER 'dragonfly'

FIGURE 12-5
Three Isoglosses in the Eastern States
SOURCE: Kurath 1949

less clear-cut. (Compare, for example, the isoglosses for the various expressions in Figure 12-3 with those in Figure 12-4.)

Dialect Boundaries   Now imagine each isogloss map drawn on a transparency and stacked one on top of the other. The result would show the extent to which the isoglosses from the different maps coincide. Isoglosses commonly "bundle" together; that is, the geographical limit for the use of one particular word (say, the word *snake feeder* for the dragonfly) often corresponds roughly to the limit for the use of another word or expression (*I want off*). Where isoglosses bundle, dialectologists draw dialect boundaries, as in Figure 12-6. A dialect boundary is simply the location of a bundle of

FIGURE 12-6
Dialect Areas in the Eastern States

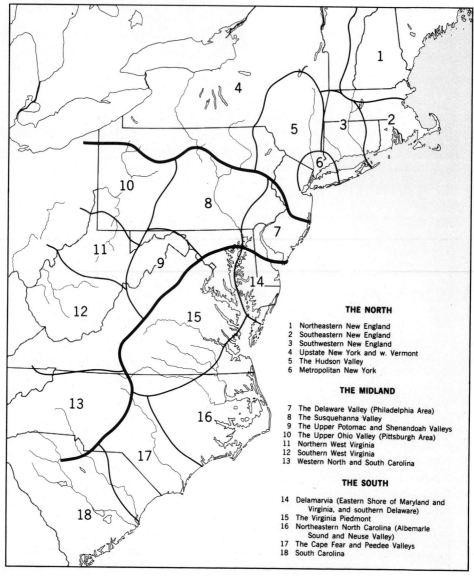

THE NORTH

1 Northeastern New England
2 Southeastern New England
3 Southwestern New England
4 Upstate New York and w. Vermont
5 The Hudson Valley
6 Metropolitan New York

THE MIDLAND

7 The Delaware Valley (Philadelphia Area)
8 The Susquehanna Valley
9 The Upper Potomac and Shenandoah Valleys
10 The Upper Ohio Valley (Pittsburgh Area)
11 Northern West Virginia
12 Southern West Virginia
13 Western North and South Carolina

THE SOUTH

14 Delamarvia (Eastern Shore of Maryland and Virginia, and southern Delaware)
15 The Virginia Piedmont
16 Northeastern North Carolina (Albemarle Sound and Neuse Valley)
17 The Cape Fear and Peedee Valleys
18 South Carolina

SOURCE: Kurath 1949

isoglosses. The map in Figure 12-6 is a distillation of dozens of maps similar to the ones shown here for 'bastard' and 'dragonfly.'

Speech patterns in the United States, as elsewhere in the world, are determined partly by the geographical and physical boundaries that inhibit communication and partly by the migration routes that were followed in settling the country. Figure 12-1 shows a line separating the North Midland from the South Midland dialect regions; it essentially follows U.S. Route 40 (now Interstate 70), which was the principal road for the migration of pioneers during the postcolonial settlement period. One oft-cited regional difference occurs in the pronunciation of the word *greasy*, which has a /z/ /grizi/ south of Route 40 but has an /s/ /grisi/ north of Route 40.

In the western part of the country, the dialect situation is considerably more complex than on the East Coast, in the South, or in the Midwest. The reason for this complexity is that the western states were settled only recently, compared to the other regions of the country, and they were settled by a greater mixture of speakers. Furthermore, a state like California is still receiving a constant influx of immigrants from many parts of the country— and the world. California is a melting pot not only of races and cultures but of dialects and languages. Extreme heterogeneity, illustrated dramatically by the California case, is not conducive to the development of a distinctive regional variety of American English.

Structural Differences Across Regional Varieties

Though vocabulary provides a convenient illustration of how regional dialects vary, the lexicon is obviously not the only area of language structure that can differ from one region to another. Varieties of a single language can differ from one another in phonology, morphology, syntax, semantics, and vocabulary, just as distinct languages do.

Besides the lexicon, some of the most salient differences across the regional dialects of the United States are found in the phonology. The pronunciation of the Standard American initial *hu* combination, as in *human* and *humor*, differs according to the following pattern:

Northern	Midland	Southern
hyumər	yumər	hyumər/yumər
hyumən	yumən	hyumən/yumən

Similarly, speakers of the Northern dialects pronounce word-initial *wh* as /hw/, while speakers of Midland and Southern varieties pronounce the same cluster /w/; this can be illustrated in the pronunciation of the words *which* and *when*.

Northern	Midland	Southern
hwɪč	wɪč	wɪč
hwɛn	wɛn	wɛn

Many patterns of variation are found in the pronunciation of vowels. It is well known, for example, that Southerners pronounce the second vowel in *admire* as /a/, where Northerners have a diphthong; speakers of Midland dialects are split between the two patterns.

Northern	Midland	Southern
ədmayr	ədmayr/ədmar	ədmar

Compared to patterns of lexical and phonological variation, the patterns of grammatical variation across American regional dialects are neither numerous nor important. Most touch on minor sentence constructions. Northern and Southern dialects, for example, have different constructions with verbs like *need* and *want*. In Southern varieties, these verbs may directly take a past participle as a complement, without an infinitive, as in the following examples:

The house needs painted badly.

The dog wants fed.

The corresponding constructions in Northern varieties are:

The house needs *to be* painted badly.

The dog wants *to be* fed.

The isogloss for this construction is approximately the same as for the *I want off* example previously described.

Many regional peculiarities are found in the use of grammatical words denoting quantities, like *all* and *any*. The word *all* is used in the South and the Midland areas to mean 'the only.'

This is all the coat I've got.
('This is the only coat I have.')

In New England, a subregion of the Northern dialect area, *all* is used to mean 'covered with.'

My hands are all greasy.
('My hands are covered with grease.')

Outside New England, the quantifying word *any* combines with *more* in many areas of the country to mean 'nowadays.'

Anymore, they build shopping malls everywhere.
('Nowadays, they build shopping malls everywhere.')

These few examples illustrate the subtle grammatical differences found across the regional dialects of American English.

The Dictionary of American Regional English

In 1985 the first volume of the *Dictionary of American Regional English* appeared. Though covering only words and expressions beginning with the letters *a, b*, and *c, DARE* (as the project and the dictionary are called) made available for the first time more information about regional words and expressions throughout the United States than had ever been known before. *DARE* had been in preparation for several decades and represents the most up-to-date and most complete knowledge of the state of American regional English.

Based on answers to 1,847 questions asked of Americans by field workers who visited 1,002 communities across the country, the computer-produced maps that *DARE* uses for exhibiting some of its findings represent not geographical space but population density. Thus the largest states are those with the largest populations. As a result, *DARE* maps appear somewhat oddly shaped.

Figure 12-7 shows the distribution of the terms *mosquito hawk* and *skeeter hawk* on a *DARE* map and on a conventional map. The word *cruller* (and slight variants) 'a twisted doughnut' has a very different distribution, as shown in the *DARE* map in Figure 12-8.

As the result of a great increase in knowledge, due to continued work on various regional dialect projects, especially *DARE*, a more accurate picture of American English dialects is now emerging, as Figure 12-9 shows. The width of the lines separating the dialects in the figure is indicative of how major the dialect boundary is. In addition, the darker the shading of a dialect area, the greater the number of lexical items that distinguish that dialect area from others. As can be seen, the farther west one goes, the fewer become the peculiar linguistic characteristics of an area; this is the result of more complex settlement patterns, with settlers coming from a greater number of dialect and language areas. The boundaries of American dialects are better established in the eastern states than in the more recently settled western ones.

Figure 12-9 indicates that the previous view of Northern, Midland, and Southern dialects needs further refining. It now appears that there are basically North and South dialects, each divided into upper and lower

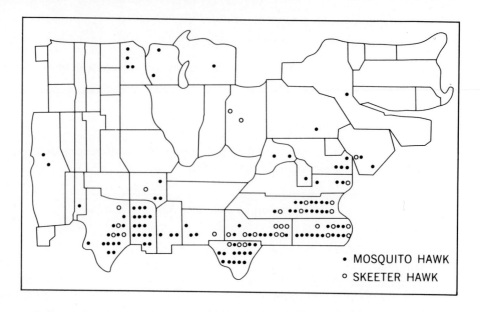

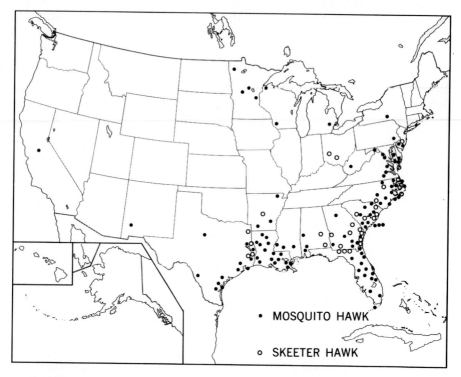

FIGURE 12-7
The Distribution of *mosquito hawk* and *skeeter hawk*
on the *DARE* Map and a Conventional Map
SOURCE: *Dictionary of American Regional English*, vol. 1, 1985

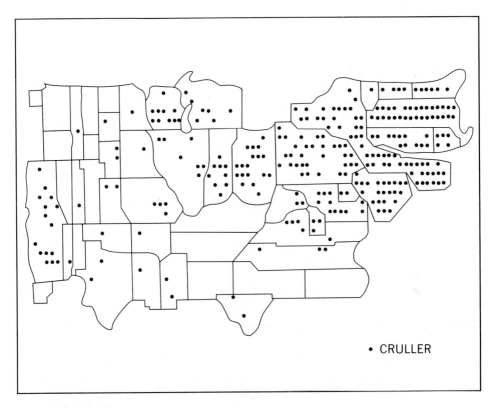

FIGURE 12-8
Distribution of *cruller* **on a** *DARE* **Map**
SOURCE: *Dictionary of American Regional English*, vol. 1, 1985

regions. In the Upper North, there are dialects in New England, the Upper Midwest, and the Northwest, with some lesser-marked dialect boundaries in the Central West and Northern California. The Southwest is also a dialect area, with Southern California having distinct characteristics. The South dialect is divided into an Upper South and Lower South, each having subdialects as well. As a comparison of Figure 12-9 with Figure 12-1 will show, our knowledge of American regional dialects has increased significantly in the last few decades.

SOCIAL VARIETIES

Just as oceans and mountains separate people and can lead eventually to distinct speech patterns, so social and political boundaries separate people and can be instrumental in promoting different speechways. To the extent that such technology as the automobile, the jet plane, the telephone, radio, and television have reduced the separating effect of physical boundaries and shortened distances between people, physical separation has become a less

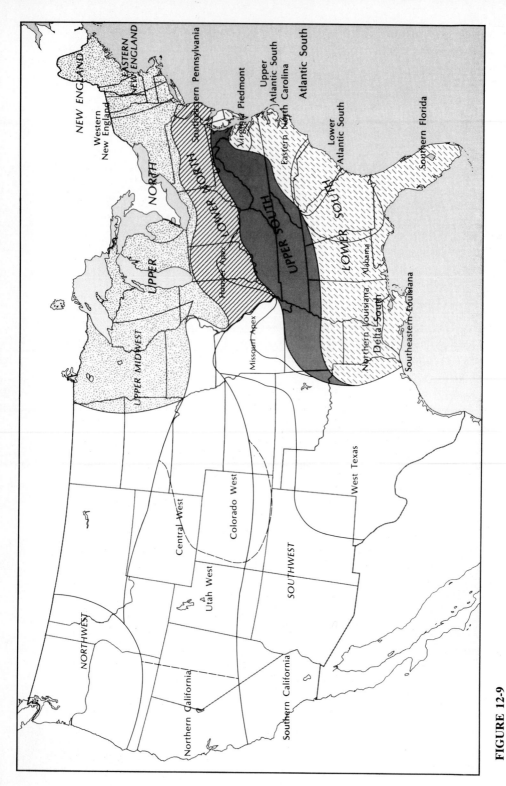

FIGURE 12-9
The Major Dialect Regions of the United States
SOURCE: Carver 1987

significant barrier to communication. Still, social barriers of various sorts continue to play a dramatic role in promoting and maintaining characteristic speech patterns among groups of people. And social barriers exist in most, if not all, societies.

Thus we can speak of **social dialects** as realistically as we have spoken of regional dialects. The social groups that claim the various social dialects as their own may identify themselves as separate socioeconomic classes or separate ethnic groups. In addition, cutting across all other social boundaries are differences in the ways women and men speak. In this section we explore several examples of how language varies across social boundaries, especially in America. As will be evident from this discussion, society can be subdivided in a multiplicity of ways: according to ethnic background, social-class affiliation, gender, and age, to name a few. Language, the mirror of society, varies across all these different boundaries.

Ethnic Varieties

Americans commonly believe that their society is essentially homogeneous. This belief is a myth. Even though Americans may be less class-conscious than, say, the British, social-group affiliation nevertheless remains extremely important. In fact, the language that each American uses serves to mark him or her as a member of particular groups, which we unconsciously learn to identify and react to as we grow up.

The most salient socially defined dialects of American English are *ethnic varieties.* Ethnicity is sometimes racial and sometimes not. For example, differences in the speech of Jewish and Italian New Yorkers have been noted, and bookstores carry books describing "Yinglish," the variety of English influenced by Yiddish speakers who have settled in America. But the social separation that leads to ethnic varieties of language is particularly noticeable in the characteristic speech patterns of urban blacks. In some cities, the speech of black residents is becoming increasingly distinct from the speech of white residents. Such a distinction between social groups is also noticeable in the characteristic speech patterns of other ethnic groups. Spanish-speaking immigrants in Los Angeles, New York, Chicago, and elsewhere have learned English as a second language, and their English is marked by a foreign accent. The children of these immigrants acquire English as a native language (and many are bilingual to some degree), but the variety of English that many Hispanic-Americans speak identifies them as being of Latin ancestry.

The discussion that follows identifies certain major characteristics of two ethnic dialects of American English: Black English and Chicano English. It is important to keep in mind that these dialects are bona fide varieties of American English like any other regional or social variety. Both Black English and Chicano English have complete grammatical systems overlapping to a very great degree with other varieties of English. And, like Standard American English, both Chicano English and Black English have several varieties each. Speakers of Black English and Chicano English do not speak the same variety in all circumstances.

While both dialects share many characteristics with Standard American English, they also exhibit certain distinctive features. Some of these features are peculiar to one or the other variety; some are shared by both of them and by other varieties of American English—though to a greater or lesser degree in one variety or another.

To think of Black English or Chicano English as an inferior variety of English or as ungrammatical English would be erroneous. Like all other social dialects, Chicano English and Black English have rules that dictate what can and cannot be said. A construction can be ungrammatical in Black English or in Chicano English just as readily as in any other variety, including Standard American English. Rules govern the structures and use of all the world's dialects, including Black English and Chicano English.

Black English   Probably the most widespread and most familiar ethnic variety of American English is Black English. Not that all black Americans are fluent speakers of Black English, but neither are all speakers of Black English black. After all, people grow up speaking the language variety spoken around them. As each of us could have grown up speaking Japanese, Swahili, or Arabic had we been born into Japanese-, Swahili-, or Arabic-speaking families, so children brought up by speakers of different regional and social varieties grow up speaking the same variety as their elders. In an ethnically diverse city like Los Angeles, one can meet teenage speakers of Black English whose foreign-born parents speak Chinese or Vietnamese. The variety of English spoken by these young Asian-Americans reflects the characteristic speechways of their friends and of the neighborhoods in which they acquired English. To underscore an obvious but often misunderstood fact, the acquisition of a particular language or language variety is as independent of one's skin color as it is of one's height or weight. People speak like the people they grow up speaking with.

The history of Black English in the United States is not completely understood, and there are conflicting theories about its origins and subsequent development. But there is no disagreement concerning its structure and functioning. It is universally recognized among scholars that Black English is simply one of many varieties of American English and that it differs in ways that are altogether parallel to the ways in which any variety differs from every other variety. Black English has characteristic phonological, morphological, and syntactic features, as well as some vocabulary of its own. In addition, speakers of Black English, like all other social groups, share characteristic ways of interacting. Black English is as rule-governed and systematic, as rich in its communicative expression and adaptability, as other varieties of English. In this section we examine some of the phonological and syntactic features of Black English; we will not discuss lexical or interactional characteristics, though the latter were touched on at the end of Chapter 10.

One of the most prominent phonological characteristics of Black English is the frequent simplification of consonant clusters, as in "des" /dɛs/ for *desk*, "pass" /pæs/ for *passed*, and "wile" /wayl/ for *wild*. This feature is not peculiar to Black English; it occurs to a lesser degree in several regional varieties of American English. In Standard English the consonant clusters in *desk* and *wild* are also commonly simplified, as in "asthem" /æsðəm/ for *ask them* and "tole" /tol/ for *told*. But consonant cluster simplification occurs more frequently and to a greater extent in Black English than in other varieties.

Another salient characteristic of Black English concerns the final stop consonants in words like *side* and *borrowed*. Speakers of Black English frequently delete some word-final stops, pronouncing *side* like *sigh* and *borrowed* like *borrow*. Even though these deletions do not occur in all words that end in consonants, they are not random either. Rather, the deletion rule is governed by the linguistic circumstances of the utterance. When a final stop consonant represents a separate morpheme (as it would in the words *followed* and *tried*), the final [d] is preserved much more frequently than when it is part of the word stem (as it would be in the words *side* and *rapid*). Another factor influencing the deletion of word-final stops is whether they occur in a syllable that is strongly stressed (as in *tried*) or weakly stressed (as in *rapid*); strongly stressed syllables tend to preserve final stops more than weakly stressed syllables do. A third factor is whether the stop has a vowel following it (as in *side angle* and *tried it*) or a consonant (as in *tried hard* and *side street*). A following vowel serves to protect the stop from being deleted; in fact, it appears to be the most significant factor in determining whether a final stop is deleted in this variety of English.

Black English distinguishes itself not only at the phonological level but also in its syntax. One prominent syntactic feature is a characteristic use of the verb *be*. Compare the uses of this verb in Black English and in Standard American English:

Black English	Standard American English
(a) That my bike.	That's my bike.
(b) The coffee cold.	The coffee's cold.
(c) The coffee be cold there.	The coffee's (always) cold there.

As sentences (a) and (b) illustrate, speakers of Black English can omit the verb *be* in the present tense whenever Standard English can use a contracted form of the verb *be*. As example (c) shows, speakers of Black English express recurring or repeated action by using the form *be*. To those Americans who are not very familiar with Black English, it sometimes seems that *be* is equivalent to Standard American English *is*, but in fact *be* in a sentence like (c) is equivalent to a verb expressing a habitual or continuous state of affairs. As the black scholar Geneva Smitherman wrote about sentences like (b) and (c), "If you the cook and *the coffee cold*, you might only just get talked about that day, but if *The coffee bees cold*, pretty soon you ain't gon have no job!"

Thus, in Black English, the verb *be* (or its inflected variant *bees*) is used to indicate continuous, repeated, or habitual action. The following examples illustrate its function further.

Black English	Standard American English
Do they be playing all day?	Do they play all day?
Yeah, the boys do be messin' around a lot.	Yeah, the boys do mess around a lot.
I see her when I bees on my way to school.	I see her when I'm on my way to school.

Another distinguishing feature of Black English is the use of the expression *it is* where Standard American English uses *there is* in the sense of 'there exists.'

Black English	Standard American English
Is it a Miss Jones in this office?	Is there a Miss Jones in this office?
She's been a wonderful wife and it's nothin' too good for her.	She's been a wonderful wife and there's nothing too good for her.

A final illustration of the distinctiveness of Black English as an ethnic variety is provided by the following examples:

Black English	Standard American English
Don't nobody never help me do my work.	Nobody ever helps me do my work.
He don't ever go nowhere.	He never goes anywhere.

These sentences contain more than one negative word. In Black English, multiple-negative constructions are grammatical, as they are in several other varieties of American English. The fact that these constructions are not grammatical in Standard English has no effect on their grammaticality in other varieties.

Chicano English   Another important ethnic dialect of American English is Chicano English, spoken by many people of Mexican descent in the major urban areas of the country and in rural areas of the Southwest. Chicano English has not been studied as much as Black English has, and our comments here are therefore somewhat general and tentative. Certain features of Chicano English also occur in other varieties of Hispanic English, such as those spoken in the Cuban community in Miami, Florida, and the Puerto Rican community in New York City.

First, note that Chicano English—like the language used by any social group—is not a single variety but many varieties, depending on the circumstances of use. As there are several varieties of Standard English and of Black English used by speakers in different parts of the country and by any given speaker in different situations, so there are varieties of Chicano English, which vary from place to place and from one set of circumstances to another. While some characteristics of Chicano English may result from the persistence of Spanish as one of the language varieties of the Hispanic-American community, Chicano English has nevertheless become a distinct variety of American English and can no longer be regarded as English spoken with a foreign accent. Chicano English is acquired as a first language by many children and is the native language of hundreds of thousands of adults. It appears to be a stable variety of American English, with its own patterns of grammar and pronunciation.

Among other well-known phonological characteristics of Chicano English is the substitution of *ch* [č] for *sh* [š], as in saying *che* [či] for *she* [ši], [čuz] (homophonous with *choose*) for *shoes* [šuz], and [spεčəli] for *specially*. This feature is so distinctive that it has become a stereotype for Mexican-Americans. There is also substitution of *sh* for *ch*, as in "preash" for *preach* and "shek" [šεk], for *check* [čεk], though this phenomenon seems not to be so stereotyped. Other phonological characteristics of Chicano English are consonant cluster simplification, as in "is" for *it's*, "kine" for *kind*, "ole" for *old*, "bes" for *best*, "un-erstan" [ʌnərstæn] for *understand*. Much of this can be represented in the phrase "It's kind of hard," which is pronounced [ɪs kanə hɑr] in Chicano English. Another major characteristic of the phonological system of Chicano English is to devoice /z/, especially in word-final position. Because of the widespread occurrence of /z/ in the inflectional morphology of English (plural and possessive nouns and third person singular present tense verbs), this salient characteristic is also stereotypical of Chicano English. Chicano English pronunciation is also characterized by the substitution of stops for the standard fricatives represented in spelling by *th*: [t] for [θ] and [d] for [ð], as in [tɪk] for *thick* and [dεn] for *then*. Still another notable phonological characteristic of Chicano English is the pronunciation of the morpheme *-ing* as [in] ("een") rather than as /ɪn/ ([ən]) or /ɪŋ/. Finally, perhaps the most prominent feature distinguishing Chicano English from other varieties of American English is its use of certain intonation patterns. These intonation patterns often strike other English speakers as uncertain or hesitant.

Chicano English is also characterized by features other than phonology, including some syntactic and lexical patterns. Chicano English often lacks the past tense marker on verbs ending in the alveolars /t/, /d/, or /n/; thus "wan" for *wanted* and "wait" for *waited*. At least in Los Angeles, *either . . . or either* instead of *either . . . or*, as in *Either I will go buy one, or either Terry will* is sometimes heard. Another feature of Chicano English is the use of prepositions such as *out from* for *away from*, as in *They drink to get out from their problems*. One final feature of Chicano English that might be mentioned is the use of multiple negation, which is also a feature of Black English and other nonstandard, nonethnic varieties of American English.

Before we leave the subject of ethnic varieties of American English, it is useful to reemphasize that many (though not all) of the customary structures of Chicano English and Black English are also characteristic of varieties of "mainstream" American English (including in some cases the standard varieties), as for example with consonant cluster simplification and multiple negation. What makes any variety salient is not one but many characteristics, some of which may be shared by several other varieties. It is worth noting that both Black English and Chicano English occur in a number of varieties along a continuum of greater and lesser similarity to Standard American English.

Socioeconomic Status Varieties

We have seen that different regional and ethnic groups tend to have characteristic speechways. New Yorkers and Bostonians speak different regional varieties, while black and white inhabitants within these cities may speak distinct ethnic varieties. Less striking in some ways, but equally significant, is the remarkable pattern of speech characteristics among different socioeconomic status groups.

New York City   To illustrate this point, we report a well-researched example. New Yorkers sometimes pronounce /r/ and sometimes drop it in words like *car, fourth,* and *beer* (when /r/ follows a vowel, either at the end of a word or preceding a consonant). The presence or absence of this post-vocalic /r/ in words like *car* and *fourth* does not change its referential meaning. The price of a "beer" and the price of the same brand of "beeah" in a given tavern are the same. A "cah pahked" in a red zone is ticketed as surely as a similarly "parked car." Taxi drivers with day-old "beards" and day-old "beahds" are equally in need of shaves. And whether one lives in New York or "New Yoahk," one still has the same mayor (or "maya"). The pronunciation of /r/ in this class of words denotes the same thing that an /r/-less pronunciation denotes. No difference in referential meaning is conveyed by pronunciations with or without /r/.

Still, the occurrence of /r/ in the pronunciations of these words is anything but random and anything but meaningless. With a keen ear for variation and a shrewd observer's eye, linguist William Labov speculated that /r/ pronunciations depended on the social-class affiliation of New Yorkers. He hypothe-

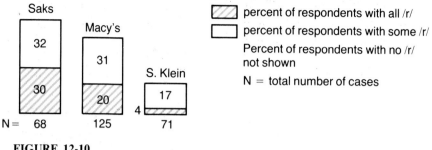

FIGURE 12-10
Overall Stratification of /r/ by Store
SOURCE: Labov 1966

sized that any two socially ranked groups of New Yorkers would differ systematically in their pronunciation of /r/, and he predicted that members of higher socioeconomic status groups would pronounce /r/ more frequently than would individuals from lower socioeconomic classes.

To test this hypothesis, Labov investigated pronunciations of /r/ among employees of three Manhattan department stores of different social rank: Saks Fifth Avenue, an expensive, upper-middle-class store; Macy's, a medium-priced, middle-class store; and S. Klein, a discount store patronized principally by working-class New Yorkers. He asked supervisors, sales clerks, and stock boys the whereabouts of merchandise he knew to be displayed and sold on the fourth floor of their store. In answer to a question like "Where can I find the lamps?" he elicited a response of *fourth floor*. Then, pretending not to have caught the answer, he said, "Excuse me?" This elicited a repeated—and presumably more careful—utterance of *fourth floor*. Each employee thus had an opportunity to pronounce post-vocalic /r/ four times (twice each in *fourth* and *floor*) in a natural and realistic setting in which language itself was not the focus of attention.

At Saks, the highest ranked of the stores, employees pronounced /r/ more often than employees did at S. Klein, the lowest-ranked store. At Macy's, the middle-ranked store, employees pronounced an intermediate number of /r/s in *fourth floor*. Figure 12-10 presents the results of Labov's survey. The shaded sections represent the percentage of speakers in a store who pronounced /r/ four times; the clear sections above the shaded area represent the percentage of employees who pronounced /r/ one, two, or three times (but not four); employees who did not pronounce any /r/ are not directly represented in the bar graph. As can be seen, 30 percent of the Saks employees pronounced all /r/, and an additional 32 percent pronounced some /r/. At Macy's, 20 percent of the employees pronounced /r/ four times, and an additional 31 percent pronounced some. At S. Klein, only 4 percent of the employees pronounced all /r/, and an additional 17 percent pronounced one, two, or three /r/s. Labov's hypothesis about the social stratification of post-vocalic /r/ was thus strikingly confirmed.

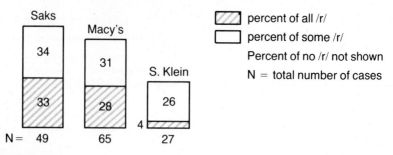

FIGURE 12-11
**Stratification of /r/ by Store for Native New York
White Saleswomen**
SOURCE: Labov 1966

There are other possible explanations for Labov's findings. Factors other than socioeconomic status might have influenced the results of his survey, as Labov himself recognized. If he happened to have spoken to more men than women in one store, or to more stock boys than sales clerks, or more blacks than whites, the difference in pronunciation of /r/ could have been the result of gender, job, or ethnic differences. Job, gender, and ethnicity could conceivably have contributed to shaping Labov's findings about the different degrees of /r/ pronunciation. To rule out the possibility that his findings reflected one of these other factors, Labov examined pronunciation among the largest homogeneous group of respondents in his sample; as it happened, there were more white female sales clerks than any other single group. Looking at their pronunciations apart from those of everyone else would eliminate the possibility of findings skewed by gender, job, or ethnicity. The results, given in Figure 12-11, reveal an overall pattern of distribution exactly similar to that for the whole sample of respondents. The white female sales clerks at Saks pronounced more /r/ than those at Macy's, who in turn pronounced more than those at S. Klein. Thus Labov could rule out the possibility that his findings reflected ethnic, gender, or in-store job differences.

In a third shuffling of the same data, Labov sought to determine whether his hypothesis would hold up in an even narrower range of social ranking than that across department stores. This time he examined the pronunciation of /r/ across the three occupational groups working in a single store. (He chose Macy's because it provided his largest sample.) Using the same hypothesis that predicted the ranking across the department stores, Labov predicted that he would find the highest percentage of /r/ pronunciation among the floorwalkers, least among stock boys, and an intermediate percentage among sales clerks. As Figure 12-12 demonstrates, that is exactly what he found. He concluded that post-vocalic /r/ pronunciation is indeed socially stratified in New York City—that higher-ranking social groups pronounce more post-vocalic /r/ than lower-ranking groups do.

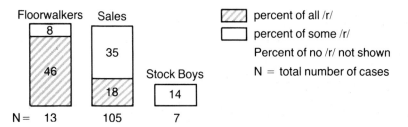

FIGURE 12-12
**Stratification of /r/ by Occupational Groups
in Macy's**
SOURCE: Labov 1966

Using his department store survey as a springboard, Labov undertook a very different kind of examination of pronunciation variants. This time, equipped with detailed sociological descriptions of individual residents of Manhattan's Lower East Side, he spent several hours with each of a couple hundred respondents there. As these New Yorkers discussed a variety of topics, Labov tape-recorded the conversations. Labov's interviewing techniques prompted his respondents to use speech samples characteristic of several different speech situations, a topic that we mention only incidentally here but will return to in detail in Chapter 13.

Among the consonants studied (besides post-vocalic /r/) were *th* in words like *thirty, through*, and *with* (New Yorkers sometimes say *thirty* with /θ/ and sometimes "tirty" with /t/); and the *th* of words like *this, those, then*, and *breathe* (the infamous "dis," "dat," "dem," and "dose" words, which have the variants /ð/ and /d/). Labov was also interested in the alternate pronunciation of *-ing* words like *running* versus *runnin'* and *talking* versus *talkin'*, which have /ɪŋ/ and /ɪn/ variants.[3] In addition, Labov examined the pronunciation of the vowels in the two word classes *coffee, soft, caught* and *bad, care, sag*. We report his findings in detail because they reveal how pronunciation differences reflect the structure of American society in one major city. Such studies can provide the basis for generalizations that can help us explain the social basis for linguistic variation in the United States.

In Labov's interviews with residents of the Lower East Side of Manhattan, he spoke with women and men, parents and children, blacks and whites, Jews and Italians. In other words, he interviewed a representative sample of Lower East Side residents. On the basis of extensive information available to him about their education, income, and occupation, Labov was able to assign each respondent to a particular socioeconomic status group. He used the education of the respondent, the income of the respondent's household, and the

---

[3] This alternation is often referred to as "dropping the *g*," but as you know from your study of phonetics in Chapter 2, the alternation is actually between an alveolar nasal /n/ and a velar nasal /ŋ/; there is no *g* to be dropped except of course in the spelling.

occupation of the principal household breadwinner as criteria for placing individuals into four distinct socioeconomic status categories: lower class, working class, lower-middle class, and upper-middle class.

As expected, upper-middle-class respondents exhibited more /r/ than lower-middle-class respondents, who in turn exhibited more than working-class respondents, who used more /r/ than lower-class respondents. Each group also pronounced more /r/ as attention paid to speech was increased in various styles. Through several graded speech registers—casual style, interview style, and reading styles—respondents in all socioeconomic groups increased the percentage of /r/ pronounced (see Chapter 13).

Remarkably, Labov found that all the variables he investigated were socially stratified: they varied significantly according to the social group of the respondent. The higher the socioeconomic status of an individual, the more likely that individual was to pronounce /r/. Each socioeconomic status group had characteristic patterns in its pronunciation of the variables, and the percentage of pronunciation of the variants was ranked in the same way as the groups themselves. The upper middle class pronounced most /θ/ for *th* (as in *thing*), most /ð/ for *th* (as in *then*), most /ɪŋ/ (as in *running*), and most /r/ (as in *car*). The lower-class respondents pronounced fewest of these variants, while the lower middle class and working class were in between, with the lower middle class pronouncing more than the working class. Such regular patterns of variation were surprising indeed, for they suggested that even subtle differences in social stratification could be reflected in language use. While it was common knowledge that differences existed in the language patterns of different social classes, no one had imagined that there would be marked quantitative differences among even very closely ranked socioeconomic groups.

The vowels were stratified in a similar way. The predicted difference in the use of vowels had to do with how high they were pronounced in the mouth. New Yorkers have several pronunciations of the first vowel in *coffee*: it ranges from the high back tense vowel [u] through the mid back vowel [ɔ] down to the low back vowel [ɑ], which is more characteristic of the speech of residents of much of the western and midwestern United States. The vowel of words in the *bad* class also varies—from low front lax [æ] to high front tense [iᵊ] with an offglide.[4] Labov's analysis carefully sorted the pronunciations into each of several discrete values depending on how high the vowels were pronounced in the mouth. (Needless to say, this required a very good ear, whose reliability was checked with acoustic phonetic machinery.)

Norwich, England   Curious about how widespread this kind of differentiation of speech patterns might be among socially stratified groups,

---

[4] A glide is created by movement of the vocal apparatus from the position used for one sound to the position used for a following sound: a transition from a vowel of one quality to the vowel of another quality. In [iᵊ], the superscript schwa represents a glide from the high front position of [i] to the mid central position of [ə]. Glides can be offglides, with the peak being on the first element (as in [iᵊ], or onglides, with the peak being on the second element (as in certain pronunciations of *spoon* [ᵘu]).

TABLE 12-1
**Percent of *-ing* Suffix Pronounced as /ɪn/ for Several
Socioeconomic Classes in Norwich and New York City**

Norwich			New York City		
Social class	Casual style	Reading style	Social class	Casual style	Reading style
MMC	28	0	UMC	5	0
LMC	42	10	LMC	32	1
UWC	87	15	WC	49	11
MWC	95	44	LC	80	22
LWC	100	66			

British linguist Peter Trudgill investigated the speech patterns of residents of Norwich, a city near the eastern coast of England. Trudgill's findings revealed patterns strikingly similar to those Labov had uncovered in New York. In Norwich, variation in syntactic as well as phonological expression was correlated with the socioeconomic status of speakers. Trudgill divided his subjects into five groups: middle-middle class (MMC), lower middle class (LMC), upper working class (UWC), middle working class (MWC), and lower working class (LWC). Table 12-1 illustrates the distribution of one phonological feature, the alternation between final /n/ and /ŋ/ in the suffix *-ing*. Data from both Labov's New York City study and Trudgill's Norwich study are given, as the comparison between the two cities is revealing.

The patterns of distribution for socioeconomic status are strikingly parallel in the two cities. Each successively higher socioeconomic status group pronounces fewer /ɪn/ than the group immediately below it in status. To put it most generally, the higher the socioeconomic status of a group, the less it will pronounce *-ing* as /ɪn/ and the more it will pronounce it as /ɪŋ/.

On the basis of evidence from these and other studies, parallel patterns of distribution may be expected for phonological variables wherever similar social structures are found. It is likely that comparable morphological and syntactic variation also exists, though evidence about variation at these levels of the grammar is scanty. What holds true of variation in English may well characterize other speech communities as well, though evidence here is also scanty.

Gender Varieties

It is a well-known fact that in many of the world's languages women and men don't speak identically. In English, for example, certain words that are closely associated with women may "sound" feminine as a result of that association. Adjectives like *lovely, darling*, and *cute* may carry feminine associations. Words that describe very precise shades of color like *mauve* and *chartreuse* are also believed to be more commonly used by women than by men. Likewise (though decreasingly so these days), certain four-letter words may surprise us when uttered by a woman. Comedian Joan Rivers has capitalized on some of these gender differences, shocking audiences by her use of taboo words generally associated with male rather than female speakers.

In some languages, the differences between women's and men's speech are considerably more dramatic than in English. Among the Koasati Indians of Louisiana, women and men use different forms of certain indicative and imperative verb forms. For example, the men's form uses an /s/ instead of the nasalization characteristic of women's forms in some verbs, as in (a) and (b) in the following examples; and the men's form sometimes adds an /s/ where the women's form ends in a vowel plus consonant, as in (c) and (d).

	Women	Men	
(a)	lakawwā̄	lakawwā́s	'he will lift it'
(b)	kā̄	ká̄s	'he is saying'
(c)	lakáw	lakáws	'he is lifting it'
(d)	íp	īps	'he is eating it'
(e)	ót	óč	'he is building a fire'

In some cases, the forms used by women are more conservative than those used by men, reflecting older forms of Koasati usage. When the research reported here was conducted fifty years ago, only middle-aged and elderly women were using women's forms. Younger women were using forms identical to those of the men. (One older man reported that the forms of the older women sounded better to him!) It is interesting to note that both men and women are familiar with the forms used by the other; when stories are told, the characters in the stories speak the forms characteristic of men or women as appropriate, no matter whether a man or woman is telling the story. Moreover, when Koasati parents correct the speech of their children, fathers may correct daughters and mothers may correct sons. Thus there is no taboo on men using women's forms or women using men's forms. Similar striking differences between the language of men and women occur in Creek and Hitchiti (two other languages of the Muskogean family), Yana (a California Indian language), Siouan, and certain Eskimo languages, as well as in Carib and other South American Indian languages.

Outside the Americas, reports of striking differences between gender varieties are cited for Chukchee (spoken in Siberia) and for Thai. In polite

Thai conversation between men and women of equal rank, women say *dič^hăn* while men say *p^hŏm* for the first person singular pronoun. Thai also has a set of particles used differently by men and women, especially in formulaic questions and responses such as 'thank you' and 'excuse me.' The polite particle used by men is *k^hráp*, while women use *k^há* or *k^hâ*. Because these politeness particles are frequently used in daily interaction, speech differences between men and women can be quite marked in Thai, despite the fact that there are very few words so differentiated.

In English, besides the lexical differences between the sexes, there are more subtle differences, some of which go largely unnoticed. One early study of variation in American speech investigated the pronunciations of the *-ing* suffix in words like *talking* and *swimming*. Such words sometimes end in an alveolar nasal /n/, sometimes in a velar nasal /ŋ/. In a semirural New England village in the mid-1950s, the speech patterns of twelve boys and twelve girls, aged three to ten were studied. Even in children that young, all but three exhibited both pronunciations in words like *running* and *talking*. Interestingly, the girls showed a higher percentage of the /ɪŋ/ forms than the boys did. The figures are given in the table.

	Preference for /ɪŋ/	/ɪn/ equal to or more frequent than /ɪŋ/
Girls	10	2
Boys	5	7

The finding that girls favor the /ɪŋ/ pronunciation over the /ɪn/ pronunciation may seem surprising, since girls and boys in this New England village (as generally in western societies) are in constant face-to-face contact with each other. The separation in the communication channels suggested earlier as the motivating factor of greatest import in the differentiation of speech patterns appears not to be an adequate explanation in this case. What then is the explanation for such differences between the speech of males and females, even from an early age?

One hypothesis suggested by a number of researchers is the "toughness" characteristic associated with working-class life styles combined with the "masculinity" characteristic associated with the /ɪn/ forms.[5] If using the term "masculinity" to explain gender differences seems to beg the question, it

---

[5] Association of /ɪn/ with masculinity may outweigh the associations with prestige and higher socioeconomic status that accompany the /ɪŋ/ variant. In fact, more prestigious speech has often been found to be preferred to a greater extent by women than by men. This fact is in accordance with sociologists' findings that women are generally more status conscious than men are. If that is so, then the preference for a less prestigious variant may in some cases be a marker of masculinity.

nevertheless hints at an important fact about gender differences in language. Gender differences have little to do with sex differences. Rather, what is important is the cultural fact of gender: what it means in a particular society to be female, what it means to be male. We are aware of gender differences as marked by hair length, clothing, jewelry use, and traditional household duties, to mention just a few. It should not be at all surprising, then, that language reflects the important social identity of one's gender role. (See the last section of Chapter 15 for a discussion of sexist language.)

Age Varieties

Everyone is aware of certain differences in the words that younger and older people use to refer to the same things. The importance of age as a social factor in language variation is most strikingly demonstrated when we listen to young children speak: two-year-old children have a very limited vocabulary, imperfect phonology, and very rudimentary syntax; five-year-old children have a much more standard syntax but a still limited vocabulary; ten-year-old children, in contrast, have a comparatively extensive vocabulary, and the structure of their utterances does not differ significantly from that of adults. Thus language evolves with age.

Leaving aside the question of how language develops in children, we note language differences between younger adults and older adults. The most striking differences are lexical. Depending on their age, our grandparents may refer to a stereo as a *hi-fi, record player, phonograph*, or *Victrola*. Similarly, the word *icebox* is still used by some people to refer to what younger generations call a *refrigerator* (see Chapter 9). We may also notice certain pronunciation differences between our grandparents and our parents or our parents and our friends. In general, older people tend to be more conservative than younger people in their speech habits: they use older words, incorporate fashionable terms less readily into their vocabulary, and use certain structures that younger generations have abandoned. There are many differences between the speechways of people belonging to different generations.

SUMMARY

With separation and distance—physical or social—people who otherwise would possess shared speechways come to speak different varieties. Given sufficient time and separation, distinct languages can arise. Conversely, the speech of people talking with one another as members of the same community can develop in unison, even tending to merge in some situations. Still, there are interesting and important linguistic differences among speakers within every speech community.

Language can vary greatly from one social group to the next, and social groups may be defined in a number of ways besides regionally. A social group may distinguish itself from the rest of the community by its distinct ethnic affiliation. A social group may also be defined in socioeconomic terms.

Females and males may also be thought of as belonging to different social groups. And individuals of particular age groups distinguish themselves from other age groups as much by their characteristic uses of language as by fashions of dress and other nonlinguistic behavior. If we combine all these different group distinctions, we obtain a complex picture of the composition of society: within a particular ethnic group, we find socioeconomic classes; members of these socioeconomic classes may be young or old, male or female. All these distinctions are reflected in language.

Whatever the social group, its language probably has distinctive characteristics that distinguish it from varieties used by other social groups. The linguistic markers that characterize social varieties may also serve as markers (or symbols) of group membership. When a black American man wants to stress his membership in his ethnic group, he may exaggerate the Black English features in his speech. If a woman wants to appear particularly feminine, she may choose to exhibit the features associated with women's speech and avoid "masculine-sounding" words and constructions. Individuals can thus take advantage of socially marked language characteristics for their own purposes.

EXERCISES

1. Distinguish between an accent and a dialect; between a dialect and a language. What is meant by a language variety? Does it make any sense to say of a language variety that "it isn't a language, but only a dialect"?

2. Examine a copy of a newspaper or magazine published in Great Britain (one or more of the following should be available in your library's current periodicals room: *The Times, The Economist, Punch, The Spectator, The Listener*) and list as many examples of differences between American and British English as you can notice on two pages. Include examples of words, syntax, spelling, and punctuation.

3. Listen carefully to the pronunciation of the principal anchors on the three major television networks. What differences can you notice in their speech? (Attempt to transcribe some of those differences if possible.) Can you determine from their speech patterns where the anchors were raised?

4. Which of the following words are you familiar with? Make two lists: one comprising those words you normally use, the other those words you don't usually use but have heard others use. With what regional or national group do you associate the words you have heard others use but don't use yourself? Compare your judgments with those of others in your class.

   dragonfly   darning needle, mosquito hawk, spindle, snake feeder, snake doctor
   pancake   fritter, hot cake, flannel cake, batter cake
   cottage cheese   curds, curd cheese, clabber cheese, dutch cheese, pot cheese
   string beans   green beans, snap beans
   earthworm   fishing worm, night crawler, angle worm, rain worm, red worm, mud worm
   lightning bug   firefly, fire bug
   baby carriage   baby buggy, baby coach, baby cab, pram

5. The following questions are part of the questionnaire used around the United States in gathering data for *DARE*. After you answer each question, compare your answers with those of your classmates. Do you and your classmates agree on the regions in which the particular variants are used? (*DARE* provides maps for answers to each of the questions.)

I. What names are used around here for:
—the part of the house below the ground floor?
—a container for coal to use in a stove?
—a small stream of water not big enough to be a river?
—a round cake of dough, cooked in deep fat, with a hole in the center?
—an oblong cake cooked in deep fat?
—a piece of cloth that a woman folds over her head and ties under her chin?
—the common worm used as bait?
—vehicles for a baby or small child, the kind it can lie down in?

II. What expressions do you have around here for:
—someone who is confused or mixed up, as in "So many things were going on at the same time that he got completely _____"?
—someone who seems to be very stupid—"He doesn't know _____"?
—a very skilled or expert person (for example at woodworking)—"He's a _____"?

How do the answers of your classmates to the last question in group I compare with this map from *DARE* for *baby buggy*?

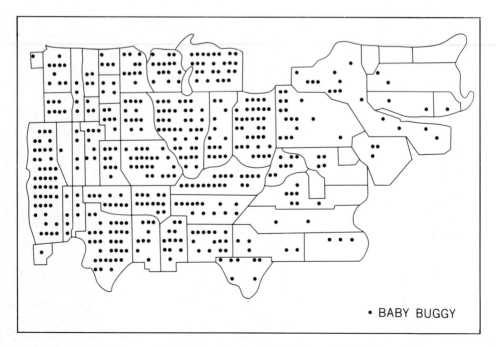

• BABY BUGGY

SOURCE: *Dictionary of American Regional English*, vol. 1, 1985

6. What was Labov's hypothesis about the distribution of /r/ in New York City, and what did he discover about its distribution in the three department stores? In your city or town, are there three stores that could be similarly investigated? What phonological features do you think are likely to be socially differentiated in your stores? Compose a question that you could ask for each feature that would uncover the data needed to confirm your hypothesis. (Be certain that the question would be a natural one for the kind of store you have in mind.) Would you ask your respondents to repeat their answers as Labov did? Explain why or why not.

7. Briefly describe how Labov eliminated the possibility that the variation he found was ascribable to racial, sex, or job status differences. How would you do the same thing in your survey?

8. Describe four features of Black English not mentioned in this chapter, including at least one phonological and one syntactic characteristic. For each characteristic, indicate whether it represents an absolute difference or a relative (that is, quantifiable) difference between Black English and Standard English.

9. List several ways in which the speech of women and the speech of men differ from one another in greetings, threats, swearing, and promises. What do you think accounts for these differences? Do you think the differences are increasing or decreasing? Explain the bases for your answers.

10. What reasons can you think of to help explain why the -*ing* variable, rather than some other potential variables, seems so marked with respect to gender?

11. Make a list of words or expressions that are used by your grandparents but not by your parents or your friends. Make another list of words that are used by your parents but not by your friends. Do you think of any of the expressions on your lists as being "old-fashioned"? Are any of the words or expressions on your lists examples that you think you will come to use as you grow older, or are they all "old-fashioned" expressions that are passing out of use? What evidence do you have for your view?

SUGGESTIONS FOR FURTHER READING

Useful general treatments of dialect are Francis (1983) and Chambers and Trudgill (1980). Most of the more general sociolinguistics books such as Hudson (1980) and Wardhaugh (1986) contain discussions of dialects and related subjects. Scherer and Giles (1979) is a collection of essays, each treating the linguistic marking of a social category such as gender, social class, or ethnicity in speech. The data and discussion of convergence in Kupwar are based on Gumperz and Wilson (1971). Labov (1972a) is a frequently cited description of Black English; Penfield and Ornstein-Galicia (1985) treats Chicano English. Other treatments of Black English include Smitherman (1977), from which some of our examples are taken, and Baugh (1985). From Labov (1966; 1972b), classic treatments of social variation, come the New York City data reported in this chapter, while the Norwich data come from Trudgill (1983). Ferguson and Heath (1981) is a collection of essays describing language among Native and other Americans: blacks, Puerto Ricans, Jews, Italian-, French-, and German-Americans, Filipinos, and others. With its emphasis on British and other European dialects, Petyt (1980) complements our treatment in this chapter. Kurath (1972) is a thorough analysis of the methods and some of the findings of dialect geography, with special emphasis on American English (including its roots in England) but with some attention to the Romance and Germanic languages as well. Brief and limited introductions to American English dialects can be found in Reed (1977) and Shuy (1967). The most comprehensive treatment of American regional variation in vocabulary has started to appear in print with Cassidy (1985). Carver (1987) is the most up-to-date overview of American English dialects, with emphasis on their cultural and historical origins. Some of the principal findings of American dialect geographers on the East Coast can be found in Kurath (1949), Atwood (1953), and Kurath and McDavid (1961). The relationship between language and the sexes is treated in Smith (1985); Thorne, Kramarae, and Henley (1983) provides an overview of research on this topic in the preceding decade, a number of individual studies, and a lengthy annotated bibliography. The data reported in this chapter on gender differences in Koasati and Thai come from Haas (1940), which also discusses Chukchee and other languages. Fischer (1958) reports the New England -*ing* data. Philips et al. (1987) is a collection of essays examining women's and men's speech in a cross-cultural perspective and gender differences in the language of children. The relationship between language and social identity is treated in Edwards (1985).

REFERENCES

Atwood, E. Bagby. 1953. *A Survey of Verb Forms in the Eastern United States* (Ann Arbor: University of Michigan Press).

Baugh, John. 1985. *Black Street Speech: Its History, Structure, and Survival* (Austin: University of Texas Press).

Carver, Craig M. 1987. *American Regional Dialects: A Word Geography* (Ann Arbor: University of Michigan Press).

Cassidy, Frederic G. (ed.). 1985. *Dictionary of American Regional English*, vol. I (Cambridge: Belknap Press of Harvard University Press).

Chambers, J. K., and Peter Trudgill. 1980. *Dialectology* (Cambridge: Cambridge University Press).

Edwards, John. 1985. *Language, Society and Identity* (New York: Basil Blackwell).

Ferguson, Charles A., and Shirley Brice Heath (eds.). 1981. *Language in the USA* (Cambridge: Cambridge University Press).

Fischer, John L. 1958. "Social Influences on the Choice of a Linguistic Variable," in *Word*, vol. 14, pp. 47–56; reprinted in Hymes (ed.), 1964, pp. 483–488.

Francis, W. Nelson. 1983. *Dialectology: An Introduction* (New York: Longman).

Gumperz, John J., and Robert Wilson. 1971. "Convergence and Creolization: A Case from the Indo-Aryan/Dravidian Border in India," in Dell Hymes (ed.), *Pidginization and Creolization of Languages* (Cambridge: Cambridge University Press), pp. 151–167.

Haas, Mary R. 1940. "Men's and Women's Speech in Koasati," *Language*, vol. 20, pp. 142–149; reprinted in Hymes (ed.), 1964, pp. 228–233.

Hudson, R. A. 1980. *Sociolinguistics* (Cambridge: Cambridge University Press).

Hymes, Dell (ed.). 1964. *Language in Culture and Society* (New York: Harper & Row).

Kurath, Hans. 1949. *A Word Geography of the Eastern United States* (Ann Arbor: University of Michigan Press).

————.1972. *Studies in Area Linguistics* (Bloomington: Indiana University Press).

Kurath, Hans, and Raven I. McDavid, Jr. 1961. *The Pronunciation of English in the Atlantic States* (Ann Arbor: University of Michigan Press).

Labov, William. 1966. *The Social Stratification of English in New York City* (Washington, D.C.: Center for Applied Linguistics).

———. 1972a. *Language in the Inner City* (Philadelphia: University of Pennsylvania Press).

———. 1972b. *Sociolinguistic Patterns* (Philadelphia: University of Pennsylvania Press).

Penfield, Joyce, and Jacob L. Ornstein-Galicia. 1985. *Chicano English: An Ethnic Contact Dialect* (Amsterdam: John Benjamins).

Petyt, K. M. 1980. *The Study of Dialect: An Introduction to Dialectology* (London: Andre Deutsch).

Philips, Susan U., Susan Steele, and Christine Tanz (eds.). 1987. *Language, Gender, and Sex in Comparative Perspective* (Cambridge: Cambridge University Press).

Reed, Carroll E. 1977. *Dialects of American English*, rev. ed. (Amherst: University of Massachusetts Press).

Scherer, Klaus R., and Howard Giles (eds.). 1979. *Social Markers in Speech* (Cambridge: Cambridge University Press).

Shuy, Roger. 1967. *Discovering American Dialects* (Champaign, Ill.: National Council of Teachers of English).

Smith, Philip M. 1985. *Language, the Sexes and Society* (Oxford: Basil Blackwell).

Smitherman, Geneva. 1977. *Talkin and Testifyin: The Language of Black America* (Boston: Houghton Mifflin).

Thorne, Barrie, Cheris Kramarae and Nancy Henley (eds.). 1983. *Language, Gender and Society* (Rowley, Mass.: Newbury House).

Trudgill, Peter. 1983. *Sociolinguistics: An Introduction to Language and Society*, rev. ed. (Harmondsworth, England: Penguin).

Wardhaugh, Ronald. 1986. *An Introduction to Sociolinguistics* (New York: Basil Blackwell).

REGISTERS:
LANGUAGE VARIATION
IN SITUATIONS
OF USE

13

INTRODUCTION: THE CLOCKS OF BALLYHOUGH

Ballyhough railway station in England has two clocks, which disagree by some six minutes. When one helpful gentleman pointed out this fact to a porter, the porter's reply was "Faith, sir, if they was to tell the same time, why would we be having two of them?" Though the porter's logic may be faulty when applied to railway clocks, it may nevertheless be applied to the many competing languages that exist throughout the world. If each were to do the same work as the others, there would be no need of more than one.

Every language (and every language variety) serves a distinct purpose. Primary among those purposes is to identify and unify the speakers whose language it is and to separate them from speakers of other languages, from members of other groups. Of course, it is possible to imagine a fantasy world in which all human beings speak exactly the same language, with no dialect variations of any kind. Men and women would speak alike; different ethnic and social class groups would speak alike; even succeeding generations would speak alike. In other words, language could not be used to mark socially salient distinctions. For better or worse, this imaginary situation is not what we find when we examine natural languages in the real world. Rather, there exists a multitude of tongues, each with several dialects, all changing continuously so that each generation speaks differently from those that precede and follow it.

In Chapter 12, we saw how language varieties reflect the social characteristics of their users and serve to mark culturally and socially salient distinctions of region, gender, social class, age, and ethnicity. In this chapter we shall discuss language variation that is associated not with the social grouping of *users* but with the situations of *use*. We will explore the varieties of language that an individual may use every day as well as those that crop up only occasionally. To take some simple examples, we do not talk to close friends the way we talk to our teachers, and we do not write to our parents in the same way we would to an attorney or a minister or an elderly aunt. In different circumstances, we vary our use of language forms to one degree or another. In some societies, different situations call for different languages altogether; in other societies, different situations call for different varieties of the same language. Language varieties that are associated with different situations of use are called **registers**.

LANGUAGE VARIATION AND MULTILINGUALISM

Though most Americans study a foreign language in school, the circumstances of that learning experience seldom lead to mastery of the language. Very few Americans are fluent enough in a foreign tongue to communicate through it when visiting Spanish-speaking, French-speaking, or German-speaking countries, to mention three commonly studied foreign languages. We are fortunate that English is spoken as a second language in so many places, because otherwise our linguistic parochialism would interfere with (if not entirely prevent) communication with speakers of even the major European tongues. With more than a hint of envy, Americans often comment on the ability of many Europeans to speak a second language or even a third.

The reasons for this discrepancy between Americans and Europeans have nothing to do with language learning ability as such. In part, the linguistic versatility of Europeans can be attributed to the fact that in a relatively small land area people have frequent occasion to meet and interact with other nationals speaking other languages. Even within a single country, more than one language may be spoken, not by immigrants but by communities in long-term residence. Tiny Switzerland is home to German, French, Italian, and Romansch, with the first three sharing official status. In Belgium, Dutch (or Flemish, as the Belgian variety of Dutch is called) and French are spoken widely.

Language Choice in a Multilingual Society

We might assume that in multilingual countries different languages are spoken by different groups of people. In fact, though, if you were to examine the use of different languages in a bilingual or multilingual community, you would notice a systematic allocation of languages across various situations of use. In a speech community employing several languages, language choice is not arbitrary. Particular settings such as school or government will usually favor a particular language, and different languages will be appropriate to different speech situations. Where one language is appropriate, another will be inappropriate. Though there may be roughly equivalent expressions in two languages, the social meaning that attaches to the use of one language generally differs from the social meaning attached to the use of another. As a result, speakers must attend to the social import of language choice, however unconsciously that choice may be made. A choice of one tongue over another signals something in the social situation, and each new speech situation has the possibility of requiring a change of language.

Linguistic Repertoires in Brussels, Tehran, and Los Angeles   The use of several varieties in two languages among government workers in the capital of Belgium illustrates the nature of language choice among various languages in one European community.

> Government functionaries in Brussels who are of Flemish origin do not always speak Dutch *to each other*, even when they all know Dutch *very* well and *equally* well. Not only are there occasions when they speak French *to each other* instead of Dutch, but there are some occasions when they speak standard Dutch and others when they use one or another regional variety of Dutch with each other. Indeed, some of them also use different varieties of French with each other as well, one variety being particularly loaded with governmental officialese, another corresponding to the non-technical conversational French of highly educated and refined circles in Belgium, and still another being not only a 'more colloquial French' but the colloquial French of those who are Flemings. All in all, these several varieties of Dutch and of French constitute the *linguistic repertoire* of certain social networks in Brussels.[1]

The language variety chosen for use in Brussels is occasioned, or triggered, by the setting in which the talk takes place, by the topic, by the social relations among the participants, and by any of several other features of the situation. In general, the use of Dutch is associated with interaction that is informal and intimate, whereas French is associated with more official or more highbrow speech situations. Given these associations, the choice of French or Dutch carries an associated social meaning in addition to the referential meaning that is conveyed.

We will use the term **linguistic repertoire**, or verbal repertoire, for the set of language varieties exhibited in the speaking and writing patterns of a speech community. As in the case of Brussels, the linguistic repertoire of any speech community may consist of several languages and may include several varieties of each language. Other linguistic repertoires besides that of Brussels can be cited, and we will describe several.

[1] Fishman (1972), pp. 47–48.

At least into the mid 1970s, there was still considerable multilingualism in the Iranian city of Tehran. Christian families spoke Armenian or Assyrian at home and in church, Persian at school, all three in different situations while playing or shopping, and Azerbaijani Turkish at shops in the bazaar. Moslem men from northwest Iran, who were working as laborers in the booming capital, spoke a variety of Persian with their supervisors at construction sites but switched to a variety of Turkish with their fellow workers and to a local Iranian dialect when they visited their home villages on holidays; in addition, they listened daily to radio broadcasts in standard Persian and heard passages from the Koran recited in Arabic. It was not uncommon for individuals of any social standing to command as many as four or five languages and to use them all in different situations.

To take another example, this one of a group using its native tongue as a foreign language, the Korean-speaking community in Los Angeles supports bilingual institutions of various sorts: banks, churches, shops, and a wide range of services from pool halls and video rentals to hotels and construction companies. At several banks all the tellers are bilingual, and in the course of a day's work they switch often between Korean and English. As the tellers alternate between Korean-speaking and English-speaking patrons, the language in which they conduct business alternates just as naturally.

The bilingual Japanese-American and Chinese-American communities in Los Angeles are older and more established than the Korean community, and all three taken together are dwarfed by the size and dispersion of the bilingual Latin-American community. Among the people of this community, Spanish is often spoken at home and in neighborhood shops as well as in church. English is generally the language of government and of education beyond a certain level of elementary school. There are not only individual radio and television programs in Spanish but several stations that broadcast exclusively in Spanish. Both locally published and imported Spanish-language newspapers are widely available. Many speakers routinely alternate between Spanish and English. Each setting generally has one language allocated to it—Spanish for home and church, English in secondary schools—though both Spanish and English are used on the playing fields and in some business interactions.

Switching Varieties Within a Language   If we examine the situation in Europe, besides switching between languages we see examples of language-internal switching. As mentioned earlier, Brussels residents switch not only between French and Dutch but also between varieties of French and between varieties of Dutch. And in Hemnes, a village in northern Norway, residents speak two quite distinct varieties of Norwegian. Ranamål is a local dialect and serves to identify speakers of that region. Bokmål, one of two forms of standard Norwegian (the other being Nynorsk), is in use in Hemnes for education, religion, government transactions, and the mass media. All members of the community control these two varieties and regard themselves at any given time as speaking one *or* the other. In general, speakers do not perceive themselves as mixing the two varieties in their speech. There are differences of pronunciation, morphology, lexicon, and syntax. We illustrate with a simple sentence meaning 'Where are you from?'

Ranamål   ke du e ifrå

Bokmål   vor ær du fra

While Bokmål is the expected variety in certain well-defined situations, the residents of Hemnes do not accept the use of Bokmål among themselves outside those situations. In situations in which Ranamål is customarily used, the employment of Bokmål would signal social distance and contempt for community spirit. In Hemnes, to use Bokmål with fellow locals is to *snakk fint* or *snakk jalat* 'put on airs.' As the researchers who report these findings write:

> Although locals show an overt preference for the dialect, they tolerate and use the standard in situations where it conveys meanings of officiality, expertise, and politeness toward strangers who are clearly segregated from their personal life.[2]

Regard for the social situation is thus important even in choosing varieties of the same language.

SPEECH SITUATIONS

As we have seen in Hemnes, Los Angeles, Brussels, and Tehran, language switching can be triggered by a change in any one of a number of situational factors, including the setting, the purpose of the communication, the person being addressed, the social relations between the interlocutors, and the topic of discussion.

Elements of the Speech Situation

If we define a speech situation as the coming together of various significant situational factors such as purpose, topic, and social relations, then each speech situation in a bilingual community will generally allow for only one of the two languages to be used. Table 13-1 illustrates this concept.

As we see from the table, in situation A a variety of Spanish is appropriate; in situation C, a variety of English. Only in the relatively rare case of situation E might an individual have a genuine choice between Spanish and English without calling attention to the language chosen. In situation E, a choice is allowed because of the conflict between intimacy (which usually requires Spanish, as in situations A or B) and a learned topic (for which English is usually preferred).

Table 13-2 charts certain aspects of a speech situation that may require a change in language variety.

[2] Blom and Gumperz (1972), pp. 433–434.

TABLE 13-1
Linguistic Repertoire

Situation	Relation of listeners	Place	Topic type	Spanish	English
A	intimate	school	not learned	×	
B	intimate	home	not learned	×	
C	not intimate	school	not learned		×
D	not intimate	home	learned		×
E	intimate	school	learned	×	×

Related to *purpose*, the kind of activity that is involved is crucial. Is one making a purchase, giving a sermon, telling a story? Each activity may have an influence on the selection of a language. Is one attempting to entertain, to report information, or to affirm a social relationship? To greet a friend or invite an aunt to dinner?

As to *setting*, one may switch from one language to another as the topic switches, from one of quite local interest, say, to one of national concern; or from something quite personal to something about university studies. The location can have influence in that a person might well use one language in a university setting but a different language in church or at home for otherwise equivalent situations. The mode—that is, whether one is speaking or writing—can certainly influence the language variety selected.

As to the *participants*, the identity of the speaker will influence the language choice. Likewise, the person being addressed will influence the choice of code. Speakers of probably all languages adapt their utterances to the age of their addressee. In some societies, the older the person, the higher his or her social standing; younger people must address older people more respectfully than they address peers. To cite another example, in French the second person singular pronoun 'you' has two forms: the grammatically singular form *tu* is used when addressing social equals or as an expression of intimacy with the addressee, while the plural form *vous* is reserved for

TABLE 13-2
Speech Situation

Purpose	Setting	Participants
Activity	Topic	Speaker
Goal	Location	Addressee
	Mode	Social relations between speaker and addressee
		Character of audience, if any

persons of higher social status or social distance. A younger person addressing an older person is expected to use *vous*, not *tu*, unless the older person is a
close relative. The French pronoun system illustrates one way in which
morphology may vary according to the age of the addressee, and similar
patterns are found in several European languages.

Also with respect to participants, it is not just the social identity of speaker
and addressee that is relevant but the roles they are playing in the particular
speech situation. A judge, for example, may speak one variety at home and
another in the courtroom. A parent who works as a teacher and has his child
for a student may speak different varieties at home and at school, even when
the topic and the addressee are the same.

The various aspects of the speech situation come together in a particular
choice of language or language variety. In each bilingual situation—whether
a general situation such as home or church or a specific one such as discussing
soccer in a cafe with one's closest friends—only one variety is usually
appropriate. In fact, people get so accustomed to speaking a particular
language in a given setting that they often have difficulty communicating in
another language in that setting, no matter how familiar that other language
may be in other settings.[3] As a result, switching between language varieties is
very common throughout the world.

Naturally, when a bilingual person switches from one language to another,
all levels of the grammar reflect that switch. To speak Spanish is to use
Spanish sounds in Spanish words formed into Spanish sentences. To switch
from Spanish to English entails using the phonology, lexicon, morphology,
and syntax of English.

REGISTERS IN A MONOLINGUAL SOCIETY

The recognition that there are settings and speech situations in multilingual
societies in which one language or another is appropriate has a direct parallel
in monolingual speech communities, in which varieties of a single language
constitute the linguistic repertoire. As in multilingual communities, mono-
linguals mark socially salient speech situations with appropriate varieties of a
language. For example, consider the difference between the full forms of
careful speech and the abbreviations and reductions characteristic of fast
speech that occur in face-to-face relaxed communication: not only workaday
contractions like *won't* and *I'll* but reduced sentences like [jityɛt] for 'Did you
eat yet?'

To take a second example, we are aware that (other aspects of the situation
being equal) we do not use the same terms in referring to certain body parts
when speaking to friends, family, and physician. The term *collarbone* might

---

[3] Exceptions to this generalization include professional translators, bilingual educators, and
certain business people regularly engaged in negotiations with members of their own and
another culture.

be used at home, while *clavicle* might be used with a physician; either could be used with friends, depending on other aspects of the particular speech situation. The choices made in different speech situations for other body parts may be much more striking.

The distribution of alternative terms for the same referent may seem arbitrary and without communicative benefit; indeed, in the case of body parts, all the terms may be known and used by all the parties under equivalent circumstances. A physician speaking with her own physician may use the term *clavicle*; with her family and friends, however, she will be expected to use the same terms the rest of us would use with equivalent addressees in parallel speech situations. When nonmedical people address a physician, they use only the terms appropriate to discussion of a medical situation.

Since all the terms would be equally well understood and could communicate referential meaning equally well, the choice of a socially appropriate variant is *cognitively* unhelpful. One may ask, then, why language forms differ in different speech situations. The answer is that different forms for the same content can indicate one's affective relationship to various aspects of the situation (setting, addressee, topic, and so on). Such variation as has lasted for centuries in a language can be assumed to be serving a fundamental need of human communication.

If one were to overhear a portion of a discussion using one set of body part terms instead of another, one could ascertain whether the speaker was addressing a physician, a friend, or a parent (even in the absence of other information about the situation). Lexical choices, in other words, not only signal cognitive content but also indicate the kind of situation in which a discussion is taking place. In fact, lexical choices help create and communicate the way a context is perceived by the interlocutors.

Thus, just as a multilingual linguistic repertoire allocates different languages over different speech situations, so does a monolingual repertoire. For all speakers—monolingual and multilingual—there is marked variation in the forms of language used for different activities, addressees, topics, and settings. These marked forms of language constitute the registers of a linguistic repertoire. By choosing among the varieties, situational variation is both created and communicated.

From a relatively young age, everyone learns to control several language varieties for use in different speech situations. No one is limited to a single variety of a single language. For some, the language varieties they control belong to one language; for others, the varieties are drawn from more than one language. Just which speech situations—which purposes, topics, addressees—prompt a different variety depends on the norms in particular cultures. In one society, the presence of in-laws may call for a different variety (as it does in several aboriginal Australian societies); in other societies, the presence of in-laws may have no independent influence on the selection of an appropriate language variety, whereas the presence of children or members of the opposite sex may be crucial. In Western societies, there are many words that people avoid saying in the presence of children.

Markers of Register

As languages and dialects differ from one another at every grammatical level, so registers can differ in vocabulary, phonology, morphology, syntax, and semantics. There may also be different interactional patterns in different speech situations—how the allocation of turns is decided, for example. In addition, there are rules governing nonlinguistic behavior such as physical proximity, face-to-face positioning, standing, and sitting that also accompany register variation; both the interactional patterns and the body language are beyond the scope of this book, and we mention them only incidentally.

When we find characteristic features of a register at one level of the grammar, we can expect to find corresponding features at other grammatical levels as well. For example, to describe the register known as legalese we must describe its characteristic lexicon, sentence structure, and semantics, as well as its characteristic terms of address, rules of interaction, and so forth.

Lexicon

As noted in the preceding chapter, language varies with region, gender, ethnicity, socioeconomic status, and age. Registers also vary along certain dimensions. For example, people generally speak (and write) in markedly different ways in formal and informal situations. Formality and informality can be seen as opposite poles of a situational continuum along which the various levels of language may vary.

Let's begin our analysis of register variation with an examination of word choice. The words that follow generally mean the same thing and can have the same referent, but it is not difficult to rank them according to their degree of formality. It would be surprising if we did not generally agree that these words should be ranked as follows, with the least formal word first: *pissed, pickled, high, drunk, intoxicated.*

Think of other terms for the state that results from having consumed too much alcohol. In one context, to suggest inebriation may require the word *intoxicated*, while in another a more appropriate expression may be *drunk* or *under the influence*. The words *bombed* and *pissed* are also sometimes used, especially by younger people in situations of considerable informality. The entries in a thesaurus can be surprising for their number: one thesaurus lists more than 125 words or phrases for 'intoxicated.' By no means are they situationally equivalent.

Not every word that can be glossed as 'inebriated' is suitable for use on all occasions when reference to intoxication is intended. Word choice can indicate quite different attitudes toward the state, the addressees, the person being described, and so on. It can also index the speech situation in which the term is being used—as intimate or distant, formal or informal, serious or jocular, and so forth. Different referring expressions for intoxication have different connotations, depending on the situations of use with which they are customarily associated. These affiliated situations of use add a dimension of meaning that is quite distinct from the referential meaning of a word. Imagine the following fictional dialogue between a judge and a defendant at an arraignment in a courtroom:

Judge: I see that the cops say you were pickled last night and were driving an old jalopy down the middle of the road. True?

Defendant: Your honor, if I might be permitted to address this allegation, I should like to report that I was neither inebriated nor under the influence of an alcoholic beverage of any kind; I imbibed no booze last evening.

Of the many possible observations about this exchange, we shall make just a few. In the first place, the judge's language seems out of place: the words *cops, pickled,* and *jalopy* (among others) strike us as bizarre, inappropriate for a judge in a courtroom. As for the defendant's response, it too seems out of place, especially following the very informal speechways of the judge; indeed, the defendant's language might well seem too formal, too elevated, even if the judge had used more formal language. There is an incongruity in the defendant's using more formal terms than the judge. It also seems odd to have the informal word *booze* used in an utterance in which the more formal *imbibed, inebriated, beverage,* and *allegation* also occur.

Compare the judge's language in the first example with the following, which is more appropriate to the speech situation.

Judge: You are charged with driving a 1982 blue Ford while under the influence of alcohol. How do you plead?

Thus we see that within a single language certain registers are appropriate to specific circumstances. Like all language varieties, registers constrain which words can be used together and which others cannot be, even though their use together would not violate grammatical constraints. These kinds of co-occurrence restrictions also apply to phonological and syntactic patterns, as we shall see.

Address Terms   Consider that appropriate forms of address differ in different situations. Judges are addressed in court as *Your Honor*, though they may well be addressed by their friends and neighbors quite differently. Each of us can be addressed in several ways: by first name (*Sally*); family name (*Smith*); family name preceded by a title (*Mister, Doctor, Professor*); the second person pronoun (*you*); terms showing respect (*Sir, Madam*). Cardinals in the Catholic church are addressed as *Your Eminence*, the Pope as *Your Holiness*, the Queen of England as *Your Majesty* (or *Mam*). At the opposite end of the scale of respect are terms of disrespect such as *you bastard* or *you son of a bitch*. Notice that a given individual may be addressed in different ways in the course of several speech situations. A judge's spouse does not normally employ *Your Honor* as a form of address, nor do parents normally address their children with a title of any sort, nor do children (of any age) normally address their parents with a title and name.

Slang   One well-known register is *slang*, the variety used in situations of extreme informality, particularly among younger people. Slang has a legitimate place in the linguistic repertoire of most speech communities. Like all registers, the effectiveness of slang depends crucially on the circumstances of its use, not on the socioeconomic or educational status of its users. In appropriate circumstances anyone can use slang. We might not expect to hear it from the Queen of England, but that is because most of us have no occasion to interact with Her Majesty in circumstances in which slang might be appropriate. Were his teammates to hear the Prince of Wales utter some slang expression in the heat of a polo match, we should not expect to see their eyebrows raised in surprise. Appropriate uses of slang are hardly noticed, irrespective of who uses it.

The observation that the effectiveness of a particular register depends not on the socioeconomic status of the user but on the circumstances of use applies equally to all registers: even the most formal varieties of English are not appropriate to all occasions, any more than a tuxedo is suited to all occasions. A tuxedo at the beach is as out of place as a bathing suit at a church wedding.

Just as informal clothing can extend its welcome from informal circumstances into somewhat more formal circumstances, so slang expressions often climb up the social ladder, becoming acceptable in more formal circumstances. The words *mob* and *pants* are among many that were considered slang at an earlier period of their history but can now be used in any circumstances. As words become used in more formal circumstances, they lose their status as slang, and other slang terms develop in their stead.[4]

It is useful to note that slang is a variety for which we have a name in English; that is, we recognize it as a register by a combination of the lexical features that it exhibits and the circumstances in which it is used. Slang differs from other registers in that it is characterized chiefly by lexical peculiarities.

Phonology

Different registers are marked not only by word choice but by all other levels of the grammar, including phonology. Recall Labov's study of New York City dialects (see Chapter 12). For various phonological variables, every socioeconomic status group pronounces more of one variant than the group ranked below it and fewer than the group ranked above it. For example, upper-middle-class New Yorkers pronounce post-vocalic /r/ more frequently than the lower middle class, the lower middle class more frequently than the working class, and the working class more frequently than the lower class. The distribution of /r/ across socioeconomic status groups is similar to the distribution of several other phonological variables including *th*

---

[4] Though this climb up the social ladder is in fact quite common for slang expressions, some slang expressions are apparently destined to remain forever suited only to the most informal circumstances. *Bones* meaning 'dice' was used by Chaucer in the fourteenth century, and *beat it* meaning 'scram' by Shakespeare.

TABLE 13-3
**Percentage of Pronunciation of *-ing* Suffix as /ɪn/
for Three Speech Situations Among Different
Socioeconomic Status Groups in New York City**

	Speech Styles		
	Casual	Careful	Reading
Lower class	80	53	22
Working class	49	31	11
Lower middle class	32	21	1
Upper middle class	5	4	0

as in *three, th* as in *then*, and *ing* as in *talking*. This kind of variation across social groups is called *dialect variation*.

Table 13-3 presents figures for the pronunciation of *-ing* as /ɪn/ in different circumstances of use. Here we are focusing not on the differences between the social groups but on the variation that occurs within a single group in different situations. The speech situations in this case consist of three kinds of interaction in the course of an interview. The style of the interview, with questions and answers, is here taken to be "careful" speech. In addition, the respondents were asked to read a set passage aloud; this "reading" style was taken to be an example of more careful speech than interview style. At the end of the interview, to prompt more relaxed speech than interview style, the interviewer asked respondents whether they had ever had a close call with death; this opening usually elicited a very relaxed, unguarded variety, here called "casual" speech.

In their casual speech, lower-class respondents pronounce the *-ing* suffix as /ɪn/ 80 percent of the time and as /ɪŋ/ the other 20 percent. In their careful speech, the occurrence of /ɪn/ drops to 53 percent, while the occurrence of /ɪŋ/ increases to 47 percent. When reading a passage aloud, the same lower-class respondents pronounce /ɪn/ only 22 percent of the time and /ɪŋ/ 78 percent. This represents a very dramatic increase of /ɪŋ/ pronunciations as the speech situation becomes increasingly formal. The same pattern exists for the other three socioeconomic groups: each class decreases its pronunciation of /ɪn/ as formality increases.

In another study, this one in the Los Angeles area, both males and females reduced the percentage of /ɪn/ in arguments, as compared with a joking speech situation. The figures are given in Table 13-4. Though men and women differ in their use of this phonological variable (as we saw in Chapter 12), both exploit it in the same way as a marker of register to signal different situations of use. Both men and women increase the percentage of /ɪn/ as they shift from arguing to joking registers.

TABLE 13-4

Percentage of *-ing* Suffix Pronounced as /ɪn/ for Two Situations of Speaking by Males and Females in Los Angeles

	Speech Styles	
	Joking	Arguing
Males	46	24
Females	28	21

The study in Norwich, England, demonstrated similar register shifting. Norwich residents of five different socioeconomic status groups all used some /ɪn/ for *-ing*. The lower working class *always* used /ɪn/ in casual speech, and the middle-middle class (the highest social group in this study) *never* used /ɪn/ in reading style. Thus, at the extremes of both socioeconomic status and degree of formality, the range of difference was 100 percent. Still, all classes used both /ɪn/ and /ɪŋ/. The figures are given in Table 13-5. The pattern in Norwich is the same as in New York City: each socioeconomic status group uses most /ɪn/ in casual speech and least in reading style, with an intermediate percentage for careful speech. It is clear that on this variable, three widely separated English-speaking communities use /ɪŋ/ differentially to mark situations of greater and lesser formality. It should be stressed that it is not the absolute percentage that marks situations but the *relative* percentage with respect to other situations. The data we have examined indicate that this situational marker is a continuous variable, able to indicate fine distinctions in degree of formality across a wide range of speech situations.

TABLE 13-5

Percentage of Pronunciation of *-ing* Suffix as /ɪn/ for Three Speech Situations and Several Socioeconomic Status Groups in Norwich, England

	Speech Styles		
	Casual	Careful	Reading
Middle-middle class	28	3	0
Lower middle class	42	15	10
Upper working class	87	74	15
Middle working class	95	88	44
Lower working class	100	98	66

TABLE 13-6
Number of Contractions per Thousand Words of
British English in Different Situations of Use

Situation of Use	Contractions
Telephone conversation with friends	59.9
Telephone conversation with business associates	49.6
Telephone conversation with strangers	48.8
Interviews	25.4
Broadcasts	21.5
Romantic fiction	19.0
Spontaneous speeches	17.8
Prepared speeches	13.3
Science fiction	6.5
Press	1.5
Academic journals	0.1
Official documents	0.0

As another example of phonological variation (or its equivalent spelling variation) with different speech situations, we examine the distribution of everyday contractions such as *can't, won't, isn't, haven't* in different situations of use, from telephone conversations between personal friends, business associates, and people who do not know one another to writing in newspapers and academic journals. Even in so straightforward a linguistic feature as contractions, English speakers exhibit differential use of forms in different speech situations. The figures in Table 13-6 are based on a large sample of written and spoken British English and represent the average number of contractions per one thousand words.

Syntax

In looking at lexical and phonological variation in different situations of use, we have seen that degrees of formality are associated with greater or lesser degrees of certain pronunciations and that certain word choices are typically more characteristic of one situation than another. Syntactic variables also mark situations of use.

As a first instance, consider the occurrence of sentence-final prepositions. You may recall from your school days that a sentence-final preposition is generally disfavored in prescriptive textbooks and by some teachers (*That's the teacher I was telling you about* as compared with *That's the teacher about whom I was telling you*). Using the same large number and wide range of texts as for contractions, the number of sentence-final prepositions per thousand prepositions for several spoken and written registers is given in Table 13-7.

TABLE 13-7
Number of Sentence-Final Prepositions per
Thousand Prepositions in Different Situations of Use

Situation of Use	Sentence-Final Prepositions	
Telephone conversation with business associates	58	
Face-to-face conversation	56	
Telephone conversation with friends	50	
Interviews	50	
Spontaneous speeches	48	Speech
Telephone conversation with strangers	44	
Broadcasts	39	
Prepared speeches	33	
Adventure fiction	23	
Science fiction	21	
Mystery fiction	20	Fiction writing
Romantic fiction	18	
General fiction	14	
Academic journals	8	
Hobbies writing	8	
Popular lore writing	5	
Press	4	Nonfiction writing
Religious writing	4	
Official documents	1	

This table does not show the same continuous incline from least formal to most formal that we saw with contractions. Instead, there is a major distinction between spoken varieties and nonfiction writing; fictional writing (which includes fictional dialogue) has intermediate values between the two. In the spoken texts, somewhere between 33 and 58 prepositions per thousand appear in sentence-final position. In nonfiction writing, however, in all situations of use, the number of final prepositions is less than for all spoken registers; the range is between 1 and 8 per thousand. Thus for this feature there is a marked difference between speech and writing.

As a second example of syntactic variation across different situations of use, examine this brief passage of *legalese*—one of the registers that is identified by name in English:

Upon request of Borrower, Lender, at Lender's option prior to full reconveyance of the Property by Trustee to Borrower, may make Future Advances to Borrower. Such Future Advances, with interest thereon, shall be secured by this Deed of Trust when evidenced by promissory notes stating that said notes are secured hereby.

This passage illustrates several of the characteristic syntactic features of legalese:

1. frequent use of passive structures: *shall be secured, are secured*
2. preference for repetition of nouns in lieu of pronouns: *Lender/at Lender's option, promissory notes/said notes, Future Advances/Such Future Advances*
3. avoidance of indefinite and definite articles: *Upon request, of/to Borrower, Lender, at Lender's, by Trustee*

Semantics

A given word often carries different meanings in different registers. Consider, for example, the word *notes*: as used in the legalese passage, *notes* means promissory notes, or IOUs. In its everyday meaning, however, *notes* refers to brief, informal written messages on any topic. Among other words with one meaning in common everyday use but with a different meaning in legal register are the following:

hearing, action, to continue, to alienate, to serve, save, party, reasonable man, executed, consideration, suit, sentence, rider, motion

Not only lawyers but also some of their clients may give specialized meanings to words. The criminal argot (now understood by a wide stripe of people, not only those with connections to the underworld) contains many words and expressions that are in common use but carry a different meaning when used in the context of crime or criminal behavior. The following two lists are illustrative (the first list is more general; the second refers specifically to the current drug world):

mob, hot, fence, excess baggage, sting, sing, rat, racket, a mark, confidence game, bug, bird cage, slammer, joint (for 'prison')

crack, coke, snow, rock, dime, pot, grass, toot, high, down, downer, speed, pusher, dealer, joint (for 'marijuana cigarette')

Each of these words and phrases is used with one meaning in everyday situations but bears a quite different meaning in the underworld.

TWO EXAMPLES OF REGISTER DIFFERENCES

Let's examine two brief passages of text as a way of illustrating the nature of register variation in some detail. We will demonstrate how the various levels of grammar come together to form a coherent register. The first illustrative passage will be immediately recognizable as legalese. While critics have remarked that it should be considered a foreign language because it is so different from ordinary writing and speaking, legalese is simply one of the many registers of English. That it may be more difficult to understand than other registers (for people not accustomed to using it) does not give grounds for considering it a foreign tongue.

This passage comes from a rider to a deed of trust. A deed of trust is an agreement that places the title to a piece of real estate in the hands of a trustee to ensure that money borrowed with the property as security or collateral will be repaid; a rider is an addition to the basic document.

	Line	Sent.
Notwithstanding anything in the Deed of Trust to the con-	1	1
trary, it is agreed that the loan secured by this Deed of Trust	2	
is made pursuant to, and shall be construed and governed by,	3	
the laws of the United States and the rules and regulations	4	
promulgated thereunder, including the federal laws, rules	5	
and regulations for federal savings and loan associations.	6	
If any paragraph, clause or provision of this Deed of Trust or	7	2
the Note or other obligations secured by this Deed of Trust	8	
is construed or interpreted by a court of competent jurisdic-	9	
tion to be void, invalid or unenforceable, such decision shall	10	
affect only those paragraphs, clauses or provisions so con-	11	
strued or interpreted and shall not affect the remaining	12	
paragraphs, clauses and provisions of this Deed of Trust or	13	
the Note or other obligations secured by this Deed of Trust.	14	

The second passage is from a 1961 interview with former President Harry Truman; Truman's questioner is author Merle Miller.

	Line	Sent.
Q. What do you consider the biggest mistake you made as	1	1
President?	2	
A. That damn fool from Texas that I first made Attorney	3	2
General and then put on the Supreme Court.	4	
I don't know what got into me.	5	3
He was no damn good as Attorney General, and on the	6	4
Supreme Court ... it doesn't seem possible, but he's	7	
been even worse.	8	
He hasn't made one right decision that I can think of.	9	5
And so when you ask me what was my biggest mistake,	10	6a
that's it.	11	
Putting Tom Clark on the Supreme Court of the United	12	6b
States.	13	
I thought maybe when he got on the Court he'd improve,	14	7
but of course, that isn't what happened.	15	
I told you when we were discussing that other fellow.	16	8a
After a certain age it's hopeless to think people are going	17	8b
to change much.[5]	18	

[5] Merle Miller, *Plain Speaking* (New York: Berkley Books, 1974), p. 242.

It is apparent at a glance how strikingly different these two passages are. Of course, the linguistic differences are not as great as those between different languages. But in some respects, these samples from different registers differ substantially from one another—certainly far more than different national varieties such as Indian English, Australian English, and Canadian English differ in the same respects.

First consider sentence length. The first passage (from the trust deed) is 139 words long and comprises two sentences. By contrast, the 135 words of the second passage occur in eight sentences. (The interviewer, in writing down Truman's words as represented here, made nine sentences of them; in our numbering of the sentences, we have used the letters *a* and *b* to indicate a combining of two of the interviewer's sentences into a single sentence so as not to exaggerate the number of separate sentences.) Thus average sentence length differs significantly in these register samples: almost 70 words for the trust deed, just under 17 for the interview.

It is instructive to examine the passages closely to discover other linguistic features that contribute to the impression of register difference. We recommend that readers review the passages and jot down as many characteristics as they can before reading the analysis that follows; note contrasting features as well as any features the passages may have in common.

Vocabulary

One easily observed difference between the passages is in their vocabulary. The deed of trust contains certain words and phrases that might seem odd if they appeared in the interview: *notwithstanding, pursuant to, thereunder, jurisdiction*. Likewise, Truman's earthy language contains certain words that would strike most of us as highly inappropriate in a legal document: *damn, fool, fellow, hopeless*, and *maybe* would stand out in a deed of trust, though they seem perfectly natural in the interview. Furthermore, while the words *no* and *good* might not individually call attention to themselves in a deed of trust, they would certainly be remarkable in the combination *no good*, and all the more so in *no damn good*.

We are not suggesting that the words we have mentioned in the trust deed could never occur in Truman's interview, or vice versa. Rather we are suggesting that, at least as they are actually used in these passages, they would seem out of place and would call attention to themselves if used in the other register. The few words that actually do occur in both passages are chiefly the simple and most common words of English—the ones that occur in all registers and might be expected to appear in nearly all sample passages: *the, of, and, a, to, it, is*, and *that*. These monosyllabic words are everyday pronouns, prepositions, conjunctions, and articles; they are among the twenty most common words of English. (The few instances of nouns and verbs that occur in both our passages will be discussed later.)

We have now seen that in the selection of words and the collocation of these words into phrases, as well as in sentence length, there are striking differences between the passages. It is useful to note that it is precisely such features—not in isolation but taken together—that help us identify passages as being particular *kinds* of text, particular language varieties suitable in different situations, particular registers.

Phonology

Besides sentence length, lexical collocations, and vocabulary, there are other distinctive characteristics of these passages, though they may not jump off the page so dramatically. It is useful to examine the passages and ask whether features of syntax, semantics, morphology, and phonology distinguish one register from the other and help us recognize the identity of each.

Since only one of the two passages originated in speech, we cannot make straightforward phonological comparisons between them, but we can analyze phonology insofar as it is reflected in spelling conventions. The trust deed originated as a written document, while Truman's words were originally spoken in answer to a question asked by a face-to-face interviewer. We do not have a phonetic transcription, but we can infer from the text that Truman exhibited frequent phonological abbreviation. Instead of full forms like *do not*, we find eight contractions even in this small sample of text: *don't, doesn't, isn't, hasn't, he's, he'd, that's*, and *it's*. In the one place in the deed of trust where a comparable form might appear, we find *it is*, not *it's*. If we were comparing two forms of spoken English and had suitable transcriptions, we could perhaps say more about phonological similarities and differences. Even comparing these two passages, however, we can observe the equivalent of phonological differences between varieties.

Morphology and Lexicon

We next ask whether there are morphological and lexical differences between the passages. We begin our analysis by examining lexical categories. In looking at nouns, prepositions, and verbs, we see that the trust deed is very "nominal," the interview much more "verbal."

Nouns and Pronouns   In roughly comparable amounts of text, the trust deed has forty nouns, the interview only seventeen. On the other hand, the interview has many more pronouns than the trust deed.

Prepositions   There is considerable difference in the exploitation of prepositions in the passages. The trust deed has nineteen prepositions, nearly twice as many as the ten that occur in the interview.

Verbs   The number of verbs in the trust deed is nine (counting the compound verbs separately), about one third the number in the Truman interview. Thus the interview is very verbal. As to particular verbs, Truman uses *think* (and *thought*), *know*, and *seem*, and his interviewer uses *consider*. Such "private" verbs have to do with internal states of the speaker or writer and are appropriate in an interview, though they would be out of place in the trust deed. Truman also employs pro-verbs of various sorts (pro-verbs take the place of other verbs, much as pro-nouns take the place of nouns): *do* and *happen*, which can be substituted for many verbs; *put* and *get*, which are more limited but still have far-ranging uses. In this short passage *got* appears twice, and Truman uses *put on* and *putting on* (the Supreme Court) instead of, say, *appointed to*. The verb *to be*—the most common in English—occurs as a main verb seven times, whereas in the trust deed it occurs four times as an auxiliary (*is agreed, is made, be construed*, and *is construed*) but just once as a main verb (*to be void*).

The following verbs of the trust deed are related to the topic of discussion and therefore to the register of the passage: *agree, construe, govern, promulgate, interpret*, and *affect*. Not related to topic but also characteristic of legalese is the use of *shall* as an auxiliary verb. While *shall* can occur in many registers of English, its use is very common in legalese.

Verb Tenses   The interview concerns the years of Truman's presidency, as the preponderance of verbs in the past tense reflects. Of the twenty-three verbs in this passage, fourteen are in the past tense; the eight present tense verbs generally make reference to the ongoing interaction or to Truman's own thought processes in the course of the interview: *what do you consider, when you ask, I don't know, I can think*. The one verb that refers to future time uses the auxiliary construction *are going to* instead of the more formal *shall* or *will*. *Shall*, on the other hand, occurs as an auxiliary in both sentences of the trust deed.

Negation   In the interview, four out of five negative morphemes occur as the separate negative adverb *not* (usually attached to the verb as a contraction); the fifth negative is the simple adverb *no* modifying the adverb *damn*. In contrast, the trust deed incorporates the elements of negation into adjectives or adverbs by the processes of derivational morphology (*invalid* and *unenforceable*) or compounding (*notwithstanding*); there is one isolated *not* (which occurs with reference to future time *shall not* and in contrast to a future positive *shall*); in addition, there are several words that have negative content built into their definitions, as in *void* and *contrary*.

Impersonal Constructions   The deed of trust is also characterized by several impersonal constructions, especially passives: *is agreed, is made, shall be construed*. Passives demote agent subjects to be objects of a preposition and in turn permit deletion of the agent. In legalese, the occurrence of agentless passives is common. In keeping with the impersonal character of this passage, there are no occurrences of first or second person pronouns and only a single occurrence of any third person pronoun: the nonreferential *it*. In contrast, the interview uses first and second person pronouns frequently: *I, me*, and *we* a total of eleven times; *you* four times; the possessive adjective *my* once.

Latinate Vocabulary   In contrast to the short everyday words of the interview, the deed of trust uses more uncommon words, as is customary in legalese. The vocabulary in the deed of trust is more "Latinate" or learned, the words themselves longer: *promulgated, construed, governed, regulations, obligations, decision, jurisdiction, provisions, void, invalid, unenforceable, remaining, secured*. There is also the markedly legal collocation *competent jurisdiction*, in which the word *competent* does not carry its ordinary meaning of 'capable' but its legal meaning of 'having proper jurisdiction over the matter to be decided.' As with many registers, words that are used elsewhere with one meaning have a different meaning in legalese. Besides *competent*, the following words in the passage have a sense quite specific to legalese: *deed, trust, obligation, decision, provisions*, and *note*, among others.

Syntax

The interview and the legal document exhibit striking syntactic differences. Sentence length is one such difference, but there are more important and more subtle examples as well.

Passive Voice   One striking feature of the deed of trust is its frequent use of the passive voice (*is agreed, is made, shall be construed and governed, is construed or interpreted*). In marked contrast, Truman and his interviewer use only active voice verbs.

Questions   It is interesting to observe that in using the form of a direct question (*When you ask me what* was *my biggest mistake*) instead of an indirect question (*When you ask me what my biggest mistake* was), Truman contributes to the overwhelming impression of informality that characterizes the passage. And though it may seem too obvious to mention, the interview naturally contains a question, a syntactic structure that not only does not appear in the trust deed but would seem very odd there.

Prepositions   Prepositions were discussed in the lexical section, but two further aspects can be mentioned here. First is the use of series of prepositional phrases in the deed of trust. Whereas in the interview there is only one instance of two prepositional phrases used consecutively (*on the Supreme Court of the United States*), the trust deed has seven of them, including one example of a sequence of three: *in the deed of Trust to the contrary*.

Second, in the interview we see an example of a sentence-final preposition (*He hasn't made one right decision that I can think of*), something that does not occur in the passage of legalese and occurs very rarely in formal writing of any kind.

Pronominalization   We have already mentioned that no first or second person pronouns appear in the trust deed, though they occur frequently in the interview. There are other differences in pronominal use as well, reflecting a major difference between the customary usage of legalese and conversation. Truman uses the pronoun *that* as a "sentence" pronoun, referring not to a noun phrase but to an entire clause, as in *that isn't what happened* and *that's it*.

The interview also exhibits frequent third person pronouns, using *he* five times in reference to Tom Clark. This can be contrasted with the repetition of full noun phrases in the trust deed, in which *Deed of Trust* occurs six times, the compound noun phrase *rules and regulations* occurs twice, and the lengthy compound noun phrase *paragraph, clause or provision* three times (once in the singular and twice in the plural). One exceptionally long noun phrase is repeated, and it contains a repetition of the noun phrase *Deed of Trust* within it: *this Deed of Trust or the Note or other obligations secured by this Deed of Trust.*

Reduced Subordinate Clauses   Another characteristic feature of legalese is the occurrence of reduced subordinate clauses, especially relative clauses. A reduced relative clause is one in which the relative pronoun and a form of the verb *to be* do not appear where they might but are instead omitted from the relative clause. In the following examples, we have inserted in parentheses the words that have been deleted.

loan (that is) secured

rules and regulations (that are) promulgated thereunder

paragraphs, clauses or provisions (that are) so construed or interpreted

Conjoining   Another syntactic feature worth noting is typical of many passages of legalese: the structure "X, Y conjunction Z." Sometimes it occurs with an additional conjunction between X and Y: "X conjunction Y conjunction Z." In legal register, X, Y, and Z can be members of almost any lexical category, most commonly nouns (or noun phrases), adjectives, or verbs; X, Y, and Z are usually members of the same lexical category. The following exemplify the pattern:

laws, rules and regulations   (nouns)

paragraph, clause or provision   (nouns)

deed of trust or the note or other obligation   (noun phrases)

void, invalid or unenforceable   (adjectives)

Sometimes variation within the X, Y, and Z constituents produces not completely parallel structures but very similar structures, as in these examples:

(a)   is made pursuant to, and shall be construed and governed by

(b)   the laws of the United States and the rules and regulations

In (a), there are two verb structures, but the second contains two conjoined verbs (*construed and governed*). In (b), we might more accurately describe the structure not as X, Y, and Z but as X and Y, with Y itself a compound M and N; thus, the X and the (M and N).

Adverbs and Adjectives   Legalese is famous for its use of words like *thereto, hereinunder*, and *wherefore*. There is only one instance of this kind of adverb in our passage (*thereunder*). A strikingly marked adjective of legalese does, however, occur in *such decision*. The adverbials of the legalese passage are phrasal (*notwithstanding anything . . .*), clausal (*If any paragraph . . . is construed*), or, when simply lexical, peculiarly legal (*thereunder*).

Truman's adverbials are quite different. When clausal, they are often introduced by *when* (*when you ask me, when he got on the court, when we were discussing*). Truman's simple adverbs commonly make reference to time (*first, then*); others are hedges of various sorts that indicate Truman's stance toward what he is saying: *of course, even worse, maybe*.

As for adjectives, Truman's are judgmental and simple: *good, worse, right, biggest, hopeless*; notice that one is a comparative (*worse*) and another a superlative (*biggest*). The use of *that* as a demonstrative adjective (*That damn fool; that other fellow*) and demonstrative pronoun (*that isn't what happened*) is rare in legalese and does not occur at all in the trust deed. The legalese adjectives, none of them among the common adjectives of English, are limiting: *federal, competent, void, invalid, unenforceable, remaining*.

Conjunctions   The Truman interview is marked by frequent occurrence of coordinating conjunctions, such as *and, but, and then, and so*, which serve chiefly to link clauses. These conjunctions are entirely lacking in the legalese passage except for *and*, which is used to link verbs, nouns, or adjectives but not clauses.

Comparing Registers

In comparing and contrasting the two passages, it is not any single feature alone that leads to our judgment about what registers they exemplify. Rather, various features occurring in combination characterize the first passage as legalese and the second passage as a spoken interview. Truman's style is so informal that it suggests a conversation rather than a formal interview: this may be partly the result of his personal style and partly the result of the interviewer's having spent many months with Truman, morning and afternoon. No doubt the interview came increasingly to resemble conversation between friends as the days passed.

We have now seen that the features of language differ from one speech situation to another. Sometimes they differ in that there is more of one feature in a given register than in another. Sometimes a feature occurs in one register almost exclusively. Sometimes the same form occurs in more than one register but with different meanings or different uses.

THE DIMENSIONS OF REGISTER VARIATION

The linguistic resources from which registers must draw their particular features produce consistent and coherent texts from a single grammatical system. It is by differentially drawing on the same grammatical resources at each level of the grammar that different texts in different registers are created.

Using computers and large data bases, linguists have begun to identify systematically which sets of linguistic features tend to co-occur in texts. Identifying and analyzing sets of co-occurring features have contributed to our understanding of the underlying dimensions of register variation and of how sets of features co-occur in the service of common functions.

Sets of Co-occurring Features

One set of linguistic features that commonly occur together in texts includes the following:

Set A
first and second person pronouns (*I, me, we, us; you*)
that deletion from subordinate clauses (*She said ∅ he lied.*)
private verbs (*think, consider, assume*)
demonstrative pronouns (*this, that, these*)
emphatics (*really, for sure*)
hedges (*kind of, more or less, maybe*)
sentence relatives (*Then he lied, <u>which</u> bothered her a lot.*)
sentence-final prepositions (*the teacher I told you <u>about</u>*)

To make this set of features more concrete, it will help to reexamine the Truman interview. First and second person pronouns go together because they commonly occur in face-to-face interaction (and in personal letters), in which there is a personalized speaker/writer addressing a particular known addressee. In such a circumstance, it is natural to express one's inner thoughts and feelings (and to inquire about the addressee's), which thus requires the use of private verbs. The use of emphatics (Truman's *damn fool, no damn good, biggest, worse*) and hedges (*of course*) is also characteristic of such interaction. The occurrence of sentence- and clause-final prepositions (*that I can think of*) marks relatively informal person-to-person speech and writing. The use of demonstrative pronouns is characteristic of a shared context between speaker and addressee, in that the addressee must be present in many instances to understand the reference of words like *that* and *these*. Many of the features in Set A do indeed occur in the brief Truman interview, even though the determination of which features occur together was based on a much larger sample of texts, not including the two we have examined here.

Another set of features that commonly occur together in texts is the following:

Set B
frequent nouns and prepositions
longer words
lexical variety
attributive adjectives (*the tall buildings*)

It is not surprising that prepositions and nouns should occur commonly together. After all, prepositional phrases include noun phrases. What is less obvious is why frequent nouns and prepositions would occur with longer words and with lexical variety. A moment's thought will help explain this pattern. Lexical variety results from using a relatively larger number of alternative words. Given that alternative words usually have somewhat different meanings (or different connotations), lexical variety generally indicates an attempt to be exact in expressing meaning or to expand the meaning of a referent already mentioned. Contrast Truman's use of different referring expressions for Tom Clark, his Supreme Court appointment. Instead of repetition of *Tom Clark* or the pronoun *he*, the use of various referring expressions permits Truman to make additional comments that expand on his opinionated description of Justice Clark. (In the deed of trust, the use of attributive adjectives—*federal laws, remaining paragraphs*—has the same function of specifying noun phrases.)

As it happens, there is a very strong tendency for the features of Set A to occur in texts in which the features of Set B do not occur, and vice versa. That is, where one finds first and second person pronouns, *that* deletion, and the other features of Set A, one does not typically find longer words, much lexical variety, frequent nouns and prepositions, or frequent attributive adjectives, the features of Set B. If you think about it, this makes sense, for it is precisely in contexts that require lexical specificity that speakers and writers have less occasion to use personal pronouns, private verbs, and the other features of Set A, and vice versa: when one is in a face-to-face interactional situation requiring the features of Set A, one does not need or have occasion to produce great lexical variety, longer words, and so on.

We can think of these two sets of features—Set A and Set B—as defining opposite poles of a single dimension of register variation. At one pole is a heavy emphasis on interaction and personal involvement; at the other pole is virtually no interaction or personal involvement but a heavy emphasis on information sharing. As with all functional dimensions of register variation, a given text will be more or less informational, more or less involved. Texts are rarely *either* informational *or* involved. Rather, any given text will fall somewhere along a continuum between extremely informational and extremely involved, though of course certain texts may fall at the extremes.

Involved Versus Informational Texts

Using the features just indicated as indexes of involved versus informational focus, the locations of several hundred texts of different kinds have been calculated along this involved/informational continuum. In Figure 13-1, average ratings for groups of similar texts have been used to locate romantic fiction texts, broadcasts, and official documents on the dimension.

In the figure, conversations of two kinds are at the involved end of the scale, while official documents (which would include legal documents like trust deeds) are at the opposite end—the informational end. Interviews are grouped with personal letters and spontaneous speeches toward the more interactive end of the scale. As you will recall, the Truman interview

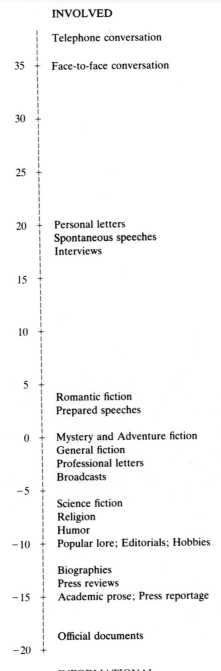

INVOLVED

35 +	Telephone conversation
	Face-to-face conversation
30 +	
25 +	
20 +	Personal letters
	Spontaneous speeches
	Interviews
15 +	
10 +	
5 +	
	Romantic fiction
	Prepared speeches
0 +	Mystery and Adventure fiction
	General fiction
	Professional letters
	Broadcasts
−5 +	
	Science fiction
	Religion
	Humor
−10 +	Popular lore; Editorials; Hobbies
	Biographies
	Press reviews
−15 +	Academic prose; Press reportage
	Official documents
−20 +	

INFORMATIONAL

FIGURE 13-1
Distribution of Texts Along Dimension 1—the
Involved/Informational Dimension
Dimension 1 Defined by Feature Sets A and B

SOURCE: Biber 1988

exhibited many examples of features that contribute to the "involved" characterization, while the trust deed showed longer words, more lexical variety, and almost twice as many prepositions. In other words, if we were to do the calculations needed to place our example texts on this scale, the Truman interview would rank high on involvement, while the trust deed would fall much more toward the informational end of the scale.

Narrative Texts

Two other sets of co-occurring features are as follows:

Set C
past tense verbs
third person pronouns
public verbs (*admit, say, write, explain*)
perfect aspect verbs (with *have* as in *have seen*)

Set D
present tense verbs
attributive adjectives

The features of Set C tend to co-occur in some texts, and the features of Set D tend to co-occur in other texts. Furthermore, like the features of Sets A and B, the features of Sets C and D tend to be complementary. That is, texts marked by frequent occurrence of the features of Set C will have a marked *absence* of the features of Set D.

The features of Set C mark texts that are narrative; those of Set D mark nonnarrative texts. As can be seen in Figure 13-2, the texts that rank toward the narrative extreme are various kinds of fiction, while official documents and broadcasts occur at the opposite pole. Our trust deed would fall at the nonnarrative end of this continuum; it has no past tense verbs, no third person pronouns, and no perfect aspect verbs.

These two dimensions can be thought of as the axes in a two-dimensional space—a plane surface on which every text can be situated. A text is situated along each dimension in accordance with the degree to which it exploits the features that define that dimension. In Figures 13-1 and 13-2, each set of texts is located according to the degree to which those texts exploit the particular features defining the dimension. Figure 13-3 illustrates the location of a few sets of texts in the two-dimensional plane.

Notice that telephone conversations rank extremely high on Dimension 1 (they are very involved) and fairly low on Dimension 2 (they are not very narrativelike). Romantic fiction, on the other hand, ranks very high on the narrative/nonnarrative dimension but not very high on the involved/informational dimension. Official documents rank toward the bottom of both dimensions.

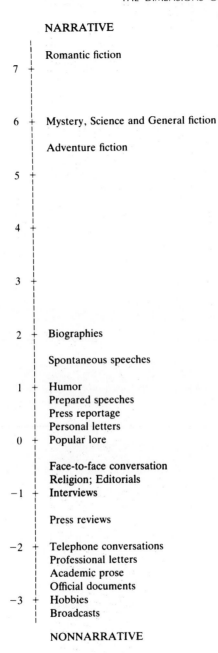

NARRATIVE

7 +	Romantic fiction
6 +	Mystery, Science and General fiction
	Adventure fiction
5 +	
4 +	
3 +	
2 +	Biographies
	Spontaneous speeches
1 +	Humor
	Prepared speeches
	Press reportage
	Personal letters
0 +	Popular lore
	Face-to-face conversation
	Religion; Editorials
−1 +	Interviews
	Press reviews
−2 +	Telephone conversations
	Professional letters
	Academic prose
	Official documents
−3 +	Hobbies
	Broadcasts

NONNARRATIVE

FIGURE 13-2
Distribution of Texts Along Dimension 2—the Narrative Dimension
Dimension 2 Defined by Feature Sets C and D

SOURCE: Adapted from Biber 1988

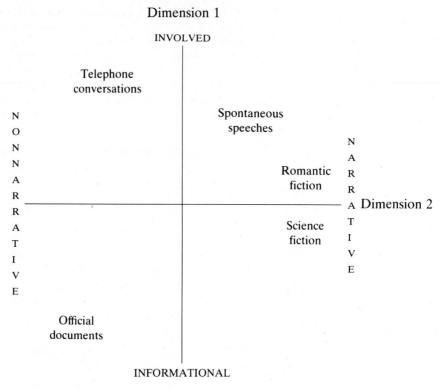

FIGURE 13-3
Distribution of Five Kinds of Texts
Along Two Dimensions of Register Variation

It is relatively straightforward to imagine adding other dimensions to represent other sets of co-occurring linguistic features. Thus a multi-dimensional "space" would be created to represent the range of textual variation. Each text (and each set of texts) could then be situated in this space according to its exploitation of the particular features defining each dimension. More than three dimensions of linguistic variation are in fact necessary in order to represent textual variation adequately, but discussion of the other dimensions is beyond the scope of this book.

SUMMARY

Three principal elements determine each situation of use: setting, purpose, and participants. As part of the setting, one must consider the topic and the location. As one wears different clothing to different places and for different activities, so one does not generally speak the same way in court and on the soccer field. As part of the purpose, one must consider such things as activity type and goals. With respect to participants, it is not only the people themselves who influence language form but the roles they are playing at a given time.

In multilingual communities, different situations of use call sometimes for different languages and sometimes for different varieties of the same language. *Registers* are language varieties appropriate for use in particular speech situations (in contrast to dialects, which are language varieties viewed with respect to their customary users as members of social groups). The set of varieties used in a speech community in various speech situations is called its *linguistic* (or verbal) *repertoire*.

In the linguistic repertoire of a monolingual community are many registers, which differ from one another in their linguistic features either in an absolute sense or (more usually) in a more or less relative sense. Each register is characterized by a set of linguistic features. The sum total of such variants (at the phonological, morphological, syntactic, and semantic levels), together with the characteristic patterns for the use of language in a particular situation, determines a register. Almost by definition, all varieties within a language draw on the same grammatical system; hence the differential exploitation of that system for marking different registers must occur in an essentially relative fashion.

A number of feature sets frequently co-occur in natural texts and can be interpreted in functional terms. Every text can be positioned with respect to every other text depending on its exploitation of the features that characterize that dimension. Taken altogether, the dimensions constitute a multidimensional space throughout which every text can be positioned with respect to every other text. It is the coming together in a single text of the various linguistic characteristics (and the implicit knowledge of their role in those functional dimensions) that allows us to recognize texts as belonging to one register or another. This same knowledge of the dimensions and of their functional roles enables us to use appropriate registers in different speech situations—in fact to help create those situations by indexing them linguistically with appropriate lexical, phonological, morphological, syntactic, and semantic choices.

EXERCISES

1. Consider the following two remarks:

   Kindly extinguish the illumination upon exiting.
   Please turn off the lights on your way out.

   The content of the directive is basically the same in both cases, but the social meanings differ markedly. Identify the features that characterize the differences between the two directives; then discuss the impression that each is likely to make and under which circumstances each might be appropriate.

2. Rank these words in order of informality: *prof, teacher, instructor, mentor, educator*. And these: *don, guru, mullah, maestro, trainer, coach*. Are any of the words in either set so informal as to be slang? Explain.

3. Tape-record a brief radio news report and a brief television news report (preferably the same news item). Transcribe the passages and compare them with one another to see what effect the two media have on the choice of linguistic features.

4. The immediate sequel to the Truman passage quoted in this chapter is this:

   Q. How do you explain the fact that he's been such a bad Justice?
   A. The main thing is . . . well, it isn't so much that he's a *bad* man. It's just that he's such a dumb son of a bitch. He's about the dumbest man I think I've ever run across. And lots of times that's the case. Being dumb's just about the worst thing there is when it comes to holding high office, and that's especially true when it's on the Supreme Court of the United States.

   As I say, I never will know what got into me when I made that appointment, and I'm as sorry as I can be for doing it. (*Plain Speaking*, p. 242).

   What does *that* refer to in *that's the case* and in *that's especially true*? What is this feature called, and in what feature set (A, B, C, or D) does it occur? What does it indicate about how the interview is aligned on Dimension 1, which is in part defined by this feature? What other features that co-occur with this feature in defining Dimension 1 also occur in the passage?

5. Look up the definition of slang in a good desk dictionary. Using the definition as a guideline, list as many slang words and expressions as you can for two of the notions in column A and two in column B.

A	B
drunk	sober
sexually carefree person	chaste person
ungenerous with money	generous with money
sloppy in appearance	neat and tidy

   (A)   What is it about the notions in column A that makes them more susceptible to slang words and expressions than those in column B?
   (B)   To the extent that you were able to cite slang terms for the items in column B, do they have negative or positive overtones?
   (C)   Does the dictionary definition of slang help explain the differential distribution of slang terms in columns A and B and the negative connotations associated with the slang terms in column B? If so, explain how. If not, revise the dictionary definition so as to accommodate what you have discovered about the connotations of slang terms.

6. Examine the following three letters. The first is a letter of recommendation for a student seeking admission to a master's degree program in linguistics, the second a letter to a magazine, and the third a personal letter from a woman to a female friend in another state. Identify the particular characteristics of each type of letter in terms of the co-occurring features on the two dimensions examined in this chapter. Then, using the features as a guide, indicate approximately where each letter might fall on the two dimensions.

Letter of Recommendation

I have known Mr. John Smith as a student in three of my courses at State, and on the basis of that acquaintance with him, it is my recommendation that he should certainly be admitted to graduate school.

John was a student of mine in Linguistics 100, where he did exceptionally well, writing a very good paper indeed. On the basis of that paper, I encouraged him to become a linguistics major and subsequently had the good fortune to have him in two more of my classes. In one of these (historical linguistics) he led the class, obviously working more insightfully than the other seventeen students enrolled. In the other course (introduction to phonology), he did less well, perhaps because he was under some financial pressure and was forced to work twenty hours a week while carrying a full academic load. In all three courses, John worked very hard, doing much more than was required.

I recommend John Smith to you without reservation of any kind. He knows what he wants to achieve and is clearly motivated to succeed in graduate school.

Editorial Letter

Your story on Afghanistan was in error when it stated that the Russian-backed coup of 1973 was bloodless. As a Peace Corps volunteer in Afghanistan at the time, I saw the bodies and blood and ducked the bullets. It was estimated that between 1,000 and 1,500 died, but it is hard to get an accurate count when a tank pulls up to the house of the shah's supporters and fires repeatedly into it from 30 feet away, or when whole households of people disappear in the middle of the night.

Personal Letter

So, what's up? Not too much going on here. I'm at work now, and it's been so slow this week. We haven't done anything. I hate it when it's so slow. The week seems like it's never going to end.

Well how have you all been? Did you get the pictures and letter I sent you? We haven't heard from you in a while. Mother has your B'day present ready to send to you and Dan's too, but no tellin when she will get around to sending it. How are the kids? Does Dan like kindergarten? Well, Al has gone off to school. I miss him so much. He left Monday to go to LLTI. It's a trade school upstate. You only have to go for two years, and he's taking air conditioning and refrigeration and then he's going to take heating.

7. In the summer of 1982 the popular song "Valley Girls" poked gentle fun at the speech of adolescent girls in the San Fernando Valley of Southern California. "Val-speak" (or "Valley Girl Talk") was characterized by such expressions as "grody to the max," "gag me with a spoon," "fer sure," "barf me out," and "like a total space cadet." Of course, Val-speak wasn't the exclusive domain of adolescent girls, and "dudes" shared some of these characteristic speech patterns.

Besides the expressions mentioned above, and an excessive use of *like* as a hedge and *totally* as an emphatic, Val-speak exhibited certain phonological characteristics. For example, /u/ and /o/ were pronounced with front vowel onglides (compare the description of offglides in footnote 4, page 412). Thus *spoon* and *dude* are pronounced something like [sp^{I}un] and [d^{I}ud], while *grody* and *totally* are pronounced [gr$^{\varepsilon}$odi] and [t$^{\varepsilon}$oDəli].

Insofar as Val-speak is characteristic of the speech of a particular age group or gender group (or a combination of these), it can be treated as a social dialect (see Chapter 12). Insofar as Val-speak is characteristic principally of certain situations of use, it can be considered a register. Because this register is appropriate in very informal settings (and has certain other situational characteristics), it could be regarded as a variety of slang.

(A)   Give several arguments for considering Val-speak a social dialect, and list the social groups that use such a dialect.
(B)   Give several arguments for considering Val-speak a register, and describe the situations of use in which that register is appropriate.
(C)   As a register, what characteristics of its use make Val-speak comparable to other registers, and what characteristics, if any, make it different in kind from other registers?

8.   Listen attentively to the language of your friends or classmates. Make a list of their characteristic words, expressions, and pronunciations. Do your friends exhibit any characteristics of Val-speak (including those described in the preceding exercise)? Which particular register or dialect of English do you (and do your friends) regard the following as characteristic of: the use of *totally* as an emphatic; *like* as a hedge; *tubular; radical*? What do you think the use of their characteristic speech patterns indicates about the way your friends (or classmates) wish to be perceived?

SUGGESTIONS FOR FURTHER READING

Joos (1962) is a brief and entertaining introduction to the notion of register, or "style," as Joos calls it; the story of the Ballyhough railway station is reported from Joos. Crystal and Davy (1969) contains chapters on the language of conversation, religion, newspaper reporting, and legal documents. Brown and Fraser (1979) surveys those elements of a speech situation influencing the form of language. The description of switching in Brussels comes from Fishman (1972), while Blom and Gumperz (1972) describes the switching that takes place between Bokmål and Ranamål in Norway. Biber (1988) is a detailed quantitative study of register variation in a computerized corpus of spoken and written English; it is the source of our discussion in the final section. Shopen and Williams (1981) is a collection of essays written for a general audience and treating discourse, the variable *-ing*, literary and other styles, and English in Los Angeles. Lambert and Tucker (1976) reports several social-psychological studies of address forms, principally in Canadian French and Puerto Rican and Colombian Spanish. Besnier (1986) surveys the literature discussing register and examines various approaches to defining register, with special attention to the dimension of formality. Chapman (1986) is an up-to-date dictionary of slang and a discussion of its nature and sources.

REFERENCES

Besnier, Niko. 1986. "Register as a Sociolinguistic Unit: Defining Formality," in Jeff Connor-Linton, Christopher J. Hall, and Mary McGinnis (eds.), *Social and Cognitive Perspectives on Language*, Southern California Occasional Papers in Linguistics, No. 11 (Los Angeles: Department of Linguistics, University of Southern California), pp. 25–63.
Biber, Douglas. 1988. *Variation Across Speech and Writing* (Cambridge: Cambridge University Press).
Blom, Jan-Petter, and John J. Gumperz. 1972. "Social Meaning in Linguistic

Structure," in John J. Gumperz and Dell Hymes (eds.), *Directions in Sociolinguistics* (New York: Holt, Rinehart and Winston), pp. 407–434.

Brown, Penelope, and Colin Fraser. 1979. "Speech as a Marker of Situation," in Klaus Scherer and Howard Giles (eds.), *Social Markers in Speech* (Cambridge: Cambridge University Press), pp. 33–62.

Chapman, Robert L. (ed.). 1986. *New Dictionary of American Slang* (New York: Harper & Row).

Crystal, David, and Derek Davy. 1969. *Investigating English Style* (London: Longman).

Fishman, Joshua A. 1972. "The Sociology of Language," in Pier Paolo Giglioli (ed.), *Language and Social Context* (New York: Penguin), pp. 45–58.

Joos, Martin. 1962. *The Five Clocks* (New York: Harcourt Brace Jovanovich).

Lambert, Wallace E., and G. Richard Tucker. 1976. *Tu, Vous, Usted: A Social-Psychological Study of Address Patterns* (Rowley, Mass.: Newbury House).

Shopen, Timothy, and Joseph M. Williams. 1981. *Style and Variables in English* (Cambridge, Mass.: Winthrop).

THE HISTORICAL DEVELOPMENT OF ENGLISH

14

A THOUSAND YEARS OF CHANGE IN ENGLISH

Nearly every secondary school student in the English-speaking world has studied the writings of William Shakespeare and Geoffrey Chaucer, two of the greatest writers ever to use English (or any language) as a poetic vehicle. You may recall that when you read Shakespeare's plays, some of his lines were opaque, as with the opening lines of *I Henry IV:*

> So shaken as we are, so wan with care,
> Find we a time for frighted peace to pant,
> And breathe short-winded accents of new broils
> To be commenced in stronds afar remote.

The fact that some of Shakespeare's lines are opaque has a simple explanation (besides the fact that they are poetry): the English spoken in and around London four centuries ago is often subtly and sometimes strikingly different from the English spoken today. Still, much of it is altogether accessible, and very little of it is so foreign that it eludes us completely. Many of the words in the brief passage just cited are familiar enough, though some are used in ways that strike the modern reader as peculiar. While the words of the opening line are mostly familiar to us and can be sorted out syntactically as poetic English, line two is a bit tougher, even though all the words (except *frighted*) exist in Modern English in exactly the same forms. (The line means 'Let us find a time for frightened peace to catch its breath.')

As the many Shakespearean productions in American and British theaters testify to, reciting Shakespeare with his sixteenth-century lexicon and syntax but with a modern pronunciation enables twentieth-century audiences to follow his plays with little difficulty. With the support of costumed actors interacting with props on a rich visual set, there is not much in *Romeo and Juliet, Henry IV*, or *King Lear* that modern audiences fail to grasp.

Far more difficult to understand than Shakespeare's English is the English of Chaucer, who lived in London two centuries earlier. Chaucer's *Canterbury Tales*, whose opening lines follow, was the first major book to be printed in England. William Caxton published it in 1476, almost a century after it was written and long after Chaucer's death in 1400.

> Whan that Aprill with his shoures soote
> The droghte of March hath perced to the roote,
> And bathed every veyne in swich licour,
> Of which vertu engendred is the flour; . . .
> Thanne longen folk to goon on pilgrimages.

Though their pronunciation differs dramatically from ours, quite a few of Chaucer's fourteenth-century words have the same written form now as they did then: *that, with, his, the, of, bathed, every, folk, pilgrimages*, along with seven or eight others in the thirty-seven words in this passage. Several others can easily be recognized, though their Modern English counterparts differ: *droghte* 'drought,' *perced* 'pierced,' *veyne* 'vein,' *vertu* 'virtue, strength,' and *flour* 'flower.' Of course, some are more opaque: *soote* 'sweet,' *swich* 'such,' *thanne* 'then,' and the verbs *longen* 'long' and *goon* 'go.' As a whole, the Chaucer passage is harder to grasp than the Shakespeare. Thus, in the two centuries between Chaucer (1340–1400) and Shakespeare (1564–1616), English changed—as languages always do. Chaucer understood language change and the arbitrariness of linguistic form for accomplishing the ends of language, as we learn in these lines from his *Troilus and Criseyde* (II, 22–26).

> Ye knowe ek, that in forme of speche is chaunge
> Withinne a thousand yeer, and wordes tho
> That hadden pris, now wonder nyce and straunge
> Us thinketh hem, and yet thei spake hem so,
> And spedde as wel in love as men now do.[1]

The English spoken in Chaucer's time is far enough removed from today's English that students often study the *Canterbury Tales* in "translation"— from fourteenth-century English into twentieth-century English. Though we

[1] You know also that in speech's form (there) is change
Within a thousand years, and words then
That had value, now wondrously foolish and strange
To us seem them, and yet they spoke them so,
And fared as well in love as men now do.

are not yet so estranged from Shakespeare's language to require a translation, editions of his plays have glosses and footnotes aplenty.

If we now examine the language of the epic poem *Beowulf*, written down almost four centuries before Chaucer lived, we are struck by the utterly foreign appearance of these forms of Old English. Indeed, speakers of Modern English cannot recognize *Beowulf* as English; it is as far removed as Dutch or German (if such impressionistic comparisons have any meaning). The *Beowulf* poet, whose identity is lost to history, composed his grim epic in the first half of the eighth century, about six hundred years before Chaucer, who surely would have found its language almost as unintelligible as modern readers do. Here are the first three lines from the *Beowulf* manuscript, written around the year 1000:

> Hwæt wē Gār-Dena   in gēardagum
> þēodcyninga   þrym gefrūnon,
> hū ðā æþelingas   ellen fremedon.[2]

No one needs to be persuaded that Old English is a "foreign" language. Scarcely a word in the passage seems familiar (though when you have finished reading this chapter, a few may not seem so formidably strange). Even some of the letters, or graphs, are different: Modern English no longer uses æ, þ, or ð. Still, an imaginative inspection may reveal that some function words remain in present-day English (*wē* = *we*, *in* = *in*, and *hū* = *how*). Perhaps you also recognized *ðā* as Modern English *the* and *Hwæt* as *what*, but it is not easy to recognize *gēardagum* as *year* and *days* or *cyninga* as *kings*. Even knowing these words, however, you would find the passage far from transparent. You would need to know the meaning of the nouns *þēod*, *þrym*, and *æþelingas* (none of which survives in Modern English), the verbs *gefrūnon* and *fremedon*, and the adjective *ellen* (here used as a noun). And given all that lexical information, the syntax of Old English would still be elusive. About a thousand years old, Old English is indeed a long way from Modern English.

THE BACKGROUND OF ENGLISH

Historical Background

Where did English come from, and how long has it been spoken in England? What are the principal ancestors of English, and what are its closest relatives?

Before the beginning of the modern era, Britain was inhabited by Celtic-speaking peoples, related to the Irish, Scots, and Welsh of today. In 55 B.C.,

---

[2] A rough word-for-word translation:
>   What! We of Spear-Danes in yore-days
>   People's-kings glory have heard,
>   How the nobles heroic-deeds did.
> A more colloquial rendering: 'Yes, we have heard of the might of the kings of the Spear-Danes in days of yore, how the chieftains carried out deeds of valor.'

Britain was invaded by Julius Caesar, but that attempt to colonize it failed, and the Romans conquered Britain only in A.D. 43. When the Roman legions withdrew in A.D. 410, the Celts, who had long been accustomed to their protection, were at the mercy of the Picts and the Scots from the north of Britain. In a profoundly important development for the English language, Vortigern, king of the Romanized Celts in Britain, sought help from three Germanic tribes, who in A.D. 449 set sail from what is today northern Germany and southern Denmark to aid the Celts. When they landed in Britain, however, they decided to settle, leaving the Celts only the remote corners—today's Scotland, Wales, and Cornwall.

The invaders spoke closely related varieties of West Germanic—the dialects that were to become English. The word *England* derives from the name of one of the tribes, the Angles: thus England, originally *Englaland*, is the 'land of the Angles.' The Old English language used by the early Germanic inhabitants of England and their offspring up to about 1100 is often called Anglo-Saxon, after two of the tribes (the Jutes were the third tribe). Early Anglo-Saxon has left no written records. The oldest surviving English-language materials come from the end of the seventh century, and there is an increasing quantity after that, giving rise to an abundant and impressive literature including *Beowulf*.

Once the Anglo-Saxon peoples had settled in Britain, there were additional onslaughts from other Germanic groups starting in A.D. 787. In the year 850, a fleet of 350 Danish ships arrived. In 867, Vikings captured York. Danes and Norwegians settled in much of eastern and northern England and from there launched attacks into the kingdom of Wessex in the southwest. In 878, after losing a major battle to King Alfred the Great of Wessex, the Danes agreed by the Treaty of Wedmore to become Christian and to remain outside Wessex in a very large section of eastern and northern England that became known as the Danelaw because it was subject to Danish law. After the treaty, Danes and Norwegians were assimilated to Anglo-Saxon life, so much so that fourteen hundred English place names are Scandinavian including all those ending in *-by* 'farm, town' (*Derby, Rugby*), *-thorp* 'village' (*Althorp*), *-thwaite* 'isolated piece of land' (*Applethwaite*), and *-toft* 'piece of ground' (*Brimtoft, Eastoft*).

Attacks from the Scandinavians continued throughout the Viking Age (roughly 750–1050), until finally King Svein of Denmark was crowned King of England and was succeeded almost immediately by his son Cnut in 1016. England was then ruled by Danish kings until 1042 when Edward the Confessor regained the throne his father, Aethelred, had lost to the Danes. The intermingling between the Anglo-Saxon invaders and the subsequent Scandinavian settlers created a mix of Germanic dialects in England that molded the particular character of the English language and distinguishes it markedly from its cousins.

English as a Germanic Language

As we said in Chapter 9, West Germanic was distinguished from two other branches of the Germanic group of Indo-European languages: from North

Germanic (which includes Swedish, Danish, and Norwegian) and from East Germanic (including only Gothic, which has since died out).

During the first millennium B.C., before the Germanic group of languages had split into three branches but after it had split from the other branches of Indo-European, Common (or Proto) Germanic developed certain characteristic features that continue in its daughter languages, setting them apart as a group from all other Indo-European varieties. Among these characteristics are features of phonology, lexicon, morphology, and syntax.

Phonology   The most striking phonological characteristic of the Germanic languages is a set of consonant correspondences found in none of the other Indo-European languages. It was Jacob Grimm, one of the Brothers Grimm of fairy-tale fame, who in 1822 formulated these correspondences in what is now called "Grimm's Law." Grimm described the regular sound shifts that had occurred within three natural classes of sounds in developing from Indo-European into Germanic.

1. voiceless stops became voiceless fricatives: p > f, t > θ, k > h (usually stated p t k > f θ h)

2. voiced stops became voiceless stops: b > p, d > t, g > k

3. voiced aspirated stops became voiced unaspirated stops: b^h > b, d^h > d, g^h > g

The impact of these changes can be seen in Figure 14-1 by examining the shift of voiceless stops in Indo-European to voiceless fricatives in Germanic.

FIGURE 14-1
Reflexes of Indo-European Voiceless Stops in Germanic and Romance

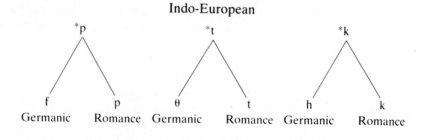

| Germanic | | Romance | |
English	Latin	French	Spanish
fish	piscis	poisson	pescado
three	tres	trois	tres
heart	cord	cœur	corazón

We illustrate this shift by citing English words that have inherited the sounds /f θ h/ from Germanic and contrasting them with corresponding words in Romance languages, which (like all the other branches of Indo-European) did not undergo these sound shifts.

Another important phonological development of Common Germanic was a shifting of stress patterns. Indo-European had variable stress on its words: a morpheme could be stressed on one syllable in the context of a given word and elsewhere in a different word. But in Common Germanic stress shifted systematically to a word's first or root syllable. Compare Modern English ˈfather, ˈfatherly, unˈfatherly, and ˈfatherless, all having stress on the root syllable in the Germanic fashion, with the Greek borrowings ˈphotograph, phoˈtographer, and photoˈgraphic, which have variable stress in the Indo-European fashion.

Lexicon The regular pattern of sound shifting described by Grimm's Law set the phonological shape of the Germanic vocabulary apart from that of other Indo-European languages (as seen in the Romance examples in Figure 14-1). In addition, the Germanic languages have a set of words found nowhere else in Indo-European. Once the Germanic tribes separated from the rest of the Indo-European peoples, any words innovated or borrowed from speakers of a non-Indo-European tongue would be distinctively Germanic within Indo-European. Among the English words found in other Germanic languages but not in any other Indo-European languages are the nouns *arm, blood, earth, finger, hand, sea*, and *wife*; the verbs *bring, drink, drive, leap*, and *run*; and the adjectives *evil, little*, and *sick*. Here are the strictly Germanic nouns from English and German (to illustrate the similarity among Germanic tongues) and from French (to illustrate the striking contrast between Germanic and Romance languages).

English	German	French
arm	Arm	bras
blood	Blut	sang
earth	Erd	terre
finger	Finger	doigt
hand	Hand	main
sea	See	mer
wife	Weib	femme

It is conceivable that these Germanic words could have existed in Indo-European and were lost in all daughter languages except Germanic, but it is hardly likely. Hence we can assume they were not inherited from Indo-European but were innovated or borrowed during the Common Germanic period.

Grammar: Morphology and Syntax   Indo-European—at least at some stages—was certainly a highly inflected language. Because Sanskrit, one of the oldest attested Indo-European languages, had eight case inflections on nouns, it is possible that Indo-European itself had eight cases (though case distinctions not in Proto-Indo-European could have arisen in the Indic branch to which Sanskrit belongs). If we assume that the rich inflectional morphology of Sanskrit reflects the complexity of Indo-European, then Indo-European nouns would have had eight cases as well as three numbers (singular, dual, and plural) and three genders (masculine, feminine, and neuter). Verbs were also highly inflected, probably for two *voices* (active and a kind of passive), four *moods* (indicative, imperative, subjunctive, and optative), and three *tenses* (present, past, and future). In addition, verbs carried markers for *person* and *number*.

The Indo-European system of indicating verb tenses was principally word internal (as in English *sing/sang/sung*). While this internal sound *gradation* (sometimes called *ablaut*) is typical of Indo-European languages, the typical English inflection [-t] (*kissed*) or [-d] (*judged*) for the past tenses is characteristically Germanic. Thus the two-tense system, with past tense marked by a dental or alveolar suffix, sets the Germanic group apart from all its Indo-European cousins.

PERIODS IN THE HISTORY OF ENGLISH

Because languages change continuously, any division into historical stages or periods is necessarily somewhat arbitrary. Nevertheless, scholars have divided the history of English into three main periods representing very different stages of the language. We now refer to the language spoken in England from the end of the seventh century to the end of the eleventh century (700–1100) as Old English (or Anglo-Saxon). The English spoken since 1450 or 1500 is called Modern English. The language spoken in between—from 1100 to 1450 or 1500—is known as Middle English. Thus *Beowulf* is written in Old English, the *Canterbury Tales* in Middle English, and *Henry IV* in (early) Modern English.

OLD ENGLISH: 700–1100

When the Angles, Saxons, and Jutes began to invade England in 449, they settled in different parts of the island. Thus four principal dialects of Old English sprang up: Northumbrian in the north (above the Humber River); Mercian in the Midlands; Kentish in the southeast; and West Saxon in the southwest (see Figure 14-2). Because Wessex was the seat of the powerful King Alfred, its dialect, West Saxon, achieved a certain status; it forms the basis of most surviving Old English literature and of the study of Old English today.

Like the classical Latin of Roman times and the German and Russian of today, Old English was a highly inflected language. It had an elaborate system

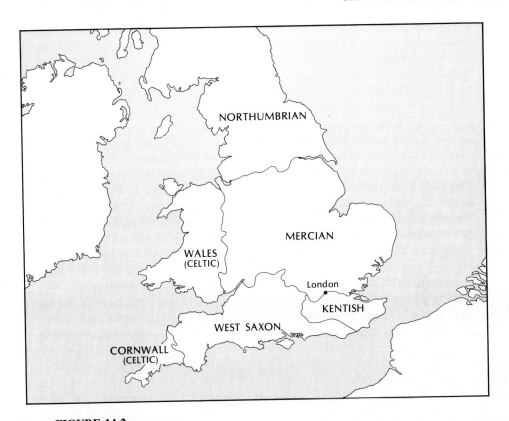

FIGURE 14-2
The Old English Dialects
SOURCE: Adapted from Samuel Moore and A. H. Marckwardt, *Historical Outlines of English Sounds and Inflections* (Ann Arbor, Mich.: George Wahr, 1951).

of inflectional suffixes on nouns, pronouns, verbs, adjectives, and even determiners. Only traces of these inflectional forms of Old English survive in Modern English.

Orthography

Only a few Old English letters differ from those of Modern English, but they occurred in some of the most frequently used words, giving Old English an exaggerated air of strangeness. Among the graphs no longer used in English are þ (thorn), ð (eth), ƿ (wynn), and æ (called ash). Editors usually let the graphs þ, ð, and æ stand in modern texts, but they almost invariably substitute *w* for wynn.

Both þ and ð (and their capitals Þ and Ð) were alternative spellings for two sounds; each graph, like Modern English *th*, represented the sounds [θ] or [ð], which were allophones of a single phoneme in Old English. Old English scribes did not assign one graph to the sound [θ] and the other to [ð] simply because, as allophones of a single phoneme, the two sounds were not perceived as different. Old English speakers were no more aware of the difference between [θ] and [ð] than Modern English speakers are aware that they are pronouncing different /p/ sounds in *pot* and *spot*. Besides, alphabetic systems ideally assign different symbols not to different sounds (allophones) but to different *distinctive* sounds (phonemes).

The graph æ, rarely used in Modern English, represented the same pronunciation in Old English that it has in the phonetic alphabet used today (the vowel of *hat*). The Old English vowel combinations *ēo* and *ēa* represented the diphthongs [ēɔ] and [ēə] respectively. The letter sequence *sc* (as in *Englisce*) is equivalent to Modern English *sh* [š]. The letter *c* represented two sounds: [k] as in *cȳpmenn* or [č] as in *æðellīce*. The letter *g* represented three sounds: [y] initially when it preceded and finally when it followed front vowels (as in *gelamp*, *gȳt*, and *Rōmānabyrig*) and [g] or [ɣ] elsewhere. The letter *y* was always a vowel. The letters *j* and *q* were not used in Old English, and *k* was rare (hence *folc* 'folk'), though the sounds they represent today did exist (compare *cwēn* 'queen' and *cēpan* 'keep'). The letter *x* was an alternative spelling of *cs*, pronounced [ks], as in *axode* 'asked.' Finally, we might mention that ꝥ 'and' was the customary representation in original manuscripts of the Old English equivalent of an ampersand sign "&."

Phonology

A good deal could be said about the Old English sound system. We shall make only a few observations about patterns that have implications for the development of Modern English. Old English had a system of long and short vowels and diphthongs, though in late Old English the diphthongs tended to become simplified to their first element. (A similar process occurs today in American dialects of the South, in which words like *time* /taym/ tend to be pronounced [tam], like the word *I* throughout the United States in a phrase like *I'm gonna* ... [amgʊnə].) The short vowels have remained relatively constant over the centuries, so that many words are pronounced today as they were in Old English: *fisc* 'fish', *æt* 'at,' *þorn* 'thorn,' *benc* 'bench,' and *him* 'him.' The long vowels, on the other hand, have undergone marked changes. Suffice it to say for now that Old English long vowels had their "continental" values, as in the following words: *stān* [stān] 'stone'; *sēon* [sēɔn] 'see'; *sōðlīce* [sōðlīčɛ] 'truly'; *būton* [būtɔn] 'without, except'; and *swīðe* [swīðɛ] 'very.'

As to consonants, Old English permitted combinations of consonants that Modern English no longer tolerates, including initial *hl-*, *hr-*, and *cn-* (/kn-/). Three pairs of sounds whose members are distinct phonemes in Modern English were allophones of single phonemes in Old English: [f] and [v]; [θ] and [ð]; and [s] and [z]. The voiceless allophones [f, θ, s] occurred at the beginning and end of words and when adjacent to voiceless sounds within words; between voiced sounds, however, the voiced allophones occurred. Thus in the nominative case of the word *wīf*, *f* represented the allophone [f]: [wīf]; but in the genitive case it represented the allophone [v]: *wifes* [wīvɛs] (note the final [s] too). The phonemes /s/ and /θ/ figure prominently in the history of English because so many inflections and so many function words contain them.

Morphology

Compounds   Old English writers (and presumably speakers) were very fond of compounding. The three lines of *Beowulf* cited earlier contain three compounds: *Gār-Dena* meaning 'spear Danes,' *gēardagum* meaning 'yore days' (that is, 'days of yore'), and *þēodcyninga* meaning 'of the kings of the people.'

Noun Inflections   Old English had several inflections for noun phrases, depending on their grammatical and semantic role in a sentence. Four principal cases could be distinguished: *nominative* (usually for subjects), *genitive* (for possessives and certain other functions), *dative* (for indirect objects and certain other functions), and *accusative* (for direct objects and objects of certain prepositions). Each noun carried a grammatical gender. Occasionally this grammatical gender reflected natural gender; *guma* 'man' and *brōðor* 'brother' were masculine, while *brȳd* 'bride' and *sweostor* 'sister' were feminine. But usually a noun's gender had nothing to do with its natural sex. For example, the nouns *mīl* 'mile,' *wist* 'feast,' and *lēaf* 'permission' were feminine; *hund* 'dog,' *hungor* 'hunger,' *wīfmann* 'woman,' and *wīngeard* 'vineyard' were masculine; and *wīf* 'woman, wife,' *manncynn* 'mankind,' and *scip* 'ship' were neuter. Thus grammatical gender is simply a grammatical category that determined the way a given noun was inflected and also determined the endings on adjectives and other constituents of the noun phrase. Old English nouns and adjectives exploited only three (sometimes four) case inflections because the nominative and accusative forms were the same.

Table 14-1 shows the paradigms for the nouns *fox* 'fox,' *lār* 'learning, lore,' *dēor* 'animal,' and *fōt* 'foot.' (Recall from Chapter 4 that a *paradigm* is simply the set of inflected forms for a particular word. For nouns, pronouns, and adjectives, the paradigms are called *declensions*.)

From the Old English *fox* declension come the only productive Modern English noun inflections: the genitive singular in -*s* and all plurals in -*s*. The *dēor* paradigm survives in uninflected modern plurals like *deer* (whose meaning has been narrowed from 'animal' to 'deer') and *sheep*, but new words never follow this pattern. The *fōt* declension has yielded a few nouns (like *foot, goose,* and *tooth; louse* and *mouse*; and *man*) whose plurals are signaled by an internal vowel change rather than by the common -*s* suffix. Modern English phrases like *a ten-foot pole* are relics of the Old English genitive plural ('a pole of ten feet'), whose form *fōta* has given rise to *foot*. Over the centuries, most nouns that had previously been inflected according to other paradigms have come to conform to the *fox* paradigm, and new nouns (with the exception of a few borrowings from other languages) are also inflected like it.

TABLE 14-1
Four Old English Noun Declensions

	Masculine 'fox'	Feminine 'learning'	Neuter 'animal'	Masculine 'foot'
Singular				
Nominative	fox	lār	dēor	fōt
Accusative	fox	lār-e	dēor	fōt
Genitive	fox-es	lār-e	dēor-es	fōt-es
Dative	fox-e	lār-e	dēor-e	fēt
Plural				
Nom./Acc.*	fox-as	lār-a	dēor	fēt
Genitive	fox-a	lār-a	dēor-a	fōt-a
Dative	fox-um	lār-um	dēor-um	fōt-um

* In laying out Old English declensions, it is customary to list the nominative and accusative singular forms separately despite their sameness but to collapse the nominative and accusative plural forms in a single line as we have done. The reason is simply that in the paradigms for articles and adjectives, the other elements of a noun phrase, the nominative and accusative are identical in the plural but not necessarily in the singular.

Articles   The Modern English definite article is simple in form. It has a single orthographic shape *the* with two standard pronunciations, [ði] before vowels and [ðə] elsewhere. In sharp contrast, the Old English demonstratives—forerunners of today's definite article—were inflected for five cases and three genders in the singular and for three cases without gender distinction in the plural (see Table 14-2). The fifth case, the instrumental, was used either with or without a preposition to indicate such semantic roles as accompaniment or instrument ('with the chieftains,' 'by an arrow').

TABLE 14-2
Old English Declension of Demonstrative 'that'

		Singular		Plural
	masculine	feminine	neuter	all genders
Nominative	sē	sēo	þæt	þā
Accusative	þone	þā	þæt	þā
Genitive	þæs	þære	þæs	þāra
Dative	þæm	þære	þæm	þæm
Instrumental	þȳ	þære	þȳ	þæm

As in Modern English, Old English indefinite noun phrases were frequently unmarked (*She writes books*), except that *sum* 'a certain' and *ān* 'one' occurred sometimes in the singular for emphasis and were inflected like adjectives.

Adjective Inflections   The Old English adjective system owes its complexity to innovations that had arisen in Common Germanic and consequently do not appear in other Indo-European languages (and have not survived into Modern English).

Old English adjectives were inflected for gender, number, and case to agree with their head noun. There were two distinct kinds of adjective declensions. When a noun phrase had as one of its constituents a highly inflected possessive pronoun or demonstrative, adjectives were declined with one set of inflections—the so-called "weak" (or *definite*) declension. In other instances, such as predicative usage (*He is tall*), when indicators of grammatical relations were few or nonexistent, the more varied forms of the "strong" (or *indefinite*) declension were required. Table 14-3 gives the indefinite and definite adjective paradigms for *gōd* 'good.' Notice that there are ten different forms of 'good' as compared to its single form in Modern English.

Nothing remains of the Old English inflectional system for adjectives. Today all adjectives occur in a single shape such as *tall, old,* and *beautiful* (except for the quite separate comparative and superlative inflections, as in

TABLE 14-3
Old English Declensions of the Adjective 'good'

	Singular			Plural		
	masc.	fem.	neut.	masc.	fem.	neut.
Indefinite						
Nom.	gōd	gōd	gōd	gōd-e	gōd	gōd
Acc.	gōd-ne	gōd-e	gōd	gōd-e	gōd	gōd
Gen.	gōd-es	gōd-re	gōd-es	gōd-ra	gōd-ra	gōd-ra
Dat.	gōd-um	gōd-re	gōd-um	gōd-um	gōd-um	gōd-um
Ins.	gōd-e	gōd-re	gōd-e	gōd-um	gōd-um	gōd-um

	masc.	fem.	neut.	all genders		
Definite						
Nom.	gōd-a	gōd-e	gōd-e	gōd-an		
Acc.	gōd-an	gōd-an	gōd-e	gōd-an		
Gen.	gōd-an	gōd-an	gōd-an	gōd-ra (gōd-ena)		
Dat.	gōd-an	gōd-an	gōd-an	gōd-um		

taller/tallest and *older/oldest*). For any gender, number, or case of the modified noun, and for both attributive (*the tall ships*) and predicative (*the ship is tall*) functions, the form of a Modern English adjective remains invariant.

Personal Pronouns   The Modern English personal pronouns preserve more of their earlier complexity than any other part of speech. The Old English paradigms for personal pronouns are given in Table 14-4, alongside their Modern English counterparts.

As can be seen, besides singulars and plurals Old English had a dual number in the first and second persons to refer to exactly two people ('we two' and 'you two'). The dual was already weakening in late Old English and eventually disappeared from English, as did the distinct number and case forms of the second person pronoun (*pū* 'thou'/*pē* 'thee' and *gē* 'ye'/*ēow* 'you' are all now *you*); the distinct dative case form for the third person singular neuter pronoun has also disappeared.

Relative Pronouns   In Old English, an invariant particle *þe* marked the introduction of relative clauses, though *þe* was often compounded with the demonstrative *sē, sēo, þæt*, as in *sē þe* (for masculine reference) and *sēo þe*

TABLE 14-4
Old English and Modern English Pronouns

	Old English					Modern English				
	first	second	third person			first	second	third person		
			masc.	fem.	neut.			masc.	fem.	neut.
Singular										
Nom.	ic	þū	hē	hēo	hit	I	you	he	she	it
Acc.	mē	þē	hine	hie	hit	me	you	him	her	it
Gen.	mīn	þīn	his	hiere	his	mine	yours	his	hers	its
Dat.	mē	þē	him	hiere	him	me	you	him	her	it
Dual										
Nom.	wit	git								
Acc.	unc	inc								
Gen.	uncer	incer								
Dat.	unc	inc								
			all genders					all genders		
Plural										
Nom.	wē	gē	hīe			we	you	they		
Acc.	ūs	ēow	hīe			us	you	them		
Gen.	ūre	ēower	hiera			ours	yours	theirs		
Dat.	ūs	ēow	him			us	you	them		

(for feminine reference) 'who, that.' The forms of the demonstrative *sē, sēo, þæt* also occurred alone as relatives:

anne æðeling se   wæs Cyneheard hāten
a   prince   Rel was Cyneheard called
'a prince who was called Cyneheard'

Old English relative clauses were also sometimes introduced by *þe* and a form of the personal pronoun:

Nis   nū cwicra nān   þe ic him mōdsefan mīnne durre āsecgan
(there) isn't now alive   no one Rel I him mind   my   dare speak
'There is no one alive now to whom I dare speak my mind.'

As this example shows, Old English relativized indirect objects. Therefore, according to the universals examined in Chapter 8, we would assume that it also relativized direct objects and subjects—which in fact it did.

Verbs and Verb Inflections   Like other Germanic languages, Old English and its descendants exhibit two types of verbs. The characteristically Germanic regular verbs have a [d] or [t] suffix in the past tense (and are called "weak"). The so-called irregular verbs (the traditional Indo-European "strong" type) show a vowel gradation (as in *sing/sang/sung*). Old English had seven patterns of irregular verbs. Table 14-5 lists the principal parts (the forms from which all other inflected forms can be derived) of the seven Old English verb classes. These illustrative words survive as irregular verbs in Modern English, but quite a few Old English irregular verbs have developed into Modern English *regular* verbs in the course of time. (*Shove, melt, wash,* and *step*, for instance, were irregular in Old English.)

Two tenses—the present and the past (sometimes called the *preterit*)—and two moods (the indicative and subjunctive) could be formed from a verb's

TABLE 14-5
Seven Classes of Old English Strong Verbs

	Infinitive	Past Sing.	Past Pl.	Past Participle	
(1)	rīdan	rād	ridon	geriden	'ride'
(2)	frēosan	frēas	fruron	gefroren	'freeze'
(3)	drincan	dranc	druncon	gedruncen	'drink'
(4)	beran	bær	bǣron	geboren	'bear'
(5)	licgan	læg	lǣgon	gelegen	'lie'
(6)	standan	stōd	stōdon	gestanden	'stand'
(7)	feallan	fēoll	fēollon	gefeallen	'fall'

TABLE 14-6
Conjugation of 'judge, deem' in Old English

	Indicative Mood	Subjunctive Mood
Present Tense		
Singular		
first person	dēm-e	
second person	dēm-st (or dēm-est)	dēm-e
third person	dēm-þ (or dēm-eþ)	
Plural		
first, second, and third	dēm-aþ	dēm-en
Past Tense		
Singular		
first	dēm-d-e	
second	dēm-d-est	dēm-d-e
third	dēm-d-e	
Plural		
first, second, and third	dēm-d-on	dēm-d-en
Gerund	tō dēm-enne (or dēm-anne)	
Present participle	dēm-ende	
Past participle	dēm-ed	

principal parts. Table 14-6 gives a typical Old English regular verb conjugation for *dēman* 'judge, deem.' (*Conjugation* is the name for a verb paradigm, parallel to *declension* for a noun paradigm.) Note that the present tense indicative had three singular forms and one plural, but the present tense subjunctive had only one singular and one plural form. Compared to the twelve distinct forms of an Old English regular verb paradigm, the Modern English paradigm has only four separate forms (*judge, judges, judged,* and *judging*) and does not include any distinctly subjunctive forms.

Compared to its elaborate Indo-European ancestors and some of its even more elaborate cousins, Old English had a simple verbal system. Old English verbs were inflected for person, number, and tense in the indicative mood and for number and tense in the subjunctive mood; the subjunctive mood was used far more frequently in Old English than it is in Modern English. Latin, by way of contrast, was inflected for active and passive *voice*, for perfective and imperfective *aspect*, and for present, past, and future *tenses*, as well as for several *moods*. Scholars are uncertain whether Latin inherited all those distinctions from Indo-European or innovated some on its own.

Inflections and Word Order

Having a rich inflectional system, Old English could rely on its morphological distinctions to indicate the grammatical relations of nouns (and, to a lesser extent, their semantic roles). Noun phrases had agreement in gender, number, and case among the demonstrative/definite article, the adjective, and the head noun; adjectives were declined, either definite or indefinite, as already described. Using some of the declensions provided in Tables 14-1, 14-2, and 14-3, and two other adjectives, we can form the following Old English noun phrases. Note that in each instance the adjective and demonstrative article must *agree* with the noun (that is, they must be inflected for the same gender, case, and number).

sē gōda fox	'the good fox' (masc. nom. sg.)
gōd dēor	'good animals' (neuter nom./acc. pl.)
þā gōdan fēt	'the good feet' (masc. nom./acc. pl.)
langra fōta	'long feet' (masc. genitive pl.)
þǣre micelan lāre	'the great learning' (fem. genitive/dative sg.)

The rich inflectional system operating within Old English noun phrases could indicate grammatical relations and certain semantic roles without having to rely on word order the way Modern English does. Word order was therefore more flexible in Old English than it can be in Modern English. Still, by the period of late Old English, word order patterns were already similar in many respects to those of Modern English. Both Old English and Modern English show a preference for SVO order (subject preceding verb preceding object) in main clauses. Modern English prefers SVO in subordinate clauses as well; Old English (like Modern German) preferred verb-final word order (SOV) in subordinate clauses.

As in Modern English, the order of elements in Old English noun phrases was usually determiner-adjective-noun: *sē gōda mann* 'the good man.' Far more frequently than in Modern English, genitives preceded nouns, as in the following:

folces weard 'people's protector'

mǣres līfes mann 'a man of splendid life'
(literally '(a) splendid life's man')

fōtes trym 'the space of a foot'
(literally '(a) foot's space')

We saw in Chapter 4 that "adpositions" can either follow or precede their nouns. Old English generally had prepositions, though pronouns often had the same form in postposition (that is, after them), as shown in this example:

sē hālga Andreas him tō cwæþ...
the holy Andrew him to said...
'St. Andrew said to him...'

Like Modern English adjectives, Old English adjectives almost uniformly preceded their head nouns (*sē foresprecena here* 'the aforesaid army'), though they could sometimes follow them:

wadu weallendu
waters surging
'surging waters'

As they do in Modern English, relative clauses, unlike adjectives, generally followed their head nouns in Old English.

ða cyningas ðe   ðone onwald hæfdon
the kings   who the   power had
'the kings who had the power'

AN OLD ENGLISH NARRATIVE TEXT

The Old English passage in Figure 14-3 originates in Bede's *Ecclesiastical History of the English People*, completed in A.D. 731 by the venerable monk and subsequently translated from Latin into English perhaps by Alfred the Great during his reign as king of Wessex (871–899). The version here is slightly edited from a later translation by the English abbot Ælfric (about 955–1020). Written in the plain style that Ælfric sometimes used, the story tells of how Gregory the Great, who reigned as pope between 590 and 604, first learned of the English as he walked through a marketplace in Rome and saw boys being sold as slaves. The passage seems as foreign as any language written in the Roman alphabet and more so than some, given its unusual letters.

Lexicon of the Text

Function Words   Focusing on such function words as prepositions, demonstratives, and pronouns, we see some notable similarities between the Old English passage and Modern English: in the prepositions *æt* 'at,' *tō* 'to,' *betwux* 'between, among,' *of* 'of, from'; in the conjunction ˥ 'and,' which occurs more than half a dozen times in the passage; in the conjunction *þā* 'then,' used frequently to introduce sentences (usually with the verb following, as in lines 1, 4, and 8 of the passage). The subordinator *þæt* (lines 8 and 17) was used exactly as it is in Modern English. Some of the personal pronouns functioned exactly as they do in Modern English (except that their

1 Ðā gelamp hit æt sumum sæle, swā swā gȳt for oft dēð,
Then happened it at a certain time as yet oft does,

2 þæt Englisce cȳpmenn brōhton heora ware tō Rōmānabyrig,
that English traders brought their wares to Rome

3 ꝶ Grēgōrius ēode be þǣre strǣt tō ðām Engliscum mannum,
and Gregory went through the street to the English men.

heora ðing scēawigende.
their things looking at.

4 Þā geseah hē betwux ðām warum cȳpecnihtas gesette,
Then saw he among the wares slaves seated

5 þā wǣron hwītes līchaman ꝶ fægeres andwlitan menn, ꝶ æðellīce gefexode.
who were of white body and of fair countenance men, and nobly haired.

6 Grēgōrius ðā behēold þǣra cnapena wlite,
Gregory then saw the boys' countenances.

7 ꝶ befrān of hwilcere þēode hī gebrōhte wǣron.
and asked from which people they brought were.

8 Þā sǣde him man þæt hī of Englalande wǣron,
Then said to him someone that they from England were.

9 ꝶ þæt ðǣre ðēode mennisc swā wlitig wǣre.
and that the people of that race so handsome were.

10 Eft ðā Grēgōrius befrān, hwæðer þæs
Again then Gregory asked, whether that

11 landes folc crīsten wǣre ðe hǣðen.
land's people Christian were or heathen.

12 Him man sǣde þæt hī hǣðene wǣron....
Him someone told that they heathen were....

13 Eft hē āxode, hū ðǣre ðēode nama wǣre þe hī of cōmon.
Later he asked, how the people's name was that they from came.

14 Him wæs geandswarod, þæt hī Angle genemnode wǣron.
To him was answered, that they Angles named were.

15 Hwæt, ðā Grēgōrius gamenode mid his wordum tō ðām naman ꝶ cwæð,
Well, then Gregory played with his words on the name and said,

16 "Rihtlīce hī sind Angle gehātene, for ðan ðe hī engla wlite habbað,
"Rightly they are Angles called, because they angels' countenances have,

17 ꝶ swilcum gedafenað þæt hī on heofonum engla gefēran bēon.
and for such it is right that they in heaven angels' companions be.

FIGURE 14-3
A Narrative Written in Old English Around the Year 1000

pronunciations have in most instances changed): *hit* 'it,' *hē* 'he,' *hī* 'they,' *him* 'him.' We can see in the verb *to be* the singular past tense inflection *-e* (*wǣre*) and the plural past tense inflection *-on* (*wǣron*).

Content Words   There is greater difference between Old English and Modern English in nouns, verbs, and adjectives than in function words, but some of this strangeness is due to inflections (*mannum* the dative plural of 'man') and much of it to spelling differences resulting from orthographic practice or pronunciation. Thus we can see in the words *Englisce, strǣt, ðing, menn*, and *nama* the earlier forms of the nouns *English, street, thing, men*, and *name*. In *brōhton, behēold, sǣde*, and *wǣre* are the etymons of the modern verbs *brought, beheld, said*, and *were*. Among other words that still exist today are *hwæðer* 'whether,' *hū* 'how,' *crīsten* 'Christian,' and *hǣðen* 'heathen.' A few others are not quite so transparent, but they can trigger a flash of recognition once the connection is pointed out: *rihtlīce* 'rightly,' *cwæð* 'quoted,' *heofonum* 'heaven,' *engla* 'angel.'

Grammar: Syntax and Morphology in the Text

Given its highly inflected nature, Old English had considerable freedom of word order. There were word order preferences for SVO in main clauses and SOV in subordinate clauses, but all orders did occur. Note, however, that the verb occurred in second position following the introductory adverb *þā* (*þā geseah hē*, line 4, and also lines 1 and 8); otherwise, it tended to occur in final position in subordinate clauses (*þæt hī hæðene wǣron*, line 12, and 1, 7, 9, 13, 14, and 17). As in Modern English, noun phrases had the order (article)-(adjective)-noun (*sumum sǣle* 'a certain time,' *þǣre strǣt* 'the street') and prepositional phrases the order preposition-adjective-noun (*æt sumum sǣle, be þǣre strǣt*).

Text Structure

One striking characteristic of Old English writing was the strong preference for linking sentences together with ⁊ 'and' and *þā* 'then,' much as is done in Modern English oral narratives. Frequent use of subordinators making explicit the relation between one clause and another (*because, since, until*) was a later development. Clauses are introduced with 'and' or 'then' often in the passage, including lines 1, 4, and 8. There are a few examples of subordination, as in *hwæðer* 'whether' in line 10 and *for ðan ðe* 'because' in line 16.

MIDDLE ENGLISH: 1100–1500

The Norman Invasion

In the year 1066, William, Duke of Normandy, sailed across the Channel to claim the English throne. After winning the Battle of Hastings, William was crowned king of England in Westminster Abbey on Christmas Day, and Anglo-Saxon England passed into history. Thus was established a Norman kingdom in England: for generations the king of England and the duke of Normandy would be one person. The Norman invasion would not only reshape England's institutions but exercise a profound effect on its language.

The Norman French spoken by the invaders quickly became the language of England's ruling class, while the lower classes remained English-speaking. Following the invasion, English had a recess from many of the duties it previously had performed. In particular, it was relieved of many of its duties in the affairs of government, the court, the church, and education; all these important activities were conducted in French. Indeed, for two centuries after the Conquest, the kings of England could not speak the language of many of their subjects, and English-speaking subjects could not understand their king. The most famous king of this period, Richard the Lion-Hearted, was in every way French: during his ten-year reign (1189–1199), he visited England only twice (both times to raise money), staying a total of less than ten months. Eventually the middle classes became bilingual, speaking to peasants in English and to the ruling classes in French.

After 1200 the situation began to change, when King John lost Normandy to King Philip of France. On both sides of the Channel, decrees were issued commanding that no one could own land in both England and France. Cut off from its Norman origins, the force that had sustained the use of French in Britain began to collapse.

Lexicon

A hundred years later, at the beginning of the fourteenth century, English came to be known again by all inhabitants of England. The language that emerged was strikingly different from the Old English used prior to the Norman invasion, at least as Old English is reflected in the surviving written documents. The vocabulary of Middle English was heavily spiced by Norman French. The English word stock was swollen by the addition of thousands of French words because speakers learning English used French words to refer to things whose English labels they didn't know. Based on calculations by the great Danish scholar Otto Jespersen, it has been estimated that approximately ten thousand French words came into English during the Middle English period, and most of them remain in use today. Especially plentiful were words pertaining to religion, government, the courts, and the army and navy, though there were also generous doses of borrowings that relate to food, fashion, and education—all the arenas in which the invaders and their successors had wielded great influence in England.

Once English had been reestablished as the language of the law, the residents of England found themselves without sufficient English terminology to carry on the activities that had been conducted for centuries in French. Hence a good many French legal terms were borrowed, including even the words *justice* and *court* (the word *law* itself, however, derives from Old English *lagu*). To discuss events in a courtroom today, the following words—all borrowed from French during the Middle English period—are used: *judgment, plea, verdict, evidence, proof, prison,* and *jail.* The actors in a courtroom now have French names: *bailiff, plaintiff, defendant, attorney, jury, juror,* and *judge.* The names of certain crimes are French, including *felony, assault, arson, larceny, fraud, libel, slander,* and *perjury,* as well as the word *crime* itself. We have cited examples only from the law, and by no means all of them; similar extensive lists of French borrowings could be provided for the other arenas.

Phonology

Vowels   The Old English long vowel /ā/ in words like *bān, stān,* and *bāt* became in Middle English long /ɔ̄/ (and in Modern English /o/) as in *boon* 'bone,' *stoon* 'stone,' and *boot* 'boat.' Other long vowels of Old English were generally maintained in Middle English unchanged. Many diphthongs were simplified in late Old English and early Middle English. Thus the words *sēon* 'see' and *bēon* 'be' were leveled to long /ē/, a sound that went on to become [i] in Modern English.

Short vowels in unstressed syllables, which had been kept distinct at least in early West Saxon, tended to merge in schwa [ə], usually written *e.*

Consonants and Consonant Clusters   The Old English initial consonant clusters /hl-/, /hn-/, /hr-/, and /kn-/ were simplified to /l/, /n/, and /r/, all losing their initial /h/ or /k/: *hlāf* 'loaf,' *hlot* 'lot,' *hnecca* 'neck,' *hnacod* 'naked,' *hrōf* 'roof,' *hræfn* 'raven,' *hring* 'ring,' *cnīf* 'knife,' *cnoll* 'knoll,' *cniht* 'boy, knight.' A phonological change of considerable consequence was the merging of word-final /-m/ and /-n/ in a single sound (/-n/) when they occurred in unstressed syllables (*foxum* > *foxun*). Significantly, unstressed syllables included all the inflections on nouns, adjectives, and verbs. By the end of the Middle English period even this /-n/ was dropped altogether (*foxun* > *foxen* > *foxe*), and of course the final *-e* was also dropped.

Morphology

Three of the phonological changes just mentioned had a profound effect on the morphology of Middle English.

1. -m > -n
2. -n > ∅
3. a, o, u, e > e [ə]   (when not stressed)

Figure 14-4 shows how, as a consequence of these sound changes, certain sets of Old English inflections merged, becoming indistinguishable in Middle English and being further reduced or dropping altogether in an early Modern English stage. As a result of these mergers, the Old English noun paradigms became greatly simplified in Middle English, and grammatical gender disappeared (see Table 14-7).

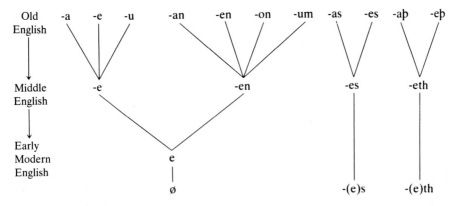

FIGURE 14-4
The Historical Reduction of English Inflections

The frequently used subject and object noun phrase forms (nominative and accusative cases) established the nominative and accusative plural form *foxes* (and the *-es* inflection for other nouns in general) throughout the plural; it also established the nominative and accusative singular throughout the singular except that the genitive in *-s* was maintained. Thus the Middle English paradigm for a noun like *fox* came to be what it is in Modern English: *fox* and *foxes* (now spelled *fox's*) in the singular and *foxes* throughout the plural (now spelled *foxes'* in the genitive).

In some of the other noun paradigms, the damage to the morphological distinctions brought on by the merging of unstressed vowels was even greater. Old English *dēor* was reduced to three forms (*deer/deeres/deere*), while *lār* was reduced to two (*loor* and *loore*), a distinction that was in turn lost when final inflected *-e* vanished about 1500.

TABLE 14-7
Four Middle English Noun Declensions

	'fox'	'lore'	'animal'	'foot'
Singular				
Nom./Acc.	fox	loor	deer	foot
Genitive	foxes	loor(e)	deeres	footes
Dative	fox(e)	loor(e)	deer(e)	foot
Plural				
Nom./Acc.	foxes	loor(e)	deer	feet
Genitive/Dative	foxes	loor(e)	deer(e)	foot(e)

We have the Modern English forms of the word *deer* (*deer* and *deer's*) from the nominative and accusative singular inflection, which were extended throughout the singular (except that the ending in -*s* has been kept in the genitive). The parallel nominative and accusative plural form extended throughout the plural (except that by analogy with all other English nouns the genitive plural is formed by adding -*s* to the form of the nominative plural).

From the *foot* declension, the origin of the Modern English forms are clear: Middle English nominative and accusative *foot* was extended throughout the singular, with the -*s* of the genitive form *footes* maintained; the nominative and accusative plural *feet* was extended throughout the plural (and, as usual, the inflected genitive is formed by adding -*s* to the nominative). Modern English expressions like *a ten-foot pole* 'a pole of ten feet' and *a three-day weekend* 'a weekend of three days' are simply relics of the Old English constructions with genitive plurals (for example, *fōta*), whose final -*a* became -*e* in Middle English and then was dropped.

Adjectives   The same merging of distinct inflections that collapsed the noun paradigms also had a devastating effect on adjectives. The only indefinite forms surviving the phonological change from Old English were *goodne* (masculine accusative singular), *goodes* (masculine and neuter genitive singular), and *goodre* (feminine genitive, dative, and instrumental singular, and genitive plural). Then *good* became the universal form for the singular. In the plural, the nominative, accusative, and dative forms for all genders became *good*, and the genitive plural also became *good* by analogy. That left only a single form in the singular and plural, namely *good*, which yielded Modern English *good* as the invariable form of the adjective (comparative and superlative forms aside).

In the definite declension, the only two forms surviving were *good* and *goodre*. Then *goodre* was re-formed by analogy (whereby one form takes on the shape of other forms in the same or another paradigm) to *good*, thus leaving only a single definite adjective form, which was the same as the indefinite. Thus a few seemingly simple phonological changes (and some analogical adaptations) reduced the complex forms of Old English adjectives to the striking simplicity of today's single forms.

Syntax

Much could be said about Middle English syntax, but the language changed so thoroughly during the four centuries of this period that a good deal of provision would have to be made for intermediate stages. Since we have described Old English and Modern English syntax at some length, suffice it to say that Middle English was a transitional period, especially with respect to the change from a reliance on inflection to a reliance on word order for a considerable amount of information about grammatical relations. As the inflections of Old English disappeared, the word order of Middle English became increasingly fixed. The communicative work that had previously been done for nouns by inflectional morphology still needed doing, and it fell principally to prepositions and word order to perform these tasks. We have already said that Old English preferred SVO word order in main clauses but often had SOV word order in subordinate clauses. The exclusive use of the SVO pattern emerged in the twelfth century and has remained part of English ever since.

A MIDDLE ENGLISH TRAVEL FABLE

We can now see how some of these features of morphology and syntax came together in Middle English prose. Figure 14-5 is a brief passage from *The Travels of John Mandeville*, a translation made from Mandeville's French work by an unknown but gifted English writer in the early fifteenth century (about the time of Chaucer's death). These travel stories, in large part fables, were extremely popular and survive in more than three hundred manuscripts. In the passage quoted here, Mandeville is describing a fabulous place called Lamary.

We analyze this passage with a view to how English of the early fifteenth century differed from today's. First of all, it should be noted that the passage is quite intelligible, though a few marked differences (and some subtle ones) can be noted between it and today's English.

Lexicon

As to vocabulary, not a single word in the passage will be unknown to readers today, though a few (such as *lond* 'land,' *hete* 'heat,' *ʒeer* 'year,' *byʒen* 'buy,' and *hem* 'them') might not be instantly recognizable. (The graph ʒ, called *yogh*, was pronounced like [y].) Not all the words borrowed from French during the Middle English period immediately took their current form, but all are nevertheless transparent (except perhaps for *clos*): *custom, strange, clothed, nature, comoun, clos, contradiccioun, contree, habundant, marchauntes*.

Morphology

Only a few inflections remain from Old English that have not survived in Modern English. For example, third person singular present tense verbs end in -(*e*)*th*: *holdeth, hath, lyketh, taketh* (but compare past tense *made*); and plural present tense verbs end in *-n* or *-en*: *gon, scornen, seyn, ben, eten, bryngen, byʒen*, and others. This *-n* or *-en* is not the direct reflex of the Old English plural form *-aþ* but has apparently been introduced from the subjunctive plural so as to maintain a distinction between the singular and the plural, which otherwise would have been lost when the unstressed vowels of the singular *-eþ* and the plural *-aþ* merged to give Middle English *-eth* for both forms. While Mandeville's translator alternates between the two spellings *þei* and *thei* for the third person plural subject pronoun, the *þ/th* forms of the objective case do not yet appear in this passage, which instead shows the objective form *hem* (lines 19, 20, and 21). Otherwise, several of the Modern

1   In þat lond is full gret hete,
     In that land is very great heat.

2   and the custom þere is such þat men and wommen gon all naked.
     and the custom there is such that men and women go all naked.

3   And þei scornen, whan thei seen ony strange folk goynge clothed.
     And they scorn, when they see any strange folk going clothed.

4   And þei seyn, þat god made Adam and Eue all naked
     And they say, that God made Adam and Eve all naked

5   and þat no man scholde schame him to schewen him such as god made him;
     and that no man should shame himself to show himself such as God made him;

6   for no thing is foul þat is of kyndely nature....
     for no thing is foul that is of natural nature....

7   And also all the lond is comoun; for all þat a man
     And also all the land is common; for all that a man

8   holdeth o ȝeer, another man hath it anoþer ȝeer,
     keeps one year, another man has it another year,

9   and euery man taketh what part þat him lyketh.
     and every man takes what part that him pleases.

10   And also all the godes of the lond ben comoun, cornes and all oþer þinges;
     And also all the goods of the land are common, grains and all other things;

11   for no þing þere is kept in clos, ne no þing þere is vndur lok,
     for no thing there is kept in a closet nor no thing there is under lock.

12   and euery man þere taketh what he wole, withouten ony contradiccioun.
     and every man there takes what he wants, without any contradiction.

13   And als riche is o man þere as is another.
     And as rich is one man there as is another.

14   But in þat contree þere is a cursed custom:
     But in that country there is a cursed custom:

15   for þei eten more gladly mannes flesch þan ony oþer flesch.
     for they eat more gladly man's flesh than any other flesh.

16   And ȝit is þat contree habundant of flesch, of fissch,
     And yet is that country abundant with flesh, with fish,

17   of cornes, of gold and syluer, and of all oþer godes.
     with grains, with gold and silver, and with all other goods.

18   Þider gon marchauntes and bryngen with hem children,
     Thither go merchants and bring with them children,

19   to selle to hem of the contree; and þei byȝen hem.
     to sell to them of the country; and they buy them.

20   And ȝif þei ben fatte, þei eten hem anon; and ȝif þei ben lene,
     And if they are fat, they eat them at once; and if they are lean,

21   þei feden hem till þei ben fatte, and þanne þei eten hem.
     they feed them until they are fat, and then they eat them.

22   And þei seyn, þat it is the best flesch and the swettest of all the world.
     And they say, that it is the best flesh and the sweetest of all the world.

FIGURE 14-5

A Travel Fable Written in Middle English Around the Year 1400

English inflections have their current form (after some slight spelling adjustments): *goynge* (= *going*), *clothed, godes* (= *goods*), *þinges* (= *things*), *marchauntes* (= *merchants*), and *swettest* (= *sweetest*). Even certain words that had kept their exceptional forms from Old English are the same in 1400 and today: *men, wommen, folk, children,* and *best.* Being among the more common words of the language they were more likely to maintain their unusual forms than were words used less frequently.

Syntax

The first notable difference in syntax occurs in line 1. Where Modern English requires a "dummy subject" (without a referent), Middle English did not: *In þat lond is* .... But note the dummy *þere* in line 14: *But in þat contree þere is* .... Another striking difference is the double negative *ne no þing* 'nor nothing' in line 11.

There are marked word order differences. Compare in line 13 this word-for-word equivalent with its current English version (which follows the slash): *And as rich is one man there as is another/And one man there is as rich as another.* Note too that the adverbial phrase *more gladly* (line 15) follows its verb instead of preceding it as it would in Modern English. Finally, note the relic of Old English verb-second word order in line 18 (*Thither go merchants*) and the prepositional phrase *with hem* in the same line, which in current English would follow the direct object *children*.

Among some of the subtler syntactic differences are the use of *scorn* intransitively (that is, without a direct object) in line 3, which is no longer possible, and the use of the nonreflexive pronoun *him* where current English would reflexivize (line 5). One final interesting difference occurs in line 9, where *him* is an object form that complements the verb *lyketh* (in a benefactive semantic role); *him lyketh* literally translates *to him* (*it*) *likes* 'it pleases him.' Since Old English times, this "impersonal" construction had not required a subject but had required a dative (or, later, objective) case form of the pronoun; it resembles the French *s'il vous plait* 'if it you pleases,' which may have influenced the now archaic formulation *if it please you* or *if it please my lord.*

We may tend to overlook some of the syntactic differences that do exist in this passage as compared to current English because we are accustomed to finding relatively conservative syntax in such places as the King James Bible and certain formal prose styles such as legalese. Still, it is fair to say that this Middle English passage, now six centuries old, is obviously English and is almost completely transparent to modern readers.

MODERN ENGLISH: 1500–PRESENT

Chapters 2–6 of this book examined the structure of twentieth-century English in detail, and there is no need to recapitulate that material here. This section focuses instead on what changes occurred in the earliest stages of Modern English to move the language from the forms we have seen in Middle English to those we know today.

Early and Late Modern English

As our analysis of Mandeville's travel fable shows, Middle English had developed many of the principal syntactic patterns we know today by the beginning of the fifteenth century. The complex inflectional system of Old English had been simplified ("destroyed" may be a more accurate description); and today's system, with fewer than ten inflections, had emerged. Most nouns that had been inflected in Old English according to various patterns now conformed to the *fox* pattern. By the time of Shakespeare, the third person plural pronouns with *th-* instead of *h-* (*they, their,* and *them*) were in general use and had been for a century; Chaucer and the Mandeville translator had used *they*, but both still used the older possessive form *her* and objective form *hem*. In addition, word order had become more fixed, essentially as it is in Modern English.

The language of the late fifteenth century is in most ways Modern English—though in so saying, one should be mindful that perhaps the principal phonological development of English vowels took place sometime between 1450 and 1650, when all the long vowels changed their quality very markedly, as we shall see. If that phonological change is not apparent, it is simply because the modern spellings of English vowels had essentially been established by the time of William Caxton, who founded his printing press in the vicinity of Westminster Abbey in 1476—before the phonological change had progressed very far at all. Caxton's spellings thus disguise the fundamental alteration that has occurred in the system of English vowels, throwing the system out of harmony with the representations that these same written vowels have in the continental languages.

Phonology: The English Vowel Shift

In the Mandeville travel passage, certain words are easily recognized by their similar spellings to Modern English. In particular, the words *gret, hete, schame*, and *foul* are similar or identical to their modern counterparts. The written similarity, however, disguises the fact that the words as *pronounced* in Chaucer's time are not likely to be recognizable to a modern listener. Sometime in the two centuries between 1450 and 1650, all the long vowels of Middle English underwent a systematic shift. Each long front vowel was raised and became pronounced like another vowel higher in the system. The same thing occurred with back vowels: each long vowel was systematically raised to be pronounced like the vowel next higher in the vowel chart. Thus /ɔ̄/ came to be pronounced /ō/, /ē/ came to be pronounced /ī/, and so on. The two highest long vowels, high front /ī/ and high back /ū/, could not be raised any farther and instead were diphthongized to /ay/ and /aw/ respectively. Thus Middle English *I* /ī/ became /ay/, *hous* /hūs/ became /haws/'house,' and so on. We can represent the situation as in Figure 14-6.

Morphology

Verbs   Of the hundreds of irregular (strong) verbs in Old English, fewer than half survive in Modern English. Of those that do, many came to be

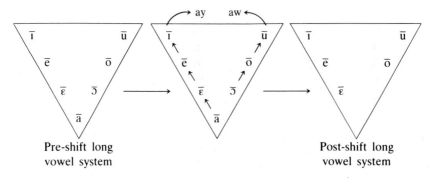

Pre-shift long
vowel system

Post-shift long
vowel system

FIGURE 14-6
The English Vowel Shift

SOURCE: Adapted from Theodora Bynon, *Historical Linguistics* (Cambridge: Cambridge University Press, 1977), p. 82.

inflected like the regular verbs, with an alveolar stop suffix rather than the vowel gradation characteristic of irregular verbs. One tally suggests that of the 333 irregular verbs of Old English, only 68 continue as irregular verbs in Modern English. Among those that have become regular over the centuries are *burn, brew, climb, flow, help,* and *walk.* Slightly more than a dozen verbs have become irregular in the history of English, including *dive,* which has recently developed a past tense form *dove* alongside the historical form *dived.* Most of us have also heard *drug* for *dragged,* as its use seems to be on the rise as well. Among other verbs that are now irregular but were formerly regular are *wear, spit,* and *dig.*

Definite Article   The initial consonant of *sē* and *sēo,* the Old English masculine and feminine nominative singular demonstratives, differed from all other forms, which began with [θ] (orthographic *þ*). *Sē* was apparently reshaped by analogy with forms having initial [θ]. By Middle English, *þe* had become the invariant definite article in the north, and its use soon spread to all dialects. Chaucer uses only *the,* pronounced [θə]. The voicing of the initial consonant as we have it today occurred because the customary lack of stress on *the* encouraged assimilation to the vowel nucleus, which of course is voiced. Such a history is somewhat surprising for what is by far the most commonly used word in Modern English.

Indefinite Article   The history of the indefinite article *a/an* is also remarkable, for while Old English did not use an indefinite article, today *a/an* is the fifth most common word in written American English.

Personal Pronouns   Though the personal pronouns retain more of their Old English diversity than any other part of speech, our earlier comparison of Old and Modern English pronouns (Table 14-4) indicates that the dual was lost entirely (starting even at the beginning of the Middle English period). During the early Modern English period, the distinction between the second person singular and plural forms—between *thou* and *thee* singular and *ye* and *you* plural—disintegrated.

Under the apparent influence of French, speakers of English began using the plural forms *ye, your*, and *you* as a sign of respect or formality, much as happens with the French pronoun *vous*, which is grammatically plural but is used to show respect and deference in addressing strangers, elders, and "betters." Among the higher social classes in England, the historical plural form *you* came to be used as a mutual sign of respect even in informal conversation between equals. In time, the singular forms all but disappeared, as did the distinction in the plural between the subject and object forms *ye* and *you*. Thus, from the six-fold distinction found in Old English and much of Middle English, Modern English has only a two-fold distinction—between *you* and *yours*.

The loss of a singular/plural distinction for *you* is a kind of accident of history, and Modern English speakers seem to find it difficult to get along without a distinctive second person plural pronoun. In fact, certain varieties of Modern English have created distinct plural forms, although these are regionally marked (*y'all* in the American South) or socially stigmatized (*yous* [yuz] or [yɪz] in New York City and *y'uns* in western Pennsylvania and the Ohio valley). Standard varieties of English have no way to mark the second person pronoun for plurality, though of course one can say such things as *you two* or *you should all think*.

Syntax

Deprived of the richness of its earlier inflectional signposts to meaning, Modern English has become an analytical language, more like Chinese than like Latin and the other early daughters of Proto-Indo-European. With nouns inflected only for the possessive case (and for number, of course), word order is now the chief signal of grammatical relations, displacing the earlier inflectional morphology. Even the fuller pronominal inflections are subordinate to the grammatical relations signaled by word order, so that *Him and me saw her at the party*, though not standard, is nevertheless not confusing in any way as to subject and object.

Why English should have advanced further than its Germanic cousins along the path to becoming an analytical language (rather than remaining an inflected language) is not clear. Possible explanations may be found in the thoroughgoing contact between the Danes and the English after the ninth century, in the French ascendance over English for numerous secular and religious purposes in the early Middle English period, and in the preservation of the vernacular chiefly in folk speech and therefore without the conservationist brake of writing for several generations in the eleventh and twelfth centuries. The influence of the Danes is particularly important: when they invaded England in the seventh and eighth centuries, the Danes spoke varieties of Germanic that must have been quite similar to the dialects spoken in England but with different inflections. It is easy to imagine that children exposed to parents using different inflectional suffixes and to friends whose inflectional suffixes were not uniform might readily look for other means to signal the differences formerly indicated by inflections.

In any case, decades before the Norman Conquest, those inflectional reductions started that became apparent when English reemerged; doubtless they had advanced further in speech than the written texts of the day indicate. Thus phonological reductions undermined the inflectional morphology, and, as inflection grew less able to signal grammatical relations and semantic roles, word order and the deployment of prepositions came to bear those communicative tasks less redundantly. Gradually, the freer word order of Old English yielded to the relatively fixed order of Modern English, whose linear arrangements are the chief carrier of grammatical functions.

Spurred by an almost total absence of inflections on nouns, Modern English syntax has evolved to permit unusually free interplay among grammatical relations and semantic roles. With nouns marked only for possessive case, and pronouns additionally for objective case, Modern English exercises minimal inflectional constraint on subject noun phrases, which are consequently free to represent an exceptionally wide range of semantic roles (as illustrated in Chapter 6, p. 203).

Lexicon

As in the course of the Middle English period, when English supplanted French and borrowed thousands of French words, so in the course of early Modern English, as English came to be used where Latin had previously been used, a great many words were borrowed from Latin (and through Latin from Greek). The words borrowed from Latin are not common words like the courtroom terminology from French but are instead learned words, reflecting the arenas in which Latin had been used. Even with these borrowings, English found itself in need of a great many more words as it spread from principally literary and personal uses into every sphere of activity. The *Oxford English Dictionary* records words from about fifty different languages borrowed into English during the first century and a half of Modern English (1500–1650), the period during which the vernacular came to replace Latin in nearly every learned arena.

Among the words that can be cited as Latin borrowings of this early Modern English period are the following: *allurement, allusion, anachronism, antipathy, antithesis, appendix, atmosphere, autograph*, and *axis* among the nouns (to stick to those beginning with *a*); *abject, agile*, and *appropriate* among the adjectives; and *adapt, alienate*, and *assassinate* among the verbs. Some of these words, though introduced to English from Latin, came originally from Greek. During the Renaissance, words were borrowed directly from Greek as well; these include *acme, anonymous, catastrophe, criterion* (and its plural, *criteria*), *idiosyncrasy, lexicon, ostracize, polemic, tantalize*, and *tonic*. Not everyone appreciated borrowed words, and many writers who used these then-strange terms were criticized for their "inkhorn" words. And not every borrowed term was equally successful; many failed to survive.

SUMMARY

English belongs to the West Germanic group of the Germanic branch of the Indo-European family. Among the major languages, its closest relatives are German and Dutch. In the course of its history, English has been greatly enriched by thousands of words borrowed from more than a hundred languages—most notably from French, as the descendants of the Norman invaders started using English in the thirteenth century, and from Latin, during the Renaissance, as the vernacular came to be used in arenas previously reserved for the classical language.

Beowulf is an epic poem of the Old English period (700–1100). Chaucer wrote during the Middle English period (1100–1500), Shakespeare early in the Modern English period (1500–present). While Old English was a highly inflected language, certain sound changes left little inflectional morphology in Middle English. Modern English is thus an analytical language, relying principally on word order to express grammatical relations that were formerly marked inflectionally.

EXERCISES

1. Modern English words that were borrowed from Latin or Greek do not show the influence of Grimm's Law (which affected only the Germanic branch of Indo-European). For many such borrowed words, English also has a related word that has been directly inherited from Indo-European through Germanic. Any such inherited word that contained an affected consonant did undergo the consonant shifts described by Grimm. For each borrowed word given below, cite an English word that is related in meaning and whose pronunciation shows the result of the consonant shift. For this exercise, focus only on the initial consonant of each word. For example, given *pedal*, you would seek a word like *foot* that has a related meaning and begins with [f] (because Indo-European [p] became [f] in Germanic).

cardiac	dual	capital	cordial
paternal	pentagon	piscatorial	canine
plenitude	dentist	triangle	decade

2. This exercise is like the preceding one, except that here we provide English words that have undergone the Germanic consonant shift and ask you to provide another English word that is likely to have been borrowed because it has a closely related meaning and does not show the results of Grimm's Law. Bear in mind that most Latin and Greek borrowings tend to be more learned and technical than the related ones inherited directly from Indo-European. Focus only on the underlined consonant. For example, given *foot*, you would cite a word that begins with *p* such as *podiatrist* 'foot doctor.'

tooth	ten	lip
hound	fire	eat

3. You know that, by the effects of Grimm's Law, Indo-European *[bʰ] became [b], and Indo-European *[gʰ] became [g] in Germanic. Latin, not being a Germanic language, did not undergo these consonant shifts. Instead, Indo-European *[bʰ] became [f] in Latin, and Indo-European *[gʰ] became [h] in Latin. We can

represent these facts in the following correspondences:

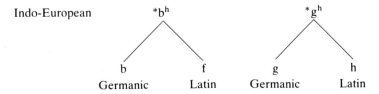

With this information, you may be able to provide an English word inherited directly from Indo-European for each of the following words, which are all borrowed from Latin. Focus on the initial consonant, and bear in mind that other changes may have affected the remainder of the word so that the resemblance is distant.

fraternity	fundamental
fragile	flare
hospitable	fracture

4. Indicate which allophone of /f/, /θ/, or /s/ was pronounced in each of the following Old English words (use the description of the allophonic distribution given on p. 464 to help you determine the correct answer): *þæt, sēo, his, ūs, wæs, æðeling* 'prince,' *frēosan* 'freeze,' *dēmst* 'judge,' *līfes* 'of life,' *þā* 'then,' *drīfan* 'drive,' *wulfas* 'wolves,' *hræfn* 'raven,' *bosm* 'bosom,' *seofon* 'seven,' *bæþ* 'bath,' *sceaft* 'shaft.'

5. (a) Identify the grammatical gender of the following Old English nouns, and then write out the full declension (all cases, singular and plural) for each of the noun phrases in which they appear; use the paradigms given in this chapter as models.

   sē stān 'the stone'
   ðæt word 'the word'
   sēo wund 'the wound'

   (b) For each of these Old English noun phrases, provide the Old English pronoun that would be used in the space given.

Sē stān, _____ is gōd.	'The stone, it is good.'
Ðæt word, _____ is gōd.	'The word, it is good.'
Sēo wund, _____ nis gōd.	'The wound, it isn't good.'

6. Compare the Old English passage on p. 473 with the Middle English passage on p. 480 and identify ways in which Middle English differs from Old English in orthography, lexicon, morphology, and word order. Provide an example from the passages to illustrate each point.

7. You have seen several words in this chapter whose meaning has changed from Old English to Modern English. One example is the word *dēor*, which meant 'animal' in Old English but has narrowed its meaning to 'deer' in Modern English. Among several other ways, words can change their meaning by becoming more specialized, as with *deer*, or becoming more generalized. Examine the Old English words and meanings that follow and note what each word has become in Modern English. State whether the word's meaning has become more specialized or more

generalized in the course of its development from Old English into Modern English.

Old English	Modern English
steorfan 'die'	starve
berēafian 'deprive of'	bereave
hlāf 'bread'	loaf
spēdan 'prosper'	speed
spellian 'speak'	spell
hund 'dog'	hound
mete 'food'	meat
wīf 'woman'	wife
dōm 'judgment'	doom
sellan 'give'	sell
tīd 'time'	tide

8. Nearly all of the words listed below were borrowed into English from other languages. Keeping in mind the character of the words and what they signify, make an educated guess as to the likely source language for each word and the approximate date of borrowing. Then, for each word, look up its origin in a good dictionary, noting for borrowed words the actual source language and the date of borrowing. For which words has no source been identified? (While the source language will be identified in most good dictionaries, the date of borrowing may not be. *Webster's Ninth New Collegiate Dictionary* does supply dates. It may be useful for different students or student groups to tackle different columns of words and then to compare their findings.)

barf	kerchief	denim	mutton
zilch	teriyaki	algebra	klutz
duffel	catsup	alarm	glitch
mai tai	hunk	a la mode	schlock
hummus	honcho	nosh	kvetch
tortilla	macho	ginger	glasnost
tandoori	moped	giraffe	kayak
ginseng	jeans	ciao	shtick
kibble	disco	karate	moussaka
bummer	dude	kimono	whiskey
dinosaur	sphere	kung fu	karma
leviathan	taffy	paparazzi	caucus
tae kwon do	dim sum	taffeta	caddy
piña colada	cadaver	falafel	goober

SUGGESTIONS FOR FURTHER READING

There are several excellent general histories of the English language. Baugh and Cable (1978)—from which our examples of French borrowings in Middle English, Latin and Greek borrowings of early Modern English, and regular and irregular verbs are taken—is superb on the external history of the language. Pyles and Algeo (1982), from which we have borrowed a few other examples, is balanced between internal and external history and complements Baugh and Cable by being stronger on the internal history. Bolton (1982) is also very good. All three include references to the more specialized books treating each period. Algeo (1982) is a workbook in the history of English. A useful and easy-to-use Old English reference grammar is Quirk and Wrenn ([1957]), from which several of our examples are taken. Especially valuable for Old English syntax and reliable as a pedagogical grammar is Mitchell and Robinson (1986). For Middle English, Mossé (1952), with grammar and texts, is useful. Good selections of texts, some with detailed apparatus, can be found in Fisher and Bornstein (1974) and Rigg (1968). Kaiser (1961) prints a large, carefully edited collection with minimal apparatus. For the early Modern English period, Barber (1976) is good on language structure, on attitudes toward borrowing and correctness, and on semantic change in the lexicon. Traugott (1972) has a helpful discussion of historical English syntax.

Background information about Indo-European is conveniently found in Philip Baldi's chapter, "Indo-European Languages," in Comrie (1987) and information about Germanic in the chapter "Germanic Languages" by John A. Hawkins in the same volume. Two excellent books about life in Anglo-Saxon Britain are Campbell et al. (1982) and Wood (1986), which have photographs of artifacts, ruins, and manuscripts; Wood's book was made to accompany a BBC television series. Evans (1986), also lavishly illustrated, describes the treasures evacuated at the site of a burial ship for a seventh-century king of one of the Anglo-Saxon kingdoms. Also useful and very readable is Laing (1982), with a bias toward the archaeological.

There are excellent recordings of English from various periods. EAV Lexington has released *A Thousand Years of English Pronunciation*, a selection of readings by Helge Kökeritz from Old, Middle, and early Modern English texts, and *Beowulf/Chaucer*, with *Beowulf* read by John C. Pope and Chaucer by Kökeritz. On the Spoken Arts label is *Beowulf*, read in Old English by Norman Davis and Nevill Coghill. Yale University Press has released a recording (manufactured by Columbia Records) with Helge Kökeritz reciting selections from Shakespeare. Finally, the National Council of Teachers of English has issued a three-record set called *The Sounds of Chaucer's English*, with a study pamphlet and script, and now available on audiocassettes. Linn and Zuber (1984) is a handy bibliography of language recordings.

REFERENCES

Algeo, John. 1982. *Problems in the Origins and Development of the English Language*, 3rd ed. (New York: Harcourt Brace Jovanovich).

Barber, Charles. 1976. *Early Modern English* (London: Andre Deutsch).

Baugh, Albert C., and Thomas Cable. 1978. *A History of the English Language*, 3rd ed. (Englewood Cliffs, N.J.: Prentice-Hall).

Bolton, W. F. 1982. *A Living Language: The History and Structure of English* (New York: Random House).

Campbell, James, Eric John, and Patrick Wormald. 1982. *The Anglo-Saxons* (Oxford: Phaidon).

Comrie, Bernard. 1987. *The World's Major Languages* (New York: Oxford University Press).

Evans, Angela Care. 1986. *The Sutton Hoo Ship Burial* (London: British Museum Publications).

Fisher, John H., and Diane Bornstein. 1974. *In Forme of Speche Is Chaunge* (Englewood Cliffs, N.J.: Prentice-Hall).

Kaiser, Rolf. 1961. *Medieval English: An Old English and Middle English Anthology* (West Berlin: Rolf Kaiser).

Laing, Lloyd and Jennifer. 1982. *Anglo-Saxon England* (London: Paladin).

Linn, Michael D., and Maarit-Hannele Zuber. 1984. *The Sound of English* (Urbana, Ill.: National Council of Teachers of English).

Mitchell, Bruce, and Fred C. Robinson. 1986. *A Guide to Old English: Revised with Prose and Verse Texts and Glossary* (New York: Basil Blackwell).

Mossé, Fernand. 1952. *A Handbook of Middle English*, translated by J. A. Walker (Baltimore: The Johns Hopkins Press).

Pyles, Thomas, and John Algeo. 1982. *The Origins and Development of the English Language*, 3rd ed. (New York: Harcourt Brace Jovanovich).

Quirk, Randolph, and C. L. Wrenn. [1957]. *An Old English Grammar* (New York: Holt, Rinehart and Winston).

Rigg, A. G. 1968. *The English Language: A Historical Reader* (New York: Appleton-Century-Crofts).

Traugott, Elizabeth Closs. 1972. *A History of English Syntax* (New York: Holt, Rinehart and Winston).

Wood, Michael. 1986. *Domesday: A Search for the Roots of England* (London: BBC Books).

LANGUAGE STANDARDS AND LANGUAGE ATTITUDES

15

INTRODUCTION

Views of the Origin of Language

A good many people in all parts of the world share a belief that the origin of language can be traced to the Garden of Eden, where the first woman and the first man spoke the original language given to them by their creator. Even among people who do not give credence to this particular story, many seem to believe that language had its origins in a paradise where its pristine form was perfectly "logical" and perfectly "grammatical." The belief is widespread that language, once pure, has in the course of history become progressively contaminated with assorted illogicalities, ungrammaticalities, and impurities.

As examples of impurities, subscribers to this view might cite such borrowed words as American *okay* and French *disco*, which have spread into many other languages. Putative illogicalities come in many shapes; double negatives are one commonly cited English example. The claim is that as two negatives yield a positive in algebra or logic (*it is not untrue* means 'it is true'), so *I don't like no one* should logically mean 'I do like someone' and *He never took none* should mean 'He took some'—which of course they don't. Alleged ungrammaticalities also come in many shapes. A commonly cited one is the use of the personal pronoun *I* in a grammatical relation other than subject, as in *just between you and I.*

Views of Language Diversity: From Babel to Babble

As to why languages differ from one another and why they change, people have different ways of explaining the facts. The Old Testament relates that before the Tower of Babel everyone spoke the same language and could understand one another without difficulty; human haughtiness eventually provoked God into punishing the people by confounding their language. Language differences among people are thus seen as a penalty for sinful behavior. Similarly, Moslems believe that God spoke to Mohammed in a form of Arabic that was by definition pure and perfect. The Koran is taken as exemplar of the purest and most grammatically perfect Arabic, while the many varieties of present-day Arabic are perceived as having arisen through the subsequent weakness and culpability of their speakers.

Professional linguists take a different approach. They see the multiplicity of languages as the product of natural historical change, the inevitable result of people bending their language to meet changing needs. As groups of people move to different places on the globe, mixing with people who speak different tongues or settling previously uninhabited areas, their language adapts to new circumstances. Meeting people with new artifacts and different views of the world and confronting unfamiliar aspects of nature invite accommodation and linguistic adaptation. As a result, individual languages have evolved quite differently around the globe—though always within the constraints imposed by the brain's ability to acquire only certain kinds of structures.

As we saw in Chapters 12 and 13, there is marked variation not only from language to language but also within a single language. Different social groups speak different varieties, and every social group controls a repertoire of registers for use in diverse speech situations. Whatever the ultimate explanation of the origins of language and whatever one's faith, it is a simple fact that language is *inherently* variable. Given the social nature of human beings, there is a powerful bias toward language variation and language diversification: language varieties mark groups of *users* and situations of *use*. Every language variety is an integral part of the social identity of its speakers and of the uses to which they put their language.

From the point of view of the discipline of linguistics, there is no basis for preferring the structure of one language variety over another. Judgments like "illogical" and "impure" are notions imported from outside the realm of language; they represent attitudes to language varieties or to particular forms of expression within particular language varieties. As to the notion of "ungrammatical," we have used it throughout this book, starring ungrammatical and unacceptable utterances. However, if speakers of English started saying *He never took none*, then linguists would say not that they were speaking ungrammatically but that the grammar of English was changing.

THE STATUS OF LANGUAGE VARIETIES

As we look around the world, it is easy to see that language varieties carry different statuses. There are national and regional language varieties, official language varieties, standard language varieties, and assorted dialect and register varieties. German, Japanese, and Somali are national languages, each associated with one or more countries. Some languages occur in various national varieties, as with Canadian French, Mexican Spanish, Lebanese Arabic, and American English. Other language varieties serve as regional languages; witness Breton in France, Catalan in Spain, and Basque in the Pyrenees between France and Spain. Then, too, some varieties are regarded not as autonomous languages but as dialects or registers: Black English and Chicano English exemplify dialects with ethnic affiliations, and "Brooklynese" is a regional dialect. Legalese and motherese are registers that occur in quite a few languages.

Languages as International Vehicles of Communication

As mentioned earlier, perhaps as many as five thousand distinct languages exist in the world. In light of this global diversity, it is sobering to examine language use at the most prominent of world bodies. At the United Nations, only Arabic, Chinese, English, French, Russian, and Spanish are used for official communication, and communication in any of these languages is translated into the other five. We want to underscore three points about the situation at the UN. First, no single language is adequate to the tasks of this august body. Second, only six languages out of five thousand have the privilege of official status. Third, what is meant by Arabic, Chinese, English, French, Russian, and Spanish differs, reflecting different situations.

This third point requires some elaboration. The "Arabic" used at the UN is Modern Standard Arabic, a variety that is not spoken in casual conversation in any Arabic-speaking country. It is a learned language used for international communication and for certain limited functions in the Arab world. "Chinese" is Mandarin Chinese, the dialect of Beijing, now standardized for use as a *lingua franca* by all Chinese people. "English" has many national varieties, all of which are acceptable in spoken communication at the UN. "Spanish" is also spoken at the UN in many national varieties. "French" is the standard European French, and "Russian" is the Moscow standard variety.

As a result of UN policy and practice, representatives of countries with official and unofficial languages other than the six must use an additional language at least at the UN. Which languages best serve a country's international needs depends on such factors as historical accident, political alliances, and patterns of trade and commerce. Given its historical connection with France, Algeria uses French (in addition to Arabic). Given its close trade ties to the United States, Japan uses English.

The six languages designated for use at the United Nations were selected partly because of their historical importance and partly for demographic reasons. They do not possess any linguistic superiority over the other languages of the world (except that their lexicons have developed words for the issues that are addressed at the UN, whereas many other languages may not have had occasion to do so). Like so much else about language choice and language use, the factors governing the selection of official UN languages are a matter of social and political organization, of practicality, and of history. They reflect nothing of the inherent properties of these tongues.

Official and National Languages

Official Languages   An official language is one that is so designated in some institutional setting (such as the World Court or the United Nations) or some political jurisdiction—a nation, state, or province. Official languages are established by law for use in certain activities such as voting, legislation, record keeping, transportation, and education.

In more than two dozen countries other than those we think of as English-speaking, English is the sole official language. This is the case in Ghana, Liberia, Nigeria, Uganda, and Zimbabwe in Africa; in Jamaica, the Bahamas, Dominica, and Barbados in the Caribbean; and in Vanuatu, Fiji, and the Solomon Islands in the Pacific. English shares official status with some other language in a score of nations including Canada (with French), Tanzania (with Swahili), Cameroon (with French), South Africa (with Afrikaans), Singapore (with Chinese, Malay, and Tamil), the Philippines (with Pilipino, the official name for Tagalog), Western Samoa (with Samoan), Kiribati (with Gilbertese), Pakistan (with Urdu), and India (with Hindi). In some countries, English holds no official status only because its widespread use in trade and government is taken for granted. Besides the United Kingdom and the United States themselves, the two Pacific island nations of Tonga and Tuvalu exemplify this situation.

Though the United States does not have an official language, certain jurisdictions do. Spanish and English are official languages of the city of Miami, Florida, an accommodation to the large number of Cuban immigrants living there. In California, English is the official language. (By a 1986 referendum, the state legislature is prohibited from making any law that "diminishes or ignores the role of English as the common language of the State of California.") French was formerly an official language in certain jurisdictions of Louisiana.

National Languages   Besides official languages, there are national languages in which the news media and other institutions operate. English in England, French in France, and Japanese in Japan may be taken as exemplars of languages that are so intimately tied to their countries that no official designation is needed. (Of course, France also has speakers of Breton, Provençal, and Alsatian, while Japan has speakers of Ainu and Okinawan.)

In some countries, a variety that no one speaks natively is used for public affairs. In the Middle East and North Africa, each region has its own variety of Arabic that native speakers acquire as a first language. Varieties such as

Algerian Arabic, Egyptian Arabic, Kuwaiti Arabic, Lebanese Arabic, and Moroccan Arabic are not completely intelligible across national boundaries. For international communication, Modern Standard Arabic is used. The descendant of Classical Arabic, Modern Standard Arabic is not spoken as a mother tongue by any identifiable group. Unlike Spanish, French, Japanese, Chinese, and Persian—in which particular regional varieties have been standardized—Modern Standard Arabic must be studied essentially as a foreign language by all Arabic speakers. Given its status as a learned language, this variety is limited in its use to specific tasks. It is used in public affairs: for lectures (except sometimes for introductory and concluding remarks) and public announcements; on radio and television; in newspapers, magazines, and books. It is not used for conversation among nationals of a single country.

Regional and Minority Languages

In many countries, different languages serve different regional needs. For example, Welsh, Irish Gaelic, and Scots Gaelic are spoken in different parts of the United Kingdom. In France, Breton is spoken in Brittany; in Spain, Catalan is spoken in Catalonia. In the United States, Spanish is widespread throughout the Southwest, French in Louisiana and parts of New England. In India, dozens of regional languages compete for attention, including Bengali and Tamil, each spoken by tens of millions of people.

Regional and minority languages are often perceived as divisive or even threatening to national unity. In Iran, when the Shah was in power, regional languages were suppressed as part of a nationalist campaign to unify diverse regional political interests. At one point, newspapers with circulations of fewer than two thousand could be published only in Persian. In Spain, Catalan, the native language of many students and teachers, was excluded from school instruction for several decades because it carried political connotations of regional autonomy that the Franco government disfavored. In France, a seventeenth-century edict still in effect decrees that all official documents be written in French. Thus regional languages and the languages of minority groups are sometimes strongly discouraged.

Languages of Limited Function

In many situations, a language variety is used that is different from the international, national, and regional languages. Latin was used until the 1960s in the liturgy of the Roman Catholic church throughout the world. Arabic serves a similar religious purpose even in the non-Arab Moslem world—in Iran and Nigeria, for example. In some countries there may be several religious languages: Latin or Armenian in the churches, Arabic in the mosques, Hebrew in the synagogues.

Pidgins (see Chapter 9) are another form of language used only in a limited set of circumstances. They would be as out of place in a home where everyone shared the native language variety as would Modern Standard Arabic in a casual conversation among family members.

Social Equality and Inequality in First Language Acquisition

The use of Modern Standard Arabic today is parallel to the use of Latin in the Middle Ages and Renaissance in that no group speaks it natively. Because this "high" variety is not a native language, no group starts life with a linguistic advantage over other groups. English plays the same role in India, where it is the nation's only politically neutral language.

The situation in the United States stands in marked contrast to these. American speakers of several regional varieties are born with an advantage over those who first acquire certain ethnic varieties such as Black English or Chicano English. The former are standardized and will serve in any spoken capacity; the latter are nonstandard varieties and are generally not permitted to function even as spoken languages in education or government. It goes without saying that written English is not "native" to anyone and must be learned; it is also a highly standardized variety.

STANDARD VARIETIES AND THE PROCESS OF STANDARDIZATION

Wherever a particular variety has official standing—as a national language, an official language, or a lingua franca used across language or dialect boundaries—that variety must be standardized to do its work adequately.

What Is a Standard Variety?

A *standard language variety* is a variety that has been designated as such and for which a set of forms has been identified and codified in dictionaries and grammars. It is a variety whose lexicon (including spelling and pronunciation), morphology, syntax, and usage have been settled (relatively speaking) and written down. Simply put, a standard language variety is one that has undergone the lengthy process of being standardized.

There are several aspects to the process of standardization:

(a)   selection of a norm

(b)   elaboration for use in different functions

(c)   restriction or elimination of diversity

(d)   codification in grammars and dictionaries

Selection   Selection of a norm generally involves the choice of a particular variety as a basis for the standard. In many cases it is a regional variety, often the dialect of the capital city. Thus Mandarin Chinese (spoken in Beijing), Parisian French, Tehran Persian, and the English spoken in and around London when Modern English was first standardized became the bases for standardization in those languages. In cases where a single regional variety cannot be selected because of political or social reasons, a blend of two or more varieties is often created. In standardizing Somali, for example, forms were carefully selected to represent both the northern and southern parts of Somalia.

Elaboration *Elaboration* has mostly to do with vocabulary; standardizers must ensure that words exist and are consistently used, especially in technical arenas such as science, health care, and equipment maintenance. There can also be elaboration (or refinement) of the writing system and occasionally of the morphology. Deliberate elaboration of syntax is rarely successful, though syntactic elaboration occurs spontaneously in the process of creolization and language change (see Chapters 9 and 14).

Restriction and Codification The *codification* of the selected norm in dictionaries and grammars is an essential step in the process of standardization, one that often involves *restriction* or elimination of certain options of expression in favor of others. Particular events can often be identified with steps along the way to codification. For English, the introduction of printing into England by Caxton in 1476 and the publication of the first great dictionary by Samuel Johnson in 1755 are notable events in the history of standardization. Noah Webster's mammoth *American Dictionary of the English Language* (1828) is a milestone in the process of standardizing American English.

From the fact that standardization is a process, it follows that any standard variety can be more or less standardized at a particular time. English, Arabic, and French are highly standardized languages with centuries-long traditions of codification and a high degree of uniformity (especially in writing). Portuguese and Persian are less standardized, Somali still less. Tuvaluan and Tongan are in the early stages of standardization. Black English and Chicano English are not standardized at all in this sense.

Who Sets Standards?

Although people commonly think the answer is obvious, it is nevertheless useful to ask who carries out the processes of standardization.

Official Standard Setters In some cases, officially appointed language guardians set the standards. France, Sweden, Italy, and Spain (among others) have language academies. The best known is the *Académie Française*, whose secretary stated in announcing a new dictionary in 1986: "I don't think there is another academy in the world that applies itself so thoroughly to guarding a language." In founding the French Academy in 1635, Cardinal Richelieu proclaimed that its principal function would be "to work with all possible care and diligence to give definite rules to our language and render it pure, eloquent and capable of dealing with arts and sciences."

The need for standard languages to be "capable of dealing with arts and sciences" is widespread. It is particularly important that terminology for technical subjects such as medicine and engineering be standardized. In most cases where languages are being standardized in developing countries today, the desire for "eloquence" is a secondary priority. The desire for "purity" varies greatly from one culture to another. The French Academy seems at times almost maniacal about foreign words contaminating the French language, and the French government imposes fines on institutions that use certain prohibited words. While English has never had an academy, its unofficial standardizers have over the centuries codified tens of thousands of borrowed words from scores of languages. As reflected in its borrowed word stock, English is probably the best-traveled language on the globe.

Many national governments appoint commissions to make recommendations concerning language standardization. Particularly in countries that lack a written standard or that have competing languages among different ethnic or tribal groups, such a body may be helpful in developing and implementing a sound, workable policy. The People's Republic of China is a recent example of a country that set up a board to modify its spelling system.

Unofficial Standard Setters Not all countries and not all languages have official standardizers of any sort. All of the standardization that English has achieved has occurred through private endeavor and the fortunate circumstances of history. Principal among the unofficial standard setters have been dictionary makers and influential printers, translators, and publishing houses. Lexicographic traditions in Britain and America reflect a centuries-long commitment to recording linguistic usage as it occurs on the lips and written pages of speakers. Certainly the great citation dictionaries such as *Webster's International* dictionaries, published by the Merriam-Webster Company, and the incomparable *Oxford English Dictionary* stand as exemplars of the descriptive tradition in lexicography.

Besides dictionary makers, other unofficial arbiters of the language include handbook writers. In contrast to the essentially descriptive approach of dictionary makers, handbook writers have been essentially prescriptive. Instead of describing current English usage as it exists in their chosen sources (books, newspapers, and magazines of reputable publishers), handbook writers have tended to provide litanies of supposed abuse and misuse of the language, with prescriptive standards that vary widely.

The most popular American handbook seems to be Strunk and White's *Elements of Style*, known simply as "Strunk and White." The book's chapter on "commonly misused" English describes certain current American expressions as "loosely used" or "annoying." One of its most frequent pieces of advice is "Avoid!" Typically, it finds *finalize* a "pompous, ambiguous verb," *meaningful* and *in the last analysis* "bankrupt," and *feature* and *factor* "hackneyed." Given the impressive sales record of this little book, "Strunk and White" is satisfying a hearty American appetite for uncomplicated and unambivalent advice—principally on what to *avoid* in English usage.

The best known and most respected handbook of usage in the English-speaking world is Fowler's *Dictionary of Modern English Usage*. Covering a great deal more territory than Strunk and White, Fowler is also far more sensitive to nuance and to the complexities of usage in different situations.

For many languages, especially those in the early stages of standardization, missionary groups can be influential. In selecting a variety and forms to be codified in preparation for translating the Bible, missionary groups can be decisive on the outcome of the process of standardization. By far the most ambitious group is the Summer Institute of Linguistics (SIL), which has produced grammars and dictionaries for many previously unstandardized languages. SIL's 207-page catalogue of publications lists languages from Abau (spoken in Papua New Guinea) to Zuque Copainala (spoken in Mexico). Under the letter A alone, three dozen languages are listed for which SIL has produced grammars, dictionaries, or readers. Such codification is extremely influential in establishing and propagating standards.

One final group of unofficial standard setters, especially in English, is the "pop grammarians": men (mostly) such as Edwin Newman, John Ciardi, John Simon, Jim Quinn, and William Safire who set up shop to comment about the state of the language (and who generally think it is sliding downhill). Their forums include radio and television shows, newspaper and magazine columns, and books. They cover the spectrum in terms of what they deem acceptable and of how they determine "correct English." At the conservative extreme, the comments of Newman and Simon are nothing if not definitive. Newman cites hundreds of "wrong" and "impossible" usages found in the nation's best newspapers and periodicals. A typical Newman comment: "'Different *than*,' rather than different *from*, is wrong. So is 'augur for.' *Augur* does not take *for* after it. It cannot take *for* after it"—the pages of his favorite newspapers and magazines to the contrary notwithstanding. Simon, having learned English as his fifth language, is perhaps understandably rigid about how the language should be used. He is downright reactionary at times. On the basis of our language use, Simon says that "most people—92 percent perhaps—are not intelligent enough to be human beings." More or less descriptive rather than prescriptive are John Ciardi and especially William Safire. Safire's popular books and weekly columns in the *New York Times Magazine* contain sensible observations about a language continuously in flux. Jim Quinn is at the liberal end of the spectrum, drawing particularly on historical precedent to justify usages under attack by other language guardians.

Description and Prescription: A Case History

Dictionaries are far and away the principal reference work in codifying information about language—about phonology, morphology, syntax, and semantics as well as spelling. As such, they are powerful regulators of linguistic behavior, at least in writing, where behavior can be planned and monitored. Even in the English-speaking world, which lacks both academy and official word book, virtually everyone speaks of looking up words in *the* dictionary. "*The* dictionary" has a place of prominence in English-speaking homes that is rivaled only by the Bible and the telephone directory. Thus dictionaries influence, guide, and regulate language choices. But who regulates dictionaries? Where does their authority derive from?

In 1961, after the last big "Webster's" was published, an intellectual and scholarly battle raged throughout much of the English-speaking world. *Webster's Third New International Dictionary* was the latest edition of the mammoth word book first published by Noah Webster himself more than a century earlier. The 1961 edition—called the *Third*—outraged many observers by what they perceived to be its policy of permissiveness. The lexicographers who compiled the dictionary correctly believed they were following a long and revered tradition of recording actual usage as it occurs in reputable speech and writing. Usage was their only authority. The dictionary's prescriptive detractors lambasted its policies and practices so savagely that its supporters were moved to call the critics' views medieval, ignorant, authoritarian, crippling, enslaving, sadistic, masochistic, and superstitious—all comments made in published discussions about a dictionary!

Among the English speakers offended by the *Third* were the members of another publishing firm. Despite having no prior experience in dictionary making, the American Heritage Company was so distressed with the *Third* that it sought to buy out the Merriam-Webster Company and suppress its new word book: "We'd go back to the Second International and speed ahead on the Fourth," the president of American Heritage said at the time. American Heritage failed in its bid to buy Merriam-Webster, and the *Third* has remained in print for more than a quarter of a century now. Though not flawless, it and its supplements provide a magnificent source of authoritative information about how the English language was and is being used in the middle quarters of the twentieth century.

Frustrated in its determination to suppress the *Third*, American Heritage decided to launch a dictionary of its own. Obviously motivated by both ideological and commercial interests, the publisher sought to "add the essential dimension of guidance ... toward grace and precision which intelligent people seek in a dictionary." When *The American Heritage Dictionary* (*AHD*) appeared in 1969, it reflected its publisher's "deep sense of responsibility as custodians of the American tradition in language as well as history." The "custodial" view announced by American Heritage represents an approach to dictionary making akin to the French Academy's. The custodial or prescriptive view has limited respect for what even reputable writers do; instead it places a premium on what such writers and others (including the prescriptivists themselves) say *ought* to be done.

The opposing view is descriptive and has characterized the best English-language dictionaries for more than two hundred years. In following this descriptive tradition, Merriam-Webster had its staff reading widely and listening to speakers in order to discover what usages to codify in the dictionary. Its readers and listeners recorded ten million examples of current usage exactly as they heard and read them. What they found is recorded in the nearly twenty-seven-hundred pages of the *Third* and in its abridged spin-offs, including the most recent, *Webster's Ninth New Collegiate Dictionary*.

The American Heritage approach was quite different. In a remarkable departure from lexicographical tradition, American Heritage empaneled a jury of arbiters whose opinions about the good, the bad, and the indifferent in English usage were tallied and reported in the dictionary. These opinions about such items as *ain't, hopefully*, and *rather unique* are incorporated into usage notes appended to some two hundred entries.

On the word *unique* and on modifying (or qualifying) it—as in phrases like *so, very, rather*, and *most unique*—*AHD*'s entry states:

> u•nique (y͞o͞o-nēk′) *adj.* **1.** Being the only one of its kind; solitary; sole: *"Man's language is unique in consisting of words"* (Julian Huxley). **2.** Being without an equal or equivalent; unparalleled: *"Your crisis is by no means unique"* (William Demby). —See Synonyms at **single.** [French, from Latin *ūnicus*, only, sole. See **oino-** in Appendix.*] —u•nique′ly *adv.* —u•nique′- ness *n.*
>
> *Usage: Unique*, in careful usage, is not preceded by adverbs that qualify it with respect to degree. Examples such as *rather unique*, with reference to a book, and *the most unique*, referring to the most unusual of a rare species of animals, are termed unacceptable by 94 per cent of the Usage Panel, on the ground that the quality described by *unique* cannot be said to vary in degree or intensity and is therefore not capable of comparison. The same objection is raised about examples in which *unique* is preceded by *more, somewhat*, and *very*. In such examples an appropriate substitute for *unique* can usually be found from among *unusual, remarkable, rare, exceptional*, or the like, which are weaker and can be qualified freely. However, *unique* can be modified by terms that do not imply degree in the sense noted: *almost* (or *nearly*) *unique; more* (or *most*) *nearly unique*.

What about the approach of a descriptive dictionary? The *Third*'s entry for *unique* lists three meanings: (1) 'sole'; (2) 'unequaled'; and (3) 'unusual' or 'notable.' The first two meanings, as you can see, are not capable of comparison: one cannot be more or less 'sole' and one cannot be more or less 'unequaled.' But in its third sense, something or someone can be more or less 'unusual' or 'notable,' and a few of the citations given in the *Third* illustrate this meaning and use: *the most unique characteristic of that environment* (from R. A. Billington), *the most unique theater in town* (from an advertisement), and (from playwright Arthur Miller) *She's the most unique person I ever met.* As far as the *Third*'s lexicographers could determine, *unique* had extended its meaning—much as other words have done in the course of their history. Now, besides meaning 'sole' and 'unequaled,' *unique* also means 'unusual' or 'notable.' So be it, the *Third*'s lexicographers must have thought; we record it as we record any other change in the language—as we find it.

It may be somewhat fairer to compare the *AHD* not with the *Third*—which is, after all, an unabridged dictionary triple the *AHD*'s size—but with *Webster's Seventh New Collegiate Dictionary*, the first Merriam-Webster abridged dictionary based on the *Third*. It is comparable to *AHD* in size, scope, and price, and in subsequent comparisons we will use it and its most recent successor (the *Ninth Collegiate*, published in 1983) as a basis of comparison with the *AHD*.

Like the larger *Third*, the *Seventh* has *no* discussion of the points in *AHD*'s usage note. It simply lets its entry for *unique* stand on its own merit, making no comment and raising no question about the status of *unique* with respect to comparison or qualification. The files on which all Merriam-Webster dictionaries are based must have shown plainly that in one of its senses *unique* was frequently compared or qualified and that *in this sense* English speakers (at least those on the American side of the Atlantic) perceived degrees of uniqueness and reflected this fact in their language. Like the *Third*, the *Seventh Collegiate* gives 'sole' and 'unequaled' as the first two senses of *unique* (and in these senses *unique* clearly cannot be compared). The *Seventh* also gives 'unusual' as a third meaning and refers readers to synonyms at *strange*. Plainly, in this third sense *unique* is capable of qualification and comparison, and the *Seventh* merely records what Merriam's lexicographers discovered in their reading and listening program. In addition to an unattributed source (*a very unique ball-point pen*), the *Seventh* cites author J. D. Salinger: *We were fairly unique, the sixty of us, in that there wasn't one good mixer in the bunch*.

By the time Merriam-Webster published the *Ninth Collegiate* in 1983, it had decided to incorporate usage notes into some of its entries in order to "provide the dictionary user with suitable guidance on the usage in question." Given the differences in the two companies' outlooks about language use, it is not surprising that American Heritage's and Merriam-Webster's usage notes are strikingly different. Here is the *Ninth Collegiate*'s entry for *unique*, including the usage note.

unique \yù-'nēk\ *adj* [F, fr. L *unicus*, fr. *unus* one — more at ONE] (1602)
1 : being the only one : SOLE ⟨his ~ concern was his own comfort⟩ ⟨I can't walk away with a ~ copy. Suppose I lost it? —Kingsley Amis⟩ ⟨the ~ factorization of a number into prime factors⟩ **2 a :** being without a like or equal : UNEQUALED ⟨could stare at the flames, each one new, violent, ~ —Robert Coover⟩ **b :** distinctively characteristic : PECULIAR 1 ⟨this is not a condition ~ to California —Ronald Reagan⟩ **3 :** UNUSUAL ⟨a very ~ ball-point pen⟩ ⟨we were fairly ~, the sixty of us, in that there wasn't one good mixer in the bunch —J.D. Salinger⟩ *syn* see STRANGE — **unique·ly** *adv* — **unique·ness** *n*
usage Many commentators have objected to the comparison or modification (as by *somewhat, almost,* or *very*) of *unique;* the statement that a thing is either unique or it is not has often been repeated by them. Objections are based chiefly on the assumption that *unique* has but a single absolute sense, an assumption contradicted by information readily available in a dictionary. *Unique* dates back to the 17th century but was little used until the end of the 18th when, according to the Oxford English Dictionary, it was reacquired from French. H.J. Todd entered it as a foreign word in his edition (1818) of Johnson's Dictionary, characterizing it as "affected and useless." Around the middle of the 19th century it ceased to be considered foreign and came into considerable popular use. With popular use came a broadening of application beyond the original two meanings (here numbered 1 and 2a). In modern use both comparison and modification are widespread and standard but are confined to the extended senses 2b and 3. When sense 1 or sense 2a is intended, *unique* is used without qualifying modifiers.

We can highlight the difference in the two approaches to lexicography by comparing the entries for *unique* in the *American Heritage Dictionary* and *Webster's Ninth New Collegiate Dictionary*. First, note that the *AHD* gives only the two senses 'sole' and 'unequaled.' The third sense—identified by Merriam-Webster as 'unusual'—represents an extension of the word's meaning (a change, if you will), which as a product of descriptive lexicography the *Ninth* records (with citations).

Second, note that the *AHD* reports the disapproving opinion of 94 percent of a panel of distinguished writers and others toward this particular extension of meaning, explaining that "the quality described by *unique* cannot be said to vary in degree or intensity and is therefore not capable of comparison." Insofar as the *AHD*'s main entry for *unique* recorded only senses that accord with this particular quality, the panel would of course be correct. But as the entry in the *Ninth* indicates, *unique* is being used in a new sense, whose quality (namely 'unusualness') can legitimately be said to vary in degree or intensity. What the American Heritage lexicographers found in their citations about the use of *unique* in this third sense must have been sufficient to have them turn to their usage panel for an opinion. This means that the sources they were checking to determine and illustrate the state of the language must have provided sufficient respectable examples (they would not have considered disreputable sources) to illustrate that the word *unique* was often compared or qualified—why else would they have gone to the panel? Perhaps some language custodian on the staff had noted the new usage, personally disliked it (or suspected others might), and decided to approach the panel. Then, having discovered that the panel disfavored this third sense of *unique*, American Heritage decided not to report it in the main entry. Instead, a usage note was provided to explain why the widespread usage of the word in its third sense was not reported in the main entry. This process exemplifies prescriptive lexicography.[1]

Prescriptive lexicography has what many regard quite rightly as the noble ambition to slow down change in the language—presumably for concern that too-rapid changes will undermine the very purpose of language to communicate. John Simon expresses this ambition directly when he says, "It is, or ought to be, possible to stop—or at least considerably delay—unnecessary change [in language]." As we saw in Chapters 9 and 14, however, language is incessantly changing. Lexicographers cannot impede change effectively.

What the Regulatory Agencies Prescribe and Proscribe

Language Choice   Throughout the world, various regulatory agencies—official and unofficial alike—often prescribe mere morphological, syntactic, and lexical uses. In some societies, however, entire languages are mandated or forbidden. Language planning groups thus determine which languages may be used and under what circumstances—for street signs, in newspapers, on radio and television broadcasts, in schools, for voting, and in court.

Orthography and Pronunciation   Regulatory agencies are sometimes charged with determining what writing system and orthography to use. Turkish changed from an Arabic script to a Roman script earlier in this century. Centuries ago, Tibetan and Vietnamese adopted new scripts to replace older ones. Hindi and Urdu—basically the same language—are

---

[1] In the second college edition of the *AHD*, published in 1982, only the same two senses of *unique* are listed in the main entry; the usage note reports that the "vast majority" of the usage panel finds unacceptable any qualification or degree of the "absolute" term *unique*.

written in two different scripts. Urdu, written in Arabic script, reflects the Islamic culture of Pakistan; Hindi, written in Devanāgarı script, reflects the Hindu culture of India.

Sometimes a revision is made in the way names and other words are represented. The Chinese government recently revised the way that Chinese words were to be spelled in Roman script. Thus *Peking* became *Beijing* and the city of Tsingtao became *Qingdao*.

As to pronunciation, there seems to be less concern about eliminating variation and more tolerance especially of regional pronunciations, in America and Britain as well as elsewhere. Still, pronunciation is often a major concern of official and unofficial standardizers. The BBC uses a handbook of Received Pronunciation (RP) especially for its on-air employees. Though it is spoken by only 3 to 5 percent of the English population, RP is a norm that carries a great deal of prestige. In the United States, despite broad tolerance for pronunciation differences, even newspapers take up the cudgel against changes in the speech of their readers. A 1984 *Los Angeles Times* editorial complained that one presidential candidate's pronunciation of *nuclear* as "NOO-kyoo-ler ... frankly grates on our ears." Politics aside, the *Times* editorial represents a typical attempt to eliminate variation in the standard variety.

Lexicon   Which words are permitted, and what definitions and uses shall they be permitted to have? English, exceptionally receptive to borrowings from other languages, boasts a distinctively cosmopolitan vocabulary (see Chapters 4 and 14). It has borrowed extensively from other Germanic tongues and from Latin and French; indeed, it has absorbed thousands of words from scores of other languages over the centuries. Recent borrowings reveal an extraordinary range of donor languages, more than seventy-five in number. French provides most items by far, followed by Japanese, Spanish, Italian, Latin, Greek, German, Yiddish, Russian, Chinese, Arabic, more than two dozen African languages, and more than three dozen other languages from all parts of the globe.

Not all languages are as open to borrowing as English is. The French Academy has bestowed watchdog status on an official *Commissariat*; in a recent guide to permissible new words, the Commissioner General of the French language points with gratitude to the work of various terminology commissions in getting the French to say *baladeur* now instead of *Walkman, disquette* instead of *floppy disk, ingénierie* instead of *engineering*. Despite a general antipathy for foreign words, the commission has accepted Japanese *kamikaze* and American *holdup*—but only because no French equivalents could be found. Of course, French speakers still commonly use English borrowings in conversation and some of their writing. Such common use of words outlawed by an official body illustrates the near impossibility of regulating language behavior by legislative fiat, especially in democratic societies.

Among the unofficial groups opposing certain words, the American guardians have waged a relentless campaign against *irregardless*, about which "No such word" is the most frequent (and most perplexing) comment. Another target is the suffix *-ize*, a derivational morpheme (see Chapter 4) that transforms nouns and adjectives into verbs. We have used this suffix several times throughout this book, sometimes over the objections of our editors: *standard/standardize; passive/passivize; relative/relativize*. The suffix has been around for a long time, originally coming into English from Greek. Many words incorporate it without having any stigma attached to them: *summarize, centralize*, and *energize* among them. But many others strike English speakers as unesthetic (at least); strong objections are voiced against *operationalize, criminalize* (and *decriminalize*), *privatize, prioritize, finalize*, and *containerize*. Needless to say, not all *-ize* words are elegant, not all are needed, and not all will survive. (*Highschoolize*, for example, had a justly brief life.) The point is that the suffix itself has an excellent pedigree (if that should matter to anyone), and it remains alive and functioning after centuries of fruitful exploitation in expanding the English word hoard.

Grammar What forms among competing forms will be given approval? To illustrate, we present some of the matters of concern to the unofficial language guardians in America, thereby indicating the kinds of grammatical questions that standardizing groups might be concerned with. As the principal focus of custodians is at the level of words, it is easiest to demonstrate grammatical concerns with them. The following two are typical: the use of the pronoun *I* in grammatical relations other than subject (*He gave one to Harry and I* or *just between you and I*) and the use of *lay* as an intransitive verb (*I laid down to take a nap* or *The dog is laying under the tree*). About *between you and I*, John Simon has written that "to avoid adding to the already raging chaos in English usage and communication, we must urgently stop *between you and I*. Otherwise it will lead us to every kind of deleterious misunderstanding."[2] *AHD*, though it did not consult its usage panel on this one, does discuss this increasingly common usage.

> The use of *I* in the objective case, typically as the second of a pair of pronouns linked by a copula (as in *between you and I*), is nonstandard, although it tends to occur frequently in speech; in the 17th century it was very common at every level of usage, including the most formal.

The *Third* also labels the usage "now chiefly substandard." Nevertheless, most of us hear this usage very widely, and we can expect dictionaries to acknowledge its use as the facts become unavoidable.

Does a Standard American English Exist?

In addressing the question of an American standard, a distinction must be drawn between writing and speech. While both written and spoken American English have been standardized, there are differences between them. There is no single monolithic standard variety of English for use in all situations.

[2] *Paradigms Lost* (New York: Penguin, 1981), p. 21.

Whereas RP (Received Pronunciation) is an acknowledged standard in England and has a name of its own, there is no single universally accepted spoken standard of pronunciation in the United States. Only network newscasters seem obliged to conform to a norm of pronunciation, showing an overwhelming preference for what has been called "network standard" (really an inland northern regional variety). On one evening news program, hints of a southern accent can be detected in the principal anchorman, but regional accents are most often heard in the speech of correspondents assigned to particular government agencies. There is also great tolerance for regional pronunciations among network weather and sports announcers. Thus there is a good deal of variation in standard American pronunciation.

The fact that several recent American presidents have spoken in marked regional accents underscores the acceptance of different pronunciations in the United States. From the South came Jimmy Carter with a distinct Georgia accent and Lyndon Johnson with a marked Texas accent. From New England came the distinct Boston pronunciation of John F. Kennedy, while Ronald Reagan and Gerald Ford speak what many regard as General American. It too is a regional accent, albeit the one commonly heard on the networks. In America, all regional pronunciations are acceptable, though certain patterns of pronunciation and certain accents may strike listeners as "folksy" or "quaint."

When Americans use a dictionary to look up pronunciations, they are most likely seeking guidance on such matters as where stress falls—which vowels are full and which are reduced to schwa. English-language dictionaries must be deliberately ambiguous in providing pronunciations. The codes provide key words as references for pronunciation; these key words, in turn, indicate not an absolute pronunciation but a class of words similarly pronounced within a regional dialect. People looking up the word *caught* will find that it has the vowel of *law*; but the vowel of *law* itself varies, so that no absolute standard is set by the dictionary's reference to another word. In contrast, looking up the word *odometer* to see whether it is, say, odo-meter [ˈodəmiDər] or o-dom-eter [oˈdaməDər] will yield a definitive answer that the second is standard. Looking up the word *nuclear*, one will find the alternatives [nukliər] and [nukyələr], sometimes with a notation indicating that the second pronunciation occurs in educated speech but is considered unacceptable by some people.

Acceptability of lexical, morphological, and syntactic choices is by no means as flexible as pronunciation variants—not in speech and especially not in writing. Whereas the pronunciation of various presidents can differ markedly, their written speeches would be virtually indistinguishable from one another—politics and style aside.

ATTITUDES TOWARD LANGUAGE VARIETIES

Chapter 12 described some of the ways in which the languages of different social groups differ from one another. Language features can come to be so closely associated with particular groups of users that the occurrence of certain features in someone's speech conjures up other characteristics of the group. To put it simply, features of a dialect come to be associated with the nonlinguistic characteristics of its speakers. If you think New Yorkers brusque, you will not be surprised when someone speaking like a New Yorker acts brusquely. Similarly, our stereotypes of British, French, Spanish, German, Chinese, and Korean people influence the way we perceive individual speakers of these languages. People tend to make judgments about other people's personality, intelligence, educational level, and even qualities of character on the basis of speech traits alone. We do it not only face to face but also on the telephone and when we hear people on tape or on the radio.

Using Guises and Disguises to Uncover Language Attitudes

To investigate unconscious attitudes, "matched guise" techniques have been developed. These are audio tapes, usually of several bilinguals reading a passage in two languages (each passage a translation of the other). The tests are structured in such a way that the listener-judges are unaware that they are listening to the same person more than once. For example, using tapes of bilinguals speaking English and French natively, researchers can disguise the fact that they are asking judges for opinions about the same person in different language "guises." Since the same person is heard twice—once in a French guise, once in an English guise—there is no actual variation in the qualities about which judges are asked to render an assessment: intelligence, friendliness, and other characteristics remain constant. What is really uncovered is the listeners' attitudes toward French and English speakers.

Matched Guises in Canada In the late 1950s, English-Canadians and French-Canadians were asked to judge personality traits of speakers of French and English. The same "perfectly bilingual" speakers read a two-minute passage in one language and its translation in the other. Because the only variable was language, any differences in the judgments of someone's intelligence would reflect the judges' general assessment of the intelligence of speakers of the languages.

It will be no surprise to learn that the English-Canadians judged the English speakers (that is, the English guises) superior on *all* traits. As judged by the English-Canadians, a person speaking English was assumed to be better looking, taller, more intelligent, more dependable, more ambitious, and more respectable than the very same person speaking French. These biases in favor of English were shared by monolingual and bilingual English-Canadians alike.

When the same tapes were presented to an equivalent group of French-Canadian students, the results were not what one might expect. The French-Canadian judges also took the English guises to be better looking, taller, more intelligent, more dependable, and more ambitious. Only on kindness and religiousness did the French-Canadian judges evaluate the French guises superior to the English guises. In fact, on all other traits, the French-Canadian judges evaluated the English guises even more superior to the French guises than the English-Canadian judges had. That the French judges shared the views of the English judges to such a remarkable degree reflected a community-wide stereotype in which French-Canadians were regarded as relatively inferior people. (Today, after more than a decade of official Canadian bilingualism and a renewed sense of positive identity among French-Canadians, the results of matched guise tests would probably be very different.)

Not all groups in contact with one another share norms of evaluation as the Canadians do. In Israel, mutual hostility exists in the attitudes of Jewish and Arab adolescents. When tapes of boys bilingual in Hebrew and Arabic were played for teenage judges unaware of the experimental structure, the Jewish and Arab listener-judges rated the guises of their own culture higher on characteristics of honesty, good-heartedness, friendliness, and acceptability in marriage.

Social Dialect Attitudes in New York City   In New York City, to determine subjective reactions to the pronunciation of several stigmatized phonological variables such as "cah" for *car* and "dem" for *them*, William Labov used an audio tape compilation of five New York women reading a total of twenty-two separate sentences, including for each woman one neutral utterance completely lacking features with stigmatized variants. Two hundred New York listener-judges were given a ranked list of jobs (from television personality to factory worker) and asked to assess the highest occupation each taped speaker could hold speaking as she did. The evaluations for each sentence were compared with the evaluation of the neutral utterance so as to discount whatever role voice characteristics might have played in the assessment, and a gauge of attitudes toward individual phonological variants was established. In Figure 15-1, the first five scales represent the five women speakers reading the neutral sentences and indicate the average occupational suitability assigned by the judges. Notice that speaker 2 improves her job suitability from salesclerk to receptionist when in the guise of speaker 8 she utters a sentence in which she consistently pronounces /r/, but she falls somewhat from that post to switchboard operator when as speaker 12 she pronounces /r/s inconsistently (that is, dropping some of them). Speaker 4 dramatically improves the perception of her job suitability from receptionist to television personality in going from the neutral utterance to one in which she pronounces /r/ consistently as speaker 9 and then falls again to receptionist with inconsistent /r/ as speaker 13.

In general, judges of all socioeconomic classes showed similar patterns of evaluation, but there were some differences, with the lower middle class generally manifesting the greatest sensitivity to the variables. Differences also existed among the responses of Jews, Italians, and blacks as well as between men and women. The more a stigmatized variant was used by a particular group, the more negative was that group's evaluation of it. Women, for example, exhibit greater stylistic variation than men (and therefore use more stigmatized forms in the most informal speech), but they showed less tolerance for the stigmatized variants in the speech of others.

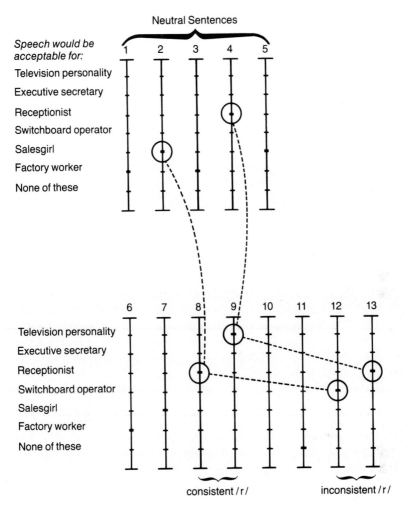

FIGURE 15–1
Subjective Evaluation Form and Patterns for /r/

SOURCE: Adapted from Labov 1972

In other aspects of his investigation, Labov found discrepancies between what a person thought correct and what he or she was observed doing in ordinary pronunciation. Here, too, there were interesting differences among social groups. Women had indexes of linguistic insecurity nearly 50 percent higher than men's scores; Jews had less linguistic insecurity as measured by this index than Italians did; and among the social classes, the working class showed the least insecurity. Labov concluded that New Yorkers manifest "a profound linguistic insecurity" and suffer from a marked linguistic self-hatred, especially among the lower middle class.

The Persistence of Stigmatized Dialects

Clearly, language varieties carry differing degrees of prestige. While the degree of stigmatization depends on the group making the judgment, norms of evaluation tend to be shared throughout a speech community. It is clear that some language varieties carry very low prestige and are stigmatized, and one wonders why such varieties don't die out. Why don't speakers give them up for more prestigious varieties?

The explanation seems to lie in the fact that one's identity—as a woman or man, as an American or Australian, as a member of a particular ethnic or socioeconomic group—is intimately bound up in the speech patterns of that group. Americans talk like other Americans; Australians talk like Australians; men speak like men and women like women. While one's sex is not a matter of choice, one's *gender* is, at least to some extent. What is considered masculine and feminine is a cultural, not a biological, matter; one can choose to behave in more or less masculine or feminine ways irrespective of one's sex. To change the way we speak is to signal changes in who we are or how we wish to be perceived. For a New Yorker transplanted to California, to start speaking like a Californian is to relinquish identity as a New Yorker. To give up speaking Black English is to replace that personal and social identity with another. To give up working-class speech patterns acquired in childhood is to take on a new identity. To take on new speech patterns is to reform oneself and present oneself anew.

Language is perhaps the major symbol of our social identity, and we have seen how remarkably fine-tuned to that identity it is. Language is not set apart from social identity and social alliances. If one wishes to identify with "nonnative" regional, socioeconomic, or ethnic groups and has sufficient contact with them, one's speech will come to resemble theirs. In fact, socially mobile individuals have been shown to exhibit pronunciation patterns more like the group toward which they are heading than like the group of current affiliation: this is true not only of individuals moving up the socioeconomic scale but also of those whose paths are pointing lower.

We can illustrate with a telling investigation of linguistic and social identity on Martha's Vineyard, an island off the coast of Massachusetts. There the vowels /ay/ and /aw/ have two principal variants, with the first element of each diphthong alternating between [a] and [ə]. Words like *night* and *why* are sometimes pronounced with [ay] and sometimes with a more centralized [əy], while words like *shout* and *how* are pronounced with [aw] or the centralized [əw]. The variants are not reflections of gender, ethnicity, or socioeconomic status; that is, they are not typical dialect features. On Martha's Vineyard, vowel centralization represents identity with traditional island values—with the island and its life. The up-island residents have more centralization than do the residents in sections catering to summer visitors. Most interestingly, young men intending to leave the island and lead lives on the mainland have least centralization, while the greatest degree of centralization was shown by a young man who had moved to the mainland but returned to Martha's

Vineyard. Thus the centralized diphthongs represent a rejection of mainland values and a positive view of the values of island life.

The importance of the symbolic value of one's language variety cannot be overestimated. In evaluating oral arguments in Britain, speakers of regional varieties rated the *quality* of an argument higher when presented in standard accent, but they found the same argument more *persuasive* when made using a regional accent.

It is easy for one group of speakers higher on the socioeconomic ladder to ask about a group of speakers lower on the ladder, "Why don't *they* start talking like *us*?" The answer is simple: *their* social identity is different, and *they* do not necessarily share the values of the higher socioeconomic groups. Some insight can be gained by thinking about gender dialects, in which the situation is less complicated. Though there have been stirrings of neutrality recently, most people still agree that everyone is entitled to a gender dialect. It is perfectly acceptable for women to speak like women and men to speak like men. Imagine men asking women to speak like them in order to get ahead in "a man's world." Imagine a woman head of a company asking her truck drivers to speak more like women to get ahead in "a woman's world." These are patently unacceptable (though not unimaginable) scenarios. Women's and men's speech patterns are equally acceptable. A nearly similar equality of status is granted to most regional varieties. Imagine a Bostonian moving to Atlanta and being told by a boss to get rid of the New England accent in order to succeed. The employee might rightly infer that the Boston origin, not the Boston accent, was at issue.

When it comes to ethnic and social-class varieties, perceptions are quite different. The widely held view is that Black English and Chicano English and the dialects of lower socioeconomic status groups cannot be employed in the schools or the professional workplace. These views reflect language attitudes; as such, they are social, not linguistic, decisions, and they are based on attitudes toward *speakers*, not *language*!

In study after study, language has been shown to be a central factor in one's identity. Asking people to change their customary language patterns is not like asking them to try on different sweaters; it is asking them to take on a new identity and to espouse the values associated with speakers of a different dialect. The principal reason that nonstandard varieties are so hearty, so resistant to the urgings of education, is simply that language varieties are deeply entwined with the identities of their speakers.

Attitudes and Second-Language Learning

Just as language attitudes pervade one's views of language users and vice versa, so they have a profound effect on one's ability to acquire a second language, especially beyond adolescence. Given that attitudes differ from group to group, the influence that attitudes have on the acquisition of a foreign or second language should not be surprising.

We must distinguish between *learning* a foreign language and *acquiring* one. Learning a foreign language is parallel to learning math or history; a body of information must be mastered. This kind of foreign language learning differs not only from first-language acquisition but also from second-language acquisition in immersion situations in which one can acquire a language in a fashion approximating (however inadequately) the environment normally surrounding first-language acquisition. Because the language variety one acquires becomes part of one's social identity, the acquisition of second languages must be seen not just as intellectual exercises but as enterprises that alter one's identity.

Scientists have long wondered whether the language acquisition device that works so well for monolingual and multilingual children might atrophy sometime during adolescence. While there is yet no definitive answer to this question, there is evidence that one's attitude toward the second language and one's motivation in undertaking the acquisition can have a profound effect on success. In acquiring a foreign language, our efforts are mediated by what Stephen Krashen calls an "affective filter"—a psychological disposition that facilitates or inhibits our natural language-acquisition capacities. Krashen maintains that if there is sufficient "comprehensible input," the acquisition of a second language, even by an adult, can proceed as effortlessly and efficiently as first-language acquisition, provided that the affective filter is not blocking the operation of these capacities.

The learning of a second (or foreign) language in school is increasingly viewed not as an intellectual or educational phenomenon but as a social-psychological phenomenon. One social psychologist describes this view well:

> In the acquisition of a second language, the student is faced with the task of not simply learning new information . . . which is part of his *own* culture but rather of *acquiring* symbolic elements of a *different* ethnolinguistic community. The new words are not simply new words for old concepts, the new grammar is not simply a new way of ordering words, the new pronunciations are not merely 'different' ways of saying things. They are characteristics of another ethnolinguistic community. Furthermore, the student is not being asked to learn about them; he is being asked to acquire them, to make them part of his own language reservoir. This involves imposing elements of another culture into one's own lifespace. As a result, the student's harmony with his own cultural community and his willingness or ability to identify with other cultural communities become important considerations in the process of second language acquisition.[3]

IDEAL LANGUAGES

Clear Communication Versus Efficient Communication

From time to time, idealists of various sorts—linguists, philosophers, and assorted others—think about ideal communication systems (see Chapter 9). Among the generally accepted criteria for an ideal language would be a

---

[3] R. C. Gardner, "Social Psychological Aspects of Second Language Acquisition," in Howard Giles and Robert St. Clair (eds.), *Language and Social Psychology* (Oxford: Basil Blackwell, 1979), pp. 193–194.

one-to-one correspondence between content and expression: a different expression for each thought (where "thought" is simply the customary way of representing a unit segment of content). We can represent this kind of ideal communication as follows:

Thought	Ideal Language	Speech
Content A	←————————→	Expression A
Content B	←————————→	Expression B
Content C	←————————→	Expression C

In this situation of a one-to-one mapping between content and expression, no ambiguity or synonymy would exist, and communication would be consistently accurate and reliable.

We can also imagine a very different kind of idealized communication: a language in which there would be just one expression corresponding to any and all content. That one expression might well be the simple form *uh* [ʌ]. With each utterance of *uh*, the content of a speaker's intended communication would be clearly conveyed to an addressee along with its illocutionary force. We can represent this communicative ideal as follows:

Thought	Ideal Language	Speech
Content A		
Content B		[ʌ]
Content C		

As with our first idealization, so with this one: no misunderstanding could arise. While the first idealization seems less far removed from actual human languages, the second, the most *efficient* of languages, would involve a degree of telepathy beyond the ability of human beings.

In practice, the various dialects and registers of all natural languages move along a continuum between these extremes of expression (never actually reaching either extreme, of course). In the circumstances of human communication, the two idealizations represent a tug of war between the forces of clear communication and those of efficient communication.

For the advantage of hearers and readers, the force of clear communication propels language in the direction of full (and thus unique) expression for content. For the advantage of speakers and writers, on the other hand, the force of efficient communication tugs in the direction of minimal expression for content. It is a simple matter: the more clear and full you are in your expression, the easier it is for me to grasp your meaning. On the other hand, as a speaker, the less I need to say in order to communicate my meaning to you, the easier my task. It is as if, for different reasons, language use were governed by a centrifugal force that teased out expression and a centripetal force that compressed it. The centrifugal force attends to the needs of addressees and interpreters, the centripetal force to the needs of speakers and writers.

When Samuel Johnson, the first great English dictionary maker, alleged that "tongues, like governments, have a natural tendency to degeneration," he was referring to the centripetal force to collapse expression. Today we can see Dr. Johnson's "degeneration" as the inevitable product of a natural bent to communicate efficiently in accordance with the cooperative principle. For the sake of efficiency, we abbreviate sentences, blend words together, use homonyms and structurally ambiguous sentences, use nouns as verbs (*water, smoke, jet*), and reduce certain sounds or skip them altogether. "Said 'e'd be 'ere" for *He said that he would be here* and [dɪjə it yɛt] or even [jityɛt] for *Did you eat yet?* are the workaday products of efficient communication in English, while [šepa] (*je ne sais pas* 'I don't know') and [šepakwa] (*je ne sais pas quoi* 'I don't know what') are two of its French manifestations.

In face-to-face communication between people who know one another well, the tolerance for abbreviated expression tends to be affordably great. Contractions like *don't, hasn't*, and *gonna* are most frequent in face-to-face conversation, decreasing in frequency as the shared context between interlocutors diminishes (see Table 13-6, p. 435). In less contextualized circumstances, linguistic expression must be fuller if communication is to succeed. Especially in certain types of writing, much must be stated explicitly that could remain implicit in conversation between people of similar background with shared assumptions.

The two forces operating on language are reasonably well balanced: the need for clear communication tends to check the urge to be efficient. Prescriptive grammarians, many schoolteachers, and untold numbers of writers of letters to the editorial page fear that centripetal efficiency will overpower the need for articulated expression, especially in writing. While insufficient explicitness can be corrected with a question in the course of conversation, readers have no ready opportunity to demand a fuller explanation from a text. Hence writers must heed the force of clarity more than speakers must.

Gender Studies and Ideal Varieties

Over the past two decades, a good deal of gender research has been spawned, in part from the feminist movement. As a result, sociologists, anthropologists, linguists, and others have become sensitized to certain subtle ways in which language reflects gender differences. In critiquing the linguistic bias of English, feminist researchers have called it a "he/man" language, alluding to the fact that the third person pronoun *he* (and *him* and *his*) and the noun *man* (with *men, men's*, and *man's*) are used in English to refer not only to males but to females and males together. The pronoun *he* and the word *man* are thus used in both sex-specific and generic contexts. While *he* and *man* can be used as referring phrases for a male being (*He told me to pay the fine*), they are also commonly used to refer to men and women—to people in general—as in the following sentences:

Everyone should wear *his* coat; it's cold out.

Man's history has not always been admirable.

The switchboard is *manned* by three volunteers.

Some have claimed that using "he/man" language in generic contexts is ambiguous and confusing. Others have made an even stronger claim that such uses tend to disenfranchise women. Supporters of this latter view point out that masculine pronouns are invariably used when *generic* references are made to doctors, lawyers, and politicians, whereas feminine pronouns are customary in references to secretaries, nurses, and schoolteachers, all less prestigious occupations.

As a result of efforts by feminist groups, some attention has been paid to creating substitute phrases for the "sexist" language of an earlier period. The effort has been directed primarily to ridding English usage of the generic use of "he/man" terms, using the phrase *he or she* instead of the generic pronoun *he*, substituting *chairperson* or *chair* for *chairman*, and talking about *people* or *humanity*—not *mankind, men*, and *man*—when referring to all people.

It is interesting to consider these attempts at linguistic reform in light of the competing forces of clear and efficient expression. Feminists are concerned, first, that English collapses expression in using *man* (and *mankind*) for both 'men' and 'women and men together' (thus losing an important content distinction) and, second, that the collapsed expression is not neutral but gives preference to one of the readings. We can represent the situation as follows:

Content	Expression
(a) 'women and men' ——————→	men
(b) 'men' ——————→	

As to the first point, *men* is sometimes used to mean 'male human beings' and sometimes to mean 'male and female human beings' (though not to mean 'female human beings'). What feminists recommend to correct this situation is a movement in the direction of a one-to-one correspondence between content and expression—distinct expression for distinct content—as follows:

Content	Expression
(a) 'women and men' ⟵⟶	people
(b) 'men' ⟵⟶	men
(c) 'women' ⟵⟶	women

The second point has to do with the particular choice of collapsed expression. Feminists claim that the expression *men* carries with it a strong tendency to prejudice interpretations in favor of 'men' instead of 'women and men,' as the expression *women* even more clearly excludes 'men.' While the collapsing of expression itself may do harm by overlooking a crucial distinction in our society (and crucial contributions by women, very often referred to along with men simply as *men*), the particular collapsing is often prejudicial, as in these examples:

Content	Expression
(a) 'doctors'	
(b) 'lawyers'	he ('male')
(c) 'politicians'	
(males and females of higher social status)	
(d) 'secretaries'	
(e) 'nurses'	she ('female')
(f) 'teachers'	
(males and females of lower social status)	

Thus the collapsing of expression to represent males and females indiscriminately is troubling enough; as in the examples, however, it is often done in a way that is socially unfair. The higher-status professions, comprising women and men, are referred to by the masculine pronoun; the lower-status professions, also including women and men, are referred to by the feminine pronoun. However much these pronominal reference patterns may reflect past social history, the feminist argument that the collapsing of expression, especially in a discriminatory fashion, does them a disservice is persuasive.

SUMMARY

The belief is widespread that languages can and should be logical and pure as well as grammatical and that languages gradually degenerate, however perfectly they began. The view of linguists is that change is natural in language and that language in use is inherently variable.

Language varieties have different statuses: there are official languages and national languages, dialects that are the native varieties of subgroups of people, and varieties like Modern Standard Arabic that are not the native language of any group but are learned for use in particular or limited functions.

Standard languages are those whose forms have been settled and codified in dictionaries and grammars. They have no inherent merit over other varieties, though their codification is essential for certain functions and often gives them a prestige over nonstandardized varieties. In the English-speaking world, handbooks and dictionaries are the chief embodiments of codification. Dictionaries generally follow an essentially *descriptive* tradition, describing the usage of reputable speakers and writers. The authors of handbooks tend to be *prescriptive*, relying on opinion and exercising personal judgment in what is prescribed and proscribed.

Speech is an important mediator in the way people perceive one another. Not only impressions of social affiliation but personal traits and even physiognomy and intelligence are conveyed by characteristics of language. For some characteristics, these impressions will be valid simply because people do indeed speak like those with whom they are socially affiliated and with whom they wish to identify. Attitudes toward languages and language forms are themselves mediated by social stereotyping. Moreover, the social characteristics of persons making a judgment can also be a biasing factor. Though not all social groups make identical judgments of the same speech patterns, there is surprising agreement in the direction of evaluation within a speech community.

One's views of oneself are also intimately linked to one's language, especially the language acquired in childhood. Adopting a second language variety—whether a standard variety of one's native language or a nonnative language—is an experience fraught with emotional overtones. The study of foreign languages cannot be equated with the study of history or math; it involves adapting to the mores of another ethnolinguistic group.

Conceptions of ideal languages tend to have either a one-to-one relationship between content and expression or a kind of telepathic function. Real language varieties vary between these two extremes of expression, with intimate conversation allowing relatively greater compression than other situations. In attempting to reform pronominal usage in English, feminists and others have attempted to establish a one-to-one correspondence between form and meaning in certain semantic fields and to ensure that where expression for different content is collapsed, it is not done in a way systematically disparaging to one sex or the other.

EXERCISES

1. Examine the following two entries for *hopefully*. What can you tell about the attitudes toward lexicography and the lexicographer's obligations from these two entries?

> **hope·ful·ly** (hōp′fə-lē) *adv.* **1**. With hope; in a hopeful manner. **2**. It is to be hoped; let us hope. See Usage note.
> **Usage:** *Hopefully*, as used to mean it is to be hoped or let us hope, is still not accepted by a substantial number of authorities on grammar and usage. The following example of *hopefully* in this sense is acceptable to only 44 per cent of the Usage Panel: *Hopefully, we shall complete our work in June.*

> **hope·ful·ly** \'hōp-fə-lē\ *adv* (1639) **1** : in a hopeful manner **2** : it is hoped
> *usage* Only the irrationally large amount of critical fire drawn by sense 2 of *hopefully* requires its particular recognition in a dictionary. Similar use of other adverbs (as *interestingly, presumably, fortunately*) as sentence modifiers is so commonplace as to excite no notice whatever. While it still arouses occasional objection, *hopefully* as a sentence modifier has been in use at least since 1932 and is well established as standard.

2. After reading the appropriate front matter describing how entries are constructed and usage labels applied, compare the entries for the following in *The American Heritage Dictionary* (*AHD*) and at least one other reputable desk dictionary: *between/among; can/may; different from/than/to; disinterested/uninterested; enthuse; finalize; to gift; imply/infer; irregardless; like/as; literally; to loan; nuclear* (pronunciation); *presently; pretty; real* and *sure* as adverbs; *wait on/wait for.*

   (a) What basis does each dictionary use for making judgments or recommendations about preferred usages? Describe in detail the nature of the usage panel judgments in the *AHD*.
   (b) Briefly describe in what ways the descriptions of usage are alike and in what ways they differ.
   (c) Which items are not treated as problematical by one or both dictionaries? Of the items that are treated in both dictionaries, describe the principal similarities and differences in the treatment of usage. Is there a basis in the approach of the two dictionaries for the differences in their treatments?
   (d) What is the validity of the *AHD*'s method of assessing preferred usage? As a potential user of the dictionary, what kind of judges, if any, would you like to see *AHD* appoint to its panel? Explain your preferences.

3. William Labov ... once said about the use of black English, "It is the goal of most black Americans to acquire full control of the standard language without giving up their own culture." ... I wonder if the good doctor might also consider the goals of those black Americans who have full control of standard English but who are every now and then troubled by that colorful, grammar-to-the-winds patois that is black English. Case in point—me.

So wrote a twenty-one-year-old black college sophomore in *Newsweek* (Dec. 27, 1982, p. 7). The student cites several features of Black English such as those described in Chapter 12.

(a) What does *patois* mean and what connotations does it carry in referring to particular language varieties? What does the phrase "grammar-to-the-winds patois" suggest about the writer's attitude toward Black English?

(b) From your study of Chapter 12, what features of Black English do you think the writer means in calling it a "grammar-to-the-winds patois"?

(c) To what extent can Black English accurately be called a "grammar-to-the-winds" speech variety? What would be the implications for communication if a speech variety were indeed "grammarless"?

(d) What would you assume to be the reason for the writer's judgments about and attitudes toward Black English? What might you explain to the student about patterns of language in every variety and about the status of particular varieties *in terms of their linguistic features*?

4. Comment on the validity of this quotation and explain your view: "If there were as many oil barons coming up from Mexico as there are farm laborers, the accents of Pancho Villa might sound more musical to American ears." [William F. Mackey in Cobarrubias and Fishman (1983), p. 186]

5. Consider the following quotation from *A Pronouncing Dictionary of American English* (John S. Kenyon and Thomas A. Knott, Springfield, Mass.: G. & C. Merriam, 1953, p. vi).

As in all trustworthy dictionaries, the editors have endeavored to base the pronunciations on actual cultivated usage. No other standard has, in point of fact, ever finally settled pronunciation. This book can be taken as a safe guide to pronunciation only insofar as we have succeeded in doing this. According to this standard, no words are, as often said, "almost universally mispronounced," for that is self-contradictory. For an editor the temptation is often strong to prefer what he thinks "ought to be" the right pronunciation; but it has to be resisted.

(a) What arguments support the view that editors should resist the temptation to record their own personal pronunciation preferences in a dictionary? What about arguments for expressing editors' personal preferences for other aspects of language such as spelling or usage? Explain your view.

(b) In what sense is it accurate to say that the phrase "almost universally mispronounced" is self-contradictory?

(c) What is meant by "cultivated usage"? Does it seem to refer to a register or a dialect (that is, to a situation of use or to a set of users)? What register(s) and what dialect(s) should a dictionary set out to describe? Explain your view.

6. Efforts to rid English of sexist usages that a large segment of society finds offensive have met with some ridicule and scorn. By inventing terms such as "personhole covers," "peopledate" (for *mandate*), and "herstory" (for *history*), a few writers and editors have attempted to poke fun at the suggestion that language has an effect on the way people perceive themselves and one another. Comment on the attitude represented by the invention of such terms. Explain what such examples indicate about how their inventors think language affects the way people perceive themselves and others.

7. Consider the following quotation from John Simon's *Paradigms Lost* (New York: Penguin, 1980, pp. 58–59) concerning Edwin Newman's book *A Civil Tongue*:

> With demonic acumen, Newman adduces 196 pages' worth of grammatical errors. Clichés, jargon, malapropisms, mixed metaphors, monstrous neologisms, unholy ambiguities, and parasitic redundancies, interspersed with his own mocking comments . . . and exhortations to do better. The examples are mostly true horrors, very funny and even more distressing . . . . Worse than a nation of shop-keepers, we have become a nation of wordmongers or word-butchers, and abuse of language whether from ignorance or obfuscation, leads, as Newman persuasively argues, to a deterioration of moral values and standards of living.

(a) Which of the types of "grammatical errors" that Simon refers to (clichés, jargon, and so on) can legitimately be called errors of grammar? What, then, are the others?

(b) Cite some errors of grammar that you have heard from nonnative speakers of English. Have you heard similar errors from native speakers? What do you think is the reason for your findings about native speakers?

(c) The point that Newman and Simon make about "abuse of language" leading to a deterioration of moral values and standards of living is a common claim of language guardians. What kinds of abuse does Simon seem to have in mind when he makes that claim? Is he correct in claiming that such abuses lead to a deterioration of moral values? Could it be the other way around? What stake could anyone have in advancing the Newman/Simon claim?

(d) Do you think that actual grammatical errors (such as nonnative speakers make) could have the same effect? Explain your position.

SUGGESTIONS FOR FURTHER READING

Fasold (1984) and Milroy and Milroy (1985) are useful treatments of several topics treated in this chapter, including attitudes, multilingualism, and standardization. Heath (1980) treats the development of the notion of Standard English, while Shaklee (1980) talks about the rise of Standard English itself. Baron (1982) reports the history of efforts at language reform in the United States. Finegan (1980) relates the history of American attitudes toward "correct" English and describes the battle waged between adherents of prescription and description over the past centuries. Bolinger (1980) is an excellent treatment of use and abuse, principally of American English. Greenbaum (1985) is a collection of articles treating the development of Standard English and attitudes toward current varieties of it in Britain, the United States, Canada, India, and elsewhere. Kachru (1986) discusses emerging standards of English around the world. Quinn (1980) is an entertaining discussion of the popular shibboleths in American English, with some eye-opening peeks at the usage of the great writers. Crystal (1984) and Mittins (1970) are brief and well-informed treatments of English usage. Ryan and Giles (1982) is a valuable survey of the empirical study of language attitudes, including second-language acquisition. Shuy and Fasold (1973) is a collection of articles about language attitudes in various North and South American contexts. Williams (1976) reports some statistically sophisticated (though easy to follow) empirical studies of attitudes, including teacher attitudes. The Martha's Vineyard and New York City studies are reported in Labov (1972). Fishman (1974) and Cobarrubias and Fishman (1983) are anthologies describing language planning efforts of many types in different parts of the world. Landau (1984) is an accessible discussion of all aspects of dictionary making by an experienced lexicographer. Collison (1982) is a historical survey of foreign-language dictionaries. Second-language acquisition, including the role of attitudes, is treated in Klein (1986) and Ellis (1986). Krashen and Terrell (1983) is worth a read by every student attempting to master a foreign language. Gardner and Lambert (1972) discusses attitudes and motivation in second-language acquisition.

REFERENCES

Baron, Dennis E. 1982. *Grammar and Good Taste* (New Haven: Yale University Press).

Bolinger, Dwight. 1980. *Language—the Loaded Weapon: The Use and Abuse of Language Today* (London: Longman).

Cobarrubias, Juan, and Joshua A. Fishman (eds.). 1983. *Progress in Language Planning: International Perspectives* (Berlin: Mouton).

Collison, Robert L. 1982. *A History of Foreign-Language Dictionaries* (London: Andre Deutsch).

Crystal, David. 1984. *Who Cares About Usage?* (New York: Penguin).

Ellis, Rod. 1986. *Understanding Second Language Acquisition* (Oxford: Oxford University Press).

Fasold, Ralph. 1984. *The Sociolinguistics of Society* (New York: Basil Blackwell).

Finegan, Edward. 1980. *Attitudes Toward English Usage: The History of a War of Words* (New York: Teachers College Press, Columbia University).

Fishman, Joshua A. (ed.). 1974. *Advances in Language Planning* (The Hague: Mouton).

Fowler, H. W. 1965. *A Dictionary of Modern English Usage*, 2nd ed. rev. by Sir Ernest Gowers (New York: Oxford University Press).

Gardner, Robert C., and Wallace E. Lambert. 1972. *Attitudes and Motivation in Second-Language Learning* (Rowley, Mass.: Newbury House).

Greenbaum, Sidney. 1985. *The English Language Today* (Oxford: Pergamon).

Heath, Shirley Brice. 1980. "Standard English: The Biography of a Symbol," in Shopen and Williams (eds.), 1980, pp. 3–62.

Kachru, Braj J. 1986. *The Alchemy of English: The Spread, Functions and Models of Non-native Englishes* (Oxford: Pergamon).

Klein, Wolfgang. 1986. *Second Language Acquisition* (Cambridge: Cambridge University Press).

Krashen, Stephen D., and Tracy D. Terrell. 1983. *The Natural Approach: Language Acquisition in the Classroom* (Hayward, Calif.: Alemany Press).

Labov, William. 1972. *Sociolinguistic Patterns* (Philadelphia: University of Pennsylvania Press).

Landau, Sidney I. 1984. *Dictionaries: The Art and Craft of Lexicography* (New York: Charles Scribner's Sons).

Milroy, James, and Lesley Milroy. 1985. *Authority in Language: Investigating Language Prescription and Standardisation* (London: Routledge & Kegan Paul).

Mittins, W. H., et al. 1970. *Attitudes to English Usage* (London: Oxford University Press).

Quinn, Jim. 1980. *American Tongue and Cheek: A Populist Guide to Our Language* (New York: Penguin).

Ryan, Ellen Bouchard, and Howard Giles (eds.). 1982. *Attitudes Towards Language Variation: Social and Applied Contexts* (London: Edward Arnold).

Shaklee, Margaret. 1980. "The Rise of Standard English," in Shopen and Williams (eds.), 1980, pp. 33–62.

Shopen, Timothy, and Joseph M. Williams (eds.). 1980. *Standards and Dialects in English* (Rowley, Mass.: Newbury House).

Shuy, Roger W., and Ralph W. Fasold (eds.). 1973. *Language Attitude: Current Trends and Prospects* (Washington, D.C.: Georgetown University Press).

Strunk, William, Jr., and E. B. White. 1979. *The Elements of Style*, 3rd ed. (New York: Macmillan).

Williams, Frederick. 1976. *Explorations of the Linguistic Attitudes of Teachers* (Rowley, Mass.: Newbury House).

GLOSSARY

This Glossary defines and explains many of the important terms used in this book. When first discussed within the text, such terms have been printed in **boldface**, to indicate that they are also in the Glossary for ease of reference. Likewise, within the definitions that follow, every special term used in explaining another term appears in **boldface** and thus points to a related Glossary entry. To locate additional discussion of a term, consult the Index.

absolute universal: a linguistic pattern at play in all languages of the world without exception. Example: "A language with voiced **stops** also has voiceless stops."

adjacency pair: a set of two consecutive, ordered turns that "go together" in a conversation, such as question/answer sequences and greeting/greeting exchanges.

affective meaning: the information conveyed by a linguistic **expression** about the attitudes and emotions of the producer toward the **content** or the context of expression; together with **social meaning**, affective meaning is sometimes called *connotation*.

affix: a **bound morpheme** that occurs attached to another **morpheme** (called the *root* or *stem*). *Prefixes* (attached to the beginning of the root or stem) and *suffixes* (attached to the end) are the most common types of affixes. Less common in the world's languages are *infixes* (inserted within the root or stem) and *circumfixes* (a part of which is attached at each end of the root or stem).

affricate: also called *stop fricative*, a sound produced when air is built up by a complete closure of the oral tract at some **place of articulation** and then released and continued like a **fricative**. Examples: English /č/ (as in *chin*) and /ǰ/ (as in *gin*).

agreement: the marking of a word (as with an **affix**) to indicate a particular grammatical relationship to another word in the sentence; a verb that *agrees* with its **subject** in **person** and **number** has a form that indicates that relationship.

allomorph: the alternant phonetic forms of a **morpheme** in particular linguistic environments. For example, the English plural morpheme has three allomorphs: [əz] (as in *buses*), [z] (*twigs*), and [s] (*cats*).

allophone: the phonetic manifestation of a **phoneme** in a particular phonological environment. Example: in English, unaspirated [p] and **aspirated** [pʰ] are allophones of the phoneme /p/ because they occur in **complementary distribution.**

alphabet: a writing system in which, ideally, each **symbol** represents a distinctive sound of the language.

alveolar: a sound articulated at the alveolar ridge, the bony ridge just behind and above the upper teeth.

ambiguous: a term used to describe an **expression** that can be interpreted in more than one way as a consequence of having more than one **constituent structure** (*John or Jack and Bill*) or more than one **referential meaning** (*river bank* and *savings bank*).

antonymy: refers to opposite meanings; words with opposite meanings are said to be *antonymous.*

appropriateness conditions: conventions that regulate the interpretation under which an **utterance** serves as a particular **speech act**, for example as a question, a promise, an invitation.

approximant: a sound produced when one articulator is close to another but the vocal tract is not sufficiently narrowed to create the audible friction that typically characterizes **consonants**; thus, *approximant* refers to a **manner of articulation**. Examples: [w], [y], [r], [l].

argument: a noun phrase that occurs with a verb as part of a proposition. For example, the verb *wash* has two arguments, a **subject** and a **direct object**, in *Alice washed the car.*

aspect: a grammatical category of verbs used to mark the way in which a situation described by a verb takes place in time, for example as continuous, repetitive, or instantaneous.

aspirated: the term applied to sounds produced accompanied by a puff of air; represented in phonetic transcription by a following raised [ʰ].

attributive adjective: an adjective that functions syntactically as part of the noun phrase whose head it modifies (*a spooky house*), as distinguished from a **predicative** adjective (*The house is spooky*).

auxiliary verb: a verb used with (or instead of) the main verb to carry certain kinds of grammatical information such as **tense** and **aspect**. In English, it is the auxiliary verb that is inverted with the **subject** in yes/no questions (*Did she fall?*) and that carries the negative element in contractions (*can't, wasn't*).

basic sentence: a sentence that has been generated without the application of any major **transformations.**

bilabial: a **place of articulation** involving both lips.

bilingualism: the state of having **competence** in more than one language.

bound morpheme: a **morpheme** that functions as part of a word but cannot stand alone as a word. Examples: -MENT (as in *establishment*), -ER (*painter*), and 'PLURAL' (*zebras*).

case: a grammatical category associated with nouns and pronouns that indicates their grammatical relationship to other elements in the **clause**, usually the verb. Example: the pronoun *I* is marked for common case, *me* for objective case, and *mine* for possessive case.

circumfix: see **affix**.

clause: a **constituent** unit of **syntax** consisting of a verb with its **argument** noun phrases; clauses can function as constituents of a sentence or can stand by themselves as **simple sentences**.

cognates: words or **morphemes** that have developed from a single, historically earlier source. Example: English *father*, German *Vater*, Spanish *padre*, and Gothic *fadar* are cognates because all have developed from the Proto-Indo-European word **pəter*. The word *cognates* is also used for languages that have a common historical ancestor. Example: English, Russian, German, Persian, and all the other **Indo-European** languages.

communicative competence: see **competence**.

comparative reconstruction: a method used in historical linguistics to uncover the structures and vocabulary of an ancestor language by drawing inferences from the evidence that remains in several daughter languages.

competence: the ability to produce and understand grammatical sentences in a language is called *grammatical competence*, and the ability to produce and interpret utterances appropriate to their context of use is called *communicative competence*.

complementary distribution: a pattern of distribution of two or more sounds that do not occur in the same position within a word in a given language. Example: in English, [pʰ] does not occur where [p] occurs (and vice versa).

complex sentence: a sentence that consists of a matrix **clause** and one or more embedded (or subordinate) clauses.

conjugation: the term used for the set of inflectional variants of a verb; also called a verb *paradigm*. Example: *go, goes, went, going, gone*. Compare with **declension**.

consonant: a sound produced by partial or complete closure of part of the vocal tract, thus obstructing the airflow through the vocal tract and creating audible friction of various kinds. Consonants are described in terms of **voicing, place of articulation**, and **manner of articulation**. Abbreviation: C.

constituent: a syntactic unit that functions as part of a larger unit within a sentence; typical constituent types are verb phrase, noun phrase, prepositional phrase, and **clause**.

constituent structure: the linear and hierarchical organization of the words of a sentence into syntactic units.

content: information that is conveyed or communicated by linguistic **expression**.

content word: a word whose primary function is to describe objects, ideas, qualities, and states of being in the world; nouns, verbs, adjectives, and adverbs are content words; opposed to **function words**.

contrastive: said of a noun phrase that is marked as being in opposition to another noun phrase in a **discourse**.

converseness: the term used to characterize a reciprocal relationship between pairs of words, as in *husband* and *wife*.

cooperative principle: the set of four maxims that describe how language users cooperate in producing and understanding **utterances** in context: maxim of quantity, maxim of quality, maxim of relevance, and maxim of orderliness.

coordinate sentence: a sentence that contains two (or more) **clauses** neither of which functions as a grammatical **constituent** of the other; the clauses of a coordinate sentence are usually joined by a coordinating conjunction such as *and* or *but* (*John went to England, and Mary went to France*).

creole: a contact language, a former **pidgin**, that has "acquired" native speakers.

cuneiform: a written symbol developed by the Sumerians and Akkadians in the Middle East around 3000 B.C.; characterized by the wedgelike shape that results from its being written on clay with a stylus.

declension: the set of all the inflectional variants of a particular noun; also called a noun *paradigm*. Example: *child, child's, children, children's*. Compare with **conjugation**.

deep structure: see **underlying structure**.

definite noun phrase: a noun phrase that is marked to indicate that the speaker assumes that the addressee is able to identify the **referent** of the noun phrase; opposed to *indefinite*. In English, definiteness and indefiniteness are marked by the choice of article (*the* versus *a*).

degree: a grammatical category associated with the extent of comparison for adjectives and adverbs; there is typically a three-way distinction of degrees: *positive* (as in *speedy*); *comparative* (*speedier* or *more speedy*), and *superlative* (*speediest* or *most speedy*).

deixis: the marking of the orientation or position of entities and situations with respect to certain points of reference such as the place (*here/there*) and time (*now/then*) of utterance.

derivational morpheme: a **morpheme** that serves to derive a word of one class or meaning from a word of another class or meaning. Examples: -MENT (as in *establishment*), which derives a noun from a verb, and RE- (*repaint*), which alters the meaning from verb (for example, 'paint') to verb 'again' ('paint again').

dialect: a language **variety** used by a particular social group, such as a regional, ethnic, socioeconomic, or gender group.

diphthong: a **vowel** sound whose production requires the tongue to start in one place and move to another. Examples: the vowel sounds [ay] in *buy* and [aw] in *bout*.

direct object: one of two kinds of objects (the other being **indirect object**); the direct object is the noun phrase in a **clause** that, together with the verb of the clause, usually forms the verb phrase **constituent**.

discourse: a sequence of sentences that "go together" to constitute a unity, as in conversations, newspaper columns, stories, personal letters, and radio interviews.

etymon: the linguistic form from which a word is historically derived.

expression: any spoken, written, or signed language; the part of language used to convey **content**.

family: see **language family**.

flap: a **manner of articulation** produced by quickly flapping the tip of the tongue against some place of articulation on the upper surface of the vocal tract, commonly the alveolar ridge, as for *t* in the American pronunciation of *metal* [mɛDəl].

free morpheme: a **morpheme** that can stand alone as a word; opposed to **bound morpheme**. Examples: ZEBRA, PAINT, PRETTY.

free variation: the term used to characterize **allophones** of a given **phoneme** that can occur in the same position in a word without altering meaning, as in the final sound of the English word *step*, which can be released [p] or unreleased [p˺] without affecting the word's meaning.

fricative: a sound made by passing a continuous stream of air through a narrowed passage in the vocal tract thereby causing turbulence, such as that created between the tip of the tongue and the alveolar ridge in the production of [s].

function words: a class of words such as **prepositions** and conjunctions whose primary role is to mark grammatical relationships between **content words** or other structures such as phrases and **clauses**.

gender: a system in which all the nouns of a language fall into one lexical class or another. Example: German has a gender system of three classes of nouns (called masculine, feminine, and neuter) whose inflections and associated noun phrase articles and adjectives vary in form for **number** and **case** in **agreement** with the gender class of the noun.

given information: **content** that has been introduced into a **discourse** and that can therefore be presumed to be at the forefront of the hearer's mind and available to ready recollection.

glottis: the narrow aperture between two folds of muscle (the vocal cords) in the **larynx**.

grammatical competence: see **competence**.

grammatical relation: the syntactic function that a noun phrase has in its **clause** (for example, as **subject** or **direct object**).

homonymy: the state of sounding the same but having different meanings; *homophonous* is sometimes used with the related meaning of 'sounding alike.'

hyponym: a term whose **referent** is included in the referent of another term. Example: *blue* is a hyponym of *color*.

iconic symbol: a nonarbitrary **symbol** that bears some resemblance to its **referent** or to a particular feature of its referent; also called *representational symbol*.

illocution: the intention that a speaker or writer has in producing a particular **utterance**. Example: the illocution of the utterance *Can you pass the salt?* is to request that the salt be passed and not (as the structure would indicate) to inquire about the addressee's ability to pass the salt.

implicational universal: a universal rule of the form "If condition P is satisfied, then conclusion Q holds."

indefinite: see **definite**.

indirect object: one of two **grammatical relations** that serve as objects, the other being a **direct object**. Indirect objects usually occur in English before the direct object (*He gave <u>the clerk</u> a rose*) but with a preposition they can occur after (*He gave a rose to <u>the clerk</u>*).

indirect speech act: an **utterance** whose **locution** (or literal meaning) and **illocution** (or intended meaning) are different. Example: *Can you pass the* *salt?* is literally a yes/no question, but it is usually uttered as a request or polite directive for action.

Indo-European: a **language family** all of whose members are descendants of an ancestral language called Proto-Indo-European, spoken probably in Central Asia about 5,000 years ago.

infix: see **affix**.

inflectional morpheme: a **morpheme** used to create variant forms of a word to mark the syntactic function of the word in its sentence. Example: the *suffix -s* (as in *paints*) indicates that the verb agrees with a third-person singular **subject**.

information structure: the level of structure at which certain elements in a sentence are highlighted or backgrounded according to their prominence in the **discourse**.

interdental: a **place of articulation** between the upper and lower teeth. Examples: *th* as in English *thin* [θ] and *then* [ð].

intransitive verb: a verb such as *smile* that does not take a **direct object**: *She smiled.*

isogloss: the geographical boundary marking the limit of the regional distribution of a particular word, pronunciation, or usage.

language family: a group of languages that are said to be genetically related to one another because they have all developed from a single ancestral language.

larynx: the part of the windpipe that houses the vocal cords; also called the *voice box* and the *Adam's apple*.

lexical field: a set of words with an identifiable semantic affinity. Example: *angry, sad, happy, exuberant, depressed.*

lexical item: a unit in the **lexicon** of a language including all its inflected forms; thus, *child, child's, children*, and *children's* taken together constitute the lexical item CHILD.

lexical semantics: the branch of **semantics** that deals with word meaning.

lexicon: the list of all words and **morphemes** of a language that is stored in a native speaker's memory; the internalized dictionary.

lingua franca: a language **variety** used for communication among groups of people who do not otherwise share a common language, as English is the lingua franca of the international scientific community.

linguistic repertoire: the set of language **varieties** (including **registers** and **dialects**) used in the speaking and writing practices of a speech community; also called *verbal repertoire.*

locution: the literal meaning of an **utterance**. Example: the locution of the utterance *Can you close the window?* is a question about the hearer's ability to close the window.

logographic writing: writing in which each **symbol** represents a word. Examples: 8 'eight' and $ 'dollar' are logographic symbols, as are Chinese characters.

manner of articulation: the way in which the airstream is obstructed in the vocal tract in the production of a sound. Example: the **stop** manner of articulation such as for [p] and [t] is produced by blocking the airstream in the oral cavity and then suddenly releasing it.

marked: the elements of a **lexical field** that have a less basic meaning. Usually, more marked elements have more precise meanings than less marked elements, can be described in terms of less marked elements, and are less frequent in natural speech. Example: *cocker spaniel* is more marked than *dog*.

metaphor: an extension of the use of a word beyond its primary meaning to describe referents that bear some similarity to the word's primary **referent**.

minimal pair: a pair of words that differ by only a single sound in the same position. Example: *look* and *took*.

modality: the category through which speakers convey their attitude toward the truth of their assertions (called epistemic modality) or express obligation, permission, or suggestion (called deontic modality); also called *mood*.

modes: channels of linguistic **expression**: speaking, writing, and signing.

morpheme: the smallest unit of language that bears meaning or serves a grammatical function. A morpheme can be a word, as with *zebra* and *paint*, or part of a word, as in *zebras* and *painted*, which contain two morphemes each (ZEBRA and 'PLURAL'; PAINT and 'PAST TENSE').

nasals: a class of sounds including the **consonants** [m] and [n] produced by lowering the velum and allowing air to pass out of the vocal tract through the nose.

nativization: the process through which a speech community adopts another speech community's language as its own and modifies the structure of that new language, thus developing a new **dialect** that becomes characteristic of that community.

natural class: a subset of sounds in the phonemic inventory of a language whose elements can all be characterized by one or a few phonetic features and that includes all sounds of the language that are characterized by these phonetic features. Example:/p t k/ form a natural class of sounds in English because the class includes all and only the voiceless **stops** in the language.

neutralized: the localized loss of a distinction between two **phonemes** that have identical **allophones** in a certain environment. Example: in American English, /t/ in *metal* and /d/ in *medal* are neutralized in that both are pronounced [D] intervocalically following a stressed syllable.

new information: **content** introduced into a **discourse** for the first time.

nonimplicational universal: a property of languages that can be stated without any conditions. Example: "All languages have at least three vowels."

nonreferential: see **referential** noun phrase.

number: a grammatical category associated principally with nouns and pronouns that indicates something about the number of **referents** for the noun or pronoun. Example: *I* and *car* are marked for singular number, while *we* and *cars* are marked for plural number.

object: see **direct object**.

oblique: a noun phrase whose **grammatical relation** in a **clause** is not that of **subject, direct object,** or **indirect object,** but marks such categories as location or time. Example: the noun phrase *the game* has an oblique grammatical relation in *He gave Joe the ball after the game.*

orthography: a spelling system.

palato-alveolar: a **place of articulation** in the oral cavity between the alveolar ridge and the palate. Example: the English sound /š/ represented by the *sh* in *shoe* is articulated in the palato-alveolar region.

paradigm: see **conjugation** and **declension**.

person: a grammatical category associated principally with pronouns to indicate whether the pronoun refers to the speaker (first person), the addressee (second person), a third party (third person), or a combination of these; verbs are sometimes marked for **agreement** with their **subject** or **object** in person.

phoneme: a distinctive and significant element in the sound system of a language. A phoneme is an abstract element (defined by a set of phonetic features) that can have alternative manifestations (called **allophones**) in particular phonological environments. Example: the English phoneme /p/ has several allophones, including [pʰ], [p˥], and [p].

phonetics: the study of sounds made in the production of human languages.

phonological rule: a rule that specifies the **allophones** of a **phoneme** and their distribution in a particular language.

phonotactic constraints: rules that specify the structure of **syllables** allowed in a particular language.

phrase-structure rule: a rule that describes the composition of **constituents** in **underlying structure**; also called *rewrite rule*. Example: the phrase-structure rule S → NP VP states that a simple sentence (or underlying **clause**) is made up of a noun phrase and a verb phrase (in that order).

pictogram: a symbolic drawing that represents an object or idea independently of the word that refers to that object or idea. Examples: the highway signs that indicate dangerous curves or merging traffic without the use of words.

pidgin: a contact language that develops in multilingual colonial situations, in which one language (commonly that of the colonizer) forms the base for a simple and generally unstable new **variety**; a pidgin is restricted in use and is not spoken natively by anyone.

place of articulation: the location in the mouth cavity where the airstream is obstructed in the production of a sound. Example: alveolar sounds such as [t] and [s] are produced by obstructing the airstream at the alveolar ridge.

polysemy: the term used to refer to multiple meanings for the same word or sentence; a word is polysemic when it has more than one meaning, as with *bank* in *river bank* and *savings bank*.

possessor: a **grammatical relation** between two nouns that are closely associated, often but not always by virtue of having a possessive relationship. Examples: *Luke's harp, the book's cover, an arm's length.*

postposition: see **preposition**.

pragmatics: a term used as an alternative to the term **information structure**; also the name of the branch of linguistics that studies information structure.

predication: the part of a **clause** that makes a statement about a particular entity. Example: *likes ice cream* is the predication made of Deborah in the clause *Deborah likes ice cream.*

predicative adjective: an adjective that serves as a complement to the verb of a **clause**; opposed to **attributive** adjective. Example: *cold* is predicative in *The coffee is cold* but attributive in *the cold coffee.*

prefix: see **affix**.

preposition: a **function word** that occurs preceding noun phrases and indicates the **semantic role** or **grammatical relation** of the noun phrase; *postpositions* serve the same purpose but occur following noun phrases. Prepositions and postpositions constitute the class of *adpositions*, differing from one another only in their placement with respect to nouns.

reference: a semantic category through which language provides information about the relationship between noun phrases and their **referents**.

referent: the entity (person, object, notion, or situation) in the world referred to by a linguistic **expression**. Example: the referent of *John's dog* is the four-legged canine belonging to John.

referential meaning: the meaning that an expression has by virtue of its ability to refer to an entity; referential meaning is contrasted with **social meaning** and **affective meaning**, and is sometimes called *denotation*.

referential noun phrase: a noun phrase that refers to a particular entity; *a good piano teacher* is referential in *Tom knows a good piano teacher* but not in *Tom wants to find a good piano teacher*.

referring expression: an **expression** that refers to an entity or situation.

register: a language **variety** associated with a particular situation of use. Examples: baby talk, legalese.

relative clause: a **clause** that is embedded in a noun phrase and serves to modify a noun. The noun that is modified by a relative clause is the *head* of the relative clause. Example: in *This is the book that I told you about*, the relative clause *that I told you about* modifies the head *book*.

repair: a sequence of turns in a conversation during which a previous **utterance** is edited, corrected, or clarified.

repertoire: see **linguistic repertoire**.

representational: see **iconic symbol**.

rewrite rule: see **phrase-structure rule**.

semantic role: the way in which the **referent** of a noun phrase is involved in the situation described by the **clause**, for example as agent, patient, or cause.

semantics: the study of the systematic ways in which languages structure meaning, especially in words and in sentences.

sign: a nonarbitrary indicator of an object or of an event, as smoke is a sign of fire; often opposed to **symbol**.

simple sentence: a sentence that contains only one **clause**.

social dialect: a language **variety** characteristic of a social group; typically, social dialects refer to characteristic ways of speaking by socioeconomic groups, gender groups, or ethnic groups, as distinct from regional dialects.

social meaning: information that words and sentences convey about the social characteristics of their producers and of the situation in which they are produced; together with **affective meaning**, social meaning is sometimes called *connotation*.

speech act: an action carried out through language, such as promising, lying, and greeting.

stop: a sound created when air is built up at a **place of articulation** in the vocal tract and suddenly released through the mouth; sometimes called *oral stops* when **nasals** are excluded.

structural description: the range of sentence structures to which a particular **transformation** may apply; a sentence that does not meet the structural description of a transformation cannot undergo the transformation.

subgroup: the term used to refer to a set of languages that belong to the same **language family** and that developed as a single language for a period of time after other subgroups had developed into separate languages; thus, Romance and Germanic are subgroups of **Indo-European**; West Germanic is the subgroup of Germanic to which English belongs; also called *branch*.

subject: a noun phrase that, together with the verb phrase, constitutes a **clause**.

subordinator: a word that marks the boundary between an embedded **clause** and its matrix clause; *that* is a subordinator in *I think that he fell*.

suffix: see **affix**.

surface form: a word's actual pronunciation, generated by the application of the **phonological rules** of a language to the **underlying form**; sometimes also said of sentences (see **underlying structure**).

surface structure: the **constituent structure** of a sentence after all relevant **transformations** have applied.

syllabic writing: writing in which each **symbol** represents a **syllable**.

syllable: a phonological unit consisting of one or more sounds, including a nucleus that is usually a **vowel**; frequent syllable types are CV and CVC.

symbol: an arbitrary representation of an object, event, or entity.

synonymous: the term used to refer to words or sentences that mean the same thing.

syntax: the structure of sentences and the study of sentence structure.

tense: a category of the verb that expresses time reference, for example as past (*walked*) or present (*walk*).

terminal string: the string of syntactic symbols (such as Det, N, V) generated by application of all applicable syntactic rules of a grammar; it is a string to which no further **transformations** can apply.

topic: the main center of attention in a sentence.

transformation: a syntactic rule that alters **constituent structure** in a systematic way; also called *transformational rule*.

transitive verb: a verb that takes a **direct object**.

trill: a **manner of articulation** characterized by the rapid (20 to 30 times per second) vibrating of an articulator caused by air passing rapidly over it (but not including vocal cord vibration).

typology: a field of inquiry that seeks to classify the languages of the world into different types according to particular structural characteristics.

underlying form: the form of a **morpheme** that is stored in the internalized **lexicon**; sometimes also said of sentences (see **underlying structure**).

underlying structure: the abstract structure of a sentence before any **transformations** have applied; specified by **phrase-structure rules**; also called *deep structure*.

universal: a linguistic pattern at play in most or all of the world's languages; see also **absolute universal** and **universal tendency**.

universal tendency: a linguistic pattern at play in most, but not all, of the world's languages; also called *relative universal*. Example: most (but *not all*) verb-final languages place adjectives before the nouns they modify.

utterance: an **expression** produced in a particular context with a particular intention.

variety: any language, **dialect**, or **register**.

velar: a **consonant** whose **place of articulation** is the velum, that is, a consonant produced by the tongue approaching or touching the roof of the mouth at the velum.

voicing: the vibration in the **larynx** caused by air from the lungs passing through the vocal cords when they are partly closed.

vowels: one of the two major classes of sounds (the other being **consonants**); vowels are articulated without complete closure in the oral cavity and without sufficient narrowing to create the friction characteristic of consonants. Abbreviation: V.

ILLUSTRATION CREDITS

Figures 2-3 and 2-4: From *A Course in Phonetics*, 2nd ed., by Peter Ladefoged, copyright © 1982 by Harcourt Brace Jovanovich, Inc. Reprinted by permission of the publisher.

Figure 3-1: Type B/65 Sonogram R Kay Elemetrics Co., Pine Brook, N.J.

Figures 9-2 and 9-4: John Terrell. 1986. *Prehistory in the Pacific Islands: A Study of Variation in Language, Customs, and Human Biology* (Cambridge, England: Cambridge University Press).

Figure 9-14: Edgar A. Gregersen. *Language in Africa: An Introductory Survey* (New York: Gordon & Breach), 1977.

Figure 9-18: Copyright © Bob Browne 1980.

Figures 11-1 and 11-2: I. J. Gelb. 1963. *A Study of Writing*, 2nd ed. (Chicago: University of Chicago Press).

Table 11-1: Albertine Gaur, *A History of Writing*, 1984, The British Library, London.

Table 11-2: Sylvia Scribner & Michael Cole, © 1981, P & F, *The Psychology of Literacy*, fig. 3.2, p. 33, Cambridge, Harvard University Press. Reprinted by permission.

Figure 12-1: Roger Shuy. 1967. *Discovering American Dialects*. Copyright © 1967 by the National Council of Teachers of English. Reprinted by permission of the publisher.

Figures 12-2, 12-3, 12-4, 12-5, and 12-6: Hans Kurath. 1949. *A Word Geography of the Eastern United States* (Ann Arbor: University of Michigan Press).

Figures 12-7 and 12-8, and page 418: *Dictionary of American Regional English*, vol. 1, 1985, Harvard University Press. Reprinted by permission.

Figure 12-9: Craig M. Carver. 1987. *American Regional Dialects: A Word Geography* (Ann Arbor: University of Michigan Press).

Figures 12-10, 12-11, and 12-12: William Labov. 1966. *The Social Stratification of English in New York City* (Washington, D.C.: Center for Applied Linguistics).

Figure 14-2: Map of Old English dialects, adapted from Samuel Moore and A. H. Marckwardt, *Historical Outlines of English Sounds and Inflections* (Ann Arbor: George Wahr, 1951). © George Wahr Publishing Co., 3041½ S. State Street, Ann Arbor, MI 48104.

Figure 15-1: Adapted from William Labov, *Sociolinguistic Patterns* (Philadelphia: University of Pennsylvania Press, 1972).

INDEX

A separate Language Index follows this general index.

Terms followed by an asterisk (*) are defined in the Glossary, on pages 523–533.

A

ablative 103–04. *See also* case*
ablaut 462
Académie Française 497–98, 500, 504
accusative 95,103–04, 465–68. *See also* case*
acquisition
  adult input 16–18
  and learning 511–12
  of morphology 87–88
  of phonology 59–62
  stages 18–20
acronym 110
address
  form of 175–76
  terms 431–32
addressee 194, 196, 216, 427–28
adjacency pair* 341–44
adjective 90–91, 444
  attributive* 90, 445
  predicative* 90
  See also comparative; superlative; word class
adposition
  postposition 91, 262
  preposition 91, 262
  See also word class
adverb 93, 196, 444. *See also* word class
Ælfric 472
affective filter 512
affix* 97, 109–10
affricate* 46
Afroasiatic 305–07
agent 201, 202, 203, 204

agentless passive 232–33
agglutinative language 122ex
agreement* 90
Alfred the Great 459, 472
allomorph* 112, 118
allophone* 62–64, 79, 464
  distribution 64–69, 79
alphabet* 362, 372, 375, 378
  Cyrillic 372–73
  International Phonetic Alphabet (IPA) 37
alveolar* 42
alveolar ridge 42
ambiguity* 98, 136, 173, 222
American Heritage Dictionary 500–03, 505
American Sign Language, and
  chimpanzees 11–12
animal communication 9–14
anomalous 173, 202
antonym* 184, 186, 191, 192, 206
appropriateness conditions* 330–31
approximant* 46
argument* 147
Aristotle 8, 90n.
articles, and definiteness 220
artificial languages 317–18
ash 463
aspect* 198
aspiration* 63–68, 71–72
assimilation 113
Athabascan 309
atlas, linguistic 390
attitude (language) 492, 505
  and second language 511–12
attributive*. *See* adjective
Australian languages 311
Austronesian 302–05
AUX 158–59
auxiliary verb* 158

B

Babel 492
baby talk 17–18
back formation 110

LANGUAGE INDEX

B 9
C 0
D 1
E 2
F 3
G 4
H 5
I 6
J 7